GREAT WRITERS STUDENT LIBRARY

THE NOVEL TO 1900

GREAT WRITERS STUDENT LIBRARY

Editor: James Vinson
Associate Editor: D. L. Kirkpatrick

GREAT WRITERS STUDENT LIBRARY

THE NOVEL TO 1900

INTRODUCTION BY
A. O. J. COCKSHUT

First published 1980 by
THE MACMILLAN PRESS LIMITED
London and Basingstoke
Associated companies in New York, Dublin
Melbourne, Johannesburg and Madras

ISBN 0333 28331 7

CONTENTS

EDITOR'S NOTE

The entry for each writer consists of a biography, a complete list of his published books, a selected list of published bibliographies and critical studies on the writer, and a signed critical essay on his work.

In the biographies, details of education, military service, and marriage(s) are generally given before the usual chronological summary of the life of the writer; awards and honours are given last.

The Publications section is meant to include all book publications, though as a rule broadsheets, single sermons and lectures, minor pamphlets, exhibition catalogues, etc. are omitted. Under the heading Collections, we have listed the most recent collections of the complete works and those of individual genres (verse, plays, novels, stories, and letters); only those collections which have some editorial authority and were issued after the writer's death are listed; on-going editions are indicated by a dash after the date of publication; often a general selection from the writer's works or a selection from the works in the individual genres listed above is included.

Titles are given in modern spelling, though the essayists were allowed to use original spelling for titles and quotations; often the titles are "short." The date given is that of the first book publication, which often followed the first periodical or anthology publication by some time; we have listed the actual year of publication, often different from that given on the title-page. No attempt has been made to indicate which works were published anonymously or pseudonymously, or which works of fiction were published in more than one volume. We have listed plays which were produced but not published, but only since 1700; librettos and musical plays are listed along with the other plays; no attempt has been made to list lost or unverified plays. Reprints of books (including facsimile editions) and revivals of plays are not listed unless a revision or change of title is involved. The most recent edited version of individual works is included if it supersedes the collected edition cited.

In the essays, short references to critical remarks refer to items cited in the Publications section or in the Reading List. Introductions, memoirs, editorial matter, etc. in works cited in the Publications section are not repeated in the Reading List.

INTRODUCTION

Aristotle taught us long ago that it is vain to seek for exact definitions of literary terms. Novels are what people agree to call novels. They are fiction, they are in prose, and they usually, but not quite always, have a degree of realism which is unequalled by any previous literary form. The sources of the English novel are multitudinous and vague. There is the desire to tell a story which is older than literature itself. There are Italian prose romances, adapted or imitated by the Elizabethans. The Spanish and French picaresque tradition is still more important. Cervantes had an immense reputation in eighteenth-century England, as titles like *The Female Quixote* and *The Spiritual Quixote* clearly show, and Fielding wrote on the title page of *Joseph Andrews* "in imitation of the manner of Cervantes, author of *Don Quixote.*"

Another strand is provided by the fable or parable, whose sources are both biblical and Greek. This develops in the eighteenth century into the novel of ideas. Often witty and intellectual, it had also as a precursor something different and immensely popular, Bunyan's *Pilgrim's Progress*. Bunyan's habit of indicating a character's nature and function by his name (which he shares with many seventeenth-century dramatists) is continued by Peacock, and later writers. On the other hand, Mme. de Lafayette's *La Princesse de Clèves* (1678) anticipates the serious psychological and analytical tradition of the English novel from Richardson onwards.

We are on more shaky ground if we try to explain why prose fiction became for the first time in the eighteenth century a major concern of some of the best writers, or why this tendency increased in the nineteenth century until Henry James could eventually claim for the novel the status of the greatest and subtlest of literary forms. It is always easy to find reasons why things were "inevitable" after they have happened. But it is most unlikely that anyone in the early eighteenth century could have foreseen this. A few indications, however (I would not dignify them with the name of causes), can be noted. There were a large and rapid increase in literacy, and a tendency for life to be lived more privately. Long, solitary communion with a book began to fit more easily than in the past into the pattern of many lives. The novel is (often) domestic, minute, and psychological rather than public, masculine, and heroic. Not only did the number of women readers increase sharply, but in the late seventeenth century, perhaps for the first time, writers had a female audience consciously in mind. *The Spectator* of Addison and Steele (1711–12) anticipates Richardson in being particularly concerned with a feminine point of view. Naturally, the emergence of a large number of women novelists was not after this very long delayed. Female poets, scholars, dramatists, and essayists were the exception until a much later period. Even vaguer and more uncertain are the connections sometimes claimed with the "rise of capitalism." But it may not be an accident that almost the first English book which is both undoubtedly a novel and a lasting literary classic, Defoe's *Robinson Crusoe* (1719), can be read as a kind of parable of economic man and an anticipation of the work of Adam Smith.

If we do not aim at an impossible rigidity of classification, and accept the fluidity of types, we may approximately divide the novels written before Scott and Jane Austen into the following types: 1) General studies of manners, where hero and plot are loosely designed to show varieties of district, class, and human type. This would include most of the work of Defoe (except *Robinson Crusoe*), Fielding, Smollett, Fanny Burney, and part of the work of Maria Edgeworth. 2) The novel of sensibility and moral instruction, of which Richardson is the great classic exponent, and Sterne, Henry Mackenzie, Mrs. Inchbald, and others are followers. (But Sterne only partly fits this category, being also the first "experimental" or "anti-novelist" novelist.) 3) The novel of ideas, which includes *Gulliver's Travels* (hardly a true novel perhaps), Johnson's *Rasselas,* and works by Godwin and, later, Peacock. 4) The novel of fantasy and excitement, including works by Horace Walpole, Mrs. Radcliffe, M. G. Lewis, and Maturin.

Inevitably the types overlap. There is an element of fantasy in Smollett which is absent in Fielding, who, however, in *Jonathan Wild,* exceptionally wrote something like a moral fable. One can learn as much, or more, from Richardson as from Fielding about eighteenth-century family structure and inheritance customs, so he, too, is in a way a novelist of manners. Mrs. Radcliffe has a serious, satirical side, though it had little to do with her popular appeal. Maria Edgeworth is at once a student of manners, a moralist, and a psychologist.

Undaunted by anomalies, however, let us take the main types one by one.

Defoe is admittedly the chief initiator of the novel of manners. He was qualified by a unique combination of minute powers of observation and moral obtuseness. *Robinson Crusoe* is successful just because the solitary hero is so literal, so limited, so brave, so resourceful, so utterly unimaginative. (James Joyce was later to say that he represented the English character better than any other literary character.) In *Moll Flanders, Colonel Jack,* and *Roxana* he gives a minutely detailed but feeling and impressionistic view of the seamy side of London and the provinces, with some excursions abroad. The heroes and heroines are curiously sensitive in one sense, and curiously insensitive in another. One can share the very sensations of the boy pickpocket, Colonel Jack, as he wonders whether his first theft will be discovered, but the moral issues involved in thieving receive superficial treatment. The repentance with which several of the books end seems hardly more than a convention. When Moll Flanders is led to think that her current lover is really her brother, she has vague memories of moral principles sufficient to tell us that she feels horrified, but she does not convince. Defoe will always appeal most to those who seek in the novel vivid impressions and sharply drawn social pictures. He disappoints the more questing and curious readers.

Fielding, partly through accidents of literary history, is by now not an easy writer to assess fairly. The excessive praise (including the manifestly absurd title "father of the English novel") lavished on him by some Victorian and later writers tends to inhibit judgment. The absurdity, of course, is seen when we recall that Defoe easily has priority in time, and Richardson is far superior in talent and originality. Indeed, Fielding's true place in the novel's history is well indicated by the fact that he begins as a *commentator* on Richardson. The central idea of *Joseph Andrews* (1742) is that Richardson's study of female virtue rewarded in *Pamela* would be transposed into uproarious comedy if a study of male chastity and female lust was substituted for the more conventional female resistance to male importunity. He combined this with transferring Don Quixote's endless progress along the roads of Spain to the familiar roads of England; and his English Quixote, Parson Adams, is at once his most charming creation and the nearest approach of a rather literal-minded man to a genuine spiritual note. Parts of the book (especially the scene where Lady Booby fails to tempt Joseph into bed) are genuinely funny, and a few scenes in which Adams appears are touching, but the construction is perfunctory and amateurish, and we never altogether forget the impression of a joke that got out of hand. *Tom Jones* (1749), Fielding's most celebrated and most overrated work, is an overlong, and morally simplistic, celebration of the "natural goodness" of its very self-satisfied and self-centred hero. But it is strong, in the traditional picaresque way, as a study of English social types encountered on many roads and in numerous inns. In the more muted and less popular final novel, *Amelia* (1751), he showed a surer moral discernment, and created a heroine who combines activity, robust strength, and patient endurance in dealing with a weak and erring, though well-meaning husband.

Though no one has ever been able to extract very much meaning from the phrase "comic epic in prose," Fielding's parade of classical learning and his elegant essay writing in the introductory chapters of *Tom Jones* helped to endow the early years of the novel with a certain much-needed traditional respectability. But this did not go to the heart of the matter. For the real obstacle to taking the novel seriously was that it was hard to see where its formal principle lay. If one can just tell a story, or a series of stories. and call it a novel, how does the resulting work claim superiority over mere anecdote? In the eighteenth century, with its admirable sense of the difficulty and the dignity of the literary craft, this must have seemed a formidable difficulty. It was Richardson, not Fielding, who pointed the way to a solution. For him, as for most great novelists since, the formal principle of the novel lay in *probability.* And that is a more difficult idea (when applied to the novel) than it may sound. To invent a situation and a set of characters to fill it in the detailed fulness which prose fiction permits is to present the reader with a challenge: "Now you know all this, can you fault the middle and later part of the work either in the logic of events or in the consistency of characters?" When he has finished explaining the *donnée,* the novelist admits defeat if he merely tries to tell us. He must show, he must convince that it would have been so, and not otherwise. And many of the most memorable moments in great novels are those where we are surprised, startled by something unexpected, which perhaps for a moment seems out of character, and then absorb the surprise as a new revelation. Then we say, "Ah, yes, in spite of everything it would have been so." Alone or almost alone of eighteenth century novelists, Richardson has this faculty of inspiring surprise and conviction simultaneously.

Richardson's first and least satisfactory novel, *Pamela* (1740), grew out of his habit of writing model letters suitable for young girls who lacked the education to write for themselves. Apart from a very few brief interjections by the author, the whole of Richardson's fiction is epistolary. In *Pamela* he gave only a single point of view, that of a virtuous servant-girl threatened by a licentious master and several venal and treacherous allies. Although Richardson had a wonderful, perhaps unprecedented, gift of conveying minute feminine observations and sensations, there is inevitably a certain monotony. And Fielding was right in the criticism he expressed both in *Joseph Andrews* and in the more outrageous skit, *Shamela:* there is a moral flaw in the work. Because the whole drift of the story is to show that Mr. B. was a sensual and unscrupulous brute and that Pamela's best hope was to escape him altogether, to find her willing, even eager, to marry him is disconcerting, and gives plausibility to the taunt that Pamela's virtue was difficult to distinguish from worldly ambition. But the originality of the book, in the freshness of its impressionism, remains. In *Clarissa Harlowe* (1747–48), which is perhaps the only novel of the eighteenth century that fully deserves the classic status we willingly accord to the great novels of the nineteenth, such objections are magnificently overcome. Clarissa, faced by an avaricious and unfeeling family with a command to marry a man she detests, runs away with Lovelace. Though she knows him to be a notorious seducer, she is convinced that she can either marry him or retain her virginity and independence under his protection. He has for a time convinced her that he really cares for her, and in a way he does. But his admiration for her character inspires him with the perverse wish to test her virtue to the limit as the representative of all that is best in woman. Eventually he rapes her when she is in a drugged condition, thinking to make amends by marriage. His real aim is to reduce the whole female sex to submission by the "conquest" of its finest flower. But she astonishes him by refusing to marry him; the moment of her loss of worldly dignity and prospects is the moment of her greatest spiritual ascendancy. Throughout one of the longest novels in the language the interest never flags and the merciless logic of events never falters. After this *Sir Charles Grandison* (1753–54), though finely constructed and full of incident, comes as something of an anti-climax. It is pleasant to remember, though, that Fielding was one of *Clarissa*'s warmest admirers.

The close connection in literary history between Fielding and Richardson has taken us away from our first category, in which Smollett and Maria Edgeworth remain to be mentioned. Until recently few critics have concurred with Scott's view that Smollett was Fielding's superior. But there is something to be said for it. His books are less well-constructed, coarser, less good-tempered. But they have a sharper wit and greater powers of invention, and contain more memorable dialogue. *Roderick Random* (1748) is the favourite of those who prefer Smollett at his most vigorous and outrageous, *Humphry Clinker* (1771), another epistolary novel, of those who welcome the milder humours of his later years. He excels in sharp caricature, and his naval portraits in particular are justly celebrated. It is much to his credit that he was the most important literary influence on one of our two greatest novelists, Dickens, a man not much prone to learn from other writers.

Maria Edgeworth, too, has the distinction of inspiring a writer greater than herself – Walter Scott. In her Irish stories she managed to combine a serious analysis of the social problems of a subject race with racy Irish humour. "The Absentee" (in *Tales of Fashionable Life,* 1812) is especially notable here. But some of her English stories, though less obviously original, are perhaps even finer in their moral discriminations, especially *Helen* (1834).

Apart from Richardson, Sterne is the most notable of the novelists of sensibility. Perhaps he would have been amused and pleased at the enigmatic character of his reputation in the two hundred years since his death, and not least in recent years. In *Tristram Shandy* (1759–67) he attempted with extraordinary success two quite different things, to draw attention by a brilliant and endlessly resourceful parody to the arbitrariness of the novel's conventions, and to convey the strange inconsequentiality of the human mind. His sensibility is really very different from Richardson's. Where Richardson's is fine and sensitive, Sterne's is outrageous. Where Richardson moves with endlessly subtle solemnity to the most terrible of all sexual events, a rape, Sterne is suggestive and flippant. He is fond of the trick of suggesting an obscene double meaning and then pretending innocently that the reader has invented it for himself. He treats time with the arbitrariness that the human imagination, with its mixture of hope, fear, memory, and invention, actually treats it. The paradox is that this revelation of the inner world of all of us comes with a shock of surprise, because the reasonable conventions of literary story-telling are so deeply engrained. Sterne sometimes has the effect that would be obtained by referring to the coarsest physical facts in the middle of a formal procession. But there is a serious side to Sterne. He is also a genuine enquirer into the hidden workings of the mind. He takes the familiar eighteenth-century commonplace about the "association of ideas" and shows it in many new guises. What appears to be random association eventually reveals a pattern. If a long book like *Tristram Shandy* were totally random it would soon become tedious. In *A Sentimental Journey,* published in 1768, the year of Sterne's death, the cult of sensibility is even more intense. For the first time, perhaps, we get the idea that strong and exquisite feeling is the great moral prerequisite. Without it all so-called virtues are cold and barren; its presence easily covers a multitude of sins. Henry Mackenzie's *The Man of Feeling* (1771) and several succeeding works by women carry this tendency to its very limit.

At this point in its history the novel was the arena of an important conflict of general ideas. The novelists, one might say, were unwittingly drawing attention to a deep contradiction in Augustan values. The great Augustans, especially Pope, Swift, and Johnson, were constantly appealing to reason and good sense and classical traditions. But they were all men of intense feelings; and in the case of the last two their strongest feelings were entirely at odds with any rational conceptions. Swift's compulsive washing, Johnson's fear of treading on the cracks of the paving stones have nothing to do with reason and good sense. It almost seemed as if literature in the first sixty years of the century could not take account of the irrationality, the violence, and the unpredictability of feeling as it exists in the human heart. It may seem to us that Sterne and the other merchants of sensibility actually experienced weaker feelings than Johnson and Swift. For that reason they did not need to be so watchful to control them, nor were they afraid of excess or of emotional collapse. They could dwell lingeringly and lovingly on feelings they perhaps only wished to have, or which they really had, but only in a mild degree. There are some posturing, some self-admiration, some claiming of unconvincing extremes of feeling, which may remind us of a weakling aggressively sticking out his manly chest. But there is also a genuine analytical exactness in charting unknown seas. After two hundred years Sterne has not lost his probing, worrying character; and it is no accident that he should have a particular appeal in an age like ours, when traditional values are under attack and literary forms fluid.

Whether or not we class *Gulliver's Travels* (1726) as a novel, it is at any rate a fiction; and it proved that a profound enquiry into fundamental ideas can be conducted by means of a fiction. Swift really reverses the tradition of the tale of the marvellous. Instead of trying to excite wonder by recounting improbable adventures, Swift recounts totally impossible things in quiet common-sense tones. In a certain very special sense the book could even be called picaresque, if we substitute Gulliver's tour round various imaginary kingdoms for the usual tour round a real society. Swift may be fantastic in the events he describes, but he is always a sober Augustan realist about the limitations of human nature. The great popularity and critical esteem of the work must have encouraged others to see in the novel of ideas a vehicle for thoughts more complex, serious, and abstract than might otherwise have been thought appropriate or feasible in prose fiction. But in saying this we must not forget that Swift was also reviving a much older tradition which includes the myths of Plato and the *Utopia* of his own special hero, Thomas More. Distinguished successors include Johnson's *Rasselas*, Godwin's *Caleb Williams*, and all the novels of Peacock. *Rasselas* is a deeply melancholy and meditative general consideration of human life. *Caleb Williams*, like the works of Bage, Holcroft, and some others tends to bring the novel of ideas back into the main stream of the novel. While *Gulliver's Travels* makes no attempt to assimilate itself to the surface realism of ordinary novels, these later works are in some ways indistinguishable from realistic fictions. Their plots are hardly more fanciful than those of Fielding. This was to be important for the novel's future. It meant that the categories of instruction, speculation, and entertainment would become less distinct, until eventually a novel like *Middlemarch* could deal with philosophical ideas in terms of the strictest realism, with exact fidelity to the contours of a real society and to individual psychology.

Peacock, however, is a different matter. His narrative is subordinate to a witty satirical comment on the ideas of the day. His friendly but probing criticisms of Byron, Shelley, Brougham, and others remain some of the most intelligent ever made; and he does not hesitate to move into a world of pure fantasy where an orangoutang can be a baronet. Typically, this uproarious joke is also a learned and witty allusion to an exploded biological theory of Lord Monboddo.

The so-called Gothic novel may be dismissed briefly because its products were all mediocre. It is perhaps more significant in the general history of taste than in the history of the novel proper. Its founder, Horace Walpole, who produced *The Castle of Otranto* in 1765, was also the builder of Strawberry Hill, a still visible landmark of the long and complex reassessment of the Middle Ages which continued for more than a hundred years. Walpole shows none of the tendency developed later by Scott to take men of distant times seriously. He merely places his story in a far country and a distant and supposedly dark time (the darkness was quite as much in the author's ignorance of history as in any historical reality) so that extraordinary and impossible events may appear more credible. The marvels of the Gothic novel, even in the best of them, Mrs. Radcliffe's, and especially in the celebrated but worthless novel of M. G. Lewis, *The Monk* (1796), tend to be crude and unconvincing assaults on the nerves. There is often a disagreeable air of sophisticated people playing down to the lowest tastes, which anticipates some kinds of popular journalism today. None of the Gothic novelists achieved what some of the romantic poets were later to attain, an imaginative recreation of a world of simple wonder and delight. Clara Reeve's *The Old English Baron* (1777) and a few passages in Mrs. Radcliffe perhaps escape the rather severe strictures given above.

The great age of the novel is inaugurated by two very different, almost contemporary geniuses, Walter Scott (1771–1832) and Jane Austen (1775–1817). It is pleasant to be able to record that they appreciated and admired each other, and, in particular, that Scott, who was a celebrated European figure when Jane Austen was still known only to few, knew in his heart which of them was the greater. Scott came to prose fiction in middle life when he was already a famous poet and man of letters. His great achievement is the imaginative recreation of the past. He was a man of wide learning and deep romantic enthusiasms, tempered by a shrewd and judicious knowledge of men and affairs. In his last great novel, *Redgauntlet* (1824), he amused himself by dividing his own youthful personality into two, and attributing the romantic features to one character and the traits of the intelligent and canny young Edinburgh lawyer to another. There was a strong strain of antiquarian curiosity in him; but in his best novels that is overlaid with a deep imaginative power to comprehend and recreate the feelings of a past age, its breathless sense of being in a transitory present moment, looking to an unknown future. Though he was bookish, his greatest works are more dependent on oral tradition than on books. This means that there is an unusually sharp division between his best works, which all deal with a period later than 1660, and his numerous excursions into a more remote past. Books like *Ivanhoe* (1819), placed in the time of Richard I, once considered exciting reading for boys, are little more now than curiosities. But he is profound, subtle, various, and exciting in his treatment of the Jacobite theme in *Waverley* (1814), *Rob Roy* (1817), and *Redgauntlet*. In another masterpiece, *Old Mortality* (1817), he brought to life the Lowland Covenanters of the time of Charles II in the struggle against Claverhouse. Claverhouse was one of Scott's personal heroes, but his fairness is such that he allows his opponents often to have the best of it in readers' sympathies. Scott's fairness is not a simple thing. It is composed not only of his kindly geniality, but also of a deep historian's sense of the limitations of human knowledge, the provisional character of action, and the unpredictability of consequences. It is also a social fairness. Some of his most dignified and impressive characters are beggars, outcasts, gypsies, and loose women. As G. K. Chesterton finely said, Scott was fond of introducing kings in disguise into his novels, but really, in Scott, every man is a king in disguise. When Meg Merrilies rebukes the laird (*Guy Mannering*, 1815) or when, in *The Antiquary* (1816), the beggar Edie Ochiltree tells the wealthy Wardour, as they watch the advancing tide, "Our riches will be soon equal," the hierarchical social order, to which Scott's natural conservatism strongly inclined him, is effortlessly overturned. A strange, alien prophetic note, of which the workaday Scott was hardly aware, is heard, and with it a new depth of meaning is found in the novel. For the first time it enters the domain previously reserved for tragic drama and poetry. A talented but rather facile poet in verse, Scott reserved his deepest poetry for his novels. As he was also immensely popular and extremely exciting to read he was able to place the tradition of the novel on a new and more extensive base. To doubt the high literary possibilities of prose fiction, to reject it as clearly inferior to poetry and drama, would become, after Scott, a judgment of manifest stupidity, though it was a stupidity of which many more would still be guilty. Above all, Scott was the first English novelist who could convey an impression of God's plenty, of inexhaustible inventiveness and variety, as Chaucer and Shakespeare had done long before in other forms. In this, he anticipates Dickens. And perhaps no one has combined so well as Scott did a sense of regret for a vanished past with a deeply intelligent analysis of the causes of change.

If Scott was not exactly the founder of a Scottish school of novelists, there was a brief flowering of interesting lesser talents during his time. James Hogg, the "Ettrick Shepherd" – one of the few self-educated contributors to the novel tradition – Susan Ferrier, and John Galt were all born within a few years of Scott, and the first two were friends and admirers, though Hogg was inclined to quarreling even with the genial Scott. Hogg's *Confessions of a Justified Sinner* (1824) is a most original work which, like Scott's best work, could only have been written about Scotland. The antinomianism of the more extreme Scots Calvinists is scathingly attacked as a kind of devil-worship in a work which, despite its tendency to melodrama, always carries conviction as a serious and intelligent comment on the perils and moral ambiguities which lurk in the simple-sounding concept of justification by faith alone. Miss Ferrier is less original and less Scottish, and resembles Maria Edgeworth in many ways. The moral structure of *Marriage* (1818) may be thought naive, but *The Inheritance* (1824) and *Destiny* (1831) are delicately plotted and have delightful humorous touches. John Galt is a various writer who ranges from intelligent sociological studies like *The Ayrshire Legatees* (1821) and *Annals of the Parish* (1821) to very complicated dramas of inheritance in *The Entail* (1822) to uproarious farce and slight comedy. Scotland was never so well depicted before or since as in the years 1815–30. It is worth emphasizing that none of these writers was a mere imitator of Scott; each contributes something personal and irreplaceable, as the Jacobean dramatists did after Shakespeare.

With Jane Austen we return to work that could only have been written in England. Easy to read and enjoy, she is by no means easy to assess or appreciate completely. Indeed, for all her continuing popularity, and all the high critical esteem she receives, it may be that her real greatness, her stature as one of the handful of English writers with some claim to be second only to Shakespeare, is still not fully felt. In part, perhaps, this is because we still feel the magnetic pull of false romantic ideas of what constitutes genius. Jane Austen never in her life had an original idea; she might have said that as the world had been going a long time any valuable idea would probably have been discovered long ago. She wholeheartedly accepted the traditional wisdom of the race, so far as it was known to her, and most of the temporary and local assumptions of her own milieu; and this milieu separated her from some of the most powerful currents of her time, such as industrialization, revolutionary politics, and the profound intuitions of the romantic poets. In spite of all this, she did not want for material, tension, drama, or conflict. If moral principles appeared to her clear and settled and, for the most part, simple, human nature was inexhaustibly rich, varied, comic, and, at times, tragic. She cannot be called conventional in a limiting sense, because her quick intelligence saw that the accepted standards of her society contained all sorts of paradoxes, conflicts, even contradictions. Some of her most conventional characters, worshippers at the shrines of the great world like Mrs. Elton and Sir Walter Elliot, are treated with a comprehensive and intelligent satirical bitterness which equals the greatest of the Augustan poets in wit and sharpness, and excels them in richness of effect and telling detail. Marriage, the immemorially traditional theme of comedy, becomes at last as serious and important a thing in literature as it is in life, without ceasing to be delightfully comic. The different purposes of marriage, its complex relation to love, to prudence, to security, to ambition, to social cohesion, provide her with an inexhaustible series of dilemmas, subtle discriminations, and fine shades. Her juvenilia already show rollicking high spirits and a precocious gift of parody. She admired and learned from some of her predecessors, especially Richardson and Maria Edgeworth, but she was inspired quite as much by a spirit of opposition to the melodramatic absurdities, the exaggerated coincidences, and the slippery morality of others, especially the Gothic novelists. Her short life, combined with some early discouragement from publishers, left her time to complete only six novels, but we feel that if she had lived to be old the simple-seeming material of daily life would have been more than sufficient for her. Her work may be divided roughly into two parts, the first associated with her birthplace, Steventon, and the second with Chawton, near Alton. The first group includes *Northanger Abbey* (1818), where the parody of Gothic novels is strongest, but is in the end subordinate to a personal theme, *Sense and Sensibility* (1811), a more serious and ambitious work which contains certain improbabilities and a roughness of texture, and *Pride and Prejudice* (1813), her most sparkling and perhaps her most popular book. *Sense and Sensibility* takes up again with renewed force and insight the old eighteenth-century debate between reason and feeling. Marianne Dashwood, the devotee of sensibility, when unhappy in love considers that she would have failed in her duty if she had not risen from her bed in the morning more in need of rest than when she lay down. She is both punished and rewarded in the end with a contented marriage to a steady, middle-aged colonel, whom she had earlier considered too old to marry at all. Her sister, Elinor, the "sensible" one, is revealed in the end as having a greater power of feeling, a greater capacity to love than her more exuberant sister. Here, and with greater subtlety in her later masterpieces, *Mansfield Park* (1814) and *Persuasion* (1818), Jane Austen with devastating and utterly convincing brilliance undercuts the conventional romantic distinction between romantic feeling and respectable insensibility. It is her correct and dutiful heroines, like Fanny Price and Anne Elliot, who love most, and who resist most stubbornly inducements to worldly-wise and profitable marriages. Characters who make the greatest parade of intense feeling, whether sincere, like Marianne Dashwood, or hypocritical, like Mrs. Elton in *Emma* (1816), are revealed in the end as limited by the shallowness of their feeling.

Jane Austen is the supreme realist, not only in her portrayal of society, but also in the more important sense that true self-knowledge, the ruthless destruction of all illusion, is the goal of her heroines. The process of education (partly self-education) is for them painful, for us both comic and deeply impressive, as well as being full of surprises. *Emma,* generally considered her greatest book, shows us this process at its most intricate, testing, and surprising. The effect is sharp and bracing as well as comic. It would be an insensitive reader who did not have twinges of self-criticism in reading Jane Austen; and we see why Henry James said that in reading her he always thought of a bright spring day with a cold east wind. True enough in general, however, this does not apply to her last great book, *Persuasion.* Her health was failing when she wrote it, and it is not as finely finished as the earlier books. But it remains her most personal and her most moving work, in which the general effect (and many of the actual scenes) are autumnal. Anne Elliot, to some tastes her most attractive heroine, is consumed with an apparently hopeless passion for a man she has rejected in youth through over-prudent advice from her dead mother's closest friend. The book has less humour and fewer memorable characters than the others, but the lack is abundantly compensated by intensity and concentration of feeling. To adapt Fielding on *Clarissa,* it is hard to read the end of *Persuasion* without tears.

The 1820's and early 1830's are a slack period in the history of the novel. Scott was writing hard, but all his best work, except *Redgauntlet,* is early and prior to 1820. Bulwer-Lytton, a writer of almost no literary merit, was popular in the 1820's, and works like *Pelham* (1828) are a comforting reminder that the worthless much-adulated best-seller is no new phenomenon in our century. The novel comes to life again with Dickens, who became famous about 1836, with the *Sketches by Boz* and *Pickwick Papers,* and who remained immensely popular until his sudden death in the middle of writing *Edwin Drood* in 1870. Dickens is a lasting object lesson in the pitfalls of contemporary criticism. He was immensely popular, he was vulgar, opinionated and ignorant, self-centred and vain. He wrote uproarious farce at times, and at times one-sided satire. Everybody read him, but few saw in him the great classic of the age. Indeed, the deeper currents of his work took several generations to discern; Lord Acton was typical of the high Victorian intellectual elite when he wrote that he was *ashamed* to remember how much more often he returned to Dickens than to George Eliot. No doubt a Jacobean of similar intellectual standing would have preferred Ben Jonson to Shakespeare. Dickens, like Shakespeare, is a perennial corrective to the stock idea that the great classic writer starves in a garret, and is recognized only by posterity. In some cases it is so, but here we have to reckon with the popular idol whose true greatness appears only gradually. Dickens's work can be loosely divided into two periods, before and after *Dombey and Son* (1848). (Dickens's habit of publishing in monthly parts over a period of up to two years added to public excitement, but led also to some very rapid and careless writing.) In the early period we have the reckless exuberance of an untutored genius, fantastic in comedy (or often farce), intensely melodramatic in "serious passages." Plot may either be neglected altogether, as in *Pickwick,* or simplistically over-insistent, as in *Oliver Twist* (1838). One is startled, overwhelmed by the sheer vitality, variety, and abundance. As George Orwell said, we know more about Mrs. Harris, a character who does not even exist than about many of the leading characters of ordinary novelists. Dickens's personal feelings and prejudices mingle freely with the creative flow. *The Old Curiosity Shop* (1840), for instance, is a prolonged and at times very sentimental meditation on death, occasioned by the loss of his beloved sister-in-law, Mary Hogarth. In *Martin Chuzzlewit* (1844), probably on the whole the best work of the early period, he incorporates his own hard feelings about America and the pirating of his books there, owing to defective copyright laws. But in characters like Crummles (*Nicholas Nickleby,* 1839), Pecksniff, and Mrs. Gamp (*Martin Chuzzlewit*) we feel the grip of the master. If Dickens had not existed we could no more replace them than we could find a substitute for Falstaff in the absence of Shakespeare. The early books give a curiously mixed impression of unique creative genius and childish petulance.

In the later period, Dickens has grown up; like many great men he was a slow developer, despite his precocity. The craftsmanship is much surer and for the first time the books seem to have a single continuing theme despite the undiminished variety. The later books are often just as funny – Mr. F.'s aunt in the generally grave and sombre *Little Dorrit* (1857) is as memorable a character of non-sensical farce as is to be found in our literature – but the humorous and serious passages no longer seem to be placed together at random. The profusion of Dickens is such that even on what is to him a subordinate topic, such as education, he can provide a variety of impressions which specialists would work in vain to rival. The old Goldsmithian village school of *The Old Curiosity Shop* leads on to the brilliantly portrayed genteel classical cram-shop, Dr. Blimber's academy in *Dombey and Son*, and the harsh utilitarian factory of facts in *Hard Times* (1854) and the pitifully ineffective dame-school of *Great Expectations* (1861). Highly-coloured though the pictures are, historians return to them again and again as the most revealing of contemporary portraits. George Santayana said that when people told him that Dickens exaggerated he thought they could have no eyes and ears. Perhaps this is not strictly true of the earliest Dickens, but of his vintage works, or of the best parts of them, it emphatically is.

There will never be agreement on the question of which is Dickens's best book. His own favourite was the partly autobiographical *David Copperfield* (1850) which, as it seems to me, he overrated. *Bleak House* (1853) is perhaps the richest and most various, and is unified by the persistent theme of the imperfections of the English legal system. But in it he dwelt, as he said, "upon the romantic side of familiar things," and the plot has fanciful and melodramatic elements. *Little Dorrit* is my personal favourite; it is a wonderfully detached recreation in depth of something originally very personal to himself, the effect of the Marshalsea – the old debtors' prison in which his father was incarcerated in 1822 – upon its inmates and their families. Those with an austere classical taste will be likely to prefer *Great Expectations* which is the most economical and coherent of his major works, involving a profound meditation on the nature of wealth, gratitude, and obligation. And I for one find no falling-off at all in his last completed work, *Our Mutual Friend* (1865), which is, among other things, a refutation of George Saintsbury's complaint that Dickens could not draw a gentleman.

In following Dickens to the end of his career we have anticipated. The Brontës take us back to the 1840's, and to a remote rural world which makes it an effort of imagination to see them as contemporaries with the bustling city life of *Dombey and Son*. The accident that three sisters were writing novels in the same household near a bleak and lonely moorland has been the cause of some critical confusion. In reality, only one of the Brontës, Emily, is a major figure in our literature, and she is perhaps the most purely original and irreplaceable, though not the greatest, of all our novelists. In her only novel, *Wuthering Heights* (1847), she achieved an extraordinary combined triumph of genius and craftsmanship. Dying at the age of thirty, she had little time to learn, but the book reads like the work of an experienced professional. However, for its readers, considerations of craft soon become secondary in the excitement of a story which is the perfect artistic equivalent of a weird but strong, coherent, and in a way appealing view of life. Emily Brontë does nothing less than challenge the whole traditional view of the nature of love previously accepted both in literature and in life. The love of Heathcliff and Catherine Earnshaw is far stronger than any normal human bond, marital, sexual, or filial. If it can be characterized in ordinary terms at all, it is an immeasurably intensified version of the love of brother and sister. (The two are not related by blood, but have been brought up together.) For the first time, perhaps, since Shakespeare, ghosts are used with the maximum of serious literary effect and the minimum of cheap thrills. Emily Brontë was also a poet, perhaps our finest woman poet, and we find that the usual purposes of the novel are being effortlessly combined with quite other ones, which, but for the actual success of this work, might well be thought incompatible. We are aware at the same time of a particular society, rough, remote, semi-barbarous, and of a cosmic conflict which requires from us – and successfully obtains from most readers – a complete suspension of disbelief in an alien system of thought and values. And yet, the book is a true novel, not a fantastic poetic drama, like (say) Hardy's *The Dynasts*. For it has the true novelistic quality of pursuing the logic of events to their end in a real social setting. After Heathcliff's death the normal workaday world, normal love and marriage, are still there and the representatives of the next generation inherit a world not in the end much altered by the cataclysms previously endured. Of Charlotte Brontë it is a little embarrassing to speak. The most overrated of our novelists, not even excepting Fielding, she found in *Jane Eyre* (1847) the trusty formula that has brought satisfaction to the bank managers of innumerable writers in women's magazines. *Villette* (1853) has greater merit, and moments of genuine intensity, but is marred by its author's solipsistic view of the world, and her narrow nationalistic and protestant prejudices. For those who easily resist her spell, the little read work *The Professor* (1857) has more appeal, being quieter, more balanced, and more coherent. Anne Brontë would probably have been forgotten if she had not shared her sisters' name.

With Disraeli we are back in the novel of ideas. He uses a graver version of the method of Peacock, and makes it topical in the rapidly changing world of the 1840's. Disraeli was as much an amateur novelist as he was a professional politician. He wrote with ease and zest ("When I want to read a novel, I write one"). In *Coningsby* (1844) and *Sybil* (1845) we are treated to a dazzling display of political ideas, loosely but agreeably linked to an improbable plot. And in the latter book, particularly, he inaugurated a new type of novel in which Dickens, Mrs. Gaskell, and Charles Kingsley were to be his followers. The Industrial Revolution had been proceeding for more than two generations when *Sybil* was published; but it had hitherto been the great absentee from the tradition of the novel (apart from one attempt by Mrs. Trollope in 1840). Disraeli's visit to industrial Lancashire was brief, but his apprehensions were very quick, and he supplemented his visit with a close study of blue books. Novel readers, mostly middle-class, and often living in the south of England, became aware of a new, exciting, and terrible world, of hunger and violence and technological change in which a new industrial world was being forged, not just for England but for the western world. Disraeli's books, with Kingsley's *Alton Locke* (1850), Dickens's *Hard Times,* and Mrs. Gaskell's *Mary Barton* (1848) and *North and South* (1855), must have led many sober citizens to question the prevailing free trade orthodoxy, which had presented, with grotesque inappropriateness, the findings of "science." These books and their authors differed in many ways, but they were at one in their refusal to accept a mechanical system as the last word on a human question, and in their perception of the folly of neglecting feeling as a potent factor in human affairs. Mrs. Gaskell was the only one of these writers who lived in the industrial north, and her picture has fine shades that the others lack.

However, Disraeli was to write other kinds of novel as well. His society or "silver spoon" novels are of little interest, but in *Tancred* (1847), especially its first part, he made witty comments on the scientific controversies of the day, and in *Lothair* (1870) he wrote a gripping though fantastic account of the English Catholic Revival (to which his political allegiance had made him more hostile than he had been in 1840's) and of the struggle for Italian unity. In *Endymion* (1880), actually written when he was Prime Minister, he produced a quieter and more satisfying meditation on the practical processes of politics, and on the hidden influence of women in an officially male preserve. A fictional version of the career of Lord Palmerston is neatly blended with his own unrivalled experience and expertise to make a book of unusual charm.

The Victorian novel, in general, has a strongly realistic tone; and there is only one major figure, after Disraeli, who proceeds without regard to the cause and effect of the workaday world. This is Lewis Carroll. In his power of creating an entire world of fantasy with its own logic he rivals Swift. But where Swift implies a comment on the human world as it is, Carroll is concerned more with abstract ideas. At the same time his two *Alice* books have deep psychological roots, and attain a kind of inner inevitability which is beyond the reach of more deliberately designed intellectual fictions, like those of Swift or Peacock. He shares with Swift the rare distinction of having composed a children's and an adult classic in the same work; and his puns have a crazy charm which suggests that they too have deep roots.

Despite her distinguished contribution to the industrial novel, Mrs. Gaskell's greatest strength lies in her domestic stories, especially *Cranford,* which first appeared in Dickens's journal *Household Words* in 1851–53, and *Wives and Daughters,* a long book not quite completed at the time of her sudden death in 1865. In the subtlety of her perception of the minutae of feeling and of social life and the moving quality of her understanding of feminine roles she is second only to Jane Austen. Her comedy is more genial than Jane Austen's but at times almost as intelligent. The logic of feelings and the logic of events are beautifully intertwined; causation has that elusive, complex gossamer quality that we find in our experience of it – very different from the heavy march of events in the average "plot." In Cynthia Kirkpatrick, she gives us perhaps the finest and fullest study in all our literature of the motivation of a wayward, capricious, and apparently irrational girl. Earlier in *Ruth* (1853) she had attempted with honesty and insight and partial success to deal with the intractable problem of the so-called "fallen woman." There are greater Victorian novelists, but few (perhaps only one, Anthony Trollope) who ring so true, who are so entirely free from posturing and self-deception, whose every sentence is a serious attempt to express a sensible thought.

In his lifetime, Thackeray was often compared to and contrasted with Dickens. The comparison, in the longer perspective of history, cannot be sustained. Much of Thackeray's best work is occasional, and many chapters in his novels are those of an agreeable though often prolix essayist rather than of a creative artist. He wrote fluent, attractive English prose, rising occasionally to true eloquence. A few scenes, like the one in *Henry Esmond* where the hero visits his mother's grave as an adult for the first time, never having known her in life, are hauntingly memorable. But Thackeray lacks the creative power, the inventiveness, and the piercing wisdom of the great artist. He is a student of manners, often, rather than of life. His amateurishness is less attractive than Disraeli's; Disraeli, after all, had a busy political life, while Thackeray was lazy, and felt a certain scepticism about the value of writing at all. His finest book, which towers above all his other work, is *Vanity Fair* (1848). It is notable especially for its subtle and moving treatment of time. He allows himself a whole generation so that the consequences of passions and hatreds, of sudden impulses and crazy quarrels, can have time to work to their distant unforeseen conclusions. And he has new things to say about the well-worn theme of the relation between an aristocracy and a merchant class hungry for social respect. Also, his meditative, sceptical mind brooded in an interesting and fruitful way on the novelist's accepted stereotypes of the good and bad woman, and showed that the motives of each might be different from what his readers thought. Though he died early, Thackeray gives us an odd sense of being played out long before. In books like *Pendennis* (1849–50) and the unfinished *Philip* (1862), he was constantly repeating himself.

With George Eliot, on the other hand, we have a novelist who never ceased to develop and experiment. She came to fiction only when she was approaching forty, and already had a reputation from her periodical writings of a woman of formidable intellectual attainments. She possessed unusually clear and poignant memories of childhood and adolescence, intensified no doubt by a bitter and lasting quarrel with her brother. Her early novels, *Adam Bede* (1859) and *The Mill on the Floss* (1860), have a kind of realistic-pastoral quality, that is, the celebration of an idyllic country landscape does not inhibit sharp realism about human motives. Fine, original, and, at times, moving as they are, they have two weaknesses: an over-literal acceptance of the superficial religious philosophy of Feuerbach, and, in the second book, a hurried melodramatic ending. But she was learning fast about the craft of fiction. In *Felix Holt* (1866), perhaps her most underrated book, she gives a brilliant and moving picture of an ageing woman brooding on the consequences of a long-past adultery, and on the fact that her son, heir to her husband's property, is not her husband's son. In this book, too, in the person of the independent minister, Lyon, we have an excellent example of her strength in what might be called religious sociology. There is rich comedy as well as insight in the scenes where he challenges the Anglican incumbent to a debate on the issues between the different creeds. In *Middlemarch* (1872), her most complex and probably her finest work, she used to fine effect the by now traditional Victorian device of the multiple plot. The book is at the same time a study in depth of the institution of marriage and a revelation of the way ordinary provincial life bears upon any person who is by nature, or who attempts to be, exceptional, in holiness, in scholarship, or in scientific achievement. It is one of the benefits of her intellectual approach that the leading male characters, especially Lydgate and Casaubon, are at least as convincing as the female, so that a number of generally accepted assumptions about women novelists are shattered. In her last novel, *Daniel Deronda*

(1876), she attempted a radical revaluation of the Jewish contribution to history and civilization. Though perhaps not entirely successful, the book certainly shows no falling-off in intellectual vigour, in psychological curiosity, or in narrative appeal. And the work has a particular interest because she analyzed a much-neglected question, the rights and claims of the cast-off mistress who is also the mother of children.

Anthony Trollope was the most prolific, and in some ways the most surprising and elusive, of the Victorian realists. He was devoted to facts, to the reality both of characters and events, and he was not, on the whole, much concerned with ideas. But he had taken to heart Bacon's aphorism that it is in accordance with probability that many improbable things will happen. He is remarkable for his extraordinary fairness, an amazing breadth of sympathy, in which he has perhaps only one equal or superior, Walter Scott. He was very far from being what he has sometimes been hastily proclaimed, "the voice of an epoch." His contemporaries, not least the great novelists, were remarkable for the strength of their feelings and the downright one-sidedness of their opinions. Trollope is kindly and sceptical, anxious to make excuses for everybody, just because he has no illusions about the poor, thin stuff of which ordinary human nature is composed or the extent to which most people depend for the limited decency of their lives upon habit and the good opinion of their neighbours. The Barsetshire novels, beginning with *The Warden* (1855), are his best-known work, but there are profounder and more original insights in later works, especially the political series centred round the Irish member, Phineas Finn, and the English aristocrat, Plantaganet Palliser. He is able to combine a deep meditation on the causes of peaceful political change, and the influence of the aristocratic Whig mentality on this, with one of the finest studies of marriage in our literature. Palliser and his wife, Lady Glencora, have married as people of their class do marry, for money and position, and also to escape from earlier entanglements. They are not apparently well-suited, he being cool, judicious, and devoted to public work, she passionate and wilful. Yet the gradual process by which they learn to understand and trust each other, pursued through several volumes, never fails to be gripping and is often surprising; and there is poignancy in the last of the series, *The Duke's Children* (1880), in which, after his wife's sudden death, the duke is confronted with three grown-up children whom he hardly knows, each presenting a different intractable problem. To illustrate Trollope's versatility and unexpectedness I would name *He Knew He Was Right* (1869) and *Mr. Scarborough's Family* (1883). In each the stage is held by a man of property and powerful character who is more or less mad, and both the psychological states and the practical consequences for others are depicted with masterly and ruthless insight.

With the death of George Eliot in 1880 and Trollope in 1882, the high Victorian novel is over, and a new phase begins, in which the novel is less concerned simply with society and character, but becomes more philosophically questing, more symbolical, more poetical even. The great names here are Meredith, who overlaps the earlier period in time, Hardy, and Henry James. Before discussing them we can briefly mention others, Surtees, our greatest sporting writer whose comedy is extraordinarily astrigent and fresh, Stevenson, a writer of real talent who never found his true medium, and Gissing, the English novel's nearest approach to the world of French naturalism. As an imitator of Scott, Stevenson is not very convincing. He is at his best, perhaps, either in a rollicking boys' story, like *Treasure Island* (1883), or in the ingenious, mannered, fantastic style of *New Arabian Nights* (1882). Here he recalls the gripping interest of plot shown earlier in the high Victorian period by Dickens's friend Wilkie Collins, who in *The Woman in White* (1860) and *Armadale* (1866) showed that melodrama conducted with perfect craftsmanship can almost attain to the status of high art.

Meredith had an immense reputation among late Victorian intellectuals, and his books have a wit and sparkle that owe something to his father-in-law, Peacock. There is no doubt about his intelligence or his versatility; yet it is not quite easy to believe that his early reputation was not inflated. He often attempts a kind of conflation of the novel of ideas à la Peacock and the realistic novel of the 1860's and 1870's. The marriage is not altogether a happy one, and the style often strikes us as mannered. Opinions will differ about the relative merits of his different styles. My personal preference would be for his more sober and realistic manner in books like *Evan Harrington* (1861) and *Beauchamp's Career* (1875). But in difficult and highly mannered works like *One of Our Conquerors* (1891) he anticipates some of the more experimental works of our own century.

Of the lesser talents of the latter part of the century, there is space to mention only two. William Hale White, sometimes known by the name of his most famous character, Mark Rutherford, was an exact and sensitive observer of dissenting communities, and rivals George Eliot in his comprehension of protestant conscience and intellectual difficulties of protestant faith. Mrs. Humphry Ward, a niece of Matthew Arnold, brought life to the dry abstractions of her uncle's theological writings, especially in her most famous work, *Robert Elsmere* (1888). She successfully attempts a wider religious scene than White, and she conveys very well the intellectual confusion characteristic of those educated late Victorians who could not finally commit themselves to either of the two logical alternatives, Catholicism or unbelief.

Finally, we have two great names. Thomas Hardy liked to think that he was a poet who wrote fiction for money; and he to some extent proved his sincerity by writing much poetry and almost no fiction in the last thirty years of his long life. All the same it is as a novelist that he is chiefly remembered; but we are never inclined to forget that they are a poet's novels. What holds us is the general, overmastering vision, the cosmic sweep in time and space, which easily triumphs over incredible coincidences and sometimes wooden dialogue. Hardy is the most visual of our great novelists, and, though he aims at a cosmic effect, he needs a recognizable locality as a basis. He is earthy, not in the least in the sense of coarse, but because it is impossible to read him without feeling the heaths and hills, the ancient barrows and earthworks of his native Dorsetshire, to be at least as real as any human presence. He is famous for pessimism, and most of his plots take a tragic turn, but except perhaps in the bitter and over-personal *Jude the Obscure* (1896) he cannot be called depressing. Sometimes, as in Marty South's lament at the end of *The Woodlanders* (1887), he rises to an austere classical dignity of pure and profound feeling that is comforting and even exhilarating rather than depressing. An uncertain craftsman, he produced no perfect work. More than any other of our great novelists (except perhaps Dickens) he requires to be read in the spirit in which he wrote; otherwise what is beautiful and touching may easily be rejected as, in common-sense terms, absurd. His symbolism seems to be only half-deliberate, but is nevertheless, at times, profound. Certain passages, such as the gambling by the light of fireflies in *The Return of the Native* (1878) or Sergeant Troy's sword flashing round Bathsheba in *Far from the Madding Crowd* (1874), haunt the memory in defiance of any rational objections. He came nearest to mastering the logic of events and presenting a single, coherent story in *The Mayor of Casterbridge* (1886). But generations of readers have found *Tess of the d'Urbervilles* (1891), despite its obvious faults, his most memorable and moving work.

With Henry James we are in a different, cosmopolitan world, the world of the highly cultivated American, to whom all Europe is an endlessly subtle and fascinating imaginary museum. His predecessors in the novel had been, for the most part, thoroughly English, and some of the greatest of them thoroughly insular. They despised or ignored literary theories. James not only knew personally the great contemporary figures of the continental novel, such as Turgenev and Flaubert, but he was convinced that the novel was a great literary form that would repay the most detailed critical and theoretical study. Yet his own attachment to England was strong, and in a notable passage of his journal, after lunching with the best literary society in Paris, he wrote of his conviction of the immense superiority of George Eliot to each of the men with whom he had just been talking. His expatriate English patriotism led him to take out British citizenship between the outbreak of war in 1914 and his death early in 1916.

His voluminous works constitute a lengthy and profound meditation on the "international theme" – the relation of America to Europe. He was more influenced, perhaps, than he knew by the New England puritanism which surrounded him in childhood. But he was very conscious of being influenced by the treasures of European culture and by the casual self-assurance of an English upper-class in the years when the social order afforded them an intelligible role. He wrote often, but not exclusively, about the rich. One of his most interesting heroes, Hyacinth in *The Princess Casamassima* (1886), is a deprived product of the London streets. James's style, light and easy in early works like *Daisy Miller* (1879) and *The Portrait of a Lady* (1881), becomes more and more intense, syntactically idiosyncratic, and, eventually, highly obscure. Some will find his great period in the comparatively simple but fresh and highly intelligent books of the 1880's; other will prefer the more difficult and symbolic works at the turn of the century, *The Wings of The Dove* (1902) and *The Golden Bowl* (1904). In each the theme of betrayal invades the super-civilized high social world. The emphasis is on the spiritual effects of betrayal on the traitor and on the generosity of those who can forgive treachery and keep their love unimpaired. Aesthetic sublety does not tempt James to blur moral categories. He succeeds in recreating the early Victorian heroine; Milly Theale and Maggie Verver are fully instructed about the wickedness of the world, but they achieve a deeper forgiveness than the innocent could plumb. In Henry James, the old, often conflicting aims of the novel, instruction, suspense, and aesthetic delight are finely reconciled. And, as the first great novelist in England who was also a distinguished critic of the novel, he prepared the way for the achievements of the twentieth century.

READING LIST

1. Bibliographies, handbooks, etc.

Block, A., *The English Novel 1740–1850: A Catalogue,* 1939, revised edition, 1961.

Black, F. G., *The Epistolary Novel in the Late Eighteenth Century: A Descriptive and Bibliographical Study,* 1940.

Summers, Montague, *A Gothic Bibliography,* 1941.

Carter, J., and Michael Sadleir, *Victorian Fiction,* 1947.

Cordasco, F., *The Eighteenth-Century Novel,* 1950.

Sadleir, Michael, *XIX Century Fiction: A Bibliographical Record,* 2 vols., 1951.

Leclaire, L., *A General Analytical Bibliography of the Regional Novelists of the British Isles 1800–1950,* 1954.

Bell, I. F., and D. B., *The English Novel 1578–1956: A Checklist of Twentieth-Century Criticisms,* 1959.

McBurney, W. H., *A Check-List of English Prose Fiction 1700–39,* 1960.

Stevenson, Lionel, *Victorian Fiction: A Guide to Research,* 1964.

Carter, J., *Victorian Detective Fiction: A Catalogue of the Collection Made by Dorothy Glover and Graham Greene,* 1966.

Beasley, Jerry C., *A Checklist of Prose Fiction Published in England 1740–1749,* 1972.

Dyson, A. E., *The English Novel,* 1974.

McNutt, Dan J., *The Eighteenth-Century Gothic Novel: An Annotated Bibliography of Criticism and Selected Texts,* 1975.

2. General Histories

Lubbock, Percy, *The Craft of Fiction,* 1921.

Muir, Edwin, *The Structure of the Novel,* 1928.

Baker, E. A., *The History of the English Novel,* vols. 3–9, 1930–39

Wagenknecht, Edward, *Cavalcade of the English Novel,* 1943, revised edition, 1954.

Liddell, Robert, *A Treatise on the Novel,* 1946.

Pritchett, V. S., *The Living Novel*, 1946.
Leavis, F. R., *The Great Tradition*, 1948.
Neill, S. D., *A Short History of the English Novel*, 1951.
Kettle, Arnold, *An Introduction to the English Novel*, 2 vols., 1951–53.
Van Ghent, Dorothy, *The English Novel: Form and Structure*, 1953.
Allen, Walter, *The English Novel: A Short Critical History*, 1954.
Tillyard, E. M. W., *The Epic Strain in the English Novel*, 1958.
Martin, H. C., *Style in Prose Fiction*, 1959.
Stevenson, Lionel, *The English Novel: A Panorama*, 1961.
Booth, Wayne C., *The Rhetoric of Fiction*, 1961.
Gregor, Ian, and B. Nicholas, *The Moral and the Story*, 1962.
Hardy, Barbara, *The Appropriate Form: An Essay on the Novel*, 1965.

3. Topics, themes, short periods, etc.
Cazamian, Louis, *Le Roman Social*, 1903; translated by Martin Fido as *The Social Novel in England 1830–1850*, 1973.
Tompkins, J. M. S., *The Popular Novel in England 1770–1800*, 1932.
Leavis, Q. D., *Fiction and the Reading Public*, 1932.
Cecil, David, *Early Victorian Novelists*, 1934, revised edition, 1964.
Rosa, M. W., *The Silver-Fork School: Novels of Fashion Preceding Vanity Fair*, 1936.
Shepperson, A. S., *The Novel in Motley: A History of the Burlesque Novel in English*, 1936.
Wright, W. F., *Sensibility in English Prose Fiction 1760–1814*, 1937.
Summers, Montague, *The Gothic Quest*, 1938.
Daiches, David, *The Novel and the Modern World*, 1940, revised edition, 1960.
Bentley, Phyllis, *The English Regional Novel*, 1942.
Tillotson, Kathleen, *Novels of the Eighteen-Forties*, 1954.
McKillop, Alan D., *The Early Masters of English Fiction*, 1956.
Thomson, P., *The Victorian Heroine*, 1956.
Watt, Ian, *The Rise of the Novel: Studies in Defoe, Richardson, and Fielding*, 1957.
Stang, Richard, *The Theory of the Novel in England 1850–70*, 1959.
Flanagan, T., *The Irish Novelists 1800–50*, 1959.
Mayo, R. D., *The English Novel in the Magazines 1740–1815*, 1962.
Hollingsworth, K., *The Newgate Novel 1830–47*, 1963.
James, Louis, *Fiction for the Working Man 1830–50*, 1963.
Sacks, S., *Fiction and the Shape of Belief*, 1964.
Spector, E. D., editor, *Essays on the 18th-Century Novel*, 1964.
Alter, Richard, *Rogue's Progress: Studies in the Picaresque Novel*, 1964.
Harvey, W. J., *Character and the Novel*, 1965.
Steeves, H. R., *Before Jane Austen: The Shaping of the English Novel in the Eighteenth Century*, 1965.
Graham, Kenneth, *English Criticism of the Novel 1865–1900*, 1965.
Karl, Frederick R., *An Age of Fiction: The Nineteenth-Century British Novel*, 1965.
Carrier, E. J., *Fiction in Public Libraries 1876–1900*, 1965.
Tillotson, Geoffrey and Kathleen, *Mid-Victorian Studies*, 1965.
Spearman, D., *The Novel and Society*, 1966.
Lodge, David, *Language of Fiction: Essays in Criticism and Verbal Analysis of the English Novel*, 1966.
Bradbrook, F.W., *Jane Austen and Her Predecessors*, 1966.
Donovan, R. A., *Shaping Vision: Imagination in the English Novel from Defoe to Dickens*, 1966.
Day, R. A., *Told in Letters*, 1966.
Howard, D., and others, *Tradition and Tolerance in Nineteenth-Century Fiction*, 1966.
Marcus, Steven, *The Other Victorians: A Study of Sexuality and Pornography in Mid-Nineteenth-Century England*, 1966.

Paulson, R., *Satire and the Novel in Eighteenth-Century England*, 1967.
Mack, Maynard, editor *Imagined Worlds: Essays on Some English Novels and Novelists in Memory of John Butt*, 1968.
Kermode, Frank, *The Sense of an Ending: Studies in the Theory of Fiction*, 1969.
Richetti, John, *Popular Fiction Before Richardson: Narrative Patterns 1700–39*, 1969.
Williams, Ioan, *The Novel and Romance 1700–1800: A Documentary Record*, 1969.
Colby, Vineta, *The Singular Anomaly: Women Novelists of the Nineteenth Century*, 1970.
Griest, Guinevere L., *Mudie's Circulating Library and the Victorian Novel*, 1970.
Harvey, J. R., *Victorian Novelists and Their Illustrators*, 1970.
Preston, J., *The Created Self: The English Novel Before Richardson*, 1970.
Watt, Ian, editor, *The Victorian Novel: Modern Essays in Criticism*, 1971.
Faber, Richard, *Proper Stations: Class in Victorian Fiction*, 1971.
Benedikz, B. S., editor, *On the Novel: A Present for Walter Allen on His 60th Birthday*, 1971.
Fleishman, Avrom, *The English Historical Novel: Walter Scott to Virginia Woolf*, 1971.
Lucas, John, editor, *Literature and Politics in the Nineteenth Century*, 1971.
Keating, P. J., *The Working Classes in Victorian Fiction*, 1971.
Platz-Waury, Elke, editor, *English Theories of the Novel* (vol. 3: nineteenth century), 1972.
Kettle, Arnold, editor, *The Nineteenth-Century Novel: Critical Essays and Documents*, 1972.
Collins, R. G., editor, *The Novel and Its Changing Form: Essays*, 1972.
Goldknopf, David, *The Life of the Novel*, 1972.
Gill, Richard, *Happy Rural Seat: The English Country House and the Literary Imagination*, 1972.
Goodin, George, editor, *The English Novel in the Nineteenth Century*, 1972.
Gose, Elliott B., Jr., *Imagination Indulged: The Irrational in the Nineteenth-Century Novel*, 1972.
Brooks, Douglas, *Number and Pattern in the Eighteenth-Century Novel*, 1973.
Mills, Nicolaus, *American and English Fiction in the Nineteenth Century: An Anti-Genre Critique and Comparison*, 1973.
Simmons, James C., *The Novelist as Historian: Essays on the Victorian Historical Novel*, 1973.
Martin, Robert B., *The Triumph of Wit: A Study of Victorian Comic Theory*, 1974.
Brissenden, R. F., *Virtue in Distress: Studies in the Novel of Sentiment from Richardson to Sade*, 1974.
Buckley, J. H., *Season of Youth: The Bildungsroman from Dickens to Golding*, 1974.
Williams, Ioan, *The Realist Novel in England: A Study in Development*, 1974.
Beer, Patricia, *Reading, I Married Him: A Study of the Women Characters of Jane Austen, Charlotte Brontë, Elizabeth Gaskell, and George Eliot*, 1974.
Colby, Vineta, *Yesterday's Women: Domestic Realism in the English Novel*, 1974.
Cunningham, Valentine, *Everywhere Spoken Against: Dissent in the Victorian Novel*, 1975.
Rothstein, Eric, *Systems of Order and Inquiry in Later Eighteenth-Century Fiction*, 1975.
Calder, Jenni, *Women and Marriage in Victorian Fiction*, 1976.
Kelly, Gary, *The English Jacobin Novel 1780–1805*, 1976.
Spacks, Patricia Meyer, *Imagining a Self: Autobiography and Novel in Eighteenth-Century England*, 1976

4. Anthologies of primary works

McBurney, W. H., editor, *Four Before Richardson: Selected English Novels 1720–27*, 1963.
Seymour-Smith, Martin, editor, *A Cupful of Tears: Sixteen Victorian Novelettes*, 1965.
Gifford, Douglas, editor, *Scottish Short Stories 1800–1900*, 1971.
Wolff, Robert Lee, editor, *Strange Stories and Other Explorations in Victorian Fiction*, 1971.
Keating, P. J., editor, *Working-Class Stories of the 1890's*, 1971.
Haining, Peter, editor, *Great British Tales of Terror: Gothic Stories of Horror and Romance 1765–1840*, 1972.
Bayley, Peter, editor, *Loves and Deaths: Novelists' Tales of the Nineteenth Century*, 1972.

AINSWORTH, William Harrison. English. Born in Manchester, 4 February 1805. Educated at Manchester Grammar School; articled to a Manchester solicitor, 1821–24; subsequently studied law in London, 1824–26. Married Anne Frances Ebers in 1826; three daughters. Publisher, in London, 1826–28; visited Switzerland and Italy, 1830; successful as a novelist from 1834; also, Editor, *Bentley's Miscellany*, London, 1839–41; Editor and Publisher, *Ainsworth's Magazine*, London, 1842–54, *The New Monthly Magazine*, London, 1845–70, and *Bentley's Miscellany*, 1854–68. *Died 3 January 1882.*

PUBLICATIONS

Fiction

December Tales, with others.   1823.
The Boetian.   1824.
Sir John Chiverton, with J. P. Aston.   1826.
Rookwood.   1834.
Crichton.   1837; revised edition, 1849; as *The Admirable Crichton,* 1927.
Jack Sheppard.   1839.
The Tower of London.   1840.
Guy Fawkes; or, The Gunpowder Treason.   1841.
Old Saint Paul's : A Tale of the Plague and the Fire.   1841.
The Miser's Daughter.   1842.
Windsor Castle.   1843.
Saint James's; or, The Court of Queen Anne.   1844.
James the Second; or, The Revolution of 1688.   1848.
The Lancashire Witches.   1849.
The Star-Chamber.   1854.
The Flitch of Bacon; or, The Custom of Dunmow.   1854.
The Spendthrift.   1857.
Mervyn Clitheroe.   1858.
Ovingdean Grange.   1860.
The Constable of the Tower.   1861.
The Lord Mayor of London; or, City Life in the Last Century.   1862.
Cardinal Pole; or, The Days of Philip and Mary.   1863.
John Law the Projector.   1864.
The Spanish Match; or, Charles Stuart at Madrid.   1865.
Auriol; or, The Elixir of Life.   1865.
The Constable de Bourbon.   1866.
Old Court.   1867.
Myddleton Pomfret.   1868.
Hilary St. Ives.   1870.
The South-Sea Bubble.   1871.
Talbot Harland.   1871.
Tower Hill.   1871.
Boscobel; or, The Royal Oak.   1872.
The Good Old Times: The Story of the Manchester Rebels of '45:   1873; as *The Manchester Rebels of the Fatal '45,* 1874.
Merry England; or, Nobles and Serfs.   1874.
The Goldsmith's Wife.   1875.
Preston Fight; or, The Insurrection of 1715.   1875.
Chetwynd Calverley.   1876.

The Leaguer of Lathom.   1876.
The Fall of Somerset.   1877.
Beatrice Tyldesley.   1878.
Beau Nash; or, Bath in the Eighteenth Century.   1879.
Stanley Brereton.   1881.

Verse

Poems by Cheviot Tichburn.   1822; as *The Maid's Revenge, and A Summer Evening's Tale, with Other Poems;* 1823; as *Works of Cheviot Tichburn,* 1825.
Monody on the Death of John Philip Kemble.   1823.
A Summer Evening Tale.   1825.
Letters from Cockney Lands.   1826.
May Fair.   1827.
Ballads, Romantic, Fantastical, and Humorous.   1855; revised edition, 1872.
The Combat of the Thirty, from a Breton Lay of the Fourteenth Century.   1859.

Other

Consideration on the Best Means of Affording Immediate Relief to the Operative Classes in the Manufacturing Districts.   1826.

Editor, *Modern Chivalry; or, A New Orlando Furioso,* by Catherine Gore.   1843.

Bibliography: *A Bibliographical Catalogue of the Published Novels and Ballads of Ainsworth* by Harold Locke, 1925.

Reading List: *Ainsworth and His Friends* by S. M. Ellis, 2 vols., 1911; *The Newgate Novel* by K. Hollingsworth, 1963; *Ainsworth* by George J. Worth, 1972.

*   *   *

Early in a long career, William Harrison Ainsworth established himself as one of the most popular Victorian novelists, responding to and helping to shape the nineteenth-century taste for historical, Gothic, and rogue fiction. His best work is to be found in such books as *Rookwood, Jack Sheppard, The Tower of London, Old Saint Paul's,* and *Windsor Castle,* but he went on wiriting, to diminishing acclaim, for nearly four more decades, finally producing forty-one novels.

Ainsworth often wrote in haste, and he lacked some of the chief artistic endowments of his major contemporaries. But the best of his novels still make rewarding reading. Each confronts the reader with a crowded, contentious, self-contained fictional world of great vitality, in the process teaching us much about the historical period it treats, and also about our own age – and ourselves. He was especially skillful at depicting man's perpetual craving for power. How power is won and, once won, how it is exercised were subjects to which he returned time and again. But Ainsworth also showed how loss of power, over oneself or others, can bring one to ruin: a very painful sort of ruin, generally, because he was under no illusion about the charity and mercy that man extends to his fellows.

Especially in his historical novels, Ainsworth demonstrates a remarkable fascination with the pomp and pageantry of court and castle. But it is clear that these are merely the outward ornaments of a world that is cruel and violent at the core, a harsh fact that seems to make it all the more urgent to retain what we can of convention and ceremonial and what little there may be of human compassion. More than the general run of nineteenth-century novelists, Ainsworth recognized the pervasiveness of the irrational side of human nature and the insistent drives to which it gives rise. Along with his ability to tell a gripping story and bring the past to vivid life, this surprisingly modern awareness gives Ainsworth a strong claim on our attention.

—George J. Worth

AUSTEN, Jane. English. Born in Steventon, near Basingstoke, Hampshire, 16 December 1775. Educated at a school in Reading, and privately. Lived a retired life with her family in Steventon, 1775–1800, Bath, 1801–06, Southampton, 1806–09, and Chawton, Hampshire, 1809–17. *Died 18 July 1817.*

PUBLICATIONS

Collections

Works, edited by R. W. Chapman. 6 vols., 1923–54.
Letters, edited by R. W. Chapman. 2 vols., 1932; revised edition, 1952; selection, 1955.
Shorter Works (selections), edited by Richard Church. 1963.

Fiction

Sense and Sensibility. 1811; edited by Claire Lamont, 1970.
Pride and Prejudice. 1813; edited by F. W. Bradbrook, 1975.
Mansfield Park. 1814; edited by John Lucas, 1970.
Emma. 1816; edited by David Lodge, 1971.
Northanger Abbey, and Persuasion. 1818; edited by John Davie, 1971.
Love and Freindship (sic), edited by G. K. Chesterton. 1922.
The Watsons, edited by A. B. Walkley. 1923; edited by Q. D. Leavis, with *Sense and Sensibility,* 1958.
Lady Susan, edited by R. W. Chapman. 1925; edited by Q. D. Leavis, with *Sense and Sensibility,* 1958.
Sanditon: Fragment of a Novel, edited by R. W. Chapman. 1925.
Volume the First, edited by R. W. Chapman. 1933.
Volume the Third, edited by R. W. Chapman. 1951.
Volume the Second, edited by B. C. Southam. 1963.

Other

Three Evening Prayers, edited by W. M. Roth. 1940.

Bibliography: *Austen: A Critical Bibliography* by R. W. Chapman, 1953.

Reading List: *Austen: Facts and Problems* by R. W. Chapman, 1948; *Austen: Irony as Defense and Discovery* by Marvin Mudrick, 1952; *Austen's Novels: A Study in Structure* by Andrew H. Wright, 1953, revised edition, 1964; *Austen's Novels: The Fabric of Dialogue* by H. S. Babb, 1962; *The Novels of Austen* by Robert Liddell, 1963; *Austen: A Collection of Critical Essays* edited by Ian Watt, 1963; *Austen: A Study of Her Artistic Development* by A. Walton Litz, 1965; *Austen: The Six Novels* by W. A. Craik, 1965; *Austen and Her Predecessors* by F. W. Bradbrook, 1966; *Austen: Critical Essays* edited by B. C. Southam, 1968; *Austen* by Douglas Bush, 1975; *Austen, Woman and Writer* by Joan Rees, 1976.

*   *   *

Jane Austen raises in a peculiarly difficult form the question "What do we mean by originality?" How is it that we can say with equal truth that she is one of the most traditional and one of the most original of all our great writers? Indeed, she is traditional in several different senses. First, she has the general assumption that the wisdom of our ancestors is justified in the experience of each generation, and (if he has the wit to see it) of each person. She would have thought any kind of innovation in religion or morality merely foolish. How could anything that was fundamentally true once ever cease to be fundamentally true? She would have thought it quite as absurd to suggest that one day apples would fall off the trees upwards as that truth, honesty, kindness, moderation, or humility could ever be outmoded. Then she was traditional too in the narrower context of English literary culture. She was steeped from early years in the writings of the Augustan classics. She accepted both their appeal to authority and tradition and their appeal to experience. She rejoiced especially in the wise synthesis of tradition and experience achieved by Johnson in his essays. She accepted without questioning the way of life of the very last generation of country squires who were truly local in their interests and concerns, and truly feudal in their social assumptions. Thirty years after her death it is a very different squirearchy that meets us in the pages of the early Victorians. Factories, railways, and Reform had brought irrevocable changes.

She was less completely traditional in her attitude to her predecessors in the art of the novel. She read them eagerly but with discrimination, sometimes with amused contempt, which can be seen not only in *Northanger Abbey* but even more in her earliest adolescent scribblings. But from Richardson, the greatest of her predecessors in fiction, she learnt how minute and subtle were the psychological possibilities open to the novelist, and from her best feminine predecessors that there was no need for the restricted social world of women to be an obstacle to the production of major art.

English literature, even in its Augustan phase, is not characteristically a product of the classical spirit, by which I mean the determination to see life steadily and whole, to understand the causes and consequences of things, and to allow personal tastes and preferences as little influence as possible. The writings of Dryden, Swift, and Johnson are steeped in personal enthusiasms and antipathies. Perhaps we should have to go back as far as Ben Jonson to find a great English writer as detached as Austen from the material of her art. Inevitably, this affected the use she made of her reading of earlier novelists. She delighted in Richardson's psychological minuteness and subtlety, and entirely shared his conviction that the domestic and feminine affords opportunities for art as rich and varied as any offered by the world of public affairs and adventures. But she rejected or did not require the exciting melodrama of his plots, and always maintained a much wider emotional distance from her heroines than he had done from Pamela and Clarissa. She had no need of any artificial excitement. She would have rejected as merely stupid Hardy's idea that unless a novelist has an unusual and exciting tale to tell (like the Ancient Mariner) he had better be silent. It is one of her most basic assumptions that ordinary humdrum daily life contains all the profundities of life, its agonizing dilemmas, its joys and disappointments, its moral dangers, and its spiritual opportunities. Nothing is dull for those who understand; even dulness and stupidity are fascinating to those gifted with the spirit of comedy.

The society of which she writes is well-meaning on the whole, decorous, and corrupt. Its decorousness may tend to mask its corruption. But the corruption is there. In *Mansfield Park*, Sir Thomas Bertram, a dignified and conscientious squire, sees no incongruity at all in selling the family living to pay his son's gambling debts; and when his second son is ordained, there is a general flurry of surprise and self-congratulation on all sides when it is decided that he should actually reside in his parish. No doubt considerations like this led Cardinal Newman, in one of the very few adverse criticisms of Jane Austen that do not merely reveal the limitations of the critic, to complain that she "has not a dream of the high Catholic ethos." Indeed, her moral standards are puzzling, both to those who base their attitudes upon the Sermon on the Mount and to those who are influenced by romantic individualism and hatred of respectable conventions. Her standards are at once moderate and exacting. She has no idea of sanctity or of any extraordinary flights of virtue. But she is ruthless in condemning those who fail to be honest, truthful, responsible, and kind. It never occurs to her that Mr. Knightley need have any higher aspirations than to be a good squire, a generous neighbour, and, in due course, a faithful husband. But nor does it ever occur to her to excuse Emma for being rude to Miss Bates, because she was hot and out of temper, because she did not really understand how much pain she was causing, or for any of the dozen reasons with which most people would try to reduce such an offence to the dimensions of a peccadillo if they had themselves been guilty of it. Jane Austen is at once easygoing and inexorable. And it is noticeable that, comparatively easy of attainment as they may seem to be, her standards do find almost every character wanting. Mr. Knightley is no exception. His normally sound moral judgment is deflected by the jealousy he feels when he imagines that Emma is in love with Frank Churchill. In an amusing and very typical aside we are told that his view of Frank's character changed completely in the half hour during which he discovered that it was he himself that Emma really loved. Similarly, the best and most appealing of all Jane Austen's heroines, Anne Elliot, is caught out when her own obsession with Captain Wentworth leads her to suppose that Lady Russell is watching him too, when in fact she has her eye fixed on an attractive shop window.

Both these failings in characters generally admirable reflect Jane Austen's intense concern with objective truth, which includes both exact self-knowledge and realism about the character and conduct of others. Knightley fails, momentarily, in both, Anne in the second only. Many more examples could be given of this ruthless pursuit of truth and uncompromising criticism of all those, however admirable otherwise, who relax even for a moment their desire to avoid self-deception. This fierce love of truth, this determination to follow it even when it is unpalatable or threatening, is one reason why Jane Austen is a challenging and disturbing writer. Other reasons are her acute sense of comedy which often makes the perceptive reader blush for himself, and her pervasive sense of the limits of human foresight. Many of her characters are clever, but almost all are either self-deceived, or much mistaken in their assessment of events, or both. A careful reading of Jane Austen should be a humbling as well as an exhilarating experience.

The exhilaration will come from the deadly accuracy of her humour and the beautiful exactness of her plots. Every character in the books is an independent being; we never feel, as we often do in the novels even of her greatest Victorian successors, that the character has for the moment become a ventriloquist's dummy. Yet the histories of all these independent beings converge into one grand, simple effect. In her less great books, *Northanger Abbey*, *Pride and Prejudice*, and *Sense and Sensibility*, there are few loose ends; in her greatest, *Emma*, *Mansfield Park*, and *Persuasion*, almost none at all. She is ruthlessly classical on a large scale as on a small. Her sentences do not waste a word and her books do not waste a scene or a character. Her career was short; no more than six years separate her first book from her death at the age of forty-one. But in that time she established beyond question her claim to be one of the two or three greatest English novelists.

—A. O. J. Cockshut

BAGE, Robert. English. Born in Darley, Derbyshire, 29 February 1728. Educated at a common school in Darley; subsequently trained in his father's paper-making business; in later life studied with a private tutor in Birmingham. Married in 1751; three sons. Established a paper mill at Elford, near Tamworth, soon after his marriage, and continued to manage the business until his death; also a partner in an iron manufactory, 1765–79; began writing in 1781. *Died 1 September 1801.*

PUBLICATIONS

Fiction

Mount Henneth. 1782.
Barham Downs. 1784.
The Fair Syrian. 1787.
James Wallace. 1788.
Man As He Is. 1792.
Hermsprong; or, Man As He Is Not. 1796; edited by Vaughan Wilkins, 1951.

*   *   *

If Robert Bage is an underrated novelist it is perhaps his own fault. He pretended that he only turned to novel-writing in middle age in order to satisfy his daughters' demands for new gowns, and then he persisted in turning out at regular intervals novels that were so entertaining that he was bound to be considered merely a talented amateur, working successfully in the vein of Fielding and Smollett. In fact, Bage continued rather than repeated the work of his predecessors in the comic novel tradition, and succeeded in adapting that tradition to the tastes, ideas, issues, and attitudes of the Age of Sensibility and the decades of the French and American Revolutions. Yet Bage was always, though in the best sense, provincial. Far removed from the life of literary London, he had to give his own intellectual and comic vitality to fictional techniques and forms perfected by others, and put them to serving his own interests, ideas, and vision of man and society. For his novels are crammed with references to new developments in science and technology (Bage was a paper manufacturer and member of the Derby Philosophical Society), to English, Irish, American, and French politics, to the philosophical, aesthetic, and religious issues of the day, to the condition of women, and to the standard subjects of social satire – luxury, fashion, "improvement," social climbing, and snobbery. All this Bage cast in the comic novel conventions of his day, coloured with his own tolerant and benevolent outlook on human folly. The seriousness of his work, then, is revealed in its overall unity, just as each of his novels has a unity of tone and theme rather than of plot and construction. And his seriousness is also demonstrated by his continual development and mastery of his chosen repertoire of conventions and techniques, and by his continual adaptation of that repertoire to ever new issues and ideas.

There is a continuous development in skill and scope from *Mount Henneth* to *Man As He Is*, and it is really only *Hermsprong; or, Man As He Is Not*, written after the French Revolution had caused a conservative reaction in England, that Bage's satire acquired a sharper bite, and a more radical view of social relations. For this reason, it is this last novel which has most to offer now, although its predecessor, *Man As He Is*, is a more copious comic fiction. Sceptical and tolerant, benevolent and satiric, comic and humane, Bage's novels manage to reconcile qualities and conventions usually at odds in the fiction of that time, and it is this unity which is perhaps his best claim to originality and to our continued interest.

—Gary Kelly

BALLANTYNE, R(obert) M(ichael). Scottish. Born in Edinburgh, 24 April 1825. Educated at Edinburgh Academy, 1835–37, and privately. Ensign, 1858, and Captain, 1860, in the Edinburgh Volunteers. Married Jane Dickson Grant in 1866; four sons and two daughters. Apprentice Clerk, Hudson's Bay Company, Canada, 1841–47; Clerk, North British Railway Company, Edinburgh, 1847–49; member of staff, Alexander Cowan and Company, paper makers, Edinburgh, 1849; Junior Partner, Thomas Constable and Company, printers, Edinburgh, 1849–55; lecturer and free-lance writer from 1855; lived in Harrow after 1883. *Died 8 February 1894.*

PUBLICATIONS

Fiction

> *Snowflakes and Sunbeams; or, The Young Fur Trader: A Tale of the Far North.*   1856.
> *Three Little Kittens.*   1856.
> *Ungava: A Tale of Esquimeaux-Land.*   1857.
> *The Coral Island: A Tale of the Pacific Ocean.*   1857.
> *Mister Fox.*   1857.
> *My Mother.*   1857; as *Chit-Chat by a Penitent Cat,* 1874.
> *The Butterfly's Ball and the Grasshopper's Feast.*   1857.
> *The Life of a Ship from the Launch to the Wreck.*   1857.
> *The Robber Kitten.*   1858.
> *Martin Rattler; or, A Boy's Adventures in the Forests of Brazil.*   1858.
> *The World of Ice; or, Adventures in the Polar Regions.*   1859.
> *Mee-a-ow! or, Good Advice to Cats and Kittens.*   1859.
> *The Dog Crusoe: A Tale of the Western Prairies.*   1861; as *The Dog Crusoe and His Master,* 1869.
> *The Gorilla Hunters: A Tale of the Wilds of Africa.*   1861.
> *The Golden Dream; or, Adventures in the Far West.*   1861.
> *The Red Eric; or, The Whaler's Last Cruise: A Tale.*   1861.
> *The Wild Man of the West: A Tale of the Rocky Mountains.*   1862.
> *Gascoyne, The Sandal-Wood Trader: A Tale of the Pacific.*   1863.
> *Fighting the Whales; or, Doings and Dangers on a Fishing Cruise.*   1863.
> *Away in the Wilderness; or, Life among the Red Indians and the Fur-Traders.*   1863.
> *Fast in the Ice; or, Adventures in the Polar Region.*   1863.
> *The Lifeboat: A Tale of Our Coast Heroes.*   1864.
> *Chasing the Sun; or, Rambles in Norway.*   1864.

Freaks on the Fells; or, Three Months' Rustication, and Why I Did Not Become a Sailor. 1864.

The Lighthouse, Being the Story of a Great Fight Between Man and the Sea. 1865.

Shifting Winds: A Tough Yarn. 1866.

Fighting the Flames: A Tale of the London Fire Brigade. 1867.

Silver Lake; or, Lost in the Snow. 1867.

Deep Down: A Tale of the Cornish Mines. 1868.

Erling the Bold: A Tale of the Norse Sea-Kings. 1869.

Sunk at Sea; or, The Adventures of Wandering Will in the Pacific. 1869.

Lost in the Forest; or, Wandering Will's Adventures in South America. 1869.

Over the Rocky Mountains; or, Wandering Will in the Land of the Red Skin. 1869.

Saved by the Lifeboat: A Tale of Wreck and Rescue on the Coast. 1869,

The Cannibal Islands; or, Captain Cook's Adventures in the South Seas. 1869.

Hunting the Lions; or, The Land of the Negro. 1869.

Digging for Gold; or, Adventures in California. 1869.

Up in the Clouds; or, Balloon Voyages. 1869.

The Battle and the Breeze; or, The Fights and Fancies of a British Tar. 1869.

The Floating Light of the Goodwin Sands: A Tale. 1870.

The Iron Horse; or, Life on the Line: A Tale of the Grand National Trunk Railway. 1871.

The Pioneers: A Tale of the Western Wilderness, Illustrative of the Adventures and Discoveries of Sir Alexander Mackenzie. 1872.

The Norsemen in the West; or, America Before Columbus: A Tale. 1872.

Life in the Red Brigade. 1873.

The Iron Horse; or, tife on the Line: A Tale of the Grand National Trunk Railway, 1871.

The Pioneers: A Tale of the Western Wilderness, Illustrative of the Adventures and Discoveries of Sir Alexander Mackenzie. 1872.

The Norsemen in the West; or, America Before Columbus: A Tale. 1872.

Life in the Read Brigade. 1873.

Black Ivory: A Tale of Adventure among the Slavers of East Africa. 1873.

The Pirate City: An Algerine Tale. 1874.

Rivers of Ice: A Tale Illustrative of Alpine Adventure and Glacier Action. 1875.

The Story of the Rock; or, Building on the Eddystone. 1875.

Under the Waves; or, Diving in Deep Waters: A Tale. 1876.

The Settler and the Savage: A Tale of Peace and War in South Africa. 1876.

In the Track of the Troops: A Tale of Modern War. 1878.

Jarwin and Cuffy: A Tale. 1878.

Philosopher Jack: A Tale of the Southern Seas. 1879.

The Lonely Island; or, The Refuge of the Mutineers. 1880.

Post Haste: A Tale of Her Majesty's Mails. 1880.

The Red Man's Revenge: A Tale of the Red River Flood. 1880.

My Doggie and I. 1881.

The Giant of the North; or, Poking Around the Pole. 1881.

The Battery and the Boiler; or, Adventures in the Laying of Submarine Electric Cables. 1882.

The Kitten Pilgrims; or, Great Battles and Grand Victories. 1882.

Dusty Diamonds Cut and Polished: A Tale of City-Arab Life and Adventure. 1883.

Battles with the Sea; or, Heroes of the Lifeboat and Rocket. 1883.

The Thorogood Family. 1883.

The Madman and the Pirate. 1883.

The Young Trawler: A Story of Life and Death and Rescue on the North Sea. 1884.

Twice Bought: A Tale of the Oregon Gold Fields. 1884.

The Rover of the Andes: A Tale of Adventure in South America. 1885.

The Island Queen; or, Dethroned by Fire and Water: A Tale of the Southern Hemisphere.   1885.
Red Rooney; or, The Last of the Crew.   1886.
The Prairie Chief: A Tale.   1886.
The Lively Poll: A Tale of the North Sea.   1886.
The Big Otter: A Tale of the Great Nor'west.   1887.
The Fugitives; or, The Tyrant Queen of Madagascar.   1887.
Blue Lights; or, Hot Work in the Soudan: A Tale of Soldier Life in Several of Its Phases.   1888.
The Middy and the Moors: An Algerine Story.   1888; as *Slave of the Moors,* 1950.
The Crew of the Water Wagtail: A Story of Newfoundland.   1889.
The Eagle Cliff: A Tale of the Western Isles.   1889.
Blown to Bits; or, The Lonely Man of Rakata: A Tale of the Malay Peninsula.   1889.
The Garret and the Garden; or, Low Life High Up, and Jeff Benson; or, The Young Coastguardsman.   1890.
Charlie to the Rescue: A Tale of the Sea and the Rockies.   1890.
The Buffalo Runners: A Tale of the Red River Plain.   1891.
The Coxwain's Bride; or, The Rising Tide: A Tale of the Sea, and Other Tales.   1891.
The Hot Swamp: A Romance of Old Albion.   1892.
Hunted and Harried: A Tale of the Scottish Covenanters.   1892.
The Walrus Hunters: A Romance of the Realms of Ice.   1893.
Reuben's Luck: A Tale of the Wild North.   1896.

Other

Hudson's Bay; or, Every-Day Life in the Wilds of North America.   1848.
The Northern Coasts of America, and the Hudson's Bay Territories: A Narrative of Discovery and Adventure, by Patrick Fraser Tytler, with continuation by Ballantyne.   1853.
Handbook to the New Gold Fields: A Full Account of the Richness and Extent of the Fraser and Thompson River Gold Mines.   1858.
Environs and Vicinity of Edinburgh.   1859.
Ships: The Great Eastern and Lesser Crafts.   1859.
The Lakes of Killarney.   1859.
How Not to Do It: A Manual for the Awkward Squad; or, A Handbook of Directions Written for the Instruction of Raw Recruits in Our Rifle Volunteer Regiments.   1859.
Discovery and Adventure in the Polar Seas and Regions, by Sir John Leslie and Hugh Murray, with continuation by Ballantyne.   1860.
The Volunteer Levee; or, The Remarkable Experiences of Ensign Sopht.   1860.
Ensign Sopht's Volunteer Almanack for 1861.   1861.
Man on the Ocean.   1862; revised edition, 1874.
Photographs of Edinburgh, with Archibald Burns.   1868.
Our Seamen: An Appeal.   1873.
The Ocean and Its Wonders.   1874.
Six Months at the Cape; or, Letters to Periwinkle from South Africa.   1878.
The Collected Works of Ensign Sopht, Late of the Volunteers.   1881.
Personal Reminiscences in Book-Making.   1893.

Editor, *Naughty Boys; or, The Sufferings of Mr. Delteil,* by Champfleury, translated by Jane Ballantyne.   1855.

Bibliography: *Ballantyne: A Bibliography of First Editions* by Eric Quayle, 1968.

Reading List: *Ballantyne the Brave: A Victorian Writer and His Family* by Eric Quayle, 1967.

*　　*　　*

R. M. Ballantyne was one of the first writers of fictional adventure tales to study original material on whatever geographical location his stories used. G. A. Henty, another adventure writer of the same period, used historical backgrounds in the manner of Sir Walter Scott; Ballantyne lived in whatever environment his plot was to deal with. Thus for *The Lifeboat*, he lived at Deal with a lifeboat crew; for *The Lighthouse*, he spent several uncomfortable weeks in the Bell Rock Lighthouse; for *Fighting the Flames*, he stayed with the London Fire Brigade, waiting for the bells to signal a fire; for *Deep Down*, he lived with the tin-miners of St. Just, Cornwall, for over three months. He endured weeks of sea-sickness on the Gull Lightship for *The Floating Light of the Goodwin Sands*, and he acted as fireman on board the tender of the London-Edinburgh express for *The Iron Horse*. The result of these and similar expeditions was a series of well over a hundred juvenile novels with a realism never before seen in works for teenage boys.

His first novel was *Snowflakes and Sunbeams* in 1856; a year later, with *The Coral Island*, he made his name as the foremost writer of adventure stories. *Coral Island* was the book R. L. Stevenson acknowledged as the formative influence on his own love of the South Seas which eventually led to his writing *Treasure Island*, with its dedicatory reference to "Ballantyne the Brave."

Ballantyne's weakness as a writer lay in his being strait-jacketed by his puritanism. Unlike Stevenson, he was unable to give his readers a romantic and exciting story that was not laced through with moralising. Too often the action in his tales slowed to a halt while his young hero fell on his knees for a stint of evangelistic soliloquizing. Nevertheless, for the children of middle- and working-class families Ballantyne opened up an exciting vista of a world spiced with romance and danger waiting to be explored. Boys in the late Victorian age learned more geography from reading his books than from their teachers, just as they learned much of their history from Henty.

Ballantyne used a well-tried formula – giving full rein to youthful emotions within the strict bounds of what then passed for Christian morality. He wrote for the age in which he lived, portraying a world in which the good were terribly good and terribly British, and the bad were terribly bad and spoke with foreign accents. To have suggested otherwise was quite unthinkable.

—Eric Quayle

BANIM, John. Irish. Born in Kilkenny, 3 April 1798; brother of the writer Michael Banim. Educated locally; subsequently studied art at the drawing academy of the Royal Dublin Society. Married in 1821; one daughter. Drawing teacher in Kilkenny; settled in Dublin, 1820, and thereafter devoted himself to literature; moved to London, 1822, and contributed to various periodicals, most notably the *Literary Register*; lived abroad for his health, 1829–35; returned to Kilkenny, 1835. Granted Civil List pension, 1836. *Died 13 August 1842.*

PUBLICATIONS

Fiction (with Michael Banim)

Tales of the O'Hara Family (*Crohoore of the Billhook, The Fetches, John Doe*).   1825;
    second series (*The Nowlans, Peter of the Castle*), 1826.
The Boyne Water.   1826.
The Anglo-Irish of the Nineteenth Century.   1828; as *Lord Clangore*, 1865.
The Croppy.   1828.
The Denounced; or, The Last Baron of Crana.   1830.
The Smuggler.   1831.
The Ghost-Hunter and His Family.   1833; as *Joe Wilson's Ghost*, 1913.
The Mayor of Wind-Gap, with *Canvassing* by Miss Martin of Ballynahinch.   1835.
The Bit o' Writin' and Other Tales.   1838.
Father Connell.   1842.

Plays

Damon and Pythias, revised by R. L. Sheil (produced 1821).   1821.
Sylla, from a play by V. J. E. de Jouy (produced 1826).
The Sergeant's Wife, music by John Godd (produced 1827).   1855(?).
The Ghost Hunter, from his own story (produced 1833).
The Duchess of Ormond (produced 1836).

Verse

The Celt's Paradise, in Four Duans.   1821.
Chaunt of the Cholera: Songs for Ireland, with Michael Banim.   1831.

Other

Revelations of the Dead Alive (essays).   1824; as *London and Its Eccentricities in the
    Year 2023*, 1845.

Bibliography: in *XIX Century Fiction: A Bibliographical Record* by Michael Sadleir, 2 vols.,
1951.

Reading List: *The Life of Banim* by P. J. Murray, 1857; *John and Michael Banim: A Study in
the Development of the Anglo-Irish Novel* by Mark D. Hawthorne, 1975.

*   *   *

In his day, John Banim had his poetry praised by Sir Walter Scott, a tragedy produced
successfully at Covent Garden, and was a prolific member, until his health gave way, of that
hard-living and overworked band of Irish journalists (prominent among them were William
Maginn and Gerald Griffin) involved in the burgeoning London literary periodical trade. He
is best remembered now for *Tales of the O'Hara Family*, written in collaboration with his
brother Michael, a rather less talented writer who did not pursue a professional literary
career.

The tales were intended to do for Ireland what Scott's fiction had done for his native land. From a documentary point of view they achieved some success. Lower levels of contemporary Irish life – peasants, bailiffs, and priests – were portrayed more intimately than ever before. But here any similarity with Scott's work ends. The tales contain the substance of history, but nothing like an adequate fictional rendering of an historical sense. For the most part the subject matter is portrayed in either sombre, or lurid, shades. Violence, often presented with maximum gothic effect, is endemic. The style is frequently strident and overheated. While such effects depict a certain truth about the psychological atmosphere of the life found in a realm of contemporary Ireland – interlaced as they are with the lore and superstitions of the people – the picture lacks the sense Scott's work offers of a whole view judiciously reached. Once Banim's work moves beyond its chosen realm, to depict life in a higher class, for example, it quickly becomes vapid and stilted. Because it achieves some degree of psychological differentiation, and a sense of depth and completeness of view, *The Nowlans* is probably the most successful of the tales. The nearest John Banim comes to emulating Scott is in his novel of the Jacobite war, *The Boyne Water*, which provides an understanding of that conflict's issues but in its prolixity makes the narrative disproportioned and unresolved. There is throughout Banim's work a distinct sense of the impossible situation as an archetype of experience, a reading of contemporary history possibly reinforced by the author's own physical and emotional suffering.

Michael Banim's contribution to the tales is not negligible, both in his provision of local colour for his London-based brother and in his actual artistic contribution. As to the extent of the latter there is a certain amount of scholarly conjecture. It is likely that John took final editorial responsibility, however, a view substantiated by the poor quality of the work Michael produced after his brother's death, the best-known piece being *The Town of the Cascades* (1864).

—George O'Brien

BARING-GOULD, Sabine. English. Born at Dix's Fields, Exeter, Devon, 28 January 1834. Educated privately, mainly abroad, and at Clare College, Cambridge, 1853–56, B.A. 1856. Married Grace Taylor in 1868 (died, 1916); five sons and nine daughters. Assistant Master at the choir school of St. Barnabas's Church, Pimlico, London, 1857, and at Hurstpierpoint College, Sussex, 1857–64; ordained deacon, 1864, and priest, 1865; Curate of Horbury, Yorkshire, 1864–66; Vicar, Dalton, Yorkshire, 1866–71; Editor, *The Sacristy* magazine, 1871–73; Rector of East Mersea, Essex, 1871–81, and Lew-Trenchard, Devon, 1881 until his death. President, Devonshire Association, 1896. Honorary Fellow, Clare College, 1918. Wrote numerous hymns, including "Onward Christian Soldiers." *Died 2 January 1924.*

PUBLICATIONS

Fiction

The Path of the Just: Tales of Holy Men and Children.   1857.
Through Flood and Flame.   1868.

In Exitu Israel. 1870.
Mehalah: A Story of the Salt Marshes. 1880; edited by C. A. McIntyre, 1950.
John Herring. 1883.
Court Royal. 1886.
Little Tu'penny. 1887.
Jack Frost's Little Prisoners. 1887.
Red Spider. 1887.
The Gaverocks. 1887.
Richard Cable, The Lightshipman. 1888.
Eve. 1888.
The Pennycomequicks. 1889.
Arminell. 1890.
Jacquetta and Other Stories. 1890.
Urith. 1891.
Margery of Quether and Other Stories. 1891.
In the Roar of the Sea. 1892.
Through All the Changing Scenes of Life. 1892.
Mrs. Curgenven of Curgenven. 1893.
Cheap Jack Zita. 1893.
The Icelander's Sword; or, The Story of Oraefadal. 1894.
Kitty Alone. 1894.
The Queen of Love. 1894.
Noémi. 1895.
Dartmoor Idylls. 1896.
The Broom-Squire. 1896.
Perpetua. 1897.
Guavas the Tinner. 1897.
Bladys of the Stewponey. 1897.
Domitia. 1898.
Pabo the Priest. 1899.
Furze Bloom: Tales of the Western Moors. 1899.
Winefred. 1900.
In a Quiet Village (stories). 1900.
The Forbishers. 1901.
Royal Georgie. 1901.
Nebo the Nailer. 1902.
Miss Quillet. 1902.
Chris of All-Sorts. 1903.
Siegfried. 1904.
In Dewisland. 1904.
Monsieur Pichelmère and Other Stories. 1905.

Play

The Red Spider, music by Learmont Drysdale, from the novel by Baring-Gould
  (produced 1898).

Verse

The Silver Store, Collected from Medieval, Christian, and Jewish Mines. 1868; revised
  edition, 1887, 1898.

Other

Iceland: Its Scenes and Sagas. 1863.
The Book of Were Wolves. 1865.
Post-Medieval Preachers. 1865.
Curious Myths of the Middle Ages. 2 vols., 1866–68.
Curiosities of the Olden Times. 1869; revised edition, 1896.
The Golden Gate: A Manual. 3 vols., 1869–70.
The Origin and Development of Religious Belief. 2 vols., 1869–70.
Legends of Old Testament Characters. 2 vols., 1871.
One Hundred Sermon Sketches for Extempore Preachers. 1871.
The Lives of the Saints. 17 vols., 1872–89; revised edition, 16 vols., 1897–98.
Village Conferences on the Creed. 1873.
How to Save Fuel. 1874.
Yorkshire Oddities, Incidents, and Strange Events. 2 vols., 1874.
The Lost and Hostile Gospels: An Essay on the Toledoth Jeschu and the Petrine and Pauline Gospels. 1874.
Some Modern Difficulties: Nine Lectures. 1875.
The Vicar of Morwenstow: Life of R. S. Hawker. 1876; revised edition, 1876, 1899.
The Mystery of Suffering: Six Lectures. 1877.
Germany Past and Present. 2 vols., 1879.
Sermons to Children. 2 vols., 1879–1907.
The Preacher's Pocket: A Packet of Sermons. 1880.
The Village Pulpit: Sermon Outlines. 2 vols., 1881.
The Seven Last Words: A Course of Sermons. 1884.
Our Parish Church: Twenty Addresses to Children. 1885.
The Passion of Jesus. 1885.
The Birth of Jesus: Eight Discourses. 1885.
Nazareth to Capernum: Ten Lectures. 1886.
Germany. 1886; revised edition, 1905.
The Trials of Jesus: Seven Discourses for Lent. 1886.
The Way of Sorrows. 1887.
Our Inheritance: An Account of the Eucharistic Service in the First Three Centuries. 1888.
The Death and Resurrection of Jesus: Ten Lectures. 1888.
Grettir the Outlaw (juvenile). 1889.
Historic Oddities and Strange Events. 2 vols., 1889–91.
Old County Life. 1890.
Conscience and Sin: Daily Meditations for Lent. 1890.
My Prague Pig and Other Stories for Children. 1890.
The Church in Germany, edited by P. H. Ditchfield. 1891.
In Troubadour Land: Provence and Languedoc. 1891.
Wagner's Parsifal at Baireuth. 1892.
The Tragedy of the Caesars. 2 vols., 1892.
Strange Survivals: Some Chapters in the History of Man. 1892.
A Book of Fairy Tales Retold. 1894.
The Deserts of Southern France. 2 vols., 1894.
The Life of Napoleon Bonaparte. 1897.
A Study of St. Paul. 1897.
The Sunday Round: Plain Village Sermons. 4 vols.,1898–99.
An Armory of the Western Counties, from Unpublished Manuscripts of the 16th Century, with R. W. Twigge. 1898.
An Old English Home and its Dependencies. 1898.
A Book of the West: Introduction to Devon and Cornwall. 2 vols., 1899.

The Crock of Gold (juvenile).   1899.
Virgin Saints and Martyrs.   1900.
A Book of Dartmoor, Brittany, North Wales, South Wales, the Riviera, the Rhine, the Cevennes, the Pyrenees.   8 vols., 1900–07.
Brittany.   1902.
A Coronation Souvenir.   1902.
Amazing Adventures.   1903.
A Book of Ghosts.   1904.
A Memorial of Lord Nelson.   1905.
Lives of the British Saints, with J. Fisher.   1907.
The Restitution of All Things; or, The Hope That Is Before Us.   1907.
Devon.   1907.
Devonshire Characters and Strange Events.   1908.
A Baring-Gould Continuous Reader, edited by G. H. Rose.   1908.
Cornish Characters and Strange Events.   1909.
A History of Sarawak under Its Two White Rajahs 1839–1908, with C. A. Bampfylde.   1909.
Cornwall.   1910.
Family Names and Their Story.   1910.
The Land of Teck and Its Neighbourhood.   1911.
Cliff Castles and Cave Dwellings of Europe.   1911.
Sheepstor.   1912.
A Book of Folk-Lore.   1913.
The Church Revival.   1914.
Thoughts of Baring-Gould, edited by H. B. Elliott.   1917.
The Evangelical Revival.   1920.
Early Reminiscences 1834–64.   1923.
My Last Few Words (sermons).   1924.
Further Reminiscences 1864–94.   1925.

Editor, *Songs and Ballads of the West.*   4 vols., 1889–91.
Editor, with H. Fleetwood Sheppard, *A Garland of Country Song: English Folk Song.*   1895.
Editor, *English Minstrelsie.*   8 vols., 1895–99.
Editor, *Old English Fairy Tales.*   1895.
Editor, *A Book of Nursery Songs and Rhymes.*   1895.
Editor, *Selected Works,* by St. Francis de Sales.   1907.

Translator, *Ernestine,* by Wilhelmine von Hillern.   1879.

Reading List: *Onward Christian Soldier: A Life of Baring-Gould* by William Purcell, 1957; "The Stature of Baring-Gould as a Novelist" by William J. Hyde in *Nineteenth Century Fiction 15,* 1961; *Baring-Gould, Writer and Folklorist* by B. H. C. Dickinson, 1970.

*   *   *

When Sabine Baring-Gould's *Mehalah* appeared in 1880, it drew praise from critics as a novel of promise and power. Swinburne found it the only work which might "challenge the comparison" with *Wuthering Heights.* The high promise remained unfulfilled, but in output – novels of country life, hymns, saints' lives, folklore, folk songs, travel books, reminiscences – Baring-Gould's career would dwarf that of most major novelists.

The chief virtue of Baring-Gould's novels is, in his own critical terms, their "colour." First there is color of setting, the tangible atmosphere of regions like the Essex salt marshes or the

Devonshire moors, and the occupations of the land from which the character of the people derives. Then there is color of character, by which he meant visibly striking figures grouped harmoniously in their environment. Many of his characters, especially women in the title roles and hero-villains such as Elijah Rebow, Farmer Drownlands, and "Captain Cruel" Coppinger, have enormous vitality. Young women were Baring-Gould's specialty. His preference for a heroine was usually a lower-class girl, orphaned or burdened with a helpless parent. Set amidst the grasping rivalries and passions of a male world, she displays uninhibited and thoroughly unconventional self-reliance.

"The character of the scenery and the character of the people determine the character of the tale." Plot was subordinate in Baring-Gould's critical intentions, yet as his output grew, he was accused of employing melodramatic formulas and self-plagiarism of characters, probably to satisfy expectations of typical novel readers "whose whole aim is distraction." Swinburne and, later, Barrie questioned unnecessary violence in his plots, but Baring-Gould was convinced of "an innate cruelty in human nature which neither Christianity, nor education, nor teetotalism will eradicate." The resultant starkness often does seem right, though interrupted sometimes by inharmonious comedy. Some virtue derives even from his faults, for Baring-Gould scarcely ever grows dull.

"There is no veneer in my work," the narrator of "Margery of Quether" asserts. Unvarnished realism is preferred, especially in the short stories, where anecdotes are not shaped by an artist so much as transcribed from the author's observations. A troubled sleeper at the Warren Inn is fascinated by moonlight illuminating an old oak chest in his room, until he looks inside the chest and discovers a corpse. Morning brings a simple explanation from his hostess: "it's only old vayther. The frost be that hard, the snow that deep, us can't carr'n yet awhile to Lydford churchyard to bury'n so us has salted'n in" (*Dartmoor Idylls*).

"If only Mr. Baring-Gould wrote less, what fine work might he not turn out!" (*Athenaeum*, 9 December 1893). The preacher, however, preferred serving God to carefully cultivating his art. With a profusion of novels he could reach the widest possible readership, "to please, perhaps to instruct." Baring-Gould is much more than a third-rate novelist – one with many first-rate talents which he persisted in exploiting in his own way.

—William J. Hyde

BECKFORD, William. English. Born in Fonthill, Wiltshire, 29 September 1759. Educated privately; studied music with Mozart; studied in Geneva, 1777–78. Married Lady Margaret Gordon in 1783 (died, 1786); two daughters. Inherited vast family fortune, 1770; visited the Low Countries and Italy, 1780, 1782; lived in Switzerland, 1783–86; Member of Parliament for Wells, 1784–90, and Hindon, 1790–94; settled near Cintra, Portugal, 1794–96; built Fonthill Abbey, 1796, and lived there until 1822, amassing a collection of books, art objects, and curios; again served as Member of Parliament for Hindon, 1806–20; moved to Bath, 1822: built Lansdowne Tower, Bath. *Died 2 May 1844.*

PUBLICATIONS

Fiction

An Arabian Tale, translated by Samuel Henley.   1786; as *Vathek* (in French), 1787;
   revised edition, 1816; edited by R. H. Lonsdale, 1970.
Modern Novel Writing; or, The Elegant Enthusiast.   1796.
Azemia: A Descriptive and Sentimental Novel.   1797.
The Episodes of Vathek, edited by Frank T. Marzials.   1912.

Other

Biographical Memoirs of Extraordinary Painters.   1780.
*Dreams, Waking Thoughts, and Incidents in a Series of Letters from Various Parts of
   Europe.*   1783; edited by Guy Chapman, as *The Travel Diaries 1,* 1928.
Epitaphs.   1825.
Italy, with Sketches of Spain and Portugal.   2 vols., 1834; revised edition, 1834; edited
   by Guy Chapman, as *The Travel Diaries 2,* 1928.
Recollections of an Excursion to the Monasteries of Alcobaca and Batalha.   1835;
   revised edition, 1840; edited by A. Parreaux, 1956.
The Vision; Liber Veritatis, edited by Guy Chapman.   1930.
Journal in Portugal and Spain 1787–88, edited by Boyd Alexander.   1954.
Life at Fonthill 1807–22, from the Correspondence, translated and edited by Boyd
   Alexander.   1957.

Translator, *The Story of Al Raoui: A Tale from the Arabic.*   1799; revised edition 1799.

Bibliography: *A Bibliography of Beckford* by Guy Chapman, 1930.

Reading List: *Beckford* by Guy Chapman, 1937; *Beckford, Auteur de Vathek* by A. Parreaux,
1960; *England's Wealthiest Son: A Study of Beckford* by Boyd Alexander, 1962; *Beckford* by
Robert J. Gemmett, 1977.

*   *   *

William Beckford's fame rests on the bizarre, pseudo-Oriental tale *Vathek* – some would
say, on the last ten to twelve pages of the book, when the caliph Vathek and the beautiful
Nouronihar descend into the subterranean caverns of Istakar to meet the Prince of Darkness,
Eblis, and their doom of hatred and unrelenting fire in their hearts. Yet even without *Vathek*
Beckford would have a minor place in English literary history, if not for his clever mixture of
art criticism and parody (in *Biographical Memoirs*) or his later satires on gothic and
sentimental novels (in *Modern Novel Writing* and *Azemia*), then certainly for his romantic
travel books about Italy and Portugal. *Dreams, Waking Thoughts, and Incidents*, suppressed
at his mother's request and later republished in abridged form as *Italy*, best displays what
Beckford called "my visionary way of gazing." It is not so much a description of place as an
artful record of impressions and sensations, in response to people, places, and especially
landscapes, which had a powerful effect on Beckford's imagination.

The genius of this eccentric collector and dilettante – "England's wealthiest son," in
Byron's phrase – is clearly strongest, however, in *Vathek* and in the three *Episodes* intended
to accompany the tale but not published until 1912. The English prose is not, in fact,
Beckford's: he wrote the tale in French, sent it to his friend, Rev. Samuel Henley, who

translated it and, against Beckford's strict orders, published it himself in 1786 as a translation of an anonymous Arabic tale. Although Vathek, with Faustian curiosity, seeks knowledge and experience at any expense, Beckford is not interested in his moral choices but in the spectacle of Vathek's pursuit of gratification. The eternal childishness and innocence of the boy Gulchenrouz has its appeal in Beckford's world, but the passionate life of Vathek leads him (and the reader) into another world of repulsive cripples and beautiful women, of black magic and ardent love, of sadism and voluptuous sweetness, and finally into a Hell of exhaustion and torment which Borges aptly called "the first truly atrocious Hell in literature."

—David McCracken

BESANT, Sir Walter. English. Born in Portsmouth, Hampshire, 14 August 1836. Educated at King's College, University of London; Christ's College, Cambridge (scholar and Prizeman exhibitioner), BA. 1859. Married Mary Foster-Barham in 1895. Senior Professor, Royal College of Mauritius, 1861–67; Secretary, 1868–85, and Honorary Secretary, 1885–1901, Palestine Exploration Fund. Advocate of social reform in the East End of London: helped found the People's Palace at Mile End. A Founder, 1884, and first Chairman, 1884–85, and, again, 1887–92, Society of Authors. Fellow, Society of Antiquaries, 1894. Knighted, 1895. *Died 9 June 1901.*

PUBLICATIONS

Fiction

> *Ready-Money Mortiboy*, with James Rice.   1872.
> *My Little Girl*, with James Rice.   1873.
> *With Harp and Crown*, with James Rice.   1875.
> *The Golden Butterfly*, with James Rice.   1876.
> *The Case of Mr. Lucraft and Other Tales*, with James Rice.   1876.
> *This Son of Vulcan*, with James Rice.   1876.
> *Such a Good Man!*, with James Rice.   1877.
> *The Monks of Thelema*, with James Rice.   1878.
> *By Celia's Arbour*, with James Rice.   1878.
> *'Twas in Trafalgar's Bay and Other Stories*, with James Rice.   1879.
> *The Seamy Side*, with James Rice.   1880.
> *The Chaplain of the Fleet*, with James Rice.   1881.
> *Sir Richard Whittington*, with James Rice.   1881.
> *The Ten Years' Tenant and Other Stories*, with James Rice.   1881.
> *The Revolt of Man.*   1882.
> *All Sorts and Conditions of Men.*   1882.
> *All in a Garden Fair.*   1883.
> *The Captain's Room.*   1883.
> *Dorothy Foster.*   1884.
> *Uncle Jack* (stories).   1885.
> *Children of Gibeon.*   1886.

Katherine Regina. 1887.
The World Went Very Well Then.   1887.
Herr Paulus. 1888.
The Inner House. 1888.
The Bell of St. Paul's. 1889.
For Faith and Freedom. 1889.
The Doubts of Dives. 1889.
To Call Her Mine. 1889.
Armorel of Lyonesse. 1890.
The Demoniac. 1890.
The Holy Rose. 1890.
Blind Love, by Wilkie Collins, completed by Besant.   1890.
St. Katherine's by the Tower.   1891.
Verbena Camellia Stephanotis (stories and essays).   1892.
The Ivory Gate. 1892.
Beyond the Dreams of Avarice.   1895.
In Deacon's Orders (stories).   1895.
The City of Refuge. 1896.
The Master Craftsman.   1896.
A Fountain Sealed. 1897.
The Changeling. 1898.
The Orange-Girl. 1899.
The Alabaster Box. 1900.
The Fourth Gentleman. 1900.
The Lady of Lynn. 1901.
A Five Years' Tryst and Other Stories.   1902.
No Other Way. 1902.

Plays

Ready-Money, with James Rice, from their own novel.   1875.
Such a Good Man, with James Rice, from their own novel (produced 1879).
The Charm, with W. H. Pollock (produced 1884).   In *The Charm ...,* 1896.
The Ballad Monger, with W. H. Pollock (produced 1887).
The Charm and Other Drawing Room Plays, with W. H. Pollock.   1896.

Other

Studies in Early French Poetry. 1868.
Jerusalem: The City of Herod and Saladin, with E. H. Palmer.   1871.
When George III Was King. 1872.
The French Humorists. 1873.
Constantinople, with W. J. Brodribb.   1879.
Gaspard de Coligny. 1879.
Rabelais. 1879.
The Life and Achievements of E. H. Palmer.   1883.
Life in an Hospital: An East End Chapter.   1883.
Twenty-One Years' Work 1865–86.   1886; revised edition, 1895.
The Eulogy of Richard Jefferies.   1888.
Fifty Years Ago. 1888.
Captain Cook. 1890.
London. 1892.

The History of London.　1893.
The Society of Authors.　1893.
Westminster.　1895.
The Rise of the Empire.　1897.
The Pen and the Book.　1899.
South London.　1899.
East London.　1901.
The Story of King Alfred.　1901.
The Strand District, with Geraldine Mitton.　1902.
Autobiography.　1902.
London in the Eighteenth Century.　1902.
London in the Time of the Stuarts.　1903.
As We Are and As We May Be.　1903.
Essays and Historiettes.　1903.
The Thames.　1903.
London in the Time of the Tudors.　1904.
Medieval London.　2 vols., 1906.
Early London: Prehistoric, Roman, Saxon, and Norman.　1908.
London in the Nineteenth Century.　1909.
London South of the Thames.　1912.
Bourbon Journal, August 1863.　1933.

Editor, with R. J. Griffiths, *Stewart's Local Examination Series.*　17 vols., 1877–82.
Editor, *The Literary Remains of C. F. T. Drake.*　1877.
Editor, with E. H. Palmer, *The Survey of Western Palestine,* by C. R. Conder.　1881.
Editor, *Readings in Rabelais.*　1883.
Editor, *The Fascination of London Series,* with Geraldine Mitton.　12 vols., 1902–08.
Editor, *The Survey of London.*　10 vols., 1901–12.

Reading List: "Besant, Novelist" by F. W. Boege, in *English Fiction in Transition 2,* 1959; "Besant on the Art of the Novel" by E. Boll, in *English Fiction in Transition 2,* 1959

*　*　*

Although Sir Walter Besant is probably the best remembered as the author of an essay on the art of fiction which brought Henry James to reply in one of the greatest essays ever written on the subject, Besant was, in his own day, a highly popular author who had his say on many issues of importance, and who was first president of the Society of Authors. An admirer of Zola, and something of a socialist, Besant wrote two widely acclaimed novels about working-class London, *All Sorts and Conditions of Men* and *Children of Gibeon.* These two works of the 1880's had a colossal influence on contemporaries, so much so indeed that Besant's recommendation for a people's palace of pleasures became a reality when in 1887 Sir Edmund Currie, taking *All Sorts and Conditions of Men* as his textbook, began a subscription which resulted in a "palace" of sorts being built.

During the same decade Besant was at work in other areas. *The Revolt of Man* is a satire on feminism, and as such it anticipates his hostile reaction to Ibsen's *The Doll's House.* In his article "The Doll's House – and After" (*English Illustrated Magazine,* January 1890), Besant conjured up a picture of the effects on Nora's family of her desertion. Her husband has degenerated into a drunkard, her son turns to a life of crime, and her daughter ends in suicide. For a man with socialist sympathies, Besant was stridently conventional about the role of women in public and private life. This is evident in another of his popular successes, *Dorothy Foster,* an historical novel which is really no more than "costume" history, and which treats the fortunes of its heroine in a sugary, romantic-sentimental manner. (It is no accident that Besant should have been an enthusiastic admirer of Anthony Hope's *The Prisoner of Zenda*.)

More substantial, perhaps, is *All in a Garden Fair*, a novel about the literary life, which Gissing admired and which may have had some influence over Gissing's novel on the subject, *New Grub Street*. *New Grub Street* is a much better novel than *All in a Garden Fair*, perhaps because Gissing was a more serious and dedicated admirer of Zola than Besant was, and his naturalism seems more authentic.

Besant, indeed, never seems to be wholly serious in his avowals of support for either naturalism or socialism. I do not find it surprising that he should have written the mawkish little tale *The Ivory Gate*, which shows a lawyer who in his business hours is very lawyer-like – tough, legalistic, dry – but who in his hours of relaxation becomes the very model of benevolence, overflowing with the milk of human kindness, and ready to put his money where his mouth is. *The Ivory Gate* owes something to *A Christmas Carol*, and perhaps to the Cheerybles of *Nicholas Nickleby*.

Besant also had a highly successful literary partnership with James Rice. In 1872 he and Rice published *Ready-Money Mortiboy*, the popularity of which resulted in a series of twelve novels. On the whole, Besant's gifts were too readily deployed in tailoring books to meet audience demand. Yet *All Sorts and Conditions of Men* retains its interest, and *Children of Gibeon* is a decent if comparatively undistinguished contribution to fiction about working-class London and the possibilities of social revolution, matters which so engaged people's attention during the 1880's.

—John Lucas

BLACKMORE, R(ichard) D(oddridge).   English.   Born in Longworth, Berkshire, 7 June 1825. Educated at Blundell's School, Tiverton; Exeter College, Oxford, matriculated 1843, B.A. 1847, M.A. 1852; worked as a tutor in the family of Sir Samuel Scott of Sundridge Park, Kent, then entered the Middle Temple, London: called to the Bar, 1852. Married Lucy Pinto Leite in 1852 (died). Settled in London; practised as a conveyancer, but gave up the law because of ill-health; Classical Master, Wellesley House School, Twickenham Common, Middlesex, 1853; built Gomer House on extensive grounds at Teddington, Middlesex, 1858, settled there, and supported himself as a market gardener. *Died 20 January 1900.*

PUBLICATIONS

Fiction

    Clara Vaughan.   1864; revised edition, 1872.
    Cradock Nowell.   1866; revised edition, 1873.
    Lorna Doone: A Romance of Exmoor.   1869; edited by R. O. Morris, 1920.
    The Maid of Sker.   1872.
    Alice Lorraine.   1875; revised edition, 1876.
    Cripps the Carrier.   1876.
    Erema; or, My Father's Sin.   1877.
    Mary Anerley.   1880.

Christowell. 1882.
The Remarkable History of Sir Thomas Upmore Bart, M.P.   1884.
Springhaven. 1887.
Kit and Kitty. 1890.
Perlycross. 1894.
Tales from the Telling-House.   1896.
Dariel. 1897.

Verse

Poems. 1854.
Epullia. 1854.
The Bugle of the Black Sea; or, The British in the East.   1855.
The Fate of Franklin.   1860.
Fringilla: Some Tales in Verse.   1895.

Other

Figaro at Hastings, St. Leonards.   1877.
Humour, Wit, and Satire. 1885.
Fotheringay and Mary Queen of Scots.   1886.
Betrothal Ring of Mary Queen of Scots 1565: A Description of the Darnley Ring.   1887.
Argyll's Highlands; or, MacCailein Mor and the Lords of Lorne, with Traditional Tales,
   edited by J. Mackay.   1902.

Translator, *The Farm and Fruit of Old: The First and Second Georgics of Virgil.*   1862.
Translator, *The Georgics of Virgil.*   1871; edited by R. S. Conway, 1932.
The

Reading List: *Blackmore: His Life and Novels* by Q. C. Burris, 1930; *Blackmore, The Author of Lorna Doone* by W. H. Dunn, 1956 (includes bibliography; supplement by J. A. Carter in *Notes and Queries*, August 1962); *The Last Victorian: Blackmore and His Novels* by Kenneth Budd, 1960.

*   *   *

Lorna Doone is the only novel by which R. D. Blackmore is now remembered, although he wrote fourteen others, beginning with *Clara Vaughan* in 1864, while living a quiet life in the house he built himself in Teddington. The appeal of *Lorna Doone* lies in its combination of an exciting story, a good deal of historical colour from the time of Monmouth's rising, and a genuine feeling for the landscape of Exmoor. It may be related to other "regional" novels like those of Scott and Hardy, but it has a robust and passionate, if at times melodramatic, atmosphere of its own.

Blackmore had some difficulty in getting *Lorna Doone* published, and at first it did not sell well, but the publication of a cheaper one-volume edition changed the situation. He himself thought that the novel owed some of its success to the fact that its appearance coincided with Queen Victoria's giving permission to her daughter Princess Louise to marry the Marquis of Lorne. It came to be believed that the novel concerned Lord Lorne's ancestors, and this encouraged many to read it out of curiosity. However this may be, the romantic story of the high-born Lorna and her lowly but ardent lover, John Ridd, embodies an archetypal romantic situation which may have had particular appeal in the changing society of the nineteenth century. Blackmore based his novel on memories of stories told by his grandfather, who used to ride across Exmoor to preach on alternate Sundays while rector of Oare, and on published accounts of the Doone family, in whose historical reality he firmly believed. The landscape descriptions present the moor as a place of mystery, and visitors attracted to the area apparently complained – according to Waldo Dunn's biography – that the moor was less dramatic and awe-inspiring than the novel had led them to believe. Blackmore's reasonable explanation, in a letter to the editor of Baedeker's *Handbook of Great Britain* in 1887, was that he "romanced" simply "for the uses of my story." And he did so to excellent effect.

Some of his later novels, like *The Maid of Sker* (Blackmore's own favourite) and *Springhaven*, also combine landscape and passion in ways that make their neglect surprising. How much the success of *Lorna Doone* owed to the Victorian tendency – which it encouraged – to equate the West Country with a particular quality of Englishness is hard to calculate, but its continuing appeal suggests the strength of the central romantic story. It is a classic of middlebrow literature, and representative of a significant tradition romanticising specific parts of the English countryside.

—Peter Faulkner

BORROW, George (Henry). English. Born in East Dereham, Norfolk, 5 July 1803. Educated at Norwich Grammar School, 1816–18; articled to a firm of Norwich solicitors, 1818–23. Married Mary Clarke in 1840. Worked as a hack writer to the publisher Sir Richard Phillips, London, 1824; travelled throughout England, often with groups of gypsies, 1825–32; Agent of the Bible Society: travelled to St. Petersburg, 1833–35, and in Spain, Portugal, and Morocco, 1835–39; also, Foreign Correspondent of the *Morning Herald*, 1837–39; lived at Oulton Broad, Norfolk, from 1840. *Died 26 July 1881.*

PUBLICATIONS

Collections

Works, edited by Clement K. Shorter.   16 vols., 1923–24.

Fiction

Tales of the Wild and Wonderful.   1825.
Lavengro: The Scholar, The Gypsy, The Priest.   1851; edited by Walter Starkie, 1961.
The Romany Rye: A Sequel to Lavengro.   1857; edited by Walter Starkie, 1949.

Other

The Zincali; or, An Account of the Gypsies of Spain, with an Original Collection of Their Songs and Poetry and a Copious Dictionary of Their Language. 2 vols., 1841; edited by Walter Starkie, 1961.

The Bible in Spain; or, The Journeys, Adventures, and Imprisonments of an Englishman in an Attempt to Circulate the Scriptures in the Peninsula. 3 vols., 1843; supplementary chapter, 1913; edited by Peter Quennell, 1959.

Wild Wales: Its People, Language, and Scenery. 3 vols., 1862.

Romano Lavo-Lil: Word-Book of the Romany; or, English Gypsy Language. 1874.

Letters to the British and Foreign Bible Society, edited by T. H. Darlow. 1911.

Letters to His Wife, Mary Borrow. 1913.

Letters to His Mother, Ann Borrow, and Other Correspondents. 1913.

Celtic Bards, Chiefs, and Kings, edited by H. G. Wright. 1928.

Editor, *Celebrated Trials and Remarkable Cases of Criminal Jurisprudence from the Earliest Records to 1825.* 6 vols., 1825.

Editor, *Evangelioa San Lucasen Guissan,* by Oteiza. 1838.

Translator, *Faustus,* by F. M. von Klinger. 1825.

Translator, *Romantic Ballads.* 1826.

Translator, *Targum; or, Metrical Translations from Thirty Languages and Dialects.* 1835.

Translator, *The Talisman,* by Pushkin. 1835.

Translator, *Embéo e Majaró Lucas.* 1837.

Translator, *The Sleeping Bard; or, Visions of the World, Death, and Hell,* by Elis Wynne. 1860.

Translator, *The Turkish Jester; or, The Pleasantries of Cogia Nasr Eddin Effendi.* 1844.

Translator, *The Death of Balder,* by Johannes Ewald. 1889.

Translator, *Russian Popular Tales.* 1904.

Translator, *The Gold Horns,* by A. G. Ohlenschläger. 1913.

Translator, *Welsh Poems and Ballads,* edited by Ernest Rhys. 1915.

Translator, *Ballads of All Nations: A Selection,* edited by R. Brinsley Johnson. 1927.

Bibliography: *A Bibliography of the Writings in Prose and Verse of Borrow* by T. J. Wise, 1914.

Reading List: *Life, Writings, and Correspondence of Borrow* by W. I. Knapp, 2 vols., 1899; *Borrow* by M. D. Armstrong, 1950; *Gypsy Borrow* by B. Vesey-Fitzgerald, 1953; *Borrow, Vagabond, Polyglotte, Agent Biblique, Ecrivain* by R. Fréchet, 1956 (includes bibliography); *Borrow* by Robert Meyers, 1966.

* * *

Though he laid claims to be considered as a novelist, George Borrow was essentially a writer of what was later to be known as travel literature. Some of his work openly purports to be of this kind; but even *Lavengro* and *The Romany Rye,* though usually described as picaresque novels, are really romanticised excursions in autobiography thinly disguised in the trappings of first-person singular narrative fiction. His literary work is to an unusual extent a direct projection of his own personality, a re-creation of his particular quiddity.

His father's itinerant life as a recruiting officer may have encouraged footloose propensities in the son, and certainly meant that his early schooling was erratic. Though he became a considerable philologist, familiar with over thirty languages and dialects and a pioneer in the study of Gypsy languages and customs, he also developed, like many self-taught scholars, a strong didactic strain which perpetually informs his writing. Fortunately he gained his education as much in the streets and market-places, in stable-yards, boxing-rings, and Gypsy camps, as in the school-room, library, or solicitor's office in which he served a brief apprenticeship; but though this give him rich, unusual, and fascinating material to write about, his readers must be prepared to accept a recurrent note of assertive punditry in Borrow's work.

Only Borrow specialists are likely to turn to his earlier publications, translations of *Faustus* and Danish ballads, the volume *Targum* which contains metrical translations from thirty languages, and the six volumes of *Celebrated Trials*, which can be dismissed as hack work. Equally, his translation of St. Luke's Gospel into Caló (the dialect of Spanish Gypsies) and his important *Romano Lavo-Lil*, or Romany word-book, are of interest mainly to philologists and folklorists. But *The Zincali*, with its vivid description of Spanish Gypsy life and customs, and *The Bible in Spain*, one of the most evocative of all descriptions of that country and its manners, are still among the best reading for the traveller in Spain. Borrow's attempts to portray the life of English Gypsies and travelling folk in *Lavengro* and *The Romany Rye* are less successful. Because he was unable to distance himself sufficiently from his material as a novelist, his characters fail to achieve independent reality within a fictional world: the narrative and the dialogue tend to reflect in monochrome Borrow's own colloquial if lively style and tone of voice. His was an egocentric and wayward talent, achieving its best expression in his travel books, including *Wild Wales*, an affectionate description of a walking holiday which is fit to stand beside *The Bible in Spain*.

—Stewart F. Sanderson

BRADDON, Mary Elizabeth. English. Born in London, 4 October 1835. Educated privately. Lived with the publisher John Maxwell in the 1860's, married him in 1874 (died); two daughters and three sons, including the novelists W. B Maxwell and Gerald Maxwell. Appeared on the stage during the 1850's as Mary Seaton; full-time writer from 1860; became wealthy as a result of the success of *Lady Audley's Secret*, 1862; contributed to various London magazines, and edited *Belgravia* from 1866, the *Belgravia Annual* from 1867, and the *Mistletoe Bough*, 1878–92. *Died 4 February 1915.*

PUBLICATIONS

Fiction

> *Three Times Dead; or, The Secret of the Heath.* 1854; as *The Trail of the Serpent,* 1861.
> *The Lady Lisle.* 1861.
> *The Captain of the Vulture.* 1862.
> *Lady Audley's Secret.* 1862.
> *Ralph the Bailiff and Other Tales.* 1862; augmented edition, 1866(?).
> *Eleanor's Victory.* 1863.
> *Aurora Floyd.* 1863.
> *John Marchmont's Legacy.* 1863.

The Doctor's Wife. 1864.
Henry Dunbar: The Story of an Outcast. 1864.
Only a Clod. 1865.
Sir Jasper's Tenant. 1865.
The Lady's Mile. 1866.
Birds of Prey. 1867.
Rupert Godwin. 1867.
Dead-Sea Fruit. 1868.
Charlotte's Inheritance. 1868.
Run to Earth. 1868.
Fenton's Quest. 1871.
The Lovels of Arden. 1871.
Robert Ainsleigh. 1872.
To the Bitter End. 1872.
Lucius Davoren; or, Publicans and Sinners. 1873.
Milly Darrell and Other Tales. 1873.
Strangers and Pilgrims. 1873.
Taken at the Flood. 1874.
Lost for Love. 1874.
Hostages to Fortune. 1875.
A Strange World. 1875.
Dead Men's Shoes. 1876.
Joshua Haggard's Daughter. 1876.
The Black Band; or, Mysteries of Midnight. 1877.
Weavers and Weft and Other Tales. 1877.
An Open Verdict. 1878.
The Cloven Foot. 1879.
Vixen. 1879.
Just As I Am. 1880.
The Story of Barbara. 1880.
Asphodel. 1881.
Mount Royal. 1882.
Flower and Weed. 1882.
Phantom Fortune. 1883.
Married in Haste. 1883.
The Golden Calf. 1883.
Under the Red Flag. 1883.
Flower and Weed and Other Tales. 1884.
Ishmael. 1884; as *An Ishmaelite,* 1884.
Wyllard's Weird. 1885.
One Thing Needful, and Cut by the County. 1886.
Mohawks. 1886.
Like and Unlike. 1887.
The Fatal Three. 1888.
The Day Will Come. 1889.
One Life, One Love. 1890.
Gerard; or, The World, The Flesh, and the Devil. 1891.
The Venetians. 1892.
All along the River (stories). 1893.
Thou Art the Man. 1894.
The Christmas Hirelings. 1894.
Sons of the Fire. 1895.
London Pride; or, When the World Was Younger. 1896.
Under Love's Rule. 1897.

Rough Justice.   1898.
In High Places.   1898.
His Darling Sin.   1899.
The Infidel: A Story of the Great Revival.   1900.
The Conflict.   1903.
A Lost Eden.   1904.
The Rose of Life.   1905.
The White House.   1906.
Her Convict.   1907.
Dead Love Has Chains.   1907.
During Her Majesty's Pleasure.   1908.
Our Adversary.   1909.
Beyond These Voices.   1910.
The Green Curtain.   1911.
Miranda.   1913.
Mary.   1916.

Plays

The Loves of Arcadia (produced 1860).
The Model Husband (produced 1868).
Griselda; or, The Patient Wife (produced 1873).
Genevieve (produced 1874).
The Missing Witness.   1880.
Dross; or, The Root of Evil.   1882.
Married Beneath Him.   1882.
Marjorie Daw.   1882.
For Better, For Worse (produced 1890).

Verse

Garibaldi and Other Poems.   1861.

Other

Boscastle, Cornwall: An English Engadine.   1881.

Editor, *The Summer Tourist: A Book for Long and Short Journeys.*   1871.
Editor, *Aladdin; or, The Wonderful Lamp.*   1880.

Reading List: *Things Past* by Michael Sadleir, 1944; *The Novels of Braddon* by B. M. Nyberg (unpublished dissertation, University of Colorado), 1965; *A Literature of Their Own* by Elaine Showalter, 1977; *Sensational Victorian: The Life and Fiction of Braddon* by Robert Lee Wolff, 1978 (includes bibliography).

*   *   *

Mary Elizabeth Braddon's literary career spanned nearly sixty years and included the publication of more than seventy novels under her own name, a large quantity of anonymous and pseudonymous work, and the editorship of several periodicals, most notably *Belgravia*;

but it was as the author of a single immensely popular novel, *Lady Audley's Secret*, that she was primarily famous among her contemporaries and is remembered today.

Along with Wilkie Collins's *The Woman in White* and Mrs. Henry Wood's *East Lynne*, *Lady Audley's Secret* inaugurated the vogue of the Sensation Novel, a controversial sub-genre that dominated the popular fiction of the 1860's. Initially, some reviewers applauded the exciting, well-made plots characteristic of the form, but as the decade progressed they became increasingly critical of the Sensation Novel's plot-dominance, its emphasis on crime and encouragement of sympathy for morally ambiguous characters, and its lack of realism despite its contemporary settings. Miss Braddon was especially criticized for the lurid melodrama of her work and her relatively frank depiction of passionate and criminal women; and, indeed, of all the Sensation Novelists she gave hostile reviewers the most opportunities, publishing seventeen novels, almost all of them sensational, in eight years. This extraordinary productivity stemmed in part from an abundant creative energy which characterized Miss Braddon's entire career, but it was also due at least in part to the sensational quality of her private life. Her relationship with John Maxwell, an enterprising publisher with five children and a wife in an asylum, involved her in his financial difficulties throughout the mid-1860's.

After 1870, Miss Braddon's domestic life (she and Maxwell were able to marry in 1874) and her novels assumed a calmer character. The humor, sharp social observation, and interest in character, only intermittent in her early work, became the leading characteristics of the later. Observing this, Michael Sadleir has argued that Miss Braddon was more than a "mere sensationalist," and that her reputation was distorted by her youthful success. In his excellent dissertation, the most extended discussion of Miss Braddon's work, B. M. Nyberg contends that her Sensation Novels are neither her best nor, considering her career as a whole, her most characteristic work; he points to *The Infidel* among her historical novels, *Strangers and Pilgrims* among her novels of manners, and *The Rose of Life* among her character novels as a more suitable basis for her literary reputation. Sadleir and Nyberg are surely right that Miss Braddon's early fame obscured her later achievement; but it is also true that her early novels attracted attention and praise from readers as diverse as Thackeray, Rossetti, Robert Louis Stevenson, and the middle-class patrons of Mudie's, and that *Lady Audley's Secret*, which helped to establish an important sub-genre and a new feminine type, perhaps understandably secured her place in literary history.

—Randolph Ivy

BRONTË, Anne. English. Born in Thornton, Yorkshire, 17 March 1820; sister of Charlotte Brontë, *q.v.*, and Emily Brontë, *q.v.*; moved with her family to Haworth, Yorkshire, 1820, and lived there for the rest of her life. Educated at home, and at Miss Wooler's School, Roehead, later at Dewsbury Moor, Yorkshire, 1835–37. Governess to the Ingham family at Blake Hall, 1839, and to the Robinson family at Thorpe Green, 1841–45. *Died 28 May 1849.*

PUBLICATIONS

Collections

Complete Poems, edited by C. K. Shorter. 1923.
The Shakespeare Head Brontë, edited by T. J. Wise and J. A. Symington. 19 vols., 1932–38.

Fiction

> *Agnes Grey,* with *Wuthering Heights,* by Emily Brontë.   1847; edited by Herbert Van
> Thal, 1966.
> *The Tenant of Wildfell Hall.*   1848.

Verse

> *Poems,* with Charlotte and Emily Brontë.   1846.
> *Self-Communion,* edited by T. J. Wise.   1900.
> *Dreams and Other Poems.*   1917.

Bibliography: *A Bibliography of the Writings in Prose and Verse of the Brontë Family* by T. J. Wise, 1917.

Reading List: *Brontë* by Winifred Gérin, 1959; *Brontë* by Ada Harrison and Derek Stanford, 1959. For other works, see the entry for Charlotte Brontë.

*   *   *

But for the impetus given her by her sisters' example, Anne Brontë might never have sought self-expression in writing fiction. As a child, led on by the enthusiasm of her favourite sister, Emily, she joined in writing some of the "Gondal" saga scripts; but her true talent lay in poetry, for which she had a life-long love. Mostly written in the prosody of hymns, and influenced by the thought and style of Cowper and Wordsworth, her favourite poets, she made no claim to originality. Writing poetry was for her the most natural outlet for the two strongest emotions of her life: religion and her love of Nature. She found consolation for the trials and sorrows of her life in the one; and her keenest joy in the other. The lines "Written on a Windy Day" are not only typical of her simple, unforced style, but evidence of her close observation of Nature's moods:

> My soul is awakened, my spirit is soaring
> And carried aloft on the wings of the breeze;
> For above and around me the wild wind is roaring,
> Arousing to rapture the earth and the seas.
>
> The long withered grass in the sunshine is glancing,
> The bare trees are tossing their branches on high;
> The dead leaves, beneath them, are merrily dancing,
> The white clouds are scudding across the blue sky.
>
> I wish I could see how the ocean is lashing
> The foam of its billows to whirlwinds of spray;
> I wish I could see how its proud waves are dashing
> And hear the roar of their thunder to-day!

Life dealt hardly with her: William Weightman, the man she could have loved and married, died young of cholera, and she mourned his loss in some memorably haunting lines that have found their place in the anthologies. Hers was a naturally elegiac talent.

Her first novel, *Agnes Grey,* was the relation of her experiences in her two posts as governess. It was highly rated by George Moore, who said of it (*Conversations in Ebury Street,* 1930) that it was "the most perfect prose narrative in English literature.... As simple and as beautiful as a muslin dress ... the one story in which style, characters and subject are in perfect keeping ...," a judgement not shared by the generality of critics and readers despite the artless charm of the writing and the imprint of truth in the incidents.

Branwell Brontë, the highly gifted brother of the Brontës, died of a mixture of drink and drugs at thirty-one after untold mental and physical suffering. Anne Brontë felt it her duty to describe unflinchingly, in *The Tenant of Wildfell Hall*, the degradation and horror of such a ruin and its effects on the family of the victim. In her novel she traces the slow degrees of Arthur Huntingdon's destruction, and the courage of his wife, Helen, in leaving him so as to rescue their son from his influence. This made scandalous reading at the time, with its strong plea for the rights of married women to protection from such husbands, and to financial independence; but its very boldness ensured the book's success. It was, with *Jane Eyre*, in the best-seller class in the Circulating Libraries. At the same time, the author's love and pity and her deep faith speak eloquently on behalf of the sinner whose death she records as the inevitable "Wages of Sin." Huntingdon's wife, who returns to nurse him through the final stages of his decay, sitting by him through his last moments, proclaims the faith the author herself strongly held – not generally accepted at the time in evangelical circles – of ultimate salvation, even for such as he: "none can imagine the miseries, bodily and mental, of that death-bed! How could I endure to think that that poor trembling soul was hurried away to everlasting torment? It would drive me mad! But, thank God, I have hope ... that through whatever purging fires the erring spirit may have to pass, whatever fate awaits it, still, it is not lost, and God, who hateth nothing that He hath made, will bless it in the end."

—Winifred Gérin

BRONTË, Charlotte. English. Born in Thornton, Yorkshire, 21 April 1816; sister of Anne Brontë, *q.v.*, and Emily Brontë, *q.v.*; moved with her family to Haworth, Yorkshire, 1820, and lived there for the rest of her life. Educated at home, at a school for clergymen's daughters, Cowan Bridge, Yorkshire, 1824–25, Miss Wooler's School, Roehead, Yorkshire, 1831–32, and at the Pensionnat Heger, Brussels, 1842. Married Arthur Bell Nicholls in 1854. Teacher at Miss Wooler's School, Roehead, later at Dewsbury Moor, Yorkshire, 1835–37, 1838; Governess to the Sidgwick family of Stonegappe, Yorkshire, 1839, and the White family of Rawdon, Yorkshire, 1841; Teacher at the Pensionnat Heger, 1843; successful as a novelist from 1847. *Died 31 March 1855.*

PUBLICATIONS

Collections

The Complete Poems, edited by C. K. Shorter. 1923.
The Shakespeare Head Brontë, edited by T. J. Wise and J. A. Symington. 19 vols., 1932–38.

Fiction

Jane Eyre: An Autobiography. 1847; edited by Margaret Smith, 1973.

Shirley. 1849; edited by Andrew and Judith Hook, 1974.
Villette. 1853; edited by Margaret Lane, 1957.
The Professor. 1857.
The Adventures of Ernest Alembert: A Fairy tale, edited by T. J. Wise. 1896.
The Moores, edited by W. R. Nicoll, with *Jane Eyre.* 1902.
The Four Wishes: A Fairy Tale, edited by C. K. Shorter. 1918.
Napoleon and the Spectre: A Ghost Story. 1919.
The Twelve Adventurers and Other Stories, edited by C. W. Hatfield. 1925.
The Spell: An Extravaganza, edited by G. E. MacLean. 1931.
Legends of Angria, edited by Fannie E. Ratchford and W. C. De Vane. 1933.
The Search after Hapiness: A Tale, edited by T. A. J. Burnett. 1969.
Five Novelettes, edited by Winifred Gérin. 1971.
Two Tales: The Secret and Lily Hart, edited by William Holtz. 1978.

Verse

Poems, with Anne and Emily Brontë. 1846.
Richard Coeur de Lion and Blondel, edited by C. K. Shorter. 1912.
Saul and Other Poems. 1913.
The Violet, edited by C. K. Shorter. 1916.
The Red Cross Knight and Other Poems. 1917.
The Swiss Emigrant's Return and Other Poems. 1917.
Latest Gleanings, edited by C. K. Shorter. 1918.
Darius Codomannus. 1920.

Bibliography: *A Bibliography of the Writings in Prose and Verse of the Brontë Family* by T. J. Wise, 1917.

Reading List: *The Brontës' Web of Childhood* by Fannie E. Ratchford, 1941; *The Accents of Persuasion: Brontë's Novels* by R. B. Martin, 1966; *Their Proper Sphere: A Study of the Brontë Sisters as Early Victorian Female Novelists* by I. S. Ewbank, 1966; *Brontë: The Evolution of Genius* by Winifred Gérin, 1967; *The Brontës: A Collection of Critical Essays* edited by Ian Gregor, 1970; *The Brontës and Their Background: Romance and Reality* by Tom Winnifrith, 1973; *Brontë: A Psychosexual Study of Her Novels* by Charles Burkhart, 1973; *The Brontës: The Critical Heritage* edited by Miriam Allott, 1974; *Charlotte: The Foreign Vision of Brontë* by Enid L. Duthie, 1975; *Brontë: The Self Conceived* by Helene Moglen, 1976.

*   *   *

Limited in her formative years to the region and residents of her father's Yorkshire moorland parish, Charlotte Brontë was essentially influenced by her reading in the periodical literature of the day – *Blackwood's Magazine,* in particular – and the leading poets of the Romantic Revival – Byron, Scott, Southey, Campbell. Her strong imagination was stimulated far in advance of her experience of life, and resulted in a precocious talent for writing. From the age of twelve she was continuously writing stories, dramas, verses, and critiques, the apprenticeship for her adult writings. Consequently, her work forms one continuous whole, the major works on which her fame rests to-day – *Jane Eyre, Shirley, Villette, The Professor* – being as securely rooted in the juvenilia as in the subsequent experiences of her life.

Her writing is marked throughout by intensity, intensity of vision in the descriptive passages, intensity of feeling in the emotional scenes. The passionate involvement of the individual in every situation endows her work, like that of her sister Emily, with the quality of poetry, even in the medium of prose. Her childish writings already show the two distinct characteristics of her work as a whole: the closely observed, scrupulously factual relation of domestic detail and the extravagant adventures of the spirit in which she ranged as in a fantasy world, whose scenario and setting were supplied by any book she happened to be reading at the time, *The Travels of Mungo Park*, say or *The Arabian Nights*. Two constant themes overlapped from the juvenilia into the adult writings: the theme of the Rival Brothers, and the theme of the Orphan Girl. The first of these originated with the Wellesley brothers, Wellington's sons, who were the protagonists of the young Brontës' earliest tales, their substitute identities. The brothers' inveterate enmity formed the main-spring of Charlotte's Angrian cycle of tales for ten years and more. Under modified identities they appear in *The Professor* as the Crimsworth brothers, and in *Shirley* as Robert and Louis Moore. Stranger still, they appear again in one of Charlotte's last sketches, "Willie Ellin," as though the potentiality of the subject still remained un-resolved. The conception of a fragile, friendless, often orphaned, girl, whose struggles in a hostile society could reflect Charlotte's own painful experiences as governess, became central to the development of her plot-patterns in the adolescent novelettes; Mina Laury, Caroline Vernon, and Elizabeth Hastings are the recognisable prototypes of their illustrious successors Jane Eyre, Lucy Snowe, and Frances Henri, the first governess-heroines in Victorian literature.

Jane Eyre became a best-seller overnight. It tells the story of an orphan girl, educated in a charitable Institution, Lowood, and engaged as governess at Thornfield Hall. There she is exposed to some heart-searching experiences in her relations with her employer, Mr. Rochester, who is, unknown to her, a married man with a mad wife. The depth of her involvement and the honesty of her mind made this love-story startling in its day, and still profoundly true in human terms to-day.

The theme of unrequited love, so central to the plots of the adolescent juvenilia, is again present in *Shirley*. What weakens the interest is the duplication of the situation: there are two pairs of lovers, Caroline Helstone and Robert Moore, Shirley Keeldar and Louis Moore. The second pair of lovers would be redundant were it not for the character of Shirley, who was reputed to be an attempt to portray Emily Brontë after her death, an act of piety that was doomed to failure. The real subject of the book is Caroline's unhappy love, which is explored with exemplary delicacy and reticence.

Of all Charlotte Brontë's novels, *Villette* is the most ambitious in scale, the richest in character, the most mature in experience. It is set in a Brussels boarding-school, closely resembling the Pensionnat Heger where the author spent two years; the heroine, Lucy Snowe, is an orphan, without relatives or friends other than a godmother, Mrs. Bretton, and her son, Dr. John Graham Bretton. Her isolation is essential to the subject of the book. It makes Lucy exceptionally vulnerable to suffering or to kindness of any sort; she responds, both to Dr. Bretton's and Professor Emanuel's kindness, with all the intensity of a lonely heart. It is again the theme of unrequited love, such as the author herself suffered for her Belgian master, the married M. Heger. In the novel there is no legal barrier to Lucy's happiness, only the jealousy of the school's Directrice, the superbly realised Mme. Beck. The emotional climate of the book is tempestuous throughout, progressing from stormy scene to stormy scene with a climax of electrical excitement that called on all the author's reserves of consummate story-telling. *Villette* is not only Charlotte Brontë's masterpiece, but one of the great Victorian novels. Here, once again, use is made throughout of natural forces at work, to heighten the sense of fate directing human destinies.

Written before all the rest of the Brontë novels, and rejected by successive publishers throughout the author's life, *The Professor* was posthumously published. In its use of a male first-person narrator, and in the revival of the Enemy-Brothers theme, the book harks back to the juvenilia. It is saved, however, by the charm of the heroine, Frances Henri, who, in Mrs. Gaskell's opinion, was "the most charming woman she ever drew," and by some humorously observed Brussels characters and scenes that foreshadow the triumph of *Villette*.

The novels are not only autobiographical in setting, but in the character and situation of the protagonists. Her heroines are marked by a code of honour and a personal fastidiousness of taste characteristic of the author herself; this, while exposing them to great mental suffering, also allows them no facile road to fulfilment and happiness. Jane Eyre, Lucy Snowe, and Shirley Keeldar are endowed with a quality of mind, a strength of will, a capacity for love that differentiates them fundamentally from the general productions of contemporary lady-novelists; they are portrayed with total honesty and courage. Charlotte Brontë and her sister Anne were among the first women novelists to claim equality between women and men in the right to declare their love. It is Jane Eyre who declares her love to Rochester before he makes his sentiments plain to her, and, by doing so, greatly shocked the first readers of the book. "Do you think, because I am poor, obscure, plain, and little, I am soulless and heartless?" she cries, believing Rochester about to marry another woman and to dismiss her; "You think wrong! – I have as much soul as you, – and full as much heart! And if God had gifted me with some beauty, and much wealth, I should have made it as hard for you to leave me, as it is now for me to leave you. I am not talking to you now through the medium of custom, conventionalities, nor even of mortal flesh: – it is my spirit that addresses your spirit; just as if both had passed through the grave, and we stood at God's feet, – equal, – as we are!"

A further distinctive element in the novels is the role given to nature in affecting the affairs of man. Writing in a wild and beautiful region in closest contact with the changing elements at all seasons of the year, Charlotte Brontë, not surprisingly, shows the influence of natural phenomena on the human situation, and uses it as a device in the plot. Witness the Aurora Borealis in *Villette* that influences Lucy Snowe to go to London, the storm that forces her to seek shelter in Ste. Gudule to make her Confession, and the storm in *Jane Eyre* that rends the old chestnut tree in presage of her broken marriage. In such passages as these, and in countless others, the poetic character of the inspiration is plainly seen, enriching the total vision of the novels with a spiritual quality that is as integral a part of their content as the narrative impetus of their plots.

—Winifred Gérin

BRONTË, Emily (Jane).   English.   Born in Thornton, Yorkshire, 30 July 1818; sister of Anne Brontë, *q.v.*, and Charlotte Brontë, *q.v.*; moved with her family to Haworth, Yorkshire, 1820, and lived there for the rest of her life. Educated at home, at a school for clergymen's daughters, Cowan Bridge, Yorkshire, 1824–25, Miss Wooler's School, Roehead, Yorkshire, 1835; Pensionnat Heger, Brussels, 1842. Taught in a school at Law Hill, Halifax, 1837–38. *Died 19 December 1848.*

PUBLICATIONS

Collections

Complete Works, edited by C. K. Shorter and W. R. Nicoll.   2 vols., 1910–11.
The Shakespeare Head Brontë, edited by T. J. Wise and J. A. Symington.   19 vols., 1932–38.
Complete Poems, edited by C. W. Hatfield.   1941.
Poems, edited by Rosemary Hartill.   1973.

Fiction

Wuthering Heights, with *Agnes Grey*, by Anne Brontë.   1847.

Verse

Poems, with Anne and Charlotte Brontë.   1846.
Two Poems, edited by Fannie E. Ratchford.   1934.
Gondal Poems, edited by Helen Brown and Joan Mott.   1938.
Gondal's Queen: A Novel in Verse, edited by Fannie E. Ratchford.   1955.

Other

Five Essays Written in French, translated by Lorine White Nagel, edited by Fannie E. Ratchford.   1948.

Bibliography: *A Bibliography of the Writings in Prose and Verse of the Brontë Family* by T. J. Wise, 1917.

Reading List: *Brontë: Her Life and Work* by Muriel Spark and Derek Stanford, 1953; *Brontë* by Winifred Gérin, 1971; *Brontë: A Critical Anthology* edited by Jean-Pierre Petit, 1973; *The Mind of Brontë* by Herbert Dingle, 1974. For other works, see the entry for Charlotte Brontë.

*   *   *

Emily Brontë's reputation might appear at first sight disproportionate to her meagre output: one novel and 193 poems. Their quality, however, is unique, so visionary and powerful as to rank her indisputably among the writers of genius.

Few influences on her writing can be traced. She was a very private person, rejecting such contacts with the world as were offered her through her sister Charlotte and her London publishers. Though her work has many affinities with the English Metaphysical poets, Traherne and Vaughan in particular, there is no evidence that she ever read them. Her reading was, on her own showing, very limited, very desultory, and without method. She reproached herself repeatedly in her diary papers for the want of "regularity" in her studies. She knew the romantic poets, Wordsworth especially, and Shakespeare, whom she often quotes. She had little schooling, falling ill whenever sent from home. All the source of her health and happiness, and the inspiration of her writing, were the moors that stretch twenty miles round about her home, Haworth, where she spent her whole life. Her intimate knowledge of the moors at all seasons of the year, and of the wild-life inhabiting them, gave her all the stimulus she needed to enrich her imagination and inspire her writing.

The nature of her poetry and of her one novel – *Wuthering Heights* – is profoundly metaphysical, nourished by the visions that she undoubtedly experienced and was able to describe with all the clarity of facts perceived. The following lines are drawn from a poem about a young captive who awaits her liberator. As with much of her poetic imagery, the awaited visitant is not a corporeal but a spiritual presence.

> He comes with western winds, with evening's wandering airs,
> With that clear dusk of heaven that brings the thickest stars;
> Winds take a pensive tone, and stars a tender fire,
> And visions rise and change which kill me with desire....

But first a hush of peace, a soundless calm descends;
The struggle of distress and fierce impatience ends;
Mute music soothes my breast – unuttered harmony
That I could never dream till earth was lost to me.

Then dawns the Invisible, the Unseen itself reveals;
My outward sense is gone, my inward essence feels –
Its wings are almost free, its home, its harbour found;
Measuring the gulf it stoops and dares the final bound!

Oh, dreadful is the check – intense the agony
When the ear begins to hear and the eye begins to see;
When the pulse begins to throb, the brain to think again,
The soul to feel the flesh and the flesh to feel the chain!

The religious terminology of much of Emily Brontë's poetry does not obscure the fact that hers was no conventional religion (despite her father's calling). So far as her intensely personal beliefs can be defined, she was a Pantheist, seeing all life as One – the Visible and the Invisible, the human, the elemental, the animal and vegetable all imbued with the same spiritual forces.

She made a marked distinction between her personal and her Gondal poetry by transcribing them in two separate and clearly marked notebooks. Through the Gondal poems runs a dramatic Saga relating to the royal houses of Angora and Almedore, who contended for the thrones of the island kingdoms of Gondal and Gaaldine, the location of the drama; the principal theme is the love-hate relationship binding the Queen of Angora, Augusta Geraldine Almeda, to her various lovers, primarily Julius Brenzaida. Under cover of this scenario, begun in childhood, Emily Brontë found the substitute identities and the adventurous actions lacking in her life, the freedom that her spirit craved. Freedom was, for her, a pre-condition of life. As she wrote in one of her personal poems:

And if I pray, the only prayer
That moves my lips for me
Is – "Leave me the heart that now I bear
And give me liberty.

Yes, as my swift days near their goal
'Tis all that I implore –
Through life and death, a chainless soul
With courage to endure."

The situations of which she wrote in the Gondal poems, often describing passionate love relations, led her early readers to suppose them autobiographical, revealing a real-life love affair. Their true context in the Gondal Saga, however, has dispelled this notion for good (the known circumstances of her life leave no room for such a relationship), though the "love-poems," like the famous lament "Cold in the earth," when placed in their right context, are seen to resemble the subject of *Wuthering Heights* so closely as to show the overall unity of her creative work.

For years before the writing of *Wuthering Heights*, the Gondal poems dealt with an orphan boy, "black of mien, savage in disposition," passionately involved with a fair girl, his superior in social standing, the very situation of Heathcliff and Catherine Earnshaw in the novel. Emily Brontë's belief in the indissoluble nature of earthly love, first treated in the poems, found its complete expression in the novel, where even the separation of death is shown as powerless to sever a spiritual connection. Catherine Earnshaw gives utterance to this Credo early in the novel when Heathcliff runs away and she is urged to forget him and make a suitable marriage with Edgar Linton: "… my great thought in living is [Heathcliff]. If all else perished, and *he* remained, I should still continue to be; and if all else remained, and he were annihilated, the universe would turn to a mighty stranger; I should not seem a part of it…. My love for Heathcliff resembles the eternal rocks beneath…. Nelly, I *am* Heathcliff!" Catherine's faith is shown as justified in the novel's end where Heathcliff even desecrates her grave so as to be buried with her; and their ghosts are ultimately seen, wandering freely together upon the hillside. The death of Heathcliff, self-induced by his longing for Catherine, is one of the most powerful and daring climaxes in English fiction.

The boldness of the conception that man is the master of his own fate is matched by her last poem, "No coward soul is mine." Addressed to the "God within my breast," she makes her declaration of faith in the universal nature of the soul inhabiting each individual:

> Though Earth and moon were gone
> And suns and universes ceased to be
> And thou wert left alone
> Every Existence would exist in thee
>
> There is not room for Death
> Nor atom that his might could render void
> Since thou art Being and Breath
> And what thou art may never be destroyed.

That is the metaphysical message of *Wuthering Heights*: the indestructibility of the spirit. Such a subject was so far removed from the general run of Victorian fiction – it belonged, if anywhere, to the Gothic tradition, still being followed by Mary Shelley with her *Valperga* (1823) in Emily Brontë's childhood – that it explains the novel's failure when first published. Only two critics, Sydney Dobell and Swinburne, praised it (in 1850 and 1883 respectively), too late to bring recognition to the author in her lifetime.

The book's curious and lasting appeal rests upon a number of qualities: the unflagging excitement of the plot; the wild moorland setting and the splendour of the descriptions; the originality of the characters; the unearthly, not to say ghostly atmosphere created by the interplay of the elements in the affairs of men; the homely background of the old house, The Heights, in which the decaying fortunes of the Earnshaw family are – literally – played out, gambled away, by the last of the line. The author's close familiarity with the local rustic types, the fiercely independent hill-farmers living about the moors, enabled her to create the old curmudgeon Joseph, the general factotum to the family, with both humour and fidelity: his permanent ill-humour and girding condemnation of his associates as all destined for Hell fire, faithfully portrays the primitive attitudes left in the wake of the Methodist Revival in Yorkshire; and acts as a counter-balance to the gothic atmosphere of much of the plot and the high Romanticism of the larger-than-life hero and heroine, Heathcliff and Catherine. In creating such a character as Joseph, Emily Brontë showed that, undoubted visionary as she was, she also had her feet firmly planted on earth.

—Winifred Gérin

BULWER-LYTTON, Edward (George Earle); 1st Baron Lytton of Knebworth. English. Born in London, 25 May 1803. Educated at Dr. Ruddock's School in Fulham, London; Dr. Hooker's School at Rottingdean, Sussex; with a Mr. Wallington,

Ealing, London, 1818–20; Trinity College, Cambridge (pensioner), 1822, and Trinity Hall, Cambridge (fellow-commoner; Chancellor's Medal for verse, 1825), 1822–25, B.A. 1826, M.A. 1835. Married Rosina Doyle Wheeler in 1827 (separated, 1836); one daughter and one son. Visited Paris, 1825, and thereafter divided his time between London and Paris; settled at Woodcot House, near Pangbourne, Berkshire, 1827, and supported himself by writing for various magazines, including *Quarterly Review*, *Keepsakes*, and *Books of Beauty*; settled in London, 1829; Editor, *New Monthly Magazine*, London, 1831–33; Liberal Member of Parliament for St. Ives, Cornwall, 1831, and for Lincoln, 1832–41; active supporter of stronger copyright laws and of the removal of taxes on literature; published, with others, *The Monthly Chronicle*, London, 1841; succeeded to the family estate at Knebworth, 1843; travelled abroad, 1849; Conservative Member of Parliament for Hertfordshire, 1852 until his elevation to the peerage, 1866; Secretary for the Colonies, 1858–59. Lord Rector of the University of Glasgow, 1856, 1858. LL.D.: Cambridge University, 1864. Created Baron Lytton, 1866. *Died 18 January 1873.*

PUBLICATIONS

Fiction

Falkland. 1827; edited by Herbert Van Thal, 1967.
Pelham. 1828; revised edition, 1839; edited by Jerome J. McGann, 1972.
The Disowned. 1828.
Devereux. 1829.
Paul Clifford. 1830.
Eugene Aram. 1832.
Asmodeus at Large. 1833.
Godolphin. 1833.
The Last Days of Pompeii. 1834; revised edition, 1835; edited by Edgar Johnson, 1956.
The Pilgrims of the Rhine. 1834.
Rienzi, The Last of the Roman Tribunes. 1835.
Ernest Maltravers. 1837.
Leila; or, The Siege of Granada. 1837.
Alice; or, The Mysteries. 1838.
Calderon, The Courtier. 1838.
Night and Morning. 1841.
Zanoni. 1842.
The Last of the Barons. 1843; edited by F. C. Romilly, 1913.
Lucretia; or, The Children of Night. 1846.
Harold, The Last of the Saxon Kings. 1848; edited by G. L. Gomme, 1906.
The Caxtons: A Family Picture. 1849.
My Novel; or, Varieties in English Life. 1852.
The Haunted and the Haunters. 1857.
What Will He Do with It? 1859.
A Strange Story. 1862; revised edition, 1863.
The Coming Race. 1871.
Kenelm Chillingly: His Adventures and Opinions. 1873.
The Parisians. 1873.
Pausanias the Spartan, edited by Bulwer-Lytton's son. 1876.

Plays

The Duchess de la Vallière (produced 1837).   1836.
The Lady of Lyons; or, Love and Pride (produced 1838).   1838.
Richelieu; or, The Conspiracy (produced 1839).   1839.
The Sea-Captain; or, The Birth-Right (produced 1839).   1839.
Money (produced 1840).   1840.
Not So Bad as We Seem; or, Many Sides to a Character (produced 1851).   1851.
The Rightful Heir (produced 1868).   1868.
Walpole; or, Every Man Has His Price.   1869.
The House of Darnley Court, revised by Charles F. Coghlan (produced 1877).
Junius Brutus; or, The Household Gods (produced 1885).

Verse

Ismael: An Oriental Tale.   1820.
Delmour; or, A Tale of a Sylphid and Other Poems.   1823.
Sculpture.   1825.
Weeds and Wild Flowers.   1826.
O'Neill; or, The Rebel.   1827.
The Siamese Twins: A Satirical Tale.   1831.
Eva, The Ill-Omened Marriage, and Other Poems.   1842.
Poems, edited by C. D. Macleod.   1845.
The New Timon.   1846.
King Arthur: An Epic Poem.   3 vols., 1848–49; revised edition, 1870.
Poetical Works.   1859; revised edition, 1865, 1873.
St. Stephen's.   1860.
The Boatman.   1864.
Lost Tales of Miletus.   1866.

Other

England and the English.   2 vols., 1833; edited by Standish Meachum, 1970.
A Letter to a Late Cabinet Minster on the Present Crisis.   1834.
The Student: A Series of Papers.   2 vols., 1835.
Athens: Its Rise and Fall.   2 vols., 1837.
Critical and Miscellaneous Works.   2 vols., 1841.
Confessions of a Water-Patient.   1846.
A Word to the Public.   1847.
Letters to John Bull Esquire.   1851.
Poetical and Dramatic Works.   5 vols., 1852–54.
Caxtonia: A Series of Essays on Life, Literature, and Manners.   2 vols., 1863.
Miscellaneous Prose Works.   3 vols., 1868.
Speeches.   2 vols., 1874.
Works.   37 vols., 1873–77.
Quarterly Essays.   1875.
Letters to His Wife, edited by Louisa Devey.   1884.
Pamphlets and Sketches.   1887.
Letters to Macready.   1911.
Bulwer and Macready: A Chronicle of the Early Victorian Theatre, edited by Charles H.
   Shattuck.   1958.

Editor, *Literary Remains of William Hazlitt.*   2 vols., 1836.

Translator, *The Poems and Ballads of Schiller.*   2 vols., 1844.
Translator, *The Odes and Epodes of Horace.*   1869.

Bibliography: *XIX Century Fiction* by Michael Sadleir, 2 vols., 1951.

Reading List: *Life, Letters, and Literary Remains,* edited by Earl of Lytton, 2 vols., 1883; *The Life of Lytton,* 2 vols., 1913, and *Bulwer-Lytton,* 1948, both by V. A. G. R. B. Lytton; *Bulwer-Lytton's Novels and Isis Unveiled* by S. B. Liljegren, 1957; *The Newgate Novel 1830–1847* by Keith Hollingsworth, 1963; "Bulwer-Lytton" by Curtis Dahl, in *Victorian Fiction* edited by Lionel Stevenson, 1960; *Bulwer-Lytton: The Fiction of New Regions* by Allen Conrad Christensen, 1977.

*   *   *

"The padded man – that wears the stays – / Who killed the girls and thrilled the boys / With dandy pathos when you wrote" – so in his biting satiric poem "The New Timon and the Poets" Tennyson characterized Edward Bulwer-Lytton, and the description had enough truth in it to cut. Both as a person and as a writer Bulwer was often stiff, affected, prolix, melodramatic, sentimental. But, as in more generous moods Tennyson and almost all his contemporaries would have admitted, this harsh judgment was far too severe and ignored the central role that Bulwer played in earlier Victorian literature. Indeed, no Victorian novelist had a more creatively stimulating influence on his fellow writers than Bulwer-Lytton. None opened so many new paths in fiction for them to follow. His *Pelham* set the character for the "silver-fork" novel of high life and offered the ideal target for Carlyle's *Sartor Resartus*; *Paul Clifford, Eugene Aram,* and *Lucretia* effectively established the "Newgate novel" of crime and criminals; *The Last Days of Pompeii* popularized the archaeological novel; *Rienzi, Harold,* and *The Last of the Barons* brought careful historical research and contemporary political reference into the English historical novel; *The Caxtons* and *What Will He Do with It?* encouraged the trend toward domestic realism; *Zanoni* and *A Strange Story* made important the novel of the occult; *The Coming Race* is central in the tradition of the utopian science-fiction novel. Dickens, Thackeray, George Eliot, Collins, and others owe him a tremendous debt.

But Bulwer-Lytton's merits are not historical only. He won a huge popularity with a wide reading public from the parlors of England to the backwoods of America. He wrote effective satires, such as *The New Timon,* and graceful essays. He was influential as a critic and as editor of *The New Monthly Magazine.* His *England and the English* was one of the most acute critiques of English culture and society. He had a moderate success as a politician and as a political pamphleteer. Though his epic and lyric poetry, his translations, and his historical writings are rightly forgotten, his plays *The Lady of Lyons* and *Richelieu,* written for the great actor-manager Macready, held the boards into the twentieth century, and still have vitality. Moreover, after a period of denigration, his fiction is gaining more and more critical respect. For behind the too frequently obfuscating diction, wordiness, and generality of his style, there are keen philosophical, political, and moral thought and a sound though currently unfashionable concept of literary art. He has much to say to the reader who will fight through his verbiage, and a number of his novels are still readable today as fascinating and exciting fiction. Though his once brilliant general fame has waned, the "padded man," whose own wife once vengefully accused him of trying to get rid of her by shutting her up in a madhouse but who held the respect and friendship of most of the English literary world of his time, still rightly deserves his just share of praise.

—Curtis Dahl

BURNEY, Fanny (Frances Burney). English. Born in King's Lynn, Norfolk, 13 June 1752; moved with her family to London, 1760. Married the French officer Alexandre d'Arblay in 1793 (died, 1818); one son and one daughter. From 1778 member of the London literary circle of Mrs. Thrale: a friend of Johnson, Burke, Sheridan, and Garrick; Second Keeper of the Robes to Queen Charlotte, 1786 until she retired with a pension, 1791; lived in France, 1802–12, 1814–15; thereafter lived in retirement in London. *Died 6 January 1840.*

PUBLICATIONS

Collections

Journals and Letters, edited by Joyce Hemlow and others.   1972–.

Fiction

Evelina; or, The History of a Young Lady's Entrance into the World.   1778; edited by Edward A. Bloom, 1968.
Cecilia; or, Memoirs of an Heiress.   1782; edited by R. B. Johnson, 1893.
Camilla; or, A Picture of Youth.   1796; revised edition, 1802; edited by Edward A. and Lillian D. Bloom, 1972.
The Wanderer; or, Female Difficulties.   1814.

Play

Edwy and Elgiva (produced 1795).   Edited by Miriam J. Benkovitz, 1957.

Other

Brief Reflections Relative to the Emigrant French Clergy.   1793.
Memoirs of Dr. Burney.   3 vols., 1832.
Diary and Letters 1778–1840, edited by Charlotte Frances Barrett.   7 vols., 1842–46; edited by Austin Dobson, 6 vols., 1904–05; selections edited by John Wain, 1960.
The Early Diary 1768–78, edited by Annie Raine Ellis.   2 vols., 1889; revised edition, 1907.

Reading List: *Poets and Story-Tellers* by David Cecil, 1949; *The History of Fanny Burney* by Joyce Hemlow, 1958; *Burney, Novelist: A Study in Technique* by Eugene White, 1960; *Burney* by Michael E. Adelstein, 1968.

*   *   *

A novel, as conceived by Fanny Burney, "is, or it ought to be a picture of supposed, but natural and probable human existence. It holds, therefore, in its hands our best affections; it exercises our imaginations; it points out the path of honour; and gives to juvenile credulity knowledge of the world, without ruin, or repentance; and the lessons of experience, without its tears." This, essentially, was the critical creed to which she adhered with the tenacity of absolute conviction. The limitations are self-evident, but within them – even granting often flawed textures of character and incident – she wrought stories that have delighted readers for two hundred years since publication of *Evelina*. Fiction was Fanny Burney's private world of imagination transposed into a filtered reality, peculiar to her ethos, which she equated with moral truthfulness. It was a truthfulness sometimes too high-flown for pragmatic tastes. Nevertheless it was compounded of respect for traditional Christian values and a sense that these values must be confirmed by individual experience, growth, and self-identity. Each of her young heroines – Evelina, Cecilia, Camilla, Juliet – is subjected to the rites of social initiation as the requisite for private discovery. Simultaneously each heroine emerges from the seclusion of self, stirring in sympathetic readers the pangs and joys of maturing. Avowedly didactic, thus, Fanny Burney was in palpable control of the feeling heart.

Although she never quite shook off the bias inculcated in proper young females that novels were morally suspect, she was unable to resist either the compulsion of her own creative spirit or the lure of literary fame and fortune. At least in her first two novels – *Evelina* and *Cecilia* – she wrote with a passionate intensity that conveys the sense of necessity indigenous in all good if not necessarily great art. And she wrote about human fallibility and nobility, about poignant and comic experience, in such a way as to encase her truths in the agreeably disguised symbols of highly entertaining narration. There is an organic impulse in the earlier novels – a union of wisdom and invention – that has insured Fanny Burney's permanent niche in literary history. By common consent she is an important transitional novelist, carrying on the traditions of Richardson, Fielding, and Smollett while creating a modest tradition of her own, and then passing that on to Jane Austen.

The architectonics of fiction never engaged her as much as its potential for edification. Certainly she was no bold innovator in structure. Having employed, and quite successfully, the epistolary format of *Evelina*, she was content thereafter to write in the more conventional episodic manner of the omniscient author. The capacious, sometimes melodramatic, structures of *Cecilia*, *Camilla*, and *The Wanderer* were better suited to authorial exhortation than were the subjective letters (even when penned by a persona like the Reverend Mr. Villars). That tendency toward didactic statement, increasingly apparent after *Evelina*, was in part deference to public taste. But it was also symptomatic of the author's view of her own craft. Periodically, however, she flashes forth in scenes whose comic dialogue remind us that Fanny Burney was dramatically talented. In at least two of her plays (unfortunately never produced) she reveals the kind of comic spirit which brightens some of the somber restraint of *Cecilia* and *The Wanderer*. Balancing that disposition toward the hortatory, therefore, is an attractive strain of wit and satire. Comic mischance, social stumbling, any manners indeed which reveal the vulgar posturings of such commoners as the Branghtons, Mrs. Mittin and Mr. Dubster, sailors and shopkeepers, are the entertaining if implicitly cruel resources of a snobbish author.

Fops and well-born cads are also targets in these novels. And they, like the vulgarians, are important to the diversity which constitutes Fanny Burney's often complex plots and informs an almost central theme: youthful innocence, often orphaned, must come to virtuous maturity despite the temptations and bad examples which confront it constantly. The heroine is especially vulnerable when, like Cecilia or Juliet, she is stranded in an alien society without financial means of her own. A Burney heroine, however, is endowed with innate goodness which causes her not only to withstand ultimate temptation but to learn from it. Some, like Evelina and Camilla, err frequently and are humiliated. But through error they gradually discover the prudence that comes with maturity, and they are assisted by the benevolent concern of guardian figures and their future husbands.

The rewards for prudent conduct may stretch belief, but they are the essence of much that we hold dear in the fairy-tale ethic. In Fanny Burney's ideal world, an excellent marriage, freedom from financial care, and the lasting love of parent or guardian become the zenith of social well-being. The rascals retreat in confusion, but they have served their purpose, giving "to juvenile credulity knowledge of the world, without ruin, or repentance; and the lessons of experience, without its tears."

—Edward A. Bloom

BUTLER, Samuel.   English.   Born at Langar Rectory, near Bingham, Nottinghamshire, 4 December 1835. Educated at Shrewsbury School, Shropshire, 1848–54; St. John's College, Cambridge, 1854–58, B.A. (honours) 1858; abandoned intention of taking holy orders; studied painting at Heatherley's School, London, 1865. Sheep farmer in the Rangitata district of New Zealand, 1859–64; returned to England, and settled in London, 1864; exhibited paintings at the Royal Academy, London, 1868–76; studied and composed music, including the cantata *Narcissus*, 1888, and the oratorio *Ulysses*, 1904. *Died 18 June 1902.*

<small>PUBLICATIONS</small>

Collections

> *Works*, edited by H. F. Jones and A. T. Bartholomew.   20 vols., 1923–26.
> *The Essential Butler*, edited by G. D. H. Cole.   1950.

Fiction

> *Erewhon; or, Over the Range.*   1872; revised edition, 1872, 1901; edited by Peter Mudford, 1970.
> *Erewhon Revisited Twenty Years Later.*   1901.
> *The Way of All Flesh*, edited by R. A. Streatfeild.   1903; edited by James Cochrane, 1966.

Verse

> *Seven Sonnets and a Psalm of Montreal*, edited by R. A. Streatfeild.   1904.

Other

> *A First Year in Canterbury Settlement.*   1863; revised edition, edited by R. A. Streatfeild, 1917; edited by A. C. Brassington and P. B. Maling, 1964.
> *The Evidence for the Resurrection of Jesus Christ As Given by the Four Evangelists.*   1865.
> *The Fair Haven: A Work in Defence of the Miraculous Element in Our Lord's Ministry upon Earth.*   1873; edited by G. Bullett, 1938.
> *Life and Habit: An Essay after a Completer View of Evolution.*   1877.
> *Evolution Old and New.*   1879.
> *Unconscious Memory.*   1880.
> *Alps and Sanctuaries of Piedmont and the Canton Ticino.*   1881.
> *Selections from Previous Works.*   1884.
> *Holbein's Dance.*   1886.
> *Luck or Cunning as the Main Means of Organic Modifications?*   1886.
> *Ex Voto: An Account of the Sacro Monte or New Jerusalem at Varallo-Sesia.*   1888; revised edition, 1889.
> *On the Trapanese Origin of the Odyssey.*   1893.
> *The Life and Letters of Dr. Samuel Butler.*   2 vols., 1896.
> *The Authoress of the Odyssey.*   1897.
> *Shakespeare's Sonnets Reconsidered, and in Part Rearranged.*   1899.

Essays on Life, Art, and Science, edited by R. A. Streatfeild. 1904.
Note-Books: Selections, edited by H. F. Jones. 1912; *Butleriana,* edited by A. T. Bartholomew, 1932; *Further Extracts,* edited by A. T. Bartholomew, 1934; *Selections,* edited by Geoffrey Keynes and Brian Hill, 1951.
God the Known and God the Unknown, edited by R. A. Streatfeild. 1909.
The Humour of Homer and Other Essays, edited by R. A. Streatfeild. 1913.
Letters Between Butler and Miss E. M. A. Savage, edited by Geoffrey Keynes and Brian Hill. 1935.
Correspondence of Butler and His Sister May, edited by Daniel F. Howard. 1962.
The Family Letters 1841–1886, edited by Arnold Silver. 1962.

Translator, *The Iliad and Odyssey of Homer.* 2 vols., 1898–1900; edited by L. R. Loomis, 2 vols., 1942–44.
Translator, *Hesiod's Works and Days.* 1924.

Bibliography: *The Career of Butler: A Bibliography* by S. B. Harkness, 1955.

Reading List: *Butler: A Memoir* by H. F. Jones, 1919; *The Triple Thinkers* by Edmund Wilson, 1938; *Butler and the Way of All Flesh* by G. D. H. Cole, 1947; *Butler* by P. N. Furbank, 1948; *Darwin and Butler: Two Versions of Evolution* by Basil Willey, 1960; *Butler* by Lee E. Holt, 1964.

*   *   *

Samuel Butler was one of the most independent minds of the later nineteenth century: his interest in social ideas links him with such Victorian sages as Carlyle, Ruskin, and Arnold, but his preference for irony and paradox brings him close to Bernard Shaw and Oscar Wilde. The fact that he is so hard to classify would undoubtedly have pleased him, but it may account for the varied and fluctuating assessments of his importance.

Erewhon is his most stimulating book. A story in the tradition of *Gulliver's Travels,* it uses its conventional Evangelical protagonist Higgs and his adventures to raise many significant lines of thought – a possible analogy between crime and disease, the inauthenticity of much contemporary religious observance, the abstractness of upper-class Classical education, the dangers of mechanisation, the extravagances of moral dogma, and, above all, the hold of conventions on the mind. And Butler does all this in a highly entertaining way. He clearly saw himself as a free-thinker, and his mission as to challenge, by argument and irony, the conventional wisdom of his day. Above all, his insight into the extent to which human beliefs are the products of social environment is impressive, especially at a time when thinkers were apt to believe in absolutes. He writes of an Erewhonian judge: "He could not emanicpate himself from, nay, it did not even occur to him to feel, the bondage of the ideas in which he had been born and bred." Butler's distinction was his awareness of the awaiting bondage.

In some cases Butler's determination not to be dragooned into orthodoxy led him to extravagances of his own. Many would feel that this is true of his protracted campaign against Darwin's idea of evolution. In a series of books including *Life and Habit, Unconscious Memory,* and *Luck or Cunning,* Butler argued that the evolutionary process was directed by some kind of life-force. He thus introduced a new and complicating note into the controversy between Science and Religion. Sometimes his love of heterodoxy led him to attack accepted assumptions irresponsibly, but there was usually enough behind his arguments to make attention to them an enlivening experience. In *The Authoress of the Odyssey* he argued from internal evidence that the poet must have been a woman, and in *Shakespeare's Sonnets* that they were addressed to a plebeian lover.

His *Note-Books* perhaps best reveal the wide range of his interests, but his best-known book is *The Way of All Flesh* which, published posthumously in 1903, dealt a massive blow to the Victorian family ideal. In it Butler mixes autobiography with experiences of his own ideas, thoroughly debunking the attitudes represented by the father, Theobald Pontifex. The book had a liberating effect on many young writers of the time, and its attitude to Victorianism underlies the criticisms of the 1920's. The early scenes have great vividness, but there are elements of complacency in the later part which mark Butler's limitations. He lived very much to himself and this comes out in the somewhat inhuman ideal which is propounded at the end. The comment made on Ernest Pontifex shows, however, a just awareness on Butler's part of how he was regarded: "With the general public he is not a favourite. He is admitted to have talent, but it is considered generally to be of a queer, unpractical kind, and no matter how serious he is, he is always accused of being in jest." Butler's jests often retain for the modern reader an interest which can no longer be accorded to the conventional wisdom of the age which he strove to educate by his paradoxes.

—Peter Faulkner

CARLETON, William.   Irish.   Born in Prillisk, Clogher, County Tyrone, 4 March 1794. Educated at various district schools, and at a classical school in Donagh, County Monaghan, 1814–16. Married; two sons. Settled in Dublin: worked as a taxidermist and as a tutor; contributed to the *Christian Examiner* and the *Dublin University Magazine*; full-time writer from 1830. Granted government pension, 1848. *Died 30 January 1869.*

PUBLICATIONS

Fiction

> *Father Butler; The Lough Dearg Pilgrim; Being Sketches of Irish Manners.*   1829.
> *Traits and Stories of the Irish Peasantry.*   1830; second series, 1833; as *Irish Life and Character*, 1860; edited by F. A. Niccolls, 1911.
> *Tales of Ireland.*   1834.
> *Fardorougha the Miser; or, The Convicts of Lisnamona.*   1839.
> *The Fawn of Spring-Vale, The Clarionet, and Other Tales.*   1841; as *Jane Sinclair*, 1843; as *The Clarionet, The Dead Boxer, and Barney Branagan*, 1850.
> *Parry Sastha; or, The History of Paddy Go-Easy and His Wife Nancy.*   1845.
> *Rody the Rover; or, The Ribbonman.*   1845.
> *The Battle of the Factions and Other Tales of Ireland.*   1845.
> *Tales and Sketches Illustrating the Character of the Irish Peasantry.*   1845; as *Irish Life and Character*, 1855.
> *Valentine M'Clutchey, The Irish Agent; or, The Chronicles of the Castle Cumber Property.*   1845.
> *Art Maguire; or, The Broken Pledge.*   1845.
> *The Black Prophet: A Tale of Irish Famine.*   1847.
> *The Emigrants of Ahadarra: A Tale of Irish Life.*   1848.

The Tithe Proctor, Being a Tale of the Tithe Rebellion in Ireland.   1849.
The Irishman at Home: Characteristic Sketches of the Irish Peasantry.   1849.
Red Hall; or, The Baronet's Daughter.   1852; as *The Black Baronet,* 1858.
The Squanders of Castle Squander.   1852.
Willy Reilly and His Dear Coleen Bawn.   1855.
Alley Sheridan and Other Stories.   1858.
The Evil Eye; or, The Black Spectre.   1860.
Redmond Count O'Hanlon, The Irish Rapparee: An Historical Tale.   1862.
The Silver Acre and Other Tales.   1862.
The Double Prophecy; or, Trials of the Heart.   1862.
The Poor Scholar, Frank Martin and the Fairies, The Country Dancing Master, and Other Irish Tales.   1869.
The Fair of Emyvale, and The Master and the Scholar.   1870.
The Red-Haired Man's Wife.   1889.

Other

The Life of Carleton, Being His Autobiography and Letters, continued by D. J. O'Donoghue.   2 vols., 1896.

Reading List: *Poor Scholar: A Study of the Works and Days of Carleton* by Benedict Kiely, 1947.

*   *   *

Patrick Kavanagh, who claimed in a BBC talk that William Carleton was one of the two great native writers of Ireland (the other being James Joyce) also remarked in his preface to Carleton's *Autobiography* (1968) that "he wrote two books and a great deal of melodramatic trash." The two books he refers to are the *Autobiography* itself and *Traits and Stories of the Irish Peasantry.*

The *Autobiography,* which Carleton left unfinished, was first published in 1896 long after his death. It tells the story, in vigorous and straightforward prose, of his early life and wanderings as a hedge-scholar. *Traits and Stories* contains a large collection of stories and descriptive sketches of Irish peasant life in the days before the great famine. They tell of courting, weddings, faction fights, and pilgrimages. Carleton reproduces, in amusing and racy dialogue, the speech of the people, with tags of Irish interspersed, and he attempts by his spelling to suggest the Irish brogue. Some of the stories, such as "The Poor Scholar," are dark and sombre, but the most characteristic are humorous. A priest describing a roasting goose in "Denis O'Shaughnessy Going to Maynooth" remarks: "it was such a goose as a priest's corpse might get up on its elbow to look at, and exclaim 'Avourneen machree, it's a thousand pities that I'm not living to have a cut at you!' "

There is much excellent and amusing writing in *Traits and Stories,* and the whole collection is a valuable source-book of social history, but Carleton was an uneven and an uneducated writer. He is often ponderous, melodramatic, or crudely moralizing. These faults are even more glaring in his novels. He wrote a great many, of which the best known are *Fardorougha the Miser, Valentine M'Clutchey, The Irish Agent, The Black Prophet: A Tale of Irish Famine,* and *The Tithe Proctor.* Melodramatic they certainly are, but it is unfair to dismiss them as trash. There are passages of sombre power that reveal the harsh lives of the Irish peasants with truth and passion.

—Alan Warner

CARROLL, Lewis. Pseudonym for Charles Lutwidge Dodgson. English. Born in Daresbury, Cheshire, 27 January 1832. Educated at a school in Richmond, Surrey, 1844–46; Rugby School, 1846–49; Christ Church, Oxford (Boultor Scholar, 1851), B.A. (first-class honours) in mathematics 1854, M.A. 1857; ordained, 1861. Fellow of Christ Church from 1855: Master of the House and Sub-Librarian, 1855; Bostock Scholar, 1855; Lecturer in Mathematics, 1856–81; Curator of the Common Room, 1882–92. *Died 14 January 1898.*

PUBLICATIONS

Collections

The Collected Verse, edited by J. F. McDermott.   1929.
The Complete Works.   1939.
The Works, edited by Roger Lancelyn Green.   1965.
*Alice in Wonderland: Authoritative Texts of Alice's Adventures in Wonderland, Through
    the Looking-Glass, The Hunting of the Snark,* edited by Donald J. Gray.   1971.
The Poems, edited by Myra Cohn Livingston.   1973.
The Letters, edited by Morton N. Cohen.   2 vols., 1978.

Fiction

Alice's Adventures in Wonderland.   1865; revised edition, 1886, 1897; edited by Roger
    Lancelyn Green, 1965.
Through the Looking-Glass, and What Alice Found There.   1871; revised edition, 1897.
Alice's Adventures Underground.   1886; edited by Martin Gardner, 1965.
The Nursery Alice.   1889; edited by Martin Gardner, 1966.

Verse

Phantasmagoria and Other Poems.   1869.
The Hunting of the Snark: An Agony in Eight Fits.   1876; edited by Martin Gardner,
    1962.
Rhyme? and Reason?   1883.
Sylvie and Bruno.   1889.
Sylvie and Bruno Concluded.   1893.
Three Sunsets and Other Poems.   1898.
For the Train: Five Poems and a Tale, edited by Hugh J. Schonfield.   1932.

Other

The Fifth Book of Euclid Treated Algebraically.   1858; revised edition, 1868.
A Syllabus of Plane Algebraical Geometry, part 1.   1860.
Notes on the First Two Books of Euclid.   1860.
Notes on the First Part of Algebra.   1861.
The Formulae of Plane Trigonometry.   1861.
An Index to "In Memoriam."   1862.
*The Enunciations of the Propositions and Corollaries with Questions in Euclid, Books 1
    and 2.*   1863; revised edition, 1873.

A Guide to the Mathematical Student, part 1. 1864.
Notes by an Oxford Chiel (The Dynamics of a Particle, with an Excursus on the New Method of Evaluation as Applied to Pi; Facts, Figures, and Fancies Relating to the Elections to the Hebdomadal Council; The New Belfrey of Christ Church, Oxford; The Vision of the Three T's: A Threnody; The Blank Cheque: A Fable). 5 vols., 1865–74.
An Elementary Treatise on Determinants. 1867.
Algebraic Formulae for Responsions. 1868.
Algebraic Formulae and Rules. 1870.
Enunciations, Euclid, 1–4. 1873.
Preliminary Algebra, and Euclid, Book 5. 1874.
Suggestions as to the Best Methods of Taking Votes. 1874.
Some Popular Fallacies about Vivisection. 1875.
Doublets: A Word Puzzle. 1879.
Euclid and His Modern Rivals. 1879; revised edition, 1885.
Lawn Tennis Tournaments: The True Method of Assigning Prizes. 1883.
Twelve Months in a Curatorship, by One Who Has Tried. 1884; revised edition, 1884.
The Principles of Parliamentary Representation. 1884.
A Tangled Tale: A Series of Mathematical Questions. 1885.
Three Years in a Curatorship. 1886.
The Game of Logic. 1886.
Curiosa Mathematica. 2 vols., 1888–93.
Symbolic Logic, part 1. 1896.
The Carroll Picture Book: A Selection from the Unpublished Writings and Drawings, edited by Stuart Dodgson Collingwood. 1899; as *Diversions and Digressions*, 1961.
Feeding the Mind. 1907.
Some Rare Carrolliana. 1924.
Six Letters, edited by W. Partington. 1924.
Novelty and Romancement. 1925.
Tour in 1867. 1928; as *The Russian Journal*, edited by J. F. McDermott, in *The Russian Journal and Other Selections*, 1935.
Two Letters to Marion. 1932.
The Rectory Umbrella, and Misch-Masch, edited by F. Milner. 1932.
Logical Nonsense, edited by Philip C. Blackburn and Lionel White. 1934.
The Russian Journal and Other Selections, edited by J. F. McDermott. 1935.
How the Boots Got Left Behind. 1943.
The Diaries, edited by Roger Lancelyn Green. 2 vols., 1954.
Carroll Observed: A Collection of Unpublished Photographs, Drawings, Poetry, and New Essays, edited by Edward Guiliano. 1976.
Symbolic Logic, parts 1–2, edited by W. W. Bartley, III. 1977.

Editor, *Euclid, Books 1–2*. 1875; revised edition, 1882.
Editor, *The Rectory Magazine*. 1976.

Bibliography: *A Handbook of the Literature of Dodgson* by S. H. Williams and F. Madan, 1931, additions by Madan, 1935.

Reading List: *Life of Carroll* by Langford Reed, 1932; *Carroll* by Derek Hudson, 1954, revised edition, 1975; *Carroll*, 1960, and *The Carroll Handbook*, 1962, both by Roger Lancelyn Green; *The Annotated Alice* edited by Martin Gardner, 1960; *Language and Carroll* by Robert D. Sutherland, 1970; *Play, Games, and Sport: The Literary Voice of Carroll* by Kathleen Blake, 1974; *Carroll and His World* by John Pudney, 1976; *Carroll: Fragments of a Looking-Glass* by Jean Gattégno, 1976.

*   *   *

If one takes the Christian names of Charles Lutwidge Dodgson and reverses them, then translates them into and out of Latin, the result is, or may be, Lewis Carroll. Some such process of transformation by logical steps takes place too between the mathematical treatises which were written in the real name, and the fantasy of Lewis Carroll. The transformation of orthodox mathematics into wonderland is a passage through the looking glass, where all is still logically related, but seen in reverse. The link is clear in the satires, published in Dodgson's name, on the University of Oxford and its works, under such titles as *New Method of Evaluation of Pi*, and the Carroll books which sought to make mathematics and logic accessible to children, whether in the form of puzzles and games, like *A Tangled Tale* and *The Game of Logic*, or directly, in *Symbolic Logic*.

No external evidence is needed, in fact, to reveal that the Alice books and Carroll's poems in *Phantasmagoria* and *The Hunting of the Snark* are the work of a mathematical logician. Given the premises which they adopt, everything about them conforms strictly to logic: I cannot have more tea if I have had none already, and Alice's answer to the Mad Hatter is not pert but pertinent. In *The Hunting of the Snark*, in particular, the nonsense is so compellingly clear and apparently full of meaning that much scholarly effort (sanctioned, one must suppose, by Carroll's frank admission that he did not know what it meant himself) has been expended on inventing meanings for it to be full of. The verses have the internal consistency – of verse. By a stunningly simple manoeuvre Carroll has taken some of the outer structures of poetry – a particular stanza form, a chorus, some incremental repetition, alliterative naming – and stood them up like a stiff suit of clothes full only of their own shape. The process is related to parody, but the result is paradoxically a comic effect which seems, because it is so abstractly conceived, to belong to some realm of pure freedom and delight. Strictly verbal consistency frees the invention from all more solid and earthbound constraints.

In the Alice books too the appearance of a divine freedom, complete originality and imaginative free play is achieved by the transformation of the known and familiar world of the child, including her books and lessons and good manners and pets, by a species of literary parody, combined with logical games. The people and creatures Alice meets are often recognisably based on the acquaintances of Alice Liddell, to whom the stories were told; but every Victorian child had access to the sources of many other parts of the books. The rhymes are parodies of familiar nursery poems by Dr. Watts and others, or, even more effectively, of adult songs and poems whose incomprehensible original words would have floated over the heads of children in Victorian drawing rooms, and were now delightfully set down for them, making sense at last. The persons encountered, who demand of Alice everchanging, mysterious forms of politeness, reflect the complex adult social world, with its formal phrases and apparently meaningless rules especially designed to plague the young. Carroll's logical extensions of the formulae of social behaviour are very like the kinds of unsuccessful attempt to understand literally what is going on that all children apply to the world around them, especially if it is governed by very formal conventions.

There are a certain clarity and hardness in Alice's logical world which appeal to the modern reader, as reflecting our notion of the innocence of the child – she is direct, positive, innocent of degrading emotional display, self-dramatisation, deceit, and role-playing which burgeon all around her; she is constantly attempting to make rational sense of the messy world of other people's emotions. Carroll too set much store by childish innocence: indeed, out of his responsiveness to the uncomplicated, prepubescent affection of his child friends, which he preferred to the taxing world of adult emotions, has sprung the modern view of him as latent paedophile, a kind of response which could be felt to justify his suspicion of the murky adult imagination. When, however, he made conscious statements of his notion of child innocence, it became narrowly Victorian and very like the central premise of his friend and fellow-fantasist George MacDonald. His outrage at child actors saying "Damme" in a production of *H.M.S. Pinafore* now seems merely a curious instance of double thinking in a man who loved theatre and took his little friends to see all kinds of shows involving the exploitation of wretched theatrical children for the sake of whimsy; but the angel-children in the Sylvie and Bruno books, and particularly Bruno's seraphic baby-talk, are very difficult for the modern reader to accept. These late books, despite some good fantasy figures and some of the best of Carroll's verse, are often made tedious by moralising as well as by the sentimentality of Bruno and his talk. It is perhaps not so strange that the success of *Alice* should have made Carroll too conscious of his responsibilities as a writer for children; and it was then inevitable that he should have reverted to the moulds of moral fiction from which *Alice* had been so excitingly altered.

—J. S. Bratton

CLELAND, John. English. Born in England; baptized in Kingston-upon-Thames, Surrey, 24 September 1710. Educated at Westminster School, London, 1721–23. Worked for the East India Company, in Bombay, 1728–40: foot soldier in the East India Company's Militia, 1728; attorney in the Bombay Mayor's Court, 1730; Writer in the Civil Service, 1731; Factor, 1734; in charge of the Mahim Customhouse, 1737; Secretary for Portuguese Affairs, 1737; Junior Merchant, 1737; Secretary of the Council, 1738–40; retired from the company and returned to London, 1741; imprisoned for debt, in Fleet Prison, 1748–49; free-lance writer from 1749; regular contributor to the *Monthly Review*, 1749–51, and to the *Public Advertiser*, 1765–87; political writer for Lord Bute's ministry in the early 1760's. *Died 23 January 1789.*

PUBLICATIONS

Fiction

Memoirs of a Woman of Pleasure.   2 vols., 1748–49; revised edition, as *Memoirs of Fanny Hill*, 1750; edited by Peter Quennell, 1963.
Memoirs of a Coxcomb; or, The History of Sir William Delamere.   1751.
The Surprises of Love, Exemplified in the Romance of a Day, and Other Stories.   1764; revised edition, 1765.
The Woman of Honour.   1768.

Plays

Titus Vespasian, from a play by Metastasio.   1754.
The Ladies' Subscription.   1755.
Tombo-Chiqui; or, The American Savage, from a play by L. F. Delisle de la Drévetière.   1758.

Other

Institutes of Health.   1761.
The Way to Things by Words and to Words by Things.   1766.
Specimen of an Etymological Vocabulary.   1768; *Additional Articles*, 1769.

Reading List: "*Fanny Hill* and Materialism" by Leo Braudy, in *Eighteenth-Century Studies 4*, 1970; " 'The Most Interesting Moving Picture': *Fanny Hill* and Comedy" by Malcolm Bradbury, in *Possibilities*, 1973; *Cleland: Images of a Life* by William H. Epstein, 1974.

* * *

In the British Library catalogue, John Cleland's name carries that most damning of literary labels, "Miscellaneous Writer"; and his reputation would probably have remained interred in the common grave of Grub-street were it not for the notoriety achieved, in its own time and ours, by his first novel, *Memoirs of a Woman of Pleasure* – better known as *Fanny Hill*. Cleland's later career reads remarkably like a scenario for the archetypal hack: he tried his hand at drama, and had one play (*Titus Vespasian*) rejected by Garrick; attempted to repeat his success in fiction, but managed only a thin follow-up to *Fanny Hill* (*Memoirs of a Coxcomb*), a standard exercise in epistolary fiction (*The Woman of Honour*), and short sentimental tales (*The Surprises of Love*); and eventually subsided into literary and political journalism. Nothing else that he wrote repeated the extraordinary *éclat* of *Fanny Hill*.

The case of *Fanny Hill* is one in which the literary historian owes a debt to the pornophile. After the novel's initial prosecution for obscenity in 1749, it went underground, retaining popularity chiefly among connoisseurs of erotica, and finally re-emerged in the wake of the liberalisation of book-censorship laws in the 1960's. Its open publication in 1963 stimulated reassessment by scholars and critics, and led to a more accurate placing of *Fanny Hill* in the contexts of mid-eighteenth-century fiction and thought rather than in the pornographic tradition: for example, Leo Braudy demonstrated that the novel may be seen as an embodiment of philosophical materialism, and Malcolm Bradbury that it is "about aesthetics as well as about sex."

Fanny Hill is certainly a novel of considerable comic dexterity and linguistic dash. It consists of the heroine's retrospective account, in two long letters to a friend, of her career as a "woman of pleasure." She belongs in that fictional enclave of embattled young provincial girls isolated in a bewildering, predatory society: she is (self-consciously) part of the sisterhood that includes Defoe's Moll Flanders, Hogarth's Moll Hackabout, and Richardson's Pamela and Clarissa – and there are thematic and verbal echoes of these throughout her narrative. On her arrival in London from Liverpool, she is snapped up by a bawd as a novice prostitute, but before her confirmation in the profession she falls in love with the handsome Charles, and runs off with him. However, Charles is forced by his father to leave England, and Fanny then becomes a high-class whore, and the latter half of the novel is largely an account of her sexual experiences in this role. Finally, she is reunited with the returned Charles in marriage. The novel therefore comprises two interlocking structures: the carnal-picaresque, in which Fanny witnesses and/or participates in, a series of polymorphous sexual episodes – with the picara's customary delight in her profession; and the sentimental-romantic, in which Fanny's first love is also her last. The relationship between Fanny and Charles is complete because it unites love *and* lust: as Fanny says, Charles makes her "happy ... by the heart, happy by the senses." This romantic perfection is comically underlined when Fanny flouts the eighteenth-century fictional convention whereby narrator and reader discreetly halt at the boudoir door on the wedding-night: Fanny insists on displaying the *full* joys of the marriage-bed.

—J. C. Hilson

COLLINS, (William) Wilkie. English. Born in London, 8 January 1824; son of the portrait painter William Collins. Educated at Maida Hill Academy, London; lived with his parents in Italy, 1836–39; articled to the London firm of Antrobus and Company, tea merchants, 1841–46; entered Lincoln's Inn, London, 1846: called to the Bar, 1849. Associated with Caroline Graver, 1859–89; and with Martha Rudd, 1868–89, two daughters and one son. Writer from 1848; also a painter: exhibited at the Royal Academy, 1849; met Charles Dickens, 1851, and contributed to, and assisted Dickens in the editing of, *Household Words*, and its successor *All the Year Round*, 1856–61; toured the United States, giving readings of his works, 1873–74. *Died 23 September 1889.*

PUBLICATIONS

Collections

Tales of Terror and the Supernatural, edited by Herbert van Thal.   1972.

Fiction

Antonia; or, The Fall of Rome.   1850.
Mr. Wray's Cash-Box; or, The Mask and the Mystery.   1851.
Basil: A Story of Modern Life.   1852; revised edition, 1862.
Hide and Seek.   1854; revised edition, 1861.
After Dark.   1856.
The Dead Secret.   1857.
The Queen of Hearts.   1859.
The Woman in White.   1860; edited by Harvey Peter Sucksmith, 1975.
No Name.   1862; edited by Herbert Van Thal, 1967.
Armadale.   1866.
The Moonstone: A Romance.   1868; edited by J. I. M. Stewart, 1966.
Man and Wife.   1870.
Poor Miss Finch.   1872.
The New Magdalen.   1873.
Miss or Mrs.? and Other Stories in Outline.   1873.
The Frozen Deep and Other Stories: Readings and Writings in America.   1874.
The Law and the Lady.   1875.
The Two Destinies.   1876.
A Shocking Story.   1878.
The Haunted Hotel (with *My Lady's Money*).   1878.
A Rogue's Life, From His Birth to His Marriage.   1879.
The Fallen Leaves.   1879.
Jezebel's Daughter.   1880.
The Black Robe.   1881.
Heart and Science.   1883.
I Say No.   1884.
The Evil Genius.   1886.
The Guilty River.   1886.
Little Novels.   1887.
The Legacy of Cain.   1888.
Blind Love, completed by Walter Besant.   1890.
The Lazy Tour of Two Idle Apprentices, No Thoroughfare, The Perils of Certain English Prisoners, with Dickens.   1890.

Plays

A Court Duel (produced 1850).
The Lighthouse, from his own story "Gabriel's Marriage" (produced 1855).
The Frozen Deep (produced 1857).   1866.
The Red Vial (produced 1858).
No Name, with W. B. Bernard, from the novel by Collins (produced 1871).   1863;
    revised edition, 1870.
Armadale, from his own novel.   1866.
No Thoroughfare, with Dickens, from their own story (produced 1867).   1867; revised
    version, 1867.
Black and White, with Charles Fechter (produced 1869).   1869.
The Woman in White, from his own novel (produced 1870).   1871.
Man and Wife, from his own novel (produced 1873).   1870.
The New Magdalen (produced 1873).   1873.
Miss Gwilt (produced 1875).   1875.
The Moonstone, from his own novel (produced 1877).   1877.
Rank and Riches (produced 1883).
The Evil Genius (produced 1885).

Other

Memoirs of the Life of William Collins, R.A., with Selections from His Journals and
    Correspondence.   2 vols., 1848.
Rambles Beyond Railways; or, Notes in Cornwell Taken A-Foot.   1851.
My Miscellanies.   2 vols., 1863.
Considerations on the Copyright Question Addressed to an American Friend.   1880.

Bibliography: Collins and Reade by M. L. Parrish, 1940; Collins and Reade: A Bibliography
of Critical Notices and Studies by F. Cordasco and K. Scott, 1949; "A Collins Check-List" by
R. V. Andrew, in English Studies in Africa 3, 1960.

Reading List: Collins: A Biography by Kenneth Robinson, 1951; Collins by Robert Ashley,
1952; The Life of Collins by Nuel P. Davis, 1956; Collins by William H. Marshall, 1970;
Collins: The Critical Heritage edited by Norman Page, 1974.

*   *   *

Though one of the most popular novelists in England and America between 1860 and
1889, Wilkie Collins is remembered today primarily for his novels of the 1860's, principally
The Woman in White and The Moonstone. After Antonia, his only historical novel, Collins's
early work reflects certain lifelong characteristics – an interest in mystery and crime; a talent
for foreboding atmosphere, effective description of scene, and intricate plots; and a belief in
the romance and drama of real life – characteristics which, along with his bonhomie, made
possible a close personal and literary relationship with Dickens. Collins served as assistant
editor of Dickens's periodicals from 1856–1861, contributing numerous essays and
collaborating with Dickens on several Christmas numbers.
    However, despite his ten-year apprenticeship and close association with Dickens, the
mature achievement of The Woman in White is remarkable. The story itself is a collection of
manuscript narratives by individual characters, no one of whom holds all the keys to the
complex mystery plot. This device enables Collins legitimately to withhold crucial
information and thus heighten suspense while at the same time developing the character of

each narrator. Particularly memorable are the villainous Count Fosco and the courageous Marian Halcombe, whose dramatic conflict so gripped the reading public that the publication of each new installment became a social event. Contemporary critics recognized *The Woman in White* as an excellent example (indeed, perhaps initiator) of an emerging and controversial sub-genre, the Sensation Novel, whose merits were debated throughout the decade. With few exceptions, the critics deplored the form's subordination of character to plot, its emphasis on crime and encouragement of sympathy for morally ambiguous characters, its combination of realism and romance, and its melodramatic style; but their strictures did not keep readers of all classes from making the Sensation Novel the dominant sub-genre of the 1860's, with Wilkie Collins its acknowledged master. Collins's next novels, *No Name* and *Armadale*, augment their sensational qualities by employing female Fosco-figures and reveal the centrality of identity mysteries in Collins's work of this period. The loss and recovery of social identity, a theme Collins explored throughout his career, constitutes the formulaic core of his (and others') Sensation Novels and is clearly related to mid-Victorian insecurities. In the characters of Ezra Jennings and Franklin Blake, Collins continues this theme in *The Moonstone*, whose superb plot led T. S. Eliot to call it "the first and greatest of English detective novels."

The marked decline in the quality of Collins's novels after *The Moonstone* is attributed by modern critics to his deteriorating health and subsequent dependence on laudanum, and to the increasing thesis-domination of his work. Among his later novels, *Man and Wife* attacks Scotch marriage laws and athleticism; *The New Magdalen* and *The Fallen Leaves*, society's treatment of reformed prostitutes. Weak though these novels are, they are the natural outgrowth of Collins's earlier thematic concerns, as he now shows society itself, rather than aggressive individualists, to be the principal cause of identity loss. In this development Collins follows the lead of Dickens, but without his range of vision and talent. Still, Collins produced two very fine novels and several others of note, and gave shape to a sub-genre that reflected major preoccupations of mid-Victorian culture. For this, and for his close connection with the many greater and lesser literary lights of his day, he deserves to be remembered.

—Randolph Ivy

CORELLI, Marie. Pseudonym for Mary Mackay. English. Born in Bayswater, London, 1 May 1855. Educated privately; studied music, and made debut as a pianist, London, 1884. Writer from 1885; settled in Stratford upon Avon, 1901. *Died 21 April 1924.*

PUBLICATIONS

Fiction

A Romance of Two Worlds. 1886.
Vendetta; or, The Story of One Forgotten. 1886.
Thelma. 1887.
Ardath. 1889.
My Wonderful Wife: A Study in Smoke. 1889.
Wormwood. 1890.

The Hired Baby and Other Stories and Social Sketches. 1891.
The Soul of Lilith. 1892.
Barabbas: A Dream of the World's Tragedy. 1893.
The Sorrows of Satan; or, The Strange Adventures of One Geoffrey Tempest, Millionaire. 1895.
Cameos: Short Stories. 1896.
The Murder of Delicia. 1896; as *Delicia*, 1917.
The Mighty Atom. 1896.
Ziska. 1897.
Jane. 1897.
Boy. 1900.
The Master-Christian. 1900.
Temporal Power. 1902.
God's Good Man. 1904.
The Strange Visitation of Josiah McNason. 1904.
The Treasure of Heaven. 1906.
Holy Orders. 1908.
The Devil's Motor. 1910.
The Life Everlasting. 1911.
Innocent: Her Fancy and His Fact. 1914.
Eyes of the Sea. 1917.
The Young Diana. 1918.
My Little Bit. 1919.
The Love of Long Ago and Other Stories. 1920.
The Secret Power. 1921.
Love − and the Philosopher. 1923.

Verse

Poems, edited by Bertha Vyver. 1925.

Other

The Silver Domino; or, Side-Whispers, Social and Literary. 1892.
Patriotism or Self-Advertisement? A Social Note on the War. 1900.
The Greatest Queen in the World: A Tribute to the Majesty of England 1837–1900. 1900.
A Christmas Greeting of Various Thoughts, Verses, and Fancies. 1901.
The Passing of the Great Queen. 1901.
The Plain Truth of the Stratford-upon-Avon Controversy. 1903.
Free Opinions Freely Expressed on Certain Phases of Modern Social Life and Conduct. 1905.
Woman or Suffragette? A Question of National Choice. 1907.
Open Confession to a Man from a Woman. 1924.

Editor, with Percy S. Brentnall and Bertha Vyver, *Stratford upon Avon Guide Book.* 1931.

Reading List: *Corelli: The Life and Death of a Best-Seller* by George Bullock, 1940; *Corelli: The Woman and the Legend* by Eileen Bigland, 1953; *Corelli: The Story of a Friendship* by W. S. Scott, 1955; *Now Barabbas Was a Rotter* (biography) by Brian Masters, 1977.

"Why *can't* I be a Marie Corelli!" Those words were uttered by Anne Sedgwick, a late-nineteenth century novelist of some talent and little popularity. She was contrasting her poor fortunes with those of the most famous best-seller of her day, beside whose achievement even those of Ouida and Elinor Glyn pale into insignificance. Even in 1909, by which time her popularity had begun to fade, her publishers rapidly sold 130,000 copies of her new book, and offered her an advance of £9,500 for the next.

How did she do it? It is not easy to answer that question. Perhaps the nearest we can come to it is by noting the fact that her stories all have an element of sensationalism in them, plus a dose of vague, mystical, other-or-ideal worldly religion; and that this was almost bound to go down well in an age which had not lost its religious impulse, even though the discoveries and arguments of Darwin and his followers had denied that impulse orthodox expression. Queen Victoria herself praised the *Sorrows of Satan*, and Amy Cruse, in *After the Victorians*, points out how often it was used as a text by fashionable preachers of the day. A Father Ignatius praised the novel to a packed congregation at the Portman Rooms, Baker Street, and wrote to Marie Corelli, calling her "a prophet of good things to come in this filthy and materialistic generation." She had thrillingly portrayed, he told her, "the utter misery of being without Christ in life and death, the daring blasphemies of popular poets and other writers, and the consequences in the lives of their readers."

Her choice of living place – Stratford upon Avon – is significant. For it appears that she really did think of herself as a writer in the class of Shakespeare, one whose house would become a literary shrine every bit as much frequented as his. Why should she not choose to live where he had lived? The vanity is touching rather than contemptible. For there was absolutely nothing fraudulent or hypocritical about Marie Corelli. From first to last she believed in her genius, believed, too, in the "reality" of the misty mysticism which blows through the pages of her books. And why should she not, when the entire nation, it seemed, agreed with her valuation of herself? True, there were dissident voices. Critics tended to be unkind. Indeed, after the cruel critical reception given to *Barabbas*, in 1893, Marie Corelli refused to allow any of her books to be sent out for review.

But anyway, criticism did not matter. Suppose a hostile reviewer were to point out the similarity between her *Soul of Lilith* and Rider Haggard's *She*, what then? The hard fact remained that *The Soul of Lilith* sold "by the ton." And suppose that same hostile reviewer were to point out that the end of her greatest best-seller, *The Mighty Atom*, bore a striking resemblance to the ending of *Jude the Obscure*? Marie Corelli could always retort that for many people her novel amounted to a new gospel, and that she had given the little Devon town of Clovelly guide-book fame, "as the scene of Miss Corelli's great novel."

Of course, she isn't a great novelist, she isn't even a good one. But her books are of interest because they clearly reflect opinions, wishes, likes and dislikes that were widely current during the last years of the nineteenth century and the early years of the twentieth. If you want to know what the man on the Clapham omnibus thought of life during those years, Marie Corelli's books will help to tell you.

—John Lucas

CRAIK, Mrs.   See MULOCK, Dinah Maria.

DEFOE, Daniel.   English.   Born in London c. 1660.   Educated at Charles Morton's Academy, London. Married Mary Tuffley; seven children. Worked as a hosiery maker, and commission merchant: bankrupt, 1692; associated with a tile works in Tilbury, which failed, 1703; Accountant to the Commissioners of the Glass Duty, 1695–99; pilloried, gaoled, and fined for *The Shortest Way with Dissenters*, 1703–04; political writer and confidential agent for Robert Harley, later Earl of Oxford, 1704–11; Editor of *The Review of the Affairs of France, and of All Europe*, 1704–13; carried out various government commissions and wrote pro-government pamphlets in the 1710's; contributed to various periodicals, and edited *The Manufacturer*, 1720, and *The Director*, 1720–21. *Died 26 April 1731.*

PUBLICATIONS

Collections

> *Novels*, edited by Sir Walter Scott.   12 vols., 1810.
> *Novels and Miscellaneous Works.*   20 vols., 1840–41.
> *Romances and Narratives*, edited by G. A. Aitken.   16 vols., 1895.
> *Works*, edited by G. H. Maynadier.   16 vols., 1903–04.
> *Novels and Selected Writings.*   14 vols., 1927–28.
> *Letters*, edited by George Harris Healey.   1955.
> *Selected Poetry and Prose*, edited by M. Schugrue.   1968.
> *Selected Writings*, edited by James T. Boulton.   1975.

Fiction

> *The Consolidator; or, Memoirs of Sundry Transactions from the World in the Moon.*   1705; selections, as *A Journey to the World in the Moon*, 1705, *A Letter from the Man in the Moon*, 1705, and *A Second and More Strange Voyage to the World in the Moon*, 1705.
> *The Memoirs of Majr. Alexander Ramkins, A Highland Officer.*   1718; edited by James T. Boulton, 1970.
> *The Life and Strange Surprising Adventures of Robinson Crusoe, of York, Mariner.*   1719; *Further Adventures*, 1719; part 1 edited by J. Donald Crowley, 1972; edited by Michael Shinagel, 1975.
> *The King of Pirates, Being an Account of the Famous Enterprises of Captain Avery.*   1719.
> *Memoirs of a Cavalier; or, A Military Journal of the Wars in Germany, and the Wars in England, 1632 to 1648.*   1720; edited by James T. Boulton, 1972.
> *The Life, Adventures, and Piraces of the Famous Captain Singleton.*   1720; edited by Shiv Kumar, 1969.
> *Serious Reflections During the Life and Surprising Adventures of Robinson Crusoe, with His Vision of the Angelic World.*   1720.
> *The History of the Life and Adventures of Mr. Duncan Campbell.*   1720; as *The Supernatural Philosopher*, by William Bond, 1728 (perhaps by Bond).
> *The Fortunes and Misfortunes of the Famous Moll Flanders.*   1722; revised edition, 1722, 1723; as *Fortune's Fickle Distribution*, 1730; as *The History of Laetitia Atkins*, 1776; edited by George A. Starr, 1972.
> *The History and Remarkable Life of the Truly Honourable Col. Jacque, Commonly Called Col. Jack.*   1722; edited by Samuel Monk, 1965.
> *A Journal of the Plague Year, 1665.*   1722; as *The History of the Great Plague in London*, 1754; edited by Louis A. Landa, 1969.

The Fortunate Mistress; or, A History of the Life and Vast Variety of Fortunes of Mademoiselle de Beleau, The Lady Roxana, in the Time of King Charles II. 1724; edited by Jane Jack, 1964.

A Narrative of All the Robberies, Escapes, etc. of John Sheppard. 1724; edited by H. Bleackley, in *Jack Sheppard,* 1933.

The History of the Remarkable Life of John Sheppard. 1724; edited by H. Bleackley, in *Jack Sheppard,* 1933.

A New Voyage round the World, by a Course Never Sailed Before. 1724.

The Life of Jonathan Wild, from His Birth to His Death. 1725.

The True and Genuine Account of the Life and Actions of the Late Jonathan Wild. 1725; edited by W. Follett, with *Jonathan Wild* by Henry Fielding, 1926.

The Four Years Voyages of Capt. George Roberts. 1726.

The Memoirs of an English Officer Who Served in the Dutch War in 1672 to the Peace of Utrecht in 1713, by Captain George Carleton. 1728; as *A True and Genuine History of the Last Two Wars,* 1740; as *The Memoirs of Cap. George Carleton,* 1743.

Verse

A New Discovery of an Old Intrigue: A Satire Leveled at Treachery and Ambition. 1691; edited by M. E. Campbell, 1938.

The Character of the Late Dr. Samuel Annesley, by Way of Elegy. 1697.

The Pacificator. 1700.

The True-Born Englishman: A Satire. 1701; revised edition, 1701, 1716.

Reformation of Manners: A Satire. 1702.

The Spanish Descent. 1702.

More Reformation: A Satire upon Himself. 1703.

A Hymn to the Pillory. 1703.

A Hymn to the Funeral Sermon. 1703.

An Elegy on the Author of The True-Born Englishman, with an Essay on the Late Storm. 1704; as *The Live Man's Elegy,* 1704.

A Hymn to Victory. 1704.

The Double Welcome: A Poem to the Duke of Marlbro. 1705.

The Diet of Poland: A Satire. 1705.

A Hymn to Peace. 1706.

Jure Divino: A Satire. 1706.

Hymn for the Thanksgiving. 1706.

The Vision. 1706.

Caledonia: A Poem in Honour of Scotland and the Scots Nation. 1706.

A Hymn to the Mob. 1715.

Other (a selection)

The Englishman's Choice and True Interest in a Vigorous Prosecution of the War Against France. 1694.

An Essay upon Projects. 1697; as *Essays upon Several Projects,* 1702.

An Enquiry into the Occasional Conformity of Dissenters. 1698.

An Argument Showing That a Standing Army Is Not Inconsistent with a Free Government. 1698.

The Poor Man's Plea for a Reformation of Manners and Suppressing Immorality in the Nation. 1698.

The Two Great Questions Considered. 1700.

The Six Distinguishing Characters of a Parliament-Man. 1701.

The Succession to the Crown of England Considered. 1701.

Good Advice to the Ladies, Shewing That as the World Goes, and Is Likely to Go, The Best Way Is for Them to Keep Unmarried. 1702; as *A Timely Caution,* 1728.

An Enquiry into Occasional Conformity. 1702.

The Shortest Way with the Dissenters; or, Proposals for the Establishment of the Church. 1702.

King William's Affection to the Church of England Examined. 1703.

The Shortest Way to Peace and Union. 1703.

A Collection of the Writings. 1703.

A True Collection of the Writings. 1703; revised edition, 1705; vol. 2, 1705.

More Short Ways with the Dissenters. 1704.

The Storm; or, A Collection of the Most Remarkable Casualties and Disasters Which Happened in the Late Dreadful Tempest. 1704.

Giving Alms No Charity, and Employing the Poor a Grievance to the Nation. 1704.

The Parallel; or, Persecution of Protestants the Shortest Way to Prevent the Growth of Popery in Ireland. 1705(?).

An Essay at Removing National Prejudices Against a Union with Scotland. 6 vols., 1706–07.

A True Relation of the Apparition of One Mrs. Veal. 1706.

The History of the Union of Great Britain. 1709.

A Collection of the Several Addresses Concerning the Conception and Birth of the Pretended Prince of Wales. 1710.

An Essay upon Public Credit. 1710.

An Essay upon Loans. 1710.

The Secret History of the October Club. 1711; part 2, 1711.

An Essay upon the Trade to Africa. 1711.

An Essay on the South Sea Trade. 1712.

A Defence of the Allies and the Late Ministry; or, Remarks upon the Tories' New Idol. 1712.

Hannibal at the Gates; or, The Progress of Jacobitism, with the Present Danger of the Pretender. 1712; revised edition, 1714.

Memoirs of Count Tariff. 1713.

An Essay on the Treaty of Commerce with France. 1713.

A Brief Account of the Present State of the African Trade. 1713.

Reasons Against the Succession of the House of Hanover. 1713.

And What If the Pretender Should Come? 1713.

An Answer to A Question That No Body Thinks of, viz, But What If the Queen Should Die? 1713.

A Letter to the Dissenters. 1713.

Memoirs of John Duke of Melfort, Being an Account of the Secret Intrigues of the Chevalier de S. George. 1714.

The Secret History of the White Staff. 1714; part 2, 1714; part 3, 1715.

A Secret History of One Year. 1714.

An Appeal to Honour and Justice, Being a True Account of His Conduct in Public Affairs (autobiography). 1715.

The Family Instructor. 2 vols., 1715–18.

The History of the Wars of His Present Majesty Charles XII, King of Sweden. 1715; revised edition, 1720.

Memoirs of the Church of Scotland. 1717.

The Conduct of Robert Walpole from the Beginning of the Reign of Queen Anne. 1717.

A Short View of the Conduct of the King of Sweden. 1717.

Memoirs of the Life and Eminent Conduct of Daniel Williams, D.D. 1718.

A History of the Last Session of the Present Parliament, with a Correct List of Both Houses. 1718.

The History of the Reign of King George.   1718.

The Anatomy of Exchange Alley; or, A System of Stock-Jobbing.   1719.

An Historical Account of the Voyages and Adventures of Sir Walter Raleigh.   1720.

Religious Courtship, Being Historical Discourses on the Necessity of Marrying Religious Husbands and Wives Only.   1722.

Due Preparations for the Plague as Well for Soul as Body.   1722.

An Impartial History of the Life and Actions of Peter Alexowitz, Czar of Muscovy.   1722.

A General History of the Robberies and Murders of the Most Notorious Pirates, by Captain Charles Johnson.   1724; part 2, as *The History of the Pirates,* 1728; edited by Manuel Schonhorn, 1972.

A Tour Thro' the Whole Island of Great Britain.   3 vols., 1724–26; edited by Pat Rogers, 1971.

An Account of the Conduct and Proceedings of the Late John Gow, Alias Smith, Captain of the Late Pirates.   1725; edited by J. R. Russell, 1890.

The Complete English Tradesman, in Familiar Letters.   2 vols., 1725–27.

A Brief Historical Account of the Lives of the Six Notorious Street-Robbers Executed at Kingston.   1726.

An Essay upon Literature; or, An Enquiry into the Antiquity and Original of Letters Proving that the Two Tables Written by the Finger of God in Mount Sinai Was the First Writing in the World.   1726.

The Political History of the Devil.   1726.

Unparalleled Cruelty; or, The Trial of Captain Jeane of Bristol Who Was Convicted for the Murder of His Cabin-Boy.   1726.

Mere Nature Delineated; or, A Body Without a Soul, Being Observations upon a Young Forester from Germany.   1726.

Some Considerations upon Street-Walkers.   1726.

A System of Magic; or, A History of the Black Art.   1726.

Conjugal Lewdness; or, Matrimonial Whoredom.   1727; as *A Treatise Concerning the Use and Abuse of the Marriage Bed,* 1727; edited by Maximillian E. Novak, 1967.

An Essay on the History and Reality of Apparitions.   1727; as *The Secrets of the Invisible World Disclosed; or, An Universal History of Apparitions,* 1728.

Augusta Triumphans; or, The Way to Make London the Most Flourishing City in the Universe.   1728; revised edition, as *The Generous Projector; or, A Friendly Proposal to Prevent Murder and Other Enormous Abuses,* 1731.

A Plan of the English Commerce, Being a Complete Prospect of the Trade of This Nation as Well the Home Trade as the Foreign.   1728; revised edition, 1730.

Atlas Maritimus and Commercialis; or, A General View of the World So Far as It Relates to Trade and Navigation.   1728.

Madagascar; or, Robert Drury's Journal During Fifteen Years Captivity on That Island, revised and partly written by Defoe.   1729.

The Complete English Gentleman, edited by K. D. Bülbring.   1890.

Of Royall Education: A Fragmentary Treatise, edited by K. D. Bülbring.   1895.

A Review of the Affairs of France, and of All Europe (other minor name changes are used; Defoe's journal covers 1704–13), edited by A. W. Secord.   22 vols., 1938; *Index* by W. L. Payne, 1948.

The Meditations (1681), edited by George Harris Healey.   1946.

The Best of Defoe's Review, edited by W. L. Payne.   1951.

The Versatile Defoe (uncollected non-fiction works), edited by Laura Curtis.   1978.

Editor, *A Collection of Miscellany Letters, Selected Out of Mist's Weekly Journal.*   4 vols., 1722.

Bibliography: *A Checklist of the Writings of Defoe* by J. R. Moore, 1960, revised edition,

1961; *New Cambridge Bibliography of English Literature 2*, 1971; "An Annotated Bibliography of Works about Defoe 1719–1974" by W. L. Payne, 3 parts, in *Bulletin of Bibliography*, 1975.

Reading List: *The Early Masters of English Fiction* by Alan D. McKillop, 1956; *Economics and the Fiction of Defoe*, 1962, and *Defoe and the Nature of Man*, 1963, both by Maximillian E. Novak; *The Rise of the Novel* by Ian Watt, 1963; *Defoe and Spiritual Autobiography*, 1965, and *Defoe and Casuistry*, 1971, both by George A. Starr; *The Reluctant Pilgrim* by J. Paul Hunter, 1966; *Defoe and Middle-Class Gentility* by Michael Shinagel, 1968; *Defoe: A Critical Study* by James Sutherland, 1971; "The Displaced Self in the Novels of Defoe" by Homer O. Brown, in *Journal of English Literary History 38*, 1971; *Defoe: The Critical Heritage* edited by Pat Rogers, 1972; *Defoe and the Novel* by Everett Zimmerman, 1975; *Defoe's Narrative: Situations and Structures* by John J. Richetti, 1975; *Defoe: A Collection of Critical Essays* edited by Max Byrd, 1976.

* * *

It is understandable that students of Daniel Defoe should draw attention to the scope and variety of his work – more than 550 separate publications, if we include pamphlets, broadsides, and occasional pieces. His journalism by itself would fill several fat volumes, with the *Review* (1704–13) extending to well over a thousand issues, all from his own hand. He was among the best informed political and economic pamphleteers of his time, and from the time of *The Shortest Way with the Dissenters* (1702) his productions in this area consistently attracted intense national comment and vociferous opposition. His early vein as a satiric poet worked itself out by about 1710, but not before works such as *The True-Born Englishman* and *Jure Divino* had provoked an immense controversy. From the beginning Defoe had the gift of exciting attention. His ghost story *The Apparition of Mrs. Veal* foreshadowed later writings on parapsychology, a century or more prior to the real currency of this genre. His collection of disaster tales, *The Storm*, brings a new actuality and reportorial skill to the conventional mode of "Providence displayed." And, at the very start of his writing career, *An Essay upon Projects* already indicates the breadth of his humanitarian concerns, along with a forceful manner of presentation sharply distinguished from the run of contemporary schemes and proposals.

But equally it is not surprising that the general reading public should have settled on his later work, the novels in particular, as a centre of interest. Something really did change in 1719 when Defoe, rising sixty, produced the first part of *Robinson Crusoe*. Up till then he had been an author of high talent, all too explicably a man famous in his own day who gave little sign of transcending the forms and subject-matter familiar to the contemporary audience. *Robinson Crusoe* is his most deeply original book, though paradoxically it is one with all kinds of roots in earlier modes of literary expression. After its appearance Defoe showed himself regularly a writer of genius. He brought a new purpose and authority to standard forms such as travel books, lives of pirates and criminals, conduct-manuals, sociological tracts, and economic surveys. To this period belongs what may well have been his favourite undertaking, the life of Sir Walter Raleigh (1720). Some of his most characteristic works appeared in a cluster around the middle of the decade. There is the boldly dramatic *General History of the Pyrates*, written under the pseudonym of Captain Charles Johnson, which did more than any other single work to create the image of piracy handed down over many generations. There is the *Tour thro' the Whole Island of Great Britain*, which turns the dull, sub-artistic genre of the guide-book into a wonderfully evocative portrait of the nation. There is still no survey of Britain which conveys so powerfully the sense of a people living and working, of a landscape and a social environment, of a way of life frozen for ever by exact observation and shrewd insight. And there is *The Complete English Tradesman*, a strange, anxious, urgent book: a vocational manual which celebrates the grandeurs of a business community but at the same time explores the miseries of its condition. It is as though an existentialist had rewritten Samuel Smiles. Other works of sharp interest include *A General History of Discoveries and Improvements* and *The Political History of the Devil*. Many people have deplored the fact that Pope saw fit to give Defoe a niche in *The Dunciad* (1728), since we know the poet retained a fair amount of admiration for his victim. Viewing the matter differently, we might instead regret the lost opportunity to instal Defoe as King of the Dunces; he was certainly the individual writer who had brought Grub Street themes and idiom into high literature.

So it is with his masterpiece, indeed. *Robinson Crusoe* can be analysed down to component parts which look like the ingredients for minor art. It draws on many traditions: the narratives of voyages and discoveries which were then so popular, the spiritual guides and manuals of right living, the biographies of puritan converts, the tales of providential escape from natural hazards. Crusoe may be plausibly interpreted as a social misfit, unwisely rebelling against the safe "middle station" to which he was born. He can equally be seen as a lone colonist, improving his state by well-planned industry and prudent measures of self-help. He has been viewed as the embodiment of capitalism, as a figure symbolising the isolation of puritan spirituality, as the precursor of nineteenth-century imperialism, as a type of the prodigal son, and much else. Not all these conflicting interpretations can be wholly correct, since they involve different readings of crucial episodes, such as the "original sin" of running away to sea, or the conversion of Friday. But the book is rich enough to contain a number of overlapping meanings, and it would be rash to discount many of the religious, economic, social, or philosophic ideas which have been discovered. The important thing in the last resort, however, is the extraordinary fictional chemistry which makes a stable compound of so many disparate elements. The heart of the book is to be found in Crusoe's sojourn on the island, particularly his early years of solitude and self-communion. Neither the framing parts of this story, nor the globe-trotting sequel of Crusoe's *Farther Adventures* attains the same power and vibrancy of expression.

If Crusoe is a naturally gregarious man, cast by fate into prolonged isolation, then the heroine of *Moll Flanders* might be described as a natural loner who is destined to float about on the tides of an alien society. Moll wants nothing more than to achieve gentility, or at the very least respectability: but first her sexual misadventures and then her criminal escapades serve to drag her into a marginal condition. The force of the novel derives from this collision in her being; her urge to conformity is cut across by the need to survive in desperate or unconventional ways. She was easily assimilated into the chapbook versions of this story, since her life-history has the diagrammatic clarity favoured in such moralistic narratives. But there is a mysterious dimension to her character, a depth of personality in the acting Moll which the reporting Moll does not seem fully to apprehend. It is this which has made the novel something of a cult in the twentieth century: significantly it was the generation of Joyce and Virginia Woolf which first seized on this added strain of psychological drama.

These two works are Defoe's most famous novels, and deservedly so. His other fiction contains much of interest, but none of the other books quite coheres as do *Crusoe* and *Moll*. For example, *Roxana* mixes several moments of intense nervous energy with some half-hearted melodrama: Defoe does not seem to have been altogether sure how much sympathy (if any) he could afford to invest in the heroine. Again, *Colonel Jack* shows signs of muddled purposes, with excellent evocation of varied social locales (notably a London childhood) and less assurance in depicting inner thoughts and feelings. Defoe was perhaps more at home with the vigorous action which informs the plot of *Captain Singleton*, *Memoirs of a Cavalier*, and *A New Voyage round the World*, the last certainly marking an improvement on the second part of *Crusoe*. There is plenty of external drama, for that matter, in *A Journal of the Plague Year*, but the interest is less narrowly concentrated on such things. Defoe manages to recreate the flurried excitement of a city under siege, and sticks particularly close to the real-life data of the Great Plague. But he deepens the treatment by presenting events through the eyes of a single observer, the saddler H. F., who is involved in the struggle for survival but sufficiently detached to afford a degree of critical detachment. The *Journal* is the most technically adroit among Defoe's works of fiction, with the possible exception of the first part of *Robinson Crusoe*. It avoids the strange *rubato* effects in narrative tempo which impair the structure of other books, and it preserves a more unified angle of vision than, say, *Colonel Jack*.

If we accept that Defoe lives on by virtue of his novels, despite the high merits of the rest of his oeuvre, then it is still difficult to locate with absolute precision the sources of his enduring power. It is not enough to define his themes – for, while the struggle to survive in a hostile environment is a rich vein of interest, such topics are hardly unique to Defoe. And his capacity to dramatise the essential *privacy* of experience, even where an individual like the saddler is caught up in public events, seems to emanate less from a sharply personal vision than from an eclectic blend of the theologies and moralities available to him. He wrote often about ordinary people *in extremis*, but at the level of basic impulse he seems to share the urge of Crusoe and Moll to return to normality at the earliest opportunity. His novels, then, present an unrivalled picture of men and women who reach fulfilment and identity under the severest pressure; but they also dramatise the yearning for a quiet life, even at the cost of losing that fulfilment.

—Pat Rogers

DICKENS, Charles (John Huffam). English. Born in Landport, Portsea, Hampshire, 7 February 1812; moved with his family to London, 1814, Chatham, Kent, 1816, and again to London, 1821. Worked in the office of a blacking factory, Hungerford Market, London, while his family was in debtor's prison; subsequently attended Wellington House Academy, Hampstead, London, 1824–27, and Mr. Dawson's school in Brunswick Square, London, 1827; largely self-educated. Married Catherine Hogarth in 1836 (separated, 1858); seven sons and three daughters. Clerk in a London law office, 1827–28; taught himself shorthand and worked as a shorthand-reporter in the Doctors Commons, 1828–30, and in Parliament for the *True Son*, 1830–32, the *Mirror of Parliament*, 1832–34, and the *Morning Chronicle*, 1835; began contributing articles to the *Monthly Magazine*, 1833, as "Boz," 1834, and to the *Evening Chronicle*, 1835–36; full-time writer from 1836; visited America, 1842; lived in Italy, 1844–45; edited the *Daily News*, London, 1846; lived in Switzerland and Paris, 1846; manager of an amateur theatrical company touring English provincial cities, 1847; Founder-Editor, *Household Words*, London, 1849–59, and its successor, *All the Year Round*, from 1859; toured Britain, reading his works, 1858–59, 1861–63, 1866–67, and 1868–70; toured America, 1867–68. *Died 9 June 1870.*

PUBLICATIONS

Collections

> *Letters,* edited by Georgina Hogarth and Mamie Dickens.   3 vols., 1880–82; revised edition, edited by Madeleine House and Graham Storey, 1965–
> *Nonesuch Dickens,* edited by Arthur Waugh and others.   23 vols., 1937–38.

Fiction

Sketches by Boz Illustrative of Every-Day Life and Every-Day People.   1836; *New Series,* 1836.

The Posthumous Papers of the Pickwick Club.   1837.

Oliver Twist; or, The Parish Boy's Progress.   1838; edited by Kathleen Tillotson, 1966.

Nicholas Nickleby.   1839; edited by Michael Slater, 1978.

Master Humphrey's Clock: The Old Curiosity Shop, Barnaby Rudge.   3 vols., 1840–41; *Barnaby Rudge* edited by Gordon W. Spence, 1973.

A Christmas Carol, Being a Ghost Story of Christmas.   1843.

Martin Chuzzlewit.   1844.

The Chimes.   1844.

The Cricket on the Hearth: A Fairy Tale of Home.   1845.

The Battle of Life: A Love Story.   1846.

The Haunted Man and the Ghost's Bargain: A Fancy for Christmas Time.   1848.

Dealings with the Firm of Dombey and Son, Wholesale, Retail, and for Exportation.   1848; edited by Alan Horsman, 1974.

David Copperfield.   1850.

Bleak House.   1853; edited by George Ford and Sylvère Monod, 1977.

Hard Times, for These Times.   1854; edited by George Ford and Sylvère Monod, 1972.

Little Dorrit.   1857; edited by John Holloway, 1967.

A Tale of Two Cities.   1859; edited by Barbara Osbourn, 1957.

Great Expectations.   1861; edited by Louise Stevens, 1966.

Our Mutual Friend.   1865; edited by Stephen Gill, 1971.

The Mystery of Edwin Drood.   1870; edited by Arthur J. Cox, 1974.

Christmas Stories from Household Words and All the Year Round, in *Works* (Charles Dickens Edition).   1874.

The Lazy Tour of Two Idle Apprentices, No Thoroughfare, The Perils of Certain English Prisoners, with Wilkie Collins.   1890.

The Christmas Books, edited by Michael Slater.   1971.

Plays

O'Thello (produced 1833).   In *Nonesuch Dickens,* 1937–38.

The Village Coquettes, music by John Hullah (produced 1836).   1836.

The Strange Gentleman (produced 1836).   1837.

Is She His Wife? or, Something Singular (produced 1837).   1837.

Mr. Nightingale's Diary, with Mark Lemon (produced 1851).   1851.

No Thoroughfare, with Wilkie Collins, from their own story (produced 1867).   1867; revised version, 1867.

The Lamplighter.   1879.

Other

American Notes for General Circulation.   2 vols., 1842; edited by John S. Whitely and Arnold Goldman, 1972.

Pictures from Italy.   1846.

Works.   17 vols., 1847–67.

A Child's History of England.   3 vols., 1852–54.

The Uncommercial Traveller.   1861.

Speeches Literary and Social, edited by R. H. Shepherd.   1870; revised edition, as *The Speeches 1841–70,* 1884.
Speeches, Letters, and Sayings.   1870.
The Mudfog Papers.   1880.
Plays and Poems, edited by R. H. Shepherd.   2 vols., 1885.
To Be Read at Dusk and Other Stories, Sketches, and Essays, edited by F. G. Kitton.   1898.
Miscellaneous Papers, edited by B. W. Matz.   2 vols., 1908.
Speeches, edited by K. J. Fielding.   1960.
Uncollected Writings from Household Words, 1850–1859, edited by Harry Stone.   1969.
Household Words: A Weekly Journal 1850–1859, edited by Anne Lohrli.   1974.
The Public Readings, edited by Philip Collins.   1975.

Editor, *The Pic Nic Papers.*   3 vols., 1841.

Bibliography: *The First Editions of the Writings of Dickens* by John C. Eckel, 1913, revised edition, 1932; *A Bibliography of the Periodical Works of Dickens* by Thomas Hatton and Arthur H. Cleaver, 1933; *A Bibliography of Dickensian Criticism 1836–1975* by R. C. Churchill, 1976.

Reading List: *The Life of Dickens* by John Forster, 3 vols., 1872–74, edited by A. J. Hoppé, 2 vols., 1966; *The Dickens World* by Humphrey House, 1941; *Dickens: His Triumph and Tragedy* by Edgar Johnson, 2 vols., 1952, revised edition, 1978; *Dickens at Work* by Kathleen Tillotson and John Butt, 1957; *Dickens: The World of His Novels* by J. Hillis Miller, 1958; *The Imagination of Dickens* by A. O. J. Cockshut, 1961; *The Flint and the Flame: The Artistry of Dickens* by Earle R. Davis, 1963; *The Dickens Theatre: A Reassessment of the Novels* by Robert Garis, 1965; *Dickens the Novelist* by Sylvère Monod, 1968; *Dickens the Novelist* by F. R. and Q. D. Leavis, 1970; *Dickens: The Critical Heritage* edited by Philip Collins, 1971; *A Reader's Guide to Dickens* by Philip Hobsbaum, 1973; *The Violent Effigy* by John Carey, 1973.

*   *   *

The greatness of Charles Dickens is of a peculiar kind, one that should give pause to highbrows. He was, at the same time, the great popular entertainer and the great artist, unrivalled in greatness in the rich tradition of the English novel except by Jane Austen. Moreover, his greatness and his popular appeal are inseparable. We hear a lot – and truly enough in certain cases – about unappreciated genius. In the generation after Dickens's death, genius starving in a garret became something of a cliché. The obverse, the successful public man, read and enjoyed by everybody, but not for many years perceived to be a wonderful classic genius, was somewhat overlooked. Matthew Arnold enjoyed Dickens like everybody else, but he could not recognize him as one of the great classics of the age, because he subconsciously expected that the great classics would be poets. Lord Acton, one of the most learned men of the age and one of the most omnivorous readers, lamented his own infirmity in that he returned so much more often to Dickens than to George Eliot. He would have been surprised, perhaps astonished, that the judgment of posterity would be that Dickens was even greater than George Eliot.

I said that the genius of Dickens and his status as popular entertainer were inseparable. The reasons for this lie deep in the man's nature. He was a born orator and actor. His lifelong enthusiasm for amateur dramatics, and the maniacal intensity with which he read aloud his own works – the excitement of the process may well have contributed to his death at the early age of 58 – were both significant. Like chess-players writers may be divided into those who "play the board" (try to make the best move objectively) and those who "play the man" (try to make the move most effective against a given opponent). Dickens was emphatically of the latter kind. He was never a pure artist. Like a great political orator, he drew strength from his audience; he delighted to please them, he accepted the validity of their judgment. It would never have occurred to him to complain that they were mistaken if some aspect of his art was unappreciated. They were the proper arbiters of his destiny whom he delighted to honour and obey.

In this he was not sycophantic or mercenary. He reverenced them partly because he was so like them. Some great writers are natural solitaries, others are learned and obscure; but Dickens was in many respects the ordinary English man of the middle-class transformed by a unique unrepeatable genius. In his own person he fulfilled and exemplified many dominant myths of the mid-nineteenth century. He was a self-made man, like the heroes of the immensely popular and influential Samuel Smiles. Without proper education, without a loving and secure home, he had made himself a household name by the time he was in his early twenties. In an age more notable perhaps than any other for deep feeling (some might say sentimentality) about childhood, he had been a rejected child, forced to find his own lodgings and earn his own living by the time he was ten years old.

Then, he was typical of his great middle-class public in being a practical man of the world, not particularly bookish, with a double share of the extraordinary exuberant energy and humour of that expansive age. Like his public, he was a bit of a philistine; his views on art were much nearer to those of the crowds who thronged the Royal Academy and admired the accuracy of Frith's *Derby Day* than they were to those of John Ruskin.

Like his public, too, he was interested in reform. Like them he was very certain that reform should work in the direction of reducing aristocratic privilege; like them he was much more dubious about extending middle-class privileges to those lower down. Like them he was very keen on a strong police force and the prevention of crime, and like them he took an unholy delight in the breathless drama of a murder story. He was an unthinking, self-righteous protestant like many of them, and just as intensely insular and as ignorant as they were of the wider European tradition. Sometimes, as in the character of Podsnap in *Our Mutual Friend*, he tried to make fun of some of these English limitations, and at times the satirical humour was excellent. But he shared many of the same characteristics.

Self-knowledge was the least of his attainments. He was sincerely convinced that the breakdown of his marriage was entirely the fault of his unoffending wife, and that he could have lived happily with almost anybody else. But no one else is likely to believe this. Like other popular writers he was deeply melodramatic. But, unlike some, there was nothing cynical or calculating in his melodramatic appeal. He never wrote down to his adoring public. In expressing their aspirations, fears, and prejudices he was simply expressing himself.

Dickens was a man of obsessions, which can be traced all through his work. He was haunted by the idea of the lonely child, because he had been one. He was haunted by the idea of the prison, because his father had been in the debtors' prison. He was deeply obsessed by the thought of violence. These themes and a few others recur constantly; but it would be a complete mistake to suppose that this makes his work repetitive. His development, and like all great artists he developed continually to the end, consists partly in the perpetual deepening and enrichment of these themes. The prison of *Pickwick Papers* is the same debtors' prison as the one in *Little Dorrit* (and the same in which his own father was confined) but as literary experiences the two could hardly be more different, and the later one is immensely the more brilliant and profound. Occasionally, two of his obsessions meet in the same passage, such as the burning of the prison by the mob in *Barnaby Rudge* (prison and violence) or the exclusion of Dorrit at night from her only home, the Marshalsea prison (prison and lonely child). Such passages often have a particularly intense power or pathos.

Balancing this constant recurrence of the same facts and ideas we have his extraordinary inventiveness, variety, and mastery of significant detail. His world is fuller and richer than other novelists' worlds. He squanders enough characters on one novel to last any other novelist for five; and then has just as many swarming into his mind for the next. His hypnotic imagination finds poetry, humour, significance in the most ordinary things. London, that terrifying, amorphous, unadministered, physically filthy Victorian London, which struck intelligent foreign visitors as almost a hell on earth, was his natural home as man and artist. He drew strength and inspiration from his long, solitary walks (often at night) through the dingiest and strangest areas. His pathos, his wild, extravagant humour, his zeal for reform, his serious indignation were all rooted in this vision of the largest and strangest city the world had ever seen, and the one with the most bizarre contrasts.

There is no space here to chart his development in detail. In general one may say that in his early works, up to about 1845, his exuberance, whether comic or melodramatic, predominates. Plots are wildly improbable; coincidences abound; deeds often lack their natural outcome. At times we seem to be almost in the world of "the omnipotence of thought," a kind of fairy-tale, not about princesses, but about orphans and chimney-sweeps and strolling players. *Dombey and Son* (1848) is a landmark of change. The old features are still present in some degree, but so are those that become more and more dominant in his later work, psychological insight, serious thought about society, and above all a sense of the consequences of things and of the complexity of moral choices. In *Nicholas Nickleby*, an early work, two philanthropical brothers diffuse joy and peace all round them by giving away their money. In *Our Mutual Friend*, his last completed novel, Boffin, a kindly man anxious to do good with his large fortune, finds himself thwarted and deceived, and unable to produce beneficial effects. The later books are in places just as funny as the earlier. But the humour is more satirical, even savage. The soaring, high-spirited nonsense of *Pickwick* is gone.

Finally, I would stress the inexhaustible variety of Dickens. In him alone among later English writers, we can, without absurdity, find a likeness to the fecundity of Shakespeare.

—A. O. J. Cockshut

DISRAELI, Benjamin; 1st Earl of Beaconsfield.   English. Born in London, 21 December 1804; son of the writer Isaac D'Israeli. Educated at a private school in Walthamstow, London; articled to Swain and Stevenson, solicitors, London, 1821; entered Lincoln's Inn, London, 1824; removed his name, 1831. Married Mrs. Wyndham Lewis in 1839 (died, 1872). Began writing in 1826; toured Spain, Italy, and the Near East, 1828–31; returned to London, and devoted himself to writing, 1831–37; contested the Parliamentary seats of High Wycombe, 1821, 1834, and Taunton, 1835; Conservative Member of Parliament for Maidstone, Kent, 1837–41, Shrewsbury, 1841–47, and Buckinghamshire, 1847 until his elevation to the House of Lords, 1876: Leader of the Young England Party of Conservatives, 1842; Chancellor of the Exchequer in Lord Derby's first government, 1852; Chancellor of the Exchequer and Leader of the House of Commons in Derby's second government, 1858–59; Chancellor of the Exchequer in Derby's third government, 1866–68: introduced and carried Reform Bill, 1867; became Prime Minister on Derby's retirement, 1868; opposed Gladstone's Irish and foreign policies, 1868–73; again Prime Minister, 1874–80: made Britain half-owner of the Suez Canal, 1875; persuaded Queen Victoria to accept title of Empress of India, 1876, and became a close friend of the Queen; attempted to check Russian influence in Eastern Europe, 1877–78; represented England at the Congress of Berlin, 1878. Created Earl of Beaconsfield, 1876; Knight of the Garter, 1878. *Died 19 April 1881.*

PUBLICATIONS

Collections

Works, edited by Edmund Gosse.   20 vols., 1904–05.

Fiction

Rumpel Stiltskin: A Dramatic Spectacle, with W. G. Meredith.   1823; edited by
   Michael Sadleir, 1952.
Vivian Grey.   5 vols., 1826–27.
The Voyage of Captain Popanilla.   1828.
The Young Duke.   1831.
Contarini Fleming: A Psychological Autobiography.   1832; as *The Young Venetian*,
   1834.
The Wondrous Tales of Alroy and the Rise of Iskander.   1832; edited by W. S.
   Northcote, 1906.
Henrietta Temple.   1837; edited by W. S. Northcote, 1906.
Venetia; or, The Poet's Daughter.   1837.
Coningsby; or, The New Generation.   1844.
Sybil; or, The Two Nations.   1845; edited by Victor Cohen, 1934.
Tancred; or, The New Crusade.   1847.
Ixion in Heaven, The Infernal Marriage, Popanilla, Count Alarcos.   1853; edited by W.
   S. Northcote, 1906.
Lothair.   1870; edited by Vernon Bogdanor, 1975.
Novels and Tales.   10 vols., 1870–71.
Endymion.   1880.
Tales and Sketches, edited by J. L. Robertson.   1891.

Play

The Tragedy of Count Alarcos (produced 1868).   1839.

Verse

The Revolutionary Epick.   1834; revised edition, 1864.
The Modern Aesop, edited by Michael Sadleir.   1928.

Other

*An Inquiry into the Plans, Progress, and Policy of the American Mining
   Companies*.   1825.
Lawyers and Legislators; or, Notes on the American Mining Companies.   1825.
The Present Stage of Mexico.   1825.
Key to Vivian Grey.   1827.
England and France; or, A Cure for the Ministerial Gallomania.   1832.
What Is He?   1833; revised edition, 1833.
The Crisis Examined.   1834.
Vindication of the English Constitution.   1835.

The Letters of Runnymede, The Spirit of Whiggism.   1836; edited by Francis Bickley, 1923.

Lord George Bentinck: A Political Biography.   1852; revised edition, 1872.

Mr. Disraeli to Colonel Rathbone.   1858.

Church and Queen: Five Speeches 1860–64.   1865.

Speeches on Parliamentary Reform 1848–66, edited by Montagu Corry.   1867.

Speeches on the Conservative Policy of the Last Thirty Years, edited by J. F. Bulley.   1870.

Selected Speeches, edited by T. E. Kebble.   2 vols., 1882.

Home Letters 1830–31, edited by Ralph Disraeli.   1885.

Correspondence with His Sister, edited by Ralph Disraeli.   1886; edited by Augustine Birrell, 1928.

Whigs and Whiggism: Political Writing, edited by William Hutcheon.   1913.

Letters to Lady Bradford and Lady Chesterfield, edited by the Marquis of Zetland.   2 vols., 1929.

The Radical Tory: Disraeli's Political Development Illustrated from His Original Writings and Speeches, edited by H. W. J. Edwards.   1937.

Letters to Frances Anne, Marchioness of Londonderry 1837–61, edited by the Marchioness of Londonderry.   1938.

Tory Democrat: Two Famous Disraeli Speeches, edited by Edward Boyle.   1950.

Notes for an Autobiography, edited by Helen M. Swartz and Marvin Swartz.   1975.

Editor, *The Works of Isaac D'Israeli.*   1858.

Bibliography: *XIX Century Fiction* by Michael Sadleir, 1951; *Disraeli's Novels Reviewed 1826–1968* edited by R. W. Stewart, 1975.

Reading List: *Hours in a Library 2* by Leslie Stephen, 1876; *The Political Novel* by M. E. Speare, 1924; *Disraeli* by Cecil Roth, 1952; *The Victorian Sage* by John Holloway, 1953; *Disraeli* by Paul Bloomfield, 1962; *Disraeli* by Robert Blake, 1966; *Disraeli* by Richard W. Davis, 1976; *Disraeli and His World* by Christopher Hibbert, 1978.

*   *   *

The novels of Benjamin Disraeli are probably little read today, and it is unlikely that anyone who is not interested in politics will turn to them for pleasure. For Disraeli is a prime example of the political novelist. It is not just that he writes, as Trollope does, about political themes, but that his best novels – *Coningsby* and *Endymion* – are political allegories. They express the political ideas through which he hoped to "educate" and transform the Conservative Party of his day; and, through the Conservative Party, England also.

Disraeli's first novel, *Aylmer Papillion*, was published when he was only 19 in 1824; unfortunately only two chapters of it remain. His early novels were written primarily in order to raise the money to satisfy his creditors; and Part 1 of *Vivian Grey*, "as hot and hurried a sketch as ever yet was penned," appeared in 1826 when Disraeli was 21. It proved to be a *succès de scandale* on account of the appearance in it of many characters from contemporary social life whom the reader could amuse himself by identifying. The novel itself however, was a cynical pot-boiler, modelled on the "silver-fork" novel of the day, in the production of which Disraeli's friend Bulwer-Lytton was such a master. *Vivian Grey's* central theme is the development and political education of a youth who possesses neither political ideals nor moral principles; his only concern is with worldly success – "Why then, the world's mine oyster," claims the epigraph of the book, "which I with sword will open." It was natural for Vivian to be identified with Disraeli himself.

Each of Disraeli's novels seems to display the same basic pattern as *Vivian Grey*, in that its theme is the development of a young man to maturity. Indeed, eight of the novels bear the name of the youth as their title. But what is striking about the novels of Disraeli's maturity – the trilogy *Coningsby*, *Sybil*, and *Tancred*; *Lothair*; and *Endymion* – is the way in which the heroes *differ* from Vivian Grey in seeking something more than worldly success.

As Kathleen Tillotson has noticed (*Novels of the Eighteen-Forties*, 1954), Disraeli's mature heroes "all *think* perhaps ineffectually, ignorantly, fitfully, but in their puzzled or impulsive way they do think, and about their social rights and responsibilities." Coningsby, Charles Egremont in *Sybil*, Tancred, Lothair, and Endymion are concerned at the degradation of the aristocratic ideal typified by the selfishness of great landed magnates such as Coningsby's grandfather Lord Monmouth or Lord Marney in *Sybil*. This degradation has ruined the Conservative Party, once a party of principle, social reform, and devotion to the interests of the people, so that it has become a party of concessionaires and place-seekers whose only *raison d'être* is the spoils of office. As he says in the General Preface to the novels, "no party was national; one was exclusive and odious, and the other liberal and cosmopolitan."

Disraeli's heroes, therefore, seek a social ideal through which they might organise their lives. This ideal is to be found through "the use of ancient forms and the restoration of the past." "That's the true spring of wisdom," Coningsby is told, "meditate over the past." Disraeli sought a re-invigoration of the feudal principle of social responsibility, since in a healthy society, in the relationship between employer and employed, "there must exist other ties than the payment and acceptance of wages." Disraeli's obsession with great houses and aristocratic munificence reflects his view of society. The great houses have a continuous and vital relationship to the past, rooted in the land. They serve a function not only for the family living in them, but also for the hierarchical and intergrated community of which they are the apex. For the ownership of a great house is, ideally, associated with precisely the virtues of generosity and social concern which are needed to regenerate England.

What Disraeli's novels offer then is a clearly thought-out and consistent philosophy of conservatism. His heroes come to understand the nature of conservatism by confronting the different philosophies which seek to explain men's duties, and the mature novels end with the hero at last equipped to face his responsibilities. Coningsby enters Parliament, Egremont in *Sybil* is confident that the seemingly impassable gulf between the two nations – the rich and the poor – can be bridged; Tancred understands that a political renewal cannot occur without a religious revival; and Lothair can assume the duties of a great landowner.

Where the novels end with the marriage of the hero, the symbolic nature of the union is made clear. Coningsby, in marrying Edith Millbank, the daughter of an industrialist, appreciates that the regeneration of the aristocracy depends upon its coming to terms with the rising force of industry; Egremont, by marrying Sybil, acts in accordance with his belief that aristocratic leadership can secure class harmony; and Lothair, in allying himself to Lady Corisande who represents the practical spirit of traditional wisdom, frees himself from the ideological fanaticisms of the Roman Catholic Church and modern nationalism.

Disraeli thus represents a genuine and vital link in the history of English conservative thought – a link between Burke and Coleridge and T. S. Eliot. His view of life was greatly influenced by Burke and Carlyle in that he believed human existence to have an impalpability that is not to be grasped in any set of abstract formulae or rules for living, such as the Utilitarians, for example, attempted to provide. "Utilitarians in politics," Disraeli argued in his early "Mutilated Diary," "are like Unitarians in religion. Both omit Imagination in their systems and Imagination governs mankind." And in *Lothair* Disraeli tells us that the philosophers "accounted for everything, except the only point on which man requires revelation." It is this insistence that life is not to be understood in terms of any dogmatic philosophy that gives Disraeli's novels their characteristic air of exuberance and optimism.

Disraeli was uninterested in the traditional furniture of the English novel. His concern with the development of character was perfunctory and his plots were melodramatic and preposterous. Yet he had a profound insight into political ideas, and succeeded in grafting a novel of political ideas on to the "silver-fork novel." This makes him *sui generis* among novelists writing in the English language.

—Vernon Bogdanor

DODGSON, Charles Lutwidge.   See CARROLL, Lewis.

DOYLE, Sir Arthur Conan.   Scottish.   Born in Edinburgh, 22 May 1859. Educated at the Hodder School, Lancashire, 1868–70, Stonyhurst College, Lancashire, 1870–75, and the Jesuit School, Feldkirch, Austria, 1875–76; studied medicine at the University of Edinburgh, 1876–81, M.B. 1881, M.D. 1885. Served as Senior Physician to a field hospital in South Africa during the Boer War, 1899–1902: knighted, 1902. Married 1) Louise Hawkins in 1885 (died, 1906), one daughter and one son; 2) Jean Leckie in 1907, two sons and one daughter. Practised medicine in Southsea, 1882–90; full-time writer from 1891; stood for Parliament as Unionist candidate for Central Edinburgh, 1900, and tariff reform candidate for the Hawick Burghs, 1906. LL.D.: University of Edinburgh, 1905. Knight of Grace of the Order of St. John of Jerusalem. *Died 7 July 1930.*

PUBLICATIONS

Collections

Great Stories, edited by John Dickson Carr.   1959.

Fiction

A Study in Scarlet.   1888.
The Mystery of Cloomber.   1889.
Micah Clarke.   1889.
Mysteries and Adventures.   1889; as *The Gully of Bluemansdyke and Other Stories,* 1893.
The Sign of Four.   1890.
The Captain of the Polestar and Other Tales.   1890.
The Firm of Girdlestone.   1890.
The White Company.   1891; edited by C. Kingsley Williams, 1934.
The Doings of Raffles Haw.   1892.
The Great Shadow.   1892; edited by Guy N. Pocock, 1940.
Beyond the City.   1892.
The Adventures of Sherlock Holmes (stories).   1892.

The Refugees. 1893.
The Memoirs of Sherlock Holmes (stories). 1893.
Round the Red Lamp, Being Facts and Fancies of Medical Life. 1894.
The Parasite. 1894.
The Stark Munro Letters. 1895.
The Exploits of Brigadier Gerard. 1896.
Rodney Stone. 1896; edited by C. Kingsley Williams, 1936.
Uncle Bernac: A Memory of the Empire. 1897.
The Tragedy of the Korosko. 1898.
A Duet, with an Occasional Chorus. 1899.
The Green Flag and Other Stories of War and Sport. 1900.
The Hound of the Baskervilles. 1902.
The Adventures of Gerard. 1903.
The Return of Sherlock Holmes (stories). 1905.
Sir Nigel. 1906.
Round the Fire Stories. 1908.
The Last Galley: Impressions and Tales. 1911.
The Case of Oscar Slater. 1912.
The Lost World. 1912.
The Poison Belt. 1913.
The Valley of Fear. 1915.
His Last Bow: Some Reminiscences of Sherlock Holmes. 1917.
Danger! and Other Stories. 1918.
The Land of Mist. 1926.
The Case-Book of Sherlock Holmes (stories). 1927.
The Maracot Deep and Other Stories. 1929.
Historical Romances. 2 vols., 1931–32.
Strange Studies from Life, edited by Peter Ruber. 1963.
The Annotated Sherlock Holmes, edited by W. S. Baring-Gould. 1968.

Plays

Jane Annie; or, The Good Conduct Prize, with J. M. Barrie, music by Ernest Ford
    (produced 1893). 1893.
Foreign Policy (produced 1893).
Waterloo (as *A Story of Waterloo,* produced 1894). 1919(?).
Halves (produced 1899).
Sherlock Holmes, with William Gillette, from works by Doyle (produced 1899). 1922.
A Duet. 1903.
Brigadier Gerard, from his own story (produced 1906).
The Fires of Fate: A Modern Morality (produced 1909).
The House of Temperley (produced 1909).
A Pot of Caviare (produced 1910). 1912.
The Speckled Band (produced 1910). 1912.
The Crown Diamond (produced 1921).

Verse

Songs of Action. 1898.
Songs of the Road. 1911.
The Guards Came Through and Other Poems. 1919.
Collected Poems. 1922.

Other

The Great Boer War. 1900.
The War in South Africa: Its Cause and Conduct. 1902.
Works. 12 vols., 1903.
Through the Magic Door. 1907.
The Crime of the Congo. 1909.
The German War: Sidelights and Reflections. 1914.
To Arms! 1914.
The British Campaign in France and Flanders. 6 vols., 1916–19.
A Visit to Three Fronts, June 1916. 1917.
The New Revelation; or, What Is Spiritualism? 1918.
The Vital Message. 1919.
The Wanderings of a Spiritualist. 1921.
The Case for Spirit Photography, with others. 1922.
The Coming of the Fairies. 1922.
Three of Them. 1923.
Our American Adventure. 1923.
Memories and Adventures. 1924.
Our Second American Adventure. 1924.
The History of Spiritualism. 2 vols., 1926.
Pheneas Speaks: Direct Spirit Communications. 1927.
Our African Winter. 1929.
The Roman Catholic Church. 1929.
The Edge of the Unknown. 1930.

Editor, *The Spiritualist's Reader.* 1924.

Bibliography: *A Bibliographical Catalogue of the Writings of Doyle* by Harold Locke, 1928.

Reading List: *Doyle: His Life and Art* by Hesketh Pearson, 1943, revised edition, 1977; *The Life of Doyle* by John Dickson Carr, 1949; *A Sherlock Holmes Commentary* by D. Martin Dakin, 1972; *The World of Sherlock Holmes* by Michael Harrison, 1973; *The Encyclopedia Sherlockiana* by Jack W. Tracy, 1977.

*   *   *

There are a few characters of fiction who step out of their books and become known almost universally. The literary eminence, or otherwise, of their creators seems to bear no relation to their fame; they range from Scrooge and Peter Pan to the Scarlet Pimpernel and Tarzan of the Apes, and probably the best known of them all is Sherlock Holmes who has been described as "the most famous man who never lived."

Even without Holmes, Sir Arthur Conan Doyle would still hold a reasonably high place in the literature of adventure stories and historical romance – perhaps between Rider Haggard and John Buchan. He himself wished to be remembered by his historical romances, notably *The White Company* and *Sir Nigel*, though these are ponderous compared to his two volumes of Napoleonic short stories, *The Exploits of Brigadier Gerard* and *The Adventures of Gerard*. In Gerard he created a really memorable and living character, a vain French brigadier, as brave as he boasts himself to be, though with an amusing touch of stupidity, who narrates his own exciting adventures in a delightfully flamboyant manner. Gerard is memorable in a way that Sir Nigel Loring and his White Company are not, in spite of Doyle's splendid narrative gift. Doyle's narrative, in fact, makes almost all his fiction eminently readable, and the sheer impetus of breathless adventure in the first half of *The Refugees* rivals Stanley Weyman's best. Besides the Gerard stories Doyle also produced an excellent volume of miscellaneous historical tales, *The Last Galley*, later issued with one additional story as *Tales of Long Ago*, which he considered the best of his unaffiliated short stories. He was certainly a master of the short story of plot rather than character, but, apart from the Holmes and Gerard collections, he was probably at his best with "Tales of Terror and Mystery" and of "Twilight and the Unseen," issued at first in various collections.

In 1912, trying to escape from Sherlock Holmes, Doyle strove to create another memorable character as different from him as possible, and wrote *The Lost World*, the first adventure of the redoubtable Professor Challenger (apparently suggested by Rider Haggard's Professor Higgs in *Queen Sheba's Ring*, 1909), just far enough from caricature to carry conviction. The story is of an expedition to a plateau in South America isolated from the rest of the world, where prehistoric animals and savages in a very early state of development still survive. It is told in a series of reports by the journalist member of the party – an excellent method of creating continual suspense – and remains one of the most popular of Doyle's books, lending itself particularly well to cinematic treatment.

Doyle used Challenger and his companions again in *The Poison Belt* in which they manage to survive an apparent blotting out of all life on Earth, though (as in his earlier story of a modern alchemist, *The Doings of Raffles Haw*) he is unable to exploit his idea to the full as perhaps the early H. G. Wells could have done. The same is true of his dabblings with the supernatural even in as exciting a story as *The Mystery of Cloomber*. By the time he came to introduce his Challenger group to Spiritualism in *The Land of Mist*, he was himself an ardent Spiritualist and produced a mere tract in the form of a novel.

But of course Doyle really lives as an important author by his long and short stories of Mr. Sherlock Holmes, the first private consulting detective, who made his rooms at 221B Baker Street, London so famous that large numbers of letters addressed to a fictitious character at a fictitious address still turn up.

Doyle did not invent the detective story or the detective. There were detectives in the novels of Dickens and Wilkie Collins, and a first "blueprint" for Holmes had admittedly appeared under the name of Dupin in several short stories by Edgar Allan Poe; moreover, M. Lecoq, an energetic French professional, had been created by Emile Gaboriau – apparently based on the actual detective Vidocq whose *Memoires* had been published in 1828. While these may have suggested conscious or subconscious ideas for the creation of Holmes the only intentional and admitted borrowing was from one of Doyle's professors at Edinburgh University, Dr. Joseph Bell, who was accustomed to detect not only ailments but also profession, antecedents, and other personal information about his patients without them speaking a single word.

The first appearance of Sherlock Holmes, *A Study in Scarlet*, created little stir among critics or readers; the second of the longer adventures, *The Sign of Four*, had more popular success, because Doyle's name had become known through the publication of his first historical romance, *Micah Clarke*, the previous year. But it was not until the *Adventures* began appearing month by month in *The Strand Magazine* in 1891 that Sherlock Holmes took the public by storm. One innovation was that each of the monthly issues included a complete story with the same chief characters instead of a single full-length story cut into monthly parts to which readers of the magazine had become accustomed; but this does not belittle Doyle's achievement in creating the first short detective story with the eccentric detective whose interest for the reader is focused on his mind rather than his soul, and who is accompanied by a companion who is a little more dull-witted than the reader is assumed to be. Doyle, the professional doctor with the scientific and analytic mind, trained to observe and report, but unable to create any but a static and undeveloping character found his perfect *métier* in Holmes and Watson. He also captured the setting and atmosphere of the period and background in a way that created some unexplained spell. This has produced the unique activities of Sherlock Holmes Societies all over the world and a library of Sherlock Holmes literature treating the four long and fifty-six short stories about him as true accounts of a real man's adventures: a kind of playtime research particularly attractive to the academic mind.

Probably most critics agree that *The Hound of the Baskervilles* is Doyle's masterpiece. Many of the short stories, including "The Speckled Band" and "Silver Blaze," are in the same class. Although Doyle describes Holmes as "the most perfect reasoning and observing machine that the world has seen," he was able to create externally a character and a period setting as unique and recognisable as the more deeply drawn characters of the great novelists.

—Roger Lancelyn Green

---

du MAURIER, George (Louis Palmella Busson).   English.   Born in Paris, 6 March 1834. Educated at the Pension Froussard, Paris, 1847–51; studied chemistry at University College, London 1851–54, then worked as an analytical chemist, in his own laboratory, London, 1854–56; returned to Paris, and studied art with Gleyre, 1856–57, and under De Keyser and Van Lerius at the Antwerp Academy, 1857–60. Married Emma Wightwick in 1863; two sons and three daughters. Settled in London, 1860, and thereafter worked as an illustrator: contributed to *Once a Week* and *Punch* from 1860, and became a member of the *Punch* table, 1864; illustrated stories for *Cornhill Magazine*, 1863–83; lived in Hampstead, London, 1870 until his death; also a writer from 1891. *Died 6 October 1896.*

PUBLICATIONS

Collections

> *The Young du Maurier: A Selection of His Letters 1860–1867,* edited by Daphne du Maurier. 1951.

Fiction

> *Peter Ibbetson.*   1892.
> *Trilby.*   1894.
> *The Martian.*   1897.

Verse

> *A Legend of Camelot.*   1898.

Other

> Drawings: *English Society at Home,* 1880; *Society Pictures,* 2 vols., 1891; *English Society,* 1897; *Social Pictorial Satire,* 1898.

Reading List: *The du Mauriers* by Daphne du Maurier, 1937; *du Maurier: His Life and Work* by D. P. Whitely, 1948; "du Maurier and the Romantic Novel" by Lionel Stevenson, in *Essays by Divers Hands 30,* 1960; *du Maurier* by Leonée Ormond, 1969.

*   *   *

George du Maurier in character and achievement can be considered as in some ways resembling a later and minor Thackeray. He knew Paris and the bohemian artistic world of Paris even better than Thackeray did, and his excellent *Punch* cartoons, which beautifully catch the social affectations of the late Victorian period, show that he was a more successful graphic artist than Thackeray if a much less important writer. Yet Thackeray's hasty sketches have sometimes a life and naturalness that du Maurier's delicate penmanship lacks. Similarly, though du Maurier recalls Thackeray in pathos verging dangerously on sentimentality, and in reminiscent humour, he has a kind of staginess (as in the melodramatic character of Svengali in *Trilby*) not found in Thackeray. *Trilby*, his second novel, turned into a successful melodrama with Beerbohm Tree in 1895, was his most famous book. His first, *Peter Ibbetson*, based on dreams, is more personal and original, as is the unfinished story of school memories, *The Martian*. Not a great writer or artist, du Maurier nevertheless catches very skilfully the daydreams of his time.

—G. S. Fraser

EDGEWORTH, Maria.   Irish/English.   Born in Black Bourton, Oxfordshire, 1 January 1767; daughter of the educationist Richard Lovell Edgeworth. Educated in Mrs. Lattaffiere's school in Derby, 1775–80, and at Mrs. Davis's school in London, 1780–82. Lived with her family in Edgeworthtown, Ireland, from 1783, and assisted her father, and later her brother, in running the family estates; collaborated with her father on educational works, 1798–1802; visited France, 1802–03, London, 1803, 1819, and France and Switzerland, 1820–21; thereafter devoted herself to the estate; frequently visited London and made occasional tours of the British Isles. *Died 22 May 1849.*

PUBLICATIONS

Collections

> *Tales and Novels.*   18 vols., 1857.
> *Selections,* edited by G. Griffin.   1918.

Fiction

> *The Parent's Assistant; or, Stories for Children.*   1796; revised edition, 1800.
> *Castle Rackrent: An Hibernian Tale.*   1800; edited by George Watson, 1964.

Early Lessons, with Richard Lovell Edgeworth.   10 vols., 1800–02; edited by L. Valentine, 1875.
Moral Tales for Young People.   1801.
Belinda.   1801; revised edition, 1810; edited by A. T. Ritchie, 1896.
The Mental Thermometer.   1801.
Popular Tales.   1804.
The Modern Griselda.   1805.
Adelaide; or, The Chateau de St. Pierre.   1806.
Leonora.   1806.
Tales of Fashionable Life.   6 vols., 1809–12.
Patronage.   1814; revised edition, in *Tales and Miscellaneous Pieces,* 1825.
Continuation of Early Lessons.   1814.
Harrington, and Ormond.   1817; edited by A. H. Johnson, 1900.
Rosamond: A Sequel to Early Lessons.   1821.
Frank: A Sequel to Early Lessons.   1822.
Harry and Lucy Concluded, Being the Last Part of Early Lessons.   1825.
Tales and Miscellaneous Pieces.   14 vols., 1825.
Helen.   1834; edited by A. T. Ritchie, 1896.

Plays

Love and Law (produced 1810).   In *Comic Dramas,* 1817.
Comic Dramas (includes *The Rose, Thistle, and Shamrock; The Two Guardians; Love and Law*).   1817.
Little Plays for Children: The Grinding Organ, Dumb Andy, The Dame School Holiday.   1827.

Other

Letters for Literary Ladies, to Which Is Added an Essay on the Noble Science of Self-Justification.   1795.
Practical Education, with Richard Lovell Edgeworth.   1798; as *Essays on Practical Education,* 1811.
Essay on Irish Bulls, with Richard Lovell Edgeworth.   1802.
Essays on Professional Education, with Richard Lovell Edgeworth.   1809.
Readings on Poetry, with Richard Lovell Edgeworth.   1816.
Memoirs of Richard Lovell Edgeworth, completed by Maria Edgeworth.   1820.
Chosen Letters, edited by F. V. Barry.   1931.
Tour in Connemara and the Martins of Ballinahinch, edited by H. E. Butler.   1950.
Letters of Edgeworth and Anna Barbauld, edited by Walter Sidney Scott.   1953.
Letters from England 1813–1844, edited by Christina Colvin.   1971.
The Education of the Heart: The Correspondence of Rachel Mordecai Lazarus and Edgeworth, edited by Edgar E. MacDonald.   1977.

Bibliography: *Edgeworth: A Bibliographical Tribute* by B. C. Salde, 1937.

Reading List: *Life and Letters of Edgeworth* by A. J. C. Hare, 2 vols., 1894; *Edgeworth* by P. H. Newby, 1950; *The Great Maria: A Portrait* by Elisabeth I. Jones, 1959; *Edgeworth the Novelist* by James Newcomer, 1967; *Edgeworth and the Public Scene: Intellect, Fine Feeling, and Landlordism in the Age of Reform* by Michael C. Hurst, 1969; *Edgeworth's Art of Prose Fiction* by Oleta Harden, 1971; *Edgeworth: A Literary Biography* by Marilyn S. Butler, 1972.

*　　*　　*

Maria Edgeworth acquired, and to some extent retains, three reputations. With her father, she contributed to the growing literature of education at the end of the eighteenth century, and wrote moral tales designed for young audiences; she was also a significant figure among those minor female novelists who surrounded Jane Austen's ascendant star; finally, she defined and virtually launched the school of Irish fiction which in turn influenced Walter Scott and established (with other Scottish novelists) the regional novel as a serious art-form.

The educational writings are now remembered at a purely academic level, though her training as the author of neat moral allegories should be considered in assessing her work as a whole. The titles of the *Tales of Fashionable Life* reveal her concentration on a singular moral problem or a single character in a specific and limited moral context – "Ennui," "Madame de Fleury," "The Dun." While she can occasionally effect a satirical charge at society with which Jane Austen might agree in principle, the two novelists differ in their methods. Maria Edgeworth retained not only the moral didacticism of the eighteenth century; she was indebted for many of her literary models to authors of the mid-century.

To call her a novelist is, to some extent, to take liberties with the term. Her best fiction was written in the shorter forms. Of the four full-length novels which are not Irish and regional, two – *Belinda* and *Patronage* – had to be extensively and uneasily revised for later editions, while a third, *Helen*, all but marks the end of her writing career. *Patronage* has, to be sure, a broad and impressive social base, and Marilyn Butler has suggested a comparison with *Mansfield Park* which by no means disgraces Maria Edgeworth. But as a contributor to English fiction, she remains firmly in the lower half of the second rank; her work is too calculated in both manner and effect, too mechanical in its methods and objectives, to sustain any profound critical analysis.

It is, of course, as an Irish regional writer that she survives in print. *Castle Rackrent* chronicles the decline of an Irish gentry family through four generations, their misfortune being related by the family retainer, Thady Quirk. Thady's muted dialect speech provides an admirable vehicle for irony, as when he declares of his beloved master's funeral "happy the man who could get but a sight of the hearse." It is significant that the tale was written originally for the amusement of her family, a circumstance which in part explains its diminished didacticism. "Ennui" is a slight affair, and should be read as a trial run for "The Absentee," usually but unfairly relegated to second place by the fame of *Castle Rackrent*. "The Absentee" advances an evident message to its readers, but didacticism is enveloped and transformed by the complex allegorical forms in which Irish history and folklore are interwoven into a "tale of fashionable life." It was "The Absentee" which sent Scott back to the incomplete manuscript of *Waverley* and so assisted at the birth of the historical novel proper. *Ormond*, as if to return the compliment, owes much to Scott; indeed its debt to literature is curiously bound up with its characterisation: the hero's moral development is charted through his reading of *Tom Jones* and *Sir Charles Grandison* – a further indication of Maria Edgeworth's eighteenth-century loyalties.

The Irish work is united and given coherence by its constant attention to the meaning of the past as a constituent of the present; even "Ennui" and "The Absentee," which deal ostensibly with contemporary society, are properly read as historical fiction. The scale of her material as an Irish novelist – the smallness and intimacy of Irish society, together with her inherited experience of political upheavals – suited Maria Edgeworth's abilities and talents. In the Irish fiction, moral worth is seen as directly related to social function, whereas the English novels tend towards abstract moral points.

Despite a reputation as an "ascendancy" novelist, Maria Edgeworth actually occupied a central position in the social system; she belonged to the middle gentry, and shared their insecurity, their Janus-like perspective. This creative ambiguity, unavailable to her as a commentator on English habits, is present in all her Irish work, and no more so than in Thady Quirk's eloquent and damning eulogies. Like Walter Scott her conservatism was a sympathetic one; in her best work, "The Absentee" and *Castle Rackrent*, she looked to history for meaning rather than consolation.

—W. J. McCormack

EGAN, Pierce.   English.   Born in London in 1772. Married in 1812; one son, the writer Pierce Egan the Younger. Known as a "reporter of sporting events" for various London newspapers by 1812; reporter for the journal printed by E. Young, 1812–23; full-time writer from 1823; Editor, *Pierce Egan's Life in London and Sporting Guide*, weekly newspaper, 1824–27, and *Pierce Egan's Weekly Courier*, 1829. *Died 3 August 1849.*

PUBLICATIONS

Fiction

Life in London; or, The Day and Night Scenes of Jerry Hawthorn, Esq., and Corinthian Tom.   1821.
The Life of an Actor.   1825.
Finish to the Adventures of Tom, Jerry, and Logic in Their Pursuits Through Life In and Out of London.   1828; edited by J. C. Hotten, 1871.
The Pilgrims of the Thames in Search of the National!   1838.

Plays

Tom and Jerry, from his own novel *Life in London* (produced 1821).
Life in Dublin (produced 1839).

Verse

The Show Folks.   1831.
Matthews's Comic Annual; or, The Snuff-Box and the Leetel Bird.   1831.
Epsom Races.   1835.

Other

The Mistress of Royalty; or, The Loves of Florizel and Perdita.   1814.
Boxiana; or, Sketches of Ancient and Modern Pugilism, vols. 1–3.   1818–21; *New Series,* 2 vols., 1828–29.
Walks Through Bath.   1819.
The Key to a Picture of the Fancy.   1819.

Sporting Anecdotes, Original and Select. 1820.
The Life and Extraordinary Adventures of S. D. Hayward. 1822.
The Fancy Togs' Man Versus Young Sadboy, The Milling Quaker. 1823.
Account of the Trial of J. Thurtell and J. Hunt. 1824.
Recollections of John Thurtell. 1824.
Account of the Trial of Mr. Fauntleroy for Forgery. 1824.
Account of the Trial of Bishop, Williams, and May for Murder. N.d.
Anecdotes of the Turf, The Chase, The Ring, and the Stage. 1827.
Book of Sports and Mirror of Life. 1832.

Reading List: *Bucks and Bruisers: Egan and Regency England* by J. C. Reid, 1971.

*   *   *

Pierce Egan made his name in 1812 as the author of a history of boxing, issued in monthly parts. *Boxiana* eventually ran to five volumes, the last published in 1829, and is a high point in sporting journalism. The later volumes record in rapid colloquial prose the fashionable heyday of boxing from the championship victory of "Gentleman" John Jackson in 1795 until his retirement as a coach of the nobility in 1824. Egan knew shorthand, and could revive a fight round-by-round; but *Boxiana* is socially as well as sportingly alert.

The same is true of Egan's work on his other main interests – crime, city life, and the theatre. He published celebrated accounts of the trials of Hayward, Thurtell and Hunt, and Fauntleroy, and made use of a casual acquaintanceship in adding *Recollections of John Thurtell* to the less personal courtroom observations. Though clearly fascinated by low-life and high crime, Egan took a moral line against the growing cult of rogue literature. He contributed to it nonetheless. As a practising journalist, he was occupationally committed to doing so. Criminals and criminality are a part of *Life in London*, which is neither quite a novel nor quite anything else. Ned Ward's *London Spy* (1698–99) is the model for this hugely successful foray into the high and low life of the city during the Regency. Egan's eye is not on narrative but on the locations, and on the episodes that ensue when Corinthian Tom, together with his friend Bob Logic, undertakes to introduce his Somerset cousin Jerry Hawthorn to London. There is some care in the juxtaposing of contrasting scenes, but the book owed its popularity to its graphic accuracy, to its carefully observed racy slang, and to Egan's appetite for the diversity of city life. A sequel, *Finish to Life in London*, sees the cautionary deaths of Bob and Tom, and Jerry's married retirement to Somerset. *Life in London* fathered a vast, sub-literary family, none of which brought any profit to Egan. His own dramatic version was less effective than William Moncrieff's *Tom and Jerry*, whose sensational run began in November 1821 at the Adelphi, and spread all over the provinces. The "Tom and Jerry" formula had a lasting appeal, independent not only of Egan's text but also of its superb illustration by Robert and George Cruikshank. Egan's last novel, *The Pilgrims of the Thames*, is a variation on it. Its new fastidiousness signals the transition from Regency to Victorian England. *The Life of an Actor*, an old-fashioned picaresque novel, is notable for Theodore Lane's hand-coloured illustrations and for the detailed information it gives about the provincial theatre. This is the world of Vincent Crummles, and the claim that, here and elsewhere, Egan influenced Dickens is plausible. Without Tom and Jerry, Boz might have sketched differently; and Dickens certainly looked to Egan as an expert on thieves' cant.

—Peter Thomson

ELIOT, George. Pseudonym for Mary Ann or Marian Evans. English. Born at Chilvers Coton, near Nuneaton, Warwickshire, 22 November 1819. Privately educated. Lived with George Henry Lewes, 1854 until he died, 1878; married J. W. Cross in 1880. Took charge of family household after the death of her mother, 1836; moved with her father to Coventry, 1841–49; lived in Geneva, 1849–50; settled in London, 1850, and began to write for the *Westminster Review*: Assistant Editor, 1851–54; lived in Germany, 1854, then returned to England; subsequently settled in Cheyne Walk, Chelsea, London. *Died 22 December 1880.*

PUBLICATIONS

Collections

>   *Works.* 21 vols., 1895.
>   *Letters*, edited by Gordon Haight. 9 vols., 1954–78.

Fiction

>   *Scenes of Clerical Life* (stories). 1858; edited by David Lodge, 1973.
>   *Adam Bede.* 1859; edited by John Paterson, 1968.
>   *The Mill on the Floss.* 1860; edited by Gordon Haight, 1961.
>   *Silas Marner, The Weaver of Raveloe.* 1861; edited by Q. D. Leavis, 1967.
>   *Romola.* 1863.
>   *Felix Holt, The Radical.* 1866; edited by Peter Coveney, 1972.
>   *Middlemarch: A Study of Provincial Life.* 1872; edited by Bert G. Hornback, 1977.
>   *Daniel Deronda.* 1876; edited by Barbara Hardy, 1967.

Verse

>   *The Spanish Gypsy.* 1868.
>   *How Lisa Loved the King.* 1869.
>   *The Legend of Jubal and Other Poems.* 1874.
>   *Complete Poems.* 1889.

Other

>   *Works.* 24 vols., 1878–85.
>   *Impressions of Theophrastus Such.* 1879.
>   *Essays and Leaves from a Note-Book,* edited by C. L. Lewes. 1884.
>   *Early Essays.* 1919.
>   *Essays*, edited by T. Pinney. 1963.

>   Translator, with Mrs. Charles Hennell, *The Life of Jesus Critically Examined*, by D. F. Strauss. 3 vols., 1846; edited by Peter C. Hodgson, 1973.
>   Translator, *The Essence of Christianity*, by Ludwig Feuerbach. 1854.

Bibliography: *Eliot: A Reference Guide* by Constance M. Fulmer, 1977.

Reading List: *Eliot's Life as Related in Her Letters and Journals* by J. W. Cross, 3 vols., 1885; *Eliot: Her Mind and Art* by Joan Bennett, 1948; *Eliot* by Robert Speaight, 1954; *The Novels of Eliot* by Barbara Hardy, 1959; *The Art of Eliot* by W. J. Harvey, 1961; *Eliot* by Walter Allen, 1964; *A Century of Eliot Criticism* edited by Gordon Haight, 1965; *Eliot: A Biography* by Gordon Haight, 1968; *Critical Essays on Eliot* edited by Barbara Hardy, 1970; *Eliot: The Critical Heritage* edited by D. R. Carroll, 1971; *Eliot: The Emergent Self* by Ruby Redinger, 1975; *Eliot: Her Beliefs and Her Art* by Neil Roberts, 1975; *The Novels of Eliot* by Robert Liddell, 1977.

*   *   *

To many of her admirers during her lifetime, George Eliot, though ranked as a novelist below Dickens and Thackeray, seemed more than a "mere" novelist. She was a maker of the moral law as no novelist had been before her, and despite the unconventional circumstances of her life her position when she died could be paralleled only by Wordsworth's a generation or so earlier. In the decades that followed everything changed. She fell with the great Victorians, and so far as there was interest in her it was largely as a figure in the history of woman's emancipation. Today, all is different again. She still has to yield to Dickens's superior genius but in critical estimation she leads all other Victorian novelists and is seen as the one nineteenth-century English novelist who can be mentioned in the same breath as Tolstoy. In England she is probably over-rated.

She came to the writing of fiction steeped in the advanced thought of Victorian England. She had translated Strauss's *Life of Jesus* and experienced in herself the full force of doubt about religion and the truth of Christianity. She was torn between the old, which she loved, and the new, which won her intellectual assent. She was, indeed, that familiar figure in English life, the radical Tory. Born into the Established Church, she had become a Calvinist Methodist as a girl, and, when intellectual honesty compelled a reluctant agnosticism upon her, it was an agnosticism that laid as remorseless a stress on morals and right behaviour as had the dissent of her youth.

Her beliefs chimed with what seemed to be evidence of the science of the day, of Darwinism as then interpreted. This gave her novels great authority at the time, though later it was to appear dated. It was too mechanistic a view of life to allow her to write tragedy, but by placing the responsibility for a man's life firmly on the moral choices of the individual she changed the nature of the English novel. Character became plot. D. H. Lawrence saw her as the first modern novelist, saying in an early letter that she was the first to start "putting all the action inside."

Her first work of fiction, *Scenes of Clerical Life*, which is made up of three long-short stories, need not detain us. What is good in them George Eliot was to do much better. *Adam Bede*, which appeared a year later, is quite another matter. A key to it is an authorial intrusion in which George Eliot comments on what in fact is one of the qualities of her own art:

> It is for this rare, precious quality of truthfulness that I delight in many Dutch paintings, which lofty-minded people despise. I find a source of delicious sympathy in these faithful pictures of a monotonous homely existence, which has been the fate of so many more among my fellow mortals than a life of pomp or of absolute indigence, of tragic suffering or of world-stirring action.

Here she is stressing the pastoral ambience of the novel, which encloses the moral action; the scenes in Mrs. Poyser's farmhouse, for instance, the harvest supper, and what has been called "the massively slow movement" of the novel in which the rhythms of life and the seasons are beautifully caught. But another key to the novel is contained in the Rev. Mr. Irwine's words: "Consequences are unpitying. Our deeds carry their terrible consequences ... consequences that are hardly ever confined to ourselves." These words define the inner action of the novel:

the fall of Hetty Sorrel, her seduction by Arthur Donnithorne, the effect of this on Adam Bede and his marriage to Dinah Morris.

But the touching, idyllic love-affair of Hetty and Arthur Donnithorne is undercut for us now by the hostile attitude of the author towards sex and sensuality. Nor, though the novel is a wonderful study of the impact of Methodism on English life, can George Eliot be said quite to succeed with Adam Bede and Dinah. The good are notoriously less easy to make convincing or attractive in fiction than the less good.

George Eliot's fiction falls naturally into two parts. *Scenes of Clerical Life, Adam Bede, The Mill on the Floss* and *Silas Marner* were all published between 1858 and 1861. *Romola* (1863) begins her second and more ambitious period, which takes in *Felix Holt, The Radical, Middlemarch,* and *Daniel Deronda.* The speed with which she wrote her first novels shows how near the surface of her mind was the vein of imagination she tapped. To write *The Mill on the Floss* she had only to remember her own childhood, for, though the background and setting have been very much altered, the novel is essentially autobiographical. As a detailed rendering of the growth of a girl to young womanhood, a girl of intellectual distinction and generously ardent feelings, Maggie Tulliver is unsurpassed. Equally brilliant in a different mode is the representation of the Tulliver family and of the Dodsons. They comprise a materialistic world given over entirely to the sense of property, self-regard and pride in family, made palatable to us only by the humour and shrewdness of George Eliot's observation.

Describing the inception of *Silas Marner*, George Eliot noted its Wordsworthian quality. Though she wrote two volumes of verse, it was only in the prose of *Silas Marner* that she achieved poetry. It is indeed of a Wordsworthian order, this story which shows "in a strong light the remedial influences of pure, natural human relations." Only in her own time could she have succeeded in telling the story of Marner without lapsing into sentimentality, and no one could have done so after her. A poor dissenting weaver is betrayed by his friend, accused of theft, loses his future wife, goes into exile in a remote country district, becomes a miser, is robbed of his gold, and in the end brought back into human fellowship by the discovery and adoption of a golden-haired baby girl. It is a small miracle, this novel of redemption; and in the wonderful conversations at the Rainbow Inn it contains George Eliot's finest delineations of rustic characters and her finest humorous writing.

In the fiction of her second period George Eliot wrote only one novel, *Middlemarch*, that can be called a success. *Romola* was an attempt at a historical novel, a recreation of Florence at the end of the fifteenth century and of the career and martyrdom of Savonarola. Enormous pains went to its making. It is crammed with solid and scholarly information and almost totally lacking in life. In writing *Romola* George Eliot had cut herself off from the source of her inspiration, which was the contemplation of the changing scene of the English Midland countryside in her time. She returned to it in *Felix Holt, The Radical.* It contains fine things but is dominated by a plot that is particularly cumbersome, almost impossible to synopsise and turning on points of law relating to inheritance which have baffled most readers. But Harold Transome is a notably impressive character creation, belonging to the company of George Eliot's formidable masculine figures, Lydgate and Grandcourt.

George Eliot's greatest novel is *Middlemarch*, a beautiful composition organised round four major plots, the story of Dorothea Brooke, the story of Lydgate's marriage, the history of Mary Garth, and the fall of the banker Bulstrode, all of them related to one another without strain. Together, they make a network that takes in the whole life and movement of opinion and events in a provincial city and its surrounding country in the years immediately before the first Reform Act of 1832. Two of the characters, Dorothea and Lydgate, are among the finest in fiction, and Dorothea in particular is a great conception. She is, as it were, a heightened Maggie Tulliver, with all Maggie's notability of aspiration but with the advantages of social position, wealth, and independence. The conception of Lydgate falls not far short; and around them are gathered as large and diverse a gallery of characters as exists in any English novel.

The failure of George Eliot's last novel, *Daniel Deronda*, is self-evident. It falls into two parts, that action centred on the imaginatively conceived character of Gwendolen and that centred on Deronda, this latter being propaganda for the establishment of a Zionist state. All the same, the novel is regarded now much more highly than it was because of the brilliance of Gwendolen Harleth as a character-creation. She is utterly different from George Eliot's other great heroines, cold, arrogant, self-willed where they are idealist, warm, and self-sacrificing. And Grandcourt, her nemesis, is no less magisterially drawn. It is plain now that George Eliot died before she had realised the full potentialities of her genius.

One aspect of her genius is shown in the influence she had on later novelists. Hardy and Lawrence are scarcely conceivable without her; a considerable part of Henry James developed out of her; and it has been surmised that *The Mill on the Floss* was in Proust's mind when he was planning *A la recherche du temps perdu*; and her continuing influence and example may be seen in the fiction of such novelists as Angus Wilson and Doris Lessing.

—Walter Allen

FERRIER, Susan (Edmonstone). Scottish. Born in Edinburgh, 7 September 1782. Educated privately. Writer from 1810; a friend of Sir Walter Scott, whom she visited in 1811, 1829, and 1831; blind in later life. *Died 5 November 1854.*

PUBLICATIONS

Collections

   Works, edited by Lady M. Sackville.   4 vols., 1928.

Fiction

   Marriage.   1818; revised edition, 1856; edited by Herbert Foltinek, 1971.
   The Inheritance.   1824; revised edition, 1857.
   Destiny; or, The Chief's Daughter.   1831; revised edition, 1841.

Reading List: *Memoir and Correspondence of Ferrier* by John Ferrier, edited by J. A. Doyle, 1898; *Ferrier of Edinburgh: A Biography* by Aline Grant, 1957; *Ferrier and John Galt* by William M. Parker, 1965.

*   *   *

At first sight, Susan Ferrier's achievement strikes us as a kind of riddle. How could a spinster who spent such an uneventful life produce novels of manners that betray considerable experience combined with a manifest insight into human affairs? True enough, her great contemporary Jane Austen also drew on a limited knowledge of the world, but she, after all, had her share of the egocentricity of the true artist, who absorbs whatever passes his way. Susan Ferrier thought but modestly of her own work, and yet there is something very professional about it, as if she had always correctly assessed her abilities. The secret may lie in her evident good sense, which we are tempted to trace to her background.

A native of Edinburgh, she had inherited something of that city's intellectual alertness and pragmatic way of reasoning. Such a mind will energetically respond to every facet of its environment. At her time Edinburgh social life still had a closeness and coherence that our age discovers only in novels, offering infinite material for the critical faculties. Further impressions were obtained from visits to aristocratic homes, and from her reading. Too clear-headed to turn into a bluestocking, she nevertheless possessed a remarkable knowledge of English and French literature. Her idiosyncratic figures, even when drawn from observation, continue the English tradition of character drawing; the French essayists, on the other hand, taught her to comprehend life in terms of moral and social patterns. This attitude must have suited her well. There is something very natural and obvious about her didacticism. A novel, in her opinion, had to include a sound moral to be worth the telling, but the lesson nowhere becomes a pretext for the tale.

Her common-sense outlook on life made her suspicious of flights of fancy, and she is never at ease when occasionally borrowing a motif from the romance tradition. Conversely, her observant mind and keen sense of humour will inevitably derive an effect from the most commonplace situation. The finest passages in her writings concern everyday events which may not even have an immediate bearing on the progress of the action. This will sometimes move haltingly, for she had little understanding of plotting, but her scenes from high and ordinary life have never failed to amuse. In her time she was commonly assigned to the "Scotch" novelists, although she can usually hold her own even outside her native sphere. What remains most striking about her work is, however, not so much its regional or descriptive character as a tangible element of plain, down-to-earth sense. In a small way she certainly helped to affirm the empirical, realistic quality that has characterized the English novel throughout the ages.

—Herbert Foltinek

FIELDING, Henry.   English.   Born in Sharpham Park, Glastonbury, Somerset, 22 April 1707; brother of Sarah Fielding, q.v. Educated at Eton College; studied letters at the University of Leyden, 1728–29; entered the Middle Temple, London, 1737: called to the Bar, 1740. Married 1) Charlotte Cradock in 1734 (died, 1744); 2) Mary Daniel in 1747. Settled in London, 1727; successful playwright, in London, 1728–37: Author/Manager, Little Theatre, Haymarket, 1737 (theatre closed as a result of Licensing Act); Editor, with James Ralph, *The Champion*, 1739–41; lawyer and novelist from 1740, also writer/editor for *The True Patriot*, 1745–46, *The Jacobite's Journal*, 1747–48, and the *Covent Garden Journal*, 1752; Principal Justice of the Peace for Middlesex and Westminster, 1748; Chairman, Westminster Quarter Sessions, 1749–53. *Died 8 October 1754.*

PUBLICATIONS

Collections

Complete Works, edited by W. E. Henley.   16 vols., 1903.
Works (Wesleyan Edition), edited by Martin C. Battestin and others.   1967–

Fiction

An Apology for the Life of Mrs. Shamela Andrews. 1741; edited by A. R. Humphreys, with *Joseph Andrews,* 1973.

The History of the Adventures of Joseph Andrews and of His Friend Mr. Abraham Adams. 1742; revised edition, 1742; edited by Martin C. Battestin, in *Works,* 1967.

The Life of Mr. Jonathan Wild the Great, in *Miscellanies.* 1743; edited by A. R. Humphreys and D. Brooks, 1973.

A Journey from This World to the Next, in *Miscellanies.* 1743; edited by Claude J. Rawson, 1973.

The History of Tom Jones, A Foundling. 1749; revised edition, 1749, 1750; edited by Fredson Bowers and Martin C. Battestin, in *Works,* 2 vols., 1975.

Amelia. 1752; revised edition, in *Works,* 1762; edited by A. R. Humphreys, 1962.

Plays

Love in Several Masques (produced 1728). 1728.

The Temple Beau (produced 1730). 1730.

The Author's Farce, and The Pleasures of the Town (produced 1730). 1730; revised version (produced 1734), 1750; 1730 version edited by Charles B. Woods, 1966.

Tom Thumb (produced 1730). 1730; revised version, as *The Tragedy of Tragedies; or, The Life and Death of Tom Thumb the Great* (produced 1731), 1731; edited by LeRoy J. Morrissey, 1970.

Rape upon Rape; or, The Justice Caught in His Own Trap (produced 1730). 1730; revised version, as *The Coffee-House Politician* (produced 1730), 1730.

The Letter-Writers; or, A New Way to Keep a Wife at Home (produced 1731). 1731.

The Welsh Opera; or, The Grey Mare the Better Horse (produced 1731). 1731; as *The Genuine Grub Street Opera,* 1731; edited by E. V. Roberts, 1968.

The Lottery (produced 1732). 1732.

The Modern Husband (produced 1732). 1732.

The Covent Garden Tragedy (produced 1732). 1732.

The Old Debauchees (produced 1732). 1732; as *The Debauchees; or, The Jesuit Caught,* 1745.

The Mock Doctor; or, The Dumb Lady Cured, from a play by Molière (produced 1732). 1732; edited by J. Hampden, 1931.

The Miser, from a play by Molière (produced 1733). 1733.

Deborah; or, A Wife for You All (produced 1733).

The Intriguing Chambermaid, from a play by J. F. Regnard (produced 1734). 1734.

Don Quixote in England (produced 1734). 1734.

An Old Man Taught Wisdom; or, The Virgin Unmasked (produced 1735). 1735.

The Universal Gallant; or, The Different Husbands (produced 1735). 1735.

Pasquin: A Dramatic Satire on the Times, Being the Rehearsal of Two Plays, Viz a Comedy Called The Election and a Tragedy Called The Life and Death of Common Sense (produced 1736). 1736; edited by O. M. Brack, Jr., and others, 1973.

Tumble-Down Dick; or, Phaeton in the Suds (produced 1736). 1736.

Eurydice (produced 1737). In *Miscellanies,* 1743.

The Historical Register for the Year 1736 (produced 1737). With *Eurydice Hissed,* 1737; revised version, 1737; edited by William W. Appleton, 1967.

Eurydice Hissed; or, A Word to the Wise (produced 1737). With *The Historical Register,* 1737; revised version 1737; edited by William W. Appleton, 1967.

Plautus, The God of Riches, with W. Young, from a play by Aristophanes. 1742.

Miss Lucy in Town: A Sequel to The Virgin Unmasqued, music by Thomas Arne (produced 1742). 1742.

The Wedding Day (produced 1743). In *Miscellanies,* 1743.
Dramatic Works. 2 vols., 1745.
The Fathers; or, The Good-Natured Man (produced 1778). 1778.

Verse

The Masquerade. 1728; edited by C. E. Jones, in *The Female Husband and Other Writings,* 1960.
The Vernon-iad. 1741.
Of True Greatness: An Epistle to George Dodington, Esq. 1741.

Other

The Champion; or, The British Mercury. 2 vols., 1741; excerpt edited by S. J. Sackett, as *The Voyages of Mr. Job Vinegar,* 1958.
The Opposition: A Vision. 1742.
A Full Vindication of the Duchess Dowager of Marlborough. 1742.
Some Papers Proper to Be Read Before the Royal Society. 1743.
Miscellanies. 3 vols., 1743; vol. 1 edited by Henry Knight Miller, in *Works,* 1972.
An Attempt Toward a Natural History of the Hanover Rat. 1744.
The Charge to the Jury. 1745.
The History of the Present Rebellion in Scotland. 1745; edited by I. K. Fletcher, 1934.
A Serious Address to the People of Great Britain, in Which the Certain Consequences of the Present Rebellion Are Fully Demonstrated. 1745.
A Dialogue Between the Devil, The Pope, and the Pretender. 1745.
The Female Husband; or, The Surprising History of Mrs. Mary, Alias Mr. George Hamilton, Taken from Her Own Mouth since Her Confinement. 1746; edited by C. E. Jones, in *The Female Husband and Other Writings,* 1960.
A Dialogue Between a Gentleman of London, Agent for Two Court Candidates, and an Honest Alderman of the Country Party. 1747.
Ovid's Art of Love, Adapted to the Present Times. 1747; as *The Lover's Assistant,* 1759.
A Proper Answer to a Late Scurrilous Libel, Entitled An Apology for the Conduct of a Late Celebrated Second-Rate Minister. 1747.
A Charge Delivered to the Grand Jury. 1749.
A True State of the Case of Bosavern Penlez, Who Suffered on Account of the Late Riot in the Strand. 1749.
An Enquiry into the Causes of the Late Increase of Robbers. 1751.
A Plan of the Universal Register Office, with John Fielding. 1752.
Examples of the Interposition of Providence in the Detection and Punishment of Murder. 1752.
A Proposal for Making an Effectual Provision for the Poor. 1753.
A Clear State of the Case of Elizabeth Canning. 1753.
The Journal of a Voyage to Lisbon. 1755; edited by A. R. Humphreys and D. Brooks, 1973.
The Covent Garden Journal, edited by G. E. Jensen. 1915.
The True Patriot, and The History of Our Own Times, edited by M. A. Locke. 1964.
Criticism, edited by Ioan Williams. 1970.
The Jacobite's Journal, edited by W. B. Coley, in *Works.* 1974.

Translator, *The Military History of Charles XII, King of Sweden,* by M. Gustavus Alderfeld. 3 vols., 1840.

Bibliography: by Martin C. Battestin, in *The English Novel* edited by A. E. Dyson, 1973.

Reading List: *The History of Fielding* by Wilbur L. Cross, 3 vols., 1918; *Fielding the Novelist: A Study in Historical Criticism* by Frederic T. Blanchard, 1926; *Fielding: His Life, Works, and Times* by F. Homes Dudden, 2 vols., 1952; *Fielding* by John Butt, 1954, revised edition, 1959; *The Moral Basis of Fielding's Art* by Martin C. Battestin, 1959; *Essays on Fielding's "Miscellanies"* by Henry Knight Miller, 1961; *Fielding's Social Pamphlets* by Marvin R. Zinker, Jr., 1966; *Fielding and the Language of Irony* by Glenn W. Hatfield, 1968; *Fielding and the Nature of the Novel* by Robert Alter, 1969; *Fielding and the Augustan Ideal under Stress* by Claude J. Rawson, 1972; *Fielding: A Critical Anthology* edited by Claude J. Rawson, 1973; *Fielding's "Tom Jones": The Novelist as Moral Philosopher* by Bernard Harrison, 1975; *Occasional Form: Fielding and the Chains of Circumstance* by J. Paul Hunter, 1975.

*   *   *

Though Henry Fielding is remembered chiefly as a novelist – as, indeed, along with Defoe and Richardson, one of the founders of the modern novel and as the author of one of the dozen or so greatest novels in English, *Tom Jones* – he began his literary career as a poet and a dramatist. A young man of twenty, without much money but with strong family connections to the Whig establishment, he came to London from the West Country in 1727 determined to make his mark as a wit and to solicit the patronage of the Court at a time when, because of the uncertain political climate following the death of George I, a talented writer might expect that his services would be appreciated by the prime minister, Sir Robert Walpole. Contrary to the usual view of Fielding as a staunch and unswerving opponent of Walpole and the Court, his earliest poems and plays reveal that when he was not actively seeking the king's and Walpole's favors he prudently adopted a neutral attitude in politics: to judge from the title of his first published work, *The Coronation: A Poem, and An Ode on the Birthday* (issued in November 1727 but now lost), he began, even in a Cibberian vein, by openly declaring his loyalty to George II; and besides several other poems soliciting Walpole's patronage in 1729–31, he dedicated to the prime minister his most ambitious, if unsuccessful, comedy, *The Modern Husband*. Indeed, as B. L. Goldgar persuasively argues in *Walpole and the Wits* (1976), of the fifteen comedies and farces which Fielding produced between 1728 – when his first play, *Love in Several Masques*, was acted at Drury Lane – and 1734 all but one were calculated shrewdly to amuse the widest possible audience without offending the Court; only in *The Welsh Opera* (1731) – a transparent political allegory satirizing not only Walpole and the leader of the Opposition, but the royal family itself – did he abandon this cautious policy, the result being, predictably, that the play was first withdrawn for revision and then suppressed.

These were the years in which Fielding established himself as London's most popular living playwright. With the exception of *The Modern Husband*, which treats rather too earnestly the disturbing theme of adultery and marital prostitution in high life, his more conventional comedies are entertaining and skillful, but by inviting comparison with the greater works of Congreve and Molière they have suffered the condescension of historians of the drama. No other critic, certainly, has endorsed Shaw's declaration that Fielding was "the greatest practising dramatist, with the single exception of Shakespeare, produced by England between the Middle Ages and the nineteenth century...." Where Fielding did shine was in the lesser modes of farce, burlesque, and satire – in *The Tragedy of Tragedies*, for example, an hilarious travesty of heroic drama, or in *The Author's Farce*, a delightful adaption of the "rehearsal play" concluding with a satiric "puppet show" performed by live actors, a work which in fact anticipates the expressionism of modern experimental drama.

Despite his reputation as the theatrical gadfly of the Court, it was only in the final three years (1734–37) of his dramatic career that Fielding moved, rather hesitantly, into the camp of the Opposition. Though he dedicated *Don Quixote in England* to Chesterfield, who had recently joined their ranks, the political satire in this play – as indeed even in *Pasquin*, which is usually said to be vehemently anti-ministerial – is in fact directed at the venality and incompetence of both parties. Only with *The Historical Register* and its after-piece *Eurydice Hiss'd* did he at last drop the mask of impartiality and, by ridiculing Walpole all too effectively, help to precipitate the Theatrical Licensing Act of 1737, which terminated his career as a playwright.

Forced by an Act of Parliament to abandon the stage, Fielding began preparing for the bar and, to supplement the meager income he would earn as a barrister, enlisted as a hackney author in the Opposition's campaign against Walpole. In this latter capacity, during his editorship of *The Champion* (1739–41), he almost certainly drafted his first work of fiction, *The Life of Jonathan Wild the Great*, a mock biography of an infamous real-life criminal whom he ironically praises for the very qualities of unscrupulous self-aggrandisement by which the prime minister himself had achieved "greatness." This work, however, which Walpole appears to have paid Fielding to suppress, was withheld from publication until 1743, a year after the Great Man's fall from power, when it was issued as part of the *Miscellanies*; by this time Fielding presumably had revised the novel substantially, generalizing the political satire and perhaps expanding the narrative to accommodate the more positive, contrasting element of Wild's relationship with the good-natured Heartfrees. Also included in the *Miscellanies* was *A Journey from This World to the Next*, a satirical fiction done in brisk imitation of Lucian.

It was not politics, however, but a quite remarkable literary event that provoked Fielding into finding his true voice as a novelist. Amused and not a little exasperated by the extraordinary success of Richardson's *Pamela* (1740), Fielding responded first by parodying the novel, hilariously, in *Shamela* (1741) and then by offering in *Joseph Andrews* (1742) his own alternative conception of the art of fiction. Though Fielding's improbably virtuous hero is meant to continue the ridicule of Richardson's indomitable virgin, *Joseph Andrews* is much more than merely another travesty of *Pamela*. Modelled in some respects on Cervantes' masterpiece, it yet enacts Fielding's own original theory of the "comic epic--poem in prose," whose subject is "the true ridiculous" in human nature, exposed in all its variety as Joseph and the amiable quixote Parson Abraham Adams journey homeward through the heart of England. In contrast to the brooding, claustrophobic world evoked in the letters of Richardson's beleaguered maidens, Fielding's is cheerful and expansive, presided over by a genial, omniscient narrator who seems a proper surrogate of that beneficent Providence celebrated by Pope in *An Essay on Man* (1733–34).

In *Joseph Andrews* Fielding founded, as he put it, a "new province of writing." *Tom Jones*, his masterpiece, fulfilled the promise of that ambitious, splendid beginning. Generations of readers have delighted in the comic adventures and nearly disastrous indiscretions of the lusty foundling boy who grows to maturity, discovers the identity of his parents, and marries the beautiful girl he has always loved – a story simple enough in outline, but crowded with entertaining characters, enlivened by the wit and humanity of the narrator, and complicated by the intricacies of an ingenious plot which Coleridge called one of the most perfect in all literature. Like most great books, moreover, *Tom Jones* offers us more than superficial pleasures: it is the realization of its author's profoundest philosophy of life, an artfully constructed model of a world abundant, orderly, and ultimately benign, as the Christian humanist tradition conceived it to be. Thus Fielding declares his subject to be "human nature" and his book to be nothing less than "a great creation of our own." His foundling hero stands for all of us: like the protagonists of romance, he is a kind of wayfaring Everyman who, having been expelled from "Paradise Hall," must through hard experience gain that knowledge of himself which will enable him to be united with the girl, Sophia, whose name signifies Wisdom. *Tom Jones* is, as few books have managed to be, the consummate expression of a particular form and conception of literary art.

With the publication of *Tom Jones* Fielding's life and work entered a new phase. As a reward for his services as publicist for the Pelham administration, he was appointed to the magistracy, an office which he exercised with an energy and diligence that shortened his life.

His new role as a public figure, working actively to preserve the peace and to improve the wretched condition of the poor, affected his art in interesting, but most critics would say regrettable, ways. *Amelia*, his last novel, is a very different book from *Tom Jones*: Fielding's tone has become darker, more monitory, in keeping with his subject – no longer the follies of men, but their errors and cupidities and the doubtful efficacy of those institutions, the law and the church, meant to preserve the social order; his narrator less frequently appears upon the stage, and his voice, wavering between anger and a maudlin sentimentality, no longer inspires confidence. Though his ostensible focus is the domestic tribulations of the feckless Captain Booth and his long-suffering wife, Fielding's true intentions are all too patently didactic: scene after scene is calculated to expose the imperfections of the penal laws, the destructiveness of infidelity, the injustices of the patronage system, and the immoralities of an effete and pleasure-loving society. To be sure, *Amelia* is less fun to read than any of Fielding's other novels, but in the starkness and candor of its social commentary it is compelling none the less. It is in fact the first true novel of social protest and reform in England, sounding themes that would not be resumed until the next century.

—Martin C. Battestin

FIELDING, Sarah. English. Born in East Stour, Dorset, 8 November 1710; sister of Henry Fielding, *q.v.* Very little is known about her life: educated privately; writer from c. 1740; in later life lived in Ryde, then in Bath. *Died 9 April 1768.*

PUBLICATIONS

Fiction

The Adventures of David Simple. 5 vols., 1744–53; edited by Malcolm Kelsall, 1969.
The Governess; or, The Little Female Academy, Being the History of Mrs. Teachum and Her Nine Girls. 1749; edited by Jill E. Grey, 1968.
The Cry: A New Dramatic Fable, with Jane Collier. 1754.
The Lives of Cleopatra and Octavia. 1757; edited by R. B. Johnson, 1928.
The History of the Countess of Dellwyn. 1759.
The History of Ophelia. 1760.

Other

Translator, *Xenophon's Memoirs of Socrates with the Defence of Socrates.* 1762.

*   *   *

Sarah Fielding was the third sister of Henry Fielding the novelist. Her best known prose fiction is *The Adventures of David Simple*, which obtained the status of a minor classic in the eighteenth century. The second edition of this "Moral Romance," as she called the tale, was extensively revised by her brother. Samuel Richardson's praise of her, in a letter to Sarah, 7

December 1756, is well known: "What a knowledge of the human heart! Well might a critical judge of writing say, as he did to me, that your late brother's knowledge of it was not (fine writer as he was) comparable to yours. His was but as the knowledge of the outside of a clockwork machine, while your's was that of all the finer springs and movements of the inside." The "critical judge" was Samuel Johnson, and an alternative version of the comparison is given in Boswell's *Life of Johnson* where it is applied to Henry Fielding and Richardson.

David Simple is an attempt to blend the variety of incident and wide diversity of character which distinguish her brother's novels with a sententious and sentimental essayist's manner close to that of Steele's *The Tatler*, which she greatly admired. David Simple, disenchanted by the hypocrisy, vanity, and duplicity of the world, sets himself in "his travels through the cities of London and Westminster" to find a true friend, and finds that friendship in marriage to Camilla. True simplicity is shown in the life without affectation, moderate in its desires, and possessed of the few and uncomplicated truths which are the foundation of eighteenth-century practical piety. In a bitterly ironical and tense sequel, however, entitled *Volume the Last*, David is also shown as a simpleton in his naive hopes for happiness and the tale ends with poverty and death.

In addition to producing other novels, Sarah Fielding also wrote a highly successful collection of moral fairy tales for children, *The Governess*, which is an important work in the history of education. She was well versed in classical literature also, and something of a blue-stocking. She was a correspondent of Richardson, met figures such as Joseph Warton and Edward Young, and came under the patronage of Henry Fielding's friend, Ralph Allen of Prior Park.

—Malcolm Kelsall

GALT, John. Scottish. Born in Irvine, Ayrshire, 2 May 1779. Educated at Irvine Grammar School; schools in Greenock; Lincoln's Inn, London, 1809–12. Married Elizabeth Tilloch in 1813; three sons. Clerk, Greenock Customs House, 1796, and for James Miller and Company, Greenock, 1796–1804; engaged in business ventures in London, 1805–08; travelled with Byron from Gibraltar to Malta, 1809; agent for a merchant in Gibraltar, 1812–13; Editor, *Political Review*, London, 1812, and *New British Theatre* monthly, London, 1814–15; Secretary, Royal Caledonian Society, 1815; regular contributor to the *Monthly Magazine*, 1817–23, and to *Blackwoods's Magazine* from 1819; lobbyist for the Edinburgh and Glasgow Union Canal Company, 1819–20, and later for other clients; Secretary, 1823–26, and Superintendent, resident in Canada, 1826–29, to the Canada Company, formed for the purchase of crown land: founded the town of Guelph, Ontario; imprisoned for debt after his return to England, 1829; Editor, *The Courier* newspaper, London, 1830; contributor to *Fraser's Magazine* from 1830; lived in Greenock, 1834 until his death. *Died 11 April 1839.*

Publications

Collections

Works, edited by D. S. Meldrum and William Roughead. 10 vols., 1936.

Poems: A Selection, edited by G. H. Needler.   1954.
Collected Poems, edited by Hamilton Baird Timothy.   1969.

Fiction

The Majolo: A Tale.   1816.
The Earthquake: A Tale.   1820.
Glenfell; or, Macdonalds and Campbells.   1820.
Annals of the Parish; or, The Chronicle of Dalmailing During the Ministry of the
    Reverend Micah Balwhidder.   1821; edited by James Kinsley, 1967.
The Ayrshire Legatees; or, The Pringle Family.   1821.
Sir Andrew Wylie of That Ilk.   1822.
The Provost.   1822; edited by Ian A. Gordon, 1973.
The Steam-Boat.   1822.
The Entail; or, The Lairds of Grippy, edited by David M. Moir.   1822; edited by Ian A.
    Gordon, 1970.
The Gathering of the West; or, We've Come to See the King, with The Ayrshire
    Legatee.   1823; edited by Bradford A. Booth, 1939.
Ringan Gilhaize; or, The Covenanters.   1823; edited by George Douglas, 1899.
The Spaewife: A Tale of the Scottish Chronicles.   1823.
Rothelan: A Romance of the English Histories (stories).   1824.
The Omen.   1826.
The Last of the Lairds; or, The Life and Opinions of Malachi Mailings, Esq., of
    Auldbiggins, completed by David M. Moir.   1826.
Lawrie Todd; or, The Settlers in the Woods.   1830; revised edition, 1849.
Southennan.   1830.
Bogle Corbet; or, The Emigrants.   1831.
The Member.   1832; edited by Ian A. Gordon, 1976.
The Radical.   1832.
Stanley Buxton; or, The Schoolfellows.   1832.
Eben Erskine; or, The Traveller.   1833.
The Stolen Child: A Tale of the Town.   1833.
The Ouranoulogos; or, The Celestial Volume.   1833.
Stories of the Study.   1833.
The Howdie and Other Tales, edited by William Roughead.   1923.
A Rich Man and Other Stories, edited by William Roughead.   1925.

Plays

The   Tragedies   of   Maddelen,   Agamemnon,   Lady   Macbeth,   Antonia,   and
    Clytemnestra.   1812.
The Apostate; Hector; Love, Honour, and Interest; The Masquerade; The Mermaid;
    Orpheus; The Prophetess; The Watchhouse; The Witness, in The New British
    Theatre.   1814–15.
The Appeal (produced 1818).   1818.

Verse

The Battle of Largs: A Gothic Poem, with Several Miscellaneous Pieces.   1804.
The Crusade.   1816.
Poems.   1833.

Efforts by an Invalid.   1835.
A Contribution to the Greenock Calamity Fund.   1835.
The Demon of Destiny and Other Poems.   1839.

Other

Cursory Reflections on Political and Commercial Topics.   1812.
Voyages and Travels in the Years 1809, 1810, and 1811.   1812.
The Life and Administration of Cardinal Wolsey.   1812.
Letters from the Levant.   1813.
The Life and Studies of Benjamin West.   2 vols., 1816–20; as *The Progress of Genius*, 1832; edited by Nathalia Wright, 1960.
The Wandering Jew; or, The Travels and Observations of Hareach the Prolonged (juvenile).   1820.
All the Voyages round the World.   1820.
A Tour of Europe and Asia.   2 vols., 1820.
George the Third, His Court and Family.   2 vols., 1820.
Pictures Historical and Biographical, Drawn from English, Scottish, and Irish History (juvenile).   2 vols., 1821.
The National Reader and Spelling Book.   2 vols., 1821.
A New General School Atlas.   1822.
The English Mother's First Catechism for Her Children.   1822.
Modern Geography and History.   1823.
The Bachelor's Wife: A Selection of Curious and Interesting Extracts (essays).   1824.
The Life of Lord Byron.   1830.
The Lives of the Players.   2 vols., 1831.
The Canadas as They at Present Commend Themselves to the Enterprise of Emigrants, Colonists, and Capitalists, edited by Andrew Picken.   1832.
The Autobiography.   2 vols., 1833.
The Literary Life and Miscellanies.   3 vols., 1834.

Editor, *The Original and Rejected Theatre,* and *The New British Theatre.*   4 vols., 1814–15.
Editor, *Diary Illustrative of the Times of George the Fourth,* vols. 3–4, by Lady Charlotte Bury.   1838.
Editor, *Records of Real Life in the Palace and Cottage,* by Harriet Pigott.   1839.

Reading List: *Galt* by Jennie W. Aberdein, 1936; *Galt and 18th Century Scottish Philosophy,* 1954, and *Galt's Scottish Stories,* 1959, both by Erik Frykman; *Susan Ferrier and Galt* by William M. Parker, 1965; *Galt: The Life of a Writer* by Ian A. Gordon, 1972.

*   *   *

John Galt was the author of well over forty volumes, ranging from novels and biography to travel, art criticism, drama, and verse. The reader has to discriminate between those (written under financial pressure) of slight literary interest and a central group of novels of distinctive quality. Recent evaluative criticism and publication for the first time of accurate texts have led to a revival of interest in Galt and a consequent revaluation of his work as a novelist.

Galt's major contribution to the novel was his sensitive and yet ironic portrayal of the rural Scotland of the late eighteenth century, a period when an agricultural society was giving way to the new industrial growth. Galt welcomed the advantages of industrial development, while at the same time regretting the passing of the old order and the decline of the rural sense of community. He had an acute ear for Scottish dialect speech and a sharp eye for eccentricities of character. The result in his best novels is an ironic blend of realistic comedy and a romantic nostalgia for a disappearing rural society. *Annals of the Parish* records fifty years of change, narrated by the shrewd parish minister Micah Balwhidder; *The Entail* is a three-generation study of obsession, the avaricious Claud and his wife Leddy Grippy (an indefatigable and loquacious survivor) both memorable portraits; in *The Last of the Lairds* the elderly Malachi Mailings wages a comic rearguard action against the new age of improvements.

The three other novels in Galt's Scottish group are variations on his main theme. In *The Ayrshire Legatees* and *The Steam-Boat* Galt transports his rural characters to metropolitan London, for the sake of comic contrast. *The Provost* (highly praised by Coleridge and regarded by Galt as his best work) is an acute study of the machiavellian politics of power, set in a small Scottish town. The theme was later expanded by Galt for a wider stage in *The Member*, the first political novel in English and a devastating study of the unreformed House of Commons. On its republication in 1976, a contemporary critic found it "comes close to the sublime on many pages." Two other Galt novels are worth noting: *Ringan Gilhaize*, a powerful historical novel written as a rebuttal of Scott's *Old Mortality*, and *Bogle Corbet*, republished in Canada in 1977 as illustrating "the first and still typical Canadian anti-hero."

Galt's characterisation and his handling of pithy Scots dialect has always ensured him a place as a comic writer. The recent revival of interest in Galt's work, following the republication of novels long out of print, has led to a concentration on the more serious sociological implications of his fiction. Galt's forte is the short "autobiographical" novel in which the central character, self-deceived, reveals himself. Though the comedy of *Annals of the Parish* continues to appeal, *The Provost* is the best example of Galt's ironic technique and skill as a novelist.

—Ian A. Gordon

GASKELL, Elizabeth (Cleghorn, née Stevenson).   English.   Born in Chelsea, London, 29 September 1810; brought up in Knutsford, Cheshire, by her aunt. Educated at Miss Byerley's school in Stratford upon Avon, 1824–27. Married the Unitarian minister William Gaskell in 1832; one son and four daughters. Lived in Manchester from 1832; contributed to Dickens's *Household Words*, 1850–58; met and became a friend of Charlotte Brontë, 1850: visited her at Haworth, 1853; organized sewing-rooms during the cotton famine of 1862–63; contributed to the *Cornhill Magazine*, 1860–65. *Died 12 November 1865.*

PUBLICATIONS

Collections

Novels and Tales, edited by C. K. Shorter.   11 vols., 1906–19.
Letters, edited by J. A. V. Chapple and Arthur Pollard.   1966.
Tales of Mystery and Horror, edited by Michael Ashley.   1978.

Fiction

Mary Barton: A Tale of Manchester Life.   1848; edited by Stephen Gill, 1970.
The Moorland Cottage.   1850.
Ruth.   1853.
Cranford.   1853;. edited by Peter Keating, with *Cousin Phillis,* 1976.
Lizzie Leigh and Other Tales.   1855.
North and South.   1855; edited by Angus Easson, 1973.
Round the Sofa.   1859; as *My Lady Ludlow and Other Tales,* 1861.
Right at Last and Other Tales.   1860.
Lois the Witch and Other Tales.   1861.
A Dark Night's Work.   1863.
Sylvia's Lovers.   1863; edited by Arthur Pollard, 1964.
Cousin Phillis.   1864; edited by Peter Keating, with *Cranford,* 1976.
Cousin Phillis and Other Tales.   1865.
The Grey Woman and Other Tales.   1865.
Wives and Daughters.   1866; edited by F. Glover Smith, 1969.

Other

The Life of Charlotte Brontë.   2 vols., 1857; revised edition, 1857; edited by Alan
    Shelston, 1975.
My Diary: The Early Years of My Daughter Marianne.   1923.

Editor, *Mabel Vaughan,* by Maria S. Cummins.   1857.

Bibliography: by Clark S. Northrup in *Gaskell* by Gerald DeWitt Sanders, 1929; *Gaskell: An Annotated Bibliography 1929–1975* by Jeffrey Welch, 1977.

Reading List: *Gaskell: Her Life and Work* by Annette B. Hopkins, 1952; *Gaskell, Novelist and Biographer* by Arthur Pollard, 1965; *Gaskell: The Basis for Reassessment* by Edgar Wright, 1965; *Gaskell, The Artist in Conflict* by Margaret L. Ganz, 1969; *Gaskell's Observation and Invention* by John G. Sharps, 1970; *Gaskell* by John McVeagh, 1970; *Gaskell and the English Provincial Novel* by Wendy A. Craik, 1974; *Gaskell: The Novel of Social Crisis* by Coral Lansburg, 1975; *Gaskell: A Biography* by Winifred Gérin, 1976.

*   *   *

The two best known works of Elizabeth Gaskell are not novels in the strictest sense of the term. *Cranford* is really a collection of short stories linked together by their common location in Cranford, modelled on the Cheshire town of Knutsford. Mrs. Gaskell wrote several other short stories, many of which, like "The Old Nurse's Story" and "Lois the Witch," have a powerful impact, but *Cranford* is marred by sentimentality, and owes much of its appeal to the consolation it offers to the elderly that their old age will be a happy one. Mrs. Gaskell's *Life of Charlotte Brontë,* in contrast, is a sad story, in which, though Mrs. Gaskell did her best to write the truth, she sometimes, as in suppressing Charlotte's love affair with Monsieur Heger, sacrificed truth in an effort to preserve Charlotte's reputation; at other times the novelist in her overcame the biographer. *Cranford* and *The Life of Charlotte Brontë* have had an important if adverse effect on Mrs. Gaskell's standing as a novelist. As a result of *Cranford* we tend to think of her as a pleasant lightweight writer of escapist fiction with little of value to offer in commenting on real life, while her biographical work has meant that we tend to look on her novels as records of social history, ignoring her artistic achievement. These slighting and contradictory verdicts can be shown to be false by an examination of her five major novels.

Mary Barton was published in the year of Revolutions, 1848, and reflects contemporary preoccupation with the threatened Chartist rebellion. Mary Barton is the daughter of a poor but respectable worker, John Barton, who is gradually driven to despair and murder by the refusal of the authorities to do anything to alleviate the condition of the workers. His victim is Harry Carson, who has tried to seduce Mary, and for a time Mary's other lover, Jem Wilson, is suspected of the murder; but Mary's aunt Esther, a prostitute, supplies evidence which points to the real murderer's guilt, and a deathbed confession by John Barton enables Jem and Mary to start a new life in Canada. Mary Barton's independence is the most notable feature of a somewhat unreal heroine; her levelheadedness in saving one lover from taking the blame for a crime her father has committed is commendable but improbable. John Barton is the real hero of the novel, and his decline is treated with compassion but without sentimentality, just as the nostalgic yearnings of the Manchester workers for the countryside before the Industrial Revolution can provide no solution to the problems of the future. Like many of Mrs. Gaskell's novels, *Mary Barton* asks many questions, but provides no easy answers.

Mrs. Gaskell's handling of prostitution in *Mary Barton* met with little adverse comment, but *Ruth* was attacked because it appeared to be sympathetic to a fallen woman. Ruth's fall from grace is delicately handled, and she appears to modern readers as almost entirely innocent, whereas her seducer Mr. Bellingham seems cruel and callow. Ruth, abandoned pregnant by Bellingham, is rescued by a dissenting clergyman and his sister. Mr. and Miss Benson pass her off as a young widow, and as such she meets with the approval of Benson's richest parishoner, Mr. Bradshaw, but her real identity is discovered when Bellingham reappears as a parliamentary candidate. Mr. Bradshaw is furious at Ruth and the Bensons, but they meet his onslaught calmly, and Ruth becomes a nurse, eventually dying through her courage in nursing Bellingham. This conclusion may seem a little contrived, just as the division between the virtuous unworldly Benson and Ruth herself, and the selfish Bellingham and self-righteous Bradshaw, is a little too clear-cut. Mrs. Gaskell is more successful with minor characters like the Benson's servant Sally, Bradshaw's daughter Jemima, and his partner Farquhar, who is initially in love with Ruth but eventually marries Jemima.

There is less black and white in Mrs. Gaskell's next novel, *North and South*, originally written as a serial for *Household Words*. Mrs. Gaskell did not get on well with Dickens, the editor of *Household Words*, but the novel does not show many traces of their differences. Margaret Hale is forced to leave Helstone, a Southern village, for the smoky metropolis of Milton, modelled on Manchester, because her father has religious doubts. These doubts are never explored, and Mr. Hale's vacillating behaviour is never overtly criticised, whereas the stubbornness of Margaret and her lover John Thornton, the rich Milton manufacturer, is more than once attacked. Eventually Margaret learns to abandon some of her Southern snobbery, and Thornton becomes a little more conciliatory to his workers, although the note of compromise on which the novel ends is not a very hopeful one. There is a melodramatic subplot involving Margaret's brother Frederick, who is accused of murder. *North and South* veers rather uneasily between the sexual struggle involving Margaret and Thornton and the social struggle involving Thornton and his workers, but in many ways this is Mrs. Gaskell's richest novel.

In *Sylvia's Lovers* Mrs. Gaskell crossed the Pennines to set her novel in Monkshaven, based on the Yorkshire port of Whitby. She also went back in time to the era of the Napoleonic wars when press-gangs seized the crews of the Yorkshire whalers to serve in the Navy. Charlie Kinraid, a dashing young sailor, is seized by the press-gang, though Philip Hepburn, Sylvia Robson's other lover, who has witnessed the incident, does not deny the general report that Charlie has been drowned. When Sylvia's father Daniel is executed for an attack on the press-gang, Sylvia reluctantly marries Philip. But she has not forgotten Charlie, and once the facts are known she turns against Philip. After melodramatically saving Charlie's life at the siege of Acre, Philip returns home unrecognized, eventually dying of poverty and gaining Sylvia's forgiveness. Between writing *North and South* and *Sylvia's Lovers* Mrs. Gaskell had been concerned with Charlotte Brontë's biography, and it is possible that it was the influence of the Brontës which led her to this attempt to give her novels the powerful romantic aura of *Wuthering Heights* and *Jane Eyre*. Charlie Kinraid is a pale imitation of Heathcliff, Sylvia's dilemma is never explored as fully as that of Jane Eyre, the melodramatic coincidences and reappearances are less convincing than parallel incidents in the Brontë novels – and yet in the dark, brooding, obsessive Hepburn, conventionally kind and, apart from his single lie about Kinraid's disappearance, scrupulously well-behaved, Mrs. Gaskell created a major character, the equal of any other in nineteenth-century fiction.

In *Wives and Daughters*, unfinished at the time of Mrs. Gaskell's death, there appears to be a retreat from high romance and social history to the homely world of Cranford, but, though set vaguely in the past, *Wives and Daughters* has a message for the confused squirearchy, who refused to read the signs of the times, and for their wives and daughters, who still lived in an unreal world where their empty beauty could win them instant admiration. The hero, Roger Hamley, a scientific explorer, and the heroine, Molly Gibson, shrewd, strong and sensitive, are admirable characters, admirably presented.

Mrs. Gaskell is hard to place. While obviously not in the first division of novelists she is equally obviously no minor figure. Her novels cover a more varied range than those of Thackeray, are better plotted than those of Dickens, and are more realistic than those of the Brontës; and yet, perhaps because she is trying to do too many things at once, she does not match any of these great names in spite of her considerable achievement.

—T. J. Winnifrith

GISSING, George (Robert).   English.   Born in Wakefield, Yorkshire, 22 November 1857. Educated at private day schools in Wakefield; Lindow Grove, a Quaker boarding school in Alderley Edge, Cheshire; Owens College, Manchester, 1872 (Ward's English Poem Prize). Married 1) Helen Harrison in 1879 (died, 1888); 2) Edith Underwood in 1891, one son; 3) Gabrielle Fleury in 1899. Clerk in Liverpool, then travelled to America, worked as a tutor and gas fitter in Boston, and travelled as far west as Chicago; failed to find work as a journalist in America, and returned to England in 1877; began writing in 1878; tutor to the sons of Frederic Harrison, 1882, then obtained other pupils and began contributing to the *Pall Mall Gazette* and other periodicals; full-time writer from 1890; lived in the South of France, 1901 until his death. *Died 28 December 1903.*

Publications

Collections

   Stories and Sketches, edited by A. C. Gissing.   1938.

Fiction

   Workers in the Dawn.   1880; edited by Robert Shafer, 1935.

The Unclassed. 1884; revised edition, 1895.
Isabel Clarendon. 1886.
Demos. 1886.
Thyrza. 1887.
A Life's Morning. 1888.
The Nether World. 1889.
The Emancipated. 1890.
New Grub Street. 1891; edited by Irving Howe, 1962.
Denzil Quarrier. 1892.
Born in Exile. 1892.
The Odd Women. 1893.
In the Year of Jubilee. 1894.
Eve's Ransom. 1895.
The Paying Guest. 1895.
Sleeping Fires. 1895.
The Whirlpool. 1897.
Human Odds and Ends: Stories and Sketches. 1898.
The Town Traveller. 1898.
The Crown of Life. 1899.
Our Friend the Charlatan. 1901.
The Private Papers of Henry Ryecroft. 1903.
Veranilda. 1904.
Will Warburton. 1905.
The House of Cobwebs and Other Stories. 1906.
An Heiress on Condition (story). 1923.
Sins of the Fathers and Other Tales, edited by Vincent Starrett. 1924.
A Victim of Circumstance and Other Stories. 1927.
A Yorkshire Lass (story). 1928.
My First Rehearsal, and My Clerical Rival, edited by Pierre Coustillas. 1970.

Verse

Hope in Vain. 1930.

Other

Charles Dickens: A Critical Study. 1898.
By the Ionian Sea: Notes of a Ramble in Southern Italy. 1901.
Letters to Edward Clodd. 1914; edited by Pierre Coustillas, 1973.
Letters to an Editor, edited by C. K. Shorter. 1915.
Critical Studies of the Works of Dickens, edited by T. Scott. 1924.
The Immortal Dickens. 1925.
Letters to Members of His Family, edited by Algernon and Ellen Gissing. 1927.
Letters to Eduard Bertz 1887–1903, edited by A. C. Young. 1961.
Gissing and H. G. Wells: Their Friendship and Correspondence, edited by R. A. Gettmann. 1961.
Commonplace Book, edited by Jacob Korg. 1962.
Letters to Gabrielle Fleury, edited by Pierre Coustillas. 1965.
Notes on Social Democracy. 1968.
Essays and Fiction, edited by Pierre Coustillas. 1970.
London and the Life of Literature in Late Victorian England: Diary 1887–1902, edited by Pierre Coustillas. 1977.

Editor, *Forster's Life of Dickens,* abridged and revised.   1903.

Bibliography: *Gissing: An Annotated Bibliography of Writings about Him* by Joseph Wolff, 1974; *Gissing: A Bibliography* by Michael Collie, 1975.

Reading List: *Gissing: Grave Comedian* by Mabel C. Donnelly, 1954; *Gissing* by A. C. Ward, 1959; *Gissing: A Critical Biography* by Jacob Korg, 1963; *Gissing: A Study in Literary Leanings* by O. H. Davis, 1966; *Gissing: The Critical Heritage* edited by Pierre Coustillas and Colin Partridge, 1972; *Gissing* (biography) by Gillian Tindall, 1973, as *The Born Exile,* 1974; *Gissing in Context* by Adrian Poole, 1975; *Gissing: A Biography,* 1977, and *The Alien Art: A Critical Study of Gissing's Novels,* 1978, both by Michael Collie.

*   *   *

There are two different ways of reading George Gissing, and, though the same reader may possibly adopt both, they are so incompatible that he will do so only by means of a deliberate choice to alter from one to the other. He can be read as a sociological novelist, a painstaking latter-day imitator of Dickens (whose work he adored) without the genius or the humour of Dickens, but like him in his vivid sense of the London scene and his subtle portrayal of class differences. Or he can be read as a tortured romantic who poured out in scorn and bitterness his disillusionment with life, his dissatisfaction with his own lot, and his contempt for all those millions, especially the poor and uneducated, who did not value art and literature above crude satisfactions.

His career was that of the talented and studious meritocrat, spoiled and thwarted in part by class inferiority and lack of opportunity, but much more by his own intemperance and unwisdom. He made two disastrous marriages; he always had a grudge. Beginning as an idealistic socialist (a side of him that produced the very early *Workers in the Dawn*) he soon reverted to extreme distrust and contempt for the class just below that in which he was born – his father was a bookish pharmaceutical chemist. He writes always as if men like himself, struggling to rise by intellect and literature, were being dragged down by a gross, ignorant, and heartless populace into an intolerable nether pit of squalor and mediocrity. Perhaps he maintained this all the more passionately because he knew in his heart that it was not so. He got a good education, won scholarships, and recklessly wasted opportunities for advancement.

One has only to think of Samuel Johnson, so similar to him in circumstances of birth and early education, so utterly unlike him in generous feeling for the poor, unfortunate, and ignorant to discount a good deal of Gissing's spleen. Yet his unfairness and one-sidedness were by no means an unmixed loss to him as a writer. Snobbery, admiration for the rich and well-born, anxiety about money, fear of the gutter are very powerful emotions; and in Gissing they found their poet. He carried them to a point of intensity where they seem to be purified of a good part of their pettiness; in the presentation of these feelings he has few equals. And so, though he is never a brilliant and often not even a lively writer, he contributes something irreplaceable to the canon of English literature.

Like most self-absorbed and socially inept young writers, he vastly overrated the effect he would have on the public. Already in the early 1880's he was a disappointed man. In *The Unclassed* he attempted, with partial success, to present an unvarnished account of the social and moral consequences of prostitution, implying a criticism of the sentimental treatment of the subject by the novelists of the generation before. With *Demos,* a bitter warning against trusting or trying to improve the poor, he attained his first modest success, and with the proceeds fulfilled the great ambition of his life in travelling to Italy and Greece. (It was very characteristic of him to describe his first sight of Vesuvius as the greatest moment of his life.) A later journey, made in the company of H. G. Wells, resulted in his nearest approach to a happy book, *By the Ionian Sea.*

The books which form the core of his achievement were written in quick succession between 1889 and 1893. *The Nether World* is a powerful and painful study of life among the London poor, more notable for indignation than for pity. In *New Grub Street*, though his personal feelings of envy and chagrin are not hidden, he achieved perhaps his most truthful and original sociological study. The title recalls the phrase commonly used for the literary world in the time of Alexander Pope, and both the similarities to this and the differences from it are presented in masterly style. One notices, when Gissing is writing in this vein, that it is the whole scene, not individual characters or incidents, that remains memorable. The author appears rather to be recording than creating. *The Odd Women* is an original study of the life of single women cut off from family ties and trying to make their way in what is still mainly a man's world.

We need not be surprised that he lost inspiration after this. He had always lacked high creative talent, and a certain weariness and repetitiveness creep into the later writing. Bad health also took its toll. But the rather slight *Private Papers of Henry Ryecroft* attained a surprising readership and remains one of his two or three best-known books. It is free from the tormented longings of so many earlier books, and presents in simple and sober style the easy, quiet, bookish life of a man with a small private income. It was a life Gissing never attained; but he may well have been wrong in his conviction that, if he had, he would have been a better writer. The anguish of his disappointment is the very stuff of his literary achievement.

—A. O. J. Cockshut

GODWIN, William.   English.   Born in Wisbech, Cambridgeshire, 3 March 1756; moved with his family to Debenham, Suffolk, 1758, and Guestwick, Norfolk, 1760. Educated at a dame school in Guestwick; Robert Akers's school at Hindolveston, 1764–67; Rev. Samuel Newton's school in Norwich, 1767–71; usher in Akers's school, 1771–72; Hoxton Academy, London, 1773–78. Married 1) the writer Mary Wollstonecraft in 1797 (died, 1797), one daughter, Mary, who married Shelley; 2) Mary Jane Clairmont in 1801, one son; three adopted children. Calvinist minister at Ware, Hertfordshire, 1778–79, and Stowmarket, Suffolk, 1780–82; began to write in 1782; on trial as minister at Beaconsfield, 1783, then gave up the ministry for a career as a writer; settled in London: contributed to the *English Review* and the *New Annual Register*, and occasionally took on pupils; became known, after 1793, as a spokesman for English radicalism; bookseller and publisher, with his wife, 1805 until they went bankrupt, 1822; full-time writer, 1824–33; Yeoman Usher of the Exchequer, 1833–36. *Died 7 April 1836.*

PUBLICATIONS

Collections

   An Enquiry Concerning Political Justice (and other writings), edited by K. Codell Carter. 1971.

Fiction

Italian Letters; or, The History of the Count de St. Julian.   1783; edited by Burton R. Pollin, 1965.
Imogen: A Pastoral Romance.   1784.
Things As They Are; or, The Adventures of Caleb Williams.   1794, revised edition, 1796, 1797, 1816, 1831; edited by David McCracken, 1970.
St. Leon: A Tale of the Sixteenth Century.   1799.
Fleetwood; or, The New Man of Feeling.   1805; revised edition, 1832.
Mandeville: A Tale of the Seventeenth Century in England.   1817.
Cloudesley.   1830.
Deloraine.   1833.

Plays

Antonio (produced 1800).   1800.
Faulkener (produced 1807).   1807.

Other

A Defence of the Rockingham Party, in Their Late Coalition with Lord North.   1783.
An Account of the Seminary That Will Be Opened at Epsom.   1783.
The History of the Life of William Pitt.   1784.
The Herald of Literature.   1784.
Sketches of History in Six Sermons.   1784.
Instructions to a Statesman, Humbly Inscribed to the Earl Temple.   1784.
An Enquiry Concerning the Principles of Political Justice and Its Influence on General Virtue and Happiness.   2 vols., 1793; edited by F. E. L. Priestley, 1946.
Considerations on Grenville's and Pitt's Bills Concerning Treasonable and Seditious Practices.   1795.
The Enquirer: Reflections on Education, Manners, and Literature.   1797.
Memoirs of the Author of A Vindication of the Rights of Woman.   1798; edited by J. M. Murray, 1980.
Thoughts Occasioned by Dr. Parr's Spital Sermon.   1801.
Life of Geoffrey Chaucer, Including Memoirs of John of Gaunt.   2 vols., 1803.
Fables Ancient and Modern Adapted for the Use of Children.   1805.
The Looking Glass: A True History of the Early Years of an Artist.   1805.
The Pantheon; or, Ancient History of the Gods of Greece and Rome (juvenile).   1806.
The History of England (juvenile).   1806.
The Life of Lady Jane Grey and Guildford Dudley Her Husband.   1806.
Essay on Sepulchres.   1809.
History of Rome (juvenile).   1809.
Dramas for Children, Imitated from the French of L. F. Jauffret.   1809.
The Lives of Edward and John Philips, Nephews and Pupils of Milton.   1815.
Letters of Verax (on Napoleon).   1815.
Letter of Advice to a Young American.   1818.
Of Population: An Answer to Mr. Malthus's Essay.   1820.
History of the Commonwealth of England from Its Commencement to the Restoration of Charles the Second.   4 vols., 1824–28.
History of Greece (juvenile).   1828.
Thoughts on Man, His Nature, Productions, and Discoveries.   1831.
Lives of the Necromancers.   1834.

The Moral Effects of Aristocracy, with *The Spirit of Monarchy*, by William Hazlitt. 1835(?).
Essays Never Before Published, edited by C. K. Paul. 1873.
Godwin and Mary: Letters of Godwin and Mary Wollstonecraft, edited by Ralph M. Wardle. 1966.
Uncollected Writings 1785–1822, edited by Jack Marken and Burton R. Pollin. 1968.

Bibliography: *Godwin: A Synoptic Bibliography* by Burton R. Pollin, 1967.

Reading List: *Godwin: His Friends and Contemporaries* (life and letters) by C. Kegan Paul, 1876; *Godwin: A Biographical Study* by George Woodcock, 1946; *Godwin: A Study in Liberalism* by D. Fleisher, 1951; *Godwin and the Age of Transition* by A. E. Rodway, 1952; *Godwin and His World* by R. G. Grylls, 1953; *Education and Enlightenment in the Works of Godwin* by Burton R. Pollin, 1962; *Godwin's Novels: Theme and Craft* by G. McCelvey, 1964; *Godwin* by E. E. and E. G. Smith, 1966; *The Philosophical Anarchism of Godwin* by John R. Clark, 1977.

* * *

William Godwin's novels exhibit a peculiar combination of rootedness in historical circumstance with universalizing, even "mythic" form. His earliest fictions, *Imogen* and *Italian Letters*, show at once his idealizing tendency, his perception of history as a form of romance, and his restless interest in the problem of how to give moral ideas fictional form. These very different experiments in resolving that problem were then forgotten as Godwin attempted to make his fame, and transform the world, through moral philosophy and "philosophical history," and when he returned to fiction he had just become the leading intellectual influence on "English Jacobinism" with his *Enquiry Concerning Political Justice* (1793). Here he had found exactly the style and form of discourse of express his mind, as he reflected on the political history of mankind, and strove to put the events of the early 1790's into a universal historical perspective, and so take the heat out of political controversy and social conflict.

But he clearly wanted a more popular, more moving form of writing to express the same historical vision, the same hopes and fears for the future, and almost immediately after finishing his treatise he began *Things As They Are*, better known by its original subtitle, *The Adventures of Caleb Williams*. Godwin turned to fiction rather than history because it was a more popular form, more universal, and, as he expressed it in an unpublished essay three years later, more open to the expression of the meaning of history because it was free from merely historical facts. And so in *Caleb Williams* Godwin uses names from the history of revolutions, and from the struggle of reason against feudal and chivalric custom. At the same time, he creates a form which embodies the materialist and necessitarian philosophy of *Political Justice*. He uses first person narrative for immediacy and retrospective inset narrative to show how circumstances have created character. He gives over much of the novel to the description of psychological states, thus combining the necessitarian "science of mind" with the psychological realism of Richardson, or his friend Elizabeth Inchbald (*A Simple Story*). Godwin also borrowed from the picaresque novel and criminal biographies, giving their form a greater coherence and intensity by turning it into "adventures of flight and pursuit," and dwelling on imprisonment as a universal metaphor for the relationship between the individual and social institutions. Finally, he enriched the symbolic structure of his narrative by using the language of religion (he was after all a lapsed Calvinist) to describe the crises of his hero's social rebellion, and his remorse. The achievement of *Caleb Williams*, then, is to unify several levels of meaning in a vision of the continuing struggle of truth against tyranny.

He could do this because, as he wrote the novel in 1793–4, he, like many others, was straining reason, knowledge, and imagination to prophesy the outcome of the age of Revolution.

By the time he wrote his next novel many of his worst fears had been realized. *St. Leon* is coloured by elegiac sentiment, the sense that the heroic age was past; in its choice of Reformation Europe as a setting, its use of historical characters from the French religious wars, and its insistence on the isolation of those whose knowledge gives them power to help mankind, the novel is a comment on events of the recent past. At the same time Godwin's historical conception was even grander here than in *Caleb Williams*, revealing his recent interest in and attempt to write heroic drama. Perhaps most significant, Godwin also used the novel to acknowledge his own and his fellow Jacobins' errors in ignoring the "domestic affections" and cultivation of individual sensibility. However, the novel is a failure because Godwin's execution, his style, fell far short of his design. It was only in his next novel, *Fleetwood*, that Godwin regained the power of his abstract and often heavy prose style, and only in *Fleetwood* did he successfully combine the themes, ideas, and attitudes of Wordsworthian Romanticism (received via Coleridge) with his own reconstructed philosophy of necessity. The price he paid, however, was a lessening of the intensity and a partial abandonment of the unity of plot and design which had been the strengths of *Caleb Williams*.

After *Fleetwood* Godwin turned to still other ways of spreading his ideas, writing and publishing children's books, history, biography, and essays such as the interesting *Essay on Sepulchres* and *Thoughts on Man*. These works all carry the same ideas into diverse literary modes, but he was most successful in the relaxed form of the long essay. His last three novels do not make any great advance on what he had already achieved in that form. *Mandeville* was largely a response to the fiction of Scott. After another long interval Godwin returned to fiction which resembles that of his momentary follower Bulwer Lytton. *Cloudesley* and *Deloraine* combine elements from *Fleetwood*, his heroic dramas, and his earliest novels. The truth is, Godwin had made his most substantial contribution to the development of the English novel in *Caleb Williams*, and, significantly, it was this novel which Godwin continued to revise for successive editions, the last of which was published as a contemporary of his very last novels. *Caleb Williams*, created in the midst of a universal historical crisis, synthesized the achievements of the English fiction of the past, and anticipated the achievements of the future.

—Gary Kelly

GOLDSMITH, Oliver.   Irish.   Born in Pallas, near Ballymahon, Longford, 10 November 1728. Educated at the village school in Lissoy, West Meath, 1734–37; Elphin School, 1738; a school in Athlone, 1739–41, and in Edgeworthstown, Longford, 1741–44; Trinity College, Dublin (sizar; Smyth exhibitioner, 1747), 1745–49 B.A. 1749; studied medicine at the University of Edinburgh, 1752–53; travelled on the Continent, in Switzerland, Italy, and France, 1753–56, and may have obtained a medical degree. Settled in London, 1756; tried unsuccessfully to support himself as a physician in Southwark; worked as an usher in Dr. Milner's classical academy in Peckham, 1756, and as a writer for Ralph Griffiths, proprietor of the *Monthly Review*, 1757–58; Editor, *The Bee*, 1759; contributed to the *British Magazine*, 1760; Editor, *The Lady's Magazine*, 1761; also worked for the publisher Edward Newbery: worked as a proof-reader and preface writer, contributed to the *Public Ledger*, 1760, and prepared a *Compendium of Biography*, 7 volumes, 1762; after 1763 earned increasingly substantial sums from his own writing; one of the founder members of Dr. Johnson's Literary Club, 1764. *Died 4 April 1774.*

PUBLICATIONS

Collections

> *Collected Letters*, edited by Katharine C. Balderston. 1928.
> *Collected Works*, edited by Arthur Friedman. 5 vols., 1966.
> *Poems and Plays*, edited by Tom Davis. 1975.

Fiction

> *The Vicar of Wakefield*. 1766; edited by Arthur Friedman, 1974.

Plays

> *The Good Natured Man* (produced 1768). 1768.
> *The Grumbler*, from a translation by Charles Sedley of a work by Brueys (produced 1773). Edited by Alice I. P. Wood, 1931.
> *She Stoops to Conquer; or, The Mistakes of a Night* (produced 1773). 1773; edited by Arthur Friedman, 1968.
> *Threnodia Augustalis, Sacred to the Memory of the Princess Dowager of Wales*, music by Mattia Vento (produced 1772). 1772.
> *The Captivity* (oratorio), in *Miscellaneous Works*. 1820.

Verse

> *The Traveller; or, A Prospect of Society*. 1764.
> *Poems for Young Ladies in Three Parts, Devotional, Moral, and Entertaining*. 1767.
> *The Deserted Village*. 1770.
> *Retaliation*. 1774.
> *The Haunch of Venison: A Poetical Epistle to Lord Clare*. 1776.

Other

> *An Enquiry into the Present State of Polite Learning in Europe*. 1759.
> *The Bee*. 1759.
> *The Mystery Revealed*. 1762.
> *The Citizen of the World; or, Letters from a Chinese Philosopher Residing in London to His Friends in the East*. 2 vols., 1762.
> *The Life of Richard Nash of Bath*. 1762.
> *An History of England in a Series of Letters from a Nobleman to His Son*. 2 vols., 1764.
> *An History of the Martyrs and Primitive Fathers of the Church*. 1764.
> *Essays*. 1765; revised edition, 1766.
> *The Present State of the British Empire in Europe, America, Africa, and Asia*. 1768.

The Roman History, from the Foundation of the City of Rome to the Destruction of the Western Empire. 2 vols., 1769; abridged edition, 1772.

The Life of Thomas Parnell. 1770.

The Life of Henry St. John, Lord Viscount Bolingbroke. 1770.

The History of England, from the Earliest Times to the Death of George II. 4 vols., 1771; abridged edition, 1774.

The Grecian History, from the Earliest State to the Death of Alexander the Great. 2 vols., 1774.

An History of the Earth and Animated Nature. 8 vols., 1774.

A Survey of Experimental Philosophy, Considered in Its Present State of Improvement. 2 vols., 1776.

Editor, *The Beauties of English Poesy.* 2 vols., 1767.

Translator, *The Memoirs of a Protestant,* by J. Marteilhe. 2 vols., 1758; edited by A. Dobson, 1895.

Translator, *Plutarch's Lives.* 4 vols., 1762.

Translator, *A Concise History of Philosophy and Philosophers,* by M. Formey. 1766.

Translator, *The Comic Romance of Scarron.* 2 vols., 1775.

Bibliography: *Goldsmith Bibliographically and Biographically Considered* by Temple Scott, 1928.

Reading List: *Goldsmith* by Ralph Wardle, 1957; *Goldsmith* by Clara M. Kirk, 1967; *Goldsmith: A Georgian Study* by Ricardo Quintana, 1967; *Life of Goldsmith* by Henry A. Dobson, 1972; *Goldsmith* by A. Lytton Sells, 1974; *Goldsmith: The Critical Heritage,* edited by George S. Rousseau, 1974; *The Notable Man: The Life and Times of Goldsmith* by John Ginger, 1977.

*   *   *

Oliver Goldsmith's reputation is made up of paradox. His blundering, improvident nature nevertheless won him the loyalty and friendship of figures like Dr. Johnson, Sir Joshua Reynolds, and Edmund Burke. While in society he was a buffoon, his writing testifies to personal charm and an ironic awareness of his own and others' absurdity. Critical opinion of his work similarly varies from acceptance of Goldsmith as the sensitive apologist for past values to appraisal of him as an accomplished social and literary satirist. Indeed, his work can operate on both levels, a fact perhaps recognised by the young Jane Austen in her *Juvenilia* when she took Goldsmith's abridgements of history for young persons as a model for her own exercise in irony.

Drifting into authorship after a mis-spent youth (as Macaulay notes in his disapproving *Life*), Goldsmith turned to hack writing, contributing articles to the *Monthly* and *Critical Reviews* from 1757. His more ambitious *Inquiry into the Present State of Polite Learning* of 1759 won him the reputation of a man of learning and elegant expression. In this last essay he reveals his fundamental dislike of the contemporary cult of sensibility which was to generate not only his own "laughing" form of comedy in the drama but also *The Vicar of Wakefield.* Meeting Smollett, then editor of the *British Magazine,* Goldsmith was encouraged to expand his contributions to literary journalism. He produced the weekly periodical *The Bee*; many papers collected and published in 1765 and 1766 as *Essays*; and, most important, the "Chinese Letters" of 1760–61 collected as *The Citizen of the World.*

The "citizen" is, of course, an Oriental traveller, observing the fashions and foibles of the *bon ton* in London with wide-eyed innocence that carries within it implicit comment and criticism not unmixed with humour. The device was borrowed from the French, notably

Montesquieu's *Lettres Persanes* (1721). In each essay the absurdities of behaviour are marked, the whole inter-woven by continuing narratives around the Man in Black, Beau Tibbs, the story of Hingo and Zelis, for instance. In many ways the ironies, improbabilities, and apparent innocence of the Chinese letters prefigure the extended prose romance of *The Vicar of Wakefield*.

This could be seen as Goldsmith's answer to Sterne's *Tristram Shandy* (1759). He had attacked Sterne's sentimental fiction as "obscene and pert" in *The Citizen*; in many ways *The Vicar* parodies Sterne's novel but with such a light hand that it has been taken on face value for many generations as the tale indeed of a family "generous, credulous, simple, and inoffensive." However, Goldsmith early establishes for the observant the manifest danger of complacency in such apparent virtues. His Yorkshire parson displays the moral duplicity of a feeling heart, for Goldsmith's approach to life and art is the opposite of Sterne's relativism and dilettante values.

Goldsmith's moral seriousness (while softened by genial good humour) dominates that other work now considered "classic," *The Deserted Village*. His earlier sortie in the genre of topographical/philosophical verse, *The Traveller*, did much to establish his reputation. It is an accomplished use of convention, where the poet climbs an eminence only to have his mind expanded into contemplation of universal questions. In *The Deserted Village*, however, the poet comes to terms with a particular social problem in a particular landscape as opposed to former abstract musings above imaginary solitudes. "Sweet Auburn" can be identified closely with the village of Nuneham Courtenay, where the local land-owner had recently moved the whole community out in order to extend and improve his landscape park. The fact becomes a catalyst for Goldsmith in a consideration of where aesthetic values and irresponsible wealth lead: a symbol taken from life and not from poetic convention.

Goldsmith's rhymed couplets have grace and ease, particularly when his verse is unlaboured, as in the prologues and epilogues to his own and others' plays. The charm and humour of these can be observed in his later poem *Retaliation*, which has a pointed raciness born out of the settling of personal scores. Always the butt of jokes in the group known as The Club, here he gets his own back with a series of comic epitaphs for the other members. Notable is that for Garrick – "On the stage he was natural, simple, affecting; Twas only that when he was off he was acting" – but he labels himself the "gooseberry fool."

As a dramatist, Goldsmith exploited both verbal dexterity and the comedy of situation, looking back to Shakespeare in the rejection of the so-called genteel comedy of Hugh Kelly or Richard Cumberland. Affected and strained in tone and action, the drama of sentiment offered to Goldsmith nothing of the "nature and humour" that he saw as the first principle of theatre. However he might despise the sentimental school, he cannot avoid using some of its conventions, the good-natured hero, of course, and the device of paired lovers, but the way these are treated is particular to himself. Together with Sheridan, Goldsmith exploits the theatrical unreality of comedy, using the stage as a separate world of experience with its own laws and therefore demanding the suspension of disbelief in order that farcical unreality might unmask farcical reality. His character Honeydew in *The Good Natured Man* has something in common with Charles Surface in *School for Scandal*, but the tone of Goldsmith's comedy is less brittle than that of Sheridan's. This mellow tone, a fundamental wholesomeness, is magnificently encapsulated in *She Stoops to Conquer*.

Goldsmith's first play met with a poor response, as being too "low" in its matter (especially the bailiffs scene), and, though *She Stoops to Conquer* was open to similar criticism, its riotous humour overcame prejudice. In short, it was good theatre and this is testified by its continuing popularity in production. Characters like Tony Lumpkin, Mrs. Hardcastle, and the old Squire have become literary personalities, while the pivot of the plot, Marlow's loss of diffidence in apparently more relaxed circumstances, holds true to human nature. The character of Kate is a liberated heroine in the Shakespearean style, contrasted as in the older comedy with a foil. One is able to relate Goldsmith's "laughing" comedy to that of Shakespeare in many ways, for the Lord of Misrule dominates both.

The range of Goldsmith's work is touched by this same humour and sensitivity, the good heart that is so easily squandered as he himself acknowledged in *The Good Natured Man*, but is just as easily extended with purpose to the reader. As Walter Scott observed, no man contrived "so well to reconcile us to human nature."

—B. C. Oliver-Morden

GORE, Catherine (Grace Frances, née Moody). English. Born in East Retford, Nottinghamshire, in 1799. Educated privately. Married Captain Charles Gore in 1823; ten children. Composer from 1827; settled in France, 1832, later returned to England. *Died 29 January 1861.*

PUBLICATIONS

Fiction

Theresa Marchmont; or, The Maid of Honour. 1824.
Richelieu; or, The Broken Heart. 1826.
The Lettre de Cachet; The Reign of Terror. 1827.
Hungarian Tales. 1829.
Romances of Real Life. 1829.
Women as They Are; or, The Manners of the Day. 1830.
Pin-Money. 1831.
The Tuileries. 1831; as *The Soldier of Lyons,* 1841.
Mothers and Daughters. 1831.
The Opera. 1832.
The Fair of Mayfair. 1832; as *The Miseries of Marriage,* 1834.
The Sketch Book of Fashion. 1833.
Polish Tales. 1833.
The Hamiltons; or, The New Era. 1834.
The Diary of a Désennuyée. 1836.
Mrs. Armytage; or, Female Domination. 1836.
Memoirs of a Peeress; or, The Days of Fox. 1837; revised edition, 1859.
Stokeshill Place; or, The Man of Business. 1837.
The Heir of Selwood; or, Three Epochs of a Life. 1838.
Mary Raymond and Other Tales. 1838.
The Woman of the World. 1838.
The Cabinet Minister. 1839.
The Courtier of the Days of Charles II, with Other Tales. 1839.
The Dowager; or, The New School for Scandal. 1840.
Preferment; or, My Uncle the Earl. 1840.
The Abbey and Other Tales. 1840.
Greville; or, A Season in Paris. 1841.
Cecil; or, The Adventures of a Coxcomb. 1841.
Cecil a Peer. 1841; as *Ormington,* 1842.
The Man of Fortune and Other Tales. 1842.

The Ambassador's Wife. 1842.
The Money-Lender. 1843; as *Abednego,* 1854.
Modern Chivalry; or, A New Orlando Furioso, edited by William Harrison
    Ainsworth. 1843.
The Banker's Wife; or, Court and City. 1843.
Agathonia. 1844.
The Birthright and Other Tales. 1844.
The Popular Member; The Wheel of Fortune. 1844.
Self. 1845.
The Story of a Royal Favourite. 1845.
The Snow Storm. 1845.
Peers and Parvenus. 1846.
New Year's Day. 1846.
Men of Capital. 1846.
The Débutante; or, The London Season. 1846.
Castles in the Air. 1847.
Temptation and Atonement and Other Tales. 1847.
The Inundation; or, Pardon and Peace. 1847.
The Diamond and the Pearl. 1848.
The Dean's Daughter; or, The Days We Live In. 1853.
The Lost Son. 1854.
Transmutation; or, The Lord and the Lout. 1854.
Progress and Prejudice. 1854.
Mammon; or, The Hardships of an Heiress. 1855.
A Life's Lessons. 1856.
The Two Aristocracies. 1857.
Heckington. 1858.

Plays

The School for Coquettes (produced 1831).
Lords and Commons (produced 1831).
The Queen's Champion, from a play by Scribe (produced 1834).   1886.
Modern Honour; or, The Sharpers of High Life (produced 1834).
The King's Seal, with James Kenney (produced 1835).   1835.
The Maid of Croissey; or, Theresa's Vow (produced 1835).   N.d.
King O'Neil; or, The Irish Brigade (produced 1835).   N.d.
King John of Austria, from a play by Casimir Delavigne (produced 1836).
A Tale of a Tub (produced 1837).
A Good Night's Rest; or, Two in the Morning (produced 1839).   1883(?).
Dacre of the South; or, The Olden Time.   1840.
Quid pro Quo; or, The Day of Dupes (produced 1844).   1844.

Verse

The Two Broken Hearts. 1823.
The Bond: A Dramatic Poem. 1824.

Other

The Historical Traveller, Comprising Narratives Connected with European History. 2
    vols., 1831.

The Rose Fancier's Manual.   1838.
Paris in 1841.   1842.
Sketches of English Character.   2 vols., 1846.
Adventures in Borneo.   1849.

Editor, *Picciola; or, Captivity Captive,* by X. B. Saintine.   1837.
Editor, *The Lover and the Husband,* by Charles de Bernard.   3 vols., 1841.
Editor, *Modern French Life.*   3 vols., 1842.
Editor, *Fascination and Other Tales.*   3 vols., 1842.
Editor, *The Queen of Denmark,* by T. C. Heiberg.   3 vols., 1846.

Bibliography: in *XIX Century Fiction* by Michael Sadleir, 2 vols., 1951.

Reading List: *The Silver-Fork School: Novels of Fashion Preceding Vanity Fair* by Matthew Whiting Rosa, 1936; *A Victorian Album* by Lucy Poate Stebbins, 1946.

*   *   *

"Silver-fork" novels, popular between 1825 and 1850, are exclusively devoted to detailed and realistic representations of fashionable life. Catherine Gore compensated for her late start in the genre in 1830 by her prolific output. In 1841 she published her masterpiece *Cecil* anonymously because her novel *Greville* appeared the same week and because her name was already staled by custom. The undisputed mistress of the fashionable novel, Mrs. Gore outdid her contemporaries in relentlessly poking fun at the world she depicted so accurately. Although conscious of the dubious literary merit of her "rubbish" – her "sickly progeniture" of lightweight fiction – Mrs. Gore sought to be an historian of the ephemera and caprices, the proprieties and vices of upper-crust society. Her basic theme is simply that of man's adjustment to his environment; behind her artistic detachment from her worldlings is a considerable and sympathetic understanding of human nature. Mrs. Gore excels in portraying the uppermost middle classes, whose unique traits are modified by their peculiar social position. She sagaciously exposes the life beneath the façade while tracing political, social, and domestic relations firmly and subtly. The masculine viewpoint and fearless energy of her novels distinguish her from Jane Austen, to whom she felt intellectually akin. Mrs. Gore's preface to *Pin-Money* expresses her "attempt to transfer the familiar narrative of Miss Austen to a higher sphere of society," and she is similar to her predecessor in her subjects, and her irony in describing many of her memorable characters. But Jane Austen's delicate clarity is very different from Mrs. Gore's elaborate verbosity.

The inexhaustibility of Mrs. Gore's imagination qualifies her literary reputation. Her satire and epigrammatic wit, however swift and subtle, are incessant, and her prose is a motley of foreign tags, quotations, allusions, pompous vocabulary, and circumlocution. The combination initially dazzles but eventually hypnotizes. Mrs. Gore's genius can easily be underestimated because of the abundance – and redundance – of her works themselves. She successfully created popular songs, etchings, comedies, dramas, melodramas, farces, poems, travel books, garden manuals, historical tales, and several novels extending beyond the confines of fashionable life. Her best books include *Mothers and Daughters, The Hamiltons, Mrs. Armytage, Cecil* and its sequel *Cecil a Peer,* and *The Banker's Wife.*

Mrs. Gore made the most of a genre whose formulaic situations and superficial characters precluded profound depth or universal appeal. She is superb at the comedy of artificial life; her style at its best is quick, elastic, and buoyant; her novels sometimes exhibit true pathos. She was famous both as a witty conversationalist and as a truthful and commonsensical writer. Bulwer claimed that her satire made Thackeray's look like caricature, while Thackeray reacted by parodying her work in his "Novels by Eminent Hands." Mrs. Gore's importance remains historical rather than literary – when her own audience tired of silver-fork novels, the critics predicted that future generations would re-discover her subject matter and restore her prestige.

—Janice M. Cauwels

GRAHAME, Kenneth. Scottish. Born in Edinburgh, 8 March 1859. Educated at St. Edward's School, Oxford, 1868–75. Married Elspeth Thomson in 1899; one son. Worked for Grahame, Currie, and Spens, parliamentary agents, London, 1875–79; Gentleman-Clerk, 1879–98, and Secretary, 1898–1908, Bank of England, London. Secretary of the New Shakespere Society, London, 1877–91. *Died 6 July 1932.*

PUBLICATIONS

Fiction

> *The Golden Age.* 1895.
> *Dream Days.* 1898; revised edition, 1899.
> *The Headswoman* (stories). 1898.
> *The Wind in the Willows.* 1908.
> *First Whisper of "The Wind in the Willows,"* edited by Elspeth Grahame. 1944.

Other

> *Pagan Papers.* 1893.
> *The Grahame Day Book,* edited by Margery Coleman. 1937.

> Editor, *Lullaby-Land: Songs of Childhood,* by Eugene Field. 1897.
> Editor, *The Cambridge Book of Poetry for Children.* 2 vols., 1916.

Reading List: *Grahame: Life, Letters, and Unpublished Work* by P. R. Chalmers, 1933; *Grahame: A Study of His Life, Work, and Times* by Peter Green, 1959 (includes bibliography); *Grahame* by Eleanor Graham, 1963.

*   *   *

Although he wrote only four books, a short story, and enough uncollected essays to fill one more volume, Kenneth Grahame can be claimed as a major author in two branches of literature. He is now best known for *The Wind in the Willows*, one of the greatest children's books in our language, but without it he would still hold a high place for his essays and stories *about* children collected in two volumes, *The Golden Age* and *Dream Days*.

These two volumes grew out of his first book, *Pagan Papers*, a collection of essays written in a literary style brought into fashion by such writers as Walter Pater and Robert Louis Stevenson, too exotic and precious for many readers today. This early volume (suitably adorned with an Aubrey Beardsley frontispiece) concluded with six sketches subtitled "The Golden Age," which were reprinted with twelve others as a separate book under that title. It was followed by *Dream Days*, containing eight longer stories.

These two collections brought about a revolution in children's literature by dealing with the contemporary child in every-day surroundings. They tell of a family of children (based on his own childhood) whose parents are dead and who are being brought up by maiden aunts – the "Olympians" – with whom they consider themselves permanently at war. The children live their own life of mingled reality and make-believe, pitying the Olympians and scoring off them whenever possible; the children accept their commands when they must, but consider them arbitrary and incomprehensible whims of an alien order of beings.

Grahame's ornate style is here perfectly suited to his subject and makes each sketch or episode into a literary jewel for the fastidious adult – "Well nigh too praiseworthy for praise," was Swinburne's famous description. Those readers to whom this ornate style appeals find the sketches a never-ending delight, and read them again and again.

Their effect on children's literature was to present childhood as a state in itself, and children as a distinct race of beings in their own right rather than as miniature adults to be guided up the steep path to Olympus: they opened the way for such writers as E. Nesbit, Arthur Ransome, and numerous lesser practitioners. But it must be stressed that these two books which hold so much of the precious essence of childhood are not books for children. It is not merely the style which puts off the child reader, but in some subtle way the deeper content which seems a kind of violation of the precious secrets of childhood, a trespassing of adult, Olympian feet into a land that they have no right to enter.

Writing *for* children, and using stories told to his own small son, Grahame conquered this other kingdom with *The Wind in the Willows* – a book loved by both adults and children, a fantasy set in a natural fairyland of the inner life of the river-side: "with his ear to the reed-stems he caught, at intervals, something of what the wind was whispering, so constantly among them." The "intervals" of prose-poetry may appeal mainly to the adult reader, but the riverside adventures of Toad and Mole and Rat and Badger (which A. A. Milne made into a play *Toad of Toad Hall*) appeal to the younger reader as well as the adult.

—Roger Lancelyn Green

GRAVES, Richard.   English.   Born in Mickleton, Gloucestershire, 4 May 1715. Educated privately, and at Roysse's Grammar School, Abingdon, Oxfordshire, 1728–32; Pembroke College, Oxford, 1732–36; All Souls College, Oxford, 1736–40, M.A. in divinity 1740; also studied medicine in London, 1736. Married Lucy Bartholomew c. 1744 (died, 1777); four sons and one daughter. Fellow of All Souls, 1736–44; chaplain to the William Fitzherbert family, at Tissington, near Ashbourne, Derbyshire, 1741–44; Curate, possibly at Aldworth, near Reading, 1744, and at Whitchurch, Oxfordshire, 1749; Rector of Claverton, near Bath, 1749 until his death; also ran a school at Claverton from the 1760's, and held the living of Croscombe, 1802–04. *Died 23 November 1804.*

PUBLICATIONS

Fiction

The Spiritual Quixote; or, The Summer's Ramble of Mr. Geoffry Wildgoose: A Comic Romance. 1773; edited by Clarence Tracy, 1967.
Columella; or, The Distressed Anchoret: A Colloquial Tale. 1779.
Eugenius; or, Anecdotes of the Golden Vale: An Embellished Narrative of Real Facts. 1785.
Plexippus; or, The Aspiring Plebeian. 1790.

Play

The Coalition; or, The Opera Rehearsed (produced 1793?). 1794.

Verse

The Love of Order: A Poetical Essay. 1773.
The Progress of Gallantry: A Poetical Essay. 1774.
Euphrosyne; or, Amusements on the Road of Life. 2 vols., 1776–80.
Lucubrations, Consisting of Essays, Reveries in Prose and Verse. 1786.
The Rout; or, A Sketch of Modern Life, from an Academic in the Metropolis to His Friend in the Country. 1789.
The Farmer's Son: A Moral Tale. 1795.

Other

A Letter from a Father to His Son at the University. 1787.
Recollections of Some Particulars in the Life of the Late William Shenstone. 1788.
The Reveries of Solitude, Consisting of Essays in Prose, A New Translation of the Muscipula, and Original Pieces in Verse. 1793.
Sermons. 1799.
Senilities; or, Solitary Amusements in Prose and Verse. 1801.
The Invalid, with the Obvious Means of Enjoying Health and a Long Life. 1804.
The Triflers; Consisting of Trifling Essays, Trifling Anecdotes, and a Few Poetical Trifles. 1805.

Editor, *The Festoon: A Collection of Epigrams, Ancient and Modern, with an Essay on That Species of Composition.* 1765; revised edition, 1767.

Translator, *Galateo; or, A Treatise on Politeness and Delicacy of Manners*, by Giovanni della Casa. 1774.
Translator, *The Sorrows of Werter*, by Goethe. 1779.
Translator, *The Heir Apparent; or, The Life of Commodus*, by Herodian. 1789.
Translator, *The Meditations of the Emperor Marcus Aurelius.* 1792.
Translator, *Hiero on the Condition of Royalty: A Conversation*, by Xenophon. 1793.

Reading List: *The Literary Career of Graves* by Charles Jarvis Hill, 1935 (includes bibliography).

Though Richard Graves habitually dismissed his writings as "trifling," all the best of them have an intellectual core. *Columella*, for example, illustrates the evils that may befall a man who steps out of the role in life proper to one of his class by withdrawing into himself. The plot of *Plexippus* was meant to show that a man of "genius, learning, or industry" is better entitled to respect than one who has only an hereditary title to boast of. *Eugenius* explores the "paradox" that modern manners are better than those of earlier times. *The Spiritual Quixote*, the first and best of the novels, is a satire on Methodism. Geoffry Wildgoose, its hero, goes out quixotically on the road to preach Whitefield's theology: faith rather than good works, the new birth, and the total depravity of the natural man. Wesley is also satirized for laying claim to apostolical grace, but, as his theological position was closer than Whitefield's to Graves's own, he is treated less severely. Wildgoose has many adventures of the *Joseph Andrews* type, and in the end is reconciled to the church of his ancestors by the experience of falling in love. Nature comes into conflict with grace, at least with grace as defined by the more austere of the Methodist preachers, and is triumphant.

Graves found it hard to develop a coherent plot in any of his novels. That of *Plexippus*, for example, is spoiled when the "man of genius" who is its hero turns out to have also been well born, and that of the *Spiritual Quixote* is weakened by many digressions and by Wildgoose's being diverted from his pious aims rather than disillusioned with them. Graves's love of a good story, which he tells well, combined with a heavy reliance on his own experience, makes his novels look like episodic memoirs. The best parts of the *Spiritual Quixote*, for example, are Mr. Rivers's interpolated story, in which the author tells the only slightly edited version of his own courtship and marriage, and the scenes in Bath and the Peak country, which are drawn from the life. Moreover, it has often been suggested that the character of Geoffry Wildgoose is modelled on that of the author's brother, Charles Caspar, who for a time was an itinerant Methodist preacher, and that several of the other characters are also based on Graves's friends and associates, just as Columella, in the novel of that name, is William Shenstone. Though many of those identifications are plausible, their implications must not be pressed too far: Columella, Wildgoose, and the others are not pictures of Graves's friends and relations, but characters created for his own fictional purposes. It is as wrong to underrate his imaginative powers as to overrate them.

Graves has a gift for striking words and clever turns of phrase, and apt allusions and quotations pour out in his books and letters. He is often too wordy; most of his works would have benefitted from cutting. Often he seems most successful in miniature forms like the epigram: *The Festoon*, which he edited, contains a number of his own epigrams as well as a collection of epigrams by others, and had a wide circulation. In his novels, the wit and the shrewd comments attract one now rather than the larger elements of design. An amusing talker, he gives the best of his works the liveliness and charm that mark the man himself.

—Clarence Tracy

GRIFFIN, Gerald. Irish.   Born in Limerick, 12 December 1803. Educated at local schools in Limerick. Lived with his brother in Adare, where he began writing, 1820–23; settled in London, to pursue a literary career, 1823; contributed to the *Literary Gazette* and other periodicals; tried, unsuccessfully, to achieve success as a dramatist; conceived of, and presented, an opera in recitative, and in English, at the English Opera-House, London, 1826; returned to Ireland, 1827; briefly studied law at the University of London, then returned to full-time writing; again returned to Ireland, 1838, and subsequently became a member of the Roman Catholic Society of Christian Brothers. *Died 12 June 1840.*

PUBLICATIONS

Collections

Poetical Works (includes the play *Gisippus*).   1926.

Fiction

Holland-Tide; or, Munster Popular Tales.   1827.
Tales of the Munster Festivals.   1827.
The Collegians; or, The Colleen Bawn: A Tale of Garryowen.   1829; edited by Padraic
   Colum, 1918.
The Rivals; Tracy's Ambition.   1830; edited by John Cronin, 1978.
The Christian Physiologist: Tales Illustrative of the Five Senses.   1830; as *The Offering
   of Friendship,* 1854.
The Invasion.   1832.
Tales of My Neighbourhood.   1835.
The Duke of Monmouth.   1836.
Talis Qualis; or, Tales of the Jury Room.   1842.
The Beautiful Queen of Leix; or, The Self-Consumed.   1853.
The Day of Trial.   1853.
The Voluptuary Cured.   1853.
The Young Milesian and the Selfish Crotarie.   1853.
The Kelp-Gatherer.   1854.
A Story of Psyche.   1854.
Card-Drawing, The Half Sir, and Suil Dhuv the Coiner.   1857.

Plays

The Noyades (produced 1826).
Gisippus; or, The Forgotten Friend (produced 1842).   1842.

Verse

Poetical Works.   1851.

Reading List: *The Life of Griffin* by D. Griffin, 1843; *Griffin, Poet, Novelist, Christian Brother*
by W. S. Gill, 1940; *Two Studies in Integrity: Griffin and the Reverend Francis Mahoney* by
Ethel Mannin, 1954; *The Irish Novelists 1800–1850* by Thomas Flanagan, 1959; *Griffin: A
Critical Biography* by John Cronin, 1978.

*   *   *

Poet, dramatist, and novelist, Gerald Griffin was among the most talented of early
nineteenth-century Irish writers, though in his lifetime one of the least successful of that
unhappy tribe. A number of poems and unpublished plays have their date of composition in
his adolescence, among them *Gisippus*, later produced by Macready. Griffin's main literary
training, however, took place in the demanding world of London hack journalism, in the
company of, among other expatriates, John Banim. Although most of his best work was done

after he quit that world, its tempo, palette, and sense of proportion remains substantially indebted to the models encountered during those years of apprenticeship, a period not generally noted for the quality of its fiction.

Today, Griffin's reputation rests almost solely on one novel, and that largely because it was the basis of Boucicault's well-known melodrama, *The Colleen Bawn*. He deserves better. The novel in question, *The Collegians*, is the most successful contemporary attempt to depict the moral range of Irish Catholic society. The story moves comparatively easily from drawing-room to cabin; the peasant characters are well differentiated, and the middle-classes seem somewhat less stilted than usual; a strictly contemporary note is dispensed with, so that psychological issues supersede historical ones, uncharacteristically for the Irish novel of the day. Moreover, in the character of Hardress Cregan, the hapless and gifted protagonist, Griffin has created one of the most complete embodiments of the cultural tensions obtaining in the Ireland of the author's own time, and from which he was far from immune. The style of *The Collegians* is needlessly uneven, and some of the episodes are preposterously melodramatic or intolerably sentimental. But its interest overrides its faults.

Griffin's other fiction is on the whole less impressive, being more flaccid in its scene-painting, less compressed in its use of documentary material, and not as well provided with a striking range of characters. Those with explicit historical themes are undoubtedly the weakest. Of the remainder, *Tracy's Ambition* is arguably the most noteworthy. Griffin also has his place in the development of the Irish short story as the intimate though somewhat formless *Tales of the Munster Festivals* shows. In general, while not in any real sense an unsung genius, Griffin has more to offer, particularly in the context of the development of Irish fiction in the nineteenth century, than has been usually recognised.

—George O'Brien

GROSSMITH, George.   English.   Born in London, 9 December 1847. Educated at the North London Collegiate School. Married Rosa Noyce in 1873 (died, 1905); two sons and two daughters. Reporter at Bow Street Police Court for *The Times*, London, 1866; made debut as an actor and singer, 1870; leading singer in the Gilbert and Sullivan Operas, at the Savoy Theatre, London, 1877–89; toured, with his own show, *Humorous and Musical Recitals*, in Britain, Ireland, Canada, and the United States, 1889–1906; retired from the stage, 1908. Composer: wrote more than 600 songs and sketches. *Died 1 March 1912.*

PUBLICATIONS

Fiction

The Diary of a Nobody, with Weedon Grossmith.   1892.

Plays

No Thoroughfare (produced 1869).
"Two" Much Alike, with A. R. Rogers (produced 1870).

Cups and Saucers, music by Grossmith (produced 1878).
Mr. Guffin's Elopement, with Arthur Law (produced 1882).
The Real Case of Hide and Seekyl (produced 1888).

Other

A Society Clown: Reminiscences. 1888.
Piano and I: Further Remembrances. 1910.
G.G. (miscellany). 1933.

*   *   *

Many people have approached the Victorian novel through George and Weedon Grossmith's *The Diary of a Nobody,* and from this deceptively simple account of the aspirations, anxieties, pleasures, and humiliations of a London clerk of the 1880's have had their first taste of the class structure and tabus of Victorian society. Mr. Pooter and his neat little wife Carrie live in modest, contented comfort in Brickfield Terrace, Holloway, in a nice six-roomed residence with little back garden and a maid servant in the basement. The Grossmiths record the Pooters' menage, their circle of irritating, sometimes embarrassing friends, their pastimes, their taste in clothes and in furniture with affectionate humour that never lapses into mockery. We watch Mr. Pooter put up the plaster of Paris stags' heads which are to give tone to the hall and are never tempted to sneer. It is a way of life that we sense was vanishing even then, to be overtaken soon by the more raffish late Victorian style represented by young Lupin Pooter and his flashy, moneyed acquaintances, but there is no sentimentality in the Grossmiths' account of it.

A child can appreciate the humour; an adult sees the poignancy: the hat that blows away as Mr. Pooter is about to address himself to a superior lady, the cabman who insults him, the young men who mock his clothes, the theatre party where the guests he so wants to impress finish by paying for the hosts – all mortifications that he survives, after the first chagrin, with undeflatable optimism. Continual re-reading can only make one marvel at the economy with which the Grossmiths convey the complexity of the Victorian class system, where everybody was in the comfortable position of being able to look down on somebody else and few (certainly none at the Pooter level) were without a higher class to which to pay tremulous deference. Their gift for characterisation was considerable; *The Diary of a Nobody* contains a gallery of portraits, some of which like the silent Mr. Padge and his "That's right" have passed into the national mythology. No doubt many of them were used by George Grossmith in his stage character sketches before they were written down for *Punch.* Few ephemeral writings of this sort have been so successfully welded together into permanent literary form. (Weedon Grossmith, who collaborated with his brother in the text, provided the illustrations.)

—Gillian Avery

HAGGARD, Sir H(enry) Rider. English. Born in Bradenham, Norfolk, 22 June 1856. Educated at Ipswich Grammar School, Suffolk; Lincoln's Inn, London, 1880–84: called to the Bar, 1884. Married Mariana Margitson in 1880; three daughters. Lived in South Africa, as Secretary to Sir Henry Bulwer, Governor of Natal, 1875–77, member of the staff of Sir

Theophilus Shepstone, Special Commissioner in the Transvaal, 1877, and Master of the High Court of the Transvaal, 1877–79; returned to England, 1879; managed his wife's estate in Norfolk from 1880; travelled throughout England investigating condition of agriculture and the rural population, 1901–02; British Government Special Commissioner to report on Salvation Army settlements in the United States, 1905; Chairman, Reclamation and Unemployed Labour Committee, Royal Commission on Coast Erosion and Afforestation, 1906–11; travelled around the world as a Member of the Dominions Royal Commission, 1912–17. Chairman of the Committee, Society of Authors, 1896–98; Vice-President, Royal Colonial Institute, 1917. Knighted, 1912; K.B.E. (Knight Commander, Order of the British Empire), 1919. *Died 14 May 1925.*

PUBLICATIONS

Fiction

Dawn.   1884.
The Witch's Head.   1885.
King Solomon's Mines.   1885.
She.   1887.
Allan Quatermain.   1887.
A Tale of Three Lions.   1887.
Mr. Meeson's Will.   1888.
Maiwa's Revenge; or, The War of the Little Hand.   1888.
My Fellow Laborer and the Wreck of the Copeland.   1888.
Colonel Quaritch, V.C.   1888.
Cleopatra.   1889.
Allan's Wife and Other Tales.   1889.
Beatrice.   1890.
The World's Desire. with Andrew Lang.   1890.
Eric Brighteyes.   1891.
Nada the Lily.   1892.
Montezuma's Daughter.   1893.
The People of the Mist.   1894.
Joan Haste.   1895.
Heart of the World.   1895.
The Wizard.   1896.
Dr. Therne.   1898.
Swallow.   1899.
Black and White Heart, and Other Stories.   1900.
Lysbeth.   1901.
Pearl Maiden.   1903.
Stella Fregelius.   1904.
The Brethren.   1904.
Ayesha: The Return of She.   1905.
The Way of the Spirit.   1906.
Benita.   1906.
Fair Margaret.   1907.
The Ghost Kings.   1908.
The Yellow God.   1908.
The Lady of Blossholme.   1909.
Morning Star.   1910.

Queen Sheba's Ring.   1910.
The Mahatma and the Hare.   1911.
Red Eve.   1911.
Marie.   1912.
Child of Storm.   1913.
The Wanderer's Necklace.   1914.
The Holy Flower.   1915; as *Allan and the Holy Flower,* 1915.
The Ivory Child.   1916.
Elissa; or, The Doom of Zimbabwe.   1917.
Finished.   1917.
Love Eternal.   1918.
Moon of Israel.   1918.
When the World Shook.   1919.
The Ancient Allan.   1920.
Smith and the Pharaohs and Other Tales.   1920.
She and Allan.   1921.
The Virgin of the Sun.   1922.
Wisdom's Daughter.   1923.
Heu-Heu; or, The Monster.   1924.
Queen of the Dawn.   1925.
Treasure of the Lake.   1926.
Allan and the Ice Gods.   1927.
Mary of Marion Isle.   1929.
Belshazzar.   1930.

Other

Cetywayo and His White Neighbours; or, Remarks on Recent Events in Zululand, Natal, and the Transvaal.   1882; revised edition, 1888.
Church and State.   1895.
The Spring of the Lion.   1899.
A Farmer's Year.   1899.
The Last Boer War.   1899.
A Winter Pilgrimage.   1901.
Rural England.   2 vols., 1902.
A Gardener's Year.   1905.
Report on the Salvation Army Colonies.   1905; revised edition, as *The Poor and the Land,* 1905.
Regeneration: An Account of the Social Work of the Salvation Army.   1910.
Rural Denmark and Its Lessons.   1911.
A Call to Arms.   1914.
The After-War Settlement and the Employment of Ex-Service Men.   1916.
The Days of My Life: An Autobiography, edited by C. J. Longman.   2 vols., 1926.

Bibliography: *A Bibliography of the Writings of Haggard* by J. E. Scott, 1947.

Reading List: *Haggard: His Life and Work* by Morton N. Cohen, 1960, revised edition, 1968, and *Kipling to Haggard: The Record of a Friendship* edited by Cohen, 1965; *Haggard: A Voice from the Infinite* by Peter Berresford Ellis, 1978.

*   *   *

The book that made H. Rider Haggard's reputation, *King Solomon's Mines*, was modelled on Stevenson's *Treasure Island*, but it substituted Africa, then still the "Dark Continent," for the Spanish main. Two years later, Haggard followed this initial success with a more unusual tale, *She*, which took African adventure beyond external reality into a land of hidden civilization where the supernatural held sway. Tribal Africa and mysterious culture soon became a Haggard speciality, and for over forty years, he spun one adventure tale after another, enthralling a vast English reading public hungry for armchair escape from a humdrum European existence. Haggard never styled himself a literary man or even a novelist, and in fact characterized himself aptly as a storyteller. He never aspired to the refinements and subtleties that might have taken his works into an artistic realm; he would not interrupt a flashy succession of incidents to delineate or develop character; nor did he take the pains to shape the spontaneous rush of words. Still, his virile imagination and his uncanny knack for telling a story with its own inner force have won him deep respect, and his brand of adventure, the first to exploit Africa in fiction, still claims a large audience.

—Morton N. Cohen

HARDY, Thomas. English. Born in Upper Bockhampton, Dorset, 2 June 1840. Educated in local schools, 1848–54, and privately, 1854–56; articled to the ecclesiastical architect, John Hicks, in Dorchester, 1856–61; studied in evening classes at King's College, London, 1861–67. Married 1) Emma Lavinia Gifford in 1874 (died, 1912); 2) Florence Emily Dugdale in 1914. Settled in London, 1861, to practice architecture, and worked as Assistant to Sir Arthur Blomfield, 1862–67; gave up architecture to become full-time writer from c. 1873; lived in Max Gate, Dorchester, after 1883. Justice of the Peace for Dorset; Member of the Council of Justice to Animals. Recipient: Royal Institute of British Architects medal, for essay, 1863; Architecture Association prize, for design, 1863; Royal Society of Literature Gold Medal, 1912. LL.D.: University of Aberdeen; University of St. Andrews; University of Bristol; Litt.D.: Cambridge University; D.Litt.: Oxford University. Honorary Fellow: Magdalene College, Cambridge; Queen's College, Oxford. Honorary Fellow of the Royal Institute of British Architects, 1920. Order of Merit, 1910. *Died 11 January 1928.*

PUBLICATIONS

Collections

New Wessex Edition of the Works.   1974–
Complete Poems, edited by James Gibson.   1976; revised *Variorum Edition*, 1978.
The Portable Hardy, edited by Julian Moynahan.   1977.
Collected Letters, edited by Richard Little Purdy and Michael Millgate.   vol. 1 (of 7), 1978.

Fiction

Desperate Remedies.   1871; revised edition, 1896, 1912.

Under the Greenwood Tree: A Rural Painting of the Dutch School. 1872; revised edition, 1896, 1912; edited by Anna Winchcombe, 1975.
A Pair of Blue Eyes. 1873; revised edition, 1895, 1912, 1920.
Ear from the Madding Crowd. 1874; revised edition, 1875, 1902; edited by James Gibson, 1975.
The Hand of Ethelberta: A Comedy in Chapters. 1876; revised edition, 1895, 1912.
The Return of the Native. 1878; revised edition, 1895, 1912; edited by Colin Temblett-Wood, 1975.
Fellow Townsmen. 1880.
The Trumpet-Major: A Tale. 1880; revised edition, 1895; edited by Ray Evans, 1975.
A Laodicean; or, The Castle of the De Stancys. 1881; revised edition, 1881, 1896, 1912.
Two on a Tower. 1882; revised edition, 1883, 1883, 1895, 1912.
The Romantic Adventures of a Milkmaid. 1883; revised edition, 1913.
The Mayor of Casterbridge: The Life and Death of a Man of Character. 1886; revised edition, 1895, 1912; edited by F. B. Pinion, 1975; edited by James K. Robinson, 1977.
The Woodlanders. 1887; revised edition, 1895, 1912; edited by F. B. Pinion, 1975.
Wessex Tales, Strange, Lively and Commonplace. 1888; revised edition, 1896, 1912.
Tess of the d'Urbervilles: A Pure Woman Faithfully Presented. 1891; revised edition, 1892, 1895, 1912; edited by Scott Elledge, 1965, revised 1977.
A Group of Noble Dames. 1891; revised edition, 1896.
Life's Little Ironies: A Set of Tales. 1894; revised edition, 1896, 1912.
Wessex Novels. 16 vols, 1895–96.
Jude the Obscure. 1896; revised edition, 1912; edited by Norman Page, 1978.
The Well-Beloved: A Sketch of Temperament. 1897; revised edition, 1912.
A Changed Man, The Waiting Supper, and Other Tales. 1913.
An Indiscretion in the Life of an Heiress. 1934; edited by Carl J. Weber, 1935.
Our Exploits at West Poley, edited by R. L. Purdy. 1952.

Plays

Far from the Madding Crowd, with J. Comyns Carr, from the novel by Hardy (produced 1882).
The Three Wayfarers, from his own story "The Three Strangers" (produced 1893). 1893; revised edition, 1935.
Tess of the d'Urbervilles, from his own novel (produced 1897; revised version, produced 1924). In *Tess in the Theatre,* edited by Marguerite Roberts, 1950.
The Dynasts: A Drama of the Napoleonic Wars. 3 vols., 1903–08; vol. 1 revised, 1904.
The Play of Saint George. 1921.
The Famous Tragedy of the Queen of Cornwall (produced 1923). 1923; revised edition, 1924.

Verse

Wessex Poems and Other Verses. 1898.
Poems of the Past and the Present. 1902; revised edition, 1902.
Time's Laughingstocks and Other Verses. 1909.
Satires of Circumstance: Lyrics and Reveries, with Miscellaneous Pieces. 1914.
Selected Poems. 1916; revised edition, as *Chosen Poems,* 1929.
Moments of Vision and Miscellaneous Poems. 1917.
Collected Poems. 1919.
Late Lyrics and Earlier, with Many Other Verses. 1922.

Human Shows, Far Phantasies, Songs, and Trifles. 1925.
Winter Words in Various Moods and Metres. 1928.

Other

The Dorset Farm Labourer, Past and Present. 1884.
Works (Wessex Edition). 24 vols., 1912–31.
Works (Mellstock Edition). 37 vols., 1919–20.
Life and Art: Essays, Notes, and Letters, edited by Ernest Brennecke, Jr. 1925.
The Early Life of Hardy 1840–91, by Florence Hardy. 1928; *The Later Years of Hardy, 1892–1928,* 1930 (dictated to his wife Florence).
Letters of Hardy, edited by Carl J. Weber. 1954.
Notebooks and Some Letters from Julia Augusta Martin, edited by Evelyn Hardy. 1955.
"Dearest Emmie": Letters to His First Wife, edited by Carl J. Weber. 1963.
The Architectural Notebook, edited by C. J. P. Beatty. 1966.
Personal Writings: Prefaces, Literary Opinions, Reminiscences, edited by Harold Orel. 1966.
One Rare Fair Woman (letters to Florence Henniker), edited by Evelyn Hardy and F. B. Pinion. 1972.
The Personal Notebooks, edited by Richard H. Taylor. 1978.

Editor, *Select Poems of William Barnes.* 1908.

Bibliography: *Hardy: A Bibliographical Study* by R. L. Purdy, 1954, revised edition, 1968; *Hardy: An Annotated Bibliography of Writings about Him* edited by Helmut E. Gerber and W. Eugene Davis, 1973.

Reading List: *Hardy of Wessex* by Carl J. Weber, 1940, revised edition, 1965; *Hardy the Novelist* by David Cecil, 1943; *Hardy: The Novels and Stories* by Albert Guerard, 1949, revised edition, 1964; *The Pattern of Hardy's Poetry* by Samuel Hynes, 1961; *Hardy: A Collection of Critical Essays* edited by Albert Guerard, 1963; *Hardy* by Irving Howe, 1967; *A Hardy Companion,* 1968, revised edition, 1976, and *Hardy: Art and Thought,* 1977, both by F. B. Pinion; *Hardy: His Career as a Novelist* by Michael Millgate, 1971; *Hardy and British Poetry* by Donald Davie, 1972; *Hardy and History* by R. J. White, 1974; *Young Hardy,* 1975, and *The Older Hardy,* 1978, both by Robert Gittings; *An Essay on Hardy* by John Bayley, 1978.

*   *   *

In his early twenties Thomas Hardy aspired to be a country curate and poet, like William Barnes. Yet, after a period of intense reading in London, he rejected belief in Providence for scientific philosophy, based largely on the writings of J. S. Mill, Darwin's *The Origin of Species,* and readings in geology and astronomy. Like Mill, Hardy was impressed with Auguste Comte's emphasis on the need for altruism and a programme of reform based on education and science. Hardy never forfeited his belief in the Christian ethic; he was convinced that there was little hope for humanity without enlightened co-operation and charity. His preface to *The Woodlanders* suggests that his conscious aim in his last major novels was to further amelioration through enlisting the sympathetic awareness of his readers. Humanitarianism combines with his scientific outlook in imaginatively visualized presentations to maintain his appeal today.

Hardy's basic ideas did not change greatly and, as his London poems of 1865–67 show, they were formed early. Events are the result primarily of circumstance or chance, which is all that is immediately apparent in an evolving network of cause-effect relationships extending through space and time. In *The Woodlanders* the "web" which is for ever weaving shows, for example, a link between the death of Mrs. Charmond and the American Civil War. Chance includes heredity and character; only when reason prevails is man free to influence the course of events. Such philosophical ideas are inherent, and sometimes explicit, in Hardy's first published novel, *Desperate Remedies*. His previous novel, *The Poor Man and the Lady* (which survives only in scenes adapted to other novels and in "An Indiscretion in the Life of an Heiress"), had been loosely constructed, and too satirical, of London society and comtemporary Christianity in particular, to gain acceptance.

In *Desperate Remedies* Hardy merged, for the sake of publication, a tragic situation with a thriller story and a complicated plot (in the manner of Wilkie Collins). Until the sensational dénouement takes over, the writing in enriched with poetical quotations and effects, Shelley's wintry image of adversity determining crisis settings, as in later Hardy novels. A reviewer's commendation of his rustic scenes led to *Under the Greenwood Tree*, which Hardy wrote rapidly, with notable economy, in a happy mood kindled by love of Emma Gifford, a church organist whose blue dress and vanity are the subject of light satire in a novel remarkable for its rustic humour. Though the story of *A Pair of Blue Eyes* was planned before Hardy's first Cornish visit, and its characters are almost wholly fictional, this tragic romance is based on Cornish memories. Often poetic in conception, it suffered from the pressures of serial demands. The heroine's crisis anticipates *Tess*. Writing anonymously for *The Cornhill Magazine*, Hardy was more ambitious in *Far from the Madding Crowd*, showing marked development in Wessex humour and the dramatization of passion. A suggestion that this pastoral work was written by George Eliot made Hardy put aside the story which became *The Woodlanders* for *The Hand of Ethelberta*, a comedy directed by Darwinian ideas and social satire. After a respite, during which he read a great deal, Hardy began *The Return of the Native*, but difficulties with magazine editors made him rewrite much in the first two books. Partly inspired by Arnold, more by Pater's essay on Winckelmann, his theme is hedonism (with a Greek slant) versus altruistic idealism. Life as something to be endured (and avoided by the hedonist) is represented by Egdon Heath. The insignificance of the individual in time (with reference to Egdon) is stressed in a number of scenes, the most important being Darwinian and closely associated with Mrs. Yeobright's death.

Hardy's next novels suggest that he was still searching for the direction his genius should take. After *The Trumpet-Major*, a story dependent for relief on traditional comic types and situations, against a background of threatened Napoleonic invasion, he experimented with a second novel of ideas in *A Laodicean*. Handicapped by prolonged illness, he failed to give artistic cohesion to the theme of Arnold's "imaginative reason," in resolving the conflict between modern technology and a *prédilection d'artiste* for the romantic splendours of the past. Mephistophelian villainy contributes to the counterplot, and continues on a minor scale in *Two on a Tower*, where the story, set against the immensities of stellar space, reveals Hardy's maturing emphasis on altruism. In *The Mayor of Casterbridge* he solved the problem of catering for weekly serialization without detriment to tragic grandeur, his standards being set by the great masterpieces of the past, from classical times onwards. Some of the most moving scenes are in prose of Biblical simplicity or in the vernacular of the unlettered poor. After Henchard's death, Whittle emerges more noble of heart than the shrewd Farfrae or the philosophical Elizabeth-Jane. Hardy had found where his deepest sympathies lay.

Thenceforward his tragedy is centred in the deprivation or ill-chance of the underprivileged: Marty South and Tess, Giles Winterborne and Jude. The tragedy of *The Woodlanders* hinges on false social values which induce Grace Melbury to marry a philanderer whose hypocrisy is veiled in Shelleyan idealism. Tess, as a victim of chance and the embodiment of Christian charity (which suffereth long), is a pure (but not perfect) woman. "Once victim, always victim" echoes Richardson's *Clarissa*, the most important creative influence on *Tess*. *Jude*, the most ambitious and complex of Hardy's tragedies, was not finished to his satisfaction. The Christminster-Crucifixion parallel seems forced at the critical juncture, and hereditary traits of Jude and Sue, with reference to marriage, are too exceptional and peripheral to create convincing tragedy, though the novel contains the most moving dramatic scenes Hardy ever wrote, possibly with his own domestic situation in mind.

He had reason at this time to realize more than ever his readiness to fall imaginatively in love with beautiful women, and he had made it the subject of his satirical fantasy *The Well-Beloved*. One result of this tendency is that his heroines are generally more attractive than his men, Henchard excepted.

Hardy's most characteristic natural settings are psychological rather than scenic, expressing the feelings or situations of his principal characters. His visualizing techniques serve to make his critical scenes more impressive and memorable.

Such was Hardy's sense of the relativity of things that he rarely lost his sense of humour, as may be seen in "A Few Crusted Characters," written as a relief from *Tess*. Among his short stories, there are several, ranging from anecdote to novelette, from humour to satire and tragedy, which rank high in Hardy's fiction.

Violent criticism of *Jude* made Hardy relinquish prose fiction, and return to poetry, sooner than he intended. He had time to prepare for *The Dynasts*, a work he had contemplated in various forms for many years. In this epic drama of the Napoleonic wars, with nations swayed by forces beyond the control of reason, Hardy regards the conflict philosophically through the Spirit of the Years, and tragically through the Spirit of the Pities. It is a work of immense scholarship and artistic proportion, containing some of Hardy's finest prose pictures and some moving lyrics. Its main weaknesses are in the verse, however, as well as in the visual and over-mechanical presentation of the Will.

Much of Hardy's early poetry (before and after his novel writing period) suggests that he did not write it with ease. Rigorously rejecting poetical lushness, he achieved an independence of style reflecting his own observation, thought, vision, and feeling. Integrity shines through his verse even when it is oddly laboured. Impressed by the best of Wordsworth and Browning, he disciplined himself to write lyrical poetry as little removed as possible from the idiom of spoken English; and it is this quality, combined with his personal appeal, which explains the hold he has on modern readers. Most of his poems (and most of his greatest) were composed after he had reached the age of seventy. The autobiographical element is considerable.

Fortified by Arnold's declaration that "what distinguishes the greatest poets is their powerful and profound application of ideas to life," Hardy used verse to promulgate beliefs which he hoped would help to prepare a way for the Positivist religion of humanity. He remained an "evolutionary meliorist" until, in his last years, the prospect of another European war made him place the blame for the Unfulfilled Intention in human affairs, not on an abstract Immanent Will, but on the folly of mankind.

His personal poetry has deeper resonances, as may be found particularly in "Poems of 1912–13," written after the death of his first wife. Hardy wrote many narrative poems in dramatic or ballad form. Unusual events and ironies of chance attracted him as much as in his prose; but more important is the poetry which he found in everyday life. "There is enough poetry in what is left, after all the false romance has been extracted, to make a sweet pattern," he affirmed. Many of his poems were composed with song-music in mind, and in stanzas demanding high manipulative skill. So imaginatively sensitive is Hardy to experience that even readers familiar with his poetry continually find something new to admire in movement, expression, or image. His finer poems are surprisingly varied and numerous; in them and elsewhere he modulates language with exquisite art to convey a living voice. The rare distinction of being both a major poet and a major novelist belongs to Thomas Hardy.

—F. B. Pinion

HAYWOOD, Eliza (née Fowler).   English.   Born in London, probably in 1693. Married Valentine Haywood in 1711 (who deserted her, 1721); two children. Writer from childhood; praised by Steele as "Sappho," 1709; actress, in Dublin, then in London, from 1715; successful as a novelist from 1724; ridiculed by Pope in the *Dunciad*, 1728; Editor, *The Female Spectator*, London, 1744–46, and *The Parrot*, London, 1746. *Died 25 February 1756.*

PUBLICATIONS

Fiction

Love in Excess; or, The Fatal Enquiry.   3 vols., 1719–20.
The British Recluse; or, The Secret History of Cleomira, Supposed Dead.   1722.
Idalia; or, The Unfortunate Mistress.   1723.
The Injured Husband; or, The Mistaken Resentment.   1723.
The Fatal Secret; or, Constancy in Distress.   1724.
Lasselia; or, The Self-Abandoned.   1724.
The Masqueraders; or, Fatal Curiosity.   1724.
The Rash Resolve; or, The Untimely Discovery.   1724.
A Spy upon the Conjuror.   1724.
The Arragonian Queen.   1724.
The Surprise; or, Constancy Rewarded.   1724.
Bath Intrigues, in Four Letters to a Friend in London.   1725.
The Unequal Conflict; or, Nature Triumphant.   1725.
Fantomina; or, Love in a Maze.   1725.
Memoirs of a Certain Island Adjacent to the Kingdom of Utopia.   1725.
The Dumb Projector.   1725.
Dalinda; or, The Double Marriage.   1725.
Fatal Fondness; or, Love Its Own Opposer.   1725.
Memoirs of the Baron de Brosse.   1725.
The City Jilt; or, The Alderman Turned Beau.   1726.
The Mercenary Lover; or, The Unfortunate Heiresses.   1726.
The Distressed Orphan; or, Love in a Madhouse.   1726(?).
The Double Marriage; or, The Fatal Release.   1726.
Cleomelia; or, The Generous Mistress.   1727.
The Fruitless Enquiry.   1727.
Letters from the Palace of Fame.   1727.
The Life of Madam De Villesache.   1727.
Love in Its Variety (stories).   1727.
The Perplexed Duchess; or, Treachery Rewarded, Being Some Memoirs of the Court of Malfy.   1727.
Philidore and Placentia; or, L'Amour Trop Delicat.   1727; edited by W. M. McBurney, in *Four Before Richardson*, 1963.
The Secret History of the Present Intrigues of the Court of Carimania.   1727.
Persecuted Virtue; or, The Cruel Lover.   1728.
The Agreeable Caledonian; or Memoirs of Signiora di Morella, A Roman Lady.   2 vols., 1728–29; as *Clementina; or, The History of an Italian Lady,* 1768.
The Disguised Prince; or, The Beautiful Parisian.   1728.
Irish Artifice; or, The History of Clarina.   1728.
The Fair Hebrew.   1729.
Love-Letters on All Occasions Lately Passed Between Persons of Distinction (stories).   1730.

Adventures of Eovaai, Princess of Ijaveo.   1736; as *The Unfortunate Princess,* 1741.
The Fortunate Foundlings, Being the Genuine History of Colonel M——rs and His Sister Madame Du P——y.   1744.
Epistles for the Ladies.   2 vols., 1749–50.
Life's Progress Through the Passions; or, The Adventures of Natura.   1748.
The History of Miss Betsy Thoughtless.   1751.
The History of Jemmy and Jenny Jessamy.   1753.
The Invisible Spy.   1755.
The Wife.   1756.
The Husband, in Answer to the Wife.   1756.

Plays

The Fair Captive, from a work by a Captain Hurst (produced 1721).   1721.
A Wife to Be Let (produced 1723).   1724.
Frederick, Duke of Brunswick-Lunenburgh (produced 1729).   1729.
The Opera of Operas; or, Tom Thumb the Great, with William Hatchett, music by Thomas Arne, from the play by Fielding (produced 1733).   1733.

Verse

Poems on Several Occasions.   1724.

Other

The Tea Table (magazine).   1724.
Works.   4 vols., 1724.
Secret Histories, Novels, and Poems.   6 vols., 1725–27.
Reflections on the Various Effects of Love.   1726.
A Present for a Servant Maid.   1743.
The Female Spectator (magazine).   4 vols., 1747; selections edited by J. B. Priestley, 1929.

Translator, *Mary Stuart, Queen of Scots.*   1725.
Translator, *La Belle Assemblée; or, The Adventures of Six Days,* by Madeleine Gomez.   1725.
Translator, *The Lady's Philosopher's Stone,* by Louis Adrien Duperron de Castera.   1725.
Translator, *L'Entretien des Beaux Esprits, Being a Sequel to La Belle Assemblée,* by Madeleine Gomez.   1734.
Translator, *The Virtuous Villagers,* by de Mouhy.   1742.
Translator, *The Busy Body: A Successful Spy.*   1742.
Translator, *Letters from a Lady of Quality to a Chevalier,* by Edme Boursault.   N.d.

Reading List: *The Life and Romance of Haywood* by George Frisbie Whicher, 1915 (includes bibliography).

*   *   *

As the successor to Aphra Behn and Mrs. Manley, Eliza Haywood was probably the most well-known and certainly the most prolific female writer of the 1720's. She began her career in 1719–20 with a novel, *Love in Excess; or, The Fatal Enquiry*, and during the decade which followed she published some forty original works, translated a number of French novellas, and wrote three plays. She seems to have turned to writing after leaving her husband, and she became a sophisticated professional writer who turned out book after book according to a clearly visible and highly successsful popular format. Her work in that busy decade took two separate if closely related forms: the secret history and the novel. Her *Memoirs of a Certain Island Adjacent to the Kingdom of Utopia* was a fairly successful imitation of Mrs. Manley's popular and notorious *New Atlantis* (1709). Both these books were collections of highly embellished gossip, scandal, and libel about prominent people of the day. Haywood's book combines sexual sensationalism with a vigorus satirical rhetoric in which Cupid denounces the perversion of his worship by avarice, adultery, and the exploitation and betrayal of women by a corrupt male-dominated society. The so-called "South-Sea Bubble" financial disaster of 1722 is the basis of Haywood's denunciations of the rich and the powerful, but the main appeal of the book was clearly the near-pornographic intensity and lurid melodrama of its recurring sexual scenes. Haywood's secret histories contain, in fact, nothing more than localized and abridged versions of the story she told over and over again in her novels, some of which were given the label of secret history as well. From *Love in Excess* through such works as *Idalia*, *Lasselia*, *The Fatal Secret*, and *Philidore and Placentia* Haywood repeated with unfailing energy and only slight variations an apparently popular formula story which featured genteel and euphemistic but effectively pornographic descriptions of female passion and male lust.

Typically, a young girl is pursued by a treacherous suitor in a complicated social or moral situation which often features incest as well as adultery. Seduction or outright rape is a standard incident, and terrible consequences invariably follow, even violent death and sometimes grim revenge on the seducer. At the center of all this operatic melodrama is the "power of love," an irresistible but destructive urge whose thrilling and forbidden intensities Haywood's novels were designed to evoke in their readers. A scene such as this one from *Love in Excess* is entirely representative of Haywood's style and method. The heroine, Melliora, is asleep: her "Gown and the rest of her Garments were white, all ungirt, and loosely flowing, discover'd a Thousand Beauties, which modish Formalities conceal." Melliora dreams of the handsome D'Elmont, and he enters to steal a chaste good-night kiss; but the scene quickly turns into a typical Haywoodian erotic moment, complicated by moral melodrama:

... he tore open his Waistcoat, and joyn'd his panting Breast to hers, with such a Tumultuous Eagerness! Seiz'd her with such a Rapidity of Transported hope Crown'd Passion, as immediately wak'd her from an imaginary Felicity, to the Approaches of a Solid One. Where have I been? (said she, just opening her Eyes) where am I? – (And then coming more perfectly to her self) Heaven! What's this? – I am D'Elmont (Cry'd the O'erjoy'd Count) the happy D'Elmont! Melliora's, the Charming Melliora's D'Elmont! O, all ye Saints, (Resum'd the surpriz'd Trembling fair) ye Ministring Angels! Whose Business 'tis to guard the Innocent! Protect and Shield my Virtue! ... Come, come no more Reluctance (Continu'd he, gathering Kisses from her soft Snowy Breast at every Word) Damp not the fires thou hast rais'd with seeming Coiness! I know thou art mine! All mine! And thus I – Yet think (said she Interrupting him, and Strugling in his Arms) think what 'tis that you wou'd do, nor for a Moments Joy, hazard your Peace for Ever. By Heaven, cry'd he: I will this Night be Master of my Wishes, no Matter what to Morrow may bring forth.

Haywood became famous for writing what the 18th century called "warm" scenes like this one, and a prefatory poem in her 1732 collected *Secret Histories, Novels and Poems* begins its praise of her thus: "Persuasion waits on all your bright Designs,/And where you point the Varying Soul Inclines:/See! Love and Friendship, the fair Theme inspires,/We glow with Zeal, we melt in soft Desires!" Not so soft, we might be tempted to add, for there is nothing very mysterious about the commercial success of Haywood's works. Her stories were English versions of the amatory novellas popular on the continent in the latter half of the 17th century, and they provided her apparently large and eager audience with a satisfying fantasy world filled with lust and pathos and with an exotic aristocratic elegance and corruption. Her stories are as rich with popular fantasies about the upper classes as they are thick with soft eroticism. They also very clearly expressed a sort of instinctive feminism, and in a strange and untypical novel called *The British Recluse* two ruined ladies articulate a coherent and eloquent response to male exploitation and go off to live together in virtuous seclusion in the country.

Haywood's novels of the 1720's are important (if virtually unreadable), for they are a symptom (and perhaps even a cause) of the increasing popularity of fiction in England during that period. The tradition of popular narrative she helped form is a key part of the literary context in which Richardson and Fielding and the other major novelists of the century were to operate in the 1740's. Mrs. Haywood herself outlived her fame and published little in the 1730's and '40's.

But she was shrewdly professional to the end and responded to the fashion created by Richardson's novels by writing two "domestic" novels, *The History of Miss Betsy Thoughtless* and *The History of Jemmy and Jenny Jessamy*, which remained popular until the end of the century.

—John Richetti

HENTY, G(eorge) A(lfred).   English.   Born in Trumpington, Cambridge, 8 December 1832. Educated at Westminster School, London, 1847–52; Caius College, Cambridge, 1852. Served in the Hospital Commisariat and the Purveyor's Department during the Crimean War: helped organize Italian hospitals, 1859; served in Belfast and Portsmouth: Turkish Order of the Medjidie. Married 1) Elizabeth Finucane in 1858, two sons and two daughters; 2) Bessie Keylock. Crimean War Correspondent, *Morning Advertiser*, London; Special Correspondent, in Europe, Africa, Asia, and North America, *The Standard*, London, 1865–76; Editor, *Union Jack* magazine, London, 1880–83, and *Beeton's Boy's Own Magazine*, London, 1888–90, and later annuals, 1890–93. *Died 16 November 1902.*

PUBLICATIONS

Fiction

> *A Search for a Secret.*   1867.
> *All But Lost.*   1869.
> *Out on the Pampas; or, The Young Settlers.*   1871.
> *The Young Franc-Tireurs and Their Adventures in the Franco-Prussian War.*   1872.
> *The Young Buglers: A Tale of the Peninsular War.*   1879.

Seaside Maidens. 1880.
In Times of Peril: A Tale of India. 1881.
The Cornet of Horse: A Tale of Marlborough's Wars. 1881.
Winning His Spurs: A Tale of the Crusades. 1882; as *The Boy Knight,* 1883; as *Fighting the Saracens,* 1892.
Facing Death; or, The Hero of the Vaughan Pit: A Tale of the Coal Mines. 1882.
Under Drake's Flag: A Tale of the Spanish Main. 1882.
With Clive in India; or, The Beginnings of an Empire. 1883.
By Sheer Pluck: A Tale of the Ashanti Wars. 1883.
Jack Archer: A Tale of the Crimea. 1883; as *The Fall of Sebastopol,* 1892.
Friends, Though Divided: A Tale of the Civil War. 1883.
True to the Old Flag: A Tale of the American War of Independence. 1884.
In Freedom's Cause: A Story of Wallace and Bruce. 1884.
St. George for England: A Tale of Cressy and Poitiers. 1884.
The Lion of the North: A Tale of the Times of Gustavus Adolphus and the Wars of Religion. 1885.
The Young Colonists. 1885.
The Dragon and the Raven; or, The Days of King Alfred. 1885.
For Name and Fame; or, Through the Afghan Passes. 1885.
Through the Fray: A Tale of the Luddite Riots. 1885.
Yarns on the Beach: A Bundle of Tales. 1885.
With Wolfe in Canada; or, The Winning of a Continent. 1886.
The Bravest of the Brave; or, With Peterborough in Spain. 1886.
A Final Reckoning: A Tale of Bush Life in Australia. 1886.
The Young Carthaginian; or, A Struggle for Empire. 1886.
Bonnie Prince Charlie: A Tale of Fontenoy and Culloden. 1887.
For the Temple: A Tale of the Fall of Jerusalem. 1887.
In the Reign of Terror: The Adventures of a Westminster Lad. 1887.
Sturdy and Strong; or, How George Andrews Made His Way. 1887.
The Cat of Bubastes: A Tale of Ancient Egypt. 1888.
The Lion of St. Mark: A Tale of Venice. 1888.
Captain Bayley's Heir: A Tale of the Gold Fields of California. 1888.
Orange and Green: A Tale of the Boyne and Limerick. 1888.
Gabriel Allen, M.P. 1888.
The Curse of Carne's Hold: A Tale of Adventure. 1889.
One of the 28th: A Tale of Waterloo. 1889.
By Pike and Dyke: A Tale of the Rise of the Dutch Republic. 1889.
Camps and Quarters, with Archibald Forbes and Charles Williams. 1889.
Tales of Daring and Dangers. 1889.
The Plague Ship. 1889.
With Lee in Virginia: A Story of the American Civil War. 1889.
A Hidden Foe. 1890.
By Right of Conquest; or, With Cortez in Mexico. 1890.
By England's Aid; or, The Freeing of the Netherlands (1585–1604). 1890.
A Chapter of Adventures; or, Through the Bombardment of Alexandria. 1890; as *The Young Midshipman: A Story of the Bombardment of Alexandria,* 1902.
Maori and Settler: A Story of the New Zealand Wars. 1890.
Redskin and Cowboy: A Tale of the Western Plains. 1891.
The Dash for Khartoum: A Tale of the Nile Expedition. 1891.
Held Fast for England: A Tale of the Siege of Gibraltar (1779–1883). 1891.
In Greek Waters: A Story of the Grecian War of Independence (1821–1827). 1892.
Beric the Briton: A Story of the Roman Invasion. 1892.
Condemned as a Nihilist: A Story of Escape from Siberia. ·1892.
The Ranche in the Valley. 1892.

A Jacobite Exile: Being the Adventures of a Young Englishman in the Service of Charles XII of Sweden. 1893.
Tales from the Works of Henty. 1893; as *Tales from Henty,* 1925.
St. Bartholomew's Eve: A Tale of the Huguenot Wars. 1893.
Through the Sikh War: A Tale of the Conquest of the Punjaub. 1893.
Rujub, The Juggler. 1893; as *In the Days of the Mutiny: A Military Novel,* 1893.
Dorothy's Double. 1894.
In the Heart of the Rockies: A Story of Adventure in Colorado. 1894.
When London Burned: A Story of Restoration Times and the Great Fire. 1894.
Wulf the Saxon: A Story of the Norman Conquest. 1894.
The Tiger of Mysore: A Story of the War with Tippoo Saib. 1895.
A Woman of the Commune: A Tale of the Two Sieges of Paris. 1895; as *Cuthbert Hartington: A Tale of the Siege of Paris,* 1899; as *A Girl of the Commune,* n.d.; as *Two Sieges of Paris; or, A Girl of the Commune,* n.d.
A Knight of the White Cross: A Tale of the Siege of Rhodes. 1895.
Through Russian Snows: A Story of Napoleon's Retreat from Moscow. 1895.
On the Irrawaddy: A Story of the First Burmese War. 1896.
At Agincourt: A Tale of the White Hoods of Paris. 1896
Bears and Decoits and Other Stories. 1896.
With Cochrane the Dauntless: A Tale of the Exploits of Lord Cochrane in South American Waters. 1896.
In Battle and Breeze: Sea Stories, with George Manville Fenn and W. Clark Russell. 1896.
With Moore at Corunna: A Tale of the South African War. 1897.
A March on London, Being the Story of Wat Tyler's Insurrection. 1897.
With Frederick the Great: A Story of the Seven Years' War. 1897.
Among Malay Pirates. 1897; as *Among the Malays,* 1900(?).
The Queen's Cup. 1897.
Colonel Thorndyke's Secret. 1898; as *The Brahmin's Treasure,* 1899.
At Aboukir and Acre: A Story of Napoleon's Invasion of Egypt. 1898.
Both Sides the Border: A Tale of Hotspur and Glendower. 1898.
Under Wellington's Command: A Tale of the Peninsular War. 1898.
The Golden Cañon. 1899.
No Surrender! A Tale of the Rising in La Vendée. 1899.
On the Spanish Main. 1899.
Won by the Sword: A Tale of the Thirty Years' War. 1899.
The Lost Heir. 1899.
In the Irish Brigade: A Tale of War in Flanders and Spain. 1900.
In the Hands of the Cave-Dwellers. 1900.
With Buller in Natal; or, A Born Leader. 1900.
Out with Garibaldi: A Story of the Liberation of Italy. 1900.
A Roving Commission; or, Through the Black Insurrection of Hayti. 1900.
The Sole Survivors. 1901.
With Roberts to Pretoria: A Tale of the South African War. 1901.
At the Point of the Bayonet: A Tale of the Mahratta War. 1901.
John Hawke's Fortune: A Story of Monmouth's Rebellion. 1901.
To Herat and Cabul: A Story of the First Afghan War. 1901.
With Kitchener in the Soudan: A Story of Atbara and Omdurman. 1902.
With the British Legion: A Story of the Carlist Wars. 1902.
The Treasure of the Incas: A Tale of Adventure in Peru. 1902.
With the Allies to Pekin: A Tale of the Relief of the Legations. 1903.
Through Three Compaingns: A Story of Chitral, Tirah, and Ashantee. 1903.
By Conduct and Courage: A Story of Nelson's Days, edited by C. G. Henty. 1904.
Gallant Deeds. 1905.

In the Hands of the Malays and Other Stories.   1905.
Redskins and Colonists; or, A Boy's Adventures in the Early Days of Virginia; Burton and Son; The Ranche in the Valley; Sole Survivors.   1905.
A Soldier's Daughter and Other Stories.   1906.

Other

The March to Magdala.   1868.
The March to Coomassie.   1874.
Those Other Animals.   1891.
The Sovereign Reader: Scenes from the Life and Reign of Queen Victoria.   1887; revised edition, as *Queen Victoria: Scenes from Her Life and Reign,* 1901.

Editor, *Our Sailors,* by William H. G. Kingston, continued by Henty.   1882.
Editor, *Our Soldiers,* by William H. G. Kingston, continued by Henty.   1886.
Editor, *Yule Logs.*   1898.
Editor, *Yule-Tide Yarns.*   1899.
Editor, *Famous Travels.*   1902.

Bibliography: *Bibliography of Henty and Hentyana* by R. S. Kennedy and B. J. Farmer, 1956; *Henty: A Bibliography* by Robert L. Dartt, 1971.

Reading List: *Henty: The Story of an Active Life* by G. Manville Fenn, 1907.

*   *   *

At the head of innumerable copies of Blackie & Sons list of books for the young stands a quotation from the *Athenaeum*: "English boys owe a debt of gratitude to Mr. Henty." It could almost claim that the very idea of "English boys," as a special breed, was his creation; how far the youths who were moulded to embody the idea should have been grateful has been a matter of some debate. Inescapably, Henty's books have been seen as an influence, the epitome of the values of British Imperialism, and powerful weapons in the transmission of its ideology. Prolific himself, Henty also had many imitators who repeated his message and his narrative patterns, with obvious historical and geographical didactic intent, and scarcely less obvious presentation of heroic character models.

Henty's work, however, was not original or even unusual in its deliberate transmission of certain cultural values; since the beginning, the overwhelming majority of writers and purchasers of children's books have had didactic intentions. Henty's adventure stories are the descendants of evangelical tracts, with a shift of emphasis from the virtues of submission, piety, and holy dying to independence, pluck, and courage, reflecting a shift in social values. Henty's artistic contribution was his invention of a formulaic narrative pattern into which old stories and subjects were absorbed and redirected. He took a young, middle-class hero (presented as typical rather than exceptional amongst Englishmen, so that the reader could readily identify with him and his successes) and placed him in exciting situations where he could exhibit his sterling qualities and have them substantially rewarded. The situations adaptable for this purpose included the exotic outposts of Empire, where the heroes of Ballantyne and Mayne Reid had fought, explored, and hunted; the sea settings long used by Marryat and W. H. G. Kingston; and even the city streets of the old industrious apprentice tale, transmuted by the influence of Samuel Smiles. All were grist to Henty's mill, and when he had exhausted these, and the military settings suggested by his personal experience as a war correspondent, he turned to history, and made the historical adventure story particularly his own. Of course he sought only local colour in the carefully correct historical incidents he used: he had neither Scott's perception of the significance of historical difference, nor Kipling's near-mystical vision of its oneness with the present. Similarly his stories of the Empire are devoid of Kipling's Indian atmosphere, and his sea stories are jolly rather than ecstatic like, say, John Masefield's. But intensities were no part of his purpose. In his better books, those with enough motor power to burn up their factual fuel and keep the adventure moving fast, he performs well the task he set himself of providing the young Englishman with an image of himself which would help him to become a self-respecting adult in the role society gave him. The passing of that society has left his books, so closely bound up with it, without a purpose, and inevitably unread.

—J. S. Bratton

HOGG, James. Scottish. Born in Ettrick, Selkirkshire, baptized 9 December 1770. Attended the local school for one year; apprentice shepherd from the age of 6; largely self-educated. Married Margaret Phillips in 1820. Shepherd at Willanslee, 1787–90, and at Yarrow, 1790–1800; poet and songwriter from 1796; managed his parents' farm at Ettrick, 1800–03; met Sir Walter Scott, who encouraged his writing and subsequently arranged for publication of his verse, 1802; shepherd at Mitchelstacks, Nithsdale, 1803–07; farmer in Dumfriesshire, 1808: went bankrupt and returned to Ettrick; settled in Edinburgh, 1810, and thereafter devoted himself to writing; Editor, *The Spy*, Edinburgh, 1810–11; inherited a farm, Altrive Lake in Yarrow, from a patron, 1816, and lived there for the rest of his life; contributor to *Blackwood's Magazine*, Edinburgh. *Died 21 November 1835.*

PUBLICATIONS

Collections

Tales and Sketches.   6 vols., 1837.
Poetical Works.   5 vols., 1838–40.
Works, Letters, and Manuscripts, edited by R. B. Adam.   1930.
Selected Poems, edited by Douglas S. Mack.   1970.

Fiction

The Hunting of Badlewe: A Dramatic Tale.   1814.
The Long Pack: A Northumbrian Tale.   1817.
The Brownie of Bodsbeck and Other Tales.   1818; *The Brownie of Bodsbeck* edited by Douglas S. Mack, 1976.
Winter Evening Tales.   1820.
The Three Perils of Man; or, War, Women, and Witchcraft: A Border Romance.   1822; as *The Siege of Roxburgh*, in *Tales and Sketches*, 1837; edited by Douglas Gifford, 1972.
The Three Perils of Woman; or, Love, Leasing, and Jealousy: A Series of Domestic Scottish Tales.   1823.
The Private Memoirs and Confessions of a Justified Sinner.   1824; as *The Suicide's Grave*, 1828; as *Confessions of a Fanatic*, in *Tales and Sketches*, 1837; edited by John Carey, 1969.

Altrive Tales Collected among the Peasantry of Scotland and from Foreign Adventurers. 1832.
Tales of the Wars of Montrose. 1835; edited by J. E. H. Thomson, 1909.
Kilmeny. 1905.

Plays

Dramatic Tales. 2 vols., 1817.
The Royal Jubilee: A Scottish Mask. 1822.

Verse

Scottish Pastorals, Poems, Songs. 1801.
The Mountain Bard, Consisting of Ballads and Songs Founded on Facts and Legendary Tales. 1807; revised edition, 1821.
The Forest Minstrel: A Selection of Songs, with others. 1810.
The Queen's Wake: A Legendary Poem. 1813.
A Selection of German Hebrew Melodies. 1815(?).
The Pilgrims of the Sun. 1815.
The Ettrick Garland, Being Two Excellent New Songs, with Scott. 1815.
Mador of the Moor. 1816.
A Border Garland. 1819(?).
Poetical Works. 4 vols., 1822.
Queen Hynde. 1825.
The Shepherd's Calendar. 2 vols., 1829.
Songs by the Ettrick Shepherd. 1831.
A Queer Book. 1832.

Other

The Shepherd's Guide, Being a Practical Treatise on the Diseases of Sheep. 1807.
Critical Remarks on the Psalms of David, with W. Tennant. 1830.
A Series of Lay Sermons on Good Principles and Good Breeding. 1834.
The Domestic Manners and Private Life of Sir Walter Scott. 1834; as *Familiar Anecdotes of Scott,* 1834.
A Tour in the Highlands in 1803: A Series of Letters to Scott. 1888.
Memoirs of the Author's Life, and Familiar Anecdotes of Scott, edited by Douglas S. Mack. 1972.

Editor, *The Poetic Mirror; or, The Living Bards of Britain.* 1816; edited by T. E. Welby, 1929.
Editor, *The Jacobite Relics of Scotland.* 2 vols., 1819–21.
Editor, *Select and Rare Scottish Melodies.* 1829.
Editor, *Songs Now First Collected.* 1831.
Editor, with William Motherwell, *The Works of Robert Burns.* 5 vols., 1834–36.

Bibliography: "Hogg" by F. E. Pierce, in *Yale University Library Gazette 5,* 1931.

Reading List: *The Ettrick Shepherd: A Biography* by H. T. Stephenson, 1922; *The Ettrick*

Shepherd by E. C. Batho, 1927; *Life and Letters of Hogg*, vol. 1, by A. L. Strout, 1946; *Hogg: A Critical Study* by L. Simpson, 1962; *Hogg* by Douglas Gifford, 1976.

*   *   *

James Hogg's masterpiece is *The Private Memoirs and Confessions of a Justified Sinner*, a novel set in Scotland at the beginning of the eighteenth century. Like Scott's *Old Mortality*, Hogg's novel deals with the political and religious conflicts between Whig and Tory, Covenanter and Royalist. The *Justified Sinner* begins with a description of the marriage of the Tory Laird of Dalcastle, George Colwan, and a fanatically religious woman of extreme Whig views. The marriage is a disastrous failure, and the couple soon agree to live apart, in different parts of the Laird's house. Two sons are born to Lady Dalcastle. The first is named George and is brought up by his father, but the Laird refuses to recognise the second boy as his own, and this child is brought up by his mother and the Rev. Robert Wringhim, a clergyman who shares her extreme religious views. Indeed, Lady Dalcastle's second son is eventually named Robert Wringhim after the man who, it is strongly implied, is his real father. The brothers Robert and George, by now young men, meet for the first time in Edinburgh during a session of the Scottish Parliament. This meeting provokes a public quarrel which sparks off a more general conflict between the Whig and Tory factions, and in due course Robert murders his brother outside a brothel. The first section of the novel, which is narrated by an "Editor" of Tory sympathies, ends when Robert contrives to make his escape from justice, after his guilt as a murderer has been established.

The second section of the novel consists of Robert Wringhim's own Private Memoirs and Confessions, in which Robert describes how he came to believe himself to be one of the elect, a "justified person" unalterably chosen by God for salvation, and incapable of falling from his justified state through any sinful act. Robert is then befriended by a mysterious stranger, Gil-Martin, who is recognised by the reader as the Devil in disguise. At Gil-Martin's instigation, Robert sets out to purify the world by murdering the enemies of true religion. His first victim is Mr. Blanchard, a worthy minister who opposes Robert's extreme theological views. Robert then murders his brother George, and he later seals his damnation by committing suicide.

The *Justified Sinner* is a complex and powerful novel, and the portrait of Robert Wringhim is remarkable for its psychological insight. Hogg's other works do not reach the same heights, although *The Brownie of Bodsbeck* and *The Three Perils of Man* are rich and vigorous (although loosely constructed) novels which are based largely on traditional folk material. Hogg also used folk material in his short stories, of which "The Brownie of the Black Haggs" is a particularly fine example.

As a poet, Hogg's best work was influenced by the eighteenth-century Scottish vernacular tradition of Ramsay, Fergusson, and Burns, as well as by the traditional ballads of his native Ettrick. Hogg made a distinguished contribution to the Scottish song tradition, and he also produced "The Witch of Fife," a magnificent comic poem based, like Burns's "Tam o' Shanter," on the distinctive feeling of the old Scottish peasantry for the supernatural. Hogg's outstanding achievement in verse, however, is probably "Kilmeny," a religious poem based on traditional folk tales of abduction to fairyland. Both "Kilmeny" and "The Witch of Fife" were included in *The Queen's Wake*, a long poem in which Hogg tells of a contest among the poets held to celebrate the return of Mary Queen of Scots from France.

—Douglas S. Mack

HOLCROFT, Thomas. English. Born in London, 10 December 1745. Self-educated. Married four times, lastly to Louisa Mercier; one son and two daughters. Worked as a stableboy in Newmarket, Suffolk, 1757–60, and in his father's cobbler's stall, London, 1761–64; taught school in Liverpool, 1764; resumed his trade of shoemaker, London, 1764–69, and contributed to the *Whitehall Evening Post*; tutor in the family of Granville Sharp, 1769; prompter at a Dublin theatre, 1770–71; strolling player in the provinces in England, 1771–78; returned to London, 1778, and thereafter a prolific writer: contributed to the *Westminster Magazine, Wit's Magazine, Town and Country*, and early numbers of the *English Review*; actor and playwright at Drury Lane Theatre, 1778–84; Correspondent in Paris for the *Morning Herald*, 1783; joined the Society for Constitutional Information, 1792: indicted for treason, imprisoned, then discharged, 1794; moved to Hamburg, 1799, and tried, unsuccessfully, to establish the *European Repository*; lived in Paris, 1801–03, then returned to London: set up a printing business with his brother-in-law, 1803, which subsequently failed. *Died 23 March 1809.*

PUBLICATIONS

Fiction

Alwyn; or, The Gentleman Comedian, with William Nicholson.   1780.
The Family Picture; or, Domestic Dialogues on Amiable Subjects.   1783.
An Amorous Tale of the Chaste Loves of Peter the Long and His Most Honoured Friend Dame Blanche Bazu.   1786.
Anna St. Ives.   1792; edited by Peter Faulkner, 1970.
The Adventures of Hugh Trevor.   1794; edited by Seamus Deane, 1973.
Memoirs of Bryan Perdue.   1805.

Plays

The Crisis; or, Love and Fear (produced 1778).
Duplicity (produced 1781).   1781; as *The Masked Friend* (produced 1796).
The Noble Peasant, music by William Shield (produced 1784).   1784.
The Follies of a Day; or, The Marriage of Figaro, from a play by Beaumarchais (produced 1784).   1785; revised version, 1881; revised version, from the opera by da Ponte, music by Mozart (produced 1819), 1819.
The Choleric Fathers, music by William Shield (produced 1785).   1785.
Sacred Dramas Written in French by la Comtesse de Genlis.   1785.
Seduction (produced 1787).   1787.
The School for Arrogance, from a play by Destouches (produced 1791).   1791.
The Road to Ruin (produced 1792).   1792; edited by Ruth I. Aldrich, 1968.
Love's Frailties (produced 1794).   1794.
Heigh-Ho! for a Husband.   1794.
The Rival Queens; or, Drury Lane and Covent Garden (produced 1794).
The Deserted Daughter, from a work by Diderot (produced 1795).   1795.
The Man of Ten Thousand (produced 1796).   1796.
The Force of Ridicule (produced 1796).
Knave or Not?, from plays by Goldoni (produced 1798).   1798.
He's Much to Blame (produced 1798).   1798.
The Inquisitor (produced 1798).   1798.
The Old Clothesman, music by Thomas Attwood (produced 1799).   Songs published 1799(?).

Deaf and Dumb; or, The Orphan Protected, from a play by de Bouilly (produced 1801).   1801.
The Escapes; or, The Water-Carrier, music by Thomas Attwood, songs by T. J. Dibdin, from an opera by J. N. Nouilly, music by Cherubini (produced 1801).
A Tale of Mystery, from a play by Pixérécourt (produced 1802).   1802.
Hear Both Sides (produced 1803).   1803.
The Lady of the Rock (produced 1805).   1805.
The Vindictive Man (produced 1806).   1806.

Verse

Elegies.   1777.
Human Happiness; or, The Sceptic.   1783.
Tales in Verse, Critical, Satirical, Humorous.   1806.

Other

A Plain and Succinct Narrative of the Late [Gordon] Riots.   1780; edited by Garland Garvey Smith, 1944.
The Trial of the Hon. George Gordon.   1781.
Memoirs of Baron de Tott, Containing the State of the Turkish Empire and the Crimea.   2 vols., 1785.
The Secret History of the Court of Berlin.   2 vols., 1789.
A Narrative of Facts Relating to a Prosecution for High Treason.   2 vols., 1795.
A Letter to William Windham on the Intemperance and Danger of His Public Conduct.   1795.
Travels from Hamburg Through Westphalia, Holland, and the Netherlands.   2 vols., 1804.
Memoirs, completed by William Hazlitt.   3 vols., 1816; edited by Elbridge Colby, as *The Life of Holcroft*, 2 vols., 1925.

Editor, *Letter on Egypt*, by Mr. Savary.   2 vols., 1786.
Editor, and Translator, *Posthumous Works of Frederick, King of Prussia.*   13 vols., 1789.
Editor, *The Theatrical Recorder.*   2 vols., 1805–06.

Translator, *Philosophical Essays with Observations on the Laws and Customs of Several Eastern Nations*, by Foucher d'Osbornville.   1784.
Translator, *Tales of the Castle*, by la Comtesse de Genlis.   5 vols., 1785.
Translator, *Caroline of Lichtfield*, by Baroness de Montolieu.   2 vols., 1786.
Translator, *Historical and Critical Memoirs of the Life and Writings of Voltaire*, by Chaudon.   1786.
Translator, *The Present State of the Empire of Morocco*, by Chenier.   2 vols., 1788.
Translator, *The Life of Baron Frederick Trenck.*   3 vols., 1788.
Translator, *Essays on Physiognomy*, by J. C. Lavater.   3 vols., 1789.
Translator, *Travels Through Germany, Switzerland, and Italy*, by Frederick Leopold, Count Stolberg.   2 vols., 1796–97.
Translator, *Herman and Dorothea*, by Goethe.   1801.

Bibliography: *A Bibliography of Holcroft* by Elbridge Colby, 1922.

Reading List: *Holcroft and the Revolutionary Novel* by Rodney M. Baine, 1965; *The English Jacobin Novel* by Gary Kelly, 1976.

*   *   *

Thomas Holcroft was a self-taught man of letters, and one of the leading radical writers of the period of the French Revolution. His early writing was mostly for the theatre, and both *The School for Arrogance* and *The Road to Ruin* were successful in combining sentimental melodrama with the new philosophy. But with changing theatrical taste, Holcroft's plays passed into an oblivion from which they are yet to be restored. He chose to use the novel form for the fuller exposition of his political outlook, an outlook clearly influenced by his friendship with William Godwin, the most famous radical intellectual of the day, and his acquaintance with other radicals like Tom Paine and Mary Wollstonecraft.

Holcroft's two major novels are *Anna St. Ives* and *The Adventures of Hugh Trevor. Anna St. Ives* may be regarded as the equivalent in fiction of Godwin's *Political Justice.* It expresses its criticism of society through the contrasting contenders for the hand of the heroine, Anna: the rationalist Frank Henley, the virtuous son of the steward of Anna's father, and the aristocratic rake Coke Clifton. Clifton is a character in the line of Richardson's Lovelace in *Clarissa,* confident, witty, and unprincipled. He is allowed to express himself with a theatrical exuberance which gives the novel some vitality: "Should I be obliged to come like Jove to Semele, in flames, and should we both be reduced to ashes in the conflict, I will enjoy her!" However, the novel has a clear doctrinaire intention, which results in the defeat of Clifton and the marriage of Frank and Anna. The extravagance of Holcroft's idealism comes out in the final conversion of Clifton himself to the high-minded radicalism of his two unfailing friends.

Hugh Trevor is less diagrammatic in its rendering of life, but no less didactic in intention. The story of Trevor's life is basically picaresque, with a variety of adventures and events, but the moral of his experiences is clear: society is corrupt, and reason must guide the individual if he is to avoid its coercions. But there is also some psychological development, which would seem to have an autobiographical origin, in Trevor's gradual development of control over his original impulsiveness. When this is allied with a vigorous satirical attack on various aspects of society, including the Church, the law and reactionary politicians, the overall effect is a novel of considerable interest. Together with *Anna,* it justifies Holcroft's claim to be considered as a significant participant in an important tradition of rationalist social idealism.

—Peter Faulkner

HOOK, Theodore (Edward).   English.   Born in London, 22 September 1788; son of the composer James Hook. Educated at private schools, and at Harrow School for one year; later attended Oxford University for two terms. Achieved fame as a boy as a writer, generally with his father, of numerous successful comic operas, 1805–11; a member of the Prince of Wales' circle; Accountant-General and Treasurer of Mauritius, 1813–17: discharged on a charge of embezzling; returned to London; attempted, unsuccessfully, to establish a magazine, *The Arcadian,* 1818–19; Editor, *John Bull,* from 1820; imprisoned for debt, London, and property confiscated, on the Mauritius charge, 1823–25; Editor, *New Monthly Magazine,* 1836–41. *Died 24 August 1841.*

PUBLICATIONS

Collections

Choice Humorous Works. 1873.

Fiction

The Man of Sorrow. 1808; as *Ned Musgrave; or, The Most Unfortunate Man in the World,* 1842.
Sayings and Doings: A Series of Sketches from Life. 9 vols., 1824–28.
Maxwell. 1830.
Gervase Skinner; or, The Sin of Economy. 1830.
Love and Pride. 1833; as *The Widow and the Marquess,* 1842.
The Parson's Daughter. 1833; revised edition, 1835.
Gilbert Gurney. 1836.
Jack Brag. 1837.
Gurney Married: A Sequel to Gilbert Gurney. 1838.
Precepts and Practice. 1840.
Births, Deaths, and Marriages. 1839; as *All in the Wrong,* 1842.
Fathers and Sons. 1842.
Peregrine Bunce; or, Settled at Last. 1842.

Plays

The Soldier's Return; or, What Can Beauty Do?, music by James Hook (produced 1805). 1805.
The Invisible Girl, music by James Hook, from a French play (produced 1806). 1806.
Catch Him Who Can!, music by James Hook (produced 1806). 1806.
Tekeli; or, The Siege of Montgatz, music by James Hook, from a play by Pixérécourt (produced 1806). 1806.
The Fortress, music by James Hook, from a play by Pixérécourt (produced 1807). 1807.
Music-Mad, music by James Hook (produced 1807). 1808.
The Siege of St. Quentin; or, Spanish Heroism, music by James Hook (produced 1808).
Killing No Murder, music by James Hook (produced 1809). 1809; revised version, as *A Day at the Inn* (produced 1823), with *The Gentleman in Black* by Mark Lemon, 1886.
Safe and Sound, music by James Hook (produced 1809). 1809.
Ass-ass-ination (produced 1810).
The Will or the Widow; or, Puns in Plenty (produced 1810).
Darkness Visible (produced 1811). 1811.
The Trial by Jury (produced 1811). 1811.
Exchange No Robbery; or, The Diamond Ring (produced 1820). 1820.
Over the Water (produced 1820).
A Joke's a Joke; or, Too Much for Friendship (produced 1830).

Other

Facts Illustrative of the Treatment of Napoleon Buonaparte in Saint Helena. 1819.
Tentamen; or, An Essay Towards the History of Whittington. 1820.

The Life of General Sir David Baird. 2 vols., 1832.
The Ramsbottom Letters. 1872; revised edition, 1874.

Editor, *Reminiscences of Michael Kelly the Singer.* 2 vols., 1826.
Editor, *Pascal Bruno*, by Dumas. 1837.
Editor, *Cousin Geoffrey, The Old Bachelor*, by H. M. G. Smythies. 3 vols., 1840.
Editor, *The French Stage and the French People*, by J. A. Benard. 1841.
Editor, *Peter Priggins*, by J. T. J. Hewlett. 3 vols., 1841.
Editor, *The Parish Clerk*, by J. T. J. Hewlett. 3 vols., 1841.

Bibliography: in *XIX Century Fiction: A Bibliographical Record* by Michael Sadleir, 2 vols., 1951.

Reading List: *Life and Remains of Hook* by R. H. D. Barham, 2 vols., 1849, revised edition, 1853, 1877; *Hook and His Novels* by M. F. Brightfield, 1928.

*   *   *

Theodore Hook is ranked as a forerunner of Charles Dickens. Like Dickens, whose vast audience he helped to cultivate, he never seems to have rested, forever compelled to supply copy, eager to observe and to inform. But with him the journalist proved stronger than the narrator, though he could spell out the human predicament and had a sure grasp of the narrative potential of a situation. In his numerous novels and novellas he never genuinely probes a relationship or fully explores a personality. Doubtless there is some curiosity and concern on his part, but very little compassion, or even engagement, goes into his lively and smooth-running accounts.

Hook makes little effort to develop a plausible action. His plots are contrived and abound in coincidence, whose spuriousness he may even ironically concede. When he resorts to the pattern of the didactic tale much is made of the avowed authenticity of the events described, while the inherent logic of the parable remains largely unheeded. His novels proper must have required more application, yet here we are again struck by a facility of composition which never integrates or even shapes the material employed.

Hook lacked creative genius, but excelled in observation. There are qualities of vividness and fluency about his sketches that will still hold us. Sometimes the documentation seems too detailed, but then his readers were avid for information of any kind, and the wide range of his descriptions makes for diversity. His realism, conversely, never amounts to a detached representation of men and manners. There is an abundance of oddities and cranks among his manifold characters, who owe more to Hook's acumen than to the literary models of his great predecessors. No incongruity would escape him, and he was too much a satirist to forego a sarcastic censure when the occasion arose. Nevertheless, his social criticism remains strangely abortive throughout. In an age striving for reforms Hook closed his eyes to any change that might disturb the social set-up. His heroes usually claim aristocratic descent or adhere to an upper-middle-class background. Anyone below that station can fulfil a minor role only, unless he offers material for caricature, and the most scathing comment is indeed reserved for the social climber.

This is not to say that his work is entirely subordinated to a purpose. There is considerable variety in his scenes and the ever present criticism is often blended with humour or even elevated to pathos. But satire and caricature remain the most striking elements of Theodore Hook's narrative style and may be assumed to have influenced the Victorian novel of manners. Indirectly, such an influence may even extend to a much later period.

—Herbert Foltinek

HOPE, Anthony. Pseudonym for Sir Anthony Hope Hawkins. English. Born in London, 9 February 1863. Educated at St. John's Foundation School, London and, subsequently, Leatherhead, Surrey; Balliol College, Oxford, 1881–85 (graduated with honours); called to the Bar, Middle Temple, London, 1887. Served the government in the Editorial and Public Branch Department, 1914–18. Married Elizabeth Somerville Sheldon in 1903; two sons and one daughter. Practised law in London, 1887–94; thereafter a full-time writer. Member of the Committee for twelve years, Chairman for four years, and a founder of the pension scheme, the Authors' Society, London. Knighted, 1918. *Died 8 July 1933.*

PUBLICATIONS

Fiction

A Man of Mark. 1890.
Father Stafford. 1891.
Mr. Witt's Widow. 1892.
A Change of Air. 1893.
Half a Hero. 1893.
Sport Royal and Other Stories. 1893.
The Dolly Dialogues. 1894.
The God in the Car. 1894.
The Indiscretion of the Duchess. 1894.
The Prisoner of Zenda. 1894.
The Chronicles of Count Antonio. 1895.
Comedies of Courtship. 1896.
The Heart of Princess Osra and Other Stories. 1896.
Phroso. 1897.
Rupert of Hentzau. 1898.
Simon Dale. 1898.
The King's Mirror. 1899.
Quisante. 1900.
Tristam of Blent. 1901.
The Intrusions of Peggy. 1902.
Double Harness. 1904.
A Servant of the Public. 1905.
Sophy of Kravonia. 1906.
Tales of Two People. 1907.
The Great Miss Driver. 1908.
Second String. 1910.
Mrs. Maxon Protests. 1911.
A Young Man's Year. 1915.
Captain Dieppe. 1918.
Beaumaroy Home from the Wars. 1919.
Lucinda. 1920.
Little Tiger. 1925.

Plays

The Price of Empire (produced 1896).
The Adventure of Lady Ursula (produced 1898). 1898.

When a Man's in Love, with Edward Rose (produced 1898).
Rupert of Hentzau, from his own novel (produced 1899).
English Nell, with Edward Rose, from the novel *Simon Dale* by Hope (produced 1900).
Pilkerton's Peerage (produced 1902).   1918.
Captain Dieppe, with Harrison Rhodes (produced 1904).
Helena's Path, with Cosmo Gordon-Lennox (produced 1910).
Love's Song (produced 1916).
The Philosopher in the Apple Orchard: A Pastoral.   1936.

Other

The New (German) Testament: Some Texts and a Commentary.   1914.
Militarism, German and British.   1915.
Why Italy Is with the Allies.   1917.
Selected Works.   10 vols., 1925.
Memories and Notes.   1927.

Reading List: *Hope and His Books* by Charles E. Mallett, 1935; "The Prisoner of the Prisoner of Zenda: Hope and the Novel of Society" by S. G. Putt, in *Essays in Criticism 6*, 1956.

*   *   *

The name of Anthony Hope creeps into histories of late Victorian literature almost by virtue of a single book, *The Prisoner of Zenda*, one of the most popular novels of the period, and indeed of all time. Yet Hope was a prolific writer, author of thirty-two works of fiction, a dozen or so plays, some political pamphlets written during World War I when he was employed by the Ministry of Information, and an autobiography. Trained as a barrister, Hope first took to writing in his spare time, achieving a modest success with a series of whimsical sketches contributed to the *Westminster Gazette*, later gathered together and published under the title *The Dolly Dialogues*. However, after the public's enthusiastic reception of *The Prisoner of Zenda* in 1894 he became a professional writer, endeavoring to repeat the success of this novel with a sequel entitled *Rupert of Hentzau*. He also wrote several other historical romances and some novels set in his own day, none of which deserves more than passing attention.

In a sense it is unfortunate that Hope turned professional, for in his evident determination to make a decent living by his pen, much of the spark went out of his writing. True, the arch humor of *The Dolly Dialogues* may strike modern readers as exceedingly tiresome and the social adventures he describes appallingly trivial, yet in this book his prose skips along at an easy pace, and at his best Hope can match the accomplished Ada Leverson, who covers the same social territory and writes in a similar vein.

Sprightliness and good humor are also apparent in *The Prisoner of Zenda*, an improbable tale concerning Rudolf Rassendyll, an English gentleman of Ruritania, who impersonates the king at his coronation, thereby thwarting a plot to remove him from the throne. Later, he falls in love with the King's betrothed; thus is described in *Rupert of Hentzau*, and there we follow the lovers' fortunes until Rassendyll finally gives up both his life and the Princess Flavia for their love and her honor. Although the reader is swept along by the swashbuckling incidents of the fast-moving plot, sharing vicariously the romantic adventures of the hero, the ironic tone of the first book prevents him from identifying too closely with the characters, thus enabling him to experience the thrills aroused by the hero's adventures and laugh at them at the same time. In *Rupert of Hentzau*, however, Hope seems to take his improbable tale more seriously. The villains become more theatrically villainous, and the misfortunes of the lovers are described with an almost misanthropic intensity. While occasional flashes of mild cynicism add life to the story, it rarely captures the high spirits of its better known forbear.

Hope belongs to that age of story-tellers described by Roger Lancelyn Green in his book *Tellers of Tales* (1965), which includes Robert Louis Stevenson and Rider Haggard, Conan Doyle and A. E. W. Mason, and, while it may be argued that his total achievement falls short of that of his more illustrious tale-telling contemporaries, his name will no doubt endure, at least as long as "Ruritania" remains a word in the English language.

—John M. Munro

HUDSON, W(illiam) H(enry).   British.   Born in Quilmes, near Buenos Aires, Argentina, 4 August 1841, of American parents; emigrated to England, 1869; naturalized, 1900. Served in the Argentinian Army, 1866. Married Emily Wingrave in 1877 (died, 1921). Naturalist: collected birds for the Smithsonian Institution and the London Zoological Society, 1866–69; settled in London, 1869, where he and his wife kept a series of unsuccessful boarding houses in Bayswater; began writing in 1880; lived in Westbourne Park, London, 1886–1921. Granted Civil List pension, 1901. Bird sanctuary erected in his memory, Hyde Park, London, 1925. *Died 18 August 1922.*

PUBLICATIONS

Collections

> *Works.*   7 vols., 1951–54.
> *Birds and Green Places: A Selection,* edited by P. E. Brown and P. H. T. Hartley.   1964.

Fiction

> *The Purple Land That England Lost: Travels and Adventures in the Banda Oriental, South America.*   1885.
> *A Crystal Age.*   1887.
> *Fan: The Story of a Young Girl's Life.*   1892.
> *El Ombú.*   1902; as *South American Sketches,* 1909; as *Tales of the Pampas,* 1916.
> *Green Mansions: A Romance of the Tropical Forest.*   1904.
> *A Little Boy Lost.*   1905.
> *Dead Man's Plack, and An Old Thorn.*   1920.

Other

> *Argentine Ornithology,* with P. L. Sclater.   2 vols., 1888–89; shortened version, as *Birds of La Plata,* 2 vols., 1920.

The Naturalist in La Plata.   1892.
Birds in a Village.   1893.
Idle Days in Patagonia.   1893.
British Birds, with Frank E. Beddard.   1895.
Birds in London.   1898.
Nature in Downland.   1900.
Birds and Man.   1901.
Hampshire Days.   1903.
The Land's End: A Naturalist's Impressions in West Cornwall.   1908.
Afoot in England.   1909.
A Shepherd's Life: Impressions of the South Wiltshire Downs.   1910.
Adventures among Birds.   1913.
Far Away and Long Ago: A History of My Early Life.   1918; revised edition, 1931.
Birds in Town and Village.   1919.
The Book of a Naturalist.   1919.
A Traveller in Little Things.   1921.
A Hind in Richmond Park, edited by Morley Roberts.   1922.
Collected Works.   24 vols., 1922–23.
Rare, Vanishing, and Lost British Birds, edited by Linda Gardiner.   1923.
153 Letters, edited by Edward Garnett.   1923; as *Letters to Garnett,* 1925.
Men, Books, and Birds, edited by Morley Roberts.   1925.
Letters to R. B. Cunninghame Graham, edited by Richard Curle.   1941.
Letters on the Ornithology of Buenos Ayres, edited by David R. Bewar.   1951.
Diary Concerning His Voyage from Buenos Aires to Southampton 1874, edited by Jorge
   Cesares.   1958.

Bibliography: *Hudson: A Bibliography* by John R. Payne, 1976.

Reading List: *Hudson* by Robert Hamilton, 1946; *Hudson's Reading* by H. F. West, 1947;
From Pampas to Hedgerows and Downs: A Study of Hudson by R. E. Haymaker, 1954;
Hudson by Ruth Tomalin, 1954; *Hudson* by John T. Frederick, 1972.

*   *   *

W. H. Hudson was a prolific writer; his collected works ran to twenty-four volumes, and
did not include all his writings. But in spite of this large production Hudson's books fall into
no more than two main thematic categories, those in which he recalls the pampas of the
Argentine where he lived as a child and a young man, and those in which he records the rural
life of England seen through the eyes of a peripatetic field naturalist. There is an underlying
link between the two groups; in his wanderings through the less spoilt areas of the English
countryside Hudson – who detested urban civilisation – was seeking to recover the simplicity
and the pristine quality of life on the pampas.
   Yet the writings relating to South America remain the most interesting of Hudson's works,
perhaps because they were written out of vivid memories that haunted the years of poverty
and solitude after Hudson came to England in 1874. They include an autobiographical
volume about childhood in Argentina (*Far Away and Long Ago*) and also Hudson's works of
fiction, *The Purple Land, Green Mansions,* and *El Ombú.*
   Hudson did not think of himself as primarily a novelist; his chosen role was that of
naturalist, and he was a pioneer in agitating for the protection of species of wild birds which
he saw vanishing from the English countryside. But his few works of fiction have an artless
power that comes from their being written in the kind of clear strong prose so many of the
nineteenth-century naturalists used in the accounts of their travels.
   The Purple Land is a narrative of revolution in Uruguay, and one has only to compare it

with Conrad's *Nostromo*, which deals with a similar situation, to realize that Hudson was a simple tale-teller rather than a true novelist. The narrative is direct but without subtlety, and the book holds one's interest to the end mainly for its recreation of remembered scenes in vividly descriptive passages. There is the same kind of authenticity about the sketches of gaucho life collected in *El Ombú*; they are too simple to be classed as short stories, and yet they give the kind of vivid sense a good travel book might present of the cruelty and deprivation – and also the enviable freedom – of the gaucho life. Hudson's most ambitious and most imaginative work of fiction is *Green Mansions*, a romance about the jungles of Venezuela, to which Hudson had never been; in the character of the bird-girl Rima, a fairy-tale figure, it clearly projects Hudson's sense of the need to achieve some kind of harmony between man and the natural world. It is through its evocation of the feel and texture of the natural world that *Green Mansions* still appeals; Hudson did not have the inventive power to make its central fantasy convincing or to validate its pantheism.

—George Woodcock

HUGHES, Thomas. English. Born in Uffington, Berkshire, 20 October 1822. Educated at Rugby School, 1834–42; Oriel College, Oxford, 1842–45 (played cricket for Oxford, 1842), B.A. 1845; entered Lincoln's Inn, London, 1845, migrated to the Inner Temple, and called to the Bar, 1848. Married Frances Ford in 1848; three sons and three daughters. Practised law in London from 1848: Queen's Counsel, 1869; associated with F. D. Maurice and the Christian Socialists who subsequently helped to create the co-operative movement: contributed to the *Christian Socialist* and *Tracts on Christian Socialism* and acted as Editor of the *Journal of Association*; Chairman of the first Co-operative Congress, 1869; helped to pass the Industrial and Provident Societies Act, 1893; involved in the founding of the Working Men's College, Great Ormond Street, London, 1854, and served as its Principal, 1872–83; Liberal Member of Parliament for Lambeth, 1865–68, and Frome, 1868–74; Founder Member of the Church Reform Union, 1870; established model community in Tennessee which proved unsuccessful, 1879; County Court Judge in Chester, 1882 until his death. *Died 22 March 1896.*

PUBLICATIONS

Fiction

> *Tom Brown's School Days, by an Old Boy.* 1857; edited by Charles Swain Thomas, 1920.
> *The Scouring of the White Horse; or, The Long Vacation Ramble of a London Clerk.* 1859.
> *Tom Brown at Oxford.* 1861.

Other

> *History of the Working Tailors' Association.* 1850.

Account of the Lock-Out of Engineers 1851–52. 1860.
Tracts for Priests and People. 1861.
The Cause of Freedom: Which Is Its Champion in America, The North or the South? 1863.
A Layman's Faith. 1868.
Alfred the Great. 3 vols., 1869.
Memoirs of a Brother. 1873.
The Old Church: What Shall We Do with It? 1878.
The Manliness of Christ. 1879.
True Manliness (selections), edited by E. E. Brown. 1880.
Rugby, Tennessee, Being Some Account of the Settlement Founded on the Cumberland Plateau by the Board of Aid to Land Ownership. 1881.
Memoir of Daniel Macmillan. 1882.
Life and Times of Peter Cooper. 1886.
James Fraser, Second Bishop of Manchester: A Memoir 1818–85. 1887.
David Livingstone. 1889.
Vacation Rambles. 1895.
Early Memories of Childhood. 1899.

Editor, *The Biglow Papers,* by James Russell Lowell. 1859.
Editor, *The Trades' Unions of England,* by Louis Philip d'Orleans. 1869.
Editor, *The Friendship of Books,* by F. D. Maurice. 1874.
Editor, with E. V. Neale, *A Manual for Co-Operators.* 1881.
Editor, *G.T.T.: Gone to Texas: Letters from Our Boys.* 1884.

Bibliography: *Charles Kingsley and Hughes: First Editions in the Library at Dormy House* by M. L. Parrish and B. K. Mann, 1936.

Reading List: *Hughes and His American Rugby* by M. B. Harmer, 1928; *Hughes: The Life of the Author of Tom Brown's School Days* by E. C. Mack and W. H. G. Armytage, 1953.

*   *   *

As a novelist Thomas Hughes is remembered for a single book. *Tom Brown's School Days* is an admirable work, written with fire and enthusiasm, presenting the reaction of an ordinary boy imbued with "animal life in its fullest measure, good nature and honest impulses, hatred of injustice and meanness, and thoughtlessness in its fullest measure," to the regime of Thomas Arnold, headmaster and reformer of Rugby, whose principles and ideals he barely understands, though he reverences him to the point of worship. From *Tom Brown* all later schoolboy literature sprang, though through the decades the Arnold ideal of Christian manliness became more and more distorted until it denoted just pluck and team-spirit – the aspects of schoolboy life that Dr. Arnold found so particularly distasteful and dangerous.

Tom Brown at Oxford never achieved such popularity. The *Saturday Review* called it a failure which gets "more dull, purposeless and depressing as it proceeds." We can read it now as a minor piece of social history, showing us university life in the 1840's, where the gentlemen commoners in their silk gowns and velvet caps dine aloof at High Table, where unpopular tutors are screwed into their rooms, and boisterous undergraduates play quoits with the college silver. It was the background presence of Dr. Arnold that had been the *raison d'être* of the *School Days*. There is no such figure to provide a solution to the problems that Tom Brown meets at Oxford. He finds it unsatisfying, a place where young men are tossed and left unsupervised and unoccupied to sow their wild oats, where the tradition of learning has largely departed leaving a vacuum for ordinary people such as himself who are not natural scholars, who feel distaste for the raffish dissipation of the idle rich, and who are not attracted to the High Church movement. Sport and mild Christian Socialism help to pass the time, but for Tom, as for the reader, the university year plods along wearily. Town and gown riots, fishing trips, boat races, and the lack-lustre romantic episodes are no substitute for the evocation of boyhood in the *School Days*; the warm friendships, the passionate hatreds, the hero-worship, and the Oxford personalities are pale shadows beside Harry East, Flashman, young Arthur.

The Scouring of the White Horse is even less successful – a sentimental lauding of the glories of the English countryside, where the manly, bluff, kindly squires work and play side by side with their loyal and devoted cottagers. Much of this is, in fact, an expansion of the earlier chapters of the *School Days*, which the far more powerful Rugby scenes tempt us to overlook.

—Gillian Avery

INCHBALD, Elizabeth (née Simpson).   English.   Born in Stanningfield, near Bury St. Edmunds, Suffolk, 15 October 1753. Married the actor and painter Joseph Inchbald in 1772 (died, 1779). Settled in London, 1772; debut as an actress, playing opposite her husband, Bristol, 1772; subsequently appeared in various Scottish towns, 1772–76, various English towns, 1776–78, and under Tate Wilkinson in Yorkshire, 1778–80; appeared on the London stage, 1780 until her retirement, 1789. *Died 1 August 1821.*

PUBLICATIONS

Fiction

> *A Simple Story.*   1791; edited by J. M. S. Tompkins, 1967.
> *Nature and Art.*   1796; edited by W. B. Scott, 1886.

Plays

> *A Mogul Tale; or, The Descent of the Balloon* (produced 1784).   1788.
> *I'll Tell You What* (produced 1785).   1786.
> *Appearance Is Against Them* (produced 1785).   1785.
> *The Widow's Vow,* from a play by Patrat (produced 1786).   1786.
> *Such Things Are* (produced 1787).   1788.
> *The Midnight Hour; or, War of Wits,* from a play by Dumaniant (produced 1787).   1787.
> *All on a Summer's Day* (produced 1787).
> *Animal Magnetism* (produced 1788).   1788(?).
> *The Child of Nature,* from a play by Mme. de Genlis (produced 1788).   1788.
> *The Married Man,* from a play by Philippe Néricault-Destouches (produced 1789).   1789.

The Hue and Cry, from a play by Dumaniant (produced 1791).
Next Door Neighbours, from plays by L. S. Mercier and Philippe Néricault-Destouches (produced 1791). 1791.
Young Men and Old Women, from a play by Gresset (produced 1792).
Every One Has His Fault (produced 1793). 1792; edited by Allardyce Nicoll in *Lesser English Comedies of the Eighteenth Century,* 1931.
The Wedding Day (produced 1794). 1794.
Wives as They Were and Maids as They Are (produced 1797). 1797.
Lovers' Vows, from a play by Kotzebue (produced 1798). 1798.
The Wise Men of the East, from a play by Kotzebue (produced 1799). 1799.
To Marry, or Not to Marry (produced 1805). 1805.
The Massacre and *A Case of Conscience,* in *Memoirs of Mrs. Inchbald* by James Boaden. 2 vols., 1833.

Other

Editor, *The British Theatre; or, A Collection of Plays with Biographical and Critical Remarks.* 25 vols., 1808.
Editor, *A Collection of Farces and Other Afterpieces.* 7 vols., 1809.
Editor, *The Modern Theatre.* 10 vols., 1809.

Bibliography: "An Inchbald Bibliography" by George L. Joughlin, in *Studies in English,* 1934.

Reading List: *Memoirs of Mrs. Inchbald* by James Boaden, 2 vols., 1833; *Inchbald and Her Circle* by Samuel R. Littlewood, 1921; *Inchbald, Novelist* by William MacKee, 1935; *Inchbald et la Comédie "Sentimentale" Anglaise au XVIII Siècle* by Françoise Moreux, 1971.

*   *   *

"Now Mrs. Inchbald was all heart," said James Boaden, her biographer, and the statement is as true of her writings as of her life. It is not the whole truth, of course; Boaden's memoir bears ample evidence of her independent spirit, her chasteness of mind and morals, her political liberalism, her candour, and her ardent and life-long pursuit of intellectual self-improvement. These too went to shape her plays and novels. Her plays reveal a fairly constant moral interest, combined with concern for domestic virtues set against the temptations of fashionable society, and working on the conventions of sentimental comedy and the social, scientific, religious, political, and literary topics of the day. She kept well abreast of changing theatrical tastes in the last two decades of the century, but constantly strove to give her slender subjects, complicated plots, and conventional characters some serious moral content. So, as the writer of an epilogue to one of her adaptations from French put it, her version had "the merit/Of giving Gallic Froth – true BRITISH SPIRIT." Her dramas, even those taken from French or German originals (such as Kotzebue's *Lovers' Vows*), were made her own not so much by their themes or techniques as by her thorough subordination of her borrowed materials to her personal version of the moral and aesthetic values of the time. As J. Taylor put it in his prologue to her last play, *To Marry or Not to Marry,* "In all, her anxious hope was still to find,/Some useful moral for the feeling mind."
    Her novels were her real achievement, however, and to them she devoted the painstaking care of the conscious artist. These fictions carry many of the same themes and techniques as her plays, and her skill at stagecraft is everywhere apparent in dialogue and the management of scenes, but what she adds in her novels to the technical proficiency of the experienced playwright is an acutely observed sentimental realism. For in both her novels, but especially

in the first, *A Simple Story*, can be felt the pressure of autobiography, of the many hours the young woman, wife, and widow had devoted not just to study, but to reflection, and to the practice of that candour which was self-knowledge. From her knowledge of herself, combined with her varied social experience, and informed by her reading in moral writers of all kinds, came that authenticity of psychological observation which made her novels so admired by the likes of William Godwin and Maria Edgeworth. For her, as for so many of the women writers of her day, moral education, the chastening of sensibility by experience, reflection, reason, and reading, was the basic form to be sought in life. In her first novel this form is given all the symmetry, deployed through parallels and contrasts in plot, character, and incident, that could be expected from a kind, even a fictitious kind, of moral discourse. In her second novel, moral education is made more of a public issue, diffused into a satire on the institutions of society, but still shaped by the kind of antithesis represented by the novel's title, *Nature and Art*. Autobiography and moral and social issues are not separate in her novels, then, but fused successfully in fictional form. It was this achievement that won her novels admiration in her own day, and makes them still worth reading now.

—Gary Kelly

JAMES, Henry. English. Born in New York City, 15 April 1843; brother of the philosopher William James; emigrated to England; naturalized, 1915. Educated at the Richard Pulling Jenks School, New York; travelled, with his family, in Europe from an early age: studied with tutors in Geneva, London, Paris, and Boulogne, 1855–58, Geneva, 1859, and Bonn, 1860; lived with his family in Newport, Rhode Island, 1860–62; attended Harvard Law School, Cambridge, Massachusetts, 1862–65. Settled with his family in Cambridge, 1866, and wrote for the *Nation* and *Atlantic Monthly*, 1866–69; toured Europe, 1869; returned to Cambridge, 1870–72: wrote art criticism for the *Atlantic Monthly*, 1871–72; lived in Europe, 1872–74, Cambridge, 1875, and Paris, 1875–76: writer for the *New York Tribune*, Paris, 1875–76; settled in London, 1876, and lived in England for the rest of his life; settled in Rye, Sussex, 1896; travelled throughout the United States, 1904–05. L.H.D.: Harvard University, 1911; Oxford University, 1912. Order of Merit, 1916. *Died 28 February 1916.*

PUBLICATIONS

Collections

Novels and Stories, edited by Percy Lubbock.   35 vols., 1921–24.
Complete Plays, edited by Leon Edel.   1949.
Complete Tales, edited by Leon Edel.   12 vols., 1962–65.
Representative Selections, revised edition, edited by Lyon N. Richardson.   1966.
Letters, edited by Leon Edel.   1974–

Fiction

A Passionate Pilgrim and Other Tales.   1875.
Roderick Hudson.   1875; edited by Leon Edel, 1960.

The American. 1877; edited by James W. Tuttleton, 1978.
Watch and Ward. 1878; edited by Leon Edel, 1960.
The Europeans: A Sketch. 1878; edited by Leon Edel, with *Washington Square,* 1967.
Daisy Miller: A Study. 1879.
An International Episode. 1879.
The Madonna of the Future and Other Tales. 1879.
Confidence. 1880; edited by Herbert Ruhm, 1962.
A Bundle of Letters. 1880.
The Diary of a Man of Fifty, and A Bundle of Letters. 1880.
Washington Square. 1881; edited by Gerald Willen, 1970.
The Portrait of a Lady. 1881; edited by Robert D. Bamberg, 1975.
The Siege of London, The Pension Beaurepas, and The Point of View. 1883; revised edition, 1884.
Novels and Tales. 14 vols., 1883.
Tales of Three Cities. 1884.
The Author of Beltraffio, Pandora, Georgina's Reasons, The Path of Duty, Four Meetings. 1885.
Stories Revived. 1885.
The Bostonians. 1886; edited by Leon Edel, 1967.
The Princess Casamassima. 1886.
The Reverberator. 1888.
The Aspern Papers, Louisa Pallant, The Modern Warning. 1888.
A London Life, The Patagonia, The Liar, Mrs. Temperly. 1889.
The Tragic Muse. 1890.
The Lesson of the Master, The Marriages, The Pupil, Brooksmith, The Solution, Sir Edmund Orme. 1892.
The Real Thing and Other Tales. 1893.
The Private Life, The Wheel of Time, Lord Beaupre, The Visits, Collaboration, Owen Wingrave. 1893.
Terminations, The Death of the Lion, The Coxon Fund, The Middle Years, The Altar of the Dead. 1895.
Embarrassments, The Figure in the Carpet, Glasses, The Next Time, The Way It Came. 1896.
The Other House. 1896.
The Spoils of Poynton. 1897; edited by Leon Edel, 1967.
What Maisie Knew. 1897; edited by Douglas Jefferson, 1966.
In the Cage. 1898; edited by Morton Dauwen Zabel, 1958.
The Two Magics, The Turn of the Screw, Covering End. 1898; *The Turn of the Screw* edited by Robert Kimbrough, 1966.
The Awkward Age. 1899; edited by Leon Edel, 1967.
The Soft Side (stories). 1900.
The Sacred Fount. 1901; edited by Leon Edel, 1953.
The Wings of the Dove. 1902; edited by J. Donald Crowley and Richard A. Hocks, 1978.
The Better Sort (stories). 1903.
The Ambassadors. 1903; edited by S. P. Rosenbaum, 1966.
The Golden Bowl. 1904.
Novels and Tales (New York Edition), revised by James. 24 vols., 1907–09.
Julia Bride. 1909.
The Finer Grain. 1910.
The Outcry. 1911.
The Ivory Tower, edited by Percy Lubbock. 1917.
The Sense of the Past, edited by Percy Lubbock. 1917.
Gabrielle de Bergerac, edited by Albert Mordell. 1918.

Travelling Companions (stories).   1919.
A Landscape Painter (stories).   1919.
Master Eustace (stories).   1920.
Eight Uncollected Tales, edited by Edna Kenton.   1950.

Plays

Daisy Miller, from his own story.   1883.
The American, from his own novel (produced 1891).   1891.
Guy Domville (produced 1895).   1894.
Theatricals (includes *Tenants, Disengaged*) (produced 1909).   1894.
Theatricals: Second Series (includes *The Album, The Reprobate*) (produced 1919).   1894.
The High Bid (produced 1908).   In *Complete Plays*, 1949.
The Saloon (produced 1911).   In *Complete Plays*, 1949.
The Outcry (produced 1917).   In *Complete Plays*, 1949.

Other

Transatlantic Sketches.   1875; revised edition, as *Foreign Parts*, 1883.
French Poets and Novelists.   1878; revised edition, 1883; edited by Leon Edel, 1964.
Hawthorne.   1879; edited by William M. Sale, Jr., 1956.
Portraits of Places.   1883.
Notes on a Collection of Drawings by George du Maurier.   1884.
A Little Tour in France.   1884.
The Art of Fiction, with Walter Besant.   1885; edited by Leon Edel, in *The House of Fiction*, 1957.
Partial Portraits.   1888.
Picture and Text.   1893.
Essays in London and Elsewhere.   1893.
William Wetmore Story and His Friends.   2 vols., 1903.
The Question of Our Speech, The Lesson of Balzac: Two Lectures.   1905.
English Hours.   1905; edited by Alma Louise Lowe, 1960.
The American Scene.   1907; edited by Leon Edel, 1968.
Views and Reviews.   1908.
Italian Hours.   1909.
The Henry James Year Book, edited by Evelyn Garnaut Smalley.   1911.
A Small Boy and Others (autobiography).   1913.
Notes of a Son and Brother (autobiography).   1914.
Notes on Novelists and Some Other Notes.   1914.
Letters to an Editor.   1916.
Within the Rim and Other Essays 1914–1915.   1919.
The Middle Years (autobiography), edited by Percy Lubbock.   1917.
Letters, edited by Percy Lubbock.   2 vols., 1920.
Notes and Reviews.   1921.
A Most Unholy Trade, Being Letters on the Drama.   1923.
Three Letters to Joseph Conrad, edited by Gerard Jean-Aubry.   1926.
Letters to Walter Berry.   1928.
Letters to A. C. Benson and Auguste Monod, edited by E. F. Benson.   1930.
Theatre and Friendship: Some James Letters, edited by Elizabeth Robins.   1932.
The Art of the Novel: Critical Prefaces, edited by R. P. Blackmur.   1934.
Notebooks, edited by F. O. Matthiessen and Kenneth B. Murdock.   1947.

The Art of Fiction and Other Essays, edited by Morris Roberts. 1948.
James and Robert Louis Stevenson: A Record of Friendship and Criticism, edited by Janet Adam Smith. 1948.
The Scenic Art: Notes on Acting and the Drama 1872–1901, edited by Allan Wade. 1948.
Daumier, Caricaturist. 1954.
Selected Letters, edited by Leon Edel, 1955.
The American Essays, edited by Leon Edel. 1956.
The Future of the Novel: Essays on the Art of the Novel, edited by Leon Edel. 1956; as *The House of Fiction*, 1957.
The Painter's Eye: Notes and Essays on the Pictorial Arts, edited by John L. Sweeney. 1956.
Parisian Sketches: Letters to the New York Tribune 1875–1876, edited by Leon Edel and Ilse Dusoir Lind. 1957.
Literary Reviews and Essays on American, English, and French Literature, edited by Albert Mordell. 1957.
James and H. G. Wells: A Record of Their Friendship, Their Debate on the Art of Fiction, and Their Quarrel, edited by Leon Edel and Gordon N. Ray. 1958.
French Writers and American Women: Essays, edited by Peter Buitenhuis. 1960.
James and John Hay: The Record of a Friendship, edited by George Monteiro. 1965.
Switzerland in the Life and Work of James: The Clare Benedict Collection of Letters from James, edited by Jörg Hasler. 1966.

Translator, *Port Tarascon*, by Alphonse Daudet. 1891.

Bibliography: *A Bibliography of James* by Leon Edel and D. H. Laurence, 1957; revised edition, 1961; in *Bibliography of American Literature* by Jacob Blanck, 1968.

Reading List: *James: The Major Phase* by F. O. Matthiessen, 1944; *James* (biography) by Leon Edel, 5 vols., 1953–72, revised edition, 2 vols., 1978; *The American James* by Quentin Anderson, 1957; *The Comic Sense of James* by Richard Poirier, 1960; *The Novels of James* by Oscar Cargill, 1961; *The Ordeal of Consciousness in James* by Dorothea Crook, 1962; *The Expanse of Vision: Essays on the Craft of James* by Lawrence B. Holland, 1964; *The Imagination of Loving: James's Legacy to the Novel* by Naomi Lebowitz, 1965; *James: A Reader's Guide* by S. Gorley Putt, 1966; *James: The Critical Heritage* edited by Roger Gard, 1968; *James* by Tony Tanner, 1968; *The Negative Imagination: Form and Perspective in the Novels of James* by Sallie Sears, 1969; *Reading James* by Louis Auchincloss, 1975; *Language and Knowledge in the Late Novels of James* by Ruth Bernard Yeazell, 1976.

*   *   *

Few who accord the novels and short stories of Henry James the attention they deserve come away from the experience unmoved by the subject matter and unenlightened by the artistry, yet it is probably true that James would be little read today if it were not for the continuing enthusiasm of individuals who discover him first as a reading assignment in a college or university course. More than almost any other great novelist, James is a writer whose best works require a sympathetic power of attention that the casual reader is not disposed to give. For most people James is an acquired taste. Unless they approach him in the right spirit they never acquire the taste at all. Yet he is certainly one of the great writers in English, one of those artists of another era who nevertheless seems most perennially modern.

His dedication to literature for fifty years from the Civil War until his death in 1916 produced a body of work of monumental scope. He never married, never carried on anything resembling a conventional courtship. His friendships were virtually all rooted in shared literary or artistic enthusiasms. He travelled – often, it seems, merely to reinvigorate himself for a new assault upon his artistic problems. With less talent and similar dedication he might have produced novels and tales that consisted mainly of the same stories retold, the same techniques exploited again and again in order to recapture prior successes. Something of this tendency resides in his work, as it does in the work of all masters, but there is also an extraordinary continual development that reaches its peak in three late masterpieces: *The Wings of the Dove, The Ambassadors*, and *The Golden Bowl*. The late work of some poets can best be read largely in the light of the education gained by studying their earlier efforts: James is one of a relatively few novelists whose work cries out to be approached in a similar manner.

"It's a complex fate being an American," James once wrote, "and one of the responsibilities it entails is fighting against a superstitious valuation of Europe." Herein is expressed the essence of the "international theme" that runs through much of his work. In a time when more than a few novelists were making capital out of the social complications that arise when individuals from one side of the Atlantic confront the natives of the other side upon their home ground, James made this subject peculiarly his own by returning to it in work after work. So doing, he lifted it outside the confines of drawing room comedy and placed it squarely at the crossroads of the two great traditions of the nineteenth-century novel in English. Among the best of James's international novels and tales are *The American, The Europeans, Daisy Miller, The Portrait of a Lady, The Wings of the Dove, The Ambassadors*, and *The Golden Bowl*. In these works the central concerns of previous novelists in English come together in a confrontation almost mythic in its implications. Simply expressed, the central concern of English novelists from Austen through Scott, Dickens, and Eliot was the accommodation of individual aspirations within the sheltering embrace of the social framework; both their social view and their art were shaped by a realistic vision of compromise. Just as simply expressed, the central concern of American novelists from Cooper through Hawthorne, Melville, and Twain, was with those individual aspirations that are incapable of accommodation within any social framework except the as-yet-unrealized American dream of perfect freedom, equality, and justice; their social view and their art were shaped by a vision that looked toward a world considerably more ideal than the world they lived in. James brought these visions together in an amalgamation inherently tragic. His best works express in metaphor how much the condition of modern man hangs continually in the balance between the European dream of social accommodation and the American dream of perfect freedom.

Closely related to the international theme is James's continual emphasis upon partial perspectives. Human knowledge, he insists, and consequently human action, is sharply limited by inescapable conditions of time and place. From Christopher Newman to Lambert Strether his Americans achieve their destiny because the perspectives forced upon them by birth and education allow them no choices except the ones they inevitably make. From Madame de Cintré to Madame de Vionnet his Europeans are similarly limited. This at least is the theory: the novel is realistic, as James most often intended it should be, when the fates of the characters follow inevitably from the conditions that surround them; it is romantic, as James sometimes allowed, when the fates evolve from conditions imposed by the author that are quite distinct from the facts of observable reality. The realistic effect that he intended for most of his novels derives from the success with which he developed techniques for objectifying the partial perspectives from which humans direct their lives.

An important part of his work is also the theme of awareness that comes too late. His people are concerned above all with the question of how to live, but most of them have not any clear idea of how to begin. Sometimes they are wealthy, like Christopher Newman in *The American*, Milly Theale in *The Wings of the Dove*, and Maggie Verver in *The Golden Bowl*. Sometimes they become wealthy, like Isabel Archer in *The Portrait of a Lady*. Sometimes they live in expectation of wealth, like Kate Croy in *The Wings of the Dove*. In most instances they have at least, like Lambert Strether in *The Ambassadors*, enough to enable them to live comfortably, though it is often true of the less attractive figures that they suppose themselves in need of more than they possess. In any event they are mostly free of the more mundane cares of life and have nearly total leisure in which to pursue happiness through courtship, marriage, liaisons, social activity, travel, the search for culture: whatever, in short, seems most attractive to them. To live most fully, James makes clear in a number of places, is to be most fully aware of one's possibilities so that one may make the best of them. Since, however, the most interesting possibilities come from human relationships which are inherently a tissue of subtle complexities, to be most fully aware is to possess a depth of sympathetic insight that comes to few people until it is too late to take advantage of it. Total freedom for James's characters involves the freedom to make social commitments different from those that all too often they make, wrongly, in bondage to some mistaken understanding, or do not make at all because, sadly, they fail to perceive the opportunity that lies before them.

A great critic, James is also a great technical experimenter. The best of his criticism is preserved in individual essays such as "The Art of Fiction" and in his *Notebooks* and the prefaces that he wrote for the New York edition of his works. All are read most profitably in conjunction with the example of his fiction. His technical experiments are most readily approached through those many fictions in which he enforces the theme of partial perspectives by contriving severely limited perspectives from which to narrate. Some of the easier works in which this theme and this method are important are the early *Daisy Miller* and the late "The Beast in the Jungle." Because Daisy is never seen except from the partial view that Winterbourne enjoys, the reader remains in danger of sharing Winterbourne's misunderstanding of her character. Because May Bartram, in "The Beast in the Jungle," is never seen except in a view accessible to Marcher, the same potential problem exists. Fundamentally simple in these works, both theme and technique become more complex in "The Aspern Papers," *The Turn of the Screw*, and *The Sacred Fount*. In all three the careful reader is aware that there may be some aspect of the truth that remains dark to the central character. In "The Aspern Papers" most readers believe they can see beyond the limited vision of the narrator; in *The Turn of the Screw* there are good reasons to suppose both that the ghosts do and do not exist; in *The Sacred Fount* the puzzle that begins the novel becomes not less but more of a puzzle as it ends. In *The Portrait of a Lady*, *The Wings of the Dove*, *The Ambassadors*, and *The Golden Bowl* the theme of partial perspectives (which involves often the theme of too late awareness) merges with the international theme to provide the substance of James's most lasting achievement.

Many of James's fictions conclude upon a sense of loss. In his deepest vision human life is fundamentally tragic because of the eternal tension between the individual's sense of his vast human opportunities and his frequently inadequate awareness of his personal limitations. Like Isabel Archer or Lambert Strether, twentieth-century readers, too, are possessed by dreams of boundless freedom. Like both, they make in the end the choices that they *can* make – which are often not at all the choices that they would make if they lived in a world in which a just and equal perfect freedom came less insistently into conflict with the requirements of social accommodation.

—George Perkins

JEFFERIES, Richard. English. Born at Coate Farm, near Swindon, Wiltshire, 6 November 1848. Educated at schools in Sydenham, Kent, and Swindon, to age 15. Married in 1874. Travelled in France, 1865, attempted unsuccessfully to travel to America, then returned to Swindon; wrote for the *North Wilts Herald*, 1866–70: became its regular reporter and local correspondent for a Gloucestershire paper; travelled in Belgium, 1870; returned to England and worked as a free-lance writer; settled in London, 1876, and wrote for the *Pall Mall Gazette;* in later life settled in Sussex. *Died 14 August 1887.*

PUBLICATIONS

Collections

> *Works,* edited by C. Henry Warren.   6 vols., 1948–49.
> *The Essential Jefferies,* edited by M. Elwin.   1948.

Fiction

> *The Scarlet Shawl.*   1874.
> *Restless Human Hearts.*   1875.
> *World's End.*   1877.
> *Wood Magic: A Fable.*   1880.
> *Greene-Ferne Farm.*   1880.
> *Bevis: The Story of a Boy.*   1882.
> *The Dewy Morn.*   1884.
> *After London; or, Wild England.*   1885.
> *Amaryllis at the Fair.*   1887.
> *The Early Fiction,* edited by G. Toplis.   1896.
> *T.T.T.*   1896.

Other

> *Reporting, Editing, and Authorship.*   1873.
> *Jack Brass, Emperor of England.*   1873.
> *A Memoir of the Goddards of North Wilts.*   1873.
> *Suez-cide! or, How Miss Britannia Bought a Dirty Puddle and Lost Her Sugarplums.*   1876.
> *The Gamekeeper at Home: Sketches of Natural History and Rural Life.*   1878.
> *Wild Life in a Southern County.*   1879.
> *The Amateur Poacher.*   1879.
> *Hodge and His Masters.*   2 vols., 1880; edited by Henry Williamson, 1937.
> *Round about a Great Estate.*   1880.
> *Nature near London.*   1883.
> *The Story of My Heart: My Autobiography.*   1883; edited by Samuel J. Looker, 1947.
> *The Life of the Fields.*   1884.
> *Red Deer.*   1884.
> *The Open Air.*   1885.
> *Field and Hedgegrow, Being the Last Essays,* edited by J. Jefferies.   1889.
> *The Toilers of the Field.*   1892.
> *Jefferies' Land: A History of Swindon and Its Environs,* edited by G. Toplis.   1896.
> *Nature and Eternity and Other Uncollected Papers.*   1907.
> *The Nature Diaries and Notebooks,* edited by Samuel J. Looker.   1941.
> *Beauty Is Immortal, Felise of "The Dewy Morn," with Some Hitherto Uncollected Essays and Manuscripts,* edited by Samuel J. Looker.   1948.

The Old House at Coate, and Hitherto Unpublished Essays, edited by Samuel J. Looker. 1948.

Reading List: *Jefferies: His Life and Work* by Edward Thomas, 1909; *Jefferies: A Tribute* edited by Samuel J. Looker, 1946; *Jefferies, Man of the Fields: A Biography and Letters* by Samuel J. Looker and Crichton Porteous, 1965; *Jefferies: A Critical Study* by W. J. Keith, 1966.

*   *   *

Richard Jefferies's earliest society novels are ill-conceived, whereas *Greene-Ferne Farm* and *The Dewy Morn* have been appreciated for their natural freshness. His last novel, *Amaryllis at the Fair*, is clearly the strongest, drawing on his family background and developed with naturalistic techniques "absolutely true to nature and fact." Characters come alive when Jefferies probes the rooted tensions within the family. Outstanding sketches appear of Farmer Iden's nervous wife, his ninety-year-old father, and Iden himself (a genius bent on failure) in his rituals of potato planting, dining, and napping after dinner, when he pretends to sleep while mice climb his knee for crumbs. As story, however, the novel is continually fragmented by digressions. Toward the close the plot breaks loose and then breaks off, and we sense the underlying frustrations of the dying author.

Jefferies's excellence is to be found in his essays on nature and rural life, most of these following one of three prevalent tendencies. Some of the earliest, such as appeared in *The Amateur Poacher*, are personal essays, enabling the reader to live over boyhood experiences with the author. Very similar are numerous familiar essays, descriptive encounters with people and landscapes, birds, animals, wild flowers, and golden wheat under a burning sun. Finally, social essays range from the early conservative letters to the *Times* on the Wiltshire labourer to the more radical views of "Rural Dynamite" or "One of the New Voters." Rural characters include farmers and gamekeepers, gipsies and poachers, and always the figures of Hodge and his field-faring women, on whose backs the burden of agricultural life rested. Jefferies the journalist strove for facts, and, as facts accumulated, his voice rose, "pleading for more humane treatment of the poor." With his sympathies grew his commitment to naturalism, culminating in "A True Tale of the Wiltshire Labourer." Yet he will best be remembered for familiar essays with their many descriptions of rural life executed in a transparent style.

The Story of My Heart is a unique contribution of the nature essayist. Plotless, lacking autobiographical facts, it searches out the spirit of life and conceives a realm of idea beyond the circle of the known. Many contributing thoughts are hardly original. Like Carlyle, Jefferies finds miracle in natural phenomena, casts off time and takes "now" for eternity, and focuses upon what Carlyle had considered the essential "Me." Like Mill or Hardy, he sees nature as ultra-human, lacking mind. Like Pater, he condemns asceticism and aims to enjoy all that is possible in life. What is original is perhaps Jefferies's uniting of nature and spirit, flesh and "soul life," not as philosophy but personal experience. The pantheist discovers that the mystery lies not in nature but in himself, and his spirit is darkened by the insights and aches of modernism. Still Jefferies looks beyond his problem: "full well aware that all has failed, ... there lives on in me an unquenchable belief, thought burning like the sun, that there is yet something to be found."

—William J. Hyde

JEROME, Jerome K(lapka).   English.   Born in Walsall, Staffordshire, 2 May 1858; grew up in London. Educated at Marylebone Grammar School, London. Served as an ambulance driver on the Western front during World War I. Married Georgina Henrietta Stanley in 1888; one daughter. Left school at 14 and worked, successively, as a railway clerk, schoolmaster, actor, and journalist; writer from 1885; Co-Founder and Editor, with Robert Barr and George Brown Burgin, *The Idler* magazine, London, 1892–97; Founding Editor, *To-Day* weekly newspaper, London, 1893–97. *Died 14 June 1927.*

PUBLICATIONS

Fiction

Three Men in a Boat (To Say Nothing of the Dog).   1889.
Told after Supper.   1891.
John Ingerfield and Other Stories.   1894.
Sketches in Lavender, Blue, and Green.   1897.
Three Men on the Bummel.   1900.
The Observations of Henry.   1901.
Paul Kelver.   1902.
American Wives and Others.   1904.
Tommy and Co.   1904.
The Passing of the Third Floor Back and Other Stories.   1907.
The Angel and the Author and Others.   1908.
Malvina of Brittany.   1916.
Anthony John: A Biography.   1923.

Plays

Barbara (produced 1886).   1886.
Sunset (produced 1888).   1888.
Fennel, from a play by François Coppée (produced 1888).   1888.
Woodbarrow Farm (produced 1888).   1921.
Pity Is Akin to Love (produced 1888).
New Lamps for Old (produced 1890).
Ruth, with A. Addison Bright (produced 1890).
What Women Will Do (produced 1890).
Birth and Breeding (produced 1890).   1895.
The Prude's Progress, with Eden Phillpotts (produced 1895).   1895.
The Rise of Dick Halward (produced 1895).
Biarritz, with Adrian Ross, music by F. O. Carr (produced 1896).
The MacHaggis, with Eden Phillpotts (produced 1897).
Miss Hobbs (produced 1899).   1902.
Tommy (produced 1906).
The Passing of the Third Floor Back, from his own story (produced 1908).   1910.
Fanny and the Servant Problem (produced 1908).   1909.
The Master of Mrs. Chilvers (produced 1911).   1911.
Esther Castways (produced 1913).
Robina in Search of a Husband (produced 1913).   1914.
The Great Gamble (produced 1914).
The Three Patriots (produced 1915).

The Celebrity (as *Cook*, produced 1917; as *The Celebrity*, produced 1928).   1926.
The Soul of Nicholas Snyders (produced 1927).   1927.

Other

The Idle Thoughts of an Idle Fellow: A Book for an Idle Holiday.   1886.
On Stage and Off: The Brief Career of a Would-Be Actor.   1888.
Stage-Land: Curious Habits and Customs of Its Inhabitants.   1889.
Diary of a Pilgrimage, and Six Essays.   1891.
Novel Notes.   1893.
The Second Thoughts of an Idle Fellow.   1898.
Tea-Table Talk.   1903.
Idle Ideas in 1905.   1905.
They and I.   1909.
All Roads Lead to Calvary.   1919.
A Miscellany of Sense and Nonsense.   1923.
My Life and Times.   1926.

Reading List: *Jerome: His Life and Works* by A. Moss, 1929; *Jerome* by W. Gutkess, 1930.

*   *   *

Jerome K. Jerome always believed that a literary gentleman whom he met in an East London park as a boy, and who refused to give his name, was Charles Dickens. He told the gentleman that what he liked in the novels of Dickens was the humour, and that his favourite character was Mr. Pickwick; and the gentleman said, "Oh, damn Mr. Pickwick.... I like him well enough – or used to. I'm a bit tired of him, that's all."

There would have been justice in this: for Jerome later accepted reluctantly that his own fame was based on his humour, and indeed on a book which is one of the worthiest successors of *The Pickwick Papers* – *Three Men in a Boat (To Say Nothing of the Dog)*. Its sequels – *Three Men on the Bummel* and *Diary of a Pilgrimage* – and his humorous journalistic essays *The Idle Thoughts of an Idle Fellow* remain enjoyable. His play *The Passing of the Third Floor Back* (about the redemption of the shabby and dubious inhabitants of a London lodging house by a man who offers them a sense of their better selves, and whom audiences think of as Christ, though Jerome preferred a vaguer identification), though sentimental, is still heard of. And *Paul Kelver*, his *David Copperfield*, an autobiographical picaresque novel set in East End, lodging house, and Bohemian London, is excellent reading, and most unjustly neglected.

But *Three Men in a Boat* is unique. Partly, as Jerome himself says, this is because of its "hopeless and incurable veracity." In fact, much of it is a record of holidays taken by Jerome with Carl Hentschel (Harris) and George Wingrave, though Montmorency the dog is imaginary; and few people can have gone on a boating, or indeed walking or camping, holiday, without something reminding them of the book. But the process whereby particular facts become universal and delightful truth is no less strange here than in any other literature. The style is important: Jerome has Chaucer's china-blue eye, a gift for portraying the principal narrator – himself – as both devastatingly naive and annihilatingly observant. The sentiment which surprises one in odd detachable passages, though rather feeble, seems to express some quite deep level of the book: perhaps the concluding reflection of Paul Kelver that "this fortress of laughter that a few of you have been set aside to guard" may, trivial as it seems, be the key to the battle against suffering. Moreover, the most obvious difference of *Three Men in a Boat* from Jerome's other anecdotal comedies is that the river journey does duty in it for a plot. Perhaps as Arthur Machen observed of *The Pickwick Papers* that its magic comes from its sharing the essential ecstasy, the withdrawal from life, of the *Odyssey* or the myth of Dionysus, so even in the less daemonic *Three Men in a Boat* the symbolic quality of the river journey may echo. Certainly no book conveys better the bursting happiness of a summer holiday: and isn't that ecstasy?

—Stephen Medcalf

JOHNSON, Samuel. English. Born in Lichfield, Staffordshire, 18 September 1709. Educated at Lichfield Grammar School, and at the Stourbridge School, to age 16; Pembroke College, Oxford, 1728–29, left without taking a degree. Married Elizabeth Porter in 1735 (died, 1752). Usher in a grammar school in Market Bosworth, Leicestershire; worked for the publisher of the *Birmingham Journal*, 1732; took pupils at Edial, Staffordshire, among them David Garrick, 1736–37; travelled with Garrick to London, and settled there, 1737; supported himself by writing for Cave's *Gentleman's Magazine*, 1734–44, for which he wrote reports on debates in Parliament, 1740–44; catalogued the library of the second Earl of Oxford, 1742; worked on his *Dictionary*, 1747–55; formed the Ivy Lane Club, 1749; Author/Editor, *The Rambler*, 1750–52; contributed to *The Adventurer*, 1753–54; arrested for debt, but released on a loan from Samuel Richardson, 1756; contributed to the *Literary Magazine*, 1756–58; wrote "The Idler" for the *Universal Chronicle*, 1758–60; moved to Inner Temple Lane, now Johnson's Buildings, 1759; pensioned by the crown, 1762; founded The Literary Club, 1764; wrote pamphlets against Wilkes, 1770, a defense of government policy in the Falkland Islands, 1771, and in America, 1775; toured Scotland with James Boswell, subsequently his biographer, 1773; travelled to Wales, 1774, and Paris, 1775; formed the Essex Head Club, 1783. M.A.: Oxford University, 1775; LL.D.: Trinity College, Dublin, 1765; Oxford University, 1775. *Died 13 December 1784.*

PUBLICATIONS

Collections

Works. 16 vols., 1903.
Letters, edited by R. W. Chapman. 3 vols., 1952.
Works, edited by A. T. Hazen and others. 1958–
Complete English Poems, edited by J. D. Fleeman. 1971.
Selected Poetry and Prose, edited by Frank Brady and William K. Wimsatt. 1977.

Fiction

The Prince of Abyssinia: A Tale. 1759; revised edition, 1759; as *The History of Rasselas, Prince of Abyssinia: An Asian Tale,* 1768; edited by Geoffrey Tillotson and Brian Jenkins, 1971.

Play

Irene (produced 1749). 1749; as *Mahomet and Irene* (produced 1749).

Verse

London: A Poem in Imitation of the Third Satire of Juvenal.   1738.
The Vanity of Human Wishes: The Tenth Satire of Juvenal Imitated.   1749.

Other

A Complete Vindication of the Licensers of the Stage.   1739.
The Life of Admiral Blake.   1740.
An Account of the Life of Mr. Richard Savage, Son of the Earl Rivers.   1744; edited by
Clarence Tracy, 1971.
An Account of the Life of John Philip Barretier.   1744.
Miscellaneous Observations on the Tragedy of Macbeth.   1745.
The Plan of a Dictionary of the English Language, Addressed to the Earl of
Chesterfield.   1747.
The Rambler.   8 vols., 1750–52; edited by A. B. Strauss and Walter Jackson Bate, in
Works, 1969.
The Adventurer, with others.   2 vols., 1753–54; in Works, 1963.
A Dictionary of the English Language.   2 vols., 1755; revised edition, 1773.
The Idler.   2 vols., 1761; edited by Walter Jackson Bate and J. M. Bullitt, in Works,
1963.
Preface to His Edition of Shakespeare's Plays.   1765.
The False Alarm.   1770.
Thoughts on the Late Transactions Respecting Falkland's Islands.   1771.
The Patriot, Addressed to the Electors of Great Britain.   1774.
Taxation No Tyranny: An Answer to the Resolutions and Address of the American
Congress.   1775.
A Journey to the Western Islands of Scotland.   1775; edited by D. L. Murray, 1931.
Prefaces, Biographical and Critical, to the Works of the English Poets.   10 vols.,
1779–81; as The Lives of the English Poets, 1781; revised edition, 1783; edited by G.
B. Hill, 3 vols., 1905; selection edited by J. P. Hardy, 1972.
Prayers and Meditations, edited by George Strahan.   1785; revised edition, 1785, 1796;
edited by D. and M. Hyde, in Works, 1958.
Debates in Parliament, edited by George Chalmers.   2 vols., 1787.
Letters to and from Johnson, by Hester Lynch Piozzo.   2 vols., 1788.
The Celebrated Letter to the Earl of Chesterfield, edited by James Boswell.   1790.
An Account of the Life of Johnson to His Eleventh Year, Written by Himself, edited by
Richard Wright.   1805.
A Diary of a Journey into North Wales in the Year 1774, edited by R. Duppa.   1816; in
Works, 1958.
Johnson: His Life in Letters, edited by David Littlejohn.   1965.
Literary Criticism, edited by R. D. Stock.   1974.

Editor, The Plays of Shakespeare.   8 vols., 1765.
Editor, The Works of Richard Savage, with an Account of the Author.   1775.

Translator, A Voyage to Abyssinia, by Father Jerome Lobo.   1735.
Translator, A Commentary on Pope's Principles of Morality; or, An Essay on Man, by
Crousaz.   1739.

Bibliography: A Bibliography of Johnson by W. P. Courtney and D. N. Smith, 1915;
Johnsonian Studies 1887–1950: A Survey and Bibliography by James L. Clifford, 1951,
supplement by M. Wahba, in Johnsonian Studies 1950–60, 1962.

Reading List: *Life of Johnson* by James Boswell, 1791, edited by R. W. Chapman, 1953; *Passionate Intelligence: Imagination and Reason in the Work of Johnson* by Arieh Sachs, 1967; *Johnson as Critic*, 1973, and *Johnson* (biography), 1974, both by John Wain; *The Ascent of Parnassus* by Arthur Bryant, 1975; *Johnson and Poetic Style* by William Edinger, 1977; *The Stylistic Life of Johnson* by William Vesterman, 1977; *Johnson* by Walter Jackson Bate, 1978.

*   *   *

Johnson was regarded in his own time as the dominant figure of the English literary world; his achievement covers an extraordinary range: he was scholar and critic, moralist and essayist, poet and prose stylist, all in the first degree of merit.

With his verse-tragedy *Irene* in his pocket, and David Garrick as travelling companion, Johnson came from Lichfield to London in 1737. *Irene* was not published and produced until 1749, and was no great success, but Johnson's heroic couplet satire *London*, based on Juvenal's third satire, appeared in 1738, on the same day as Pope's *Epilogue to the Satires*. *London* criticises the values of the city in general, and of Whig London in particular; here Johnson wears Pope's mantle of the conservative (and Tory) satirist. Johnson's first London years were spent partly in the company of such Grub Street inhabitants as Richard Savage; the *Account of the Life of Richard Savage* is a product of this friendship, and is an important early essay by Johnson in the art of biography.

Johnson turned again to verse satire in *The Vanity of Human Wishes*, based on Juvenal's tenth satire. This poem, Johnson's greatest, states a favourite theme: the inevitable unhappiness of human existence whatever choice in life is made. In turn Johnson considers mankind's yearnings for the various gifts of power, learning, military fame, long life, beauty, even virtue, and gives a melancholy account, with individual examples, of the misfortunes attendant upon each. This is not, however, mere pessimism. Johnson's Christian modification of Juvenal's stoic "mens sana in corpore sano" finds in religious faith a hard-fought-for consolation: "Still raise for good the supplicating voice,/But leave to heav'n the measure and the choice."

The theme of *Rasselas*, a moral tale set in Abyssinia and Egypt which has some similarities with Voltaire's *Candide*, is again the choice of life. Johnson's princely young hero escapes, with his sister and the poet Imlac, from the secluded innocence of the Happy Valley, and makes trial of various schemes of life. One after another the delusions and inconveniences of the pastoral life and the hermit's life, the life of the stoic and the life "according to nature," the family life and the scholar's life, are exposed. Life is found to be "every where a state in which much is to be endured, and little to be enjoyed"; the moral enforced is that no choice can be happy, but a choice must be made. Johnson may perhaps be seen returning to this theme with greater hope in his moving brief elegy "On the Death of Dr. Robert Levet" (1783), whose central message is that man finds fulfilment in the steady daily application of his particular talent: "The modest wants of ev'ry day/The toil of ev'ry day supplied."

It was with the 208 issues of *The Rambler* (1750–52), periodical essays on the pattern established earlier in the century by *The Spectator* and *The Tatler*, though more serious in tone and content, that Johnson became a major literary figure in contemporary estimation. In *The Rambler*, explicitly, it was Johnson's intention "to inculcate wisdom or piety," to teach both a reasonable and a religious attitude to life, dealing with topics as fundamental to human experience as youth and old age, marriage and death, grief and sorrow. In a small number of the *Rambler* essays Johnson is a literary critic, considering notably the topics of the novel (issue 4), biography (60), prejudice and the rules in criticism (93, 156, 158), and tragedy and comedy (125). Johnson's essays in *The Adventurer* and *The Idler* are in a rather lighter vein.

In the periodical essays and *Rasselas* may already be found the characteristic Johnsonian prose style, legislative and authoritative, often imitated, though far more flexible and exact than facile imitation would suggest. Careful judgements of life are crystallised in a precisely chosen diction, and ideas are given their relations by the balanced rhythms of clause echoing clause within the sentence. To this Johnson's weighty and pointed heroic couplets in *The Vanity of Human Wishes* and *London* are a poetic equivalent.

The reputation begun by *The Rambler* was established, in a different field, by the *Dictionary*, a triumph of individual scholarship and labour. Johnson as a lexicographer is distinguished by his accurate definitions of the meanings of words, and by his use of the historical principle. Words are illustrated by passages chosen not only for their semantic aptness, but also for their literary and moral qualities. The choice of passages reveals the enormous range of Johnson's reading, and, strikingly, his admiration for and knowledge of Elizabethan literature. The *Dictionary* is more descriptive than prescriptive; though he acknowledged that "there is in constancy and stability a general and lasting advantage," Johnson was too realistic to believe (with Swift, for example), that it is possible to fix and enforce linguistic usage.

Johnson's next major project was his edition of Shakespeare, remarkable for a commentary which shows Johnson's response to have been not only informed but also sometimes intensely personal, and for the theoretically and historically important preface. In the preface Johnson judges Shakespeare in a partly conservative light, approving of his "just representations of general nature" (a neo-classical position Johnson had already enunciated in the tenth chapter of *Rasselas*), and disapproving of his failure to provide a consistent and complete moral vision. Johnson shows a robust open-mindedness in defending Shakespeare against accusations that he mixes dramatic kinds and fails to observe the unities. Shakespeare's plays "are not in the rigorous and critical sense either tragedies or comedies" because they depict the mingled conditions of real life. The unities of time and place need not be observed because "the spectators are always in their senses and know ... that the stage is only a stage, and that the players are only players." Johnson rejects arbitrary prescription, steadily insisting that the primary aim of literature is a moral one, to be secured through delighting the reader: "there is always an appeal open from criticism to nature. The end of writing is to instruct; the end of poetry is to instruct by pleasing."

Johnson's literary output decreased in the late 1760's and 1770's. This is the period of gladiatorial conversation and literary dictatorship portrayed by James Boswell, whom Johnson had met in 1763. Johnson's main arena was the Club, founded at Joshua Reynolds's suggestion in 1764 and including, at its inception or in later years, many of the most eminent literary men of the time, among them Goldsmith and Garrick, Boswell and Burke, Edward Gibbon and Adam Smith.

To these years belong Johnson's most significant political writings, eloquent expressions of a personally consistent and conscientious conservatism. In *The False Alarm* Johnson defends Parliament's refusal to seat the radical John Wilkes. In *Taxation No Tyranny* he asserts the right of the British government to impose taxes upon the American colonists.

The *Journey to the Western Islands of Scotland* is a record of the tour, dangerous and adventurous for so old a man, that Johnson undertook with Boswell in 1773. If Johnson's account lacks the anecdotal vividness of Boswell's, there is here nonetheless the accustomed Johnsonian nobility of general moral reflection, in a social and physical landscape new to his experience.

Perhaps Johnson's greatest literary achievement came towards the end of his life, when he was commissioned by a group of London booksellers to provide a set of introductory essays for a collection of the works of the English poets. Each of the *Lives* consists of a detailed biography and brief character sketch, and a critical account of the poet. These critical passages are the fruition of a lifetime's reading and hard thought, providing a judicial assessment of the English poetic tradition against the twin standards of delight and truth to nature. Not surprisingly, Johnson's "great tradition" (though he has a wide range of interest and liking) is the line of satirical and ethical heroic couplet verse originating with Denham and Waller and perfected by Dryden and Pope, clear in expression and moral in intent. His aversion is poetry, whether by John Donne or Thomas Gray, which in his opinion fails to promote truth or express its meanings perspicuously. Though Johnson admired Milton's verse, and especially *Paradise Lost*, even so great a poem as *Lycidas* is attacked for what

Johnson considered its harsh and unpleasing diction and metre, and its submergence of true feeling in an artificial pastoral allegory. Though the modern critical consensus does not accept all of Johnson's valuations, his criticism has the crucial virtues of exact and generally sympathetic understanding of what he reads, and the constant application of a systematic literary judgement. Johnson may seem to us sometimes too unwilling to compromise with historical relativism, or apparently insensitive to such of our favourite literary values as irony, ambiguity, imagination, and metaphor; yet his criticism is the work of a great and superbly stocked mind, always identifying the major questions, and the modern who takes issue with him needs to be armed with reasons.

—Marcus Walsh

KINGSLEY, Charles.   English.   Born in Holne, Devonshire, 12 June 1819; brother of the writer Henry Kingsley. Educated in preparatory school in Clifton, Bristol, 1831–33; Helston Grammar School, Cornwall, 1833–35; King's College School, London, 1835–38; Magdalene College, Cambridge, 1838–42, B.A. (honours) in classics 1842, M.A. 1860. Married Fanny Grenfell in 1844; two daughters and two sons. Took holy orders: Curate, 1842–44, and Rector, 1844 until his death, Eversley, Hampshire; Lecturer at Queen's College, London, 1848; Regius Professor of Modern History, Cambridge University, 1860–69; History Tutor to the Prince of Wales, 1861; toured the West Indies, 1869–70; Canon of Chester Cathedral, 1869–73; made a lecture tour of the United States, 1873–74; Canon of Westminster Abbey, London, and Chaplain to the Queen, 1873–75. *Died 23 January 1875.*

PUBLICATIONS

Collections

Works.   28 vols., 1880–85.

Fiction

Alton Locke, Tailor and Poet: An Autobiography.   1850.
Yeast: A Problem.   1851.
Hypatia; or, New Foes with an Old Face.   1853.
Westward Ho! or, The Voyages and Adventures of Sir Amyas Leigh.   1855; edited by M. W. and G. Thomas, 1957.
Two Years Ago.   1857.
The Water-Babies: A Fairy Tale for a Land-Baby.   1863; edited by Robert Harding, with *The Heroes,* 1947.
Hereward the Wake, "Last of the English."   1866; edited by Herbert Van Thal, 1967.
The Tutor's Story, completed by Mary St. Leger Harrison.   1916.

Play

The Saint's Tragedy. 1848.

Verse

Andromeda and Other Poems. 1858.
Poems: Collected Edition. 1872; revised edition, 1878, 1880, 1884.

Other

Twenty-Five Village Sermons. 1849; revised edition, as *Town and Country Sermons,* 1861.
Cheap Clothes and Nasty. 1850.
Phaethon; or, Loose Thoughts for Loose Thinkers. 1852.
Sermons on National Subjects. 2 vols., 1852–54; revised edition, as *The King of the Earth and Other Sermons,* 1872.
Alexandria and Her Schools. 1854.
Who Causes Pestilence? 1854.
Glaucus; or, The Wonders of the Shore. 1855; revised edition, 1856, 1858.
Sermons for the Times. 1855.
Sermons for Sailors. 1855; as *Sea Sermons,* 1885.
The Heroes; or, Greek Fairy Tales for My Children, illustrated by the author. 1855; edited by M. W. and G. Thomas, 1961.
Miscellanies. 2 vols., 1859.
The Good News of God: Sermons. 1859.
The Gospel of the Pentateuch: A Set of Parish Sermons. 1863.
Hints to Stammerers, by a Minute Philosopher. 1864.
The Roman and the Teuton (lectures). 1864.
Mr. Kingsley and Dr. Newman: A Correspondence on the Question Whether Dr. Newman Teaches That Truth Is No Virtue. 1864.
David: Four Sermons. 1865; revised edition, 1874.
Three Lectures. 1867.
The Water of Life and Other Sermons. 1867.
Discipline and Other Sermons. 1868.
The Hermits. 3 vols., 1868.
Madam How and Lady Why; or, First Lessons in Earth-Lore for Children. 1870.
At Last: A Christmas in the West Indies. 2 vols., 1871.
Town Geology. 1872.
Plays and Puritans, and Other Historical Essays. 1873.
Prose Idylls New and Old. 1873.
Westminster Sermons. 1874.
Health and Education. 1874.
Lectures Delivered in America in 1874. 1875.
Letters to Young Men on Betting and Gambling. 1877.
True Words for Brave Men. 1878.
All Saints' Day and Other Sermons, edited by W. Harrison. 1878.
From Death to Life: Fragments of Teaching to a Village Congregation with Letters on the Life after Death, edited by Frances E. Kingsley. 1887.
Words of Advice to Schoolboys, edited by E. F. Johns. 1912.
American Notes: Letters from a Lecture Tour in 1874, edited by R. B. Martin. 1958.

Editor, *South by West; or, Winter in the Rocky Mountains and Spring in Mexico.* 1874.

Bibliography: *Kingsley and Thomas Hughes: First Editions in the Library at Dormy House* by M. L. Parrish and B. K. Mann, 1936.

Reading List: *Kingsley: His Letters and Memories of His Life* by Frances E. Kingsley, 2 vols., 1877; *Kingsley* by Margaret Farrand Thorp, 1937; *Kingsley and His Ideas* by Guy Kendall, 1947; *Canon Kingsley* by Una Pope-Hennessy, 1948; *Apologia pro Kingsley* by P. J. Fitzpatrick, 1969; *The Beast and the Monk: A Life of Kingsley* by Susan Chitty, 1974; *Kingsley; The Lion of Eversley* by Brenda Colloms, 1975.

*   *   *

Gerard Manley Hopkins once wittily remarked that whenever he thought of Charles Kingsley – and we may be sure it would not be too often – he imagined a man leaping up from the table, with his mouth full of bread and cheese, spluttering that he wasn't going to have any more of this damned nonsense. Probably at the forefront of Hopkins's mind was Kingsley's rash attack on Newman for going over from Anglicanism to Rome (the attack brought in reply one of the great apologies of all time, *Apologia Pro Sua Vita*), but there is a sense in which Kingsley is *always* rash.

Kingsley deserves some credit for being the founder, in the 1840's, with his subtler friend, the Rev. F. D. Maurice, of "muscular Christianity," which also became known as Christian Socialism. Both men were alarmed by the drift away from the Anglican church among working-class men; and the 1851 Religious Census confirmed just how few working-class people went to church. Kingsley rightly held the church itself to blame for this state of affairs. He saw that industrialisation had created enormous problems for its victims – as working-class people were thought of – and that the church had dismally failed to address itself to any of the problems. Kingsley had a genuine compassion for the working-classes, and he wanted fuller and happier lives to be open to them – "a life of bathhouses and cricket" as contemporaries perhaps unkindly referred to it.

A stream of novels and essays came from Kingsley's fatally fluent pen, nearly all of them concerned with the effort to reconcile class to class, to explain people to each other, to preach the brotherhood of man. *The Water-Babies* is a children's story with an adult meaning: Tom is to be understood as a social outcast, a version of Oliver Twist or the chimney sweep of Blake's great poem in *Songs of Innocence*, and Kingsley wanted his audience to be shocked into pity and compassion over his fate. The same is true of *Alton Locke*, perhaps his best and certainly his most often discussed novel. It is told by the eponymous hero, a chartist tailor, and, as I have pointed out in my essay in *Tradition and Tolerance in Nineteenth Century Fiction*, Kingsley goes out of his way to insist on Alton's being a blood brother of the middle-class audience which might be expected to read the novel. As a result, of course, he ends up by denying any conditioning factors in Alton's life that could explain his character or actions. Alton is simply an "Englishman."

Kingsley's naive form of patriotism comes out in his historical writings, which nowadays have an embarrassingly jingoistic air to them. No wonder that serious historians were appalled when he was appointed to the chair of history at Cambridge. Even Kingsley seems to have had some doubts about the wisdom of his appointment, and he was not a man given to self-doubt. Had he been, he would undoubtedly have written better books. As it is, we may be grateful to him for so vigorously drawing attention to problems and complexities which finer minds than his found difficult to understand or resolve.

—John Lucas

KIPLING, (Joseph) Rudyard. English. Born in Bombay, India, 30 December 1865, of English parents. Educated at the United Services College, Westward Ho!, Devon, 1878–82. Married Caroline Starr Balestier in 1892; three children. Assistant Editor, *Civil and Military Gazette*, Lahore, 1882–87; Editor and Contributor, "Week's News," *Pioneer*, Allahabad, 1887–89; returned to England, and settled in London: full-time writer from 1889; lived in Brattleboro, Vermont, 1892–96, then returned to England; settled in Burwash, Sussex, 1902. Rector, University of St. Andrews, 1922–25. Recipient: Nobel Prize for Literature, 1907; Royal Society of Literature Gold Medal, 1926. LL.D.: McGill University, Montreal, 1899; D.Litt.: University of Durham, 1907; Oxford University, 1907; Cambridge University, 1908; University of Edinburgh, 1920; the Sorbonne, Paris, 1921; University of Strasbourg, 1921; D.Phil.: University of Athens, 1924. Honorary Fellow, Magdalene College, Cambridge, 1932. Associate Member, Académie des Sciences Morales et Politiques, 1933. Refused the Poet Laureateship, 1895, and the Order of Merit. *Died 18 January 1936.*

PUBLICATIONS

Collections

Complete Works (Sussex Edition). 35 vols., 1937–39; as *Collected Works* (Burwash Edition), 28 vols., 1941.
Verse: Definitive Edition. 1940.
The Best Short Stories, edited by Randall Jarrell. 1961; as *In the Vernacular: The English in India* and *The English in England*, 2 vols., 1963.
Stories and Poems, edited by Roger Lancelyn Green. 1970.
Short Stories, edited by Andrew Rutherford. 1971.
Selected Verse, edited by James Cochrane. 1977.

Fiction

Plain Tales from the Hills. 1888.
Soldiers Three: A Collection of Stories. 1888.
The Stories of the Gadsbys: A Tale Without a Plot. 1888.
In Black and White. 1888.
Under the Deodars. 1888; revised edition, 1890.
The Phantom 'Rickshaw and Other Tales. 1888; revised edition, 1890.
Wee Willie Winkie and Other Child Stories. 1888; revised edition, 1890.
The Light That Failed. 1890.
The Courting of Dinah Shadd and Other Stories. 1890.
Mine Own People. 1891.
The Naulahka: A Story of West and East, with Wolcott Balestier. 1892.
Many Inventions. 1893.
Soldier Tales. 1896; as *Soldier Stories,* 1896.
The Day's Work. 1898.
The Kipling Reader. 1900; as *Selected Stories,* 1925.
Traffics and Discoveries. 1904.
Actions and Reactions. 1909.
Abaft the Funnel. 1909.
A Diversity of Creatures. 1917.
Selected Stories, edited by William Lyon Phelps. 1921.
Debits and Credits. 1926.

Selected Stories. 1929.
Thy Servant a Dog, Told by Boots.   1930; revised edition, as Thy Servant a Dog and
   Other Dog Stories, 1938.
Humorous Tales.   1931.
Animal Stories.   1932.
Limits and Renewals.   1932.
All the Mowgli Stories.   1933.
Collected Dog Stories.   1934.

Play

The Harbour Watch (produced 1913; revised version, as Gow's Watch, produced 1924).

Verse

Schoolboy Lyrics.   1881.
Echoes, with Alice Kipling.   1884.
Departmental Ditties and Other Verses.   1886.
Departmental Ditties, Barrack-Room Ballads, and Other Verse.   1890.
Barrack-Room Ballads and Other Verses.   1892.
Ballads and Barrack-Room Ballads.   1893.
The Seven Seas.   1896.
Recessional.   1897.
An Almanac of Twelve Sports.   1898.
Poems, edited by Wallace Rice.   1899.
Recessional and Other Poems.   1899.
The Absent-Minded Beggar.   1899.
With Number Three, Surgical and Medical, and New Poems.   1900.
Occasional Poems.   1900.
The Five Nations.   1903.
The Muse among the Motors.   1904.
Collected Verse.   1907.
A History of England (verse only), with C. R. L. Fletcher.   1911; revised edition, 1930.
Songs from Books.   1912.
Twenty Poems.   1918.
The Years Between.   1919.
Verse: Inclusive Edition, 1885–1918.   3 vols., 1919; revised edition, 1921, 1927, 1933.
A Kipling Anthology: Verse.   1922.
A Choice of Songs.   1925.
Sea and Sussex.   1926.
Songs of the Sea.   1927.
Poems 1886–1929.   3 vols., 1929.
Selected Poems.   1931.
East of Suez, Being a Selection of Eastern Verses.   1931.
The Complete Barrack-Room Ballads, edited by C. E. Carrington.   1973.

Other

Quartette, with others.   1885.
The City of Dreadful Night and Other Sketches.   1890.
The City of Dreadful Night and Other Places.   1891.

The Smith Administration.   1891.
Letters of Marque.   1891.
American Notes, with *The Bottle Imp,* by Robert Louis Stevenson.   1891.
The Jungle Book (juvenile).   1894; *The Second Jungle Book,* 1895.
Out of India: Things I Saw, and Failed to See, in Certain Days and Nights at Jeypore and Elsewhere.   1895.
The Kipling Birthday Book, edited by Joseph Finn.   1896.
"Captain Courageous": A Story of the Grand Banks (juvenile).   1897; edited by J. de L. Ferguson, 1959.
A Fleet in Being: Notes on Two Trips with the Channel Squadron.   1898.
Stalky & Co. (juvenile).   1899; revised edition, as *The Complete Stalky & Co.,* 1929; edited by Steven Marcus, 1962.
From Sea to Sea: Letters of Travel.   1899; as *From Sea to Sea and Other Sketches,* 1900.
Works (Swastika Edition).   15 vols., 1899.
Kim (juvenile).   1901.
Just So Stories for Little Children.   1902.
Puck of Pook's Hill (juvenile).   1906.
Letters to the Family (Notes on a Recent Trip to Canada).   1908.
Kipling Stories and Poems Every Child Should Know, edited by Mary E. Burt and W. T. Chapin.   1909.
Rewards and Fairies (juvenile).   1910.
The Kipling Reader.   1912.
The New Army in Training.   1915.
France at War.   1915.
The Fringes of the Fleet.   1915.
Tales of "The Trade."   1916.
Sea Warfare.   1916.
The War in the Mountains.   1917.
The Eyes of Asia.   1918.
The Graves of the Fallen.   1919.
Letters of Travel (1892–1913).   1920.
A Kipling Anthology: Prose.   1922.
Land and Sea Tales for Scouts and Guides.   1923.
The Irish Guards in the Great War.   2 vols., 1923.
Works (Mandalay Edition).   26 vols., 1925–26.
A Book of Words: Selections from Speeches and Addresses Delivered Between 1906 and 1927.   1928.
The One Volume Kipling.   1928.
Souvenirs of France.   1933.
Ham and the Porcupine (juvenile).   1935.
A Kipling Pageant.   1935.
Something of Myself for My Friends Known and Unknown.   1937.
Letters from Japan, edited by Donald Richie and Yoshimori Harashima.   1962.
Kipling to Rider Haggard: The Record of a Friendship, edited by Morton Cohen.   1965.

Bibliography: *Kipling: A Bibliographical Catalogue* by J. McG. Stewart, edited by A. W. Keats, 1959; "Kipling: An Annotated Bibliography of Writings about Him" by H. E. Gerber and E. Lauterbach, in *English Fiction in Transition 3,* 1960, and *8,* 1965.

Reading List: *Kipling: His Life and Work* by C. E. Carrington, 1955; *A Reader's Guide to Kipling's Work* by Roger Lancelyn Green, 1961, and *Kipling: The Critical Heritage* edited by Green, 1971; *Kipling's Mind and Art* edited by Andrew Rutherford, 1964; *Kipling and the*

Critics edited by E. L. Gilbert, 1965; *Kipling* by J. I. M. Stewart, 1966; *Kipling: Realist and Fabulist* by Bonamy Dobrée, 1967; *Kipling and His World* by Kingsley Amis, 1975; *Kipling: The Glass, The Shadow, and the Fire* by Philip Mason, 1975; *The Strange Ride of Kipling: His Life and Works* by Angus Wilson, 1977.

*   *   *

T. S. Eliot called Rudyard Kipling "the most inscrutable of authors ... a writer impossible to belittle." On the face of it, it was an extraordinary judgement to pass on an author who was the idol of the plain, philistine, notably non-literary public, suggesting that he was as difficult, almost as hermetic to popular understanding as Eliot himself might be construed to be, and that if it was impossible to belittle him it had not been for want of many people trying. As the celebrant of British imperialism and "the white man's burden," which was one of his own phrases, in his lifetime Kipling was anathema to all good liberals both with a large and a small initial letter, and even today, forty years after his death, fairness to him is not easy.

Part of the difficulty in making a judgement lies in the complexity of his character, part in the disconcerting range of his subject-matter. It is impossible to read *Plain Tales from the Hills* without being forced partially to agree with the nineteenth-century critic who accused him of honouring "everywhere the brute and the bully." At the same time it is impossible not to be struck with the warmth of his sympathy both for children and for those men and women, white and brown alike, caught up in interracial sexual relations, as in "Without Benefit of Clergy." He appears, indeed, in these stories as, to borrow Bagehot's phrase for Dickens, the "special correspondent for posterity" reporting the day-to-day life of the British Raj in the last decades of Victoria's reign. That he was an unillusioned observer of the nature of imperialism emerges clearly in what is probably the finest of his Indian stories, "The Man Born to Be King," in which two down-at-heel adventurers seize a country to the north of Afghanistan and only fail to establish a dynasty there because of the character-defects of one of them. It is an ironically grim fable on the nature of empire-building.

Though in his lifetime Kipling was seen as above all a writer about India, in fact he spent less than ten years of his adult life in the country, and it seems clear that his imagination widened and deepened after leaving it. His range is extraordinary, so much so that it is impossible to pick out any one story as typical of Kipling; instead, there are peaks of excellence, each *sui generis*, and in a narrow space all one can do is give instances. There is "Mrs. Bathurst," a study in sexual magic, and, in its subtlety and indirection and mastery of the rendering of character through dialogue, possibly the most remarkable story in the language. It compels realisation that Kipling was not only a modern but at times even a modernist writer.

There are the great mythopoeic stories of Sussex life, in particular "Friendly Brook," a story very pagan in tone about what in effect is a local deity of the kind we find in Latin poetry, and "The Wish-House," a beautiful story of self-sacrifice in which something like an instance of ancient folk-lore is astonishingly invented. There are stories based in scientific invention, such as "The Eye of Allah," in which the microscope is invented – and smashed to bits – in a medieval monastery, and "Wireless," in which an early experiment in transmission by radio is magically tied up with the presence of an apothecary's assistant, whose mind in a trance is invaded by the spirit of John Keats. There are stories of morbid psychology like the chilling and in my view often misunderstood "Mary Postgate." There is the haunting story of phantom children, "They," which so influenced Eliot in the writing of "Burnt Norton."

That he was the greatest of English short-story writers can scarcely be doubted. He was never a successful novelist, though *Kim* is a case on its own, a wonderfully sympathetic evocation of Indian native life. He was, obviously, one of the great children's writers, and it was precisely in such works as *The Jungle Book*, *Puck of Pook's Hill* and *Stalky & Co.* that he most unambiguously dramatised his moral values, what he called the Law, which "lesser breeds" were without. Above all, perhaps, with his younger contemporaries Joyce and

Lawrence, with whom one feels he would have had little sympathy, he was one of the undisputed masters of specifically modern English prose.

A definitive critical estimate of Kipling as a poet is still awaited. He stood apart from the general poetic theories and practice current in his lifetime and forged his own characteristic expression in poems like "Danny Deever" and "Mandalay" out of the music hall ballad, which he brought into literature. His most famous poem, "Recessional," is obviously one of the great hymns. He was in a very real sense that rarest of beings, a genuine popular poet, and whatever his final place in our poetry may prove to be, one thing is certain. More lines and phrases from his verse have passed into the common mind and speech than those of any other English poet of the century.

—Walter Allen

LE FANU, (Joseph) Sheridan. Irish. Born in Dublin, 28 August 1814. Educated privately, and at Trinity College, Dublin, 1833–37; called to the Irish Bar, 1839, but never practised. Married Susan Bennett in 1843 (died, 1858). Member of the staff of the *Dublin University Magazine* from 1837: Editor and Proprietor, 1861–69; purchased the Dublin newspaper *The Warder*, 1839, and subsequently took over the *Evening Packet* and later the *Dublin Evening Mail*. Active in radical conservative politics, 1838–48. Went into semi-retirement on wife's death. *Died 7 February 1873.*

PUBLICATIONS

Collections

The Poems, edited by A. P. Groves. 1896.
Madam Crowl's Ghost and Other Tales of Mystery, edited by M. R. James. 1923.
Ghost Stories and Mysteries, edited by E. F. Bleiler. 1975.

Fiction

The Cock and Anchor, Being a Chronicle of Old Dublin City. 1845; edited by B. S. Le Fanu, 1895.
The Fortunes of Colonel Torlogh O'Brien. 1847.
Ghost Stories and Tales of Mystery. 1851.
The House by the Church-Yard. 1863.
Wylder's Hand. 1864.
Uncle Silas: A Tale of Bartram-Haugh. 1864.
Guy Deverell. 1865.
All in the Dark. 1866.
The Tenants of Malory. 1867.

A Lost Name. 1868.
Haunted Lives. 1868.
The Wyvern Mystery. 1869.
Checkmate. 1871.
The Rose and the Key. 1871.
Chronicles of Golden Friars (stories). 1871.
In a Glass Darkly (stories). 1872.
Willing to Die. 1873.
The Purcell Papers (stories). 1880.

Reading List: *Wilkie Collins, Le Fanu, and Others* by Stewart M. Ellis, 1931 (includes bibliography); *Le Fanu* by Nelson Browne, 1951; "Le Fanu's *Richard Marston* (1848): The History of an Anglo-Irish Text" by W. J. McCormack, in *1848: The Sociology of Literature* edited by Francis Barker and others, 1978.

                    *   *   *

Sheridan Le Fanu is best understood as Maria Edgeworth's successor as a novelist of the Irish gentry. Like her, he is preoccupied with the past; but whereas she attempts imaginatively to reconstitute the past, Le Fanu sees it as an inexorable pressure on the present. Given his recurring and anxious concern with religious speculation, we may say that he substitutes the patterns of original sin for the dynamics of history.

This anxiety is given a Gothic expression in the stories of 1838–40, later collected as *The Purcell Papers*. With the short-lived political optimism of the early 1840's, Le Fanu wrote two historical novels, *The Cock and Anchor* and *Torlogh O'Brien*, in which a diminished interest in the supernatural is paralleled by a more flexible approach to Irish history and the possibility of social change. The events of 1848, however, combined with a deteriorating domestic life – the two are mordantly reflected in "Richard Marston" – destroyed Le Fanu's new found (and perhaps fragile) confidence. It was only fifteen years later that he resumed an active career as a novelist.

A ten-year frenzy of activity began with *The House by the Church-Yard*, which retains an Irish historical setting. From *Wylder's Hand* and *Uncle Silas* onwards he was obliged for commercial reasons to use a contemporary English setting. In *Uncle Silas*, this imposition is transformed into a further dimension of exile and dislocation, but the remaining novels – loosely identifiable with the "sensational" school of Wilkie Collins and Charles Reade – are of negligible interest. Among the later fiction the tales in *Chronicles of Golden Friars* and *In a Glass Darkly* are Le Fanu's most controlled and impressive work.

The principal difference between the full-length novels and these tales lies in the explicit operation of supernatural agencies in the short fiction. The novels recurringly present a hero whose fate is conditioned by a past offence against society or family; the tales translate this plot into the terms of a sensational theology. The overriding pattern, however, is one of implosion, of diffused self-destruction. *Uncle Silas* describes Hell and the condition of the damned as "depraved gregariousness, and isolation too"; the words also aptly describe the diminished status of the Irish ascendancy in the Victorian period, as reflected in Le Fanu's life and work.

—W. J. McCormack

LENNOX, Charlotte (née Ramsay). English.   Born in New York, possibly in Albany, c.
1729–30. Went to England, 1743, and remained there for the rest of her life. Married
Alexander Lennox in 1747 (died c. 1797), one son and one daughter. Appeared on the stage,
1749–50; thereafter supported herself by writing and translating; befriended by Samuel
Johnson and Richardson; Editor, *Lady's Museum*, London, 1760–61. Granted Royal
Literary Fund pension, 1792. *Died 4 January 1804.*

PUBLICATIONS

Fiction

The Life of Harriot Stuart.   1750.
The Female Quixote; or, The Adventures of Arabella.   1752; edited by Margaret
    Dalziel, 1970.
Henrietta.   1758.
Sophia.   1762.
The History of the Marquis of Lussan and Isabella.   1764.
Euphemia.   1790.

Plays

Philander: A Dramatic Pastoral.   1757.
Oedipus, Electra, and *Philoctetes,* in *The Greek Theatre.*   3 vols., 1759.
The Sister, from her own novel *Henrietta* (produced 1769).   1769.
Old City Manners, from *Eastward Ho* by Jonson, Chapman, and Marston (produced
    1775).   1775.

Verse

Poems on Several Occasions.   1747.

Other

*Shakespeare Illustrated; or, The Novels and Histories, on Which the Plays Are Founded,
    Collected and Translated.*   3 vols., 1753–54.
The Lady's Museum, 1760–61 (periodical).   2 vols., 1760–61 (some material not by
    Lennox).

Translator, *The Memoirs of the Countess of Bercy.*   1756.
Translator, *The Memoirs of M. de Bethune, Duke of Sully.*   1756.
Translator, *Memoirs for the History of Madame de Maintenon,* by L. Angliviel de la
    Beaumelle.   1757.
Translator, *Meditations and Penitential Prayers,* by the Duchess de la Vallière.   1774.

Reading List: *Lennox: An Eighteenth-Century Lady of Letters* by Miriam R. Small, 1935; *The
First American Novelist?* by G. H. Maynadier, 1940; *The Mystery of Lennox, First Novelist of
Colonial America* by Philippe Séjourné, 1967.

*   *   *

Charlotte Lennox's reputation is based on a single novel, *The Female Quixote*, and, although she wrote other work of some merit, her strength as an author is closely related to her insight into the mind of her Quixotic Arabella, living in a private world constructed out of the French heroic romances written in the previous century, where pure and constant passion inspires deeds of prodigious valour. Her first novel, *Harriot Stuart*, also has a romantic heroine, familiar with the attentions of admirers whose ardour was incompatible with the prosaic decencies of common life, but the element of self-delusion is less prominent. Almost anything might happen in the wilds of New York province, where Charlotte Lennox spent her childhood, and where the most attractive part of the novel is set. In *The Female Quixote* the heroine's illusions are elaborately conjured up, and artfully juxtaposed with the world of rural England and the manners of polite society. For much of the time (and here one detects the influence of her friend Samuel Johnson) the novel might be taken as a long case-history from the files of a psychiatrist. But although Arabella's preconceptions lead her continually astray, they also sustain a character that is in many ways admirable. She is benevolent, generous, and – romance apart – sufficiently intelligent. She is contrasted favourably with the petty-minded and ungenerous Miss Glanville, whose sanity could never be in doubt. The novel is evidence of a contemporary fascination with "enthusiasm" and the pleasures of imagination.

A later work, *Henrietta*, reduces the devotee of romance to a mere object of satire. Miss Woodby's passion for "violent friendships" anticipates the pretensions of Isabella Thorpe in Jane Austen's *Northanger Abbey*. The heroine herself is a sensible young woman whose perceptions are sharpened by her inferior and dependent station in life. *Sophia* provides another variation on the author's favourite theme, with a heroine whose unwearied application to reading produces only good sense and virtue.

Charlotte Lennox also wrote a few pieces for the stage. *The Sister*, based on part of *Henrietta*, includes a fine elderly female Quixote (Lady Autumn), but it is otherwise undistinguished.

—Geoffrey Carnall

LEVER, Charles (James).   Irish.   Born in Dublin, 31 August 1806. Educated at Trinity College, Dublin, 1823–28; studied medicine in Göttingen; awarded M.B. by Trinity College, 1831. Married Catherine Baker in 1833 (died, 1870); one daughter. Served as a surgeon on an emigrant ship to Canada, 1828, then practised medicine in various Irish towns; physician for the Board of Health in County Clare; dispensary doctor at Port Stewart; practised in Brussels, 1839–42; Editor, *Dublin University Magazine*, 1842–45; lived in Italy from 1845: Vice-Consul at Spezia, 1858–67, and Consul at Trieste, 1867–72. *Died 1 June 1872.*

PUBLICATIONS

Collections

Fiction

The Confessions of Harry Lorrequer. 1839; edited by L. S. Benjamin, 1907.
Charles O'Malley, The Irish Dragoon. 1841.
Our Mess (Jack Hinton and Tom Burke of "Ours"). 3 vols., 1843–44.
Arthur O'Leary: His Wanderings and Ponderings in Many Lands. 1844; as *Adventures of Arthur O'Leary,* 1856.
St. Patrick's Eve. 1845.
Nuts and Nutcrackers. 1845.
Tales of the Trains. 1845.
The O'Donoghue. 1845.
The Knight of Gwynne. 1847.
The Martins of Gro' Martin. 1847.
Diary and Notes of Horace Templeton, Late Secretary of Legation at —. 1848.
Confessions of Con Cregan, The Irish Gil Blas. 1849.
Roland Cashel. 1850.
The Daltons; or, Three Roads in Life. 2 vols., 1850–52.
Maurice Tierney. 1852.
The Dodd Family Abroad. 2 vols., 1852–54.
Sir Jasper Carew: His Life and Experiences. 1855.
The Fortunes of Glencore. 1857.
Davenport Dunn; or, The Man of the Day. 1859.
One of Them. 1861.
A Day's Ride. 1863.
Barrington. 1863.
Luttrell of Arran. 1863.
Cornelius O'Dowd upon Men, Women, and Other Things in General. 3 vols., 1864–65.
A Rent in the Cloud. 1865.
Tony Butler. 1865.
Sir Brook Fossbrooke. 1866.
The Bramleighs of Bishop's Folly. 1868.
Paul Gosslett's Confessions in Law and the Civil Service. 1868.
The Boy of Norcott's. 1869.
Lord Kilgobbin. 1872.
The Military Novels. 9 vols., n.d.
Gerald Fitzgerald the Chevalier. 1899.

Reading List: *Lever: His Life in His Letters* by Edmund Downey, 2 vols., 1906; "Lever" by Roger McHugh, in *Studies 27,* 1938; *Dr. Quicksilver: The Life of Lever* by Lionel Stevenson, 1939.

*   *   *

Charles Lever wrote some thirty novels in the thirty-five years between 1837 and 1872. His early novels, *Harry Lorrequer, Charles O'Malley,* and *Jack Hinton,* were light-hearted, full of incident, sometimes farcical, always ebullient; they have been attacked by Irish literary critics – and politicians – for their stage-Irish characters, their presentation of the lighter side of garrison life in Ireland. When Lever left Ireland in 1845 the attacks largely ceased. He then began to write novels with more historical than military interest, he explored the social and political milieu of Europe, and he deepened his understanding of. life and capacity for comment on it. He also developed his style and novelistic techniques in the middle 1840's and 1850's. Thus *Roland Cashel* and *Sir Jasper Carew* take a broad view of Irish problems, while *The Knight of Gwynne,* which owed something to Lever's friendship with Maria Edgeworth, examines the extravagant recklessness which sapped the foundations of the Anglo-Irish. His characters are now more realistic, more balanced.

Shaw's preface to *Major Barbara* acknowledges his debt to Lever's poignant sense of the tragi-comedy of Ireland – most developed in his middle period – his ironic, impartial view of the conflict between life and romantic imagination. But Yeats, Lady Gregory, and more recent commentators seem only to have noticed (and disliked) the stage-Irish element in his work. Had they read *Barrington*, *Sir Brook Fossbrooke*, and *Lord Kilgobbin*, which give a full and tragic view of Ireland in the latter part of the nineteenth century? These novels are influenced in their scope by Scott and Balzac, and convey a sense that the ascendancy's power had long vanished, a fierce indignation about the faults of British administration, and a melancholic foreboding of great catastrophe to come.

—A. Norman Jeffares

LEWIS, Matthew Gregory ("Monk" Lewis). English. Born in London, 9 July 1775. Educated at Dr. Fountaine's School, London; Westminster School, London; Christ Church, Oxford. Writer from 1791; visited Weimar, and met Goethe, 1792–93; Attaché to the British Embassy in The Hague, 1794–95; famous as a writer from the age of 20; Member of Parliament for Hindon, Wiltshire, 1796–1802; inherited his father's properties, 1812; visited his estates in Jamaica, to arrange for the welfare of his slaves, 1815–16; visited Byron and Shelley in Geneva, 1816; toured Italy, 1817. *Died 14 May 1818.*

PUBLICATIONS

Collections

Tales in Verse of Terror and Wonder, edited by L. E. Smith.   1925.

Fiction

The Monk: A Romance.   1796; expurgated edition, as *Ambrosio; or, The Monk*, 1798; edited by Howard Anderson, 1973.
Romantic Tales.   1808.

Plays

Village Virtue: A Dramatic Satire.   1796.
The Minister, from a play by Schiller.   1797; revised version, as *The Harper's Daughter; or, Love and Ambition* (produced 1803), 1813.
The Castle Spectre, music by Michael Kelly (produced 1797).   1798.
Rolla; or, The Peruvian Hero, from a play by Kotzebue.   1799.

The Twins; or, Is It He or His Brother? (produced 1799). Edited by Karl S. Guthke, in *Huntington Library Quarterly 25*, 1962.
The East Indian, from a play by Kotzebue (produced 1799). 1800; as *Rivers; or, The East Indian*, 1800; as *Rich and Poor* (produced 1812), n.d.
Adelmorn the Outlaw, music by Michael Kelly (produced 1801). 1801.
Alfonso, King of Castile (produced 1802). 1801.
The Captive (produced 1803). In *Life and Correspondence* by Margaret Baron-Wilson, 2 vols., 1839.
Rugantino: The Bravo of Venice, from a play by Pixérécourt. 1805.
Adelgitha; or, The Fruits of a Single Error, music by Michael Kelly (produced 1807). 1806.
The Wood Demon; or, The Clock Has Struck, music by Michael Kelly (produced 1807); revised version, as *One O'Clock! or, The Knight and the Wood Demon*, music by Michael Kelly and M. P. King (produced 1811).
Venoni; or, The Novice of St. Mark's, music by Michael Kelly, from a play by Bouhet (produced 1808). 1809.
Raymond and Agnes (produced 1809). N.d.
Temper; or, The Domestic Tyrant (produced 1809).
Timour the Tartar (produced 1811). 1811.
The Enchanted Fire of the Invisible Island; or, The Golden Gallery (produced 1824).

Verse

Tales of Terror, with others. 1799.
The Love of Gain: A Poem Imitated from Juvenal. 1799.
Tales of Wonder, written and collected by Lewis and others. 2 vols., 1801.
Monody on the Death of Sir John Moore. 1809.
Poems. 1812.
The Isle of Devils: A Historical Tale Founded on an Anecdote in the Annals of Portugal. 1827.
Crazy Jane. 1830(?).

Other

Journal of a West India Proprietor Kept During a Residence in the Island of Jamaica. 1834; as *Journal of a Residence among the Negroes in the West Indies*, 1845; edited by M. Wilson, 1929.

Translator, *The Bravo of Venice: A Romance*, by J. H. D. Zschokke. 1805; abridged edition, as *Rugantino: The Bravo of Venice*, 1805.
Translator, *Feudal Tyrants; or, The Counts of Carlsheim and Sargans: A Romance, Taken from the German.* 4 vols., 1806.
Translator, *The Four Facardins*, by Count Anthony Hamilton, in *Fairy Tales and Romances.* 1849.

Bibliography: in *Gothic Bibliography* by Montague Summers, 1941.

Reading List: *Life and Correspondence* by Margaret Baron-Wilson, 2 vols., 1839; Introduction by John Berryman to *The Monk*, 1952; *A Life of Lewis* by Louis F. Peck, 1961.

*   *   *

The Monk, written by a nineteen-year-old diplomat as a stay against boredom, established the fame and notoriety of Matthew Gregory Lewis, a humane, generous, rather boring little man who could scarcely be more different from his creation, with its horrific reveling in lust, incest, rape, murder, and the supernatural. In spite of the defects of a sometimes wooden style, only loosely connected episodes, and lack of depth in character, *The Monk* is a prime specimen of the Gothic horror novel, with genuine energy and lasting power. Set during the time of the Inquisition in Spain and Germany, the novel explores the mysterious evils that lie beneath the surface of normal reality. Ambrosio, the eloquent, pious monk at the peak of his career, has within him elements of vanity, hypocrisy, and lust which explode beyond control as he becomes entangled in a web of complicated events: the illicit love of Raymond and Agnes, the heartless, criminal power of a prioress, and the devoted, ultimately diabolical, passion of Matilda, who has entered Ambrosio's service disguised as a page. Lewis's narration of the progress of Ambrosio's destruction, as his lust leads him to atrocious crimes, minutely described, assumes a vigor which impels the reader into the realm of shocking chaos and nightmarish evil.

No other of Lewis's works approached the success of *The Monk*, but Lewis's literary accomplishments do not end with that novel. Some of his dramas were popular for a time, but none has been revived; his favorite forms were tragedy and what he called "Grand Romantic Melo-Drama." The most successful, *The Castle Spectre*, is typically Gothic, with an ancient castle, underground passages, a gloomy dungeon, a bloody ghost, and elaborate light and sound effects for maximum shock and melodrama. His poems have considerable merit, displaying great variety in subject and technique, often with striking rhythmic power. Sir Walter Scott said of Lewis, "He had the finest ear for the rhythm of verse I ever heard – finer even than Byron's." He was also an accomplished translator and adaptor of French and German, and orally translated Goethe's *Faust* while visiting Byron in Italy. The posthumous *Journal of a West India Proprietor*, a record of Lewis's visits to Jamaica to oversee property inherited from his father, shows Lewis as a sensible, humane observer of human life. Totally unlike his Gothic productions, it is – according to Coleridge, who found *The Monk* too "minutely libidinous" and blasphemous – "by far his best work."

—David McCracken

LOVER, Samuel.   Irish.   Born in Dublin, 24 February 1797. Educated privately. Married 1) Miss Berrel in 1827 (died, 1847); 2) Miss Wandby in 1852. Worked in his father's stock brokerage, Dublin, but left to become a painter: miniaturist, marine painter, and illustrator, in Dublin, 1818–33: elected to the Royal Hibernian Academy, 1828, and became its Secretary, 1830; exhibited at the Academy, 1832, and at the Royal Academy, London, 1833; also a song writer, librettist, and singer, from 1818; a Founder, 1833, and contributor to the *Dublin University Magazine*; settled in London, 1835: worked as a painter, and contributed to various periodicals; one of the founders of *Bentley's Miscellany*; gave up painting because of failing eyesight, 1844; devised a one-man show of his own works, "Irish Evenings," and presented it in London, 1844–46, and in America, 1846–48; returned to London, and devised a second one-man show, "Paddy's Portfolio," 1848, then resumed his earlier occupation of opera librettist; devoted himself mainly to song writing, 1852–64; retired to Dublin. *Died 6 July 1868.*

PUBLICATIONS

Collections

Poetical Works. 1880.
Collected Writings, edited by J. J. Roche.   10 vols., 1901–13.
Works, edited by J. J. Roche.   6 vols., 1902.

Fiction

Legends and Stories of Ireland.   2 vols., 1831–34; edited by D. J. O'Donoghue, 1899.
Rory O'More: A National Romance.   1837; revised edition, 1839; edited by D. J. O'Donoghue, 1898.
Handy Andy.   1842; edited by E. Rhys, 1907; abridgement edited by Sean O'Faolain, 1945.
Treasure Trove.   1844; as *He Would Be a Gentleman; or, Treasure Trove,* 1877; edited by D. J. O'Donoghue, 1899.
Tom Crosbie and His Friends.   1878.
Further Stories of Ireland, edited by D. J. O'Donoghue.   1899.

Plays

Grana Uile; or, The Island Queen, music by William Penson (produced 1832).
The Beau Isle (produced 1835).
The Olympic Pic-Nic (produced 1835).
Rory O'More, from his own novel (produced 1837).   N.d.
The White Horse of the Peppers (produced 1838).   1838.
The Hall Porter (produced 1839).   1839.
The Happy Man (produced 1839).   1858(?).
Snap Apple Night; or, A Kick-Up in Kerry (produced 1839).
The Greek Boy (produced 1840).   1884.
Il Paddy Whack in Italia (produced 1841).   N.d.
The Sentinel of the Alma (produced 1854).
Barney the Baron; or, The Haunted Chamber (produced 1857).   With *The Happy Man,* 1883.
MacCarthy More; or Possession Nine Points of the Law (produced 1861).   N.d.
Barney the Baron; The Happy Man.   1883.

Verse

Songs and Ballads.   1839.
The Low Back Car.   1855.
Metrical Tales and Other Poems.   1860.
Original Songs for the Rifle Volunteers, with C. Mackay and T. Miller.   1861.

Other

The Parson's Horn-Book.   2 vols., 1831.

Editor, *Popular Tales and Legends of the Irish Peasantry.* 1834.
Editor, *The Lyrics of Ireland.* 1858; as *Poems of Ireland,* 1884.
Editor, *Rival Rhymes in Honour of Burns.* 1859.

Reading List: *The Life of Lover: Artistic, Literary, and Musical* by W. B. Bernard, 2 vols., 1874; *Lover* by Andrew J. Symington, 1880.

*   *   *

It was Samuel Lover's misfortune that the publication of his best known novel, *Handy Andy,* coincided with the emergence of an articulate cultural nationalism in the Young Ireland movement. The novel was a harmless, and indeed remains a humorous, exercise in stage-Irish comedy, but the new self-conscious dignity of Irish public opinion rejected Lover's work as a travesty. Despite this hostile reception in his homeland, he is probably remembered principally for *Handy Andy.* An earlier novel, *Rory O'More,* deserves more attention; by taking the name of a leading aristocratic insurgent of the 1641 rebellion, and giving it to a humble character in a novel centred on the 1798 rebellion, Lover was attempting to make a general statement about Irish history and the manner in which fiction treats it. The conceit, however, was rather better managed than the execution of the novel as a whole.

If present-day interest in Lover is expressed principally by critics concerned with the development of the novel in nineteenth-century Ireland, in his time he had a reputation in Great Britain and America as an entertainer who produced drama, ballad poetry, and song with equal facility. Together with his collection of folksong and his paintings, his work is a large if ill-organised monument to Victorian industry and prolixity. The central problem, affecting the fiction with special gravity, was Lover's uncertain notion of what Irish culture was and how it might be presented to the world. Too often he concentrated on the question of presentation, and accepted hand-me-down notions of national character and humour.

—W. J. McCormack

MacDONALD, George. Scottish. Born near Huntly, Aberdeenshire, 10 December 1824. Educated at King's College, University of Aberdeen, 1840–45, M.A. 1845; Congregationalist Theological College, Highbury, London, 1848–50. Married Louisa Powell in 1850 (died, 1902); eleven children. Private tutor in London, 1845–48; Minister, Trinity Congregational Church, Arundel, Sussex, 1850–53; lecturer and preacher in Manchester, 1855–56, Hastings, Sussex, 1857–59, and London, from 1859; Editor, with Norman MacLeod, *Good Words for the Young* magazine, 1870–72; lectured in England and America, 1872; lived in Bordighera, Italy in later life. LL.D.: University of Aberdeen, 1868. Granted Civil List pension, 1877. *Died 18 September 1905.*

PUBLICATIONS

Collections

MacDonald: An Anthology, edited by C. S. Lewis. 1946.
The Light Princess and Other Tales of Fantasy, edited by Roger Lancelyn Green. 1961.
The Gifts of the Child Christ: Fairy Tales and Stories for the Childlike, edited by Glenn
    Edward Sadler. 2 vols., 1973.

Fiction

Phantastes: A Faerie Romance for Men and Women. 1858.
David Elginbrod. 1863.
Adela Cathcart. 1864.
*The Portent: A Story of the Inner Vision of the Highlanders, Commonly Called the Second
    Sight.* 1864.
Alec Forbes of Howglen. 1865.
Annals of a Quiet Neighbourhood. 1867.
Dealings with the Fairies. 1867.
Guild Court. 1867.
Robert Falconer. 1868.
The Seaboard Parish. 1868.
At the Back of the North Wind. 1870.
Ranald Bannerman's Boyhood. 1871.
The Princess and the Goblin. 1871.
The Vicar's Daughter: An Autobiographical Story. 1871.
Wilfrid Cumbermede. 1872.
Gutta-Percha Willie, The Working Genius. 1873.
The Wise Woman: A Parable. 1875; as *A Double Story*, 1876; as *The Lost Princess*,
    1895; edited by Elizabeth Yates, 1965.
Malcolm. 1875.
St. George and St. Michael. 1876.
Thomas Wingfield, Curate. 1876.
The Marquis of Lossie. 1877.
Sir Gibbie. 1879; edited by Elizabeth Yates, 1965.
Paul Faber, Surgeon. 1879.
Mary Marston. 1881.
Warlock o' Glen Warlock. 1881; as *Castle Warlock: A Homely Romance*, 1882.
Weighed and Wanting. 1882.
The Princess and the Curdie. 1882.
The Gifts of the Child Christ and Other Tales. 1882; as *Stephen Archer and Other
    Tales*, 1883.
Donal Grant. 1883.
What's Mine's Mine. 1886.
Home Again. 1887.
The Elect Lady. 1888.
A Rough Shaking. 1890.
There and Back. 1891.
The Flight of the Shadow. 1891.
Heather and Snow. 1893.
The Light Princess and Other Fairy Tales. 1893.
Lilith: A Romance. 1895.

Salted with Fire. 1897.
Far above Rubies (stories). 1899.
The Fairy Tales, edited by Greville MacDonald. 5 vols., 1904.

Verse

Within and Without: A Dramatic Poem. 1855.
Poems. 1857.
A Hidden Life and Other Poems. 1864.
The Disciple and Other Poems. 1867.
Dramatic and Miscellaneous Poems. 2 vols., 1876.
A Book of Strife, in the Form of the Diary of an Old Soul. 1880.
A Threefold Cord: Poems by Three Friends, with John Hill MacDonald and Greville Matheson, edited by George MacDonald. 1883.
The Poetical Works. 2 vols., 1893.
Rampolli: Growths from a Long-Planted Root, Being Translations Chiefly from the German, Along with a "Year's Diary of an Old Soul." 1897.

Other

Unspoken Sermons. 3 vols., 1867–89.
The Miracles of Our Lord. 1870.
Works of Fancy and Imagination. 10 vols., 1871.
England's Antiphon. 1874.
Orts. 1882; as *The Imagination and Other Essays,* 1883; revised edition, as *A Dish of Orts,* 1893.
The Tragedie of Hamlet, Prince of Denmark: A Study of the Text of the Folio of 1623. 1885.
The Hope of the Gospel (sermons). 1892.
The Hope of the Universe. 1896.

Editor, *A Cabinet of Gems, Cut and Polished by Sir Philip Sidney, Now for the More Radiance Presented Without Their Setting.* 1892.

Translator, *Twelve of the Spiritual Songs of Novalis.* 1851.
Translator, *Exotics: A Translation of the Spiritual Songs of Novalis, The Hymn Book of Luther, and Other Poems from the German and Italian.* 1876.

Bibliography: *A Centennial Bibliography of MacDonald* by John Malcolm Bullock, 1925.

Reading List: *MacDonald and His Wife* by Greville MacDonald, 1924; *The Visionary Novels of MacDonald* by A. Freemantle, 1954; *The Golden Key: A Study of the Fiction of MacDonald* by R. L. Wolfe, 1961.

*   *   *

George MacDonald wrote fairy tales and fantasies for adults and children. Modern writers like C. S. Lewis and J. R. R. Tolkien have asserted his importance in inspiring their own fantasy worlds. He in turn drew upon the visionary writing of Crashaw, Novalis, and Fouqué, and fairy-tale and legend. He sought to establish allegorical or parabolic ways of writing through which he could give the strength of traditional image and symbolism to his own moral vision, and impress its beauty on readers. Such a method is, even for as delicate an imagination as MacDonald's, fraught with problems: the simple moral lessons of the fairy-tale may be conveyed successfully even by the self-conscious imitator of the form, as MacDonald does most elegantly in the Princess stories and the tales of *Dealings with the Fairies*; but the other-worlds he constructs out of strings of parables and verses in *Phantastes* and *Lilith* can be confusing and inconsistent on a symbolic level, and indeed the symbolic power of the writing becomes dissociated from the philosophy it is intended to express.

The centre of this philosophy was MacDonald's belief in the importance of the child and a childlike approach to life and death, to human relationships, and to God. His vision of the child was as holy idiot, humankind in a natural loving relationship with all creation and its Creator. To express this idea, parable forms and fairy-tales, relegated by the wordly-wise to the entertainment of children, were an obvious choice. He also, however, embodied his message in the child hero of more conventional stories. *At the Back of the North Wind* includes both homely detail of Diamond's family life and his spiritual adventures with the North Wind; as in *Lilith*, the door between the two is in fact the door between this unsatisfactory life and the real life beyond death, and Diamond's trips with North Wind culminate in his permanent translation to the land at her back. This is MacDonald's personal version of the common tract story in which the poor child is released after much instructive suffering into a better world; his imaginative realisation of death as a cold, awesome, but loving preceptress lifts the commonplace to a different plane, but its origin is clear. The writer's own faith was founded upon a Scottish Calvinist upbringing, and other novels such as *Sir Gibbie* and *David Elginbrod* concentrate on the rich texture of Scottish life, with its simple piety, as the cradle of his holy innocents. In *Sir Gibbie*, as in *A Rough Shaking*, the rather fay saintliness of the central character is made interesting for the reader by its ability to preserve him unharmed through perilous adventures. Similarly, we are held by conventional novelists' tools of description and characterisation in MacDonald's autobiographically based novels like *Ranald Bannerman's Boyhood* and *Robert Falconer*. It is in the fantasies, however, that the modern reader finds the child-worship of this peculiarly Victorian imagination expresses itself with lasting effectiveness.

—J. S. Bratton

MACKENZIE, Henry. Scottish. Born in Edinburgh, 26 August 1745. Educated at Edinburgh High School, and the University of Edinburgh. Married Penuel Grant in 1776; eleven children. Articled to a solicitor, George Inglis, in Redhall, to learn the exchequer business; went to London to learn English exchequer practice in 1765, then returned to Edinburgh: became a partner of Inglis, whom he later succeeded as attorney for the crown in Scotland; wrote, unsuccessfully, for the Edinburgh and London stage, 1773–89; Editor, *The Mirror*, Edinburgh, 1779–80, and *The Lounger*, Edinburgh, 1785–87; wrote extensively on contemporary politics, supporting the "constitutional cause"; Comptroller of Taxes for Scotland, 1804 until his death. One of the first members of the Royal Society of Edinburgh; Member of the Highland Society of Scotland: chairman of its committee to enquire into the authenticity of the Ossian poems. *Died 14 January 1831.*

PUBLICATIONS

Fiction

The Man of Feeling. 1771; edited by Brian Vickers, 1967.
The Man of the World. 1773.
Julia de Roubigné. 1777.

Plays

The Prince of Tunis (produced 1773). 1773.
The Shipwreck; or, Fatal Curiosity, from the play *Fatal Curiosity* by Lillo (produced 1784). 1784.
The Force of Fashion (produced 1789).
Virginia; or, The Roman Father. 1820(?).

Verse

The Pursuits of Happiness. 1771.

Other

Letters of Brutus to Certain Celebrated Political Characters. 1791.
Works. 3 vols., 1807.
Miscellaneous Works. 3 vols., 1819.
Account of the Life and Writings of John Home. 1822.
Anecdotes and Egotisms, edited by Harold W. Thompson. 1927.
Letters to Elizabeth Rose of Kilravock, on Literature, Events, and People, 1768–1815, edited by Horst W. Drescher. 1967.

Editor, *The Life of Thomas Paine,* by Francis Oldys. 1793.

Reading List: *A Scottish Man of Feeling* by Harold W. Thompson, 1931; *Mackenzie* by Gerard A. Barker, 1975.

*   *   *

Although Henry Mackenzie's influence spread in various directions, he is remembered today as a minor novelist who profited from a major trend. The novel that made and preserves his fame is *The Man of Feeling,* an episodic story in the same sentimental vein as Goldsmith's *The Vicar of Wakefield* (1766) and Sterne's *Sentimental Journey* (1768). *The Man of Feeling,* the story of the mortally sensitive Harley, who, after a series of encounters in London with ruined maidens, pathetic Bedlamites, an old soldier, and a grieving family, returns to his country home and swoons to death because his favorite, Miss Walton, requites his love, was immensely popular. This brief synopsis sounds reductive and pejorative, and by today's standards and tastes *The Man of Feeling* is indeed melodramatic and incredible. But perhaps because of the popularity of such writers as Sterne and Goldsmith, perhaps because of the growing cult of the individual, or because of Pelagian-latitudinarian trends in eighteenth-century Christianity, or because of some combination of these, it made Mackenzie, for two or three decades, a popular and influential man of letters.

Mackenzie wrote two other novels, *The Man of the World* and *Julia de Roubigné*. Neither received the acclaim of *The Man of Feeling*, although *Julia de Roubigné* drew some applause. The generic influence of Samuel Richardson is apparent in both – in *The Man of the World* Mackenzie attempts to create in Sindall a counterpart to Harley in *The Man of Feeling*, a genteel villain like Lovelace in *Clarissa*. *Julia de Roubigné* has a more credible plot than *The Man of the World* and is in the epistolary style, a structural strategy resulting in a sense of psychological immediacy, as in Richardson at his best.

Although he lived until 1831, Mackenzie's "creative" writing career had effectively ended by around 1800. Declining health and increased involvement in his career as a lawyer were probably the reasons. His *Letters of Brutus* were topical and soon forgotten. He remained widely respected, however, particularly in the polite literary circles of Edinburgh, as a critic of perceptive taste. He was influential in furthering the reputations of Burns and Scott at crucial points early in their careers, and his "Account of the German Theatre" (1790) helped augment the growing popularity in Great Britain of German authors, Schiller in particular. His critical biography of the playwright John Home (1822) is sympathetic and intelligent. Mackenzie was very much a man of his times and was sensitive and thoughtful in literary matters. His canon includes poetry of the ballad-revival sort as well as dramatic tragedy and comedy. But he remained unassuming, modest, and, after some early success, not highly ambitious.

—Paul D. McGlynn

MACLEOD, Fiona. See **SHARP, William**

MALLOCK, William Hurrell. English. Born in Cheriton Bishop, Devon, 7 February 1849. Educated privately under Reverend Philpot at Littlehampton; Balliol College, Oxford (Newdigate Prize, 1871), 1869–74, degrees 1871, 1874. Novelist and political and philosophical polemicist from 1875; lectured in the United States, 1907. *Died 2 April 1923.*

PUBLICATIONS

Fiction

> *The New Republic; or, Culture, Faith, and Philosophy in an English Country House.* 1877; edited by John Lucas, 1975.
> *The New Paul and Virginia; or, Positivism on an Island.* 1878.

A Romance of the Nineteenth Century. 1881.
The Old Order Changes. 1886.
A Human Document. 1892.
The Heart of Life. 1895.
The Individualist. 1899.
The Veil of the Temple; or, From Night to Twilight. 1904.
An Immortal Soul. 1908.

Verse

Poems. 1867.
The Parting of the Ways: A Poetic Epistle. 1867.
The Isthmus of Suez. 1871.
Poems. 1880.
Verses. 1893.
Lucretius on Life and Death. 1900.

Other

Every Man His Own Poet; or, The Inspired Singer's Recipe Book. 1872.
Is Life Worth Living? (essays). 1879.
Social Equality: A Short Study in a Missing Science. 1882.
Atheism and the Value of Life: Five Studies in Contemporary Literature. 1884.
Property and Progress; or, A Brief Enquiry into Contemporary Social Agitation in England. 1884.
In an Enchanted Island; or, A Winter Retreat in Cyprus. 1889.
The Landlords and the National Income: A Chart Showing the Proportion Borne by the Rental of the Landlords to the Gross Income of the People. 1884.
Labour and the Popular Welfare. 1893.
Studies of Contemporary Superstition. 1895.
Classes and Masses; or, Wealth, Wages, and Welfare in the United Kingdom: A Handbook of Social Facts for Political Thinkers and Speakers. 1896.
Aristocracy and Evolution. 1898.
Doctrine and Doctrinal Disruption, Being an Examination of the Intellectual Position of the Church of England. 1900.
Religion as a Credible Doctrine. 1902.
The Fiscal Dispute Made Easy. 1903.
The Reconstruction of Belief. 1905.
A Critical Examination of Socialism. 1907.
The Nation as a Business Firm: An Attempt to Cut a Path Through the Jungle. 1910.
Social Reform as Related to Realities and Delusions: An Examination of the Increase and Distribution of Wealth from 1801 to 1910. 1914.
The Limits of Pure Democracy. 1819; abridgement, as *Democracy,* 1924.
Capital, War, and Wages: Three Questions in Outline. 1918.
Memoirs of Life and Literature. 1920.

Editor, *Lucretius* (selections). 1878.
Editor, *Letters, Remains, and Memoirs of E. A. Seymour, 12th Duke of Somerset.* 1893.

Reading List: *The Novels of Mallock* by Amy B. Adams, 1934; "The Novels of Mallock" by Charles C. Nickerson, in *English Literature in Transition 6,* 1963 (includes bibliography);

Literature and Politics in the Nineteenth Century by John Lucas, 1971.

*   *   *

William Hurrell Mallock became an overnight sensation with his first published work, *The New Republic*. He continued to find readers and stir controversy throughout the closing years of the nineteenth century, but died virtually forgotten in 1923. Byron asserted that he was born for opposition, and the same may be said of Mallock. Fortunately for Byron, he died before old age could make some of his attitudes irrelevant. Unfortunately for Mallock, he did not. As a result, he often gives the impression in his later years of tilting at windmills or, worse, of fighting a purely phantom enemy.

Mallock was by nature, one might say, a conservative in politics, in literature, and in religious matters. Although he never became a Catholic, he revered the Roman church; he loathed the Broad Church movement, and had a lasting contempt for its leaders, especially for Jowett, Master of Mallock's college, Balliol, even when those leaders were dead or superseded. He had an equally strong detestation for Liberals in politics, and he thought that all socialists were either madmen or frauds. In literary matters he admired the Roman poets and satirists, had little good to say of nineteenth-century writers, and thought Swinburne should have been horsewhipped for his *Songs Before Sunrise*. In short, Mallock appears as everyone's favourite caricature of the crusty, out-of-touch blimp, growling his way through a life of almost comic irrelevance.

Yet Mallock at his best is a formidable satirist, an important spokesman for Conservatism, and an elegant essayist, whose *In an Enchanted Island* must be one of the best travel books ever written. In a long life, he published volumes of poetry, novels, political treatises, works of religious polemic, social critiques, collections of literary criticism: in fact, there was scarcely anything that he did not touch on at some time or another. At the end of his life he published *Memoirs of Life and Literature*, a typically contentious, witty volume, full of valuable anecdotes.

His masterpiece is undoubtedly *The New Republic*. It is a *roman à clef* in which Mallock brilliantly holds up for inspection and, usually, ridicule, the ideas and beliefs of famous contemporaries. Among them are Jowett, Matthew Arnold, Walter Pater, Thomas Huxley and William Tyndall. (For a full list of the characters, and a key to their originals, the reader should consult my edition of the work, 1975.) Only one man is allowed to escape censure. John Ruskin appears lightly disguised as Mr. Herbert, breathing woe and damnation to his assembled audience. Ruskin was delighted by the portrait and told a friend that Mallock understood him better than any man living. Mallock himself came to have doubts about Ruskin, mostly because of Ruskin's interest in working-class politics (he took particular exception to *Unto This Last* and *Fors Clavigera*), and in his later works tended to play the role of Mr. Herbert himself. That is to say that, whether writing novel, polemic, or straightforward propaganda, he appears as the prophet of doom, telling his audience how unhappy they are because God is being killed off, how unfortunate because society is being levelled down to a common greyness, how lacking in cultural resource because the great writers of the past are increasingly neglected. It was a role he clearly enjoyed.

Mallock is often outrageous, frequently silly, and sometimes shrill and spiteful. But he is always readable, and at his best he is a weighty adversary.

—John Lucas

MANLEY, Delariviere; also known as Mary Manley. English. Born in the Channel Islands, probably in Jersey, 7 April 1663. Married her cousin John Manley c. 1688 (already married; subsequently deserted her; died, 1714). Lived with the Duchess of Cleveland, then travelled in England, 1694–96; writer from 1695; involved in an attempt to defraud the estate of a man named Pheasant, 1705; wrote romances from 1705; arrested for libel (*New Atalantis*), 1709, released 1710; contributed to *The Examiner* from 1711. *Died 11 July 1724.*

PUBLICATIONS

Collections

> *Novels (The Secret History of Queen Zarah and the Zarazians, The New Atalantis, Memoirs of Europe, The Adventures of Rivella),* edited by Patricia Köster. 2 vols., 1971.

Fiction

> *Letters, to Which Is Added a Letter from a Supposed Nun in Portugal.* 1696; as *A Stage-Coach Journey to Exeter,* 1725.
> *The Secret History of Queen Zarah and the Zarazians.* 1705.
> *The Lady's Packet of Letters, Taken from Her by a French Privateer in Her Passage to Holland.* 1707.
> *Secret Memoirs and Manners of Several Persons of Quality of Both Sexes from the New Atalantis, an Island in the Mediterranean.* 1709.
> *Memoirs of Europe, Towards the Close of the Eighth Century.* 1710.
> *Court Intrigues.* 1711.
> *The Adventures of Rivella; or, The History of the Author of the Atalantis.* 1714.
> *The Power of Love,* in *Seven Novels.* 1720.

Plays

> *The Lost Lover; or, The Jealous* (produced 1696). 1696.
> *The Royal Mischief* (produced 1696). 1696.
> *Almyna; or, The Arabian Vow* (produced 1706). 1707.
> *Lucius, The First Christian King of Britain* (produced 1717). 1717.

Other

> *A True Narrative of the Examination of the Marquis de Guiscard.* 1711.
> *A True Relation of the Intended Riot on Queen Elizabeth's Birthday.* 1711.
> *A Modest Inquiry.* 1714.

Reading List: *Five Queer Women* by Walter and Clare Jerrold, 1929; *Popular Fiction Before Richardson* by John Richetti, 1969.

*　　*　　*

Delariviere Manley achieved fame and notoriety in 1709 with the publication of *Secret Memoirs and Manners of several Persons of Quality of Both Sexes from the New Atalantis*, a collection of scandalous narratives about prominent Whig nobles and politicians. The enormous success of this book is easy to understand; the scandals it provided were mostly sexual, and Manley had a talent for the vivid rendition of what the 18th century called "warm" scenes. Like many sensational and erotic narratives of the age, *The New Atalantis* has an elaborate moral facade and claims to be an outraged satiric attack on the corruption of the times. Manley begins Part II by calling her book a satire "on different Subjects, Tales, Stories, and Characters of Invention, after the Manner of Lucian, who copy'd from Varro." The best parts of the book are precisely the satiric ones, those recurring and energetic denunciations of the age which add up to a lively and often grotesque panorama of intrigue, lust, betrayal, and even crime. Manley's stories were based on some facts, and the book was designed as Tory political propaganda to undermine public confidence in the Whig ministry, which fell from power in 1710. But *The New Atalantis* was reprinted several times until 1736, long after its political scandals had faded, suggesting that Manley's real achievement was the effective imagining of a mythical world of corruption and immorality in which readers found satisfactions that were neither satiric nor political.

In a way, Manley's abilities as a writer of narrative lagged behind her intelligence as a satirist and political writer. She wrote an interesting preface to her 1705 scandal novel about the Duchess of Marlborough, *The History of Queen Zarah*, in which she speaks with sense and clarity of the need for the probable and the natural in those "little histories" such as her book which she claims are now replacing the once popular French romances. And yet the characters in *Queen Zarah* are monsters of vice, the language they speak rhetorically swollen, and the scenes and actions depicted are wildly exaggerated. In *The Adventures of Rivella*, a thinly fictionalized version of her own curiously melodramatic private life (seduced into a bigamous marriage by her cousin and then deserted), Manley manages a restrained and even touching account of female suffering. But her other books are of little intrinsic literary value; they are vigorous and often lively but clumsy and generally incoherent narratives. Though she apparently aspired to narrative virtues such as consistency of character and probability of situation which the masters of the English novel were shortly to achieve, Manley could only describe a world of blasted female innocence and brutal male lust. But she managed to present such moral and sexual melodrama very effectively, and her works give us access to an imaginary world which had a powerful hold on a large audience for a good part of the 18th century.

—John Richetti

MARRYAT, Frederick. English.   Born in Westminster, London, 10 July 1792. Educated privately. Married Catherine Shairp in 1819; four sons and seven daughters, including the novelist Florence Marryat. Joined the Royal Navy, 1806; sailed as a midshipman on the *Impérieuse*, under Lord Cochrane, 1806–09, in the flagship *Centaur*, in the Mediterranean, 1810, and on the *Aeolus* and *Spartan* in the West Indies and off the coast of North America, 1811–12; sailed to the West Indies on the *Espiègle*, 1813; Lieutenant of the *Newcastle*, off the coast of North America, 1814 until invalided home, 1815; appointed Commander, 1815; commanded othe sloop *Beaver* cruising off St. Helena to guard against the escape of Napoleon, 1820–22; involved in suppression of Channel smuggling, on the *Rosario*, 1822; sailed in the *Larne* to the East Indies, 1823, and served in the Burmese war: Senior Naval Officer at Rangoon, 1824; commanded expedition up the Bassein River, 1825; appointed

Captain of the *Tees*, 1825, and returned in her to England, 1826: C.B. (Companion, Order of the Bath), for services in Burma, 1826; commanded the *Adriadne* in the Atlantic service, 1828 until he retired to devote himself to writing, 1830; Editor, *Metropolitan Magazine*, London, 1832–35; lived in Brussels, 1836, Canada and the United States, 1837–39, and London, 1839–43; settled on a farm, Langham Manor, in Norfolk, 1843. Recipient: Royal Humane Society gold medal, 1818. Fellow of the Royal Society, 1819; Member, Legion of Honour, 1833. *Died 9 August 1848.*

PUBLICATIONS

Collections

> *Novels,* edited by R. Brimley Johnson.   24 vols., 1896–98; revised edition, 26 vols., 1929–30.

Fiction

> *The Naval Officer; or, Scenes and Adventures in the Life of Frank Mildmay.*   1829.
> *The King's Own.*   1830.
> *Newton Forster; or, The Merchant Service.*   1832.
> *Peter Simple.*   3 vols., 1833–34.
> *Jacob Faithful.*   1834.
> *The Pacha of Many Tales.*   1835.
> *Japhet in Search of a Father.*   4 vols., 1835–36.
> *The Diary of a Blasé.*   1836; as *Diary on the Continent,* in *Olla Podrida,* 1840.
> *The Pirate, and The Three Cutters.*   1836; as *Stories of the Sea,* 1836.
> *Mr. Midshipman Easy.*   1836.
> *Snarleyyow; or, The Dog Fiend.*   1837; as *The Dog Fiend,* 1847.
> *The Phantom Ship.*   1839; edited by M. W. Disher, 1948.
> *Olla Podrida* (stories).   1840.
> *Poor Jack.*   1840.
> *Masterman Ready; or, The Wreck of the Pacific, Written for Young People.*   3 vols., 1841–42.
> *Joseph Rushbrook; or, The Poacher.*   1841; as *The Poacher,* 1846.
> *Percival Keene.*   1842.
> *The Settlers in Canada, Written for Young People.*   1844; edited by O. Warner, 1956.
> *The Mission; or, Scenes in Africa.*   1845.
> *The Privateer's-Man One Hundred Years Ago.*   1846.
> *The Children of the New Forest.*   1847.
> *The Little Savage,* completed by Frank S. Marryat.   2 vols., 1848–49.

Other

> *A Code of Signals for the Use of Vessels Employed in the Merchant Services.*   1817; revised edition, 1837, 1841.
> *A Suggestion for the Abolition of the Present System of Impressment in the Naval Service.*   1822.
> *The Floral Telegraph: A New Mode of Communication by Floral Signals.*   1836 (possibly not by Marryat).

The Diary in America, with Remarks on Its Institutions. 6 vols., 1839; edited by Sydney Jackman, 1963.
Narrative of the Travels and Adventures of Monsieur Violet in California, Sonora, and Western Texas. 1853; as *Travels and Romantic Adventures of Monsieur Violet among the Snake Indians,* 1843.
Valerie: An Autobiography (not completed by Marryat). 2 vols., 1849.

Reading List: *Life and Letters of Marryat* by F. Church, 1872; *Marryat and the Old Navy* by Christopher Lloyd, 1939; *Marryat: A Rediscovery* by O. Warner, 1953; *Marryat: L'Homme et l'Oeuvre* by Maurice P. Gautier, 1973.

*   *   *

Though he is remembered as a children's author, Frederick Marryat began his fiction-writing as a novelist, and before that spent over twenty years at sea. His earliest books, in fact, are pamphlets on naval subjects. The material for his fiction was a career in the exotic world of Nelson's navy, the source of the potent English myth of Jack Tar: his writing owed little, therefore, to the latest literary fashions. One may perhaps compare him to Scott, who also felt himself to be an amateur, and was similarly reduced to writing desperately for money to maintain that position in his latter days. Neither author can be read with pleasure unless one accepts the convention of expansive, slow-moving story-telling. Scott's novels develop more profoundly within this plan, but Marryat was not without insights into contemporary concerns. Like Scott, he found history imaginatively exciting, and recreated it vividly; and he showed the Romantic sense of the importance of childhood and education, inflected towards a concern for moral training rather than in the Wordsworthian mystical direction, but still imaginatively handled. In, for example, *The Little Savage* the Rousseau-inspired motif of the child growing up cut off from civilisation is treated with considerable psychological grasp.
It was his concern for the accuracy of information conveyed to the young which led Marryat to writing for children: he was disgusted at the fantastic seamanship of *The Swiss Family Robinson,* and set out to improve upon it in *Masterman Ready.* Victorian boys were very lucky in this, for it opened to them the whole range of his sea stories, and his writing for children is itself free from the condescension and over-simplification of many boys' books. The novels are racy and vigorous, full of facts; the children's writing has a layer of simple piety, but also the charm of real information and practical instructions. In this he shows a grasp of the primitive bases of narrative satisfaction: his books all deal with situations in which he can make absorbing use of practical detail. The model may well be Defoe. He uses the desert-island story, where civilisation is rebuilt from nothing, in *Masterman Ready* and *The Little Savage;* he uses, in *The Settlers in Canada* and *The Children of the New Forest,* the similar outline of a civilised family improvising in a wild and dangerous setting; and in *Poor Jack* he takes the alternative design of a deprived individual living like a savage in the jungle of the city, as in Defoe's *Colonel Jack.* And always, like Defoe, Marryat tells us the details of how they did it, how it worked, and what it cost. In this kind of book looseness of design is not important: Carlyle's criticism of Marryat's writing as concerned with trivia is less true to our experience than Dr. Johnson's remark that no one ever put down *Robinson Crusoe* without wishing it was longer. Marryat's writing may be uneven, ill-planned, rambling – but it is also absorbing and delightful.

—J. S. Bratton

MARTINEAU, Harriet. English. Born in Norwich, Norfolk, 12 June 1802; sister of the theologian James Martineau. Educated at home, and at the Reverend Perry's school, in Norwich, to age 15, then continued classical studies on her own. Became partially deaf while still in her teens, and suffered from poor health for all of her life; writer from 1821; went through long illness and was left destitute, 1829; lived in London, 1832–39; became successful writer; visited America, 1834–36; invalid at Tynemouth, 1839–44; settled at Clappersgate, Westmorland, 1845; became a friend of Wordsworth's; visited Egypt and Palestine, 1846–47; regular contributor to the *Daily News*, London, 1852–66; also contributed to the *Edinburgh Review* from 1859. Refused government pension, 1841, 1873. *Died 27 June 1876.*

PUBLICATIONS

Fiction

Five Years of Youth; or, Sense and Sentiment. 1831.
Illustrations of Political Economy (stories). 9 vols., 1832–34.
Poor Laws and Paupers Illustrated. 4 vols., 1833–34.
Illustrations of Taxation. 1834.
Deerbrook. 1839.
The Hour and the Man. 1841.
The Playfellow, Containing The Settlers at Home, Feats on the Fiord, The Peasant and the Prince, The Crofton Boys. 4 vols., 1841.
The Rioters. N.d.
Dawn Island. 1845.
Forest and Game-Law Tales. 3 vols., 1845–46.
The Billow and the Rock. 1846.
Merdhen, The Manor and the Eyrie, and Old Landmarks and Old Laws. 1852.
The Hampdens: A Historiette. 1880.

Other

Devotional Exercises for the Use of Young Persons. 1823; revised edition, as *Devotional Exercises, To Which Is Added A Guide to the Study of the Scriptures,* 1832.
Addresses with Prayers and Original Hymns for the Use of Families. 1826.
Essential Faith of the Universal Church Deduced from Sacred Records. 1831.
The Faith as Unfolded by Many Prophets: An Essay Addressed to the Disciples of Mohammed. 1832.
Providence as Manifested Through Israel. 1832.
Miscellanies. 2 vols., 1836.
Society in America. 3 vols., 1837; edited by Seymour Martin Lipset, 1968.
A Retrospect of Western Travel. 3 vols., 1838.
How to Observe: Morals and Manners. 1838.
Guides to Service. 1839(?).
The Martyr Age of the United States of America. 1840.
Life in the Sick-Room; or, Essays by an Invalid. 1844.
Letters on Mesmerism. 1845.
Eastern Life, Past and Present. 3 vols., 1848.
Household Education. 1849.
History of England During the Thirty Years' Peace 1816–46. 2 vols., 1849–50; revised edition, 1855.

Two Letters on Cow-Keeping.   1850(?).
Letters on the Laws of Man's Nature and Development, with H. G. Atkinson.   1851.
Introduction to the History of the Peace from 1800 to 1815.   1851.
Half a Century of the British Empire: A History of the Kingdom and the People from 1800 to 1850, part 1.   1851.
Letters from Ireland.   1853.
Complete Guide to the Lakes.   1854.
Guide to Windermere, with Tours of Neighbouring Lakes and Other Interesting Places.   1854.
The Factory Controversy: A Warning Against Meddling Legislation.   1855.
A History of the American Compromises.   1856.
Corporate Traditions and National Rights: Local Dues on Shipping.   1857.
Guide to Keswick and Its Environs.   1857.
Suggestions Towards the Future Government of India.   1858.
Endowed Schools of Ireland.   1859.
England and Her Soldiers.   1859.
Survey of the Lake District.   1860.
Health, Husbandry, and Handicraft.   1861.
Biographical Sketches.   1869; revised edition, 1876.
Autobiography.   3 vols., 1877.

Editor, *Traditions of Palestine.*   1830.

Translator, *The Positive Philosophy of Auguste Comte.*   2 vols., 1853.

Bibliography: "Martineau: A Bibliography of the Separately Printed Books" by J.'B. Rivlin, in *Bulletin of the New York Public Library,* 1946–47.

Reading List: *Martineau: An Example of Victorian Conflict* by Narola E. Rivenburg, 1932; *Martineau* by John C. Nevill, 1943; *The Life and Work of Martineau* by Vera Wheatley, 1957; *Martineau: A Radical Victorian* by Robert K. Webb, 1960; *Martineau* by Florence F. Miller, 1972.

*   *   *

A writer of eclectic works and of unflagging enthusiasms, Harriet Martineau was a novelist, political economist, journalist, travel writer, essayist, historian, translator, editor, and autobiographer. Her prodigious writing sometimes resulted in works of uneven quality but she never limited her pursuits, which ranged from children's books like *The Playfellow* to studies on the future government of India and the soldiers of England. Throughout her long, illness-plagued life – she was born without a sense of smell, gradually lost her hearing and was an invalid for five years until cured by mesmerism – Harriet Martineau was a teacher. Two curious but fascinating books describe her illness and miraculous recovery: *Life in the Sickroom* and *Letters on Mesmerism.* Literature for Harriet Martineau was a didactic vehicle to explain to readers the complex workings of society or the individual. She wrote books on American society, English morals, and Middle East religions. No subject was too arcane, no topic too abstruse for her popularizing.

The greatest success of Harriet Martineau was *Illustrations of Political Economy,* one of her earliest books. It was a series of stories that exemplified various economic principles. Summaries of the doctrinal points appear at the end of each fictional adventure. Demands for a free money market, for example, is the subject of "Berkely the Banker" while the argument for free trade is the theme of "The Loom and the Lugger." *Elements of Political Economy* by James Mill was the major source for Martineau's economic concepts. *Illustrations of Political*

Economy was immensely popular, went through numerous printings and established Martineau as a prominent literary figure in London. She continued to be successful with short fictional tracts for social and political issues such as *Poor Laws and Paupers Illustrated* and *Forest and Game-Law Tales*. Her most sustained, mature attempt at novel writing was *Deerbrook*, a didactic novel of English provincial life that shares certain general similarities with the work of Jane Austen and George Eliot.

Harriet Martineau was brought up a devout Unitarian but became a Free Thinker with an enthusiasm for science. In 1853 she translated Comte's influential work on Positivist philosophy. Her greatest subject, however, was herself, and her most significant work is her candid *Autobiography* begun in 1855 at the beginning of what she thought to be a fatal illness. The work did not appear until 1877, following her death. This lively, critical book, replete with comments on the major intellectual figures of the age and the difficulties of maintaining a literary career, is one of the most important autobiographies by a woman in the nineteenth century. With her energy, optimism, and passions, Harriet Martineau remains a vibrant although at times eccentric embodiment of the woman as Victorian man-of-letters.

—I. B. Nadel

MASON, A(lfred) E(dward) W(oodley). English. Born in Camberwell, London, 7 May 1865. Educated at Dulwich College, London, 1878–84; Trinity College, Oxford (exhibitioner in classics, 1887), 1884–87, degrees in classics 1886, 1888. Served with the Royal Marine Light Infantry in World War I, and was involved in secret service missions in Spain, Morocco, and Mexico: Major. Actor, in provincial touring companies, 1888–94; writer from 1895; Liberal Member of Parliament for Coventry, 1906–10. Honorary Fellow of Trinity College, 1943. *Died 22 November 1948.*

PUBLICATIONS

Fiction

> *A Romance of Wastdale.* 1895.
> *The Courtship of Morrice Buckler: A Romance.* 1896.
> *Lawrence Clavering.* 1897.
> *The Philanderers.* 1897.
> *Miranda of the Balcony.* 1899.
> *Parson Kelly,* with Andrew Lang. 1899.
> *The Watchers.* 1899.
> *Clementina.* 1901.
> *Ensign Knightley and Other Stories.* 1901.
> *The Four Feathers.* 1902.
> *The Truants.* 1904.
> *The Broken Road.* 1907.
> *Running Water.* 1907.
> *At the Villa Rose.* 1910.
> *The Clock.* 1910.

Making Good.   1910.
The Turnstile.   1912.
The Witness for the Defence.   1913.
The Affair at the Semiramis Hotel.   1917.
The Four Corners of the World (stories).   1917.
The Episode of the Thermometer.   1918.
The Summons.   1920.
The Winding Stair.   1923.
The House of the Arrow.   1924.
No Other Tiger.   1927.
The Prisoner in the Opal.   1928.
The Dean's Elbow.   1930.
The Three Gentlemen.   1932.
The Sapphire.   1933.
Dilemmas (stories).   1934.
They Wouldn't Be Chessmen.   1935.
Fire over England.   1936.
The Drum.   1937.
Königsmark.   1938.
The Secret Fear.   1940.
Muck and Amber.   1942.
The House in Lordship Lane.   1946.

Plays

Blanche de Malètroit, from the story by R. L. Stevenson (produced 1894).   1894.
The Courtship of Morrice Buckler, with Isabel Bateman, from the novel by Mason (produced 1897).
Marjory Strode (produced 1908).
Col. Smith (produced 1909).
The Witness for the Defence (produced 1911).   1913.
Open Windows (produced 1913).
Green Stockings.   1914.
At the Villa Rose, from his own novel (produced 1920).   1928.
Running Water (produced 1922).
The House of the Arrow, from his own novel (produced 1928).
No Other Tiger, from his own novel (produced 1928).
A Present from Margate, with Ian Hay (produced 1933).   1934.

Other

The Royal Exchange.   1920.
Sir George Alexander and the St. James's Theatre.   1935.
The Life of Francis Drake.   1941.

Reading List: *Mason: The Adventures of a Story Teller* by Roger Lancelyn Green, 1952 (includes bibliography).

*   *   *

To think of A. E. W. Mason is to think of the swift, breathless, joyous rush of the adventures which he described so well – backed by the authenticity of his own adventurous life. After five years as an actor he turned to literature, achieving sudden fame with his second book, the swashbuckling *Courtship of Morrice Buckler*, followed by several others of the kind, and contemporary "adventure novels," the best known being *Miranda of the Balcony*. A more subtle Jacobite romance, *Parson Kelly*, which he wrote with Andrew Lang, and its companion, *Clementina*, ended Mason's first period of historical romances.

By now he was able to go adventuring himself, notably into the Sudan not long after the Battle of Omdurman, which gave him the setting for his best-known book, *The Four Feathers*. This is an adventure story which is also a psychological study – notably of the hero, Harry Feversham, who, believing himself to be a coward, resigns his commission in the Army when his regiment is ordered on active service, and discovers while regaining his honour and his fiancée that he is braver than most when the actual moment of action comes. It contains also a character, John Durrance, who nearly usurps the role of hero as his powers of observation grow after he has become blind and he develops unexpected powers of detection.

This idea of detection by noticing reactions of all sorts in the people observed or suspected led Mason to the creation of his French detective, Inspector Hanaud, who made his first appearance in *At the Villa Rose* and reached his greatest powers in *The House of the Arrow* and *The Prisoner in the Opal*. These show the development of the detective story into the detective novel – the detailed presentation and study in depth of the characters, criminal and otherwise, concerned in the ingenious and exciting mystery to be solved.

Mason's other interests and experiences supplied the vivid setting for other novels and romances, most of them of a high level. His prowess as a mountaineer – sixteen hours on the Brenva Ridge of Mont Blanc – resulted in *Running Water*; his skill as a yachtsman, his early explorations in Morocco, his five years as Liberal M.P. for Coventry, his experiences in M.I.5 in the First World War – each inspired one or more books.

Towards the end of his life he turned back to historical fiction. His fine romance of the Spanish Armada, *Fire over England*, was made into one of the most popular films of its day. But his historical novel *Musk and Amber*, concerning the fortunes of an English nobleman who becomes one of the great *castrati* singers in an eighteenth-century setting in England and Venice, and achieves his vengeance on the man who sold him to this fate to cheat him of his inheritance, touches his highest peak. He will surely be remembered for this, for *The Four Feathers*, and for the best of the Inspector Hanaud stories.

—Roger Lancelyn Green

MATURIN, Charles Robert. Irish. Born in Dublin in 1782. Educated at Trinity College, Dublin, B.A. 1800. Married Henrietta Kingsbury in 1802; two sons. Took holy orders; served as Curate of Loughrea, and afterwards of St. Peter's, Dublin; also maintained a school in addition to his curacy, 1807–13; writer from 1806. *Died 30 October 1824.*

PUBLICATIONS

Fiction

Fatal Revenge; or, The Family of Montorio. 1807.

The Wild Irish Boy. 1808.
The Milesian Chief: A Romance. 1812.
Women; or, Pour et Contre. 1818.
Melmoth the Wanderer: A Tale. 1820; edited by Alethea Hayter, 1977.
The Albigenses: A Romance. 1824.
Leixlip Castle. 1825.

Plays

Bertram; or, The Castle of St. Aldobrand (produced 1816). 1816.
Manuel (produced 1817). 1817.
Fredolfo (produced 1819). 1819.
Osmyn the Renegade; or, The Siege of Salerno (produced 1830).

Verse

Lines on the Battle of Waterloo: A Prize Poem. 1816.

Other

Sermons. 1819.
Five Sermons on the Errors of the Roman Catholic Church. 1824.
The Correspondence of Scott and Maturin, edited by F. E. Ratchford and W. H. McCarthy. 1937.

Reading List: *Maturin* by Dale Kramer, 1973; *Maturin: L'Homme et l'Oeuvre* by Claude Fierobe, 2 vols., 1974.

*   *   *

Charles Robert Maturin's *Melmoth the Wanderer* has every right to be considered the finest Gothic novel in English. Earlier, Maturin had been known as a novelist – Walter Scott praised *Fatal Revenge* in the *Quarterly Review* in May 1810 – and as a playwright – Edmund Kean made a success in *Bertram* at Drury Lane – but his literary fortunes had then declined. His two later plays, *Manuel* and *Fredolfo*, failed, and Coleridge published a scathing criticism of *Bertram* in *Biographia Literaria* in 1817. But *Melmoth* was to fascinate Baudelaire, who referred to "la grande création satanique du révérend Maturin" and proposed to translate it into French; and as late as 1965 André Breton the Surrealist wrote an introduction for a new translation into French.

The success of *Melmoth* lies in its emotional intensity. The structure is far from tight, but offers a good opportunity for Maturin's best effects. The hero sells his soul to the devil in return for longer life, and the events of the novel concern his attempts to find and persuade others in moments of intense suffering and despair to change places with him. The resulting stories vary in time from the seventeenth century onwards and in place from the West Coast of Ireland to a romantic island in the Indian Ocean. But the reader's persistent awareness of Melmoth's plight gives unity and also a sense of the inevitable.

Earlier Gothic novels like *The Castle of Otranto* or *The Mysteries of Udolpho* often give an impression of fantasy, of the author's playing a literary game. But *Melmoth* is a much more disturbing work in which sadism and violence are conveyed in such a way that they cannot be ignored. The description of the death of the parricide monk, torn to pieces by the mob in view of hidden, frightened Monçada, is particularly horrifying, and its power is no doubt related to the fact that it was based partly on Maturin's memories of street violence in Dublin. He had no need to invent aspects of human wickedness; he knew them from observation and experience. The scene ends: "The officer who headed the troop dashed his horse's hoofs into a bloody formless mass, and demanded, 'Where was the victim?' He was answered, 'Beneath your horse's feet'; and they departed."

It is arguable that the Gothic novel is a limited form because of its concentration on the darker aspects of experience and its tendency to melodrama. In *Melmoth the Wanderer* Maturin was able to take the form to its limits because of the intensity of his feelings and the intermittent poetic power of his prose.

—Peter Faulkner

MEREDITH, George. English. Born in Portsmouth, Hampshire, 12 February 1828. Educated at Paul's Church School, Southsea, Hampshire; Moravian School, Neuwied sur Rhine, Germany, 1843–44; articled to a solicitor in London, 1845. Married 1) Mary Ellen Nicholls, daughter of the novelist Thomas Love Peacock, in 1849 (died, 1861), one son; 2) Marie Vulliamy in 1864 (died, 1885), one son and one daughter. Abandoned the law for journalism; settled in London, then in Surrey; writer from 1848; with others, edited *The Monthly Observer*, London, 1848–49; contributed to *Chambers Journal*, London, 1849, and to *Fraser's Magazine*, London, 1851–52; leader writer for the *Ipswich Journal* from 1860; literary adviser to Chapman and Hall, publishers, London, 1862–94; Special Foreign Correspondent for the London *Morning Post* during the Austro-Italian War, 1866; Editor, 1867–68, and Contributor, 1867–1909, *Fortnightly Review*, London; lectured on comedy at the London Institution, 1877. Recipient: Royal Society of Literature gold medal, 1905. President, Society of Authors, 1892; Vice-President, London Library, 1902. Order of Merit, 1905. *Died 18 May 1909.*

PUBLICATIONS

Collections

> *Works.* 27 vols., 1909–11.
> *Letters,* edited by C. L. Cline. 3 vols., 1968.
> *Poems,* edited by Phyllis B. Bartlett. 2 vols., 1977.

Fiction

> *The Shaving of Shagpat: An Arabian Entertainment.* 1855; edited by F. M. Meynell, 1955.
> *Farina: A Legend of Cologne.* 1857.

The Ordeal of Richard Feverel: A History of Father and Son. 1859; revised edition, 1878; edited by Norman Kelvin, 1961.
Evan Harrington; or, He Would Be a Gentleman. 1861; edited by G. F. Reynolds, 1922.
Emilia in England. 1864; as *Sandra Belloni,* 1886.
Rhoda Fleming. 1865.
Vittoria. 1867.
The Adventures of Harry Richmond. 1871.
Beauchamp's Career. 1875; edited by G. M. Young, 1950.
The House on the Beach. 1877.
The Egoist: A Comedy in Narrative. 1879; edited by Robert M. Adams, 1977.
The Tragic Comedians. 1880; revised edition, edited by C. K. Shorter, 1891.
Diana of the Crossways. 1885.
The Case of General Ople and Lady Camper. 1890.
The Tale of Chloe. 1890.
One of Our Conquerors. 1891.
Lord Ormont and His Aminta. 1894.
The Tale of Chloe and Other Stories. 1894.
The Amazing Marriage. 1895.
(Novels). 39 vols., 1896–1912 (includes miscellaneous prose and bibliography).
Short Stories. 1898.
Celt and Saxon. 1910.

Play

The Sentimentalists (produced 1910).

Verse

Poems. 1851.
Modern Love, and Poems of the English Roadside, with Poems and Ballads. 1862; revised edition, 1892.
Poems and Lyrics of the Joy of Earth. 1883.
Ballads and Poems of Tragic Life. 1887.
A Reading of Earth. 1888.
Jump-to-Glory Jane: A Poem. 1889.
Poems: The Empty Purse, with Odes to the Comic Spirit, to Youth in Memory, and Verses. 1892.
Selected Poems. 1897.
Odes in Contribution to the Song of French History. 1898.
A Reading of Life. 1901.
Last Poems. 1909.
Poems Written in Early Youth, Poems from Modern Love, and Scattered Poems. 1909.

Other

Works. 34 vols., 1896.
An Essay on Comedy and the Uses of the Comic Spirit. 1897; edited by Lane Cooper, 1956.
Up to the Midnight: A Series of Dialogues Contributed to the Graphic. 1913.
The Contributions to the Monthly Observer, edited by H. Buxton Forman. 1928.

Bibliography: *A Bibliography of the Writings in Prose and Verse by Meredith*, 1922, and *Meredithiana*, 1924, both by H. Buxton Forman; supplement by H. Lewis Sawin, in *Bulletin of Bibliography*, 1955.

Reading List: *Meredith: Les Cinquante Premières Années* by René Galland, 1923; *The Ordeal of Meredith* by Lionel Stevenson, 1954; *Meredith: His Life and Work* by Jack Lindsay, 1956; *A Troubled Eden: Nature and Society in the Works of Meredith* by Norman Kelvin, 1961; *Meredith and English Comedy* by V. S. Pritchett, 1970; *Meredith: The Critical Heritage* edited by Ioan Williams, 1971; *Meredith Now* edited by Ian Fletcher, 1971; *The Readable People of Meredith* by Judith Wilt, 1975; *Meredith: His Life and Lost Love* by David Williams, 1977.

*   *   *

In the year before his death, George Meredith, in an interview with Constantin Photiadès, remarked, "my name is celebrated, but no one reads my books." Never greatly popular in his own day, Meredith's work was nonetheless singular.

His first notable achievement was *The Ordeal of Richard Feverel*. Sir Austen Feverel, bruised by his wife's infidelity and desertion, applies the Great Shaddock Dogma, a woman-hating doctrine, to the scientific education of his son, Richard. Designed to bring him through the puppy-love stage, the Blossoming Season, and the Magnetic Age free from the temptations of Eve, or "the Apple Disease," it has disastrous consequences. Richard marries Lucy Desborough without permission, leaves her temporarily to gain his father's approbation, engages meanwhile in rescuing fallen women – and falls himself. A tragic dénouement points up the insufferability of imposing a rigid code or of systematizing human beings. Yet, at the end, incorrigible Sir Austen is plotting a program for his grandson. *The Ordeal* is stylistically unique, an amalgam of high and low comedy, of romance, and of tragicomedy. In addition to the interesting narrative structure, the epigrammatic and aphoristic wit, and the comic dialogue, there are numerous memorable characters, fewer autobiographical and more purely literary creations than in his later works. The unbalanced ones are Sir Austen's parasites – Adrian Harley, a seedy intellectual; the purely physical Algernon; and Uncle Hippias, a hypochondriacal dipsomaniac. Those who read earth right are Mrs. Berry, Lucy's counsellor ("Kissing don't last. Cookery do"); the independent, determined, and intuitive Lucy; and Austin Wentworth, Richard's spiritual guide. Finally, the cryptic and fluid symbolism of the "ordeal" broadening as the novel progresses, lends the masterful touch.

In the comic romance *Evan Harrington*, Meredith adopted a form – the *Bildungsroman* – and a subject – the illusions of class distinction – which he followed to an extent in *Emilia in England*, *The Adventures of Harry Richmond*, and *Beauchamp's Career*. Ashamed of his birth and aspiring to social status, Evan, brought ultimately to realize the distinction between a true gentleman and a sham, is able to acknowledge his lowly origins as son of a tailor. Meredith, drawing many of the characters from his family and acquaintances, suggests not merely class snobbery, but the broader scope of Carlyle's *Sartor Resartus*, as he had done in the earlier allegorical work *The Shaving of Shagpat*.

Modern Love (1862), a sequence of near-sonnets, is a psychological analysis of incompatibility in marriage. The wife has taken a lover; the husband, whose ego is battered, takes a mistress in retaliation. The study centers on the anguish and hypocrisy of physical closeness without mental communion:

> Like sculptured effigies they might be seen
> Upon their marriage-tomb, the sword between;
> Each wishing for the sword that severs all.

Love, "the crowning sun," had initially brought a oneness to intelligence and instinct; but they looked backward instead of forward and love became physical: "We are betrayed by what is false within." They at last hold "honest speech," but the wife, unable to act rationally, commits suicide to free her husband for the other woman. The omniscient narrator summarizes with a probable cause of the personal tragedy:

> Then each applied to each the fatal knife,
> Deep questioning, which probes to endless dole.
> Ah, what a dusty answer gets the soul
> When hot for certainties in this our life!

Modern Love is Meredith's most perceptive psychological study, written in his most penetrating language.

Emilia in England still displays some freshness, but the thematic thrust against sentimentalism and social climbing is a common one, and, increasingly thereafter, Meredith's work is, with a few exceptions, tired writing. *Vittoria*, the sequel to *Emilia*, deals with the Italian struggle for independence, and places the central character, now an opera diva, at the mercy of revolutionary events. *Harry Richmond* casts some oblique cross-cultural light on England through Harry's love for a German princess, Ottilia. *Beauchamp's Career* is a philosophic-political novel, with Carlyle's *Heroes and Hero Worship* in mind. Young Nevil enters politics as a Liberal, paralleling Meredith's own sympathies. This work, like many others, is flawed by a contemptuous, suspense-destroying, retrogressive narrative technique.

An Essay on Comedy gives Meredith's conception of comedy as a corrective device for pointing out right action based on reason rather than on sentimentality. Unlike satire or ridicule, it is detached and Olympian, so that it calls forth no resentment, only "volleys of silvery laughter."

The Egoist is a sustained high comedy of manners, with a style as fitted to the vain and shallow egoist, Sir Willoughby Patterne, as his trousers: "*You see he has a leg.*" While seeking a worthy match, he exercises *le driot de seigneur* by trifling with Laetitia·Dale. Clara Middleton, his bride elect, gradually detects his artificial sentiment, and breaks off with him. To save face, he proposes to Laetitia, who, with delightful irony, forces him to accept her on her own terms as a disillusioned critic of his faults. There is no narrative-impeding straining for the witty phrase and comic situation of his lesser works in this novel, usually considered his masterpiece.

"The Woods of Westermain," a poem of 1883, comes closest to consolidating Meredith's optimistic evolutionary theory emerging from his total canon. "Blood and brain and spirit, three .../ Join for true felicity." Instincts, intellect, and spirit are interdependent and derive nourishment and grow like the roots, limbs, and leaves on a tree. Any failure to read earth right results in imbalance of character, the anti-social disease of egoism. Such a theory perhaps explains the limitations of Meredith's work: the stereotyping of characters in terms of defects and the restriction to personal limitations within the social veneer. As an explanation of evil, it lacks cosmic import and complexity.

Nevertheless, as an unconventional, anti-Victorian experimentalist, as a humanistic free thinker, as a liberal reformer who championed equality for women, democratic political institutions, and freedom for oppressed nations – despite the fact that many of his other causes are now outdated – Meredith left to the reader of today three works of great distinction – *The Ordeal of Richard Feverel*, *Modern Love*, and *The Egoist*.

—Wesley D. Sweetser

MOORE, George (Augustus). Irish. Born at Moore Hall, Ballyglass, County Mayo, 24 February 1852; son of the landowner and politician G. H. Moore; moved with his family to London, 1869. Educated at Oscott College, Birmingham, 1861–69, then studied with an army tutor in London; studied painting at the Académie Julian, Paris, 1873–74. Lived in Paris, 1873–74, 1875–79; returned to London, 1880, and gave up painting for literature; wrote for the *Spectator* and the *Examiner*; art critic for the *Speaker*, 1891–95; settled in Ireland, and lived at Moore Hall and in Dublin, 1899–1911; High Sheriff of Mayo, 1905; returned to London, 1911. *Died 21 January 1933.*

PUBLICATIONS

Collections

> *Works* (Carra Edition). 21 vols., 1922–24.
> *Works* (Uniform Edition). 20 vols., 1924–33.
> *Works* (Ebury Edition). 20 vols., 1937.

Fiction

> *A Modern Lover.* 1883; revised edition, 1885; as *Lewis Seymour and Some Women,* 1917.
> *A Mummer's Wife.* 1884; revised edition, 1886, 1917; as *An Actor's Wife,* 1889.
> *A Drama in Muslin: A Realistic Novel.* 1886; revised edition, as *Muslin,* 1915.
> *A Mere Accident.* 1887.
> *Spring Days: A Realistic Novel – A Prelude to Don Juan.* 1888; revised edition, 1912; as *Shifting Love,* 1891.
> *Mike Fletcher.* 1889.
> *Vain Fortune.* 1891; revised edition, 1892, 1895.
> *Esther Waters.* 1894; revised edition, 1899, 1920.
> *Celibates* (stories). 1895.
> *Evelyn Innes.* 1898; revised edition, 1898, 1901, 1908.
> *Sister Theresa.* 1901; revised edition, 1909.
> *The Untilled Field* (stories). 1903; revised edition, 1903, 1914, 1926, 1931.
> *The Lake.* 1905; revised edition, 1906, 1921.
> *Memoirs of My Dead Life.* 1906; revised edition, 1921.
> *The Brook Kerith: A Syrian Story.* 1916; revised edition, 1927.
> *Héloise and Abélard.* 1921; *Fragments,* 1921.
> *In Single Strictness* (stories). 1922; revised edition, 1923; as *Celibate Lives,* 1927.
> *Peronnik the Fool* (story). 1926; revised edition, 1928.
> *Ulick and Soracha.* 1926.
> *A Flood* (story). 1930.
> *Aphrodite in Aulis.* 1930; revised edition, 1931.

Plays

> *Martin Luther,* with Bernard Lopez. 1879.
> *The Fashionable Beauty,* with J. M. Glover (produced 1885).
> *The Honeymoon in Eclipse* (produced 1888).
> *Thérèse Raquin,* from a play by A. Texeira de Mattos from the novel by Zola (produced 1891).

The Strike at Arlingford (produced 1893). 1893.
Journeys End in Lovers Meeting, with John Oliver Hobbes (produced 1894).
The Bending of the Bough (produced 1900). 1900.
Diarmuid and Grania, with W. B. Yeats (produced 1901). 1951; edited by Anthony Farrow, 1974.
Esther Waters, from his own novel (produced 1911). 1913.
The Apostle. 1911; revised version, as *The Passing of the Essenes* (produced 1930), 1930.
Elizabeth Cooper (produced 1913). 1913; revised version, as *The Coming of Gabrielle* (produced 1923), 1920.
The Making of an Immortal (produced 1928). 1927.

Verse

Flowers of Passion. 1877.
Pagan Poems. 1881.

Other

Literature at Nurse; or, Circulating Morals. 1885.
Parnell and His Island. 1887.
Confessions of a Young Man. 1888; revised edition, 1889, 1904, 1917, 1926.
Impressions and Opinions. 1891; revised edition, 1913.
Modern Painting. 1893; revised edition, 1896.
The Royal Academy. 1895.
Memoirs of My Dead Life. 1906; revised edition, 1921.
Reminiscences of the Impressionist Painters. 1906.
Hail and Farewell: A Trilogy (Ave, Salve, Vale) (autobiography). 3 vols., 1911–14. revised edition, 1925.
A Story-Teller's Holiday. 1918; revised edition, 2 vols., 1928.
Avowals (autobiography). 1919.
Moore Versus Harris (correspondence with Frank Harris). 1921.
Conversations in Ebury Street (autobiography). 1924; revised edition, 1930.
Letters to Edouard Dujardin 1866–1922 (in French), translated by John Eglinton. 1929.
The Talking Pine. 1931.
A Communication to My Friends. 1933.
Letters (to John Eglinton). 1942.
Letters to Lady Cunard 1895–1933, edited by Rupert Hart-Davis. 1957.
Moore in Transition: Letters to T. Fisher Unwin and Lena Milman 1894–1910. 1968.

Editor, *Pure Poetry: An Anthology.* 1924.
Translator, *The Pastoral Loves of Daphnis and Chloe*, by Longus. 1924.

Bibliography: *A Bibliography of Moore* by Edwin Gilcher, 1970.

Reading List: *The Life of Moore* by Joseph M. Hone, 1936 (includes bibliography); *Moore: A Reconsideration* by Malcolm J. Brown, 1955; *GM: Memories of Moore* by Nancy Cunard, 1956; *Moore* by A. Norman Jeffares, 1965; *Moore: L'Homme et l'Oeuvre* by J. C. Noel, 1966; *Moore: The Artist's Vision, The Storyteller's Art* by Janet Dunleavy, 1973.

*   *   *

George Moore's kaleidoscopic literary enthusiasms, his quirky use of self-parody, and his seemingly compulsive redrafting of a protean "canon" make him something of an anomaly to literary historians, both as an author and a personality. The eldest son of a wealthy Irish landowner and M.P., he grew up an awkward, ill-educated boy, the despair of his parents and, sometimes, himself. Upon coming of age, he inherited the family estate and immediately asserted independence by leaving for Paris to study art; there he lived seven years, picking up a haphazard, bohemian education in the studios and cafes of Montmartre. He spent most of the next twenty years in England, largely in London, where he established a mercurial reputation as an obstreperously avant-garde novelist and art critic. Then in 1900 he moved to Dublin to contribute his knowledge of literature and the theater to the Irish cultural renaissance. Eventually estranged from the Irish literary establishment, he returned after ten years to London to settle into an active old age, turning out controversial reminiscences and historical novels narrated in a gradually developed, distinctive prose style, the "melodic line" of his last years.

Though Moore resists facile assessment, his work is historically important – particularly his novels, short stories, and criticism/memoirs – because it mirrors significant aesthetic and technical changes in English prose fiction over a nearly fifty-year span. Both in subject and in structure his fiction champions three major late nineteenth-century art movements – Aestheticism, Naturalism, and Impressionism – and reflects his involvement in a wide spectrum of social and aesthetic "causes" – feminism and the Irish problem (*A Drama in Muslin*), the attack on the values of the middle-class English "villa" (*Spring Days*), the introduction of Ibsenesque drama in England (*Vain Fortune*), the turn-of-the-century enthusiasm for Wagnerian opera (*Evelyn Innes*), the stimulation of an endemic Irish literature (*The Untilled Field*), the pursuit of a stream-of-consciousness narrative style (*The Lake*), to name but the most obvious. Among his five books of memoirs his first, *Confessions of a Young Man*, is a revealing period piece of literary and aesthetic criticism, in its original version. Of the others, the three volumes of *Hail and Farewell* maintain interest because of their puckish blend of Irish literary gossip, lampoons, and sometimes shrewd, sometimes irascible literary criticism (those volumes stirred up wide contemporary reaction and turned most of Moore's Irish friends into acquaintances). Unfortunately, Moore blurred the topical significance of all of his works by rewriting nearly every one (often several times) in his later method and from a later perspective, and his selecting from among them three quite different collected editions.

His fiction can be divided roughly into three chronological periods: the first, an experimental blend of French and English realism and Aestheticism, ends with his best-known novel, *Esther Waters*, 1894; the second, an attempt at an amorphous psychological "intentionalism," fades into the third, that of his "melodic line," sometime after his epistolary novel, *The Lake*, 1905, and before his biblical-historical novel, *The Brook Kerith*, 1916. Within these three periods fall Moore's fifteen proto-novels and five collections of short stories. Several transcend a purely historical interest to emerge important for their own sake.

One is his second novel, *A Mummer's Wife*, the first openly avowed English attempt at doctrinaire French naturalism. It was a *succès de scandale*, and its rejection by the circulating libraries allowed Moore to attack publicly the artistic assumptions behind their monopoly. The novel itself contains two powerful character studies in the actor Dick Lennox and his dipsomaniac wife, Kate, and is narrated with uncommon structural unity. Indeed, what is remarkable about the original version is how well Moore combines a Zolaesque attention to structure and detail with a Balzacian depth of authorial comment. His next novel, *A Drama in Muslin*, also has a life of its own. In it Moore reveals the tawdry values of the Irish gentry through the lives of five girls on display in the Irish marriage mart as set against the background of their strife-torn country in the early 1880's. Arnold Bennett, for example, commended it (in *Fame and Fiction*) "as a brilliant instance of the modern tendency to bring history, sociology and morals within the dominion of the novelist's art." But by far the best and most popular of Moore's novels is *Esther Waters*. It is the story of an English servant girl who, sustained by a simple religious faith, rears her illegitimate son to manhood against heavy odds. Moore tells her story with quiet realism and tight structural unity, with each detail, each character contributing to the overall thematic pattern of Esther's muted victory over circumstances. That pattern proved a landmark in the development of thematic form in the English realistic novel.

Another literary landmark was his collection of short stories about the Irish, *The Untilled Field*. Influenced somewhat by Turgenev, he explored in most of those stories a theme of human loneliness amid the spiritual and cultural wasteland of contemporary Ireland. That theme and its inherent tone of melancholy profoundly affected the modern Irish short story. A melancholy tone is also integral to his final prose style, a languid, continuously flowing narrative line that blends dialogue with interior monologue with authorial commentary, *The Brook Kerith* being the best-known example. In that novel, through Joseph of Arimathea Moore traces the life of Jesus after he is presumably nursed back to health after being crucified; the story culminates in Jesus's ironically accidental encounter with the Christian fanatic Paul. It was, of course, another *succès de scandale*, but it also contains several powerful character studies set against a thoughtfully evoked historical background, a narrative synthesis that succeeds, for the most part, because of Moore's unique late style, his final landmark achievement.

—Jay Jernigan

MOORE, John.   Scottish.   Born in Stirling, baptized 7 December 1729; moved with his mother to Glasgow, 1737. Educated at Glasgow Grammar School; studied medicine at the University of Glasgow, and w..s simultaneously apprenticed to the surgeon John Gordon; qualified, 1747; studied in Paris, 1749–51; awarded M.D., University of Glasgow, 1770. Married Miss Simson in 1757; one daughter and five sons. Surgeon's mate in the Duke of Argyll's Regiment, serving at hospitals in Maestricht, 1747; Assistant to the Surgeon of the Coldstream Guards, at Flushing and Breda, 1748–49; Surgeon to the British Ambassador in Paris, 1749–51; practised in Glasgow with his former teacher John Gordon, 1751–53, then on his own, 1753–72; travelled with the Duke of Hamilton on the Continent, 1772–78; practised in London from 1778. *Died 21 January 1802.*

PUBLICATIONS

Collections

Works, with *Memoirs* by Robert Anderson.   7 vols., 1820.

Fiction

Zeluco: Various Views of Human Nature.   1789.
Edward: Various Views of Human Nature.   1796.
Mordaunt, Being Sketches of Life, Character, and Manners in Various Countries, Including the Memoirs of a French Lady of Quality.   1800; edited by W. L. Renwick, 1965.

Other

A View of Society and Manners in France, Switzerland, and Germany. 2 vols., 1779.
A View of Society and Manners in Italy. 2 vols., 1781.
Medical Sketches. 1786.
A Journal During a Residence in France. 2 vols., 1793–94.
A View of the Causes and Progress of the French Revolution. 2 vols., 1795.
Memoirs (of Smollett), and A View of the Commencement and Progress of Romance, in
    Works of Smollett. 1797.

Reading List: The Popular Novel in England 1770–1800 by J. M. S. Tompkins, 1932.

*   *   *

John Moore, described by Smollett's Jery Melford in Humphry Clinker as "an eminent surgeon ... a merry facetious companion, sensible and shrewd, with a considerable fund of humour," carried the Augustan literary tradition through to the end of the eighteenth century. His first publications, A View of Society and Manners in France, Switzerland, and Germany and A View of Society and Manners in Italy were the fruits of his thoughtful observations while travelling as physician to the Duke of Hamilton on a conventional Grand Tour. He then went on to write three novels, which combine the same kind of observant manner with their fictional elements.

Zeluco was the most exotic of these novels, and the only one to be reprinted in the nineteenth century. The account of Southern Italy is probably its main interest for the modern reader, but it was the villain Zeluco whose melodramatic panache and bad end appealed to popular taste. In Edward Moore wrote about English society, with a plot suggested by Marivaux's La Vie de Marianne, which perhaps accounts for the novel's lack of cohesion, but in Mordaunt he achieved a balanced expression of his interests.

Mordaunt is subtitled Sketches of Life, Character, and Manners in Various Countries, Including the Memoirs of a French Lady of Quality. In the first volume, Mordaunt is held in Switzerland by a sprained ankle, and so has leisure for a correspondence which ranges interestingly over such topics as German military discipline, the leaders of the French Revolution, the sensationalism of German plays and ballads, and the sobriety of the Spanish court. On his recovery he rescues a French lady in Paris and takes her to London, and the Marquise's story constitutes Moore's Whig critique of the Revolution, with the destruction of the Gironde seen as the abandonment of constructive idealism. The final volume tells of Mordaunt's gradually overcoming his hostility to marriage with the aid of the virtuous and lovely Horatia Clifford and – more incisively – the entrapping of the arrogant aristocrat Deanport by a designing young woman from York, despite his ambitious mother the Countess. Moore shows a wit worthy of Fielding in a scene in which Lady Deanport's declamation about charity is interrupted by a beggar, who is dismissed as an "idle, intruding vagabond" before the panegyric on benevolence can be concluded.

Good humour and good sense are the qualities of Moore's novels, especially Mordaunt, which kept alive a certain masculine flavour in an era when the novel form was largely the preserve of women, who sometimes brought to it a sentimentality to which Moore is, at his best, a bracing antidote.

—Peter Faulkner

MORE, Hannah.   English.   Born in Stapleton, Gloucestershire, near Bristol, 2 February 1745. Educated at her eldest sister's boarding school in Bristol; subsequently lived with her four sisters in a house in Bristol, and taught at the school. Visited London, 1774, and became acquainted with Garrick and his wife, Burke, Reynolds, and Dr. Johnson; enjoyed success as a playwright; lived with Garrick's wife after his death in 1779, and from that time came increasingly to devote herself to reform and religious issues; moved to Cowslip Green, near Bristol, 1787; became acquainted with John Newton and Wilberforce, 1787; set up Sunday schools in Cheddar, 1789; after 1792 issued a series of "cheap repository tracts," which led to the formation of the Religious Tract Society, 1799; continued writing religious/moral treatises until 1819. *Died 7 September 1833.*

PUBLICATIONS

Fiction

Village Politics.   1792.
Cheap Repository Tracts (49 titles).   1795–97; revised version, as *Stories for the Middle Ranks of Society, and Tales for the Common People*, 1818.
Coelebs in Search of a Wife.   1808.

Plays

A Search after Happiness: A Pastoral Drama.   1766(?); revised edition, 1796.
The Inflexible Captive (produced 1774).   1774.
Percy (produced 1777).   1778.
The Fatal Falsehood (produced 1779).   1779.
Sacred Dramas, Chiefly Intended for Young Persons, and Sensibility: A Poem (includes *Moses in the Bulrushes, Belshazzar, David and Goliath, Daniel).*   1782.

Verse

Sir Eldred of the Bower and The Bleeding Rock: Two Legendary Tales.   1776.
Ode to Dragon, Mr. Garrick's House-Dog at Hampton.   1777.
Florio: A Tale for Fine Gentlemen and Fine Ladies, and The Bas Bleu; or, Conversation.   1786.
Slavery.   1788.
Bishop Bonner's Ghost.   1789.
Poems.   1816.
The Twelfth of August; or, The Feast of Freedom.   1819; as *The Feast of Freedom; or, The Abolition of Domestic Slavery in Ceylon,* 1827.
Bible Rhymes on the Names of All the Books of the Old and New Testaments.   1821; revised edition, 1822.

Other

Essays on Various Subjects, Principally Designed for Young Ladies.   1777.
Thoughts on the Importance of the Manners of the Great to General Society.   1788.
An Estimate of the Religion of the Fashionable World.   1791.

Remarks on the Speech of M. Dumont on the Subjects of Religion and Education.   1793.
Questions and Answers for the Mendip and Sunday Schools.   1795.
Strictures on the Modern System of Female Education.   2 vols., 1799.
Works.   8 vols., 1801; revised edition, 19 vols., 1818–19; 11 vols., 1830.
Hints Towards Forming the Character of a Young Princess.   2 vols., 1805.
Practical Piety.   2 vols., 1811.
Christian Morals.   2 vols., 1813.
An Essay on the Character and Practical Writings of St. Paul.   2 vols., 1815.
Moral Sketches of Prevailing Opinions and Manners.   1819.
Letters to Zachary Macaulay, edited by A. Roberts.   1860.
Letters, edited by R. B. Johnson.   1925.

Editor, *The Spirit of Prayer.*   1825.

Reading List: *Memoirs of the Life and Correspondence of Mrs. More* by W. Roberts, 4 vols., 1834; *More,* by Charlotte Yonge, 1888; *More* by Annette B. Meakin, 1911; *More's Interest in Education and Government* by L. W. Courtney, 1929; *More's Cheap Repository Tracts in America* by Harry B. Weiss, 1946; *More and Her Circle* by Mary A. Hopkins, 1947; *More* by Mary Gwladys Jones, 1952; *Fiction for the Working Man* by Louis James, 1963.

*   *   *

Hannah More was the main literary exponent of the Evangelical movement within the Church of England in the later eighteenth and early nineteenth centuries, the ally of Wilberforce in his campaign for the moral improvement of the country. Her literary career began, however, in the freer atmosphere of the 1770's in London, where she associated with the Blue-Stockings, Mrs. Montagu's literary ladies, and with such celebrities as Burke, Reynolds, Walpole, Dr. Johnson, and Garrick. Garrick's friendship encouraged her to write *Percy,* which was successfully performed by him in 1777, but after his death she became increasingly involved in philanthropical and religious activity, and she refrained from even attending the revival of her play in 1787.

In her mood of increasing seriousness she became friendly with the Evangelical Bishop Porteus, and with the young Wilberforce himself, publishing in 1788 a criticism of the manners of the upper classes and a poem attacking the Slave Trade – a mainstay of the economy of Bristol, near which town she lived. On a visit to Cheddar with Wilberforce, she was so distressed by the lack of religious provision for the poor that she devoted her considerable energies to establishing a Sunday School, and became very involved in this attempt to provide religious education of a kind suited to the lower orders. For her political position was thoroughly conservative, and she responded to the French Revolution with horror. In 1792 she published *Village Politics,* an attack on the new radical ideas. She continued with an immensely successful series of *Cheap Repository Tracts* inculcating her political philosophy. The tracts were widely distributed, and their success helped to lead to the formation of the Religious Tract Society in 1799, part of the strenuous attempt by the religious and political establishment to contain the rising tide of social criticism and discontent.

Hannah More is more interesting as a representative figure in a significant social movement than exciting as a writer, but the *Tracts* are clear, and based on observation as well as ideology: they would not have been so widely known unless their unsophisticated readers had found something in them to hold their interest. Her *Strictures on the Modern System of*

Female Education criticises both the narrowness of the prevailing system and the feminism of Mary Wollstonecraft, whose *Vindication of the Rights of Women* had appeared in 1792. Her most substantial fictional work, *Coelebs in Search of a Wife*, attacks the looseness of Regency morals and suggests the Evangelical ideal. Her attitudes thus form a significant part of the background to such a novel as Jane Austen's *Mansfield Park*, but the deliberately didactic Hannah More lacked the irony with which Jane Austen tempered her moral idealism.

—Peter Faulkner

MORGAN, Lady (Sydney Morgan, née Owenson). Irish. Born in Dublin in 1783; daughter of the actor Robert Owenson. Educated in various schools in or near Dublin. Married Sir Thomas Charles Morgan in 1812 (died, 1843). Supported her family by working as a governess in the family of Featherstone, at Bracklin Castle, Westmeath, 1798–1800; may also have appeared on the stage; writer from 1801; later became a member of the household of the Marquis of Abercorn until her marriage; settled in Dublin, 1814; travelled in England, France, and Italy, 1818–20, France, 1829, and Belgium, 1835; granted a pension from Lord Melbourne, 1837; wrote for the *Athenaeum*, London, 1837–38; settled in London, 1839, and thereafter ceased to write. *Died 14 April 1859.*

PUBLICATIONS

Fiction

St. Clair; or, The Heiress of Desmond. 1803; revised edition, 1812.
The Novice of St. Dominick. 1805.
The Wild Irish Girl: A National Tale. 1806.
Patriotic Sketches of Ireland, Written in Connaught. 1807.
Woman; or, Ida of Athens. 1809.
The Missionary: An Indian Tale. 1811; revised edition, as Luxima, The Prophetess: A Tale of India, 1859.
O'Donnel: A National Tale. 1814; revised edition, 1835.
Florence Macarthy: An Irish Tale. 1818.
The O'Briens and the O'Flahertys: A National Tale. 1827; edited by R. Shelton Mackenzie, 1856.
Dramatic Scenes from Real Life. 1833.
The Princess: or, The Beguine. 1835.

Verse

Poems. 1801.
Twelve Original Hibernian Melodies. 1805.
The Lay of an Irish Harp; or, Metrical Fragments. 1807.
The Mohawks: A Satirical Poem, with Sir Charles Morgan. 1822.

Other

A Few Reflections (on Irish theatre). 1804.
France. 2 vols., 1817; revised edition, 1818.
Italy. 2 vols., 1821; revised edition, 3 vols., 1821.
Letters to the Reviewers of Italy. 1821.
The Life and Times of Salvator Rosa. 2 vols., 1824.
Absenteeism. 1825.
The Book of the Boudoir (autobiographical sketches). 2 vols., 1829.
France in 1829–30. 2 vols., 1830.
Woman and Her Master. 2 vols., 1840.
The Book Without a Name, with Sir Charles Morgan. 2 vols., 1841.
Letter to Cardinal Wiseman. 1851.
Passages from My Autobiography. 1859.
An Odd Volume, Extracted from an Autobiography. 1859.
Memoirs: Autobiography, Diaries, and Correspondence, edited by W. Hepworth
   Dixon. 2 vols., 1862.

Reading List: *The Friends, Foes, and Adventures of Lady Morgan* by William John
Fitzpatrick, 1859; *The Wild Irish Girl: The Life of Lady Morgan* by Lionel Stevenson, 1936.

*   *   *

The daughter of a well-known Irish actor, Robert Owenson, renowned in his day for playing the lovable stage-Irishman, Lady Morgan added to his bequest of sentimentality a histrionic flair of her own to become one of the literary curiosities of the age. Her first and greatest success, *The Wild Irish Girl*, encouraged her to don the cloak and take up the harp of her heroine, Glorvina, by which name she was known to habitués of Regency salons, whom she entertained with sad songs of Erin (anticipating, incidentally, the success of Thomas Moore some years later). She became an apologist for Irish nationalism, based on the distinctiveness of native Irish culture, thereby giving picturesque stimulus to a train of thought which has adherents yet. She developed Jacobin leanings. She became the object of scurrilous attacks by John Wilson Croker (himself Irish) of the *Quarterly Review*, and of extravagant patronage. Perhaps most importantly of all, in her own view, she became notorious.

Of her many literary productions, the most important are her Irish novels, and, for good or ill, except for Macpherson's *Ossian* they must be held most responsible for introducing Ireland to Romanticism. These novels, of which the most impressive feature is their passages of natural description, are set in a land which time has half-forgotten, peopled by remote, hill-dwelling clans led by men of fierce honour. Their themes are expressive of Ireland in the aftermath of the Act of Union – dispossession, defensiveness, social impotence. These afflictions are not presented as being important for themselves but as being the basis for a series of impossible escapes and resolutions. The novels portray deliverance from Irish reality, and as such are interesting early examples of Irish nationalist mythology. Their style is suitably rhetorical and rhapsodic. The most interesting – because of its uncharacteristic treatment of near-contemporary issues – is *The O'Briens and the O'Flahertys*.

Despite the widespread success of these and many of her other productions (notably *France*), Lady Morgan's career seems as much part of the history of taste as it is of literary history. Her contribution to Irish literature, though not without interest, is essentially spurious. The self-mythologising of her later works, her theatricality and sense of publicity, the novelty of her propaganda, even her quite original sensitivity to the moods of the literary marketplace, all seem to diminish her status as a writer, while at the same time emphasising her unique and phenomenal career.

—George O'Brien

MORRISON, Arthur. English. Born in Kent, 1 November 1863. Educated in Kent schools. Married Elizabeth Adelaide Thatcher in 1892; one son. Journalist in London from the early 1880's; member of the staff of the *National Observer* during Henley's editorship; full-time writer from 1894; collector of Chinese and Japanese paintings which were acquired by the British Museum in 1913; Chief Inspector of the Special Constabulary of Epping Forest, Essex, during World War I. Fellow, and Member of the Council, of the Royal Society of Literature. *Died 4 December 1945.*

PUBLICATIONS

Fiction

The Shadows Around Us: Authentic Tales of the Supernatural.   1891.
Martin Hewitt, Investigator (stories).   1894.
Tales of Mean Streets.   1894.
Chronicles of Martin Hewitt.   1895.
Zig-Zags at the Zoo.   1895.
A Child of the Jago.   1896; edited by P. J. Keating, 1969.
Adventures of Martin Hewitt: Third Series.   1896.
The Dorrington Deed-Box (stories).   1897.
To London Town.   1899.
Cunning Murrell.   1900.
The Hole in the Wall.   1902.
The Red Triangle, Being Some Further Chronicles of Martin Hewitt.   1903.
The Green Eye of Goona: Stories of a Case of Tokay.   1904; as *The Green Diamond,* 1904.
Divers Vanities (stories).   1905.
Green Ginger (stories).   1909.
(Stories).   1929.
Fiddle O'Dreams (stories).   1933.

Plays

That Brute Simmons, with Herbert C. Sargent, from the story by Morrison (produced 1904).   1904.
The Dumb-Cake, with Richard Pryce, from a story by Morrison (produced 1907).   1907.
A Stroke of Business, with Horace Newte (produced 1907).

Other

The Painters of Japan. 2 vols., 1911.

Reading List: "A Study of Morrison" by J. Bell, in *Essays and Studies 5,* 1952; *Four Realist Novelists* by Vincent Brome, 1965.

*   *   *

Arthur Morrison was perhaps the best of that group of writers – others were Israel Zangwill, Barry Pain, W. Pett Ridge, and Edwin Pugh – who in the last decade of the nineteenth century examined lower middle- and working-class London life more or less realistically in fiction. His reputation rests securely on *Tales of Mean Streets,* a collection of short stories, and on his novels *A Child of the Jago* and *The Hole in the Wall,* though he wrote several detective stories. The world he deals with is the East End, Stepney and Bethnal Green specifically. It has largely gone now, destroyed by the town-planners at the turn of the century and by Hitler's bombers forty years later, but it survives in a sentence in which Morrison describes the mean streets of his *Tales:* "And the effect is that of *stables."*

The stories are notably sardonic and contemptuous of their subject, very *fin-de-siècle.* Morrison's East End is anything but sentimentalised; we are never allowed to forget that the police patrol it in threes; the author's aim is to expose conditions. In *A Child of the Jago* he tells the story of a young thief in Bethnal Green. The picture it gives of street wars is unique and terrifying. As art, however, it is inferior to *The Hole in the Wall,* in which the story is shown mainly through the eyes of a child. Stephen Kemp goes to live with his grand-father, who keeps a pub at Wapping, and gradually discovers that the old man, whom he adores, is in fact a receiver of stolen goods. The old man comes by a wallet containing £800 which has been stolen from a murdered shipowner, and the plot turns on the attempts of various criminal characters to get the money back. The execution of the plot is as grim and relentless as anything in Zola, and gains greatly in effectiveness in being recorded through a child's eye. Morrison was a collector of Japanese prints – his collection is now in the British Museum – and it has been suggested that the clarity and restraint that mark the novel were derived from their study.

One thing must be borne in mind, particularly since Zola has been referred to. Morrison was a realist, but very much an English realist; the characters in his fiction are like nothing in Naturalism. And just as the dockland of *The Hole in the Wall,* the river and the fogs, remind us of the setting of *Our Mutual Friend,* so the characters, Captain Kemp, Mr. Cripps, Mrs. Grimes and the rest, seem either Dickens characters by nature or characters conceived by a novelist so deeply steeped in the Dickens tradition that automatically he turns his creations into Dickens figures. They look like them and speak like them, and though this does not undercut Morrison's genuinely realistic quality, it does remind us, as Wells and Bennett do a decade later, that realism in English fiction has native English as well as French roots.

—Walter Allen

MULOCK, Dinah Maria; also known as Mrs. Craik.   English.   Born in Stoke-on-Trent, Staffordshire, 20 April 1826. Educated privately and in local schools. Married the publisher George Lillie Craik in 1865. Settled in London, 1846; thereafter a full-time writer; lived in Bromley, Kent, from 1865. *Died 12 October 1887.*

PUBLICATIONS

Fiction

The Ogilvies. 1849.
Cola Monti; or, The Story of a Genius. 1849.
Olive. 1850.
The Head of the Family. 1852.
Bread upon the Waters: A Governess's Life. 1852.
Avillion and Other Tales. 1853.
A Hero: Philip's Book. 1853.
Agatha's Husband. 1853.
The Little Lychetts. 1855.
John Halifax, Gentleman. 1856.
Nothing New: Tales. 1857.
A Life for a Life. 1859.
Romantic Tales. 1859.
Domestic Stories. 1860.
Studies from Life. 1860.
Mistress and Maid. 1862.
Christian's Mistake. 1865.
A Noble Life. 1866.
How to Win Love; or, Rhoda's Lesson: A Story for the Young. 1866(?).
Two Marriages. 1867.
The Woman's Kingdom. 1869.
A Brave Lady. 1870.
The Unkind Word and Other Stories. 1870.
Twenty Years Ago, from the Journal of a Girl in Her Teens. 1871.
Hannah. 1872.
Is It True? Tales Curious and Wonderful. 1872.
My Mother and I. 1874.
Will Denbigh, Nobleman. 1877.
The Laurel Bush. 1877.
Young Mrs. Jardine. 1879.
His Little Mother and Other Tales. 1881.
Miss Tommy. 1884.
Work for the Idle Hands. 1886.
King Arthur: Not a Love Story. 1886.
An Unknown Country. 1887.

Verse

Poems. 1859.
Thirty Years: Poems New and Old. 1881; as *Poems,* 1888.

Other

Alice Learmont: A Fairy Tale (juvenile). 1852; revised edition, 1884.
A Woman's Thoughts about Women. 1858.
Our Year: A Child's Book. 1860.
The Fairy Book: The Best Popular Fairy Stories Selected and Rendered Anew. 1863.

A New Year's Gift to Sick Children. 1865.
Fair France: Impressions of a Traveller. 1871.
Little Sunshine's Holiday (juvenile). 1871.
The Adventures of a Brownie as Told to My Child. 1872.
The Little Lame Prince (juvenile). 1875.
Sermons Out of Church. 1875.
Children's Poetry. 1881.
Plain Speaking. 1882.
An Unsentimental Journey Through Cornwall. 1884.
About Money and Other Things. 1886.
Fifty Golden Years: Incidents in the Queen's Reign. 1887.
Concerning Men and Other Papers. 1888.

Editor, *A Legacy, Being the Life and Remains of John Martin.* 2 vols., 1878.

Translator, *M. de Barante,* by F. P. G. Guizot. 1867.
Translator, *A French Country Family,* by H. de Witt. 1867.
Translator, *A Parisian Family,* by H. de Witt. 1871.
Translator, *An Only Sister,* by H. de Witt. 1873.

Reading List: "The Author of *John Halifax, Gentleman*" by A. L. Reade, in *Notes and Queries* 9, 1951.

*   *   *

"*John Halifax* may fairly be taken as 'standing' for Mrs. Craik," in the opinion of Richard Brimley Johnson (*The Women Novelists*, 1918). More modern readers would be unlikely to demur. "The Authoress of John Halifax, Gentleman," as Dinah Maria Mulock (Mrs. Craik) appeared on countless subsequent title pages, produced more than fifty volumes during her career – novels, stories for young people, poems, short stories, and miscellaneous articles and sketches. Yet her reputation, such as it is, rests on an idealistic, sentimental tale of a tanner's apprentice of obscure birth who rises by his own efforts to become a "gentleman" and in so doing proves that the essence of gentility is not social but moral. Johnson quite rightly sees *John Halifax, Gentleman* in Mrs. Craik's happiest vein of stories for young persons, rather than as a conventional novel. In the course of his steady rise, the hero quells a bread riot, foils a rigged election in a rotten borough, and successfully introduces a steam engine into his mills with the support of his workmen, thus fixing the novel in the pre-Reform Bill era. Copious references to contemporary events and personalities, including the Napoleonic Wars, the abolition of slavery, the death of Perceval, the Luddite riots, and the appearance in the novel itself of Lady Hamilton, Dr. Jenner, Mrs. Siddons, and Charles Kemble, further establish the book's period flavour.

Mrs. Craik's penchant for deliberately placing her novels is reflected also in *A Life for a Life*, which more than one of her contemporaries regarded as equal if not superior to *John Halifax*. This is the story of an army surgeon in the immediate post-Crimean period who sells his commission and becomes immersed in prison reform. Unfortunately any interest which might have been generated by the unusual epistolary style of the novel, involving both a masculine and a feminine narrator, is more than mitigated by the plot, a typical mixture of thwarted love and a dark past involving a murder. Other novels like *Agatha's Husband* and *The Head of the Family*, more domestic in setting, are equally marred by this all too familiar formula of frustrated or undeclared love, false marriages, and even escape from shipwreck.

Mrs. Craik published two volumes of poetry during her life, of which the two best known poems are "Philip My King" and "Douglas, Douglas, Tender and True," both of which were occasionally anthologized. Of her miscellaneous work the most notable is *A Woman's*

Thoughts about Women, not a radical statement of women's rights but a practical assessment of the status quo, advocating more activity and purpose for women, but in their accepted spheres of teaching, writing, painting, and public entertainment.

—Joanne Shattock

OLIPHANT, Margaret (Oliphant, née Wilson). Scottish. Born in Wallyford, Midlothian, 4 April 1828. Married Francis Wilson Oliphant in 1852; two sons. Full-time writer from 1849; regular contributor to *Blackwood's Magazine*, Edinburgh, 1852 until her death. *Died 25 June 1897.*

PUBLICATIONS

Fiction

Passages in the Life of Mrs. Margaret Maitland.   1849.
Caleb Field: A Tale of the Puritans.   1851.
Merkland; or, Self-Sacrifice.   1851.
Memoirs and Resolutions of Adam Graeme of Mossgray.   1852.
Katie Stewart.   1853.
Harry Muir: A Story of Scottish Life.   1853.
The Quiet Heart.   1854.
Magdalen Hepburn.   1854.
Lilliesleaf.   1855.
Zaidee.   1856.
The Athelings; or, The Three Gifts.   1857.
The Days of My Life.   1857.
Sundays.   1858.
The Laird of Norlaw.   1858.
Orphans.   1858.
Agnes Hopetoun's Schools and Holidays.   1859.
Lucy Crofton.   1860.
The House on the Moor.   1861.
The Last of the Mortimers.   1862.
Chronicles of Carlingford: The Rector and the Doctor's Family, Salem Chapel, The Perpetual Curate, Miss Marjoribanks, Phoebe, Junior.   14 vols., 1863–76.
Heart and Cross.   1863.
Agnes.   1865.
A Son of the Soil.   1865.
Madonna Mary.   1866.
The Brownlows.   1868.
The Minister's Wife.   1869.
John: A Love Story.   1870.

The Three Brothers. 1870.
Squire Arden. 1871.
At His Gates. 1872.
Ombra. 1872.
May. 1873.
Innocent. 1873.
A Rose in June. 1874.
For Love and Life. 1874.
The Story of Valentine and His Brother. 1875.
Whiteladies. 1875.
The Curate in Charge. 1876.
Carità. 1877.
Mrs. Arthur. 1877.
Young Musgrave. 1877.
The Primrose Path: A Chapter in the Annals of the Kingdom of Fife. 1878.
The Fugitives. 1879.
Within the Precincts. 1879.
The Two Mrs. Scudamores (stories). 1879.
The Greatest Heiress in England. 1879.
A Beleaguered City, with *The Awakening*, by Katharine S. Macquoid. 1879.
He That Will Not When He May. 1880.
Harry Joscelyn. 1881.
In Trust: The Story of a Lady and Her Lover. 1881.
A Little Pilgrim. 1882.
Hester. 1883.
It Was a Lover and His Lass. 1883.
The Ladies Lindores. 1883.
Sir Tom. 1883.
The Wizard's Son. 1883.
Two Stories of the Seen and the Unseen (*Old Lady Mary, The Open Door*). 1885.
Madam. 1885.
Oliver's Bride. 1885.
The Prodigals and Their Inheritance. 1885.
A Country Gentleman and His Family. 1886.
Effie Ogilvie: The Story of a Young Life. 1886.
A House Divided Against Itself. 1886.
A Poor Gentleman. 1886.
The Son of His Father. 1886.
The Land of Darkness, along with Some Further Chapters in the Experience of the Little Pilgrims. 1888.
Joyce. 1888.
The Second Son, with Thomas Bailey Aldrich. 1888.
Cousin Mary. 1888.
Neighbours on the Green: A Collection of Stories. 1889.
Lady Car. 1889.
Kirsteen: The Story of a Scotch Family Seventy Years Ago. 1890.
The Duke's Daughter, and The Fugitives. 1890.
Sons and Daughters. 1890.
The Mystery of Mrs. Blencarrow. 1890.
Janet. 1891.
The Railway Man and His Children. 1891.
The Heir Presumptive and the Heir Apparent. 1891
Diana Trelawney. 1892; as *Diana*, 1892.
The Cuckoo in the Nest. 1892.

The Marriage of Elinor.   1892.
Lady William.   1893.
The Sorceress.   1893.
A House in Bloomsbury.   1894.
Who Was Lost and Is Found.   1894.
Sir Robert's Fortune.   1894.
Two Strangers.   1894.
Old Mrs. Tredgold.   1895.
The Two Marys (stories).   1896.
The Unjust Steward; or, The Minister's Debt.   1896.
The Lady's Walk (stories).   1897.
The Ways of Life: Two Stories.   1897.
A Widow's Tale and Other Stories.   1898.
That Little Cutty and Two Other Stories.   1898.

Other

The Life of Edward Irving, Minister of the National Scotch Church, London.   2 vols.,
    1862.
Francis of Assisi.   1868.
Historical Sketches of the Reign of George Second.   2 vols., 1869.
Memoir of Count de Montalembert: A Chapter of Recent French History.   1872.
The Makers of Florence: Dante, Giotto, Savonarola, and Their City.   1876.
Dress.   1876.
Dante.   1877.
Molière, with F. Tarver.   1879.
The Queen.   1880.
Cervantes.   1880.
*The Literary History of England in the End of the Eighteenth and the Beginning of the
    Nineteenth Century.*   3 vols., 1882.
Sheridan.   1883.
The Makers of Venice: Doges, Conquerors, Painters, and Men of Letters.   1887.
A Memoir of the Life of John Tulloch.   1888.
Royal Edinburgh: Her Saints, Kings, Prophets, and Poets.   1890.
Jerusalem, The Holy City: Its History and Hope.   1891; reprinted in part as *The House
    of David,* 1891.
Memoir of the Life of Laurence Oliphant and Alice Oliphant, His Wife.   1891.
The Victorian Age of English Literature, with F. R. Oliphant.   2 vols., 1892.
Thomas Chalmers, Preacher, Philosopher, and Statesman.   1893.
Historical Sketches of the Reign of Queen Anne.   1894; as *Historical Characters,* 1894.
A Child's History of Scotland.   1895; as *A History of Scotland for the Young,* 1895.
The Makers of Modern Rome.   1895.
Jeanne d'Arc: Her Life and Death.   1896.
*Annals of a Publishing House: William Blackwood and His Sons, Their Magazine and
    Friends.*   2 vols., 1897.
The Autobiography and Letters, edited by Mrs. Harry Coghill.   1899; revised edition,
    1899.
Queen Victoria: A Personal Sketch.   1901.

Editor, *Memoirs of the Life of Anna Jameson,* by Geraldine Macpherson.   1878.

Reading List: "A Valiant Woman" by Katherine Moore, in *Blackwood's Magazine,* 1958;

"Oliphant" by M. Lockhead, in *Quarterly Review*, 1961; *Everywhere Spoken Against* by Valentine Cunningham, 1975.

*   *   *

Margaret Oliphant was a minor writer in the best sense of that term. Her work at its finest displayed talent of a high order in a narrow range. What was not on a minor scale was her output – a prodigious number of novels, short stories, reviews, literary history, and biography – a monument to a full-time career as a woman of letters. The *Autobiography and Letters* is an attractive and moving document of such a literary life, of a talent forced into regular production in order to support a family virtually until her death.

Her contributions to *Blackwood's* over forty-six years represent the bulk of this effort. At its best her literary criticism is anything but hack work, perceptive assessments of a working novelist on her contemporaries. Several of her biographical sketches, on Edward Irving, and on John Tulloch, emerged as full scale biographies. Her literary histories, particularly *The Victorian Age of English Literature*, written with F. R. Oliphant, contains a wealth of detail and judgment which only a gargantuan amount of reading could have produced. But the best of her non-fiction, and probably the best known, is *Annals of a Publishing House: William Blackwood and His Sons, Their Magazine and Friends*, still the standard work on the publishing house and its famous magazine, and one of the most thorough studies of nineteenth-century publishing and periodical production.

But Mrs. Oliphant's reputation rests mainly and justifiably on her novels, ranging from early stories of Scottish life, *Passages in the Life of Mrs. Margaret Maitland* and *Katie Stewart*, to the blatant pot-boilers of the last years. Two notable strands emerge, the Scottish novels and the Chronicles of Carlingford. Of the later Scottish stories probably the best is *Kirsteen*, the story of a girl, driven from her highland home by a puritanical father, who establishes herself with full independence as a milliner in London – a heroine who exemplified Mrs. Oliphant's belief in the resourcefulness and independence of her sex.

But her place in literary history would have been secure had she written nothing but the Chronicles of Carlingford, stories of English provincial life set in a mythical town where everything is dominated by church and chapel. The novels were written hurriedly and sometimes during periods of acute personal stress. Yet despite these pressures the threads of the plots and the major characters for the entire series were established in the first two stories, "The Rector" and "The Doctor," published in three volumes as *The Rector and the Doctor's Family*. Mrs. Oliphant's fame as the chronicler of evangelical life rests on the disproportionate reputation of *Salem Chapel*, the second but by no means the best of the novels, which presents a series of affectionate portraits of a group of bacon and cheese merchants, poulterers, greengrocers, and dairymen, the pillars of the institution of the title. Their tea meetings, evening lectures, and congregational machinations over an erring pastor form the basis of the novel (unfortunately seriously marred by a "sensational" subplot), one of the few occasions in fiction where this stratum of society is so fully described. Mrs. Oliphant later confessed that much of her material was drawn from her observations of chapel life in Liverpool where she lived during the early years of her marriage. But she is equally acute on other spheres of clerical life – on the anxieties of an Oxford don unable to cope with the demands of parish life, on the agonies of the family of a High Churchman determined to abandon the Church of England for Rome, and on the trials of an impecunious clergyman, again of High Church persuasion, who is denied the family living in the gift of his evangelical aunts. *Miss Marjoribanks* and *Phoebe, Junior* concentrate on the laity of Carlingford – Miss Marjoribanks, the strong-willed, independent daughter of the town's doctor, and the much later life of the grandaughter of the butterman of Salem Chapel, raised in the highest echelons of metropolitan nonconformity in a style quite undreamed of by her grandparents.

Parallels with Trollope are almost irresistible, and in the case of one plot and title, quite apparent. So great was the fame of the Chronicles that George Eliot was forced to state publically that she was not the author. But despite obvious comparisons with more illustrious contemporaries Mrs. Oliphant's work retains a flavour, wit, and poise very much its own.

—Joanne Shattock

OPIE, Amelia (née Alderson).   English.   Born in Norwich, Norfolk, 12 November 1769. Married the painter John Opie in 1798. Writer from childhood, and novelist from 1800; a friend of Sydney Smith, Sheridan, and Madame de Stael; became a Quaker in 1825, and thereafter wrote only moral tracts and articles. *Died 2 December 1853.*

PUBLICATIONS

Fiction

Dangers of Coquetry.   1790.
The Father and Daughter: A Tale, with An Epistle from the Maid of Corinth and Other Poetical Pieces.   1801.
Adeline Mowbray; or, The Mother and Daughter.   1804.
Simple Tales.   1806.
Temper; or, Domestic Scenes.   1812.
Tales of Real Life.   1813.
Valentine's Eve.   1816.
New Tales.   1818.
Tales of the Heart.   1820.
Madeline.   1822.
Illustrations of Lying, in All Its Branches.   1825.
Tales of the Pemberton Family, for the Use of Children.   1825.
Miscellaneous Tales.   12 vols., 1845–47.

Verse

Twelve Hindoo Airs, music by E. S. Biggs.   1800(?); *Second Set,* 1800(?).
Poems.   1802.
Elegy to the Memory of the Late Duke of Bedford.   1802.
The Warrior's Return and Other Poems.   1808.
Lays for the Dead.   1834.

Other

Detraction Displayed. 1828; as *A Cure for Scandal,* 1839.
Works. 2 vols., 1835.
Works. 3 vols., 1841.
Memorials of the Life of Opie, from Her Letters, Diaries and Other Manuscripts, edited by Cecilia Lucy Brightwell. 1854.

Editor, *Lectures on Painting,* by John Opie. 1809.

Reading List: *Amelia Opie, Worldling and Friend* by M. E. Macgregor, 1933 (includes bibliography); *Amelia: The Tale of a Plain Friend* by J. Menzies-Wilson and H. Lloyd, 1937.

*   *   *

Amelia Opie deliberately wrote "tales" and not novels. She had no interest in "strong character, comic situation, bustle, and variety of incident" (preface to *The Father and Daughter*). Like many women novelists of the eighteenth century she was only interested in situations of intense emotion, and, in spite of the fact that her many volumes of tales present a fair range of character, incident, dialogue, and narrative mode, there is one basic situation which recurs again and again. A heroine of sensibility leaves or is banished from home, due to her own moral inadequacies or those of home itself (a severe or profligate parent); the result of her departure is a series of scenes of remorse, as the plot moves crookedly, usually with the help of breathtaking coincidences, through these passages of penitence to a grand reconciliation; and the heroine finally arrives "home" sadder and wiser, though home often proves to be but death's door.

The tales (and many of the poems) deal in separations, then – daughter from father (*The Father and Daughter*), daughter from mother (*Adeline Mowbray*), wife from husband (*Valentine's Eve*) – and in secret sorrows, suspicions, and unfavourable appearances ("The Black Velvet Pelisse" in *Simple Tales*), often arranged around the question of the chasteness of the heroine, and always tied up with her good or bad moral judgment. The theme arose from Mrs. Opie's own relationship with her mother, and is portrayed with directness, poignancy, and intensity in her early poem "In Memory of My Mother" (1791), a kind of miniature of the structure of feeling found in most of her tales. But she did not, in her life or her fiction, give way to morbid sensibility, and what is interesting is what she did, as a writer, with this biographical *donnée*. She had a sense of humour, an active and observant mind, and a fascination for anecdotes, and much of her own experience of the social and historical world of Norwich and London during several decades of political and intellectual crisis finds its way into her fiction. Her tales refer to a wide range of the issues, ideas, and events of the day, from Sensibility to East Anglian windstorms, from war and economic distress to the latest cut of a coat, and they show the influence of her father, of William Godwin, the Dissenting culture to which she belonged, and the events of the French Revolution, viewed typologically. All this is transposed into her writing, and all too thoroughly rendered in the language and conventions of both the literature of Sensibility and the popular but "serious" fiction of the day. Like her celebrated singing voice, Mrs. Opie's fictional voice is limited in range, and unable to extend itself over any span of effort, but it is clear, simple, personal, and in its own time was considered quite moving.

—Gary Kelly

OUIDA. Pseudonym for Marie Louise de la Ramée.   English.   Born in Bury St. Edmunds, Suffolk, 1 January 1839. Educated privately. Lived in London, 1857–71; writer from c. 1860; contributed to *Bentley's Miscellany, Fortnightly Review, Nineteenth Century, North American Review*, etc.; lived in or near Florence, 1871–93, and in or near Lucca, Italy, 1894 until her death. Granted Civil List pension. *Died 25 January 1908.*

PUBLICATIONS

Fiction

Held in Bondage.   1863.
Strathmore.   1865.
Chandos.   1866.
Under Two Flags.   1867.
Cecil Castlemaine's Gage and Other Novelettes.   1867.
Idalia.   1867.
Tricotrin.   1869.
Puck.   1870.
Folle-Farine.   1871.
Pascarel.   1873.
Two Little Wooden Shoes.   1874.
Signa.   1875.
In a Winter City.   1876.
Ariadne: The Story of a Dream.   1877.
Friendship.   1878.
Moths.   1880.
Pipistrello and Other Stories.   1880.
A Village Commune.   1881.
In Maremma.   1882.
Frescoes: Dramatic Sketches.   1883.
Wanda.   1883.
Princess Napraxine.   1884.
A Rainy June.   1885.
Othmar.   1885.
Don Gesualdo.   1886.
A House Party.   1887.
Guilderoy.   1889.
Ruffino (stories).   1890.
Syrlin.   1890.
Santa Barbara (stories).   1891.
The Tower of Taddeo.   1892.
Two Offenders (stories).   1894.
The Silver Christ, and A Lemon Tree.   1894.
Toxin.   1895.
Le Selve and Other Tales.   1896.
An Altruist.   1897.
The Massarenes.   1897.
La Strega and Other Stories.   1899.
The Waters of Edera.   1900.
Street Dust and Other Stories.   1901.
Helianthus (unfinished).   1908.

Other

A Dog of Flanders and Other Stories (juvenile).   1872.
Bimbi: Stories for Children.   1882.
The New Priesthood: A Protest Against Vivisection.   1893.
Views and Opinions.   1895.
Dogs.   1897.
Critical Studies.   1900.

Reading List: *Ouida: A Study in Ostentation* by Yvonne ffrench, 1938; *Ouida: The Passionate Victorian* by Eileen Bigland, 1950; *The Fine and the Wicked: The Life and Times of Ouida* by Monica Stirling, 1957.

*   *   *

Ouida has suffered a cruel, ironical fate. Her novels, stories, and essays have been largely forgotten while her life has become a legend. The mere mention of the name of Ouida evokes a dismissive smile or sneer; very few people have read her novels, and she is associated with highly fanciful and idealised descriptions of guardsmen. Yet Ruskin praised her, and Max Beerbohm was one of her most enthusiastic and serious admirers.

Her novels are infused with a European spirit; they are far removed from the insular and at times provincial novels of many of her English predecessors and contemporaries. If, after reading Charlotte Brontë, say, or Mrs. Gaskell, you plunge into a novel of Ouida, you seem to breathe the air of a wider, more civilised, more amusing world. The conversation sparkles, and you are treated to a cascade of wit. Nor did Ouida herself greatly revere the established English novelists of her time. She said Besant's stories contained too much Dickens and water, and felt Dickens's influence was generally too strong on later writers.

Under Two Flags is the finest of her novels about the Brigade of Guards and the life of its officers; it was also her greatest popular success. She carefully and deliberately built up an idealised picture of the Guards officer's life complete with an impecunious hero, a forged promissory note, and an illegitimate girl named Cigarette, a mascot of the Foreign Legion. *Moths*, too, has an international setting, and is brilliantly witty. In *Princess Napraxine, Othmar*, and *Frescoes*, we are reminded of the novels of Ronald Firbank. In *Princess Napraxine* – the title could well have been chosen by Firbank himself – we find the same world of fantasy, the strange juxtaposition of words as in a mosaic, the capacity to transport the reader into the world of the unconscious; indeed, she anticipated Firbank in many ways, and these are perhaps the novels which are most readable today.

Altogether different are her novels of Italian peasant life. She undoubtedly had an insight into the character of the Italian peasant, and in *A Village Commune, Ariadne, In Maremma*, and *Don Gesualdo* she describes peasant life in ways that foreshadow the realistic works of Verga and D'Annunzio. In *A Village Commune* she sets out to champion the cause of a small village against the over-powering Italian bureaucracy; the novel aroused great controversy, and many Italians took strong exception to it.

In many ways Ouida was ahead of her time. Her essays are trenchant and to the point. Her opposition to the spread of industrialism, to conscription, militarism, and colonialism, are in some ways prophetic. At the same time she had a genuine love of Italy and the Italian countryside, and her descriptions of landscape are unrivalled.

—Ian Greenlees

PALTOCK, Robert. English. Born in Westminster, London, in 1697. Studied law. Married Anna Skinner (died, 1767); two sons and two daughters. Attorney: lived in Clement's Inn, London, for several years; moved to Lambeth, London, c. 1759; writer from 1750. *Died 20 March 1767.*

PUBLICATIONS

Fiction

> *The Life and Adventures of Peter Wilkins, A Cornish Man, Relating Particularly to His Shipwreck near the South Pole.* 1750; edited by Christopher Bentley, 1973.

Reading List: *The Imaginary Voyage in Prose Fiction* by Philip Babcock Gove, 1941 (includes bibliography); *Voyages to the Moon* by Marjorie Hope Nicholson, 1948.

*   *   *

The only work for which Robert Paltock is remembered is *The Life and Adventures of Peter Wilkins*, a novel which appeared in 1750. Until 1835 his identity lurked behind the initials R. P., and even these bafflingly appeared as R. S. on the original title page. Ascription to Paltock of one and sometimes two or three other works is extremely dubious. It is therefore a measure of the attractions of *Peter Wilkins* that it emerged brightly from these authorial obscurities and has captivated occasional readers for two centuries.

The story purports to have been dictated to the author by the eponymous narrator, and it has at first something of the raconteur's mere chronological onwardness that we find in Defoe. A series of episodic adventures establishes, as in *Robinson Crusoe*, a register of realism and a sturdy reliability of witness which will render more persuasive the fantasies of a never-never land that are to follow. Cast away in Antarctic latitudes Wilkins is sportively visited by flocks of Flying Indians, and one of them, an enchanting maiden named Youwarkee, unnoticed by her soaring friends, falls from the blue into his enraptured arms. The means of flight have been acquired biologically: a cloak-like integument, called a "graundee," sheathing the body, may be sprung open into a sort of kite. (The aerodynamic details were soberly demonstrated in the first edition by engravings, reproduced in the 1973 edition.)

Alone in their earthly paradise Peter and Youwarkee live out a long idyll of chastest courtship and then of godly domestic bliss among their many children. Paltock's little Eden charmingly dismisses Marvell's sentiment that "Two paradises 'twere in one/To live in paradise alone."

There follows now a major development of the novel when Wilkins and his family, who have at length been visited by several of Youwarkee's people, fly away to her homeland. (Peter is borne aloft in a chair, complete with safety-belt, by eight Indians.) If the earlier part is a connubial *Robinson Crusoe*, this latter part is a bland *Gulliver's Travels*; and the domestic Eden may be ironically related to the political Utopia. In the stone-age culture of the Indians, Peter's technological knowledge gives him enormous power and prestige which he exerts in every sphere of life (most dramatically in warfare), convinced that the Christian basis of his enlightenment gives his interventions a missionary justification.

In its own day *Peter Wilkins* was sufficiently acceptable, in the prolific genre of the Voyage Imaginaire or Robinsonade, to be immediately reprinted and soon translated into French and German. Then it was hailed during the Romantic era as a work of striking imaginative power by such men as Coleridge, Scott, Shelley, Lamb, and Leigh Hunt. Latterly it has acquired new interest as a document indicative of European imperial assumptions that were already beginning to impose "progressive" regimes by the destruction of alternative cultures all over the world.

—R. A. Copland

PEACOCK, Thomas Love. English. Born in Weymouth, Dorset, 18 October 1785; moved with his mother to Chertsey, Surrey, 1788. Educated at Mr. Wicks' school in Englefield Green, Surrey. Married Jane Gryffydh in 1820 (died, 1852); four children. Settled in London, 1802, continued his studies on his own, and worked for merchants to support himself while writing; Secretary to Sir Home Riggs Popham, at Flushing, 1808–09; lived in North Wales, 1810–11; met Shelley, 1812, accompanied him on a visit to Edinburgh, 1813, and settled near him at Great Marlow, 1816; received a pension from Shelley; subsequently acted as the executor of Shelley's estate; joined the East India Company, London, 1819: Chief Examiner, 1836 until he retired, 1856; contributed to *Fraser's Magazine* until 1860. Lived in Halliford, near Shepperton, Middlesex. *Died 23 January 1866.*

PUBLICATIONS

Collections

> *Works,* edited by H. F. B. Brett-Smith and C. E. Jones.   10 vols., 1924–34.
> *The Novels,* edited by David Garnett.   1948.
> *A Selection,* edited by H. L. B. Moody.   1966.

Novels

> *Headlong Hall.*   1816; revised edition, 1816, 1823, 1837.
> *Melincourt.*   1817.
> *Nightmare Abbey.*   1818; revised edition, 1837; edited by Raymond Wright, with *Crotchet Castle,* 1969.
> *Maid Marian.*   1822; revised edition, 1837.
> *The Misfortunes of Elphin.*   1829.
> *Crotchet Castle.*   1831; edited by Raymond Wright, with *Nightmare Abbey,* 1969.
> *Gryll Grange.*   1861.

Plays

> *Plays* (includes *The Dilettanti, The Three Doctors, The Circle of Leda*), edited by A. B. Young.   1910.

Verse

The Monks of St. Marks. 1804.
Palmyra and Other Poems. 1806.
The Genius of the Thames: A Lyrical Poem in Two Parts. 1810.
The Genius of the Thames, Palmyra, and Other Poems. 1812.
The Philosophy of Melancholy: A Poem in Four Parts, with a Mythological One. 1812.
Sir Hornbook; or, Childe Launcelot's Expedition: A Grammatico-Allegorical Ballad. 1813.
Sir Proteus: A Satirical Ballad. 1814.
The Round Table; or, King Arthur's Feast. 1817.
Rhododaphne; or, The Thessalian Spell. 1818.
The Stable Boy. 1820.
Paper Money Lyrics and Other Poems. 1837.
Songs from the Novels. 1902.
A Bill for the Better Promotion of Oppression on the Sabbath Day. 1926.

Other

The Four Ages of Poetry. 1863; edited by J. E. Jordan, 1965.
A Whitebait Dinner at Lovegrove's at Blackwall (Greek and Latin text by Peacock, English version by John Cam Hobhouse). 1851.
Calidore and Miscellanea, edited by Richard Garnett. 1891.
Memoirs of Shelley, with Shelley's Letters to Peacock, edited by H. F. B. Brett-Smith. 1909; edited by Humbert Wolfe, in *The Life of Shelley* by Peacock, Hogg, and Trelawny, 1933.
Letters to Edward Hookham and Shelley, with Fragments of Unpublished Manuscripts, edited by Richard Garnett. 1910.
Memoirs of Shelley and Other Essays and Reviews, edited by Howard Mills. 1970.

Translator, *Gl'Ingannati, The Deceived: A Comedy Performed at Siena in 1531, and Aelia Laelia Crispis.* 1862; edited by H. H. Furness, in *New Variorum Edition of Shakespeare,* vol. 13, 1901.

Reading List: *The Critical Reputation of Peacock* by Bill Read, 1959 (includes bibliography); *Peacock* by J. I. M. Stewart, 1963; *Peacock* by Lionel Madden, 1967; *Peacock: His Circle and His Age* by Howard Mills, 1968; *His Fine Wit: A Study of Peacock* by Carl Dawson, 1970; *Peacock* (biography) by Felix Felton, 1973.

*   *   *

Thomas Love Peacock is one of the small number of writers who have created a totally personal and idiosyncratic type of fiction. Whatever he may have owed to Aristophanes, or Rabelais, or Voltaire, or Robert Bage, Peacock wrote novels unique in their blend of comedy and the play of ideas. *Headlong Hall* and *Melincourt* established this pattern, with their caricature characters like Squire Headlong, Mr. Milestone, Sir Oran Haut-Ton (the nearly-human parliamentary candidate) and Sir Telegraph Paxarett, who indulge in much conversation in which each is able to reveal his particular preoccupation (though Sir Oran maintains an impressive silence). The clash of ideas is usually so extreme that a kind of intellectual farce ensues. In *Nightmare Abbey*, *Crotchet Castle* and *Gryll Grange* Peacock exploited his form to the best effect, while *Maid Marian* and *The Misfortunes of Elphin* are more historical and more romantic.

Nightmare Abbey centres on a rendering of Peacock's friend Shelley in the character of Scythrop Glowry, a young man unable to make up his mind between the charms of two young ladies; but the interest is in the interplay of ideas between a number of entertaining characters, including Mr. Flosky, the transcendental philosopher (a caricature of Coleridge), and Mr. Cypress, the melancholy poet (based on Byron). Through the amusing dialogue Peacock suggests the latent absurdity of the romantic commitment to extremes. His own attitude may be inferred as based on the supremacy of common sense.

In fact some critics have felt that Peacock's scepticism about ideals amounts to a species of clever Philistinism, with no positive creative elements. But the evidence of the novels, and especially *Crotchet Castle*, is that the humour aroused by the extravagances of the contrasting characters constitutes a value of its own, from which the ideals of toleration and humanity emerge unscathed. Peacock's intelligent awareness of his own time is shown in *Crotchet Castle* by his choice of characters, who are well suited to satisfy their host's curiosity over current issues; Mr. Crotchet explains why he has invited his guests: "The sentimental against the rational, the intuitive against the inductive, the ornamental against the useful, the intense against the tranquil, the romantic against the classical; these are great and interesting controversies, which I should like, before I die, to see satisfactorily settled." The reader must not share Mr. Crotchet's eagerness for certainties if he is to enjoy the novel, but he will find in the Scots economist Mr. MacQuedy, the Utopian Mr. Toogood, the operatic Mr. Trillo, and the Gothic enthusiast Mr. Chainmail amusing exemplifications of contemporary interests. Peacock deals neatly with the problem of ending his novels by including an element of romance – in this case between Captain Fitzchrome and Lady Clarinda – which can find its consummation in music (Peacock is adept at providing suitable songs) and in marriage.

The most vivid presence in *Crotchet Castle*, though, is undoubtedly the genial *bon viveur* Dr. Folliott, whose robust common sense and addiction to the Classics offer a sane contrast to the evanescent enthusiasms of the other guests. He is a similar type of character to the Reverend Doctor Opimian in *Gryll Grange*, written some thirty years later but in precisely the same style as the earlier novels. Here Peacock is still astute and lively in his dismissal of the system-mongers, who were building the commercial world which the Victorians have bequeathed to later generations. Peacock's criticisms here have something of the mellowness of old age, and there is an attractive Elysian quality about the setting in the unenclosed New Forest. By this time Meredith had married Peacock's daughter, and Meredith was to give a sardonic picture of the old man as Dr. Middleton, the father of the heroine of *The Egoist*, ready to sacrifice his daughter for another glass of the exquisite Patterne port. The central characters of Peacock's creation, however, strike us as achieving a sound balance between humanity and hedonism, and so contribute to that sense of good order which gives strength to the comic structures of his novels.

The comedy of ideas has no better English practitioner, and although it may be a limited form, it is one which combines civilisation and entertainment in equal measure. Peacock thus fully deserves the tribute of F. R. Leavis's footnote in *The Great Tradition* where he is praised for having created books "that have permanent life as light reading – indefinitely re-readable – for minds with mature interests."

—Peter Faulkner

QUILLER-COUCH, Sir Arthur (Thomas). Pseudonym: "Q." English. Born in Bodmin, Cornwall, 21 November 1863. Educated at Newton Abbot, Devon; Clifton College, Bristol; Trinity College, Oxford, 1882–86, honours degrees in classics, 1884, 1886. Married Louisa Amelia Hicks in 1889; one son and one daughter. Lecturer in Classics at Trinity College, 1886–87, then settled in London; worked as a free-lance journalist and for the publishing firm of Cassell: Assistant Editor of Cassell's Liberal weekly *The Speaker*, 1890–92, and contributor until 1899; settled in Fowey, Cornwall, 1892, and continued to work as a free-lance journalist until 1912; Fellow of Jesus College, Cambridge, and King Edward VII Professor of English, Cambridge University, 1912–44: with H. M. Chadwick and Dr. Hugh Fraser Stewart, established an independent honours school of English literature at Cambridge, 1917; Editor, King's Treasuries of Literature series, Dent, publishers, London, from 1920. Mayor of Fowey, 1937–38; also Justice of the Peace and County Alderman, Cornwall. Litt.D.: University of Bristol, 1912; LL.D.: University of Aberdeen, 1927; University of Edinburgh, 1930. Honorary Fellow, Trinity College, Oxford, 1926. Fellow, and Member of the Academic Committee, Royal Society of Literature. Knighted, 1910. *Died 12 May 1944.*

PUBLICATIONS

Fiction

Dead Man's Rock. 1887.
The Astonishing History of Troy Town. 1888; as *Troy Town*, 1928.
The Splendid Spur. 1889.
Noughts and Crosses: Stories, Studies, and Sketches. 1891.
The Blue Pavilions. 1891.
I Saw Three Ships and Other Winter's Tales. 1892.
The Delectable Duchy: Stories, Studies, and Sketches. 1893.
Fairy Tales, Far and Near. 1895.
Wandering Heath: Stories, Studies, and Sketches. 1895.
Ia: A Love Story. 1895.
St. Ives, Being the Adventures of a French Prisoner in England, with Robert Louis
    Stevenson (completed by Quiller-Couch). 1897.
The Ship of Stars. 1899.
Old Fires and Profitable Ghosts (stories). 1900.
The Laird's Luck and Other Fireside Tales. 1901.
The Westcotes. 1902.
The White Wolf and Other Fireside Tales. 1902.
The Adventures of Harry Revel. 1903.
Two Sides of the Face: Midwinter Tales. 1903.
The Collaborators; or, The Comedy That Wrote Itself. 1903.
Hetty Wesley. 1903.
Fort Amity. 1904.
Shakespeare's Christmas and Other Stories. 1904.
Shining Ferry. 1905.
Sir John Constantine. 1906.
The Mayor of Troy. 1906.
Poison Island. 1906.
Major Vigoureux. 1907.
Merry-Garden and Other Stories. 1907.
True Tilda. 1909.

Corporal Sam and Other Stories. 1910.
Lady Good for Nothing: A Man's Portrait of a Woman. 1910.
Brother Copas. 1911.
The Sleeping Beauty and Other Tales from the Old French. 1911.
Hocken and Hunken: A Tale of Troy. 1912.
My Best Book (stories). 1912.
In Powder and Crinoline: Old Fairy Tales Retold. 1913; as *The Twelve Dancing Princesses and Other Fairy Tales,* 1923.
News from the Duchy (stories). 1913.
Nicky-Nan, Reservist. 1915.
Mortallone and Aunt Trinidad: Tales of the Spanish Main. 1917.
Foe-Farrell: A Romance. 1918.
Selected Stories. 1921.
Tales and Romances. 30 vols., 1928.
Q's Mystery Stories. 1937.
Shorter Stories. 1946.
Castle Dor, completed by Daphne du Maurier. 1962.

Verse

Athens. 1881.
Green Bays: Verses and Parodies. 1893; revised edition, 1930.
Poems and Ballads. 1896.
The Vigil of Venus and Other Poems. 1912.
Poems. 1929.

Other

The Warwickshire Avon, illustrated by Alfred Parsons. 1891.
Adventures in Criticism. 1896.
Historical Tales from Shakespeare. 1899.
From a Cornish Window. 1906.
The Roll Call of Honour. 1912.
Poetry. 1914.
On the Art of Writing (lectures). 1916.
Memoir of Arthur John Butler. 1917.
Notes on Shakespeare's Workmanship. 1917; as *Shakespeare's Workmanship,* 1918.
Studies in Literature. 3 vols., 1918–29.
On the Art of Reading (lectures). 1920.
Charles Dickens and Other Victorians. 1925.
The Age of Chaucer. 1926.
A Lecture on Lectures. 1927.
A Further Approach to Shakespeare. 1934.
The Poet as Citizen and Other Papers. 1934.
The Jubilee of County Councils 1899–1939. 1939.
Cambridge Lectures. 1943.
Memories and Opinions: An Unfinished Autobiography, edited by S. C. Roberts. 1944.
Q Anthology, edited by Frederick Brittain. 1948.

Editor, *The Golden Pomp: A Procession of English Lyrics from Surrey To Shirley.* 1895.
Editor, *The Story of the Sea.* 2 vols., 1895–96.
Editor, *English Sonnets.* 1897; revised edition, 1935.

Editor, *A Fowey Garland.*   1899.
Editor, *The Oxford Book of English Verse 1250–1900.*   1900; revised edition, 1939.
Editor, The World of Adventure: A Collection of Stirring Scenes (*The Black, Blue, Brown, Green, Grey,* and *Red Adventure Book*).   6 vols., 1904–05.
Editor, *The Pilgrim's Way: A Little Scrip of Good Counsel for Travellers.*   1906.
Editor, *Select English Classics.*   32 vols., 1908–12.
Editor, *The Oxford Book of Ballads.*   1910.
Editor, *The Oxford Book of Victorian Verse.*   1912.
Editor, with J. Dover Wilson, *Plays,* by Shakespeare (Comedies in New Cambridge Edition).   14 vols., 1921–31.
Editor, *A Bible Anthology.*   1922.
Editor, *The Oxford Book of English Prose.*   1925.
Editor, with A. Nairne and T. R. Glover, *The Cambridge Shorter Bible.*   1928.
Editor, *Felicities of Thomas Traherne.*   1934.

Translator, with Paul M. Francke, *A Blot of Ink,* by René Bazin.   1892.

Reading List: *The Q Tradition* by Basil Willey, 1946; *Quiller-Couch: A Biographical Study of Q* by Frederick Brittain, 1947 (includes bibliography).

*   *   *

My first introduction to Arthur Quiller-Couch ("Q") was encountering in 1945 his books *On the Art of Writing* and *On the Art of Reading,* and wondering why the lectures I was hearing at McGill were not as sensible and stimulating as those of an earlier generation at Cambridge. Q's classical quotations and erudite allusions may have sounded a bit more pompous in the 1940's than they did when first delivered, but there were a genuine enthusiasm and a desire to offer truly practical advice. Others also stressed "plain words" in writing, and were perhaps better critics of literature, but few had Q's light touch with verse parody that contrived to be both imitation and devastating criticism. Perhaps his greatest contribution to scholarship was to bring to general and critical attention the poets he featured in his thoughtful anthologies (including *The Oxford Book of English Verse*). Though not exceptionally innovative, they were sound and widely used, and it is through them, and not his strictly critical works, that he made his useful contribution to the modern view of poetry.
    Entertaining poet and influential critic that he was, it was in his own fiction that he did his best work. There is a wild Cornish romanticism in *Dead Man's Rock* and *The Astonishing History of Troy Town,* while *The Splendid Spur* and *The Ship of Stars* rival Neil Munro in catching the manner of Robert Louis Stevenson, and are, I think, better than Munro's *John Splendid* (1898). In fact, Q was chosen to finish *St. Ives,* the novel left incomplete at the death of Stevenson, and he did an admirable job in proving himself a master spinner of yarns. (His own unfinished novel, *Castle Dor,* was completed by another Cornish writer, Daphne du Maurier.)
    It is as a writer of romantic fiction, and not as a critic, anthologist, journalist, professor, or local politician, that he has a small but secure place in history.

—Leonard R. N. Ashley

RADCLIFFE, Ann (née Ward). English. Born in London, 9 July 1764. Educated privately. Married William Radcliffe, subsequently editor of the *English Chronicle*, in 1787. Writer, 1789–1797; thereafter lived in retirement. *Died 7 February 1823.*

PUBLICATIONS

Collections

Poetical Works. 2 vols., 1834.
Novels. 1877.

Fiction

The Castles of Athlin and Dunbayne: A Highland Story. 1789.
A Sicilian Romance. 1790.
The Romance of the Forest, Interspersed with Some Pieces of Poetry. 1791.
The Mysteries of Udolpho: A Romance, Interspersed with Some Pieces of Poetry. 1794; edited by Bonamy Dobrée, 1966.
The Italian; or, The Confessional of the Black Penitents: A Romance. 1797; edited by Frederick Garber, 1968.
Gaston de Blondeville; or, The Court of Henry III Keeping Festival in Ardenne; St. Alban's Abbey: A Metrical Tale; with Some Metrical Pieces. 1826.

Verse

Poems. 1815.

Other

A Journey Made in the Summer of 1794 Through Holland and the Western Frontier of Germany. 1795.

Bibliography: in *Gothic Bibliography* by Montague Summers, 1941.

Reading List: *Radcliffe* by Aline Grant, 1952; *Sublimity in the Novels of Radcliffe: A Study of the Influence of Burke's Enquiry* by M. Ware, 1963.

*   *   *

Ann Radcliffe's novels are concerned with terror and reason, in their late eighteenth-century significations. She is uninterested in complex characterizations, rational plot, natural dialogue, or social themes. Instead, she tries to throw her idealized heroines into the greatest perplexity and fear as often and for as many reasons as possible, before she finally elucidates all obscurities, dispels all fears, and explains all mysteries. Thus she uses geographical and historical distance to achieve exotic effects, and her settings exploit most of the types of the sublime and picturesque set out in the standard treatises on those subjects. Her stories concern concealed or afflicted relationships between idealized heroes and heroines and virtuous but ineffectual parents or guardians on one hand, and vicious and tyrannical persecutors on the other. Her plots are unprogressive, rely heavily on various devices of retardation, function on the principle of linked complications, and are terminated by a *deus ex machina* or a grand coincidence. Her characters, with the exception of Schedoni in *The Italian*, are abstract and uninteresting; she cares little for individual psychology, only for opportunities to describe inner conflicts, or various ways of overthrowing reason by means of sublimity and terror. The only other modes of sensibility that interest her are the moral and aesthetic tastes of her heroes and heroines, seen in her descriptions of their responses to music, ruins, or picturesque nature. Dialogue too is abstract and artificial, and, where it is impassioned, relies heavily on the rhetorical clichés of heroic drama.

And so the novels are static in form. There is no development of character or theme, no argument embodied in a concatenation of character and circumstance, only a repetition in diverse forms of mystery, obscurity, terror, and perplexity, until finally what is feared – rape, murder, or some forced action such as marriage or transfer of property – is evaded. The double movement in the novels is from mystery and confinement to knowledge and freedom, as temperance, fortitude, chastity, and family loyalty triumph over passion, egotism, pride, and licentiousness. But the victory of reason and self-control over mystery and excess is guaranteed right from the beginning by the narrative voice. Even-tempered, lucid, and balanced, it rarely breaks down into expressiveness, and, through apparent mysteries, confusions, and terrors, works out the same values, and the same view of man and society, which are presented in the contemporaneous novel of manners and social life.

The tension between terror and reason, then, is the dominant characteristic of Mrs. Radcliffe's fiction. It was the source of her enormous popularity and she continued to develop the skill and complexity of her treatment of it from *The Castles of Athlin and Dunbayne* to *The Mysteries of Udolpho*. *The Italian* was probably meant as a criticism of the mass of inferior imitators of her own achievement, and therefore probably an afterthought, while *Gaston de Blondeville* and the verse romance *St. Alban's Abbey* were unsuccessful attempts to develop fictional modes different from that she had perfected, and exhausted, with *Udolpho* and *The Italian*.

—Gary Kelly

READE, Charles. English. Born in Ipsden, Oxfordshire, 8 June 1814. Educated privately by a clergyman at Rose Hill, near Iffley, 1822–27, and at the private school of Rev. Hearn at Staines, Middlesex, 1827–29; Magdalen College, Oxford, 1831–35, B.A. 1835, M.A. 1838, D.C.L. 1847; entered Lincoln's Inn, London, 1836; Vinerian Fellow, 1842; called to the Bar, 1843. Fellow of Magdalen College, Oxford, 1835 until his death, and held the posts of Bursar, 1844 (re-elected, 1849), Dean of Arts, 1845, and Vice-President, 1851; writer from 1850; thereafter gradually withdrew from university life and lived mainly in London. *Died 11 April 1884.*

PUBLICATIONS

Collections

(Works). 17 vols., 1895,

Fiction

Peg Woffington. 1852; edited by Emma Gollancz, 1901.
Christie Johnstone. 1853.
Clouds and Sunshine; Art: A Dramatic Tale. 1855.
It Is Never Too Late to Mend. 1856.
The Course of True Love Never Did Run Smooth (stories). 1857.
Propria Quae Maribus: A Jeu d'Esprit, and The Box Tunnel: A Fact. 1857.
White Lies. 1857; as *Double Marriage; or, White Lies,* 1868.
Cream (stories). 1858.
A Good Fight and Other Tales. 1859; *A Good Fight* edited by Andrew Lang, 1910.
Love Me Little, Love Me Long. 1859.
The Cloister and the Hearth. 1861.
Hard Cash. 1863.
Griffith Gaunt; or, Jealousy. 1866.
Foul Play, with Dion Boucicault. 1868.
Put Yourself in His Place. 1870.
A Terrible Temptation. 1871.
The Wandering Heir. 1872.
A Simpleton. 1873.
The Jilt. 1877.
A Woman-Hater. 1877.
Golden Crowns: Sunday Stories. 1877.
Singleheart and Doubleface. 1882.
Good Stories of Man and Other Animals. 1884.
The Jilt and Other Stories. 1884.
A Perilous Secret. 1884.

Plays

The Ladies' Battle; or, Un Duel en Amour, from a play by Scribe (produced 1851). 1851.
Peregrine Pickle, from the novel by Smollett (produced 1854). 1851.
Angelo, from the play by Victor Hugo (produced 1851). 1851.
Rachel the Reaper, from a work by George Sand (as *A Village Tale,* produced 1852; revised version, as *Rachel the Reaper,* produced 1872). 1871.
The Lost Husband, from a play by A. A. Bourgeois and A. M. B. Gaudichot Masson (produced 1852). 1852.
Masks and Faces; or, Before and Behind the Curtain, with Tom Taylor (produced 1852). 1854; edited by George Rowell, in *Nineteenth-Century Plays,* 1953.
Gold! (produced 1853). 1853.
The Courier of Lyons; or, The Attack upon the Mail, from a work by Moreau, Siraudin, and Delacour (produced 1854). 1854; as *The Lyons Mail* (produced 1877), 1895.
The King's Rival, with Tom Taylor (produced 1854). 1854.
Honour Before Titles; or, Nobs and Snobs (produced 1854).
Two Loves and a Life (produced 1854). 1854.
Nance Oldfield, from a play by Fournier (as *Art,* produced 1855; revised version, as *An Actress by Daylight,* produced 1871; as *Nance Oldfield,* produced 1883). 1883.
Poverty and Pride, from a play by Edward Brisebarre and Eugene Nus. 1856.
The First Printer, with Tom Taylor (produced 1856).
The Hypochondriac, from a play by Molière (produced 1858; as *The Robust Invalid,* produced 1870). 1857.
Le Faubourg Saint-Germain. 1859.

It's Never Too Late to Mend, from his own novel (produced 1864). 1865; edited by Léone Rives, 1940.

The Prurient Prude. 1866.

Dora, from a poem by Tennyson (produced 1867). 1867.

The Double Marriage, from a play by August Maquet (produced 1867). 1867; revised version (produced 1868).

Foul Play, with Dion Boucicault, from their own novel (produced 1868; revised version, produced 1868). 1871; revised by Reade, 1883; revised version, as *Our Seamen* (produced 1874); as *The Scuttled Ship* (produced 1877).

The Well-Born Workman; or, A Man of the Day, from his novel *Put Yourself in His Place* (as *Put Yourself in His Place,* produced 1870; as *Free Labour,* produced 1870). 1878.

Kate Peyton; or, Jealousy, from his novel *Griffith Gaunt* (produced 1867; as *Kate Peyton's Lovers,* produced 1873). 1872.

Shilly Shally, from the novel *Ralph the Heir* by Anthony Trollope (produced 1872).

The Wandering Heir, from his own novel (produced 1873).

Joan, from the novel *That Lass o' Lowries* by Frances Hodgson Burnett (produced 1878).

The Countess and the Dancer, from a play by Sardou (as *Jealousy,* produced 1878; revised version, as *The Countess and the Dancer,* produced 1886). 1883.

Drink, from a play by Zola, Busnach, and Gastineau (produced 1879).

Love and Money, with Henry Pettitt (produced 1882). 1883.

Single Heart and Double Face (produced 1882); as *Double Faces* (produced 1883).

Other

It Is Never Too Late to Mend: Proofs of Its Prison Revelations. 1859.

Monopoly Versus Property. 1860.

The Eighth Commandment. 1860.

To the Editor of the Daily Globe, Toronto: A Reply to Criticism. 1871.

The Legal Vocabulary. 1872.

Cremona Violins. 1873.

A Hero and a Martyr: A True and Accurate Account of the Heroic Feats and Sad Calamity of James Lambert. 1874.

Trade Malice: A Personal Narrative, and The Wandering Heir. 1875.

The Coming Man (letters). 1878.

Dora; or, The History of a Play. 1878.

Readiana: Comments on Current Events. 1882.

Bible Characters. 1888.

Bibliography: *Collins and Reade* by M. L. Parrish, 1940; *Collins and Reade: A Bibliography of Critical Notices and Studies* by Francesco Cordasco and Kenneth Scott, 1949.

Reading List: *Dickens, Reade, and Collins: Sensation Novelists* by W. C. Phillips, 1919; *Reade: A Biography* by Malcolm Elwin, 1931; *The Making of The Cloister and the Hearth* by Albert Morton Turner, 1938; *Reade: Sa Vie, Ses Romans* by Léone Rives, 1940 (includes bibliography); *Reade: A Study in Victorian Authorship* by Wayne Burns, 1961; *Reade* by Elton E. Smith, 1977.

*   *   *

William Dean Howells placed his finger on the pulse of Charles Reade's claim to greatness and his singular weakness: "he might have been the master of a great school of English realism; but ... he remained content to use the materials of realism and produce the effect of romanticism" (*My Literary Passions*, 1895). Nothing could be clearer than his excessive devotion to realism. His playscripts bristled with suggestions for stage business (*Gold*), descriptions of ingenious and realistic settings (*Dora*), and the most explicit stage directions (*The Scuttled Ship*). He thanked the London *Times* for news items that provided the plots for four of his most popular novels: *It Is Never Too Late to Mend, Hard Cash, Put Yourself in His Place*, and *A Terrible Temptation*. In his study he never got beyond arm's reach of his compendious notebooks, his index files, and the five-foot-tall notecards that leaned against his walls like screens. He frequently contended that true fiction should be as "solid" with fact as non-fiction.

But Reade's absorbed interest in facts was always hostage to essentially old-fashioned, sentimental ideals. Plays and novels both follow the same pattern: evil appears to triumph and good to fail, but do not fear – at the eleventh hour the kaleidoscope will be shaken by a Celestial Hand, and all the pieces will fall into rightful place and correct relationship.

Ironically, it was his taste for melodrama that makes his plays unplayed in an age dominated by that most melodramatic of media – television. In the novel it separated him from his greater contemporaries, Thackeray, Eliot, and Dickens, and linked him with the lesser purveyors of the "sensation novel," Collins, Bulwer-Lytton, and Braddon. Indeed so little did he differentiate between stage and novel that six of his plays were rewritten as novels (*Rachel the Reaper, Masks and Faces, Gold, Foul Play, Jealousy, Singleheart and Doubleface*), and in his prose fiction the acid test of a passage was to consider how it would play on the stage.

His best and most enduring novel, *The Cloister and the Hearth*, exactly exemplifies the tension between realism and romanticism. The Erasmus *Compendium* of 1524 provided the historical facts; seventy-nine medieval studies filled in the realistic background. The Erasmus autobiographical fragment was full of stirring event and Reade was the great master of eventful narrative. The plot was one long picaresque journey, and Reade liked to send his heroes far from home. The catastrophe was borne by a fraudulent letter, and Reade's novels are full of false letters bearing evil news. The hero of the *Compendium* and *The Cloister and the Hearth* is a semi-historical figure; but is he not equally as much another of that long line of Reade's "Resourceful Heroes"? And the heroine, frank, honest, faithful, is as Victorian as fifteenth-century Dutch. The author who loved fact found the perfect fact, and Reade's masterpiece resulted.

—Elton E. Smith

REEVE, Clara. English. Born in Ipswich, Suffolk, 23 January 1729. Educated at home. Settled with her family in Colchester, Essex, 1755; thereafter a full-time writer. *Died 3 December 1807.*

PUBLICATIONS

Fiction

The Champion of Virtue: A Gothic Story. 1777; as *The Old English Baron,* 1778; edited by James Trainer, 1967.

The Two Mentors: A Modern Story. 1783.
The Exiles; or, Memoirs of the Count de Cronstadt. 1788.
The School for Widows. 1791.
Memoirs of Sir Roger de Clarendon, A Natural Son of Edward the Black Prince. 1793.
Destination; or, Memoirs of a Private Family. 1799.

Verse

Original Poems on Several Occasions. 1769.

Other

The Progress of Romance Through Times, Countries, and Manners. 2 vols., 1785.
Plans for Education, with Remarks on the Systems of Other Writers. 1792.

Translator, *The Phoenix*, by John Barclay. 1772.

*   *   *

The name of Clara Reeve is today associated almost exclusively with two works, one of them a gothic adventure story, the other a literary-historical review presented in dialogue form. The gothic story published under Reeve's name in 1778 as *The Old English Baron* had a year previously appeared anonymously as *The Champion of Virtue*, purporting to be an edition of an ancient manuscript. This device points back to the example of Horace Walpole in the preface to *The Castle of Otranto*, and although the pretence is no longer sustained in the second edition of Clara's novel, the preface openly confesses that "this story is the literary offspring of the Castle of Otranto, written upon the same plan, with a design to unite the most attractive and interesting circumstances of the ancient Romance and modern Novel." What is new is her stated intention to lessen the violent impact of Walpole's supernatural machinery which, she believed, dissolved the book's enchantment. Her pursuit of moderation embraced not only the presentation of the supernatural, but also the emotions and temperaments of the principal characters, whose function is most succinctly outlined in the exhortation that "this awful spectacle be a lesson to all present, that though wickedness may triumph for a season, a day of retribution will come!"

It is in her second major work, *The Progress of Romance*, that she discusses the process of development from romance to novel and presents in the form of a historical review "through times, countries and manners" a clear indication of her own ideals. The criteria include the portrayal of everyday events in familiar language, naturalness of manner, probability, simplicity, and moral improvement. Any analysis of her novels would show her concern with the promotion of social and domestic virtues, as in her second novel, *The Two Mentors*, where innate goodness triumphs over the worst that misguided education and evil advisers can do, up to her final work, *Destination; or, Memoirs of a Private Family*, with its high moral and didactic tone, again in a specifically educational context. As a convinced believer in the power of the written word to influence the mind, particularly of the young and immature, for good or evil, Reeve wrote in the circumspect and demure style to be expected of the modest gentlewoman that she was. (J. K. Reeves cites the use of the phrase "antiquated virgin" as evidence that Reeve was not the authoress at least of part of the novel *Fatherless Fanny* which was attributed to her, since he believed her incapable of coining such a phrase.) The absence of passion, the holding-back of the imagination, the fear of excess which characterise her work leave the reader with a feeling of a benevolent writer almost afraid of herself and of the possibility of giving offence or of weakening the moral fibre of society. Sir Walter Scott's verdict on her, with all that it does not say, still seems very appropriate: "The various novels of Clara Reeve are all marked by excellent good sense, pure morality, and a competent command of those qualities which constitute a good romance."

—James Trainer

RICHARDSON, Samuel. English. Born in Derbyshire in 1689. Little is known about his education: may have attended Christ's Hospital or Merchant Taylors' School. Married 1) Martha Wilde (died, 1731), five sons and one daughter; 2) Elizabeth Leake, one son and five daughters. Apprenticed to the stationer John Wilde, in London, 1706; thereafter worked for several years as a compositor and corrector in a London printing office; proprietor of his own printing firm in Fleet Street, afterwards in Salisbury Court, 1719 until the end of his life; became printer of the *Journals* of the House of Commons (26 volumes), of the *Daily Journal*, 1736–37, and the *Daily Gazetteer*, 1738; Master of the Stationers' Company, 1754; built new printing offices in Salisbury Court, 1755; bought half the patent of "law printer to his majesty," 1760. *Died 4 July 1761.*

PUBLICATIONS

Collections

The Novels. 18 vols., 1929–31.

Fiction

Pamela; or, Virtue Rewarded. 1740; second part, 1741; edited by M. Kinkead-Weekes, 1962.
Clarissa; or, The History of a Young Lady. 7 vols., 1747–48; augmented edition, 1749; edited by John Butt, 1962.
The History of Sir Charles Grandison. 7 vols., 1753–54; edited by Jocelyn Harris, 1972.

Other

The Apprentice's Vade Mecum. 1733; edited by Alan D. McKillop, 1975.
A Seasonable Examination of the Pleas and Pretensions of the Proprietors of, and Subscribers to, Play-Houses, Erected in Defiance of the Royal Licence. 1735.
Aesop's Fables. 1739.
Letters Written to and for Particular Friends, Directing the Requisite Style and Forms to Be Observed in Writing Familiar Letters. 1741; edited by B. W. Downs, as *Familiar Letters on Important Occasions,* 1928.

The Correspondence of Richardson, edited by Anna Laetitia Barbauld.   6 vols., 1806.
Selected Letters, edited by John Carroll.   1964.
The Richardson–Stinstra Correspondence, and Stinstra's Prefaces to Clarissa, edited by
William C. Slattery.   1969.

Editor, with others, *The Negotiations of Sir Thomas Roe, in His Embassy to the Ottoman
Porte*.   1740.
Editor, *A Tour Through the Whole Island of Great Britain*, by Daniel Defoe.   4 vols.,
1742.

Bibliography: *Richardson: A Bibliographical Record of His Literary Career with Historical
Notes* by W. M. Sale, 1936; *Richardson: A List of Critical Studies 1896–1946* by Francesco
Cordasco, 1948.

Reading List: *Richardson, Printer and Novelist*, 1936, and *Early Masters of English Fiction*,
1956, both by Alan D. McKillop; *Richardson* by R. Brissenden, 1958; *Richardson* by A.
Kearney, 1968; *Richardson: A Biography* by T. C. Duncan Eaves and Ben D. Kimpel, 1971;
Richardson and the Eighteenth-Century Puritan Character by Cynthia Griffin Wolff, 1972;
Richardson: Dramatic Novelist by M. Kinkead-Weekes, 1973; *A Natural Passion: A Study of
the Novels by Richardson* by Margaret A. Doody, 1974.

*   *   *

Samuel Richardson is generally regarded as one of the founders of the English novel, and
Pamela is one of the first authentically novelistic narratives in English. The reasons for this
primacy are partly technical, as Richardson developed a method for rendering the
psychological reality of his central character which has no equal in previous fiction. *Pamela* is
an epistolary novel, a collection of letters which Richardson claims to be editing written to
her parents by a young servant girl. Using letters to tell a story was not in itself a new strategy
in 1740, but Richardson's originality lies in the detailed intensity with which Pamela's letters
dramatize her situation and personality. Those letters are a young girl's record of a sexual
ordeal, as she tells her parents the long story of her master's attempts first to seduce and then
to rape her. The trials of persecuted female virtue were a popular theme in the early 18th
century, the subject of numerous plays and novels which provided for their audience a
mixture of moral pathos and erotic sensation. Like those works, *Pamela* presents isolated and
improbably pure female innocence versus powerful and ruthless male lust. Richardson,
however, transcends those sexual stereotypes by the simple but inspired device whereby
Pamela tells her own story as it happens and in that process of immediate transcription
reveals a personality which is far more complex than those of the paragons of popular
literature. Indeed, some readers (including some of Richardson's 18th-century critics) have
accused Pamela of hypocrisy and selfish calculation, of faking her innocence and holding out
for marriage. Such criticism confirms Richardson's achievement, for Pamela is a complex
and potentially contradictory character, self-consciously pure and innocent and at the same
time strong and self-possessed, terrified of sex and yet clearly attracted to her master, humble
and submissive to her social superiors and yet morally proud and socially ambitious. Those
contradictions and the interesting personality they define are what Richardson managed
brilliantly to convey in *Pamela*, although he might not have recognized this description of his
book.

In all his novels, Richardson's intentions were strongly didactic and religious. *Pamela*
grew out of a project undertaken at the request of several booksellers to compile a collection
of model letters which uneducated persons could use on specific occasions. One of those
imagined occasions required a letter written by her parents to a young female servant whose
master had tried to seduce her. Richardson's imagination was fired by that hint, and he wrote

Pamela in several months of intense activity. That intensity is apparent in the novel, and the remarkable complexity of its main character seems to be the result of Richardson's strong identification with her. Pamela describes events, situations, and emotions in careful detail as they happen to her; her letters sometimes turn into a spontaneous journal and she writes "instantaneous description," as Richardson later described his technique for making his characters come alive. Readers experience the world from Pamela's excited participation in it, and the effect is of immediacy and suspenseful, dramatic urgency. Richardson renders Pamela as a terrified teen-ager, menaced by her master's sexual violence, bewildered by her own ambivalence, and cut off from any effective legal redress against her persecutors. But Richardson also presents her as a moral heroine, trusting in God and praying for the spiritual strength to resist her own inclinations and to reform her master. Pamela triumphs in the end, as her Mr. B. becomes an adoring spouse and to the disgust of many modern readers "virtue" is rewarded, as the book's subtitle promises. The last pages of *Pamela* are thick with didacticism and moral sentiments, but Richardson is a pioneer of the realistic novel precisely because he shows us how religious belief and moral will interact with psychological and social factors which threaten to overwhelm them.

Pamela was a great success, so much so that several spurious continuations were published, and Richardson felt compelled to write his own sequel in which the now-married Pamela deals with her husband's infatuation with another woman. This second part of *Pamela* is virtually unreadable but marks in some ways an important step in Richardson's development as a self-consciously skillful novelist. The crude moral melodrama of the original story gives way to more complicated questions of manners, and this volume has a more varied cast of correspondents, each of whom writes letters according to character. This increased complexity of social situation and variety of character looks forward to Richardson's second and greatest work, *Clarissa; or, The History of a Young Lady.*

Clarissa is an immense work, the longest novel in the language, and yet its plot is simple enough in outline. Clarissa Harlowe is the beautiful and saintly daughter of an enormously wealthy but untitled family who press her to marry a man she despises, Roger Solmes. His rival is a young aristocratic rake, Robert Lovelace, who has entered the family circle as the suitor of Clarissa's sister, Arabella. Attracted by Clarissa's beauty and intrigued by her virtue, Lovelace declines to pursue his suit for Arabella and is challenged to a duel on this account by the brother in the family, James. After wounding James, Lovelace begins to court Clarissa, to the consternation and implacable opposition of the family. Lovelace corresponds secretly with Clarissa and tricks her into running away with him. Most of this occurs at the very beginning of the novel, and most of the letters revolve around Lovelace's attempts to seduce Clarissa. Eventually, he drugs and rapes her in the brothel where he is his prisoner; but Clarissa escapes soon after and dies with slow dignity in the course of several hundred pages, resisting Lovelace's offers of marriage and surrounded by tearful and worshipping admirers who marvel at her serene goodness. The book ends with Lovelace's death in a duel with her cousin, Colonel Morden.

As in *Pamela*, this melodramatic story is told in letters which describe events that have just happened, and again Richardson's special achievement is a dramatization of complicated personal and social relationships that leaves simple melodrama far behind. In place of the single viewpoint of *Pamela*'s letters, *Clarissa* is told by various characters, each of whom has a distinctive style as a writer and a special perspective on the action. The hundreds of letters which make up the novel are a constantly varied and shifting set of voices, and the scenes the letters describe are sharply observed and run from a witty comedy of manners to pathos and tragedy of the highest kind. Richardson's immersion in each of his large cast of characters is masterful, and in the case of Clarissa and Lovelace leads to a richness and complexity without parallel in previous fiction.

Clarissa is as good as she is beautiful, and yet her resistance to her family's demands and to Lovelace's seductions is carried out with a diplomatic skill and persuasive power that justify in one sense their claims that she is self-willed and bent upon her own pleasure. Indeed, for modern readers perhaps the book's most compelling feature is the buried sexuality implicit in

Clarissa's strong aversion to Solmes and her cautious attraction to Lovelace. To read her letters is to experience a profoundly troubled personality struggling to resolve a tangle of conflicting emotions and allegiances. Lovelace possesses an equally complex personality, overtly self-obsessed and flamboyant in asserting its needs for sex and power. Richardson's art lets us see that Lovelace plays his role of aristocratic libertine insecurely and self-consciously. He is attracted and enraged by Clarissa's virtuous resistance and driven to revealing extremes of love and hatred. In fact, the greatness of *Clarissa* can be measured by its powerfully exact revelation of the divided personalities of its two main characters. The protracted struggle between them is a contest not simply of wills but an extravaganza of competing literary styles and modes of self-understanding and presentation. Richardson's revolutionary perfection of the epistolary novel enabled him to depict a world where the subjective forces of individual will and consciousness can be observed trying to shape and even to master objective social and historical forces which resist such manipulation.

Richardson thought of the dying Clarissa as a Christian martyr and a tragic heroine destroyed by an irreligious and materialistic culture. Her slow and intensely rendered death is genuinely moving even for modern readers; it is also a novelistically appropriate action, since it is her way as a character in a novel of re-asserting control over the world and justifying herself. *Clarissa* remains a novel of tragic status because it successfully dramatizes psychological and social conflicts that we now can understand were not resolvable. To some extent, the conflict between Clarissa and Lovelace is between complex individuals whose complexity is the result of their status as representatives of different social classes at a moment of historical transition. For Richardson and the 18th-century middle-classes who were his readers, Lovelace is a projection of an outlawed egoism and sexuality which they located in a dangerous opposing way of life; he represents energies they believed in suppressing. Clarissa is a character who heroically suppresses those same energies and rejects any personal or social ambitions, but she is also an embodiment of a purified and spiritualized middle-class individualism which is in its own way imperious and ambitious. In her heroic resistance and death, she aspires to remake the world in her own image.

In spite of Clarissa's heroism, many readers found themselves drawn to the irrepressible Lovelace, and in subsequent editions of the book Richardson tried to make him less attractive, partly by revisions and partly by footnotes instructing the reader not to be fooled by Lovelace's charms. Richardson's last novel, *Sir Charles Grandison* was his attempt to produce a virtuous hero as a contrast to Lovelace. Although it has found very few modern readers, *Grandison* was a successful and influential work until the middle of the 19th century. It features an even wider variety of scenes and characters than *Clarissa*, as Sir Charles spends a good deal of his time in Italy courting the beautiful Clementina della Porretta. There is melodrama here as well in the tortured refusal of that pious lady to marry the Protestant Sir Charles because of his religion and in the hero's rescue of his wife-to-be, Harriet Byron, from an abduction carried out by a villainous rake, Sir Hargrave Pollexfen. But the main charm of the book for its 18th-century audience was its reconciliation of upper-class gentility and a perfect moral delicacy. The psychological intensity and tragic social conflicts of *Clarissa* give way to the unfailing goodness of Sir Charles, to a neat and satisfying dramatization of moral sentiments, and to a mild comedy of manners which were to set the tone for the English novel for the next fifty years.

—John Richetti

RUTHERFORD, Mark. Pseudonym for William Hale White. English. Born in Bedford, 22 December 1831. Educated at Bedford Modern School; studied for the ministry at the Countess of Huntingdon's College, Cheshunt, and at New College, St. John's Wood,

London (expelled); in later years preached in Unitarian chapels. Married 1) Harriet Arthur in 1856 (died, 1891), five sons and one daughter; 2) Dorothy Vernon in 1911. Entered the Civil Service as a Clerk in the Office of the Registrar-General, Somerset House, London, 1854; transferred to the Admiralty, 1858: Assistant Director of Contracts, 1879 until he retired, 1891; briefly served as Registrar of Births, Marriages, and Deaths for the Borough of Marylebone; London Correspondent for *The Scotsman. Died 14 March 1913.*

PUBLICATIONS

Fiction

The Autobiography of Mark Rutherford, Dissenting Minister. 1881.
Mark Rutherford's Deliverance, Being the Second Part of His Autobiography. 1885; revised edition, 1888.
The Revolution in Tanner's Lane. 1887.
Miriam's Schooling and Other Papers. 1890.
Catharine Furze. 1893.
Clara Hopgood. 1896.

Other

An Argument for an Extension of the Franchise. 1866.
A Dream of Two Dimensions. 1884.
The Inner Life of the House of Commons. 2 vols., 1897.
A Description of the Wordsworth and Coleridge Manuscripts in the Possession of Mr. T. North Longman. 1897.
An Examination of the Charge of Apostasy Against Wordsworth. 1898.
Pages from a Journal, with Other Papers. 1900; *More Pages, with Other Papers,* 1910; *Last Pages,* edited by Dorothy V. White, 1915.
John Bunyan. 1904.
The Early Life of Mark Rutherford (William Hale White) (autobiography). 1913.
Letters to Three Friends, edited by Dorothy V. White. 1924.

Editor, *Selections from Dr. Johnson's Rambler.* 1907.
Editor, *The Life of John Sterling,* by Thomas Carlyle. 1907.

Translator, *Ethic,* by Spinoza. 1893.
Translator, *Tractatus de Intellectus Emendatione,* by Spinoza. 1895.

Bibliography: *Rutherford: A Bibliography of First Editions* by S. Nowell-Smith, 1930.

Reading List: *Religion and Art of White* by W. H. Stone, 1954; *Rutherford: A Biography of White* by C. M. MacLean, 1955; *White (Rutherford)* by I. Stock, 1956; "The Novels of Rutherford" by P. Thomson, in *Essays in Criticism 14,* 1964; *The Literature of Change: Studies in the Nineteenth-Century Provincial Novel* (on Rutherford, Gaskell, and Hardy) by John Lucas, 1978.

*   *   *

Mark Rutherford (the pseudonym of William Hale White) was the author of six novels and some notes and journals. His work provides a fine example of the puritan temper that is widespread in English thought and character. Growing up in Victorian Bedfordshire, deeply rooted in the traditions of radical dissent, he freely acknowledged his spiritual kinship with John Bunyan. At the same time no contemporary dissenting creed could satisfy him, and he was expelled from his theological college for doubting the literal truth of the Bible. He is therefore a puritan outside the chapel walls and, with Bunyan, one of the rare examples of the Puritan as novelist. If nothing else, his writing serves to remind us that a puritan need not be a bore or a philistine.

His novels are close to his own experience and distinguished by a profound moral earnestness. Best known are his first two books, *The Autobiography of Mark Rutherford* and its sequel *Mark Rutherford's Deliverance*. Of the remaining novels, *The Revolution in Tanner's Lane* is the most wide-ranging and powerful, but each of the others, *Miriam's Schooling, Catharine Furze, Clara Hopgood*, has something to recommend it. The Mark Rutherford of *The Autobiography* and *Deliverance* grows up in a narrow provincial Victorian world. He becomes a dissenting minister but is appalled at the narrow illiberal life of the chapel community and turns away from it in search of a more genuine salvation. He is profoundly influenced by Wordsworth and he finally finds peace in a kind of stoic, humanist deism. Although the writer's interest is mainly in inner experience he has a shrewd eye for the details of outward life also. He sharply observed and accurately recalled the social scene, and he gives us vivid and authentic glimpses of the life of non-comformist communities in provincial towns. The puritan honesty and integrity of his mind give a fine clarity and purity to his prose. He has qualities of directness and simplicity that are rare in the Victorian period. Although he admired Carlyle, his own writing belongs rather to the tradition of Bunyan, Defoe, and Cobbett.

—Alan Warner

SCOTT, Sir Walter. Scottish. Born in Edinburgh, 15 August 1771; spent his childhood in the Border country. Educated at Edinburgh High School, and the University of Edinburgh; studied law as a clerk in his father's law office; admitted to the Faculty of Advocates, 1792. Married Charlotte Charpentier in 1797 (died, 1826); four children. Writer from 1796; Sheriff-Depute of Selkirkshire, 1799–1832; Clerk of the Court of Session, 1806–30; joined his brother and James Ballantyne as a partner in a printing company, Edinburgh, 1804, which went bankrupt in 1826, involving him in the discharge of its debts for the rest of his life; founded the *Quarterly Review*, 1809; built and lived at Abbotsford from 1812. Created a baronet, 1820. *Died 21 September 1832.*

PUBLICATIONS

Collections

Poetical Works, edited by J. G. Lockhart. 12 vols., 1833–34; edited by J. Logie Robertson, 1904.
Miscellaneous Prose Works, edited by J. G. Lockhart. 28 vols., 1834–36; 2 additional vols., 1871.
The Letters, edited by Herbert Grierson. 12 vols., 1932–37.

Short Stories.   1934.
Selected Poems, edited by Thomas Crawford.   1972.

Fiction

Waverley; or, 'Tis Sixty Years Since.   1814.
Guy Mannering; or, The Astrologer.   1815.
The Antiquary.   1816.
The Black Dwarf, Old Mortality.   1817; *Old Mortality* edited by Angus Calder, 1975.
Rob Roy.   1817.
The Heart of Mid-Lothian.   1818.
The Bride of Lammermoor; A Legend of Montrose.   1819.
Ivanhoe: A Romance.   1819.
The Monastery.   1820.
The Abbot; or, The Heir of Avenel.   1820.
Kenilworth: A Romance.   1821; edited by David Daiches, 1966.
The Pirate.   1821.
The Fortunes of Nigel.   1822.
Peveril of the Peak.   1823.
Quentin Durward.   1823; edited by M. W. and G. Thomas, 1966.
St. Ronan's Well.   1823.
Redgauntlet: A Tale of the Eighteenth Century.   1824.
Tales of the Crusaders (The Betrothed, The Talisman).   1825.
Woodstock; or, The Cavalier.   1826.
Chronicles of the Canongate: First Series: The Highland Widow, The Two Drovers, The Surgeon's Daughter.   1827; *Second Series: The Fair Maid of Perth,* 1828.
My Aunt Margaret's Mirror, The Tapestried Chamber, Death of the Laird's Jock, A Scene at Abbotsford.   1829.
Anne of Geierstein; or, The Maiden of the Mist.   1829.
Waverley Novels (Scott's final revision).   48 vols., 1829–33.
Count Robert of Paris, Castle Dangerous.   1832.

Plays

Goetz of Berlichingen, with The Iron Hand, by Goethe.   1799.
Guy Mannering; or, The Gipsy's Prophecy, with Daniel Terry, music by Henry Bishop and others, from the novel by Scott (produced 1816).   1816.
Halidon Hill: A Dramatic Sketch from Scottish History.   1822.
MacDuff's Cross, in *A Collection of Poems,* edited by Joanna Baillie.   1823.
The House of Aspen (produced 1829).   In *Poetical Works,* 1830.
Auchindrane; or, The Ayrshire Tragedy (produced 1830).   In *The Doom of Devorgoil; Auchindrane,* 1830.
The Doom of Devorgoil: A Melo-Drama; Auchindrane; or, The Ayrshire Tragedy.   1830.

Verse

The Chase, and William and Helen: Two Ballads from the German of Gottfried Augustus Bürger.   1796.
The Eve of Saint John: A Border Ballad.   1800.
The Lay of the Last Minstrel.   1805.

Ballads and Lyrical Pieces. 1806.
Marmion: A Tale of Flodden Field. 1808.
The Lady of the Lake. 1810.
The Vision of Don Roderick. 1811.
Rokeby. 1813.
The Bridal of Triermain; or, The Vale of St. John, in Three Cantos. 1813.
The Lord of the Isles. 1815.
The Field of Waterloo. 1815.
The Ettrick Garland, Being Two Excellent New Songs, with James Hogg. 1815.
Harold the Dauntless. 1817.
New Love-Poems, edited by Davidson Cook. 1932.

Other

Paul's Letters to His Kinsfolk. 1816.
The Visionary. 1819.
Provincial Antiquities of Scotland. 2 vols., 1826.
The Life of Napoleon Buonaparte: Emperor of the French, with a Preliminary View of the French Revolution. 9 vols., 1827.
Tales of a Grandfather, Being Stories Taken from Scottish History. 9 vols., 1827–29.
Miscellaneous Prose Works. 6 vols., 1827.
Religious Discourses by a Layman. 1828.
The History of Scotland. 2 vols., 1829–30.
Letters on Demonology and Witchcraft. 1830.
Tales of a Grandfather, Being Stories Taken from the History of France. 3 vols., 1830.
Letters Addressed to Rev. R. Polwhele, D. Gilbert, F. Douce. 1832.
Letters Between James Ellis and Scott. 1850.
Journal 1825–32, edited by D. Douglas. 2 vols., 1890; edited by W. E. K. Anderson, 1972.
Familiar Letters, edited by D. Douglas. 2 vols., 1894.
The Letters of Scott and Charles Kirkpatrick Sharpe to Robert Chambers, 1821–45. 1903.
The Private Letter-Books, edited by W. Partington. 1930.
Sir Walter's Postbag: More Stories and Sidelights from the Collection in the Brotherton Library, edited by W. Partington. 1932.
Some Unpublished Letters from the Collection in the Brotherton Library, edited by J. A. Symington. 1932.
The Correspondence of Scott and Charles Robert Maturin, edited by F. E. Ratchford and W. H. McCarthy. 1937.
Private Letters of the Seventeenth Century, edited by D. Grant. 1948.

Editor, *An Apology for Tales of Terror.* 1799.
Editor, *Minstrelsy of the Scottish Border.* 2 vols., 1802; edited by Alfred Noyes, 1908.
Editor, *Sir Tristrem: A Metrical Romance,* by Thomas of Ercildoune. 1804.
Editor, *Original Memoirs Written During the Great Civil War,* by Sir H. Slingsby and Captain Hodgson. 1804.
Editor, *The Works of John Dryden.* 18 vols., 1808 (*Life of Dryden* published separately, 1808, edited by Bernard Kreissman, 1963).
Editor, *Memoirs of Captain George Carleton.* 1808.
Editor, *Queenhoo-Hall: A Romance, and Ancient Times: A Drama,* by Joseph Strutt. 4 vols., 1808.
Editor, *Memoirs of Robert Cary, Earl of Monmouth, and Fragmenta Regalia,* by Sir Robert Naunton. 1808.

Editor, *A Collection of Scarce and Valuable Tracts.* 13 vols., 1809–15.
Editor, *English Minstrelsy, Being a Collection of Fugitive Poetry.* 2 vols., 1810.
Editor, *The Poetical Works of Anna Seward.* 3 vols., 1810.
Editor, *Memoirs of Count Grammont,* by Anthony Hamilton. 2 vols., 1811.
Editor, *The Castle of Otranto,* by Horace Walpole. 1811.
Editor, *Secret History of the Court of King James the First.* 2 vols., 1811.
Editor, *The Works of Jonathan Swift.* 19 vols., 1814 (*Memoirs of Swift* published separately, 1826).
Editor, *The Letting of Humours Blood in the Head Vaine,* by S. Rowlands. 1814.
Editor, *Memorie of the Somervilles.* 2 vols., 1815.
Editor, *Trivial Poems and Triolets,* by Patrick Carey. 1820.
Editor, *Memorials of the Haliburtons.* 1820.
Editor, *Northern Memoirs Writ in the Year 1658,* by Richard Franck. 1821.
Editor, *Ballantyne's Novelist's Library.* 10 vols., 1821–24 (*Lives of the Novelists* published separately, 2 vols., 1825).
Editor, *Chronological Notes of Scottish Affairs from the Diary of Lord Fountainhall.* 1822.
Editor, *Military Memoirs of the Great Civil War,* by John Gwynne. 1822.
Editor, *Lays of the Lindsays.* 1824.
Editor, *Auld Robin Gray: A Ballad,* by Lady Anne Barnard. 1825.
Editor, with D. Laing, *The Bannatyne Miscellany.* 1827.
Editor, *Memoirs of the Marchioness de la Rochejaquelein.* 1827.
Editor, *Proceedings in the Court-Martial Held upon John, Master of Sinclair, 1708.* 1829.
Editor, *Memorials of George Bannatyne, 1545–1608.* 1829.
Editor, *Trial of Duncan Terig and Alexander Bane Macdonald, 1754.* 1831.
Editor, *Memoirs of the Insurrection in Scotland in 1715,* by John, Master of Sinclair. 1858.

Bibliography: *Bibliography of the Waverley Novels* by G. Worthington, 1930; "A Bibliography of the Poetical Works of Scott 1796–1832" by W. Ruff, in *Transactions of the Edinburgh Bibliographical Society 1,* 1938; *A Bibliography of Scott: A Classified and Annotated List of Books and Articles Relating to His Life and Works 1797–1940* by J. C. Corson, 1943.

Reading List: *Scott as a Critic of Literature* by M. Ball, 1907; *Scott: A New Life* by Herbert Grierson, 1938; *Scott* by Una Pope-Hennessy, 1948; *Scott: His Life and Personality* by H. Pearson, 1954; *Scott* by Ian Jack, 1958; *The Heyday of Scott* by Donald Davie, 1961; *Witchcraft and Demonology in Scott's Fiction* by C. O. Parsons, 1964; *Scott* by T. Crawford, 1965; *Scott's Novels* by F. R. Hart, 1966; *Scott: The Great Unknown* by Edgar Johnson, 2 vols., 1970; *The Wizard of the North: The Life of Scott* by Carola Oman, 1973; *"The Siege of Malta" Rediscovered* by Donald E. Sultana, 1977.

* * *

Walter Scott was born in Edinburgh in 1771. His father, who is affectionately satirized as Saunders Fairford, the "good old-fashioned man of method" in *Redgauntlet,* was a respected solicitor. His mother, the daughter of a well-known medical professor at the University, had brains and character, and it is tempting to believe that from her Scott inherited the ability which put him for a time at the very top of the tree. He had his education at the High School of Edinburgh and at Edinburgh University. Of formative importance, however, were the months he spent at his paternal grandfather's Border farm as a small boy recuperating from the illness (probably poliomyelitis) which left him permanently lame. The tales he heard there of old, unhappy, far-off things, and the skirmishes in which his own ancestors had fought, lit in him the love of the Scottish past which was the enduring passion of his life.

As Sheriff of Selkirkshire and a Clerk of the Court of Session, Scott was obliged to divide his time between Edinburgh and his Sherifdom; and it was near Selkirk that he built Abbotsford, the "Conundrum Castle" of a house which he embellished with all manner of historical trophies and curiosities. His two official salaries combined to give him a modest competence. They were not, however, enough to let him live in the style of the wealthier Edinburgh lawyers, the *noblesse de la robe* so important to Scottish society, nor of the landowners of the Border country round Abbotsford. That, literature alone could provide.

The literary task to which he devoted his youth was the collection of the Border ballads. His taste had run that way since early youth; he loved the country through whose remoter parts he rode in the quest for those who could recite or sing to him the old songs he wanted; he had a fantastically retentive memory and above all the endearing faculty of talking easily to people of all kinds. *The Minstrelsy of the Scottish Border*, inspired by the example of Percy's *Reliques*, is not, by modern standards, scholarly. There are valuable discursive notes, but modern imitations are accorded a place alongside genuine ballads, and Scott was not interested in variant readings, nor above improving or adding a verse or two. Nonetheless *The Minstrelsy* confirmed Scott's bent towards the historic past, and it established his reputation as a rising man.

One poem, originally intended for the *Minstrelsy*, grew under Scott's hand into his first major independent work. *The Lay of the Last Minstrel* is a narrative poem of magic and border chivalry which, although imperfect in construction and seldom rising to real poetry, exactly struck the growing taste for the mediaeval and the supernatural. The poem's successors *Marmion* and *The Lady of the Lake* were also instantly successful; *Rokeby*, *The Lord of the Isles*, and *Harold the Dauntless* were less so.

Although the range of Scott's poetry is narrow, it has considerable merits. It is muscular, manly verse; its galloping rhythms suit his subjects, and it passes the first test of narrative verse that it should tell the story well. The narrative poetry reaches its heights in moments of action:

> The stubborn spearmen still made good,
> Their Dark, impenetrable wood,
> Each stepping where his comrade stood,
> The instant that he fell

or in the elegiac sadness:

> Of the stern strife, and carnage drear,
>   Of Flodden's fatal field,
> Where shiver'd was fair Scotland's spear,
>   And broken was her shield.

Scott's best-known poems, however, are the songs interspersed with the narrative in both poems and novels. Thousands who have never read Scott are familiar with Schubert's settings of "Ave Maria" and the other lyrics from *The Lady of the Lake*.

In July 1814 a three-volume novel entitled *Waverley* was published anonymously in Edinburgh. Within five weeks it had sold out, and by the following January it was into its fifth edition. If Scott's real motive had been to protect his reputation as a poet should the novel fail, he had no need to keep up the mystery; but speculation about the unknown author amused him, and he did not acknowledge his authorship of the Waverley novels, which were published at the rate of two a year, until twelve years later.

Scott's reputation has suffered from judgements based on the mass of his work rather than the best of it. At his best – in *The Antiquary*, *Rob Roy*, *Old Mortality*, *The Heart of Mid-Lothian*, *The Bride of Lammermoor*, and *Redgauntlet* (some would add *Waverley*, *Guy*

Mannering and *The Fair Maid of Perth*) – he was writing of a country whose history and people he knew intimately. *Redgauntlet* begins in the Edinburgh of his youth; the trial of Effie Deans is set in a court-room he knew well; Scott's grandmother remembered being carried as a child to a covenanters' field-preaching, and Scott himself had talked with a man who had been "out" with the Jacobites in 1715 and 1745. The Scottish novels are Scott's real achievement. They inspired writers as diverse as Hugo, George Eliot, Tolstoy, and James Fenimore Cooper. In a sense, they created Scotland as it is known today. They introduced to the world a new form of fiction, the historical novel.

The great historical characters – James VI, Cromwell, Mary and Elizabeth, Prince Charlie, Rob Roy – are seldom central to the novels in which they appear, for Scott's technique is to follow the fortunes of an ordinary man caught up in great events, but they are striking portraits of breathing, fallible human beings. "Sir Walter not only invented the historical novel," says Trevelyan, "but he enlarged the scope and revolutionized the study of history itself." After reading the Waverley novels men could no longer content themselves with broad generalizations about the past; Scott had taught them that it was peopled by real men and women.

As a creator of character his range is enormous. He is the first novelist in English to bring the lower orders of society to life on the page, not as figures of fun but as part of humanity. Fairservice, Ochiltree, Mucklebackit, Balderstone and Davie Deans – as well as Bailie Jarvie the merchant, lawyers like Pleydell and Fairfold, and small lairds like Dumbiedykes – are both of their age and for all time.

Scott's marvellous command of the Scottish dialect, his eye for the telling detail, and the humorous yet affectionate way in which he allows his characters to reveal themselves in speech, led his contemporaries to compare him with Shakespeare. "Not fit to tie his brogues," was Scott's characteristic disclaimer. In one respect, however, he is Shakespeare's superior. His common people – his servants and gardeners and beggars – are better. To Shakespeare they are seen *de haut en bas*. There is no similar condescension in Scott.

The subtleties of Jane Austen, whom he greatly admired, were not within Scott's range. As he said in his *Journal*, his was "the Big Bow-wow strain" of writing, and he prided himself on his "hurried frankness of composition." As a story-teller, he is at his best over the shorter distance of "Wandering Willie's Tale" in *Redgauntlet* or of great scenes like the trials of McIvor and Cuddie Headrigg, the appeal of Jeanie Deans to Queen Caroline, or the fight in the Clachan of Aberfoyle.

Again and again he returns to the conflict between old ways and new. By temperament and by upbringing Scott was both a romantic and a realist. In the novels he thrills to the Jacobite past; but he settles ultimately for the age of reason, for Hume and Adam Smith rather than Rob Roy and Charles Edward Stuart. The tension of opposites characteristic of eighteenth-century Scotland remains his theme in the novels set further back in time or further off in place: Cavaliers and Roundheads in *Woodstock*, Saxons and Normans in *Ivanhoe*, Royalists and Covenanters in *Old Mortality*. The truth, for Scott, habitually lies somewhere between the extremes. He is one of the sanest of great writers.

"The greatest figure he ever drew is in the *Journal*," wrote John Buchan, "and it is the man Walter Scott." In 1825, when Scott began to keep a journal, his reputation was at its height. A few months later the slump of 1826 ruined his printer and publisher and, in those days before limited liablity, Scott himself. Legally he could have declared himself bankrupt, but he would not. "My own right hand shall do it," he said, and he set himself to work, mornings and evenings, week days and Sundays, term time and holidays, to pay off the joint debt of £126,000. Thanks mainly to the collected editions of his work to which he contributed notes, the debt was finally paid off, but Scott himself, hastened to an early grave by worry and overwork, did not live to see it. Carlyle's famous sentence was fully earned: "No sounder piece of British manhood was put together in that eighteenth century of Time."

—W. E. K. Anderson

SHARP, William. Pseudonym: Fiona Macleod. Scottish. Born in Paisley, Renfrewshire, 12 September 1855. Educated at Blair Lodge School, Paisley, to 1868; Glasgow Academy, 1868–71; University of Glasgow, 1871–74. Married his cousin Elizabeth Amelia Sharp in 1884. Clerk in a law office in Glasgow, 1874–76; travelled to Australia, 1876–78; Clerk in the City of Melbourne Bank, London, 1878–81; thereafter supported himself by writing; visited Italy, and studied art, 1883–84; appointed Art Critic of the *Glasgow Herald*, 1884; Editor, *Canterbury Poets* series, 1884–90, and *Biographies of Great Writers* series, 1887–90; visited the United States and Canada, 1889; lived in Rome, 1890–91; again visited America, 1891–92; settled at Phenice Croft, Sussex, 1892; Editor, *The Pagan Review* (one number), 1892; wrote mystical prose and verse as Fiona Macleod from 1893. *Died 14 December 1905.*

PUBLICATIONS

Collections

    Writings, edited by Elizabeth Amelia Sharp.   7 vols., 1909–10.

Fiction

    The Sport of Chance.   1888.
    Children of Tomorrow: A Romance.   1889.
    A Fellowe and His Wife, with B. W. Howard.   1892.
    Pharais: A Romance of the Isles.   1894.
    The Mountain Lovers.   1895.
    The Sin-Eater and Other Tales.   1895.
    The Washer of the Ford and Other Legendary Moralities.   1896.
    Green Fire: A Romance.   1896.
    Madge o' the Pool, The Gypsy Christ, and Other Tales.   1896.
    Wives in Exile.   1896.
    The Laughter of Peterkin: A Retelling of Old Tales of the Celtic Wonderland.   1897.
    The Shorter Stories.   1897.
    Silence Farm.   1899.

Plays

    The House of Usna (produced 1900).   1903.
    The Immortal Hour (produced 1914).   1907.

Verse

    The Human Inheritance, The New Hope, Motherhood.   1882.
    Earth's Voices, Transcripts from Nature, Sospitra, and Other Poems.   1884.
    Romantic Ballads and Poems of Phantasy.   1888.
    Sospiri di Roma.   1891.
    From the Hills of Dream: Mountain Songs and Island Runes.   1896; revised edition, as *Threnodies and Songs, and Later Poems*, 1907.
    Songs and Poems, Old and New.   1909.

Other

D. G. Rossetti: A Record and a Study.   1882.
Life of Shelley.   1887.
Life of Heinrich Heine.   1888.
Life of Robert Browning.   1890.
The Life and Letters of Joseph Severn.   1892.
The Pagan Review (periodical), edited by W. H. Brooks.   1892.
Fair Women in Painting and Poetry.   1894.
Vistas.   1894.
Ecce Puella and Other Prose Imaginings.   1896.
The Dominion of Dreams.   1899.
The Divine Adventure, Iona, By Sundown Shores: Studies in Spiritual History.   1900.
Progress of Art in the Century.   1902.
The Winged Destiny: Studies in the Spiritual History of the Gael.   1904.
Literary Geography.   1904.
Where the Forest Murmurs: Nature Essays.   1906.
Poems and Dramas.   1910.

Editor, *The Songs, Poems, and Sonnets of Shakespeare.*   1885.
Editor, *Great English Painters*, by Allan Cunningham.   1886.
Editor, *Sonnets of This Century.*   1886.
Editor, *Song-Tide*, by P. B. Marston.   1888.
Editor, *American Sonnets.*   1889.
Editor, *Essays on Men and Women*, by Sainte-Beuve.   1890.
Editor, *Great Odes, English and American.*   1890.

Reading List: *William Sharp (Fiona Macleod): A Memoir Compiled by His Wife* by Elizabeth Amelia Sharp, 1912 (includes bibliography).

*   *   *

When William Sharp moved to London in 1878 from his family home in Glasgow, he was intent upon becoming a poet. He soon came under the influence of Dante Gabriel Rossetti and his circle, and that influence is apparent in his first volume of poems, *The Human Inheritance*. For the rest of the decade, he persisted with poetry, but earned his living as a critic, editor, and biographer. Other volumes of verse appeared during the 1880's but only in the phantasy poems of *Romantic Ballads and Poems of Phantasy* are there signs of the economy of language and the distinctive voice that characterized the poems he wrote in the late 1890's and published as Fiona Macleod.

During three months in Italy, he wrote a group of poems unlike any he had done, *Sospiri di Roma*. These poems are musical, sensuous, and filled with colorful, vivid imagery. They also portray with regret the ravages time has inflicted upon ancient Roman civilization, and inflicts always upon youthful love and passion. With echoes of Swinburne, these poems foreshadow a dominant motif of English poetry during the decade that was beginning.

The creative period which produced the works of Fiona Macleod began in 1894 with *Pharais: A Romance of the Isles*, which Sharp issued under that pseudonym. His original intent was to impart authenticity to the Celtic romance, and increase its chances for a favorable critical reception. The pseudonym had the effect of stimulating Sharp's imagination and releasing his deeper feelings. Although he continued until his death in 1905 to publish criticism and fictional works as William Sharp, he wrote most movingly and effectively as Fiona Macleod.

Pharais was followed by two other romances, *The Mountain Lovers* and *Green Fire*, but even as Fiona Macleod Sharp had trouble sustaining the reader's interest, or his own, through long narratives. They tend to break into vignettes. The best Fiona Macleod prose is in the short tales he collected in *The Sin-Eater* and *The Washer of the Ford*. Retellings of stories heard among the natives in the West of Scotland, these stories project the bleakness as well as the superstitions and the sense of mystery that characterized the lives of the people in the West. Celtic myths and legends inform the daily lives of the people in the tales. If Sharp frequently confused or misused the details of those legends, so, we may presume, did his informants. Many of these stories are compelling and moving even when their style becomes excessively florid.

The Fiona Macleod prose turned gradually to the essay form. With *The Divine Adventure*, *The Winged Destiny*, and *Where the Forest Murmurs*, the phantom author became a Celtic seer. These works are not without interest, but their philosophic content is thin and dated, and they lack the crisp reality and emotional power of the better tales.

Sharp's best work appeared in the poems in the successive editions of Fiona Macleod's *From the Hills of Dream*. The poems in this volume vary in quality; a few are very good. Just as Sharp's imagination had been quickened in Italy by the broken remains of Roman life and culture, so it was moved by the Celtic past of the western shores and islands of Scotland and the failures of love and loss of life he encountered there. In the poems of Fiona Macleod, Sharp turned from the strong musical cadences and brilliant imagery of *Sospiri di Roma* to the quieter, subtler music of the early Yeats. That more restrained voice produced greater control; and it more nearly suited the lamenting voices he heard and the dreary lives he observed in the West of Scotland. The best Fiona Macleod poems are marked by economy and precision of diction and a fine-tuned sense of the irony inherent in the loss of hope and the failure of dreams.

—William F. Halloran

SHELLEY, Mary (Wollstonecraft).   English.   Born in Somers Town, London, 30 August 1797; daughter of the writers William Godwin, *q.v.*, and Mary Wollstonecraft Godwin. Married the poet Percy Bysshe Shelley in 1816 (died, 1822); two sons and one daughter. Lived in Dundee, 1812, 1813–14, then returned to London; eloped to the Continent with Shelley, 1814; writer from 1816; after Shelley's death lived at Genoa with the Leigh Hunts, 1822–23, then returned to England; supported herself by writing fiction and contributing to periodical. Travelled in Germany, 1840–41, and Italy, 1842– 43. *Died 1 February 1851.*

PUBLICATIONS

Collections

   Letters, edited by Frederick L. Jones.   2 vols., 1944.
   Collected Tales and Stories, edited by Charles E. Robinson.   1976.

Fiction

   Frankenstein; or, The Modern Prometheus.   1818; revised edition, 1831; edited by M.
   K. Joseph, 1969; 1818 edition edited by James Rieger, 1974.

Valperga; or, The Life and Adventures of Castruccio, Prince of Lucca.   1823.
The Last Man.   1826; edited by Hugh J. Luke, 1965.
The Fortunes of Perkin Warbeck: A Romance.   1830; revised edition, 1830.
Lodore.   1835.
Falkner.   1837.
Mathilda, edited by Elizabeth Nitchie.   1959.

Plays

Proserpine and Midas: Mythological Dramas, edited by A. Koszul.   1922.

Verse

The Choice: A Poem on Shelley's Death, edited by H. Buxton Forman.   1876.

Other

History of a Six Weeks' Tour Through a Part of France, Switzerland, Germany, and Holland, with Percy Bysshe Shelley.   1817; abridgement edited by C. I. Elton, 1894.
Rambles in Germany and Italy in 1840, 1842, and 1843.   2 vols., 1844.
Shelley and Mary: A Collection of Letters and Documents of a Biographical Character.   3 vols., 1882.
Letters, Mostly Unpublished, edited by Henry H. Harper.   1918.
Journal, edited by Frederick L. Jones.   1947.
My Best Mary: The Selected Letters, edited by Muriel Spark and Derek Stanford.   1953.

Editor, *Posthumous Poems*, by Percy Bysshe Shelley.   1824.
Editor, *The Poetical Works of Percy Bysshe Shelley.*   4 vols., 1839.
Editor, *Essays, Letters from Abroad, Translations, and Fragments*, by Percy Bysshe Shelley.   2 vols., 1840.

Reading List: *Child of Light: A Reassessment of Shelley* by Muriel Spark, 1951; *Shelley Author of Frankenstein* by Elizabeth Nitchie, 1953; *Shelley* by E. Bigland, 1959; *Shelley dans Son Oeuvre* by Jean de Palaccio, 1969; *Shelley's Frankenstein: Tracing the Myth* by Christopher Small, 1973; *Shelley's Mary: A Life of Mary Godwin Shelley* by Margaret Leighton, 1973.

*   *   *

In a busy life as professional author, Mary Shelley wrote seven novels and some two dozen short stories, as well as travel-books, biographies, and reviews. Of all this, *The Last Man*, a least, deserves to survive for its sombre apocalyptic vision; yet Mary Shelley is remembered for one book only, *Frankenstein*, which she wrote at the age of nineteen. Its special quality owes much to the stimulating influence of Byron and Shelley on a lively young mind, though it is a book that neither of them could have written. Even its technical faults create complexity, and its unresolved ideas turn what might have been a moralistic Gothic tale into a work of mythology.

The novel, as its subtitle indicates, is a reworking of the Prometheus-creator theme in modern setting, using sensational reports of galvanism to supply fire from heaven. It then becomes a parable of the Creator's responsibility for mankind, and more specifically of the scientist's power to restructure nature. Neither Frankenstein nor the Monster that he brings to life is inherently evil: Frankenstein is a noble character, surrounded and inspired by examples of benevolence, and the Monster is initially a noble savage who responds to the benign influence of nature. Yet Frankenstein, having created the Monster, cannot fulfil his obligations to his creature, who tells him, "I was benevolent and good; misery made me a fiend. Make me happy, and I shall again be virtuous."

The title-page quotation is the anguished question of Milton's Adam to his God: "Did I request thee, Maker, from my clay/To mould Me man?" Initially it is the Monster who asks this, and even forgives Frankenstein for his desertion, asking only to be given an Eve of his own kind and allowed to withdraw to the wilderness. Only when Frankenstein reneges on this does the Monster become, not Adam, but a fallen Satan who destroys everyone connected with his maker. But the Monster, as "demon," is also an anti-self, like Blake's Spectre, and this is expressed in the dream-like chase with which the story concludes. Frankenstein too has eaten the apple of knowledge and been expelled from Paradise; he in turn can confront his Maker with the same tragic question.

The ideas which Mary Shelley absorbed from her friends reflected their interest in the new scientific speculations on the nature and origin of life which were just beginning to take shape. In the next century and a half these were to transform our understanding of the world and our capacity to act upon it. By a rare feat of imaginative insight, she was able to suggest the two main consequences of this, an obscure or absent God and an ambivalent technology. Her handling of them has entered popular consciousness through continual reworking, imitation, and parody. If these have overlaid and sometimes debased the original, this is the price one pays for creating a myth.

—M. K. Joseph

SHORTHOUSE, Joseph Henry. English. Born in Birmingham, 9 September 1834. Educated at Grove House, Tottenham, London. Married Sarah Scott in 1857. Worked in his father's chemical business in Birmingham all his life; writer from 1880. *Died 4 March 1903.*

PUBLICATIONS

Fiction

John Inglesant: A Romance. 1880.
The Little Schoolmaster Mark: A Spiritual Romance. 2 vols., 1883–84.
Sir Percival: A Story of the Past and the Present. 1886.
A Teacher of the Violin and Other Tales. 1888.
The Countess Eve. 1888.
Blanche, Lady Falaise. 1891.

Other

On the Platonism of Wordsworth. 1882.

Reading List: *The Life and Letters of Shorthouse*, edited by Sarah Shorthouse, 2 vols., 1905; *The Historical, Philosophical, and Religious Aspects of John Inglesant* by M. Polak, 1934; *"John Inglesant* and Its Author" by M. Bishop, in *Essays by Divers Hands*, 1958.

*   *   *

In the eyes of more than one of his contemporaries Joseph Henry Shorthouse was unquestionably *homo unius libri* (P. E. More, *Shelburne Essays III*, 1905). More recent admirers have tended to agree. *John Inglesant*, the work of a reclusive Birmingham vitriol manufacturer, caught the public imagination in much the same way that Mrs. Humphry Ward's *Robert Elsmere* was to do a few years later. Having worked on the book for more than ten years, Shorthouse had a hundred copies privately printed and circulated in 1880. He would have let the matter rest, professing himself content that one hundred educated persons had read his work, had not Mrs. Ward seen the novel and drawn it to the attention of Alexander Macmillan, who published it commercially in 1881. Although it never achieved the enormous popular success of Mrs. Ward's novel, *John Inglesant* was seized upon by literary and intellectual circles, and Shorthouse appropriately lionized. Lord Acton declared he had read "nothing more thoughtful and suggestive since *Middlemarch*" (*Letters to Mary Gladstone*, 1904), and as the ultimate seal of approval Gladstone was photographed with a volume of the novel on his knee.

Nineteenth-century readers saw in this seventeenth-century spiritual odyssey an analogue of their own dilemma in the wake of the Oxford Movement. John Inglesant, the hero, is brought up a member of the English church in a family with strong Catholic sympathies. Because of this background he is trained by a Jesuit to act as a mediator between the English and Roman churches. In a series of adventures, many of them undertaken in support of Charles I, he becomes friendly with the followers of Nicholas Ferrar at Little Gidding, and later spends much of his time in Italy where he becomes a disciple of the quietist Molinos. Eventually he returns to England and the English church.

Nearly half the novel takes place in Italy, a detailed and evocative setting which was commented on by contemporary readers, particularly as Shorthouse was known never to have left England during his lifetime. The entire work, both the English and Italian sections, is saturated with seventeenth-century sources, the product, it was acknowledged, of years of reading. Rumblings about the book's accuracy, by Acton and others, continued until 1925, when W. K. Fleming, in an article in the *Quarterly Review*, showed that not only was Shorthouse immersed in seventeenth-century sources, the novel was an extraordinary collage of them. Fleming uncovered almost verbatim borrowings from Anthony à Wood, Aubrey's *Lives*, Burton's *Anatomy of Melancholy*, and Evelyn's *Diary*. The last in particular was relied on extensively for the Italian scenes. In the course of Inglesant's colloquy with the philosopher Hobbes, eleven lines of the *Leviathan* appeared directly. Much of the section showing the influence of Henry More the Platonist was taken blatantly from Ward's *Life of More*.

But such a "discovery" was anything but the unveiling of a gigantic literary hoax. Irrespective of Shorthouse's dubious methods the novel remains fascinating for its plot and historical colouring. Graham Hough (*New Statesman*, 3 August 1946) quite rightly places it in the picaresque tradition, a deliberate journey of the hero through the major political and intellectual circles of his time with corresponding adventures in each. Hough is perhaps too cynical in arguing that the novel has no conclusion, that Inglesant is always convinced by the last person with whom he speaks, and that he ends up in the Church of England because the novel happens to stop when he returns to England. Readers from Acton onwards, however, have commented on Inglesant's thinness as a character. We never quite come to grips with the peculiar personality which lends itself to be trained as a go-between of the two major churches without, it would appear, wholeheartedly committing himself to either. Certainly his abrupt return to England when Molinos is disgraced does not carry with it the comfort of firm conviction. Nevertheless the work remains one of the most interesting of the religious novels of the Victorian period as well as a unique "literary curiosity."

Shorthouse failed to sustain the literary momentum generated by John Inglesant. His later works, of which *The Little Schoolmaster Mark* and *Sir Percival* are the best known, are pallid fables of almost childlike simplicity. In all his work, but particularly in the later novels, it is possible to trace the faint influence of Hawthorne, his favourite author from the days of his youth.

—Joanne Shattock

SMITH, Charlotte (née Turner). English. Born in London, 4 May 1749. Educated in local schools to age 12. Married Benjamin Smith in 1765 (separated, 1787); twelve children. Imprisoned with her husband for debt, 1783–84; settled in Normandy, 1784; full-time writer from 1787. *Died 28 October 1806.*

PUBLICATIONS

Fiction

Emmeline, The Orphan of the Castle. 1788; edited by Anne Henry Ehrenpreis, 1971.
Ethelinde; or, The Recluse of the Lake. 1789.
Celestina. 1791.
Desmond. 1792.
The Old Manor House. 1793; edited by Anne Henry Ehrenpreis, 1969.
The Wanderings of Warwick. 1794.
The Banished Man. 1794.
Montalbert. 1795.
Marchmont. 1796.
The Young Philosopher. 1798.
Letters of a Solitary Wanderer (stories). 5 vols., 1800–02.

Play

What Is She? (produced 1799). 1799.

Verse

Elegiac Sonnets and Other Sonnets. 1784; augmented edition, 1786; 2 vols., 1789–97.
The Emigrants. 1793.
Beachy Head, with Other Poems. 1807.

Other

Rural Walks, in Dialogues for Young Persons. 2 vols., 1795.
Rambles Further: A Continuation of Rural Walks. 2 vols., 1796.

A Narrative of the Loss near Weymouth.   1796.
Minor Morals, Interspersed with Original Stories (juvenile).   2 vols., 1798.
Conversations Introducing Poetry, for the Use of Children.   2 vols., 1804.
History of England, in a Series of Letters to a Young Lady, vols. 1 and 2.   1806.
The Natural History of Birds (juvenile).   2 vols., 1807.

Translator, *Manon Lescaut,* by Prévost.   2 vols., 1786.
Translator, *The Romance of Real Life,* by Gayot de Pitaval.   1787.

Reading List: *The Popular Novel in England* by J. M. S. Tompkins, 1932, revised edition, 1969; *Smith, Poet and Novelist* by Florence M. A. Hilbish, 1941.

*   *   *

It was as a poet that Charlotte Smith wished to be remembered; she undertook novel-writing only because it was more profitable. She attained considerable proficiency in her sonnets, and, although purists objected to their non-Petrarchan form, they were admired by William Lisle Bowles, Wordsworth, and Coleridge. The best of them can still be read with pleasure. Her poems are suffused with a pensive melancholy that sometimes verges on the morbid, but her observation of nature is precisely and sensitively rendered. Generally the scene – a ruined castle, a barren island, a riverside meadow – suggests her present misery as contrasted with her former happiness.

If the *Elegiac Sonnets* contain her best poetic output, *The Emigrants* – a portrait of victims of the French Revolution – illustrates Mrs. Smith's liberal sympathies. Both here and in *Beachy Head* she paints the seaside background in Sussex with careful attention to detail.

As a novelist Mrs. Smith defies classification as "Gothic" – though she flirted with Radcliffean effects – or "Revolutionary" – though she sympathized with the radical views of William Godwin and his circle. She was obsessed, as they were, with the poor, the oppressed, and the ill-educated; and her novels – sometimes explicitly, more often implicitly through characterization – embody these concerns. Her first novel, *Emmeline,* a sentimental tale of thwarted love that was derived from Fanny Burney's *Cecilia,* was followed by two others in the same mode. But with *Desmond* (1792) she broke away to produce a work of avowed propaganda. In it she argued that conditions in revolutionary France were preferable to those under the old regime, and she used her title character as an instrument to chastise the abuses of English government. Two years later, in *The Banished Man,* Mrs. Smith expressed very different views when the bloodiness of revolutionary events had tempered her liberalism. And in her third didactic novel inspired by the Revolution, *The Young Philosopher,* she sought an intellectual justification, through her Rousseauesque hero, for the turmoil in France.

Her best novel, *The Old Manor House,* is marked by vigorous characterization and a plot that depends less on coincidence and artifice than on actions which derive directly from character. Walter Scott thought Mrs. Rayland – a capricious, domineering old snob – "without a rival." Mrs. Smith's descriptions of English landscape, in this novel and others, are unusual for their understated realism. Even more admirable is her moral realism: like her hero Fielding, she was intolerant of cant and pretension. Despite her tendency to heavy-handed satire, she possessed an underlying tolerance that commands our admiration.

—Anne Henry Ehrenpreis

SMOLLETT, Tobias (George).   Scottish.   Born in Dalquhurn, Dunbartonshire, baptized 19 March 1721. Educated at Dumbarton Grammar School; studied medicine at the University of Glasgow, and apprenticed to William Stirling and John Gordon, Glasgow surgeons, 1736–39; awarded M.D. by Marischal College, Aberdeen, 1750. Married Anne Lascelles, probably in 1747; one daughter. Settled in London, 1739; sailed as a surgeon on the *Cumberland* in Ogle's West Indian Squadron, 1741–43; set up as a surgeon in Downing Street, London, 1744; writer from 1747; moved to Bath, 1751; returned to London, 1753; Founding Editor, *The Critical Review*, 1756–63: imprisoned for libel, 1759; Editor, *The British Magazine*, 1760–62, and *The Briton*, 1762–63; lived in Nice, 1763–65, and in Italy, 1769–71. *Died 17 September 1771.*

PUBLICATIONS

Collections

Works, edited by W. E. Henley and Thomas Seccombe.   12 vols., 1899–1901.
Novels.   11 vols., 1925–26.
Selected Writings, edited by Arthur Calder-Marshall.   1950.
Letters, edited by Lewis M. Knapp.   1970.

Fiction

The Adventures of Roderick Random.   1748.
The Adventures of Peregrine Pickle, in Which Are Included Memoirs of a Lady of Quality.   1751; revised edition, 1758; edited by James L. Clifford, 1964.
The Adventures of Ferdinand, Count Fathom.   1753; edited by Damian Grant, 1971.
The Life and Adventures of Sir Launcelot Greaves.   1762; edited by David L. Evans, 1973.
The History and Adventures of an Atom.   1769.
The Expedition of Humphry Clinker.   1771; edited by André Parreaux, 1968.

Plays

The Regicide; or, James the First of Scotland.   1749.
The Reprisal; or, The Tars of Old England (produced 1757).   1757.

Verse

Advice: A Satire.   1746.
Reproof: A Satire.   1747.
Ode to Independence.   1773.

Other

An Essay on the External Use of Water.   1752; edited by Claude E. Jones, in *Bulletin of the Institute of the History of Medicine,* 1935.
A Complete History of England, Deduced from the Descent of Julius Caesar to the Treaty

of Aix la Chapelle 1748. 4 vols., 1757–58; *Continuation of the Complete History of England*, 4 vols., 1760–61.

Travels Through France and Italy, Containing Observations on Character, Customs, Religion, Government, Police, Commerce, Arts, and Antiquities, with a Particular Description of the Town, Territory, and Climate of Nice. 2 vols., 1766; edited by Thomas Seccombe, 1907.

Editor, *A Treatise on the Theory and Practice of Midwifery*, by W. Smellie. 1751.
Editor, *A Collection of Cases and Observations in Midwifery*, by W. Smellie. 1754.
Editor, *Travels Through Different Cities of Germany, Italy, Greece, and Several Parts of Asia*, by Alex Drummond. 1754.
Editor, *A Compendium of Authentic and Entertaining Voyages, Digested in a Chronological Series.* 7 vols., 1756.
Editor and Translator, with Thomas Francklin, *The Works of Voltaire.* 38 vols., 1761–74; *Candide and Other Tales*, edited by James Thornton, 1937.
Editor, *The Present State of All Nations, Containing a Geographical, Natural, Commercial, and Political History of All the Countries in the Known World.* 8 vols., 1768–69.

Translator, *The Adventures of Gil Blas of Santillane*, by Le Sage. 4 vols., 1748.
Translator, *Select Essays on Commerce, Agriculture, Mines, Fisheries, and Other Useful Subjects.* 1754.
Translator, *The History and Adventures of the Renowned Don Quixote*, by Cervantes. 2 vols., 1755.
Translator, *The Adventures of Telemachus, The Son of Ulysses*, by Fénelon. 2 vols., 1776.
Translator, *Select Essays, Containing the Manner of Raising and Dressing Flax and Hemp, Collected from the Dictionary of Arts and Sciences.* 1777.

Bibliography: *Smollett Criticism, 1925–45*, and *1770–1924* by F. Cordasco, 2 vols., 1947–48.

Reading List: *The Later Career of Smollett* by Louis L. Martz, 1942; *Smollett, Traveller-Novelist* by George M. Kahrl, 1945; *Smollett's Reputation as a Novelist* by F. W. Boege, 1947 (includes bibliography); *Smollett: Doctor of Men and Manners* by Lewis M. Knapp, 1949; *Smollett* by Laurence Brander, 1951; *Radical Doctor Smollett* by Donald J. Bruce, 1964; *The Tradition of Smollett* by Robert Giddings, 1967; *Smollett* by R. D. Spector, 1969; *The Novels of Smollett* by Paul-Gabriel Boucé, translated 1976.

*   *   *

Labels like "novelist" and "novel" are at best problematic, and at worst dangerous, when applied to the writers and fictions of the eighteenth century. Not only did these words have different meanings than they do today, but none of the great quintumvirate – Defoe, Richardson, Fielding, Sterne, and Smollett – would have conceived of himself as "a novelist"; the literary output of all five covers most of the major literary kinds. The youngest of them, Tobias Smollett, comes closest to being a "professional" writer of fiction, though even his *œuvre* is staggeringly broad: he was dramatist, poet, journalist, historian, travel-writer, and translator as well as "novelist." What distinguishes him from the others is that he seems to have been working towards a concept of the novel as an autonomous literary kind. In his Dedication to *Ferdinand Count Fathom*, he presents the following definition:

A novel is a large, diffused picture, comprehending the characters of life, disposed in different groups, and exhibited in various attitudes, for the purposes of an uniform plan, and general occurrence, to which every individual figure is subservient. But this plan cannot be executed with propriety, probability, or success, without a principal personage to attract the attention, unite the incidents, unwind the clue of the labyrinth, and at last close the scene, by virtue of his own importance.

This provides an important frame for the consideration of Smollett's own work. However faulty the execution, he was clearly engaged in the development of a theory of the novel and in its application.

Four of Smollett's novels have the word "adventures" in their titles, and that fact serves to identify the mode in which he characteristically worked. Samuel Johnson's *Dictionary* defines "adventure" as "an enterprise in which something must be left to hazard"; and Smollett's fictive world is ruled and misruled by hazard and fortune. His heroes attempt in different ways, and with varying degrees of success, to order their risky, deceptive, and sometimes hostile environments. The literary co-ordinates of this anarchic world are Cervantes's *Don Quixote* and LeSage's *Gil Blas*, both of which Smollett translated. From them he derives his journey-structures, his satiric vision of society, and his fascination with the psychology of quixotism, the solipsistic delusions which he sees as controlling all human minds.

In the Preface to *The Adventures of Roderick Random*, Smollett specifically cites *Don Quixote* and *Gil Blas* as his models for his own first attempt at combining romance and satire into fiction. His overall purpose in the first-person narrative of Roderick's escapades is, he writes, to show "modest merit struggling with every difficulty to which a friendless orphan is exposed, from his own want of experience as well as from the selfishness, envy, malice and base indifference of mankind." Most readers probably find the self-centred, revengeful, angry young man at the centre of this story less sympathetic than Smollett seems to have hoped. Roderick is a young Scotsman who (like Smollett) takes the high road to London only to find fame and fortune harder to come by than he expected. After a series of urban misadventures, he is press-ganged aboard a man of war, where the chicanery, corruption, and violence are only a more intense version of life on shore. Smollett eventually extricates his hero from a world which threatens to swamp him by the romance-device of the reappearing father, whom Roderick happens upon in Paraguay. Restored to his identity and estate, he can now marry his flawless romance-heroine, Narcissa.

In *The Adventures of Peregrine Pickle*, Smollett takes a figure not unlike Roderick and subjects him to the scrutiny of a third-person narrator. Like Fielding in *Tom Jones* (to which *Peregrine Pickle* bears some affinity – indeed, Smollett intemperately accused Fielding of purloining his ideas), Smollett in *Peregrine Pickle* attempts a substantial definition of the nature of true heroism. But Tom Jones is a good man who appears to be a rogue; Peregrine *is* a rogue and a trickster, albeit with a good heart and conscience buried under a penchant for elaborate and often nasty practical jokes. These two sides of his nature co-exist rather uneasily, and Smollett as narrator fails to exert the unifying, controlling influence of Fielding's narrative voice. Peregrine's career is plotted as a moral education, a struggle between reason and passion in which the former gradually emerges victor, though not always convincingly. As in *Roderick Random*, much of the book's frenetic energy is generated by its gallery of minor characters, particularly such naval grotesques as Commodore Trunnion and Tom Pipes.

The next two novels, *The Adventures of Ferdinand, Count Fathom* and *The Adventures of Sir Launcelot Greaves*, are experiments with different kinds of heroes. Ferdinand is an unalloyed villain, born to a camp-following whore in the midst of a war, and committed in later life to a Hobbesian vision of the human condition as a state of warfare. Like Peregrine Pickle he thrives on cheating and gulling those around him; but his unmitigated viciousness draws no sympathy from the reader. Fathom is born evil, not corrupted by society, and he cannot therefore be reformed by education. Smollett can save him only by an implausible and sentimental conversion following the exposure of his villainy at the end of the novel. By contrast, Sir Launcelot Greaves is a good and sane man in a world of badmen and madmen. A *rational* quixote, he roams the roads of mid-eighteenth-century England and affords Smollett a lively satiric vehicle for renewing his perennially scathing attacks on such contemporary institutions as the law, the prison system, and the literary establishment.

Smollett's last book, *The Expedition of Humphry Clinker*, differs from its predecessors in form, tone, and purpose right from its title-page. It is an *expedition*, not a series of adventures. The distinction is clear from Johnson's definition of "expedition": "a march or voyage with martial intentions." Matthew Bramble's journey is a consciously undertaken campaign for better health, and, while he is not exempt from hazard and accident, his route is clearly plotted from his Gloucestershire estate to Bath, London, Scotland, and back. From the first, too, the primary impulse of *Humphry Clinker* is comic rather than satiric. Its hero is the most fully developed example of the "benevolent misanthrope" type who had appeared in some of the earlier novels. Outwardly a sour critic of men, manners, and institutions, Matt Bramble is in reality good-hearted, compassionate, and magnanimous. Bramble's nostalgia for the lost world of his youth affords Smollett a sounding-board for his critique of modern life, but the attitude of mind the book recommends is a mellower and more tolerant one. This is underlined by Smollett's choice of the letter-method of narration: five of Bramble's party, of both sexes and different social standing, send accounts of persons, places, and events to friends. Each correspondent is limited by his or her own experience and point of view, and only the reader has the evidence to piece together a complete version of the expedition free from "the falsifying medium of prejudice and passion." The fusion of the Fieldingesque journey-structure with Richardson's epistolary technique points to another of Smollett's purposes in *Humphry Clinker*. The novel is an affectionate critical pastiche of the themes and conventions of eighteenth-century fiction (including those of Smollett's own earlier novels). *Humphry Clinker* self-consciously employs an eponymous hero whose role is secondary (compare *Joseph Andrews*), a romance-plot turning on revelations of true identity, and a multiple-marriage ending. The last of these encapsulates Smollett's shrewdest critical point. The last word on the four marriages which end the novel is given to the marvellously malapropistic Welsh maidservant, Win Jenkins, who, as so often, reaches truth *via* an orthographic vagary. When the marriage-knots are all tied, intending to write "our society is to separate," she produces "our satiety is to suppurate." There could be no more devastating comment on the happy-ever-after myth which ended so many eighteenth-century novels with marriage. It is a pity that Smollett did not live to attempt a post-marital study like Fielding's *Amelia*.

—J. C. Hilson

STERNE, Laurence. English. Born in Clonmel, County Tipperary, Ireland, 24 November 1713, of an English Army family; as a child lived at various regimental posts in England and Ireland. Educated at a school in Halifax, Yorkshire, 1723–31; Jesus College, Cambridge, 1733–36 (sizar, 1733; scholar, 1734), matriculated 1735, B.A. 1737, M.A. 1740. Married Elizabeth Lumley in 1741 (separated, 1764), two daughters. Ordained Deacon, 1737: Curate of St. Ives, Huntingdonshire, 1737; Assistant Curate, Catton, Yorkshire, 1738; Ordained priest, 1738; Rector of Sutton-in-the-Forest, Yorkshire, 1738, and the adjoining parish Stillington from 1743 (retained both livings all his life; lived in Sutton until 1760); Prebendary of York Cathedral from 1741; writer from 1758; visited London, 1760: vilified by other writers for indecency (*Tristram Shandy*); received perpetual curacy of Coxwold, Yorkshire, and settled there, 1760; lived in France, 1762–64; travelled in France and Italy, 1765–66; met Mrs. Eliza Draper, 1767; lived in London, 1767. *Died 18 March 1768.*

Publications

Collections

> *Works,* edited by Wilbur L. Cross.   12 vols., 1904.
> *Works.*   7 vols., 1926–27.
> *Letters,* edited by Lewis P. Curtis.   1935.

Fiction

> *A Political Romance.*   1759; edited by Ian Jack, with *A Sentimental Journey* and *Journal to Eliza,* 1968.
> *The Life and Opinions of Tristram Shandy, Gentleman.*   9 vols., 1759–67; edited by James Aiken Work, 1940.
> *A Sentimental Journey Through France and Italy, by Mr. Yorick.*   1768; edited by Gardner D. Stout, Jr., 1967.

Other

> *The Sermons of Mr. Yorick.*   7 vols., 1760–69; selection edited by Marjorie David, 1973.
> *Letters to His Most Intimate Friends, with a Fragment in the Manner of Rabelais, to Which Are Prefixed Memoirs of His Life and Family Written by Himself.*   3 vols., 1775.

Bibliography: *Sterne in the Twentieth Century: An Essay and a Bibliography of Sternean Studies 1900–1965* by Lodwick Hartley, 1966, revised edition, 1968.

Reading List: *Life and Times of Sterne* by Wilbur L. Cross, 1909, revised edition, 1929; *The Politicks of Sterne* by Lewis P. Curtis, 1929; *Early Masters of English Fiction* by Alan D. McKillop, 1956; *Sterne: De l'Homme à l'Oeuvre* by Henri Fluchère, 1961, translated as *Sterne from Tristram to Yorick,* 1965; *Sterne* by W. S. Piper, 1965; *Sterne's Comedy of Moral Sentiment,* 1966, and *Sterne: The Early and Middle Years,* 1975, both by Arthur Cash, and *The Winged Skull* edited by Cash and J. M. Stedmond, 1971; *Sterne: A Collection of Critical Essays* edited by John Traugott, 1968; *Wild Excursions: The Life and Fiction of Sterne* by David Thompson, 1972; *Sterne: The Critical Heritage* edited by Alan B. Howes, 1974.

*   *   *

Tristram Shandy and *Sentimental Journey* brought Sterne immediate fame and notoriety and have continued to provoke controversy. He has been praised by some as the most innovative novelist of the eighteenth century, a humorist of genius, while damned by others as affected, shallow, and indecent. Nietzsche called Sterne "the freest writer of all times," and indeed both his novels play fast and loose with narrative conventions. The liberties of *Tristram Shandy* may strike readers as especially bewildering. What should we make of a book filled with Rabelaisian wit, in which digressions overwhelm plot, in which events and reflections seem governed by whim, in which chronology is so elastic that the novel ends several years before it begins, and in which the hero scarcely appears? First chapters normally serve to orient readers; the opening chapter of *Tristram Shandy,* with Mrs. Shandy's seemingly pointless question about winding the family clock, works to disorient us, to signal that we have entered a new world and must learn to find our way. As we read on we begin to see that the narrative is not, in fact, disjointed or random, that the story has its own principles of associative coherence.

Tristram Shandy ignores chronology because the treatment of time is psychological. Events unfold as they present themselves to Tristram's mind; the length of particular episodes depends on the number of memories, feelings, and ideas a given action or conversation evokes. The smallest incident may thus be whole chapters in the telling. The fluidity of Sterne's transitions from one subject to the next has encouraged comparisons of his method to stream-of-consciousness. Such comparisons are misleading, however, because everything presented in the novel assumes an audience. What we have in *Tristram Shandy*, and later in *Sentimental Journey*, is not interior monologue, not the flow of unspoken thoughts, but something closer to uninhibited conversation. Tristram addresses the reader as a new acquaintance who must be teased and cajoled into an understanding of how to read his book. A reader must learn, for example, that the digressions only appear to lead away from the story; usually they circle back to it in ingenious, instructive ways. As Tristram explains, "my work is digressive, and it is progressive too, – and at the same time." If Tristram interrupts Toby in mid-sentence for a thirty page excursion, that digression is by no means irrelevant. It tells us things about Toby which shed light on his singular character and which make us better able to appreciate what he has to say when Tristram finally returns to him.

Sterne's characters are no less striking than his devices of narrative. Walter, with his preposterous theories of names and noses, the gentle Toby with his passion for model fortifications, seem as single-minded as any humorous character of Jonsonian comedy. But as Sterne develops them they are neither so one-dimensional, nor so purely ridiculous. If Sterne delights in odd behavior, he wants also to know what lies behind it. He traces Toby's hobbyhorse to the days when, convalescing from a serious wound received at the siege of Namur, Toby tries to tell visitors precisely what has happened to him. First he buys a map of Namur, then he consults books on military science. One thing leads to another; before long he can think of nothing except battles. Character, Sterne suggests, is shaped by circumstances more than by choice. Men are at the mercy of events, and "the wisest men in all ages, not excepting *Solomon* himself," have had hobbyhorses. The hobbies of Walter and Toby may strike us as laughable, yet who can say that they are any more silly, or more avoidable, than those of the other characters, or any more silly than our own? In *Tristram Shandy* distinctions between the sensible and the ridiculous rapidly lose force.

Hobbyhorses do make communications between characters difficult. When every man perceives the world in an intensely personal way, how can talk fail to be at cross purposes? But Sterne steers clear of despairing reflections on human isolation. A spirit of genial tolerance informs his novel. At Shandy Hall the bonds of affection are strong enough to hold people together. Besides, breakdowns in communications are not always recognized: "He was a very great man! added my uncle *Toby*; (meaning *Stevinus*) – He was so, brother *Toby*, said my father, (meaning *Piereskius*)." The lives of Sterne's characters have little to do with their understanding of other people; they derive deepest satisfaction from their hobbyhorses. In this sense the world of *Tristram Shandy* borders on the solipsistic. Like Joyce or Virginia Woolf, Sterne stresses the primacy of subjective experience. It is not action that matters, it is the way actions are perceived. Toby may be only an invalid on half-pay, yet in imagination he is again a soldier fighting his country's battles. War games for him transcend play; they are a patriotic obligation.

We must remember that the full title of Sterne's novel is *The Life and Opinions of Tristram Shandy, Gentleman*. Tristram may scarcely appear as a character, but through his "opinions" he is everywhere; every scene is filtered through his consciousness. He says little about what has happened to him, a great deal about how he thinks and feels. We come, finally, to be on a more intimate footing with him than with many characters in fiction about whose activities we know far more. The sensibility revealed is a curious and often disconcerting amalgam of his father's licentious wit and out-of-the-way learning and his uncle's readiness to shed kindly tears. Tristram can solicit sympathy for a lovelorn maiden one moment and use her for a laugh the next: "MARIA look'd wistfully for some time at me, and then at her goat – and then at me – and then at her goat again, and so on alternately – Well, *Maria*, said I softly – What resemblance do you find?" Should we take Maria seriously or as a joke? is Sterne, at bottom, a sentimentalist or a jester? Nietzsche thought that at bottom he was *both*, and that the most striking evidence of his freedom as a writer lay precisely in the lightening ease with which he could move from pathos to mockery.

Though *Sentimental Journey* is a far less eccentric novel than *Tristram Shandy* it too celebrates private sensibility and is complicated by still subtler ambiguities. Parson Yorick's account of his travels through France transmutes small events – an encounter with a mendicant friar, conversation with a grisette, dinner with a peasant family – into richly imagined experiences. Yorick cares nothing for sights. He is a connoisseur of feeling. "Was I in a desert," he declares, "I would find out wherewith in it to call forth my affections." No reader would doubt him for a minute. What does raise doubt is the extent to which those affections are sincere. As in *Tristram Shandy* it is hard to determine just where Sterne stands. We can take a hint from Yorick's name and find evidence aplenty that he is a sentimental fool, even an outright fraud. At the theatre in Paris he trembles with pity for a dwarf whose view of the stage is blocked by an enormous German, but he lifts not a finger to help him. While he does try to release the caged starling that has been taught to cry "I can't get out," he abandons the attempt at the first difficulty, and later gives the bird away, cage and all.

Yet Sterne does not always undercut Yorick's feelings. There is nothing ludicrous, surely, about his admiration for the peasants of the Bourbonnais. If Yorick is a fool he is a fool of uncommon charm and insight. He knows, for instance, that his kindness to the *fille de chambre* who visits him in his room is to some degree self-serving. But he defends himself with a question which compels the reader to examine the purity of his own motives and to consider whether motives *need* be pure: "If Nature has so wove her web of kindness, that some threads of love and desire are entangled with the piece – must the whole web be rent in drawing them out?" Sterne is ever an enemy to hasty judgment and facile moralizing. *A Sentimental Journey* and *Tristram Shandy* invite us to look at the world anew, to find complexity and strangeness in the familiar, and to recognize that what seems excessive or odd may have closer ties to ordinary experience than we have thought.

—Michael DePorte

STEVENSON, Robert Louis (Robert Lewis Balfour Stevenson). Scottish. Born in Edinburgh, 13 November 1850. Educated at the Edinburgh Academy; studied engineering at the University of Edinburgh, 1866–71, then studied law in the office of Skene, Edwards, and Gordon, Edinburgh: called to the Scottish Bar, 1875, but never practised. Married Fanny Vandegrift Osbourne in 1880; two step-children, including the writer Lloyd Osbourne. Travelled and lived on the Continent, chiefly in France, 1875–80; writer from 1876; contributed to the *Cornhill Magazine*, 1876–82; travelled widely, partly in search for a cure for tuberculosis, from 1880: lived in Davos, Switzerland, Hyères, France, Bournemouth, England, and the South Seas; settled in Samoa, 1888. *Died 3 December 1894.*

PUBLICATIONS

Collections

The Letters of Stevenson to His Family and Friends, edited by Sidney Colvin.   2 vols., 1899; revised edition, 4 vols., 1911.

Works (Vailima Edition), edited by Lloyd Osbourne and Fanny Stevenson. 26 vols., 1922–23.
Selected Writings, edited by Saxe Commins. 1947.
Collected Poems, edited by Janet Adam Smith. 1950.
Essays, edited by Malcolm Elwin. 1950.

Fiction

New Arabian Nights (stories). 1882.
Treasure Island. 1883.
More New Arabian Nights: The Dynamiter, with Fanny Stevenson. 1885.
Prince Otto: A Romance. 1885.
Strange Case of Dr. Jekyll and Mr. Hyde. 1886.
Kidnapped, Being Memoirs of the Adventures of David Balfour in the Year 1751. 1886.
The Merry Men and Other Tales and Fables. 1887.
The Misadventures of John Nicholson: A Christmas Story. 1887.
The Black Arrow: A Tale of the Two Roses. 1888.
The Master of Ballantrae: A Winter's Tale. 1889.
The Wrong Box, with Lloyd Osbourne. 1889.
The Wrecker, with Lloyd Osbourne. 1892.
Catriona: A Sequel to Kidnapped. 1893; as *David Balfour*, 1893.
The Bottle Imp (stories). 1893(?).
Island Nights' Entertainments (stories). 1893.
The Ebb-Tide: A Trio and Quartette (stories), with Lloyd Osbourne. 1894.
The Body-Snatcher (stories). 1895.
The Amateur Emigrant from the Clyde to Sandy Hook (stories). 1895.
The Strange Case of Dr. Jekyll and Mr. Hyde, with Other Fables. 1896.
Fables. 1896.
Weir of Hermiston. 1896.
St. Ives, Being the Adventures of a French Prisoner in England, completed by Arthur Quiller-Couch. 1897.
The Waif Woman (stories). 1916.
When the Devil Was Well (stories). 1921.
The Suicide Club and Other Stories, edited by J. Kenneth White. 1970.

Plays

Deacon Brodie; or, The Double Life: A Melodrama, with W. E. Henley (produced 1882). 1880.
Admiral Guinea: A Melodrama, with W. E. Henley (produced 1890). 1884.
Beau Austin, with W. E. Henley (produced 1890). 1884.
Macaire: A Melodramatic Farce, with W. E. Henley (produced 1900). 1885.
The Hanging Judge, with Fanny Stevenson. 1887; edited by Edmund Gosse, 1914.
Monmouth, edited by Charles Vale. 1928.

Verse

Penny Whistles (juvenile). 1883.
A Child's Garden of Verses. 1885.
Underwoods. 1887.
Ticonderoga. 1887.

Ballads. 1890.
Songs of Travel and Other Verses. 1895.
Poems Hitherto Unpublished, edited by George S. Hellman. 2 vols., 1916; as *New Poems and Variant Readings*, 1918; additional volume, edited by Hellman and William P. Trent, 1921.

Other

The Pentland Rising: A Page of History, 1666. 1866.
The Charity Bazaar: An Allegorical Dialogue. 1871.
An Appeal to the Clergy. 1875.
An Inland Voyage. 1878.
Edinburgh: Picturesque Notes. 1879.
Travels with a Donkey in the Cévennes. 1879.
Virginibus Puerisque and Other Papers. 1881.
Familiar Studies of Men and Books. 1882.
The Silverado Squatters: Sketches from a Californian Mountain. 1883.
Memoirs and Portraits. 1887.
Thomas Stevenson, Civil Engineer. 1887.
Memoir of Fleeming Jenkin. 1887.
Father Damien: An Open Letter to the Reverend Dr. Hyde of Honolulu. 1890.
The South Seas: A Record of Three Cruises. 1890.
Across the Plains, with Other Memories and Essays, edited by Sidney Colvin. 1892.
A Footnote to History: Eight Years of Trouble in Samoa. 1892.
The Works (Edinburgh Edition), edited by Sidney Colvin. 28 vols., 1894–98.
In the South Seas. 1896.
A Mountain Town in France: A Fragment. 1896.
The Morality of the Profession of Letters. 1899.
Essays and Criticisms. 1903.
Prayers Written at Vailima. 1903.
Essays of Travel. 1905.
Essays in the Art of Writing. 1905.
Lay Morals and Other Papers. 1911.
Records of a Family of Engineers. 1912; unfinished chapters edited by J. Christian Bat, 1930.
Memoirs of Himself. 1912.
Some Letters, edited by Lloyd Osbourne. 1914.
On the Choice of a Profession. 1916.
Diogenes in London. 1920.
Hitherto Unpublished Prose Writings, edited by Henry H. Harper. 1921.
Stevenson's Workshop, with Twenty-Nine MS. Facsimiles, edited by William P. Trent. 1921.
Confessions of a Unionist: An Unpublished "Talk on Things Current," Written in the Year 1888, edited by F. V. Livingston. 1921.
The Best Thing in Edinburgh, edited by Katharine D. Osbourne. 1923.
The Castaways of Soledad, edited by George S. Hellman. 1928.
Henry James and Stevenson: A Record of Friendship and Criticism, edited by Janet Adam Smith. 1948.
Silverado Journal, edited by J. E. Jordan. 1954.
RLS: Stevenson's Letters to Charles Baxter, edited by De Lancey Ferguson and M. Waingrow. 1956.
From Scotland to Silverado, edited by J. D. Hart. 1966.
Travels in Hawaii, edited by A. Grove Day. 1973.

The Cévennes Journal: Notes on a Journey Through the French Highlands.   1978.

Bibliography: *The Stevenson Library of E. J. Beinecke* by G. L. McKay, 6 vols., 1951–64.

Reading List: *Stevenson,* 1947, and *Stevenson and His World,* 1973, both by David Daiches; *Voyage to Windward: The Life of Stevenson* by J. C. Furnas, 1951; *Portrait of a Rebel: The Life and Work of Stevenson* by Richard Aldington, 1957; *Stevenson and the Fiction of Adventure* by Robert Kiely, 1964; *Stevenson and the Romantic Tradition* by Edwin M. Eigner, 1966; *Stevenson* by James Pope-Hennessy, 1974; *Stevenson* by Paul M. Binding, 1974.

*   *   *

Robert Louis Stevenson was, in the best sense of that 19th century term, a man of letters. Unlike most of their kind, however, he achieved high distinction as a novelist, as an essayist, and as a poetic miniaturist.

His early novels are adventure stories, of which *Treasure Island* first won his fame. It is, by any standards, a masterly piece of story-telling, cleverly constructed, vividly drawn, and grasping the reader's attention from beginning to end. Taking an adult viewpoint, it has sometimes been criticised on the ground that the virtuous are saved almost by accident, by a boy who is hardly aware of what he is doing. It seems to me wrong to suggest that the story's resolution implies on this account some kind of Calvinistic ambiguity in Stevenson's make-up, though his understanding of the warp and woof of the temper of Calvinism was to be reflected in his last masterpiece.

The Black Arrow, though by no means "tushery" – the word Stevenson invented to define the false jargon usually to be found in historical novels set in mediaeval times – does not succeed in creating the sense of atmosphere which raises *Kidnapped* somewhat beyond the level of expert fabling for the young. The desire to provide adventure at boys' level was no doubt the prime intention in *Kidnapped,* the aftermath of Jacobitism and the affair of the Red Fox simply the historical springboard for the chase over Kinlochrannoch and the other strongly portrayed and fast-moving action scenes. But just as, in the six best Waverley novels, Scott dealt with the great moments of confrontation in Scottish history, in *Kidnapped* Stevenson shows himself capable of continuing Scott's tradition. What makes an historic novel worthwhile, as opposed to "tushery" or fancy-dress flummery, is its creation of credible tensions. The tension that holds *Kidnapped* together comes from an acute portrayal of constant clashes of conflicting loyalties, an age-old Scottish dilemma: that of the young Whig, David Balfour, for his romantic Jacobite friend, Alan Breck; that of the clansmen for Breck himself; that of Macpherson for his clan; and that of Breck for the King over the Water. Breck and Balfour are both moderately well drawn, and so is the Scrooge-like eccentric, miserly Uncle Ebenezer. The style throughout is mellifluous, Stevenson's instinctive ability to balance vocables within a period, and periods within a sentence, refined to suit the demands of fast action. The novel thus, to some extent, escapes the charge of being mannered – the style counting for more than the content – commonly applied to his earlier books, and to the sequel *Catriona,* which suffers not only from less vigorous action, but from its author's inability almost to the end of his life to create convincingly the character of a young woman.

Popular as these books are, especially with young people, Stevenson's reputation as a great writer rests not upon them. but on a handful of other works: *Dr. Jekyll and Mr. Hyde,* that macabre tale based on the double life of Edinburgh's notorious Deacon Brodie, and an excursion into the darker reaches of the Calvinist psyche; the fine Scots study in the exercise of the powers of darkness that is "Thrawn Janet" (in *The Merry Men*), a forerunner in miniature to Stevenson's masterful *Weir of Hermiston*; another story powerfully told, "The

Beach of Falesá" from *Island Nights' Entertainment*; and his two late novels, *The Master of Ballantrae* and *Weir of Hermiston*.

Superficially, *The Master of Ballantrae* might appear to be yet another exercise in the swashbuckling vein of his earlier Scottish romances. Yet it is much more than that. For all its inequalities, and its thoroughly unsatisfactory ending – a fault to which the author admitted – it marks Stevenson's first success in the creating of character for its own sake, rather than the provision of characters who depend upon the action to give them their dimensions. The Durie brothers are interesting for what they are, rather than for what they do. Alison Graeme, later Mrs. Henry Durie, is in many ways Stevenson's first reasonably convincing woman. There is the cleverly handled device of triple narrative. The fact that all three narrators are in different ways biased provides a kind of verisimilitude with the confusion of daily life, which rarely allows three people who have witnessed even the same single incident to repeat it in terms that exactly correspond.

Good though the best things in *The Master of Ballantrae* are – not least being their evocation of Scottish scenery and weather – *Weir of Hermiston* is an enormous leap forward. Based on the life-story of the "hanging judge", Robert MacQueen, Lord Braxfield, the novel includes one of the great moments in Scottish fiction – Lord Weir's confrontation with his more sensitive but weaker son, Archie, after a courtroom scene. These two central characters apart, the complete success of the two Kirsties, aunt and niece, the free and frequent handling of Scots, and the telling economy of the writing combine to make the unfinished torso a masterpiece, the first depiction in fiction of the strength and the weakness of a clever man moulded by the hereditary effects of Scots Calvinism.

Much of Stevenson's prose output took the form of travel-books, like *Travels with a Donkey in the Cévennes* and *The Silverado Squatters*, or collections of essays, the most famous being *Virginibus Puerisque* and *Familiar Studies of Men and Books*. As a travel-writer, his eye was sharp, the setting down of his observations and reactions unfailingly elegant. His letter "to maidens and boys" derived its title from Horace, and comprises gracefully expressed common sense which might do much to ease the hurt of youth, were youth a condition capable of rational remedy.

Much of Stevenson's poetry shows a concern with style for its own sake, as in the well-known "Romance," where the prospect of a woman washing herself "white" in "dewfall at night" is prettily ridiculous. Yet the poem had become popular because of its graceful clarity. Escapism, usually kept in check in his fiction, is given freer rein in his verse. Perhaps for this reason his most delightful things are to be found in *A Child's Garden of Verses*, and in such expression of homeward longing as "In the Highlands" and "To S. R. Crockett."

Stevenson's poems in Scots helped to keep the language alive in the last quarter of the 19th century, and are certainly above the general ruck of rhyming vernacular sentimentality being produced at that time. The "Standard Habbie" stanza, however, seems to have affected him with a parochialism not usually manifested in his work.

Although his reputation has been somewhat down-valued during the past fifty years, he is still affectionately regarded in Scotland as belonging to the company of Burns and Scott, if perhaps not quite on the level of either of them.

—Maurice Lindsay

STOKER, Bram. Irish. Born Abraham Stoker in Dublin, 8 November 1847. Educated in a private school in Dublin; Trinity College, Dublin, 1866–70, B.A. 1870; entered Middle Temple, London: called to the Bar, 1890. Married Florence Anne Lemon Balcombe in 1878;

one son. Civil Servant in Dublin, 1867–77; Drama Critic, *Dublin Mail*, 1871–78; Editor, The Halfpenny Press, Dublin, 1874; settled in London: Acting Manager for Henry Irving, 1878–1905, and Manager of Irving's Lyceum chain, 1878–1902; writer from 1880. President, Philosophical Society. *Died 20 April 1912.*

PUBLICATIONS

Collections

The Stoker Bedside Companion: Stories of Fantasy and Horror, edited by Charles Osborne. 1973.

Fiction

Under the Sunset (juvenile). 1881.
The Snake's Pass. 1890.
Crooken Sands. 1894.
The Watter's Mou'. 1894.
The Shoulder of Shasta. 1895.
Dracula. 1897.
Miss Betty. 1898.
The Mystery of the Sea. 1902.
The Jewel of Seven Stars. 1903.
The Man. 1905.
Lady Athlyne. 1908.
Snowbound: The Record of a Theatrical Touring Party. 1908.
The Lady of the Shroud. 1909.
The Lair of the White Worm. 1911.
Dracula's Guest and Other Weird Stories. 1914.

Other

The Duties of Clerks of Petty Sessions in Ireland. 1879.
Personal Reminiscences of Henry Irving. 2 vols., 1906.
Famous Imposters. 1910.

Reading List: *The Dracula Myth* by Gabriel Ronay, 1972; *The Annotated Dracula* by Leonard Wolf, 1975; *The Man Who Wrote Dracula: A Biography of Stoker* by Daniel Farson, 1975.

*   *   *

Cinema-goers are more familiar with Dracula's name than readers of literature with that of his creator, Bram Stoker. Apart from the much-filmed novel, Stoker's fiction is a noxious *pot-pourri* of plagiarism – "The Judge's House" and "Dracula's Guest" are borrowed from Le Fanu – racism, and semi-conscious sexual titillation, the entire tincture being then suspended in sadistic violence and pseudo magic.

Yet even to its readers *Dracula* manages to stand above this dubious standard. Its principal theme, vampirism, had a longish history dating from the days of Byron and Polidori; its incidental concern with fetishism – the vampire can be repelled not only with the sign of the cross but with the physical application of the consecrated wafer to cracks in masonry – touches with its rough texture on the raw spot of Victorian religious unease. These purely external factors, however, do not wholly account for the novel's survival. In *Dracula* Stoker adapted the device more subtly employed by Wilkie Collins of attributing various strands of his narrative to various narrators; in Collins it contributes to a psychological mystery; in Stoker it heightens a fearful ignorance. The incorporation of telegrams, extracts from letters and diaries, even the use of broken English and transliterated short-hand, helps the author to disguise the appalling lack of coherent style which marks his other work. The result is an ever-shifting, discontinuous chronicle of fascination and pursuit, where sexual, religious, racial, and historical obsessions are intermittently indulged in and deplored.

The contrast between seemingly respectable London and the timeless horror of Transylvania is an integral part of Stoker's structure. Together with the virulent anti-Negro tirades of *The Lair of the White Worm*, this juxtaposition reminds us that the author was a contemporary of Conan Doyle and Rider Haggard, and wrote during the hey-day of British jingoism and colonial exploitation.

—W. J. McCormack

SURTEES, R(obert) S(mith).   English.   Born in Durham in 1803. Educated at Durham Grammar School until 1819; articled to a Durham solicitor, 1819, and subsequently qualified. Married Elizabeth Jane Fenwick in 1841; one son and two daughters. Settled in London, and bought a law partnership, then had difficulty in recovering the purchase money; took rooms in Lincoln's Inn, and began contributing to *Sporting Magazine* to support himself; also compiled a manual for horse buyers, 1830; Founder, with Rudolph Ackermann, 1831, and Editor, 1831–36, *New Sporting Magazine*; succeeded to his father's estate in Durham, 1838; became Justice of the Peace for Durham, Major of the Durham Militia, and High Sheriff of Durham, 1856. *Died 16 March 1864.*

PUBLICATIONS

Collections

Novels.   10 vols., 1929–30.
Hunting Scenes, edited by Lionel Gough.   1953.

Fiction

Jorrocks' Jaunts and Jollities; or, The Hunting, Racing, Driving, Sailing, Eating, Eccentric, and Extravagant Exploits of That Renowned Sporting Citizen, Mr. John Jorrocks.   1838; revised edition, 1869.

Handley Cross; or, The Spa Hunt.   1843.
Hillingdon Hall; or, The Cockney Squire.   1845.
Hawbuck Grange; or, The Sporting Adventures of Thomas Scott, Esq.   1847.
Mr. Sponge's Sporting Tour.   1853.
"Ask Mamma"; or, The Richest Commoner in England.   1858.
Plain or Ringlets.   1860.
Mr. Romford's Hounds.   1864.
Young Tom Hall, edited by E. D. Cuming.   1926.

Other

The Horseman's Manual.   1831.
The Analysis of the Hunting Field, Being a Series of Sketches of the Principal Characters That Compose One.   1846.
Surtees by Himself and E. D. Cuming.   1924.
Town and Country Papers, edited by E. D. Cuming.   1929.

Reading List: *Surtees: A Critical Study* by Frederick Watson, 1933; *Surtees* (biography) by Leonard Cooper, 1952; *The England of Nimrod and Surtees* by Edward W. Bovill, 1959; *Surtees* by Horst W. Drescher, 1961; *A Jorrocks Handbook* by Robert L. W. Collison, 1964; *The Deathless Train: The Life and Work of Surtees* by David R. Johnston-Jones, 1974.

*   *   *

R. S. Surtees is *the* novelist of hunting, and is best remembered for his creation of Jorrocks, who may well have suggested the idea of Pickwick to Dickens. The contributions to *The New Sporting Magazine* (1831–34) which were collected as *Jorrocks' Jaunts and Jollities* are a series of picaresque adventures of the London grocer turned hunting-man. Fat, outspoken, self-confident and often comic, Jorrocks had in *Handley Cross,* Surtees's next novel, a foil in James Pigg, hard-riding and hard-drinking huntsman, but Pigg is more than this; he is also a "character" in his own right. *Handley Cross* creates a world of its own, a setting within a newly fashionable watering-place, possibly based on Leamington. In this novel also the characters display a greater fullness than in its predecessor. Surtees's third novel was *Hillingdon Hall,* which has didactic leanings; it has been called "a handbook to the farmer's progress."

Hawbuck Grange, like *Jorrocks,* also appeared as "Sporting Sketches" and·is, if anything, even looser than *Jorrocks.* Its central character, Tom Scott, is much less rumbustious than Jorrocks – a decent, honest hunting farmer; and a new element in Surtees is Scott's love-affair, but it does not come to anything.

The next novel, *Mr. Sponge's Sporting Tour,* is more powerful, with its main figure, "a good, pushing, free-and-easy sort of man, wishing to be a gentleman without knowing how," and a number of others – Benjamin Buckram, Jack Spraggon, Mr. Jogglebury Crowdey and Facey Romford – among Surtees's most memorable characters. It is here too that Lucy Glitters first appears, though her triumph will come later in *Mr. Romford's Hounds.* This, his last novel, is much better than its two predecessors, *Ask Mamma* and *Plain or Ringlets?* His one other novel, *Young Tom Hall,* was serialised in 1851–52, but not published complete until 1926.

Surtees's characters and dialogue are full-blooded; his plots are episodic, sometimes disjointed, but always vigorous; he is full of comedy and satire. His greatest quality is zest.

—Arthur Pollard

SWIFT, Jonathan. English. Born in Dublin, Ireland, 30 November 1667, of English parents. Educated at Kilkenny Grammar School, 1674–82; Trinity College, Dublin, 1682–88. Married Esther (Stella) Johnson in 1716 (died, 1728). Companion and Secretary to Sir William Temple at Moor Park, Farnham, Surrey, 1689–91, 1691–94, 1695–99; writer from 1695; ordained in the Anglican Church, in Dublin, 1695, and held first living at Kilroot, Northern Ireland, until 1698; Chaplain to the Earl of Berkeley, Lord Lieutenant of Ireland, 1700; vicar of Laracor; Prebend, St. Patrick's Cathedral, Dublin, 1701; editor of several volumes of Temple's works during the 1700's; aligned with the Tory ministry of Oxford and Bolingbroke, 1710: lived in London, wrote political pamphlets, and contributed to *The Examiner*, 1710–14; Dean of St. Patrick's Cathedral, Dublin, from 1713; a leader of the Irish resistance movement from 1724; visited London, 1726, 1727, but otherwise resided in Dublin until his death. D.D.: University of Dublin, 1701. *Died 19 October 1745.*

PUBLICATIONS

Collections

Poems, edited by Harold Williams. 3 vols., 1937.
Prose Works, edited by Herbert Davis. 14 vols., 1939–68.
Gulliver's Travels and Other Writings, edited by Louis A. Landa. 1960.
The Correspondence, edited by Harold Williams. 5 vols., 1963–65.
A Tale of a Tub and Other Satires, edited by Kathleen Williams. 1975.
Selected Poems, edited by C. H. Sisson. 1977.

Fiction

A Tale of a Tub, Written for the Universal Improvement of Mankind, to Which Is Added an Account of a Battle Between the Ancient and Modern Books in St. James's Library. 1704; revised edition, 1710; edited by G. C. Guthkelch and D. N. Smith, 1958.
Travels into Several Remote Nations of the World, by Captain Lemuel Gulliver. 1726; revised edition, 1735; edited by Angus Ross, 1972.

Verse

Baucis and Philemon, Imitated from Ovid. 1709.
Part of the Seventh Epistle of the First Book of Horace Imitated. 1713.
The First Ode of the Second Book of Horace Paraphrased. 1713.
The Bubble. 1721.
Cadenus and Vanessa. 1726.
Miscellanies in Prose and Verse, with others. 4 vols., 1727–32.
Horace, Book I, Ode XIV, Paraphrased. 1730.
The Lady's Dressing Room, to Which Is Added A Poem on Cutting Down the Old Thorn at Market Hill. 1732.
An Elegy on Dicky and Dolly. 1732.
The Life and Genuine Character of Doctor Swift, Written by Himself. 1733.
On Poetry: A Rhapsody. 1733.
An Epistle to a Lady. 1734.
A Beautiful Young Nymph Going to Bed, Written for the Honour of the Fair Sex. 1734.

An Imitation of the Sixth Satire of the Second Book of Horace, completed by Pope. 1738.
Verses on the Death of Dr. Swift. 1739.

Other

A Discourse of the Contests and Dissensions Between the Nobles and the Commons in Athens and Rome. 1701; edited by F. H. Ellis, 1967.
Predictions for the Year 1708. 1708.
A Project for the Advancement of Religion and the Reformation of Manners. 1709.
A New Journey to Paris. 1711.
The Conduct of the Allies. 1711.
Some Remarks on the Barrier Treaty. 1712.
A Proposal for Correcting, Improving, and Ascertaining the English Tongue. 1712.
Mr. Collin's Discourse of Free-Thinking. 1713.
The Public Spirit of the Whigs. 1714.
A Proposal for the Universal Use of Irish Manufacture. 1720.
Fraud Detected; or, The Hibernian Patriot, Containing All the Drapier's Letters to the People of Ireland. 1725; as The Hibernian Patriot, 1730.
A Short View of the Present State of Ireland. 1728.
A Modest Proposal for Preventing the Children of Poor People from Being Burthen to Their Parents or the Country. 1729.
An Examination of Certain Abuses, Corruptions, and Enormities in the City of Dublin. 1732.
The Works. 1735.
A Complete Collection of Genteel and Ingenious Conversation. 1738; edited by E. Partridge, 1963.
Some Free Thoughts upon the Present State of Affairs, Written in the Year 1714. 1741.
Three Sermons. 1744.
Directions to Servants. 1745.
The Last Will and Testament of Swift. 1746.
Brotherly Love: A Sermon. 1754.
The History of the Four Last Years of the Queen. 1758.

Editor, Letters Written by Sir William Temple and Other Ministers of State. 3 vols., 1700–03.
Editor, Miscellanea: The Third Part, by William Temple. 1701.
Editor, Memoirs: Part III, by William Temple. 1709.

Bibliography: A Bibliography of the Writings of Swift by H. Teerink, 1937, revised edition, edited by Arthur H. Scounten, 1963; A Bibliography of Swift Studies 1945–1965 by J. J. Stathis, 1967.

Reading List: The Mind and Art of Swift by Ricardo Quintana, 1936; The Sin of Wit by Maurice Johnson, 1950; Swift: The Man, His Works, and the Age by Irvin Ehrenpreis, 2 vols. (of 3), 1962–67; Swift and the Satirist's Art by E. W. Rosenheim, Jr., 1963; Swift and the Age of Compromise by Kathleen Williams, 1968, and Swift: The Critical Heritage edited by Williams, 1970; Swift: A Critical Introduction by Denis Donoghue, 1969; Swift edited by C. J. Rawson, 1971, and Gulliver and the Gentle Reader by Rawson, 1973.

*   *   *

Jonathan Swift began as a poet, and wrote many poems throughout his life. His poetic achievement has been overshadowed by his major prose satires, but deserves to be recognised. After a brief early period of Cowleyan odes, Swift abandoned "serious" or "lofty" styles (both terms are his own), and became one of the masters in a great English tradition of "light" verse, informal but far from trivial, which includes the works of Skelton, Samuel Butler, Prior, Byron, and Auden. Byron admired him especially, and said he "beats us all hollow." Swift seldom wrote what he called "serious Couplets," avoiding a form which his friend Pope was bringing to a high refinement of precision and masterfulness. He preferred looser and more popular metres, and most often the loose octosyllabic couplet chiefly associated with Butler's *Hudibras*, a poem Swift greatly admired. These looser forms reflected the disorders of life, rather than seeming to subdue or iron out these disorders within the reassuring contours of a style which overtly proclaimed the author's triumphant and clarifying mastery. Even the few poems which, exceptionally, Swift wrote in the heroic couplet, the "Description of the Morning" and the "Description of a City Shower," tend to flatten that eloquently patterned metre into an idiom of bare realistic notation, registering the chaotic and unstructured energies of common city scenes rather than any sense of the satirist's control.

These two poems also parody some conventions of grand poetic description, and Swift's impulse to undercut the loftier orderings of "serious" poets runs through virtually all his work as a poet. The celebrated "excremental" poems ("The Lady's Dressing Room," "A Beautiful Young Nymph Going to Bed," "Strephon and Chloe," "Cassinus and Peter") are among other things parodies of the false idealisations of love-poetry. The famous plaintive cry that "Celia, Celia, Celia shits," which occurs in two of the poems and has shocked healthy-minded readers like D. H. Lawrence and Aldous Huxley, has this dimension of parody, although more than mere parody is at work. The words are too playful to support any simple view that Swift hated the human body or was a misogynist. Through his foolish Strephons, Swift mocks those who cannot accept the physical facts and seek refuge in idealising poeticisms. But he also tells us that the body is ugly and perishable, and that in matters of love and of friendship the moral and intellectual virtues are a sounder guide. These themes also run through many non-scatological poems which he wrote to women friends, notably the moving and tender poems to Stella and the archly self-justifying "Cadenus and Vanessa."

The latter, a defence of his role in a one-sided love-affair, is one of several autobiographical poems which Swift, at various periods, wrote as apologies for some aspect of his private or public life. Of these, the most interesting are "The Author upon Himself" and *Verses on the Death of Dr. Swift*. The latter is perhaps his best-known poem, a comprehensive and in many places light-hearted and low-key defence of his literary and political career, rising towards the end to a pitch of self-praise which some readers have found distasteful. *An Epistle to a Lady* is a revealing poem about Swift's unwillingness to write in a "lofty Stile"; and *On Poetry: A Rapsody*, whose title implies a similar point, is in the main an angry and witty account of the world of bad poets and hireling politicians.

In the 1730's Swift also wrote a series of angry poems on Irish affairs, of which "The Legion Club" is the best known. These attacks on prominent public men in Ireland sometimes have the force of ritual curses, and are perhaps the only places where Swift attempts what is often (and almost always wrongly) attributed to him, a Juvenalian grandeur of denunciation.

Swift's earliest major work is the prose *Tale of a Tub* (published 1704, but began about 1696 and largely written by 1700), a brilliantly inventive and disturbing display of his satiric powers. It is the last and greatest English contribution to the long Renaissance debate on the relative merits of the Ancients and the Moderns. Through a deliberately diffuse and all-embracing parody, the *Tale* mimics the laxity, muddle, and arrogance of Modern thought, both in religion and in the various branches of literature and learning. This parody is sometimes very specific, as when Dryden's garrulous self-importance, or the mystical nonsense of some "*dark* Author" like Thomas Vaughan, is mocked. But it extends beyond specific examples to the whole contemporaneous republic of bad authors and to all deviant religions, which for Swift meant mainly the dissenting sects and Roman Catholicism. The cumulative force of its many-sided and probing irony reaches even further, however, transcending parody altogether and turning into a comprehensive anatomy of modern culture and indeed of human folly in general. Many readers, from Swift's time to our own, have felt that its effect was so destructive as to undermine even those things to which Swift claimed to be expressing loyalty, including the Church of England and indeed religion itself. Swift defended himself against such charges, but they stuck, and were to damage his career as a churchman. Whether or not Swift's defense is wholly accepted, the work shows Swift's deep and characteristic tendency to put his most powerful energies into the destructive or critical side of his vision, leaving the positive values to emerge by implication from the wreckage. The *Tale* was published with two accompanying pieces, *The Battle of the Books* and the *Discourse Concerning the Mechanical Operation of the Spirit*. The first extends the *Tale's* satire on learning, the second on religious abuses.

In the years after 1704, Swift wrote a number of tracts on matters of religion and ecclesiastical politics. Of these, the "Argument Against Abolishing Christianity," has exceptional distinction as an ironic *tour de force*, subtle, inventive, slippery and playful, yet charged with an urgency of purpose and a sense of cherished values under threat.

During the period of Swift's early fame, 1710–14, Swift became a protégé of Harley and wrote many political tracts in support of his Tory ministry and of the controversial Peace of Utrecht. Harley put him in charge of the *Examiner*, for which he wrote some of his best brief polemical pieces, notably against the Duke of Marlborough, hero of the war against France. Of his other political writings in this period perhaps the most important is *The Conduct of the Allies*. Swift was one of the members of the Scriblerus club, a group of satirical wits associated with Harley (now Earl of Oxford), whose other regular members were Pope, Gay, Arbuthnot, and Thomas Parnell. The Club mostly met in 1714, and was effectively dispersed after Queen Anne's death in that year and the consequent collapse of the Tory administration. But the Club's activities not only resulted in the collectively composed *Memoirs of Martinus Scriblerus* (which Pope published much later, in 1741), but also influenced other writings by individual Scriblerians, including *Gulliver's Travels* (1726), and Pope's *Dunciad* (1728). In 1713, Swift became Dean of St. Patrick's Cathedral in Dublin, the highest preferment he could achieve in the Church. He regarded it as a blow to his hopes, and thought of his native Ireland as a place of exile.

After the Queen's death in 1714, he remained in Ireland for almost the whole of his life, and became actively involved in Irish political affairs. His Irish writings of the 1720's and (to a lesser degree) the 1730's earn him his honoured place as a defender of Ireland's rights. He was one of a series of great Anglo-Irishmen who fought to relieve Ireland's wrongs at the hands of the English oppressor: the list includes Charles Stewart Parnell and W. B. Yeats. The most important literary text among Swift's Irish writings is *A Modest Proposal*, an ironic pamphlet advocating the selling of Irish infants for food as a means of helping the economy. This *Proposal* is the climax of a whole series of tracts, which included *A Proposal for the Universal Use of Irish Manufacture*, the *Drapier's Letters*, and *A Short View of the State of Ireland*, in which the economic and political weaknesses of Ireland are bitterly exposed, and remedies suggested. The common view that these works are mainly or entirely anti-English is only partially true. It is becoming increasingly recognised that Swift was also concerned to expose the Irish for their failure to help themselves: their slavish temperament, economic fecklessness, commercial disreputability, the draining of the country's resources by absentee landlords. These criticisms underlie *A Modest Proposal*, which is more accurately read as a cry of exasperation against Irishmen of all classes and parties than as an attack on the English oppressor (although it is that too). Swift disliked the Irish while feeling called upon to defend their political rights. He thought of himself as English, accidentally "dropped" in Ireland by birth and kept there by an unhappy turn in his career. But he fought powerfully for Irish interests, achieved some practical successes (especially with the *Drapier's Letters*), and became and has remained a national hero.

Gulliver's Travels was published in 1726. It bears strong traces of Swift's involvement in

Irish affairs. But its reach is, of course, much wider. Like *A Tale of a Tub*, it has a framework of parody (in this case mainly of travel-books), but its principal satiric concerns, unlike those of the *Tale*, are not in themselves enshrined in the parody. Neither work deals merely with bad books, and both are concerned with a fundamental exploration of the nature of man. But in the *Tale*, the follies of unregulated intellect and impulse are directly expressed in the kind of book and the features of style which Swift mimics, whereas in *Gulliver's Travels* the travel-book format is mainly a convenient framework for a consideration of human nature which is only marginally concerned with the character of travel-writers.

In the first two books, an allegory of human pride begins to establish itself. The tiny Lilliputians of Book I are a minuscule and self-important replica of the society of England; the giants of Book II demonstrate that in the eyes of larger creatures we ourselves seem as ludicrous as the Lilliputians seem to us. The two Books have a complementary relationship which is forceful and clear: a neat balancing of narrative structures which supports and illustrates the basic satiric irony, and is able to accommodate a wide range of detailed satiric observation about English and European mores and institutions.

This exceptionally tidy structural arrangement gives way in the rest of the work to something more complex and less predictable. Book III takes us to a miscellany of strange lands, all of them inhabited by humans of normal size, and between them illustrating particular social and political institutions (repressive government, insane and inhumane scientific research projects, wild follies of intellect). If the schematic relationship between Books I and II is not continued, much of Book III adds to or develops the exposure of particular human characteristics and institutions which had begun in the earlier books. But towards the end of Book III a new note is struck. Gulliver visits the land of the Struldbruggs, who have the gift of immortality but without perpetual youth. The horror which these hideous creatures arouse as they decay into increasing senility is no longer primarily concerned with moral culpability. It is a portrayal of certain grim features of the human situation which are independent of good and evil.

In Book IV the satire becomes absolute, transcending all mere particularities of vice and folly of the kind encountered so far. The savage Yahoos have most of the vices and follies satirised earlier, but they embody a sense of the radical ugliness of the human animal, in his moral and his physical nature, which amounts (or so it seems to many readers) to a more fundamental disenchantment. The Houyhnhnms, the horse-shaped rulers of the humanoid Yahoos, are by contrast absolutely reasonable and virtuous, as the Yahoos are absolutely irrational and vicious. Swift said that he wished to disprove the traditional definition of man as a "rational animal," and he did so partly by enshrining an ideal rationality in a beast commonly named in philosophical discourse as an example of the non-rational animal: the horse. Swift's analysis has usually been considered a bleak and disturbing one, although some recent critics have held that Swift really believed that man both was and ought to be a creature who came somewhere between Yahoo and Houyhnhnm, a liberal and humane though fallible creature of the sort exemplified by the good Portuguese captain, who appears briefly near the end. This latter view seems to me misguided.

—C. J. Rawson

THACKERAY, William Makepeace. English. Born in Calcutta, India, 18 July 1811, of English parents; sent to England, 1817. Educated at schools in Hampshire, and Chiswick, London; Charterhouse, London, 1822–28; Trinity College, Cambridge, 1829–30, left without taking a degree; travelled abroad and visited Goethe at Weimar, 1830–31; entered Middle Temple, London, 1831, but soon abandoned legal studies. Married Isabella Shawe in 1836 (separated from her, when she went insane, 1842); three daughters. Purchased *The National Standard*, London, 1833, and became its editor until it failed, 1834; settled in Paris to study drawing, 1834–37: published satirical drawings, 1836; Paris Correspondent for *The Constitutional*, London, 1836–37; returned to England, 1837; thereafter a full-time writer; contributed to *The Times* and *Fraser's Magazine*; contributed articles and drawings to *Punch*, 1842–54; published an annual "Christmas Book," 1846–50; lectured on the "English Humourists," 1851, and lectured in America, 1852–53, 1855; stood for Parliament as Liberal candidate for Oxford, 1857; Editor, *Cornhill Magazine*, 1860–62. *Died 24 December 1863.*

PUBLICATIONS

Collections

Works, edited by George Saintsbury.   17 vols., 1908.
The Letters and Private Papers, edited by Gordon N. Ray.   4 vols., 1946.

Fiction

The Second Funeral of Napoleon, in Three Letters to Miss Smith of London, and The Chronicle of the Drum.   1841.
Jeames's Diary.   1846.
Mrs. Perkins's Ball.   1847.
Vanity Fair: A Novel Without a Hero.   1848; revised edition, 1853, 1863; edited by Geoffrey and Kathleen Tillotson, 1963.
The Great Hoggarty Diamond.   1848; as *The History of Samuel Titmarsh and the Great Hoggarty Diamond*, 1849.
Our Street.   1848.
The History of Pendennis: His Fortunes and Misfortunes, His Friends and His Greatest Enemy.   2 vols., 1849–50; revised edition, 1863; edited by Donald Hawes, 1972.
Doctor Birch and His Young Friends.   1849.
The Kickleburys on the Rhine.   1850.
Stubbs's Calendar; or, The Fatal Boots.   1850.
Rebecca and Rowena: A Romance upon Romance.   1850.
The History of Henry Esmond, Esq.   1852; revised edition, 1858; edited by Gordon N. Ray, 1950.
Men's Wives.   1852.
The Luck of Barry Lyndon: A Romance of the Last Century.   2 vols., 1852–53; revised edition, as *The Memoirs of Barry Lyndon, Esq.*, 1856; edited by Martin J. Anisman, 1970.
The Newcomes: Memoirs of a Most Respectable Family.   2 vols., 1854–55; revised edition, 1863.
The Rose and the Ring; or, The History of Prince Giglio and Prince Bulbo: A Fireside Pantomime for Great and Small Children.   1855; edited by Gordon N. Ray, 1947.
The Virginians: A Tale of the Last Century.   2 vols., 1858–59; revised edition, 1863; edited by George Saintsbury and J. L. Robinson, 1911.

Lovel the Widower.   1860; revised edition, 1861.
The Adventures of Philip on His Way Through the World.   1862.
Denis Duval.   1864.

Verse

The Loving Ballad of Lord Bateman.   1839.

Other

The Yellowplush Correspondence.   1838.
The Paris Sketch Book.   2 vols., 1840.
Comic Tales and Sketches.   2 vols., 1841.
The Irish Sketch Book.   2 vols., 1843.
Notes of a Journey from Cornhill to Grand Cairo, by Way of Lisbon, Athens, Constantinople, and Jerusalem, Performed in the Steamers of the Penninsular and Oriental Company.   1846.
The Book of Snobs.   1848; complete edition, 1852; edited by John Sutherland, 1978.
Miscellanies: Prose and Verse.   2 vols., 1849–51.
The Confessions of Fitz-Boodle, and Some Passages in the Life of Major Gahagan.   1852.
A Shabby Genteel Story and Other Tales.   1852.
Punch's Prize Novelists, The Fat Contributor, and Travels in London.   1853.
The English Humourists of the Eighteenth Century: A Series of Lectures.   1853; revised edition, 1853; edited by W. L. Phelps, 1900.
Miscellanies: Prose and Verse.   4 vols., 1855–57.
Christmas Books.   1857.
The Four Georges: Sketches of Manners, Morals, Court and Town Life.   1860.
Roundabout Papers.   1863; edited by J. E. Wells, 1925.
Early and Late Papers, edited by J. T. Fields.   1867.
Miscellanies, vol. 5.   1870.
The Students' Quarter; or, Paris Five and Thirty Years Since.   1874.
The Orphan of Pimlico and Other Sketches, Fragments, and Drawings.   1876.
Sultan Stork and Other Stories and Sketches (1829–1844), edited by R. H. Shepherd.   1887.
Reading a Poem.   1891.
Loose Sketches, An Eastern Adventure.   1894.
The Hitherto Unidentified Contributions to Punch, with a Complete Authoritative Bibliography from 1845 to 1848, edited by M. H. Spielmann.   1899.
Writings in the National Standard and the Constitutional, edited by W. T. Spencer.   1899.
Stray Papers, edited by Lewis Melville.   1901.
The New Sketch Book, Being Essays from the Foreign Quarterly Review, edited by R. S. Garnett.   1906.
Contributions to the Morning Chronicle, edited by Gordon N. Ray.   1955.

Bibliography: *A Thackeray Library* by Henry Sayre Van Duzer, 1919.

Reading List: *Thackeray: A Biography* by Lewis Melville, 2 vols., 1910; *Thackeray: A Critical Portrait* by J. W. Dodds, 1941; *Thackeray: A Reconsideration* by J. Y. T. Grieg, 1950; *Thackeray: The Sentimental Cynic* by L. Ennis, 1950; *Thackeray the Novelist* by

Geoffrey Tillotson, 1954; *Thackeray* by Gordon N. Ray, 2 vols., 1955–58; *Thackeray and the Form of Fiction* by J. Loofbourow, 1964; *Thackeray: A Collection of Critical Essays* edited by Alexander Welsh, 1968; *Thackeray: The Major Novels* by Juliet MacMaster, 1971; *The Exposure of Luxury: Radical Themes in Thackeray* by Barbara Hardy, 1972; *Thackeray at Work* by John Sutherland, 1974; *Thackeray: Prodigal Genius* by John Carey, 1977; *The Language of Thackeray* by K. C. Phillips, 1978.

* * *

One of the main problems which faces the critic of Thackeray is to determine exactly where the decline sets in, and how damaging that decline was. John Carey is most severe and locates the critical point at 1848, consigning all the mature novels into an inferior place. Carey relishes the savagely satirical early Thackeray of *Barry Lyndon* and *The Book of Snobs*. The post-*Vanity Fair* fiction represents a "disastrous collapse ... into gentlemanliness and cordiality." In Carey's diagnosis the calamities of Thackeray's youth were formative of his genius; separation from his mother, exclusion from his class as a ruined young man, and a tragic marriage may have been painful, but they were the making of a great writer. After *Vanity Fair* "he was destroyed by success." Whether or not this is true, Thackeray was certainly damaged severely in health after 1849 and not always capable of giving his best, even if he had been so disposed. Nonetheless most commentators would see the first three full-sized novels, *Vanity Fair*, *Pendennis*, and *Esmond*, as constituting a sustained major achievement. Gordon Ray's authoritative opinion as the official biographer is that it was only at this stage of his career that Thackeray developed a mature moral vision commensurate with the panoramic range of his fiction and the energy of his satire. *Esmond*, coming at the end of this brilliant five-year period, is also uniquely interesting in being the only major novel which Thackeray wrote entire before publication, appearing as it did in the traditional three volumes rather than as a serial in the magazines or in monthly thirty-two page numbers. The "three-decker" *Esmond* is arguably more carefully executed than Thackeray's other month-to-month writing. The last novels have their supporters, too, and some recent scholars seem inclined to value the whole of Thackeray's output – even the previously maligned *The Virginians* and *Philip* where Thackeray's art is at its most relaxed and loose-knit.

It helps to section Thackeray's career into manageable units. The early phase (1837–47) is rich, heterogeneous, and composed of short pieces of writing for the journals and relatively slim books. (Much of this writing was published in book form only years later.) Since the convention of nineteenth-century magazine writing imposed anonymity on contributors, Thackeray turned a handicap into advantage by cultivating a virtuosity in comic pseudonyms. (His favourite persona was the amiable Michael Angelo Titmarsh; others include Ikey Solomons, Mr. Snob, Our Fat Contributor, Yellowplush, Jeames de la Pluche.) "Writing for his life" meant doing whatever work would pay, for whatever journal would hire him – whether the grand *Edinburgh Review* or Colburn's sublimely snobbish *New Monthly Magazine*. The range of Thackeray's writing at this stage of his life is bewildering. It includes historical and sociological essays, reviewing, reportage (the magnificent "Going to See a Man Hanged," *Fraser's Magazine*, August 1840, should be cited), travel books, literary polemics (especially against Bulwer-Lytton), burlesques (notably the famous 1847 *Punch* parodies, later collected as *Novels by Eminent Hands*), novellas, and illustration work (Thackeray was actually considered as a potential illustrator for *Pickwick Papers*; much of his early work is self-illustrated as are the major novels *Vanity Fair*, *Pendennis*, and *The Virginians*).

Thackeray's versatility at this stage of his writing life is extraordinary. Up to 1847 and the decisive triumph of *Vanity Fair*, it would have been difficult to foresee precisely what career this brilliant man would succeed in – if indeed his restless and often bitter temperament would allow him to succeed in anything. With hindsight, however, we can see two substantial blocks of work in this first decade's writing. First is the material Thackeray contributed to *Fraser's Magazine*, which comprises the bulk of the early fiction. Although

Thackeray himself underrated or disavowed this work in later life it remains a major achievement in its own right. It is also clear that the tory-radical tone of *Fraser's* suited Thackeray the reviewer and essayist, and some of his best work of this kind was done in Fraser's columns. His involvement with *Fraser's* diminished in the early 1840's as his other great connection, with *Punch* (founded 1841), began. Thackeray was a staff writer for *Punch* for a number of years and the weekly journal furnished innumerable comic opportunities for his pen and pencil. In addition to myriad squibs (many of which are probably still unidentified) there are longer serial offerings, one of which, *The Snobs of England* (1846–47, later *The Book of Snobs*), stands out. The critique of "snobbery" (a term which Thackeray made current in its familiar sense) organises the often undisciplined hostilities of the younger Thackeray into a coherent analysis of English society. It leads naturally on to the novel whose opening numbers overlapped with *Snobs'* final chapters, *Vanity Fair*. Regrettably, however, *Snobs*, like all Thackeray's *Punch* work, is now more recondite than his *Fraser's* contributions by virtue of the topicality which weekly publication encouraged.

Vanity Fair deserves to be considered a transitional phase of Thackeray's career all by itself. It marks the turning point in his writing career, and possibly his personal life as well. *Vanity Fair* can be seen itself as a novel balanced between two views of life, embodied in the heroines – Becky all intelligence and no heart, Amelia all heart and no intelligence. Thackeray's supposed sympathies and antipathies for the personages in this novel have furnished rich critical debate. Nonetheless it is safe to say that with all its ambiguities this is his great achievement. In the omniscient manner that he was to make his own, Thackeray follows the fortunes of an intertwining group of characters over two decades, offering, in passing, a wonderfully solid panorama of early nineteenth-century England. (Like most mid-nineteenth-century novelists Thackeray preferred to antedate the action of his novels.) For the first time Thackeray indulges expansively in the famous "sermoning," stepping down, as he says, to speak with the reader confidentially. Yet the scenic and narrative responsibilities of the novelist are not evaded as, arguably, they are in some later novels.

After *Vanity Fair* Thackeray's novels conform to a characteristic pattern. All follow the career of a young man (more or less based on Thackeray himself) making his way through the world, gaining a wife and an education in life en route. Two settings predominate, early nineteenth century and eighteenth century. As an historical novelist Thackeray has affinities with Scott; his acquaintance with the eighteenth century was intimate and unforced. (At the time of his death his library was largely composed of volumes from the eighteenth century which he collected with a connoisseur's taste.) *Esmond*, *The Virginians*, *Denis Duval* and the two sets of lectures testify to his ambition, late in life, to write a history of Queen Anne's time. Unfortunately the only substantial realisation of this ambition was the house in Palace Green, Kensington, which was designed to his specification in the Queen Anne style, and to which he moved a year before his death.

It was denied to Thackeray to give up writing fiction; he needed the money too much. Bradbury and Evans paid him £60 a number for *Vanity Fair*, £100 a number for *Pendennis*, £200 a number for *The Newcomes*, and £250 for *The Virginians*. Even at these prices Thackeray was never really comfortably off, and he was facing something of a crisis in 1859, after Bradbury and Evans lost money on his American historical novel. At this stage the dynamic publisher George Smith (who had published *Esmond*, paying £1,200) re-entered Thackeray's professional life. He was made editor of the newly founded *Cornhill Magazine* at a princely salary, which made the last years of his life the most prosperous. Thackeray did not write top-rate fiction for Smith (though *Lovel the Widower* has recently found favour with the critics). On the other hand he did provide for the magazine the magnificent series of essays collected as *The Roundabout Papers*. These benign reflections on life are the best things of their kind Thackeray ever wrote.

—John Sutherland

TROLLOPE, Anthony.   English.   Born in London, 24 April 1815; son of the novelist Frances Trollope. Educated at Harrow School, 1822–25, 1831–33, and Winchester College, 1825–30. Married Rose Heseltine in 1844; two sons. Classical usher in a school in Brussels; joined the British Post Office, 1834: Surveyor's Clerk, later Deputy Surveyor, in Bangher, Clonmel, and Belfast, Northern Ireland, 1841–54; Chief Surveyor, Dublin, 1854–59; Chief Surveyor of the Eastern District, London, 1859–67: suggested the use of letter boxes; made official journeys to the West Indies, 1858, Egypt, 1858, and the United States, 1862; writer from 1843; one of the founders of the *Fortnightly Review*, 1865; Editor, *St. Paul's Magazine*, 1867–70; stood for Parliament as Liberal candidate for Beverley, 1868; travelled in Australia and New Zealand, 1871–72, and South Africa, 1878. *Died 6 December 1882.*

PUBLICATIONS

Collections

> *The Trollope Reader,* edited by Esther Cloudman Dunn and Marion E. Dodd.   1947.
> *Oxford Trollope,* edited by Michael Sadleir and Frederick Page.   15 vols., 1948–54.
> *Letters,* edited by Bradford A. Booth.   1951.

Fiction

> *The Macdermotts of Ballycloran.*   1847.
> *The Kellys and the O'Kellys; or, Landlords and Tenants: A Tale of Irish Life.*   1848.
> *La Vendée: A Historical Romance.*   1850.
> *The Warden.*   1855.
> *Barchester Towers.*   1857.
> *The Three Clerks.*   1858.
> *Doctor Thorne.*   1858.
> *The Bertrams.*   1859.
> *Castle Richmond.*   1860.
> *Framley Parsonage.*   1861.
> *Tales of All Countries.*   2 vols., 1861–63.
> *Orley Farm.*   2 vols., 1861–62.
> *The Struggles of Brown, Jones, and Robinson, by One of the Firm.*   1862.
> *Rachel Ray.*   1863.
> *The Small House at Allington.*   1864.
> *Can You Forgive Her?*   1864.
> *Miss Mackenzie.*   1865.
> *The Belton Estate.*   1866.
> *The Claverings.*   1867(?).
> *Nina Balatka.*   1867.
> *The Last Chronicle of Barset.*   1867; edited by Peter Fairclough, 1967.
> *Lotta Schmidt and Other Stories.*   1867.
> *Linda Tressel.*   1868.
> *Phineas Finn, The Irish Member.*   1869.
> *He Knew He Was Right.*   1869.
> *The Vicar of Bullhampton.*   1870.
> *An Editor's Tales.*   1870.
> *Sir Harry Hotspur of Humblethwaite.*   1870.
> *Mary Gresley.*   1871.

Ralph the Heir. 1871.
The Golden Lion of Granpère. 1872.
The Eustace Diamonds. 1872.
Lady Anna. 1873.
Phineas Redux. 1874.
Harry Heathcote of Gangoil: A Tale of Australian Bush Life. 1874.
The Way We Live Now. 1875.
The Prime Minister. 1876.
The American Senator. 1877.
Christmas at Thompson Hall. 1877; as *Thompson Hall,* 1885.
Is He Popenjoy? 1878.
How the Mastiffs Went to Iceland. 1878.
The Lady of Launay. 1878.
An Eye for an Eye. 1879.
John Caldigate. 1879.
Cousin Henry. 1879.
The Duke's Children. 1880.
Dr. Wortle's School. 1881.
Ayala's Angel. 1881.
Why Frau Frohmann Raised Her Prices and Other Stories. 1881.
The Fixed Period. 1882.
Marion Fay. 1882.
Kept in the Dark. 1882.
Not If I Know It. 1883.
The Two Heroines of Plumplington. 1882.
Mr. Scarborough's Family. 1883.
The Landleaguers. 1883.
An Old Man's Love. 1884.

Plays

Did He Steal It? 1869; edited by R. H. Taylor, 1952.
The Noble Jilt, edited by Michael Sadleir. 1923.

Other

The West Indies and the Spanish Main. 1859.
North America. 2 vols., 1862; edited by Robert Mason, 1968.
Hunting Sketches. 1865.
Travelling Sketches. 1866.
Clergymen of the Church of England. 1866.
The Commentaries of Caesar. 1870.
Australia and New Zealand. 2 vols., 1873; *Australia* edited by P. D. Edwards and R.
   B. Joyce, 1967.
Iceland. 1878.
South Africa. 2 vols., 1878; revised abridgement, 1879.
Thackeray. 1879.
The Life of Cicero. 2 vols., 1880.
Lord Palmerston. 1882.
An Autobiography, edited by H. M. Trollope. 2 vols., 1883; edited by Michael Sadleir,
   1947.
London Tradesmen, edited by Michael Sadleir. 1927.

Four Lectures, edited by Morris L. Parrish. 1938.
The Tireless Traveller: Twenty Letters to the Liverpool Mercury, 1875, edited by Bradford A. Booth. 1941.
The New Zealander, edited by N. John Hall. 1972.

Editor, *British Sports and Pastimes.* 1868.

Bibliography: *Trollope: A Bibliography* by Michael Sadleir, 1928, revised edition, 1934.

Reading List: *Trollope: A Commentary* by Michael Sadleir, 1927, revised edition, 1945; *Trollope* by B. C. Brown, 1950; *Trollope: A Critical Study* by A. O. J. Cockshut, 1955; *Trollope: Aspects of His Life and Work* by Bradford A. Booth, 1958; *The Changing World of Trollope* by Robert M. Pohlemus, 1968; *Trollope's Political Novels,* 1968, and *Trollope,* 1978, both by Arthur Pollard; *Trollope: The Critical Heritage* edited by Donald Smalley, 1969; *A Guide to Trollope* by Winifred and James Gerould, 1975; *Trollope: His Life and Art* by C. P. Snow, 1975; *The Novels of Trollope* by James R. Kincaid, 1977; *Trollope's Later Novels* by Robert Tracy, 1978.

*   *   *

Anthony Trollope was the most prolific of the great Victorian novelists. He produced 47 novels, more than any of his major contemporaries. The system behind Trollope's unremitting industry was revealed in his *Autobiography,* where he attributed his success to getting up early and writing by the clock; he aimed to do three hours work before breakfast, composing 250 words every quarter an hour. The *Autobiography* also tots up Trollope's literary earnings which then amounted to nearly £70,000; at his peak he could command £3,000 for a three volume work. He describes this total as "comfortable, but not splendid." The early hours were necessary because for the first 24 years of his writing life he was also an official of the General Post Office in which he rose from scruffy beginnings to a high position. His extensive journeys on business were turned to authorial advantage: he continued to write on board ship and even in trains. Trollope's travel books, short stories, journalism, and other non-fictional work filled out a life of intense activity. The solidity and wide range of Trollope's fiction partly rests on the thorough knowledge of the world thus gained. Trollope also had before him the example of his mother, who had made herself into a best-selling author after the bankruptcy of his father; his brother T. A. Trollope also became a well-known writer.

Although reticent about such matters as his marriage and a near-fatal illness, the *Autobiography* is generally notable for its candour, and Trollope would probably have felt it dishonest to suppress any account of the methods by which his staggering output was kept up. For those who take a romantic view of authorship, Trollope's insistence that writing novels is a trade like any other – shoe-making, for instance – will seem philistine. How can genuine art be combined with clock-watching? How can a writer who finishes one book only to start immediately on the next (as Trollope often did) be inspired or even serious? Trollope's industry might be excused on the grounds that he was simply writing for the market; he was certainly lucky in that a market for his kind of fiction was readily available. Even though three-volume novels were expensive, the circulating libraries spread the reputation and ensured the sales of authors who were prepared to work within mid-Victorian conventions and restraints, as Trollope largely was (although in one novel, *The Vicar of Bullhampton,* he did take a fallen woman as his subject). But the market was clearly not Trollope's only consideration; if it had been, he would not have glutted it so recklessly by over-production. In reality, his apparently effortless production was made possible by the incessant, even addictive activity of his imagination. Trollope was able to write so much so quickly because of the intense vitality of the people in his mind.

The origins of this fantasy-life lay in Trollope's unhappy youth. He had been miserable at both the schools he went to (Winchester and Harrow); his family hovered between gentility and destitution; he was separated for long periods from his mother and left with an increasingly unbalanced father. When he got a clerkship in the General Post Office he had to make his own way in London with little moral or economic support. For ten years he kept a journal (later destroyed) which taught him facility of expression, but more important for the future novelist was his habit of making up stories for himself. Although daydreams, these narratives were nevertheless bound by the laws of probability – "nothing impossible was ever introduced" – and were carried on for months and even years at a time. In this way Trollope learned "to dwell on a work created by my own imagination, and to live in a world altogether outside the world of my own material life."

When Trollope wrote about other novelists his main concern is the extent to which they knew their own personages; for him, fiction meant living with his characters "in the full reality of established intimacy." They should be with the author "as he lies down to sleep, and as he wakes from his dreams." At the same time, these imaginary creations must not be exempted from the conditions of ordinary life: "on the last day of each month recorded, every person in his novel should be a month older than on the first."

With these criteria in mind, it is easy to see why Trollope's greatest achievements as a novelist depend on the completeness with which his characters are understood, an understanding which includes the ways in which their innate qualities are affected by the passage of time. A natural result of this was his unprecedented development of the novel series. His two sequences of inter-connected novels – the Barchester novels and the Palliser series – occupied him intermittently for twenty-four years of his writing life. *The Warden*, the first of the Barchester books, was actually the fourth Trollope wrote, following two Irish novels and a historical romance. It was topical, satirical, and some of the original reviewers thought it "clever." Its successor, *Barchester Towers*, develops Trollope's command of social comedy, while the next in the sequence, *Doctor Thorne*, finds Trollope grappling with a plot given him by his brother (elaborate plots were not favoured by Trollope since they brought excitement at the cost of truth to life). These novels have always been popular, but the later books in the series show an increasingly masterly command of character in action, which is not the less revealing for being precipitated by conventional dilemmas, mostly concerning love and marriage, but often involving the over-riding difficulty of how to make one's way in the world successfully but honestly. Throughout Trollope's work, characters show an almost obsessive concern with their own integrity, a concern equally apparent in their love-lives and in their professional struggles. It is in *Framley Parsonage*, *The Small House at Allington* and *The Last Chronicle of Barset*, too, that Trollope begins to reap the full advantage of his characters' reappearance. Mr. Crawley, who enters in the first of these, is developed in *The Last Chronicle* into a figure of near-tragic power. It is typical of the realism of Trollope's method that his superbly conveyed anguish is caused by something as trivial as a mislaid cheque for £20 which he is accused of stealing. Mr. Crawley does not go exactly mad, but neither is he always quite sane; he is the most striking of a number of characters in Trollope's work (Louis Trevelyan in *He Knew He Was Right* is another) whose instability is analysed with an unflustered empathy quite remarkable for its period.

The last two Barchester novels are also linked by the story of Lily Dale, jilted in the first of them, and unable even in the second to console herself with the faithful admiration of John Eames. It is a tribute to Trollope's ability to create people that seemed real that for the rest of his life he continued to get letters begging him to unite the couple at last – although, as Trollope himself pointed out, it is precisely because Lily can't get over her troubles that she is endearing. Eames's experiences as a civil servant have been said to reflect Trollope's own, but the character is not given privileged treatment or portrayed with particular intensity (as, say, the autobiographical characters of David Copperfield and Maggie Tulliver are by Dickens and George Eliot). Trollope's innate modesty did not allow him to think of himself as someone special.

This does not mean that he lacked self-assertion – he was noted in life for his bluster – or ambition. He nursed for a long time an "almost insane" desire to get into Parliament; at the age of 53 he unsuccessfully contested Beverley in Yorkshire as a Liberal. His longing to sit in the House of Commons was frustrated to good literary effect, since it resulted in the Palliser series. Trollope's interest, however, is much more in the behaviour of men in political life (and in the women who influence them) than in political ideas. There is virtually no propaganda in Trollope's as there is in Disraeli's fiction, which Trollope scorned. The two public careers that Trollope follows most closely are those of a young Irish member, Phineas Finn, whose means are slender and who depends on getting office, and Plantagenet Palliser, heir to the immense wealth of the Duke of Omnium whom he later succeeds. Plantagenet's acute sense of public responsibility leads him, in *The Prime Minister*, to head a coalition government – a task which calls for just that gift for personal relationships which, for all his genuine nobility, he lacks (and which his wife possesses so abundantly). The novel provides what is perhaps Trollope's most searching study of the interaction of private temperament and public pressure. Palliser was partly designed by Trollope as the type of the English gentleman but, though he is never less than that, his behaviour towards his wife and children, as presented in *Can You Forgive Her?* and *The Duke's Children*, is shown with a subtle understanding of the contradictions in his personality which far outruns any merely didactic intention. Palliser's rectitude and vulnerability are constantly exposed to the volatile and reckless spontaneities of his wife, Lady Glencora. They irritate each other because their personalities are so different, but they also need each other for the same reason. Their marriage, as chronicled through the whole sequence of novels, is deeply established in Trollope's imagination, so that he finds it easy, in many of its critical passages, simply to transcribe the characters' own words, rather than intervene and analyse as the theoretically all-seeing author. Trollope's personal intrusions in his own books are far from being a full guide to his characters' natures and how we should think about them; in his best work, it is the dialogue, the dramatisation, that reveals most fully the life that his books contain. Trollope rightly regarded the string of characters that run through the Palliser novels as the best work he ever did; certainly the Palliser marriage is studied with an intimacy of understanding and a lack of pretension that perhaps no other novelist of his period can match.

Part of its reality comes from the densely populated social world which Trollope accumulates round it. The great length of many of his novels allowed Trollope plenty of room in which to run several stories concurrently. The connections between these narratives are sometimes tenuous, and modern critical attempts to show that they all relate to some abstract theme or master-idea have often seemed implausible. What has attracted readers, both in his own time and subsequently, has rather been Trollope's inexhaustible interest in and capacity to register familiar fact and daily habit. Trollope knew that no-one is unimportant to himself; he treats his characters with the respect that is their due. As Henry James put it, in what is perhaps still the best essay yet written on Trollope (in *Partial Portraits*, 1888), "His great, his inestimable merit was his complete appreciation of the usual." What might be added to this generous tribute is the proviso that for Trollope "the usual" was an extraordinarily hospitable category. Trollope lived with his characters on their terms rather than on his, and as a result his fictional world has a far wider range of temperament and variety of personality than the conventional format of his novels might lead one to suppose.

—Stephen Wall

WALPOLE, Horace (or Horatio); 4th Earl of Orford. English. Born in London, 24 September 1717; son of the politician Sir Robert Walpole. Educated at Eton College, 1727–34; King's College, Cambridge, 1735–39, left without taking a degree. Travelled in France and Italy, with the poet Thomas Gray, 1739–41, then returned to England and settled in London; Member of Parliament for Callington, Cornwall, 1741–53, Castle Rising, Norfolk, 1754–57, and King's Lynn, Norfolk, 1757–67; purchased an estate at Twickenham, Middlesex, 1747, which he subsequently named Strawberry Hill and gradually gothicized, 1753–76; established a printing press at Strawberry Hill, on which he printed his own works and those of other authors, 1757–89; visited Paris, 1765, 1767, 1775; succeeded to the earldom of Orford, 1791. *Died 2 March 1797.*

PUBLICATIONS

Collections

> *Works,* edited by Mary Berry and others. 9 vols., 1798–1825.
> *Letters,* edited by Mrs. Paget Toynbee. 16 vols., 1903–05; supplement edited by Paget Toynbee, 3 vols., 1918–25.
> *Fugitive Verses,* edited by W. S. Lewis. 1931.
> *Correspondence,* edited by W. S. Lewis and others. 1937 –

Fiction

> *The Castle of Otranto.* 1765; edited by W. S. Lewis, 1964.
> *Hieroglyphic Tales.* 1785.

Plays

> *The Mysterious Mother.* 1768; edited by Montague Summers, with *The Castle of Otranto,* 1924.
> *Nature Will Prevail* (produced 1778). In *Works,* 1798.
> *The Fashionable Friends* (produced 1802). 1802.

Other

> *The Lesson for the Day.* 1742.
> *The Beauties.* 1746.
> *Epilogue to Tamerlane.* 1746.
> *Aedes Walpolianae.* 1747; revised edition, 1752.
> *A Letter from Xo Ho.* 1757.
> *Fugitive Pieces in Verse and Prose.* 1758; augmented edition, 1770.
> *A Catalogue of the Royal and Noble Authors of England, Scotland, and Ireland.* 2 vols., 1758; *Postscript,* 1786.
> *A Dialogue Between Two Great Ladies.* 1760.
> *Catalogue of the Pictures and Drawings in the Holbein Chamber.* 1760.
> *Catalogue of the Pictures of the Duke of Devonshire.* 1760.
> *Anecdotes of Painting in England, and A Catalogue of Engravers* (based on material collected by G. Vertue). 4 vols., 1762–63; additional vol. of *Anecdotes,* 1780;

additional vol. of *Anecdotes* edited by F. W. Hilles and P. B. Daghlian, 1937.
The Magpie and Her Brood. 1764.
An Account of the Giants Lately Discovered. 1766.
Historic Doubts on Richard III. 1768; edited by P. M. Kendall, 1965.
A Description of the Villa of Horace Walpole. 1774.
Essay on Modern Gardening. 1785; edited by W. S. Lewis, 1931.
Notes to the Portraits at Woburn Abbey. 1800.
Reminiscences Written for Mary and Agnes Berry. 1805; edited by Paget Toynbee, 1924.
Memoirs of the Last Ten Years of the Reign of George II, edited by Lord Holland. 2 vols., 1822.
Memoirs of George III, edited by Denis Le Marchant. 4 vols., 1845; edited by G. F. R. Barker, 1894.
Journal of George III, edited by J. Doran. 2 vols., 1859; as *Last Journals,* edited by A. Francis Steuart, 1910.
Manuscript Common-Place Book, edited by W. S. Lewis. 1927.
Memoirs and Portraits (selection), edited by Matthew Hodgart. 1963; revised edition, 1963.
Miscellany 1786–1795, edited by Lars E. Troide. 1978.

Editor, *The Life of Lord Herbert of Cherbury Written by Himself.* 1765.

Bibliography: *A Bibliography of Walpole* by Allen T. Hazen, 1948.

Reading List: *The Life of Walpole* by Stephen Gwynn, 1932; *Walpole and the English Novel* by K. K. Mehrota, 1934; *Walpole* by R. W. Ketton-Cremer, 1940; *Walpole's Memoirs* by Gerrit P. Judd, 1959; *Walpole* by W. S. Lewis, 1961; "Walpole" by Bonamy Dobrée, in *Restoration and Eighteenth Century Literature: Essays in Honor of A. D. McKillop* edited by Carroll Camden, 1963; *Walpole: Writer, Politician, and Connoisseur: Essays* edited by Warren H. Smith, 1968; *Walpole* by Martin Kallich, 1971.

*   *   *

Horace Walpole is significant for his contributions to history, literature, and art. His literary reputation rests principally on his letters (about 6000 in the correspondence, 4000 by Walpole himself) in which he vividly chronicles his times. On his continental tour he had initiated his friendship with Sir Horace Mann with whom, for example, he corresponded regularly for nearly fifty years. In a visit to Paris, 1765, he met Madame du Deffand whose friendship was confirmed in an extensive correspondence till her death in 1780. Other correspondents were William Mason, the poet and biographer of Gray; William Cole, the antiquary; and, among many others, George Montagu, his friend at Eton.

At Eton Walpole had made many lasting friends, among them the politician Henry Seymour Conway and the poet Thomas Gray. Gray accompanied Walpole on his tour, and his early poems were first published at Walpole's press at Strawberry Hill. At King's College, Cambridge, Walpole came under the influence of Conyers Middleton, whose deistic rationalism he adopted and maintained throughout his life. Walpole's "Verses in Memory of Henry VI, the Founder of King's College, Cambridge" praises the Gothic college chapel, providing evidence of a very early esthetic commitment to the Gothic architectural style. In his verse "Epistle to Ashton," Walpole emphasizes his distaste for religious bigotry and fanaticism.

In addition to his letters, Walpole also kept numerous journals in which he presented his well-informed views on the politics of the reigns of George II and George III for forty years, 1751–1791. With Burke and Conway, Walpole opposed the war against the American colonies; and, later, he believed Burke was right to oppose the egalitarian ideals of the French Revolution. In the realm of art, Walpole was a taste-maker with his innovative transformation of his country estate into the celebrated Gothic restoration at Strawberry Hill. His *Anecdotes of Painting* is a standard source of information about English art before 1750.

In his two most important literary works, the novel *The Castle of Otranto* and the tragedy *The Mysterious Mother*, Walpole exploited the possibility of violence and the supernatural in the medieval milieu, thereby setting the taste for the Gothic in narrative and drama. The chief feature of this romantic literature is terror, terror effected by the atmospheric gloom of a forbidding castle and all its appurtenances calculated to produce sensation, chilling and thrilling: skeletons and haunting ghosts in secret rooms, trap doors with creaking hinges, dark corridors, threats of violence, pursuit of a lovely damsel in distress by a satanic and lustful villain, and the like. In the novel the tyrannical villain is inexplicably motivated to sadistic cruelty, thereby creating the suspense that inevitably explodes in a catastrophic climax. In his play, Walpole evokes terror through an artful priest and horror by grounding the action upon incest, which turns out to be the mysterious sin haunting the gloomy castle.

Ironically, Walpole's esthetic medievalism resulted in the tarnishing of his reputation. For when Chatterton attempted in 1769 to make the author of *Otranto* and the builder of Strawberry Hill his patron, only to be rejected, Walpole was blamed for his untimely death as an apparent suicide. In view of what is known of Walpole's generous character, his reputation as a cold and heartless aristocrat is undeserved.

—Martin Kallich

WARD, Mrs. Humphry (née Mary Augusta Arnold).   English. Born in Hobart, Tasmania, 11 June 1851, of English parents; grand-daughter of Dr. Arnold of Rugby, and niece of the poet Matthew Arnold; returned to England with her family, 1856. Educated in English boarding schools, 1858–67. Married Thomas Humphry Ward in 1872; one son and two daughters. Settled in Oxford with her family, 1867, and continued her studies on her own; contributed to the *Dictionary of Christian Biography*, 1877; Secretary to Somerville College, Oxford, 1879; moved to London, 1881; contributed to *The Times, Pall Mall Gazette*, and *Macmillan's Magazine*; founded a social settlement at University Hall, Gordon Square, 1890, which developed into the Passmore Edwards Settlement, 1897; Founder, Women's National Anti-Suffrage League, 1908; appointed one of the first 7 women magistrates, 1920. LL.D.: University of Edinburgh. *Died 24 March 1920.*

PUBLICATIONS

Fiction

  Milly and Olly; or, A Holiday among the Mountains (juvenile).   1881.
  Miss Bretherton.   1884.
  Robert Elsmere.   1888.
  The History of David Grieve.   1892.
  Marcella.   1894.
  The Story of Bessie Costrell.   1895.

Sir George Tressady. 1896.
Helbeck of Bannisdale. 1898.
Eleanor. 1900.
Lady Rose's Daughter. 1903.
The Marriage of William Ashe. 1905.
Fenwick's Career. 1906.
Diana Mallory. 1908.
Daphne; or, Marriage à la Mode. 1909.
Canadian Born. 1910.
The Case of Richard Meynell. 1911.
The Mating of Lydia. 1913.
The Coryston Family. 1913.
Delia Blanchflower. 1915.
Eltham House. 1915.
A Great Success. 1916.
Lady Connie. 1916.
Missing. 1917.
Cousin Philip. 1919.
Harvest. 1920; as *Love's Harvest,* 1929.

Plays

Eleanor, from her own novel (produced 1902). 1903; (revised version produced 1905).
Agatha, with L. N. Parker, from the novel *Lady Rose's Daughter* by Mrs. Ward (produced 1905). 1904.
The Marriage of William Ashe, with Margaret Mayo, from the novel by Mrs. Ward (produced 1908).

Other

The Play-Time of the Poor. 1906.
William Thomas Arnold, Journalist and Historian, with C. E. Montague. 1907.
Letters to My Neighbours on the Present Election. 1910; revised edition, 1910.
Writings. 16 vols., 1911–12.
England's Effort: Six Letters to an American Friend. 1916.
Towards the Goal. 1917.
A Writer's Recollections. 1918.
The War and Elizabeth. 1918.
Fields of Victory. 1919.

Translator, *Amiel's Journal.* 2 vols., 1885.

Reading List: *The Life of Mrs. Ward* by Janet P. Trevelyan, 1923; "Mrs. Ward and the Victorian Ideal" by C. Lederer, in *Nineteenth-Century Fiction 6,* 1951; *Mrs. Ward* by Enid Huws Jones, 1973.

*   *   *

Mrs. Humphry Ward was the granddaughter of Thomas Arnold and the niece of Matthew Arnold, and she displays in her novels the moral earnestness of both her grandfather and her uncle. Her own father, Thomas Arnold, Jr., whose flirtation with Roman Catholicism was an embarrassment to his family, may have influenced her in portraying many of her heroes as men tormented by indecision and religious doubt. The most notable hero of this kind is Robert Elsmere. His struggle to resist the intellectual pressure to abandon orthodoxy in favour of humanitarian secular religion, very much on the same lines as that preached by Matthew Arnold, was recorded in *Robert Elsmere*, an instant best-seller. *Robert Elsmere* is less impressive as a novel than as a record of religious doubt, although the predicament of Robert Elsmere's wife, Catherine, who appears in a sequel, *The Case of Richard Meynell*, is outlined with great sensitivity. On the other hand a sub-plot involving a love affair between Catherine's sister Rose and a dreary Oxford don, Langham, is a distinctly lightweight affair. Sub-plots are also an irritation in *The History of David Grieve*, the record of a working man's struggle to rise in the world while abandoning the support of orthodox religion. *Helbeck of Bannisdale* is considered by many as Mrs. Ward's best novel, in that the love affair between the sceptical Laura Fountain and the devout Catholic, Alan Helbeck, is an integral part of the novel's religious investigation.

Mrs. Ward's later novels are more concerned with social than religious issues. *Marcella*, *Sir George Tressady*, and *Lady Rose's Daughter* were all concerned with the need to do something for the poor, a cause in which Mrs. Ward herself laboured strongly, although she resisted any radical solution, just as she was opposed to the Suffragette movement. The anti-suffragette novels, *Delia Blanchflower* and *Cousin Philip*, like the novels in favour of social reform, are marred by too much propaganda in favour of or against a cause, long since won and lost, but in spite of this propaganda element Mrs. Humphry Ward deserves more credit than she now receives.

—T. J. Winnifrith

YONGE, Charlotte (Mary).   English.   Born in Otterbourne, Hampshire, 13 August 1823, and lived there for the rest of her life. Writer from 1837; Editor, 1851–90, and Assistant Editor, 1891–95, *The Monthly Packet*; Editor, *The Monthly Paper of Sunday Teaching*, 1860–75, and *Mothers in Council*, 1890–1900. *Died 24 March 1901.*

PUBLICATIONS

Fiction

> *Le Château de Melville: ou, Récreations du Cabinet d'Etude.*   1838.
> *Abbey Church; or, Self-Control and Self-Conceit.*   1844.
> *Scenes and Characters; or, Eighteen Months at Beechcroft.*   1847; as *Beechcroft*, 1871.
> *Henrietta's Wish; or, Domineering.*   1850.
> *Kenneth; or, The Rear Guard of the Grand Army.*   1850.
> *Langley School.*   1850.
> *The Two Guardians; or, Home in This World.*   1852.
> *The Heir of Redclyffe.*   1853.
> *The Herb of the Field.*   1853.
> *The Castle Builders; or, The Deferred Confirmation.*   1854.
> *Heartsease; or, The Brother's Wife.*   1854.

The Little Duke; or, Richard the Fearless.   1854; as *Richard the Fearless,* 1856.
The History of Sir Thomas Thumb.   1855.
The Lances of Lynwood.   1855.
The Railroad Children.   1855.
Ben Sylvester's Word.   1856.
The Daisy Chain; or, Aspirations: A Family Chronicle.   1856.
Harriet and Her Sister.   1856.
Leonard the Lion-Heart.   1856.
Dynevor Terrace; or, The Clue of Life.   1857.
The Christmas Mummers.   1858.
Friarswood Post Office.   1860.
Hopes and Fears; or, Scenes from the Life of a Spinster.   1860.
The Mice at Play.   1860.
The Strayed Falcon.   1860.
The Pigeon Pie.   1860.
The Stokesley Secret.   1861.
The Young Stepmother; or, A Chronicle of Mistakes.   1861.
Countess Kate.   1862.
Sea Spleenwort and Other Stories.   1862.
Last Heartsease Leaves.   1862 (?).
The Trial: More Links of the Daisy Chain.   1864.
The Wars of Wapsburgh.   1864.
The Clever Woman of the Family.   1865.
The Dove in the Eagle's Nest.   1866.
The Prince and the Page: A Story of the Last Crusade.   1866.
The Danvers Papers: An Invention.   1867.
The Six Cushions.   1867.
The Chaplet of Pearls; or, The White and Black Ribaumont.   1868.
Kaffir Land; or, New Ground.   1868.
The Caged Lion.   1870.
Little Lucy's Wonderful Globe.   1871.
P's and Q's; or, The Question of Putting Upon.   1872.
The Pillars of the House; or, Under Wode, Under Rode.   1873.
Lady Hester; or, Ursula's Narrative.   1874.
My Young Alcides: A Faded Photograph.   1875.
The Three Brides.   1876.
The Disturbing Element; or, Chronicles of the Blue-Bell Society.   1878.
Burnt Out: A Story for Mothers' Meetings.   1879.
Magnus Bonum; or, Mother Carey's Brood.   1879.
Bye-Words: A Collection of Tales New and Old.   1880.
Love and Life: An Old Story in Eighteenth-Century Costume.   1880.
Mary and Norah; or, Queen Katharine's School, with *Nelly and Margaret.*   1880(?).
Cheap Jack.   1881.
Frank's Debt.   1881.
Lads and Lasses of Langley.   1881.
Wolf.   1881.
Given to Hospitality.   1882.
Langley Little Ones: Six Stories.   1882.
Pickle and His Page Boy; or, Unlooked For.   1882.
Sowing and Sewing: A Sexagesima Story.   1882.
Unknown to History: A Story of the Captivity of Mary of Scotland.   1882.
Stray Pearls: Memoirs of Margaret de Ribaumont, Viscountess of Bellaise.   1883.
Langley Adventures.   1884.
The Armourer's 'Prentices.   1884.

Nuttie's Father.   1885.
The Two Sides of the Shield.   1885.
Astray: A Tale of a Country Town, with others.   1886.
Chantry House.   1886.
The Little Rick-Burners.   1886.
A Modern Telemachus.   1886.
Under the Storm; or, Steadfast's Charge.   1887.
Beechcroft at Rockstone.   1888.
Nurse's Memories.   1888.
Our New Mistress; or, Changes at Brookfield Earl.   1888.
The Cunning Woman's Grandson: A Tale of Cheddar a Hundred Years Ago.   1889.
A Reputed Changeling; or, Three Seventh Years Two Centuries Ago.   1889.
The Slaves of Sabinus: Jew and Gentile.   1890.
More Bywords (stories and poems).   1890.
The Constable's Tower; or, The Times of Magna Carta.   1891.
Two Penniless Princesses.   1891.
The Cross Roads; or, A Choice in Life.   1892.
That Stick.   1892.
Grisly Grisell; or, The Laidly Lady of Whitburn: A Tale of the Wars of the Roses.   1893.
Strolling Players: A Harmony of Contrasts, with Christabel Coleridge.   1893.
The Treasures in the Marshes.   1893.
The Cook and the Captive; or, Attalus the Hostage.   1894.
The Rubies of St. Lô.   1894.
The Carbonels.   1895.
The Long Vacation.   1895.
The Release; or, Caroline's French Kindred.   1896.
The Wardship of Steepcombe.   1896.
The Pilgrimage of the Ben Beriah.   1897.
Founded on Paper; or, Uphill and Downhill Between the Two Jubilees.   1897.
The Patriots of Palestine: A Story of the Maccabees.   1898.
Scenes from "Kenneth."   1899.
The Herd Boy and His Hermit.   1899.
The Making of a Missionary; or, Daydreams in Earnest.   1900.
Modern Broods; or, Developments Unlooked For.   1900.

Plays

The Apple of Discord.   1864.
Historical Dramas.   1864.

Verse

Verses on the Gospel for Sundays and Holidays.   1880.

Other

Kings of England: A History for Young Children.   1848.
Landmarks of History.   3 vols., 1852–57.
The Instructive Picture Book; or, Lessons from the Vegetable World.   1857.
The Chosen People: A Compendium of Sacred and Church History for School Children.   1861.

A History of Christian Names. 1863; revised edition, 1884.
A Book of Golden Deeds of All Times and All Lands. 1864.
Cameos from English History. 9 vols., 1868–99.
The Pupils of St. John the Divine. 1868.
A Book of Worthies, Gathered from the Old Histories and Now Written Out Anew. 1869.
Keynotes of the First Lessons for Every Day in the Year. 1869.
Musings over the "Christian Year" and "Lyra Innocentium." 1871.
A Parallel History of France and England. 1871.
Pioneers and Founders; or, Recent Works in the Mission Field. 1871.
Scripture Readings for Schools, with Comments. 5 vols., 1871–79.
Questions on the Prayer-Book [Collects, Epistles, Gospels, Psalms]. 5 vols., 1872–81.
In Memoriam Bishop Patteson. 1872.
Aunt Charlotte's Stories of English [French, Bible, Greek, German, Roman] History for the Little One. 6 vols., 1873–77; as *Young Folks' History,* 6 vols., 1878–80.
Life of John Coleridge Patteson, Missionary Bishop to the Melanesian Islands. 2 vols., 1874.
Hints on the Religious Education of Children of the Wealthier Classes. N.d.
Womankind. 1875.
Eighteen Centuries of Beginnings of Church History. 1876.
The Story of the Christians and the Moors in Spain. 1878.
Short English Grammar for Use in Schools. 1879.
Aunt Charlotte's Evenings at Home with the Poets. 1880.
How to Teach the New Testament. 1881.
Practical Work in Sunday Schools. 1881.
English History Reading Books. 6 vols., 1881–83; as *Westminster Historical Reading Books,* 6 vols., 1891–92.
Talks about the Laws We Live Under; or, At Langley Night-School. 1882.
A Pictorial History of the World's Great Nations. 1882.
Aunt Charlotte's Stories of American History, with J. H. Hastings Weld. 1883.
English Church History. 1883.
Landmarks of Recent History 1770–1883. 1883.
The Daisy Chain Birthday Book, edited by Eadgyth. 1884.
A Key to the Waverley Novels, vol. 1. 1885.
Teachings on the Catechism: For the Little Ones. 1886.
The Victorian Half-Century: A Jubilee Book. 1886.
What Books to Lend and What to Give. 1887.
Hannah More (biography). 1888.
Preparation of Prayer-Book Lessons. 1888.
Conversations on the Prayer Book. 1888.
Deacon's Book of Dates: A Manual of the World's Chief Historical Landmarks and an Outline of Universal History. 1888.
Life of H.R.H. the Prince Consort. 1890.
Seven Heroines of Christendom. 1891.
Simple Stories Relating to English History. 1891.
Twelve Stories from Early English History. 1891.
Twenty Stories and Biographies from 1066 to 1485. 1891.
Old Times at Otterbourne. 1891.
An Old Woman's Outlook in a Hampshire Village. 1892.
The Hanoverian [Tudor, Stuart] Period, with Biographies of Leading Persons. 3 vols., 1892.
Chimes for Mothers: A Reading for Each Week in the Year. 1893.
The Girl's Little Book. 1893.
The Story of Easter. 1894.
John Keble's Parishes: A History of Hursley and Otterbourne. 1898.

Reasons Why I Am a Catholic and Not a Roman Catholic.   1901.

Editor, *Biographies of Good Women.*   2 vols., 1862–65.
Editor, *Readings from Standard Authors.*   1864.
Editor, with E. Sewell, *Historical Selections: A Series of Readings in English and European History.*   2 vols., 1868–70; as *European History*, 2 vols., 1872–73.
Editor, *A Storehouse of Stories.*   2 vols., 1870–72.
Editor, *Beneath the Cross: Readings for Children in Our Lord's Seven Sayings.*   1881.
Editor, *Historical Ballads.*   3 vols., 1882–83.
Editor, *Shakespeare's Plays for Schools, Abridged and Annotated.*   1883.
Editor, *Higher Reading Book for Schools, Colleges and General Use.*   1885.
Editor, *Chips from the Royal Image Being Fragments of the "Eikon Basilike" of Charles I*, by A. E. M. Anderson Morshead.   1887.

Translator, *Marie Thérèse de Lamourous, Foundress of the House of La Miséricorde at Bordeaux*, by Abbé Pouget.   1858.
Translator, *Two Years of School Life*, by Elise de Pressensé.   1869.
Translator, *The Population of an Old Pear Tree; or, Stories of Insect Life*, by E. van Bruyssel.   1870.
Translator, *Life and Adventures of Count Beugnot, Minister of State under Napoleon I*, by Count H. d'Ideville.   1871.
Translator, *Dames of High Estate*, by H. de Witt.   1872.
Translator, *Recollections of a Page at the Court of Louis XVI*, by Felix Count de France d'Hézecques.   1873.
Translator, *Recollections of Colonel de Gonville.*   1875.
Translator, *A Man of Other Days: Recollections of the Marquis Henry Joseph Costa de Beauregard.*   1877.
Translator, *The Youth of Queen Elizabeth, 1533–58*, by L. Wiesener.   2 vols., 1879.
Translator, *Catherine of Aragon, and the Sources of the English Reformation*, by Albert du Boys.   1881.
Translator, *Behind the Hedges; or, The War in the Vendee*, by H. de Witt.   1882.
Translator, *Sparks of Light for Every Day*, by H. de Witt.   1882.

Reading List: *Yonge: Her Life and Letters* by Christabel Coleridge, 1903; *Yonge: The Story of an Uneventful Life* by Georgina Battiscombe, 1943; *Victorian Best-Seller* by Margaret Mare and Alicia C. Percival, 1947; *A Chaplet for Yonge* edited by Georgina Battiscombe and Marghanita Laski, 1965.

*   *   *

The world that Charlotte Yonge describes is one that was small and rarified even in her time; she shows us a Tory squirearchy served by a loyal, dutiful, and unambitious tenantry; an upper middle class of unimpeachable descent, high-principled, highly educated, and High Church. She herself never cared to stray beyond these confines. She once ventured in middle age as far as France, to stay with a family who were as nearly the equivalent of her own family as French Protestants could be. Otherwise her whole life was passed in the Hampshire village near Winchester where she had been born. Here she devoted herself to her parents and to the parish organizations to which her writing, voluminous though it was, came second in her mind.

She disliked any ideas that she suspected might disturb the equilibrium of the old order which she upheld so staunchly. She abhorred, for instance, extreme Protestantism, the Roman church, biblical criticism, women's rights, socialism; she disapproved of the novels of Dickens and George Eliot. Her literary career spanned some 50 years, but she did not develop with them. To the end she clung to outmoded early Victorian proprieties, and wrote from the viewpoint of the dutiful daughter, true to the rules of conduct that her mother and John Keble, who had prepared her for confirmation, had laid down for her.

Within these limitations she succeeded, nevertheless, in creating a wholly credible society. We can walk in the landscapes she describes, and listen to those eager young women and high-minded young men enthusiastically discussing medieval chivalry, the poems of Southey, Schiller, foreign missions, a new project for the parish school, and know that these indeed are the voices of such families as Bishop Moberly's and her own cousinhood. Her gift for characterisation makes the reader overlook the formlessness of the plot which usually – outside the historical fiction, intended for younger readers – takes the form of domestic chronicles, many of whose personalities reappear as minor characters in other sagas. She particularly favoured huge families where the mother is dead; one remembers, for instance, the Mays of *The Daisy Chain* and *The Trial*, and the Underwoods of *The Pillars of the House*. She excelled at presenting young women, though she was never able to follow them very successfully into courtship or marriage, and it was for young, unmarried women that her adult works were specifically written, urging them to dedicate themselves to the welfare of their families (the needs of their parents being paramount). But she has left some shrewdly observed male portraits. Most memorable is the testy, impetuous Dr. May, but there are many more, including a wide range of clerics, bluff country squires, even worthless scapegraces like Arthur Martindale in *Heartsease* (though betting and extravagance are the only vices she can impute to them).

None of her novels was received with greater enthusiasm than *The Heir of Redclyffe* in 1853, which was eagerly read by bishops, undergraduates, guards officers, and royalty. It fitted the early Victorian mood, making virtue, self-sacrifice, and piety seem infinitely romantic. She maintained this ardent spirit in her later works, but, though to the end she had a large and devoted readership, it was among an older generation who, like her, preferred to look back with nostalgia.

—Gillian Avery

ZANGWILL, Israel. English. Born in the East End of London, 21 January 1864. Educated at schools in Plymouth and Bristol; Jews' Free School, Spitalfields, London; University of London, B.A. (honours). Married the writer Edith Ayrton in 1903; two sons and one daughter. Taught at the Jews' Free School, then worked as a journalist; edited the humorous periodical *Ariel*; writer from 1881. President, Jewish Territorial Organisation for the Settlement of Jews Within the British Empire, Jewish Historical Society, and Jewish Drama League. *Died 1 August 1926.*

PUBLICATIONS

Fiction

The Premier and the Painter, with Louis Cowen.   1888.
The Bachelors' Club.   1891.

The Big Bow Mystery. 1892.
Children of the Ghetto. 1892; reprinted in part as *Grandchildren of the Ghetto,* 1914.
The Old Maid's Club. 1892.
Ghetto Tragedies. 1893.
The King of Schnorrers: Grotesques and Fantasies. 1894.
Joseph the Dreamer. 1895.
The Master. 1895.
The Celibates' Club. 1898.
Dreamers of the Ghetto. 1898.
They That Walk in Darkness: Ghetto Tragedies. 1899.
The Mantle of Elijah. 1900.
The Grey Wig: Stories and Novelettes. 1903.
Ghetto Comedies. 1907.
Jinny the Carrier. 1919.

Plays

The Great Demonstration, with Louis Cowen (produced 1892). 1892.
Aladdin at Sea (produced 1893).
The Lady Journalist (produced 1893).
Six Persons (produced 1893). 1899.
Threepenny Bits (produced 1895).
Children of the Ghetto, from his own novel (produced 1899).
The Revolted Daughter (produced 1901).
Merely Mary Ann, from his own novel (produced 1904). 1921.
The Melting Pot (produced 1912). 1909.
The War God (produced 1911). 1911.
The Next Religion. 1912.
Plaster Saints (produced 1914). 1914.
The Moment Before: A Psychical Melodrama (produced 1916).
Too Much Money (produced 1918). 1924.
The Cockpit. 1921.
The Forcing House; or, The Cockpit Continued (produced 1926). 1922.
We Moderns (produced 1922). 1926.
The King of Schnorrers, from his own novel (produced 1925).

Verse

Blind Children. 1903.

Other

Without Prejudice. 1896.
Italian Fantasies. 1910.
The War for the World. 1916.
The Voice of Jerusalem. 1920.
Works. 14 vols., 1925.
Speeches, Articles, and Letters, edited by Maurice Simon. 1937.

Translator, *Selected Religious Poems,* by ben Judah Aben Gabirol Solomon. 1924.

Bibliography: "Zangwill: A Selected Bibliography" by A. Peterson, in *Bulletin of Bibliography 23,* 1961.

Reading List: *Zangwill: A Biography* by Joseph Leftwich, 1957; *Zangwill: A Study* by Maurice Wohlgelernter, 1964; *Zangwill* by Elsie Bonita Adams, 1971.

*   *   *

Israel Zangwill was a Jew in England. As such, he attempted, in great measure successfully, to integrate in his life and works the best of both civilizations, projecting them later to his people and all mankind. This he accomplished because of his versatility, a great deal of industry, and a conceit strong enough to enable him to disregard superiors, equals, and critics, as well as the fancied demands of the public. A child of two worlds, he was able to extend universally the boundaries of both these ideas he loved passionately: the Jewish and the English.

Born to poor immigrants in London's East End, he made a brief attempt at teaching, and then collaborated with a friend in writing one of the shilling books popular at the time. Some short stories and a long essay, "English Judaism," brought him to the attention of the newly organized Jewish Publication Society of America which invited him to produce a "big" Jewish novel. Accepting, Zangwill wrote *Children of the Ghetto,* an instant success which "woke all England to applause; with a bound Zangwill was on the heights."

From those heights flowed a stream of books – all reflecting the polarity within his own mind between the two worlds through which he forever moved: the Jewish and the English. For his proved to be, indeed, the antipodal mind that reveals admiration for apparently contradictory ideas. On the one hand, he wrote works which extol the belief that the ghetto, in which as a writer he seemed most successful, was no dungeon to the Jew as had been pictured by his contemporaries. In fact, Zangwill's dreamers of the ghetto, the flower of the Jewish intelligence, were often able to exchange the narrow life of their ghetto for the unrestricted ways of the outside world. On the other hand, Zangwill published some significant works of literary criticism, non-ghetto fiction, and drama with the declared attempt "to build Jerusalem in England's 'green and pleasant land,' " and, also, the world. For central to Zangwill's aesthetic is the basic concept that it is the duty of the artist *not* to divorce art from life but, rather, in the great war for the world, to use it to benefit mankind. In these works, as well as in his many essays, speeches, and articles, he is anxious not only to preach social humanism but to act as the conscience of mankind. The importance of art, he believed, necessitates that the artist sacrifice himself, a sacrifice which will, however, grant him not only truth but love. These must, he argued, inevitably improve the condition of man and mankind.

If, as Ben Jonson said, "in short circles life may perfect be," Zangwill's circles, marked, paradoxically, by the imaginary inner walls of the ghetto and the unchained world beyond, carried a light that, if not bright, was always illuminating. That light was spread by a dreamer whose soul, because it constantly assumed a dualistic form, was that of a Jewish Englishman.

—Maurice Wohlgelernter

NOTES ON CONTRIBUTORS

ALLEN, Walter. Novelist and Literary Critic. Author of six novels (the most recent being *All in a Lifetime*, 1959); several critical works, including *Arnold Bennett*, 1948; *Reading a Novel*, 1949 (revised, 1956); *Joyce Cary*, 1953 (revised, 1971); *The English Novel*, 1954; *Six Great Novelists*, 1955; *The Novel Today*, 1955 (revised, 1966); *George Eliot*, 1964; and *The Modern Novel in Britain and the United States*, 1964; and of travel books, social history, and books for children. Editor of *Writers on Writing*, 1948, and of *The Roaring Queen* by Wyndham Lewis, 1973, Has taught at several universities in Britain, the United States, and Canada, and been an editor of the *New Statesman*. **Essays:** George Eliot; Rudyard Kipling; Arthur Morrison.

ANDERSON, W. E. K. Headmaster, Shrewsbury School, Shropshire. Editor of *The Journal of Sir Walter Scott*, 1972. **Essay:** Sir Walter Scott.

ASHLEY, Leonard R. N. Professor of English, Brooklyn College, City University of New York. Author of *Colley Cibber*, 1965; *19-Century British Drama*, 1967; *Authorship and Evidence: A Study of Attribution and the Renaissance Drama*, 1968; *History of the Short Story*, 1968; *George Peele: The Man and His Work*, 1970. Editor of the *Enriched Classics* series, several anthologies of fiction and drama, and a number of facsimile editions. **Essay:** Sir Arthur Quiller-Couch.

AVERY, Gillian. Author of more than 15 books for children (the most recent being *Huck and Her Time Machine*, 1977, and *Mouldy's Orphan*, 1978), and of critical works for adults, including *Mrs. Ewing*, 1961, *Nineteenth-Century Children* (with Angela Bull), 1965, and *Childhood's Pattern*, 1975. Editor of several anthologies for children and of works by Mrs. Ewing, Andrew Lang, Charlotte Yonge, Frances Hodgson Burnett, Mrs. Molesworth, E. V. Lucas, and other writers. **Essays:** George Grossmith; Thomas Hughes; Charlotte Yonge.

BATTESTIN, Martin C. William R. Kenan, Jr., Professor of English, University of Virginia, Charlottesville. Author of *The Moral Basis of Fielding's Art*, 1959, *The Providence of Wit: Aspects of Form in Augustan Literature and the Arts*, 1974, and a forthcoming biography of Fielding. Editor of the Wesleyan Edition of Fielding's works, and of *Joseph Andrews*, *Tom Jones*, and *Amelia*. **Essay:** Henry Fielding.

BLOOM, Edward A. Professor of English, Brown University, Providence, Rhode Island; Editor of *Novel: A Forum on Fiction*. Author of *Samuel Johnson in Grub Street*, 1957; *The Order of Poetry* (with C. H. Philbrick and E. M. Blistein), 1961; *Willa Cather's Gift of Sympathy* (with Lillian D. Bloom), 1962; *The Order of Fiction*, 1964; *Joseph Addison's Sociable Animal* (with Lillian D. Bloom), 1971. Editor of *The Letters and Journals of Frances Burney*, vol. 8 (with Lillian D. Bloom), 1978. **Essay:** Fanny Burney.

BOGDANOR, Vernon. Fellow and Tutor in Politics, Brasenose College, Oxford; Review Editor, *Political Studies*. Author of *Devolution*, 1978, and of articles in *The Conservative Opportunity*, 1976, and *Parliamentary Affairs*, *Political Quarterly*, and other periodicals. Editor of *The Age of Affluence, 1951–1964*, 1970, and *Lothair*, by Disraeli, 1974. **Essay:** Benjamin Disraeli.

BRATTON, J. S. Lecturer in English, Bedford College, University of London. Author of *The Victorian Popular Ballad*, 1975. **Essays:** Lewis Carroll; G. A. Henty; George MacDonald; Frederick Marryat.

CARNALL, Geoffrey. Reader in English Literature, University of Edinburgh. Author of *Robert Southey and His Age*, 1960, *Robert Southey*, 1964, and *The Mid-Eighteenth Century* (with John Butt), a volume in the Oxford History of English Literature, 1978. **Essay:** Charlotte Lennox.

CAUWELS, Janice M. Visiting Assistant Professor of English, University of Minnesota, Minneapolis. Author of "Authorial 'Caprice' vs. Editorial 'Calculation': The Text of Elizabeth Inchbald's *Nature and Art*," in *Publications of the Bibliographical Society of America*. **Essay:** Catherine Gore.

COCKSHUT, A. O. J. G. M. Young Lecturer in Nineteenth-Century Literature, Oxford University. Author of *Anthony Trollope: A Critical Study*, 1955; *Anglican Attitudes*, 1959; *The Imagination of Charles Dickens*, 1961; *The Unbelievers: English Agnostic Thought, 1840–90*, 1964; *The Achievement of Walter Scott*, 1969; *Truth to Life*, 1974. **Essays:** Jane Austen; Charles Dickens; George Gissing.

COHEN, Morton N. Professor of English, City University of New York. Author of *Rider Haggard: His Life and Work*, 1960 (revised, 1968). Editor of *Kipling to Haggard: The Record of a Friendship*, 1965, and *The Letters of Lewis Carroll*, 2 vols., 1978. **Essay:** H. Rider Haggard.

COPLAND, R. A. Former Member of the Department of English, University of Canterbury, Christchurch, New Zealand. **Essay:** Robert Paltock.

DAHL, Curtis. Samuel Valentine Cole Professor of English, Wheaton College, Norton, Massachusetts. Author of *Robert Montgomery Bird*, 1966, and of articles on William Cullen Bryant, Edward Bulwer-Lytton, and Benjamin Disraeli. **Essay:** Edward Bulwer-Lytton.

DePORTE, Michael. Associate Professor of English, University of New Hampshire, Durham. Author of *Nightmares and Hobbyhorses: Swift, Sterne, and Augustan Ideas of Madness*, 1974, a chapter on William Davenant in *The Later Jacobean and Caroline Dramatists* edited by Terence P. Logan and Denzell S. Smith, 1978, and an article on Byron in *Modern Language Quarterly*, 1972. Editor of *Enthusiasmus Triumphatus* by Henry More, 1966, *Discourse on Madness* by Thomas Tryon, 1973 and *Lucida Intervalla* by James Carkesse (forthcoming). **Essay:** Laurence Sterne.

EHRENPREIS, Anne Henry. Private Scholar. Editor of *The Literary Ballad*, 1966; *The Old Manor House*, 1969, and *Emmeline*, 1971, both by Charlotte Smith; *Northanger Abbey* by Jane Austen, 1972. **Essay:** Charlotte Smith.

FAULKNER, Peter. Member of the Department of English, University of Exeter, Devon. Author of *William Morris and W. B. Yeats*, 1962; *Yeats and the Irish Eighteenth Century*, 1965; *Humanism in the English Novel*, 1976; *Modernism*, 1977. Editor of *William Morris: The Critical Heritage*, 1973, and of works by Morris. **Essays:** R. D. Blackmore; Samuel Butler; Thomas Holcroft; Charles Robert Maturin; John Moore; Hannah More; Thomas Love Peacock.

FOLTINEK, Herbert. Professor of English and American Literature, University of Vienna. Author of *Vorstufen zum Viktorianischen Realismus*, 1968, *Fieldings Tom Jones und das österreichische Drama*, 1976, and articles in periodicals. Editor of *Arthur Schnitzler: Grosse Szene*, 1959, and *Marriage* by Susan Ferrier, 1971. **Essays:** Susan Ferrier; Theodore Hook.

FRASER, G. S.   Reader in Modern English Literature, University of Leicester. Author several books of verse, the most recent being *Conditions,* 1969; travel books; critical studies of Yeats, Dylan Thomas, Pound, Durrell, and Pope; and of *The Modern Writer and His World,* 1953, *Vision and Rhetoric,* 1959, and *Metre, Rhythm, and Free Verse,* 1970. Editor of works by Keith Douglas and Robert Burns, and of verse anthologies. **Essay:** George du Maurier.

GÉRIN, Winifred.   Biographer and Critic. Author of *Anne Brontë,* 1959; *Branwell Brontë,* 1961; *Charlotte Brontë,* 1967; *Horatia Nelson,* 1970; *Emily Brontë,* 1971; *The Brontës,* 2 vols., 1973; *Elizabeth Gaskell: A Biography,* 1976. Editor of *Five Novelettes* by Charlotte Brontë, 1971. **Essays:** Anne Brontë; Charlotte Brontë; Emily Brontë.

GORDON, Ian A.   Professor of English, University of Wellington, 1936–74. Has taught at the University of Leeds and the University of Edinburgh. Author of *John Skelton,* 1943; *The Teaching of English,* 1947; *Katherine Mansfield,* 1954; *The Movement of English Prose,* 1966; *John Galt,* 1972. Editor of *English Prose Technique,* 1948, and of works by William Shenstone, John Galt, and Katherine Mansfield. **Essay:** John Galt.

GREEN, Roger Lancelyn.   Author of more than 50 books including fiction and verse for children and adults, retellings of folk and fairy tales, and critical studies of Andrew Lang, A. E. W. Mason, Lewis Carroll, J. M. Barrie, Mrs. Molesworth, C. S. Lewis, and Rudyard Kipling; also editor of works by these authors and others, and translator of plays by Sophocles. **Essays:** Arthur Conan Doyle; Kenneth Grahame; A. E. W. Mason.

GREENLEES, Ian.   Director of the British Institute, Florence. Author of *Norman Douglas,* 1957. **Essay:** Ouida.

HALLORAN, William F.   Dean of the College of Letters and Science, University of Wisconsin, Milwaukee. **Essay:** William Sharp.

HILSON, J. C.   Lecturer in English, University of Leicester. Editor of *Augustan Worlds* (with M. M. B. Jones and J. R. Watson), 1978, and *An Essay on Historical Composition* by James Moor, 1978. Author of articles on Hume, Richardson, Smollett, and Conrad. **Essays:** John Cleland; Tobias Smollett.

HYDE, William J.   Professor of English, University of Wisconsin, La Crosse. Author of articles on George Eliot, Hardy, Richard Jefferies, and Sabine Baring-Gould, in *PMLA, Victorian Studies, Victorian Newsletter,* and other periodicals. **Essays:** Sabine Baring-Gould; Richard Jefferies.

IVY, Randolph.   Director of the Randolph Macon Woman's College Program at Reading, England. **Essays:** Mary Elizabeth Braddon; Wilkie Collins.

JEFFARES, A. Norman.   Professor of English Studies, University of Stirling, Scotland: Editor of *Ariel: A Review of International English Literature,* and General Editor of the Writers and Critics series and the New Oxford English series. Past Editor of *A Review of English Studies.* Author of *Yeats: Man and Poet,* 1949; *Seven Centuries of Poetry,* 1956; *A Commentary on the Collected Poems* (1958) and *Collected Plays* (1975) *of Yeats.* Editor of *Restoration Comedy,* 1974, and *Yeats: The Critical Heritage,* 1977. **Essay:** Charles Lever.

JERNIGAN, Jay.   Professor of English, Eastern Michigan University, Ypsilanti: Associate Editor of *The Journal of Narrative Technique.* Author of *Henry Demarest Lloyd,* 1976, and of articles on George Moore and Yeats in *Michigan Academician, Bulletin of the New York Public Library,* and *Kansas Quarterly.* **Essay:** George Moore.

JOSEPH, M. K. Professor of English, University of Auckland, New Zealand. Author of books of verse, most recently *Inscription on a Paper Dart,* 1974; novels, most recently *A Soldier's Tale,* 1976; and of *Byron the Poet,* 1964. Editor of *Frankenstein* by Mary Shelley, 1969. **Essay:** Mary Shelley.

KALLICH, Martin. Professor of English, Northern Illinois University, De Kalb. Author of *The Psychological Milieu of Lytton Strachey,* 1961; *The American Revolution Through British Eyes* (with others), 1962; *Heav'n's First Law: Rhetoric and Order in Pope's Essay on Man,* 1967; *Oedipus: Myth and Drama* (with others), 1968; *The Other End of the Egg: Religious Satire in Gulliver's Travels,* 1970; *The Association of Ideas and Critical Theory in 18th-Century England,* 1970; *Horace Walpole,* 1971; *The Book of the Sonnet* (with others), 1972. **Essay:** Horace Walpole.

KELLY, Gary. Member of the Department of English, University of Alberta, Edmonton. Author of *The English Jacobin Novel 1780–1805,* 1976. Editor of *Mary, and The Wrongs of Women* by Mary Wollstonecraft, 1976. **Essays:** Robert Bage; William Godwin; Elizabeth Inchbald; Amelia Opie; Ann Radcliffe.

KELSALL, Malcolm. Professor of English, University College, Cardiff; Advisory Editor of *Byron Journal.* Editor of *The Adventures of David Simple* by Sarah Fielding, 1969, *Venice Preserved* by Thomas Otway, 1969, and *Love for Love* by William Congreve, 1970. **Essay:** Sarah Fielding.

LINDSAY, Maurice. Director of the Scottish Civic Trust, Glasgow, and Managing Editor of *The Scottish Review.* Author of several books of verse, the most recent being *Walking Without an Overcoat,* 1977; plays; travel and historical works; and critical studies including *Robert Burns: The Man, His Work, The Legend,* 1954 (revised, 1968), *The Burns Encyclopedia,* 1959 (revised, 1970), and *A History of Scottish Literature,* 1977. Editor of the Saltire Modern Poets series, several anthologies of Scottish writing, and works by Sir Alexander Gray, Sir David Lyndsay, Marion Angus, and John Davidson. **Essay:** Robert Louis Stevenson.

LUCAS, John. Professor of English and Drama, Loughborough University, Leicestershire; Advisory Editor of *Victorian Studies, Literature and History,* and *Journal of European Studies.* Author of *Tradition and Tolerance in 19th-Century Fiction,* 1966; *The Melancholy Man: A Study of Dickens,* 1970; *Arnold Bennett,* 1975; *Egilssaga: The Poems,* 1975; *The Literature of Change,* 1977; *The 1930's: Challenge to Orthodoxy,* 1978. Editor of *Literature and Politics in the 19th Century,* 1971, and of works by George Crabbe and Jane Austen. **Essays:** Sir Walter Besant; Marie Corelli; Charles Kingsley; William Hurrell Mallock.

MACK, Douglas S. Assistant Librarian, University of Stirling Library, Scotland; Editor of *The Bibliotheck.* **Essay:** James Hogg.

McCORMACK, W. J. Member of the Faculty, School of English, University of Leeds. Editor of *A Festschrift for Francis Stuart on His Seventieth Birthday,* 1972. **Essays:** Maria Edgeworth; Sheridan Le Fanu; Samuel Lover; Bram Stoker.

McCRACKEN, David. Associate Professor of English, University of Washington, Seattle. Author of articles on Samuel Johnson, William Godwin, Edmund Burke, and others, in *Modern Philology, Philological Quarterly, Yearbook of English Studies, Western Speech Communications,* and other periodicals. Editor of *Caleb Williams* by William Godwin, 1970. **Essays:** William Beckford; Matthew Gregory Lewis.

McGLYNN, Paul D. Member of the Department of English, Eastern Michigan University, Ypsilanti. **Essay:** Henry Mackenzie.

MEDCALF, Stephen. Member of the Faculty, School of European Studies, University of Sussex, Brighton. Author of articles on G. K. Chesterton, P. G. Wodehouse, William Golding, and other writers. Editor of *The Vanity of Dogmatizing: The Three Versions* by Joseph Glanvill, 1970. **Essay:** Jerome K. Jerome.

MUNRO, John M. Professor of English, American University of Beirut, Lebanon. Author of *English Poetry in Transition, 1968; Arthur Symons, 1969; Decadent Poetry in the 1890's, 1970; The Royal Aquarium: Failure of a Victorian Compromise, 1971; James Elroy Flecker, 1976; A Mutual Concern, 1977;* and other books. Editor of *Selected Poems of Theo. Marzials,* 1973. **Essay:** Anthony Hope.

NADEL, I. B. Associate Professor of English, University of British Columbia, Vancouver. Author of articles on Victorian writing and Jewish fiction in *University of Toronto Quarterly, Criticism, Mosaic, Midstream, Event,* and other periodicals. **Essay:** Harriet Martineau.

O'BRIEN, George. Lecturer in English, University of Warwick. **Essays:** John Banim; Gerald Griffin; Lady Morgan.

OLIVER-MORDEN, B. C. Teacher at the Open University and the University of Keele. Editor of the 18th-Century section of *The Year's Work in English 1973.* **Essay:** Oliver Goldsmith.

PERKINS, George. Professor of English, Eastern Michigan University, Ypsilanti. Author or editor of *Writing Clear Prose, 1964; Varieties of Prose, 1966; The Theory of the American Novel, 1970; Realistic American Short Fiction, 1972; American Poetic Theory, 1972; The American Tradition in Literature* (with others), fourth edition, 1974. **Essay:** Henry James.

PINION, F. B. Former Sub-Dean and Reader in English Studies, University of Sheffield; Editor of the *Thomas Hardy Society Review.* Author of *A Hardy Companion, 1968; A Jane Austen Companion, 1973; A Brontë Companion, 1975; A Commentary on the Poems of Hardy, 1976; Hardy: Art and Thought, 1977.* Editor of *Two on a Tower* by Hardy, and of Hardy's complete short stories. **Essay:** Thomas Hardy.

POLLARD, Arthur. Professor of English, University of Hull, Yorkshire. Author of *Mrs. Gaskell, Novelist and Biographer,* 1965, and *Anthony Trollope,* 1978. Editor of *The Letters of Mrs. Gaskell* (with J. A. V. Chapple), 1966; *The Victorians* (Sphere History of Literature in English), 1970; *Crabbe: The Critical Heritage,* 1972; *Thackeray: Vanity Fair* (casebook), 1978. **Essay:** R. S. Surtees.

QUAYLE, Eric. Free-lance Writer. Author of *Ballantyne the Brave,* 1967, and a bibliography of Ballantyne; *The Ruin of Sir Walter Scott,* 1968; *The Collector's Book of Books, Children's Books, Detective Fiction,* and *Boys' Stories,* 4 vols., 1971–73; *Old Cook Books: An Illustrated History,* 1978. **Essay:** R. M. Ballantyne.

RAWSON, C. J. Professor of English, University of Warwick, Coventry: Joint Editor of *Modern Language Review* and *Yearbook of English Studies,* and General Editor of the Unwin Critical Library. Author of *Henry Fielding, 1968; Fielding and the Augustan Ideal under Stress, 1972; Gulliver and the Gentle Reader, 1973; Focus: Swift, 1978.* Editor of *Fielding: A Critical Anthology,* 1973, and *Yeats and the Anglo-Irish Literature: Critical Essays* by Peter Ure, 1973. **Essay:** Jonathan Swift.

RICHETTI, John. Professor of English, Rutgers University, New Brunswick, New Jersey. Author of *Popular Fiction Before Richardson: Narrative Patterns 1700–1739*, 1969, and *Defoe's Narratives: Situations and Structures*, 1975. **Essays:** Eliza Haywood: Delariviere Manley; Samuel Richardson.

ROGERS, Pat. Professor of English, University of Bristol. Author of *Grub Street: Studies in a Subculture*, 1972, and *The Augustan Vision*, 1974. Editor of *A Tour Through Great Britain* by Daniel Defoe, 1971, *Defoe: The Critical Heritage*, 1972, and *The Eighteenth Century*, 1978. **Essay:** Daniel Defoe.

SANDERSON, Stewart F. Director of the Institute of Dialect and Folk Life Studies, University of Leeds. Author of *Hemingway*, 1961 (revised, 1970), and of many articles on British and comparative folklore and ethnology, and on modern literature. Editor of *The Secret Common-Wealth* by Robert Kirk, 1970, and *The Linguistic Atlas of England* (with others), 1978. **Essay:** George Borrow.

SHATTOCK, Joanne. Bibliographer, Victorian Studies Centre, University of Leicester. Author of articles on Victorian periodicals and reviewing, literary piracy, and the public readings of Dickens and Thackeray; contributor to *The Wellesley Index to Victorian Periodicals*. Currently editing *The Perpetual Curate* by Mrs. Oliphant, and a volume on Victorian periodicals. **Essays:** Dinah Maria Mulock; Margaret Oliphant; Joseph Henry Shorthouse.

SMITH, Elton E. Professor of English and Bible, University of South Florida, Tampa. Author of *"The Two Voices": A Tennyson Study*, 1964; *William Godwin* (with Esther Marian Greenwell Smith), 1965; *Louis MacNeice*, 1970; *"The Angry Young Men" of the Thirties*, 1975; *Charles Reade*, 1977. **Essay:** Charles Reade.

SUTHERLAND, John. Member of the Department of English, University College, London. Author of *Thackeray at Work*, 1974. Editor, with Michael Greenfield, of *Henry Esmond* by Thackeray, 1970. **Essay:** William Makepeace Thackeray.

SWEETSER, Wesley D. Professor of English, State University of New York, Oswego. Author of *Arthur Machen*, 1964, *A Bibliography of Machen* (with A. Goldstone), 1965, and *Ralph Hodgson: A Bibliography*, 1974. **Essay:** George Meredith.

THOMSON, Peter. Professor of Drama, University of Exeter, Devon. Author of *Ideas in Action*, 1977. Editor of *Julius Caesar* by Shakespeare, 1970; *Essays on Nineteenth-Century British Theatre* (with Kenneth Richards), 1971; *The Eighteenth-Century English Stage*, 1973; *Lord Byron's Family*, 1975. **Essay:** Pierce Egan.

TRACY, Clarence. Visiting Professor of English, University of Toronto. Author of *Artificial Bastard: The Life of Richard Savage*, 1953. Editor of *Poetical Works of Richard Savage*, 1962; *The Spiritual Quixote* by Richard Graves, 1968; *Browning's Mind and Art: Essays*, 1968; *Johnson's Life of Savage*, 1971; *The Rape Observed* by Alexander Pope, 1974. **Essay:** Richard Graves.

TRAINER, James. Professor of German, University of Stirling, Scotland. Editor of *The Old English Baron* by Clara Reeve, 1967. **Essay:** Clara Reeve.

WALL, Stephen. Fellow of Keble College, Oxford; Co-Editor of *Essays in Criticism*. Editor of *Charles Dickens: A Critical Anthology*, 1970. **Essay:** Anthony Trollope.

WALSH, Marcus. Lecturer in English, University of Birmingham. Editor of *The Religious Poetry of Christopher Smart*, 1972. **Essay:** Samuel Johnson.

WARNER, Alan.   Professor of English, New University of Ulster, Coleraine. Author of *A Short Guide to English Sytle*, 1961, *Clay Is the Word* (on Patrick Kavanagh), 1961; *William Allingham*, 1975. **Essays:** William Carleton; Mark Rutherford.

WINNIFRITH, T. J.   Member of the Department of English, University of Warwick, Coventry. Author of *The Brontës and Their Background: Romance and Reality*, 1973. **Essays:** Elizabeth Gaskell; Mrs. Humphry Ward.

WOHLGELERNTER, Maurice.   Professor of English, Baruch College, City University of New York. Author of *Israel Zangwill: A Study*, 1964, and *Frank O'Connor: An Introduction*, 1977. Editor of *History, Philosophy, and Spiritual Democracy: Essays in Honor of Joseph L. Blau*, 1979. **Essay:** Israel Zangwill.

WOODCOCK, George.   Free-lance Writer, Lecturer, and Editor. Author of verse (*Selected Poems*, 1967), plays, travel books, biographies, and works on history and politics; critical works include *William Godwin*, 1946, *The Incomparable Aphra*, 1948, *The Paradox of Oscar Wilde*, 1949, *The Crystal Spirit* (on Orwell), 1966, *Hugh MacLennan*, 1969, *Odysseus Ever Returning: Canadian Writers and Writing*, 1970, *Mordecai Richler*, 1970, *Dawn and the Darkest Hour* (on Aldous Huxley), 1972, *Herbert Read*, 1972, and *Thomas Merton*, 1978. Editor of anthologies, and of works by Charles Lamb, Malcolm Lowry, Wyndham Lewis, and others. **Essay:** W. H. Hudson.

WORTH, George J.   Professor and Chairman of the Department of English, University of Kansas, Lawrence. Author of *John Hannay: His Life and Works*, 1964. Editor of *Six Studies in Nineteenth-Century English Literature and Thought* (with Harold Orel), 1962. **Essay:** William Harrison Ainsworth.